ZAGAT SURVEY

Back in 1979, we never imagined that an idea born during a wine-fueled dinner with friends would take us on an adventure that's lasted three decades – and counting.

The idea – that the collective opinions of avid consumers can be more accurate than the judgments of an individual critic – led to a hobby involving friends rating NYC restaurants. And that hobby grew into Zagat Survey, which today has over 350,000 participants worldwide weighing in on everything from airlines, bars, dining and golf to hotels, movies, shopping, tourist attractions and more.

By giving consumers a voice, we – and our surveyors – had unwittingly joined a revolution whose concepts (user-generated content, social networking) were largely unknown 30 years ago. However, those concepts caught fire with the rise of the Internet and have since transformed not only restaurant criticism but also virtually every aspect of the media, and we feel lucky to have been at the start of it all.

And that wasn't the only revolution we happily stumbled into. Our first survey was published as a revolution began to reshape the culinary landscape. Thanks to a host of converging trends – the declining supremacy of old-school formal restaurants; the growing sophistication of diners; the availability of ever-more diverse cuisines and techniques; the improved range and quality of ingredients; the rise of chefs as rock stars – dining out has never been better or more exciting, and we've been privileged to witness its progress through the eyes of our surveyors. And it's still going strong.

As we celebrate Zagat's 30th year, we'd like to thank everyone who has participated in our surveys. We've enjoyed hearing and sharing your frank opinions and look forward to doing so for many years to come. As we always say, our guides and online content are really "yours."

We'd also like to express our gratitude by supporting **Action Against Hunger,** an organization that works to meet the needs of the hungry in over 40 countries. To find out more, visit www.zagat.com/action.

Nina and Tim Zagat

ZAGAT®

CELEBRATING 30 YEARS

San Francisco Bay Area Restaurants 2010

LOCAL EDITOR
Meesha Halm
STAFF EDITOR
Karen Hudes

Published and distributed by
Zagat Survey, LLC
4 Columbus Circle
New York, NY 10019
T: 212.977.6000
E: sanfran@zagat.com
www.zagat.com

ACKNOWLEDGMENTS

We thank Jon, Olive and Jude Fox, Gayle Keck and Sharron Wood, as well as the following members of our staff: Josh Rogers (senior associate editor), Christina Livadiotis (assistant editor), Brian Albert, Sean Beachell, Maryanne Bertollo, Jane Chang, Sandy Cheng, Reni Chin, Larry Cohn, John Deiner, Alison Flick, Jeff Freier, Justin Hartung, Roy Jacob, Garth Johnston, Cynthia Kilian, Natalie Lebert, Mike Liao, Andre Pilette, Becky Ruthenburg, Jacqueline Wasilczyk, Yoji Yamaguchi, Sharon Yates, Anna Zappia and Kyle Zolner.

The reviews in this guide are based on public opinion surveys. The ratings reflect the average scores given by the survey participants who voted on each establishment. The text is based on quotes from, or paraphrasings of, the surveyors' comments. Phone numbers, addresses and other factual data were correct to the best of our knowledge when published in this guide.

Our guides are printed using environmentally preferable inks containing 20%, by weight, renewable resources on papers sourced from well-managed forests. Deluxe editions are covered with Skivertex Recover® Double containing a minimum of 30% post-consumer waste fiber.

SUSTAINABLE FORESTRY INITIATIVE

Certified Chain of Custody
Promoting Sustainable Forest Management
www.sfiprogram.org

PWC-SFICOC-260

ENVIROINK™

The inks used to print the body of this publication contain a minimum of 20%, by weight, renewable resources.

Maps © 2009 GeoNova Publishing, Inc.

Contents

Ratings & Symbols

Zagat Top Spot	Name	Symbols	Cuisine	Zagat Ratings			
				FOOD	DECOR	SERVICE	COST

Area, Address & Contact

Ƶ Tim & Nina's ◑ *Seafood*   ▽ 23 | 9 | 13 | $15

Embarcadero | 999 Mission St. (The Embarcadero) | 415-555-7233 | www.zagat.com

Review, surveyor comments in quotes

Open "more or less when T and N feel like it", this bit of unembellished Embarcadero ectoplasm excels at seafood with Asian-Argentinean-Albanian accents; the staff seems "fresh off the boat", and while the view of the garbage barges is "a drag", no one balks at the "beneficent" "bottom-feeder prices."

Ratings

Food, Decor and **Service** are rated on the Zagat 0 to 30 scale.

0	–	9	poor to fair
10	–	15	fair to good
16	–	19	good to very good
20	–	25	very good to excellent
26	–	30	extraordinary to perfection
	▽		low response	less reliable

Cost

Our surveyors' estimated price of a dinner with one drink and tip. Lunch is usually 25 to 30% less. For unrated **newcomers** or **write-ins,** the price range is shown as follows:

I	$25 and below	E	$41 to $65
M	$26 to $40	VE	$66 or above

Symbols

Ƶ	highest ratings, popularity and importance
◑	serves after 11 PM
Ƨ	closed on Sunday
M	closed on Monday
⊘	no credit cards accepted

Maps

Index maps show restaurants with the highest Food ratings in those areas.

About This Survey

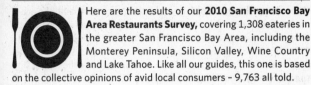

Here are the results of our **2010 San Francisco Bay Area Restaurants Survey,** covering 1,308 eateries in the greater San Francisco Bay Area, including the Monterey Peninsula, Silicon Valley, Wine Country and Lake Tahoe. Like all our guides, this one is based on the collective opinions of avid local consumers – 9,763 all told.

WHO PARTICIPATED: Input from these enthusiasts forms the basis for the ratings and reviews in this guide (their comments are shown in quotation marks within the reviews). Of these surveyors, 45% are women, 55% are men; they range in age from the 20s to the 60s. Collectively they bring roughly 1.4 million annual meals' worth of experience to this Survey. We sincerely thank each of these participants – this book is really "theirs."

HELPFUL LISTS: Our top lists and indexes should help you find exactly the right place for any occasion. See Most Popular (page 7), Key Newcomers (page 9), Top Ratings (pages 10–14), Best Buys (pages 15–17) and the 44 handy indexes starting on page 243.

OUR EDITOR: Special thanks go to our local editor, Meesha Halm, who is a Bay Area restaurant critic, cookbook author and dedicated momnivore.

ABOUT ZAGAT: This marks our 30th year reporting on the shared experiences of consumers like you. What started in 1979 as a hobby has come a long way. Today we have over 350,000 surveyors and now cover airlines, bars, dining, entertaining, fast food, golf, hotels, movies, music, resorts, shopping, spas, theater and tourist attractions in over 100 countries.

INTERACTIVE: Up-to-the-minute news about restaurant openings plus menus, photos and more are free on **ZAGAT.com** and the award-winning **ZAGAT.mobi** (for web-enabled mobile devices). They make it possible to contact thousands of places with just one click.

AVAILABILITY: Zagat guides are available in all major bookstores as well as on **ZAGAT.com.** You can also access our content when on the go via **ZAGAT.mobi** and **ZAGAT TO GO** (for smartphones).

FEEDBACK: To improve this guide, we invite your comments about any aspect of our performance. Tell us if we missed a deserving restaurant or if you feel that we got something wrong. Just contact us at **sanfran@zagat.com.**

BE A SURVEYOR: We invite you to join any of our surveys at **ZAGAT.com.** If you share your experiences with us, you'll receive a choice of rewards in exchange.

New York, NY
September 23, 2009

Nina and Tim Zagat

What's New

With a crippled state budget and over 11% unemployment, the economy has hit the Bay Area hard, and restaurants have felt the impact. Though the average cost per meal rose only 1.8% since last year (to $39.40), 52% of surveyors say they're dining out less. On the upside, 62% are taking advantage of prix fixe deals and other recession specials (see our Best Buys lists on pages 15–17), 36% find it's easier to score a hard-to-get reservation and 40% feel their patronage is more appreciated and rewarded than before.

REFRESHER COURSE: Gary Danko reclaimed the No. 1 spot for Food – edging out two north of SF standouts, **Cyrus** and the **French Laundry** (which held the title last year) – and also finished at the top of the Service and Most Popular rankings. One reason for Danko's continued popularity even in these leaner times: it offers a choice of prix fixe price points as well as an even more accessible à la carte bar menu. Other high-end restaurants taking a similar approach include Nob Hill's **Ritz-Carlton Dining Room,** which added both an à la carte and a bar menu this year, and Downtown's **Masa's,** where an abbreviated three-course menu is now available upon request.

INDIE ACTION: While million-dollar ventures by big-name chefs, such as Michael Chiarello's **Bottega** in Yountville and Gastón Acurio's **La Mar Cebicheria Peruana** on the Embarcadero, generated big buzz, some of the most intriguing newcomers came from boot-strapping fine-dining refugees. Lafayette's **Artisan Bistro,** Oakland's **Commis** and the Mission's **Saison** – opened by alums of **Coi, Manresa** and SoCal's **Stonehill Tavern,** respectively – all earned foodie cred while forgoing formality and flash.

BAR BITES: Increasingly on the cutting edge, Oakland is seeing a new wave of gourmet watering holes, such as the aperitivo-and-salumi-outpost **Adesso,** the tapas-wielding **Barlata** and the Cal-Med **Sidebar** (by **Zax Tavern** alums). All are fueling the dressed-down gastropub trend, as are the Marina's **Tipsy Pig** and chef Michael Mina's new venture, **RN74,** a high-tech wine bar presided over by a blue jeans–clad staff.

SLOW FAST FOOD: While 42% of respondents report eating out at less expensive places, 73% feel it's still important to eat green, i.e. local, organic and sustainably raised fare. Hence the openings of all-natural hot dog stands **Let's Be Frank** and **Showdogs,** and the eco-minded Mex **Nopalito.** Pizzerias are growing ever more earth-conscious too, with the arrivals of the Mission's **Flour + Water** and Sebastopol's **Pizzavino 707.**

TWEET EATS: Bay Area diners are more plugged-in than ever: 52% make reservations online and avid eaters track the whereabouts of stealth mobile street vendors such as **Chez Spencer**'s truck, **Sam's Chowder House**'s ChowderMobile and **Incanto** chef Chris Cosentino's Salumi Cycle via their websites, e-mail and Twitter accounts.

San Francisco, CA
September 23, 2009

Meesha Halm

Most Popular

These places are plotted on the map at the back of this book. Places outside of San Francisco are marked as: E=East of SF; N=North; and S=South. When a restaurant has locations both inside and out of the city limits, we include the notation SF as well.

1. Gary Danko | *American*
2. Boulevard | *American*
3. French Laundry/N | *Amer./Fr.*
4. Slanted Door | *Vietnamese*
5. Chez Panisse/E | *Cal./Med.*
6. Cyrus/N | *French*
7. Kokkari Estiatorio | *Greek*
8. Zuni Café | *Mediterranean*
9. Chez Panisse Café/E | *Cal.*
10. A16 | *Italian*
11. Michael Mina* | *American*
12. Delfina | *Italian*
13. Yank Sing | *Chinese*
14. Aqua | *Seafood*
15. Bouchon/N | *French*
16. In-N-Out/E/N/S/SF | *Burgers*
17. Fleur de Lys | *Cal./French*
18. Quince | *French/Italian*
19. Auberge Soleil/N | *Cal./Fr.*
20. Perbacco | *Italian*
21. Tadich Grill | *Seafood*
22. Farallon | *Seafood*
23. Jardinière | *Cal./French*
24. Bistro Jeanty/N | *French*
25. Absinthe | *French/Med.*
26. Chapeau! | *French*
27. Ritz-Carlton Din. Rm. | *Fr.*
28. Acquerello | *Italian*
29. Evvia/S | *Greek*
30. House of Prime Rib | *Amer.*
31. ad hoc/N | *American*
32. Greens | *Vegetarian*
33. Mustards Grill/N | *Amer./Cal.*
34. Buckeye/N | *Amer./BBQ*
35. Redd/N | *Californian*
36. Zachary's Pizza/E | *Pizza*
37. Aziza | *Moroccan*
38. Ame | *American*
39. BIX | *American/French*
40. Manresa*/S | *American*
41. Scoma's/N/SF | *Seafood*
42. Sushi Ran/N | *Japanese*
43. La Folie | *French*
44. Chow/Park Chow/E/SF | *Amer.*
45. Hog Island/N/SF | *Seafood*
46. Burma Superstar | *Burmese*
47. Amber India/S/SF | *Indian*
48. Tartine Bakery* | *Bakery*
49. Foreign Cinema | *Cal./Med.*
50. Range | *American*

It's obvious that many of the above restaurants are among the San Francisco area's most expensive, but if popularity were calibrated to price, we suspect that a number of other restaurants would join their ranks. Thus, we have added lists of Best Buys and Prix Fixe Bargains on pages 15–17.

* Indicates a tie with restaurant above

KEY NEWCOMERS

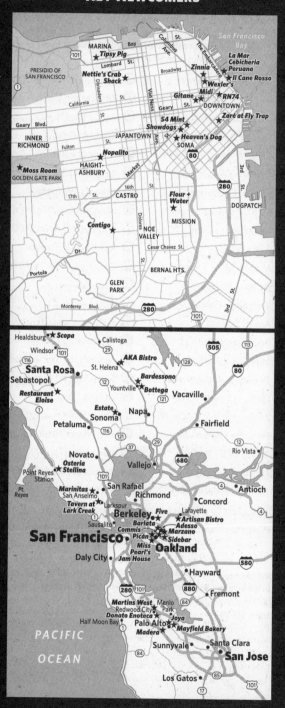

Menus, photos, voting and more – free at ZAGAT.com

Key Newcomers

Our editors' take on the year's top arrivals. See page 308 for a full list.

Adesso | *Italian*

AKA Bistro | *American*

Artisan Bistro | *Cal./Fr.*

Bardessono | *American*

Barlata | *Spanish*

Bottega | *Italian*

Commis | *American/French*

Contigo | *Spanish*

Donato Enoteca | *Italian*

Estate | *Cal./Italian*

54 Mint | *Italian*

Five | *American/Cal.*

Flour + Water | *Italian*

Gitane | *French/Spanish*

Heaven's Dog | *Chinese*

Il Cane Rosso | *Italian*

Joya Restaurant | *Pan-Latin*

La Mar Cebicheria | *Peruvian*

Madera | *American*

Marinitas | *Pan-Latin*

Martins West | *British*

Marzano | *Italian/Pizza*

Mayfield Bakery | *Bakery/Cal.*

Midi | *American/French*

Miss Pearl's Jam | *Caribbean*

Moss Room | *Cal./Med.*

Nettie's Crab | *Cal./Seafood*

Nopalito | *Mexican*

Osteria Stellina | *Italian*

Picán | *Southern*

Restaurant Eloise | *Fr./Med.*

RN74 | *French*

Scopa | *Italian*

Showdogs | *Hot Dogs*

Sidebar | *Californian*

Tavern at Lark Creek | *Amer.*

Tipsy Pig | *American*

Wexler's | *BBQ*

Zaré at Fly Trap | *Cal./Med.*

Zinnia | *American*

Following the closure of longtime business-dining magnets such as **Postrio, Jeanty at Jack's** and **Jack Falstaff,** nimble restaurateurs are ushering in a slate of more affordable start-ups. This fall, **Perbacco** spin-off **Barbacco** and Hubert Keller's **Burger Bar** at Macy's are set to debut Downtown, as is **Cotogna,** the casual sib that will be adjacent to the relocating **Quince.** Meanwhile, SoMa is greeting the new gourmet sandwich stand **Carte415** and North Beach is welcoming **Naked Lunch** by rising chef Ian Begg, as the Mission whets its appetite for the pizza-slinging **Pi Bar** and reopening **Limón.**

Over the bridge, Oakland is outshining much of the city proper with a slew of newcomers. **Lake Chalet** is poised to revive the restored historic Lake Merritt Boat House, cult hit **Pizzaiolo** is readying a Grand Avenue spin-off, and on the revitalized Jack London Square waterfront, a new gourmet marketplace three times the size of SF's Ferry Building is expected to open early in 2010, flanked by over 15 new restaurants including **Bracina** by Daniel Patterson (**Coi**), **Pizzeria Zanna Bianca** by Richard Corbo (ex **Ducca**) and the Pan-American grill **Bocanova** by Rick Hackett (**MarketBar**); the latter is leading the rest of the complex with a fall 2009 launch.

Top Food Ratings Overall

Excludes places with low votes, unless indicated by a ▽.

29	Gary Danko	*American*
	Cyrus/N	*French*
	French Laundry/N	*Amer./Fr.*
28	Kiss Seafood	*Japanese*
	Acquerello	*Italian*
	La Folie	*French*
	Masa's	*French*
	Erna's Elderberry/E	*Cal./Fr.*
	Kaygetsu/S	*Japanese*
	Chez Panisse/E	*Cal./Med.*
	Sushi Ran/N	*Japanese*
	Coi	*Californian/French*
27	Fleur de Lys	*Cal./French*
	Michael Mina	*American*
	Marinus/S	*French*
	Manresa/S	*American*
	Chez Panisse Café/E	*Cal.*
	Terra/N	*American*
	Boulevard	*American*
	Applewood Inn/N	*Cal.*

	Canteen	*Californian*
	Wolfdale's*/E	*Californian*
	Quince	*French/Italian*
	Ritz-Carlton Din. Rm.	*French*
	Le Papillon/S	*French*
	Tartine	*Bakery*
	Rivoli/E	*Californian/Med.*
	Redd/N	*Californian*
	Kokkari Estiatorio	*Greek*
	Cafe Gibraltar/S	*Med.*
	House	*Asian Fusion*
	Sierra Mar/S	*Cal./Eclectic*
26	Étoile/N	*Californian*
	Passionfish*/S	*Cal./Seafood*
	La Forêt/S	*Continental/Fr.*
	Aziza	*Moroccan*
	Aqua	*Seafood*
	Cheese Board/E	*Bakery/Pizza*
	La Toque/N	*French*
	Farmhouse Inn/Rest./N	*Cal.*

BY CUISINE

AMERICAN (NEW)

29	Gary Danko
	French Laundry/N
27	Michael Mina
	Manresa/S
	Terra/N

AMERICAN (TRAD.)

26	ad hoc/N
25	Mama's Wash. Sq.
24	Maverick
	Rutherford Grill/N
23	Chloe's Cafe

ASIAN FUSION

27	House
25	Koo
24	Bushi-tei
	Flying Fish Grill/S
23	Eos Rest./Wine Bar

BARBECUE

23	Buckeye Roadhouse/N
	Bo's Barbecue/E
22	BarBersQ/N
21	Baby Blues BBQ
20	Everett & Jones/E

BURGERS

22	In-N-Out/E/N/S/SF
	Taylor's Automatic/N/SF
21	Joe's Cable Car
19	BurgerMeister/S/SF
	Barney's/E/N/SF

CAJUN/CREOLE/SOUL

24	Brenda's French
22	1300 on Fillmore
21	Chenery Park
	farmerbrown
19	Home of Chicken/Waffles/E

CALIFORNIAN

28	Erna's Elderberry/E
	Chez Panisse/E
	Coi
27	Fleur de Lys
	Chez Panisse Café/E

CHINESE

25	Yank Sing
24	Ton Kiang
	O'mei/S
23	Great China/E
	Tai Pan/S

CONTINENTAL

26 La Forêt/S
23 Anton & Michel/S
Ecco/S
19 Bella Vista/S

DIM SUM

25 Yank Sing
24 Ton Kiang
23 Koi
22 Fook Yuen Seafood
Good Luck Dim Sum

ECLECTIC

27 Sierra Mar/S
26 Willi's Wine Bar/N
25 Avatar's/N
Firefly
24 Willow Wood Mkt./N

FRENCH

29 Cyrus/N
28 Masa's
La Folie
27 Fleur de Lys
Marinus/S

FRENCH (BISTRO)

26 Chapeau!
Mirepoix/N
Bouchon/N
25 K&L Bistro/N
Syrah/N

INDIAN

25 Ajanta/E
24 Amber India/S/SF
Vik's Chaat Corner/E
23 Shalimar/E/S/SF
Indian Oven

ITALIAN

28 Acquerello
27 Quince
26 Delfina
Picco/N
25 Santi/N

JAPANESE

28 Kiss Seafood
Kaygetsu/S
Sushi Ran/N
26 Sushi Zone
Zushi Puzzle

MED./GREEK

27 Rivoli/E
Kokkari Estiatorio
Cafe Gibraltar/S
26 Evvia/S
Lalime's/E

MEXICAN

25 La Taqueria
24 Tamarindo Antojeria/E
Tacubaya/E
23 El Metate
Don Pico's/S

MIDDLE EASTERN

25 Saha
23 Truly Mediterranean
Helmand Palace
Dish Dash/S
22 Kabul Afghan/S

PERUVIAN

25 Mochica
23 La Mar Cebicheria
Limón Peruvian
22 Destino
19 Fresca

PIZZA

26 Cheese Board Collective/E
25 Pizzaiolo/E
Little Star Pizza
Tommaso's
Pizzeria Picco/N

SANDWICHES

25 Sentinel
Gayle's Bakery/S
Downtown Bakery/N
Saigon Sandwiches
23 Cheese Steak Shop/E/N/S

SEAFOOD

26 Passionfish/S
Aqua
Swan Oyster Depot
Bar Crudo
25 Hog Island Oyster

SPANISH/BASQUE

25 Piperade
Zarzuela
22 Basque Cultural Ctr./S
24 Fringale
19 ZuZu/N

STEAK

26 Seasons
25 Harris'
   Alexander's Steak/S
24 Morton's Steak/S/SF
   Cole's Chop House/N

THAI

25 Manora's Thai
24 Thep Phanom Thai
23 Thai House
   Soi Four/E
   Marnee Thai

VEGETARIAN

26 Ubuntu/N
25 Millennium
24 Greens
21 Udupi Palace/E/S/SF
19 Cha-Ya Vegetarian/E

VIETNAMESE

26 Tamarine/S
   Slanted Door
25 Bodega Bistro
   Saigon Sandwiches
24 Thanh Long

BY SPECIAL FEATURE

BREAKFAST

26 Auberge du Soleil/N
25 Boulette's Larder
   Dottie's True Blue
24 Campton Place
23 Chloe's Cafe

BRUNCH

26 La Forêt/S
25 Zuni Café
24 Navio/S
23 Foreign Cinema
20 Garden Court

CHILD-FRIENDLY

22 Taylor's Automatic/N/SF
21 Picante Cocina/E
   Pizza Antica/E/N/S
   Joe's Cable Car
   Chow/Park Chow/E/SF
17 Pomodoro/E/S/SF

HOTEL DINING

28 Masa's
      (Vintage Court)
   Erna's Elderberry/E
      (Château du Sureau)
27 Michael Mina
      (Westin St. Francis)
   Marinus/S
      (Bernardus Lodge)
   Ritz-Carlton Din. Rm.

NEWCOMERS (RATED)

25 Bottega/N
23 Zinnia
   La Mar Cebicheria
   Marzano/E
   Nopalito

OPEN LATE

25 nopa
23 Beretta
21 Heaven's Dog
20 Globe
   Oola

SMALL PLATES

26 Willi's Wine Bar/N
   Picco/N
   Tamarine/S
24 Willi's Seafood/N
   Underwood Bar/N

TRENDY

26 Slanted Door
25 nopa
23 Foreign Cinema
   Beretta
   Dosa

WINE BARS

23 bacar
   Eos Rest./Wine Bar
20 Cav Wine Bar
   Uva Enoteca
19 Bin 38

WINNING WINE LISTS

29 Gary Danko
   Cyrus/N
   French Laundry/N
28 Acquerello
   La Folie

WORTH A TRIP

29 Cyrus/N
   French Laundry/N
28 Erna's Elderberry/E
   Chez Panisse/E
27 Marinus/S

Top Decor Overall

29 Sierra Mar/S	Spruce
Garden Court	Étoile/N
	Sutro's at Cliff Hse.
28 Ahwahnee Din. Rm./E	Plumed Horse/S
Auberge du Soleil/N	Gitane
Pacific's Edge/S	BIX
	Kokkari Estiatorio
27 Cyrus/N	Tonga Room
Erna's Elderberry/E	Seasons
Navio/S	Roy's/S
Marinus/S	Ana Mandara
Farallon	Jardinière
Ritz-Carlton Din. Rm.	El Paseo/N
French Laundry/N	
Madrona Manor/N	**25** Boulevard
Gary Danko	1300 on Fillmore
Fleur de Lys	Silks
	Meadowood Rest./N
26 Big 4	EPIC Roasthouse
Rotunda	Campton Place
Farm/N	Press/N
Bottega/N	
Waterbar	

OUTDOORS

Auberge du Soleil/N	Murray Circle/N
EPIC Roasthouse	Nepenthe/S
Étoile/N	Sam's Chowder Hse./S
Foreign Cinema	Sunnyside Resort/E
Lake Chalet/E	Tra Vigne/N
Martini House/N	Waterbar

ROMANCE

Aziza	Fleur de Lys
Cafe Jacqueline	La Forêt/S
Casanova/S	Madrona Manor/N
Chez Spencer	Marinus/S
Ecco/S	Shadowbrook/S
El Paseo/N	supperclub

ROOMS

Aziza	Foreign Cinema
bacar	One Market
Boulette's Larder	Perbacco
Boulevard	Slanted Door
Farallon	Spruce
Fleur de Lys	Waterbar

VIEWS

Ahwahnee Din. Rm./E	Guaymas/N
Albion River Inn/N	Navio/S
Beach Chalet	Pacific's Edge/S
Carnelian Room	Sierra Mar/S
Christy Hill/E	Slanted Door
Greens	Sutro's at Cliff Hse.

Top Service Overall

29 Gary Danko	Wolfdale's/E
28 Cyrus/N	El Paseo/N
Ritz-Carlton Din. Rm.	Étoile/N
French Laundry/N	Sierra Mar/S
27 Masa's	Chantilly/S
Erna's Elderberry/E	Auberge du Soleil/N
La Folie	Boulevard
Coi	Sent Sovi/S
Acquerello	Quince
Seasons	**25** Ame
Manresa/S	Albona Rist.
Chez Panisse/E	La Forêt/S
Fleur de Lys	Farmhouse Inn/Rest./N
Kiss Seafood	Campton Place
Le Papillon*/S	Kaygetsu/S
26 Meadowood Rest./N	Applewood Inn/N
Michael Mina	Fresh Cream/S
La Toque/N	Rivoli/E
Marinus/S	BayWolf/E
Madrona Manor/N	Jardinière

Best Buys Overall

BAKERIES/CAFES

27 Tartine Bakery
23 Blue Bottle Café
22 La Boulange/N/SF
   Rose's Cafe
   Emporio Rulli/N/SF
21 Calafia/S
20 Plant Cafe Organic
19 Mayfield Bakery/S

DINERS

25 Dottie's True Blue
23 Bette's Oceanview/E
22 Taylor's Automatic/N/SF
20 Pine Cone Diner/N▽
19 Jimmy Bean's/E
   Sears Fine Food
   St. Francis
18 FatApple's/E

EARLY-BIRD

27 Cafe Gibraltar/S
26 Chapeau!
24 Farallon
   Capannina
23 Chez Papa
   Wente Vineyards/E
   rnm restaurant
22 Le P'tit Laurent
20 Alamo Square

HOLE-IN-THE-WALL

25 Rosamunde Grill
   Burma Superstar/E/SF
23 Truly Mediterranean
   Shalimar/E/S/SF
   Shanghai Dumpling
22 Tu Lan
   Cha-Ya Vegetarian/E/SF
21 A La Turca

LOW/NO CORKAGE FEE

24 Dry Creek Kitchen/N
   fig cafe & winebar/N
   Tra Vigne/N
22 Market/N▽
20 Fish & Farm
19 Indigo
   Healdsburg B&G/N
   Zinsvalley/N▽

NOODLE SHOPS

23 San Tung
21 Citrus Club
   Osha Thai
19 Hotei
17 Mifune

PRIX FIXE LUNCH

27 Chez Panisse Café/E ($25)
25 K&L Bistro/N ($20)
   Ajanta/E ($12)
   Zitune/S ($24)
   Piperade ($23)
24 Sanraku ($11)
   Vik's Chaat Corner/E ($6)
23 Tommy Toy's ($23)

PRIX FIXE DINNER

27 Chez Panisse Café/E ($27)
   Cafe Gibraltar/S ($20)
26 Mirepoix/N ($26)
25 K&L Bistro/N ($29)
   Ajanta/E ($17)
24 Grasing's Coastal/S ($30)
   Isa ($24)
23 Unicorn Pan Asian ($17)

TAQUERIAS

25 La Taqueria
   Taqueria Tlaquepaque/S▽
24 Tamarindo Antojeria/E
   Tacubaya/E
23 Little Chihuahua▽
   El Metate
   Taqueria Can-Cun
22 Nick's Crispy Tacos

TOP CHEF BARGAINS

27 Chez Panisse Café/E
25 Sentinel
24 Pizzeria Delfina
   Corso Trattoria/E
22 Bocadillos
   Out the Door
20 Mijita
－ Il Cane Rosso

BEST BUYS: BANG FOR THE BUCK

In order of Bang for the Buck rating.

1. Saigon Sandwiches
2. In-N-Out/E/N/S/SF
3. El Metate
4. Arinell Pizza/E/SF
5. Blue Bottle
6. Rosamunde Grill
7. Sentinel
8. La Corneta/S/SF
9. Taqueria Can-Cun
10. Caspers Hot Dogs/E
11. Cheese Board Collective/E
12. Papalote Mexican
13. La Taqueria
14. Gioia Pizzeria/E
15. Cheese Steak Shop/E/N/S/SF
16. Pancho Villa/S/SF
17. Mixt Greens
18. Cactus Taqueria/E
19. Blue Barn Gourmet
20. Kasa Indian Eatery
21. Boogaloos
22. Truly Mediterranean
23. Nick's Crispy Tacos
24. Best-o-Burger
25. La Boulange/N/SF
26. Tartine Bakery
27. Red's Java House
28. Pluto's Fresh Food/S/SF
29. La Cumbre Taqueria/S/SF
30. Good Luck Dim Sum
31. Jay's Cheesesteak
32. Dottie's True Blue
33. Downtown Bakery/N
34. Burger Joint/S/SF
35. Mama's Royal Cafe/E
36. St. Francis
37. Jimtown Store/N
38. Tacubaya/E
39. Gayle's Bakery/S
40. Sol Food/N

BEST BUYS: OTHER GOOD VALUES

Alamo Square
A La Turca
Alice's
Angkor Borei
Asqew Grill/E/N/SF
Avatar's/N
Axum Cafe
BarBersQ/N
Bodega Bistro
Bovolo/N
Brenda's
Burma Superstar/E/SF
Cafe Citti/N
Cha-Ya Vegetarian/E/SF
Chow/Park Chow/E/SF
Delessio
Emmy's Spaghetti/N/SF
FatApple's/E
fig cafe & winebar/N
Firefly
Flying Fish Grill/S
Green Chile Kitchen
grégoire/E
Juan's Place/E

King of Thai
Krung Thai/S
Le Charm Bistro
Le Cheval/E
Little Star Pizza
Mario's Bohemian
Mendo Bistro/N
Mijita
Moki's Sushi
My Tofu House
Nopalito
Out the Door
Pacific Catch/N/SF
Picante Cocina/E
Pizzeria Delfina
Pizzeria Tra Vigne/N
Sai Jai Thai
Shanghai Dumpling
Taylor's Automatic/N/SF
Ti Couz
Udupi Palace/E/S/SF
Underdog Hot Dog∇
Vik's Chaat Corner/E
Willow Wood Mkt./N

Menus, photos, voting and more - free at ZAGAT.com

PRIX FIXE BARGAINS

Since hours may be limited and prices can change, please call ahead to confirm.

DINNER ($30 & UNDER)

Ajanta/E	$17	Garibaldis/E/SF	30
Amber Bistro/E	30	Grasing's Coastal/S	30
Axum Cafe	17	Hyde St. Bistro	30
Baker St. Bistro	17	Il Davide/N	30
Basque Cultural Ctr./S	20	Isa	24
Bistro Liaison/E	28	Jimmy Bean's/E	12
Bistro St. Germain	20	K&L Bistro/N	29
Boonville Hotel/N	30	Kan Zaman	13
Bridges/E	27	La Provence	29
Cafe Bastille	25	Le Charm Bistro	30
Cafe Gibraltar/S	20	MarketBar	27
Caffe Delle Stelle	26	Mirepoix/N	26
Charcuterie/N	20	Shabu-Sen	28
Chez Panisse Café/E	27	Tajine	30
Côté Sud	30	Town's End	23
Cuvée/N	30	Unicorn Pan Asian	17
Duck Club/E	30	Yankee Pier/N	20
1550 Hyde Café	30	Zazie	24

LUNCH ($25 & UNDER)

Absinthe	$16	La Terrasse	22
Ajanta/E	12	MarketBar	25
Ana Mandara	25	Maya	20
B44	22	Meadowood Grill/N	25
Bistro Liaison/E	17	One Market	23
BIX	25	Pakwan/E	11
Brother's Korean	9	Piperade	23
Cafe Bastille	18	Sanraku	11
Chez Panisse Café/E	25	Scoma's	24
Citron/E	21	Shanghai 1930	13
E&O Trading Co./N/SF	17/19	South Food + Wine Bar	22
Espetus Churrascaria/S/SF	24	Tarpy's Roadhouse/S	9
Garibaldis/E	15	Tommy Toy's	23
Grand Pu Bah	14	Vik's Chaat Corner/E	6
Hurley's/N	18	Waterbar	24
Il Davide/N	10	Yankee Pier/N	14
Isobune/S	9	Zibibbo/S	19
Junnoon/S	18	Zitune/S	24
K&L Bistro/N	20	Zucca/S	13

CITY OF SAN FRANCISCO

Top Food Ratings

Excludes places with low votes.

29	Gary Danko | *American*
28	Kiss Seafood | *Japanese*
	Acquerello | *Italian*
	La Folie | *French*
	Masa's | *French*
	Coi | *Californian/French*
27	Fleur de Lys | *Californian/French*
	Michael Mina | *American*
	Boulevard | *American*
	Canteen | *Californian*
	Quince| *French/Italian*
	Ritz-Carlton Din. Rm. | *French*
	Tartine | *Bakery*
	Kokkari Estiatorio | *Greek*
	House | *Asian Fusion*

26	Aziza | *Moroccan*
	Aqua | *Seafood*
	Richmond Rest. | *Cal.*
	Sushi Zone | *Japanese*
	Range | *American*
	Delfina | *Italian*
	Chapeau! | *French*
	Swan Oyster Depot | *Seafood*
	Ame | *American*
	Chez Spencer | *French*
	Bar Crudo | *Seafood*
	Jardinière | *Californian/French*
	Seasons | *Seafood/Steak*
	Slanted Door | *Vietnamese*
	Zushi Puzzle | *Japanese*

BY CUISINE

AMERICAN (NEW)

29	Gary Danko
27	Michael Mina
	Boulevard
26	Range
	Ame

AMERICAN (TRAD.)

25	Mama's Wash. Sq.
24	Maverick
23	BIX
22	Liberty Café
	Taylor's Automatic

ASIAN FUSION

27	House
25	Koo
24	Bushi-tei
23	Eos Rest./Wine Bar
21	CAFÉ KATi

BAKERIES

27	Tartine Bakery
25	Mama's Wash. Sq.
22	Liberty Café
	La Boulange
21	Citizen Cake

BURGERS

22	In-N-Out
	Taylor's Automatic
21	Joe's Cable Car
19	BurgerMeister
	Barney's

CALIFORNIAN

28	Coi
27	Canteen
26	Richmond Rest.
25	Woodward's Garden
	nopa

CHINESE

25	Yank Sing
24	Ton Kiang
23	R & G Lounge
	Tommy Toy's
	San Tung

FRENCH

28	La Folie
27	Fleur de Lys
	Ritz-Carlton Din. Rm.
26	Chez Spencer
	Jardinière

FRENCH (BISTRO)

26	Chapeau!
24	L'Ardoise
	Fringale
23	South Park Cafe
	Chez Papa

INDIAN/PAKISTANI

24	Amber India
23	Shalimar
	Indian Oven
	Dosa
22	Roti Indian Bistro

Menus, photos, voting and more - free at ZAGAT.com

ITALIAN

28	Acquerello
27	Quince
26	Delfina
25	Perbacco
24	La Ciccia

JAPANESE

28	Kiss Seafood
26	Sushi Zone
	Zushi Puzzle
	Kabuto
25	Sebo

MED./GREEK

27	Kokkari Estiatorio
26	Frascati
25	Zuni Café
24	Bar Tartine
23	Foreign Cinema

MEXICAN

25	La Taqueria
23	El Metate
	Taqueria Can-Cun
	Nopalito
	Mamacita

MIDDLE EASTERN

25	Saha
23	Truly Mediterranean
	Helmand Palace
22	Bursa Kebab
21	A La Turca

NOODLES

23	San Tung
21	Citrus Club
	Osha Thai
19	Hotei
17	Mifune

PERUVIAN

| 25 | Mochica |
| 23 | La Mar Cebicheria |

	Limón Rotisserie
22	Fresca
	Destino

PIZZA

25	Little Star Pizza
	Tommaso's
	Pizzetta 211
24	Pizzeria Delfina
	Gialina

SEAFOOD

26	Aqua
	Swan Oyster Depot
	Bar Crudo
	Seasons
25	Hog Island Oyster

SPANISH/BASQUE

25	Piperade
	Zarzuela
24	Fringale
22	Bocadillos
	Gitane

STEAK

26	Seasons
25	Harris'
24	Morton's
	House of Prime Rib
23	Ruth's Chris

TAPAS (SPANISH)

25	Zarzuela
22	Bocadillos
21	Alegrias
	Iluna Basque
20	Ramblas

VIETNAMESE

26	Slanted Door
25	Bodega Bistro
24	Thanh Long
23	Crustacean
22	Tu Lan

BY SPECIAL FEATURE

BREAKFAST

25	Boulette's Larder
	Dottie's True Blue
	Mama's Wash. Sq.
24	Campton Place
23	Chloe's Cafe

BRUNCH

27	Canteen
	Zuni Café
23	Foreign Cinema
22	Zazie
20	Garden Court

CHILD-FRIENDLY

25	Dottie's True Blue
	Yank Sing
	Mama's Wash. Sq.
	Tommaso's
	La Taqueria

NEWCOMERS (RATED)

23	Zinnia
	La Mar Cebicheria
	Nopalito
22	Zaré at Fly Trap
	Gitane

OPEN LATE

25	nopa
23	Beretta
	Shalimar
	Brother's Korean
	Thai House

OUTDOOR SEATING

26	Chez Spencer
24	Isa
23	Foreign Cinema
20	Waterbar
	EPIC Roasthouse

PEOPLE-WATCHING

27	Boulevard
26	Jardinière
25	Zuni Café
24	Town Hall
23	BIX

POWER SCENES

27	Boulevard
26	Aqua
25	Spruce

	Perbacco
22	One Market

ROMANCE

28	Acquerello
27	Fleur de Lys
26	Aziza
	Chez Spencer
25	Cafe Jacqueline

SMALL PLATES

24	Isa
	Pesce
23	Terzo
	rnm restaurant
	Oyaji

TASTING MENUS

29	Gary Danko
28	Masa's
	Coi
27	Michael Mina
	Ritz-Carlton

TRENDY

26	Slanted Door
25	nopa
23	Foreign Cinema
	Beretta
	Dosa

WINNING WINE LISTS

29	Gary Danko
28	Acquerello
27	Michael Mina
	Boulevard
23	bacar

BY LOCATION

CASTRO/NOE VALLEY

26	Sushi Zone
25	Firefly
24	La Ciccia
	Incanto
	L'Ardoise

CHINATOWN

23	R & G Lounge
22	Hunan Home/Garden
	Oriental Pearl
	House of Nanking
21	Yuet Lee

COW HOLLOW/ MARINA

26	Zushi Puzzle
25	A16
24	Capannina
	Greens
	Isa

DOWNTOWN

28	Masa's
27	Michael Mina
	Canteen
	Quince
	Kokkari Estiatorio

EMBARCADERO

27 Boulevard
26 Slanted Door
25 Boulette's Larder
   Hog Island Oyster
24 Ozumo

FISHERMAN'S WHARF

29 Gary Danko
23 Grandeho Kamekyo
22 Scoma's
   In-N-Out
   Ana Mandara

HAIGHT-ASHBURY/ COLE VALLEY

23 Grandeho Kamekyo
   Eos Rest./Wine Bar
22 La Boulange
   Alembic
   Zazie

HAYES VALLEY

25 Zuni Café
   Sebo
24 Bar Jules
23 Domo Sushi
   Hayes St. Grill

LOWER HAIGHT

25 Rosamunde Grill
24 Thep Phanom Thai
23 Indian Oven
   rnm restaurant
20 Memphis Minnie's

MISSION

27 Tartine Bakery
26 Range
   Delfina
   Chez Spencer
25 Woodward's Garden

NOB & RUSSIAN HILLS

28 La Folie
27 Fleur de Lys
   Ritz-Carlton Din. Rm.
26 Frascati
25 Zarzuela

NORTH BEACH

28 Coi
27 House
25 Mama's Wash. Sq.
   Cafe Jacqueline
   Tommaso's

PACIFIC HEIGHTS/ JAPANTOWN

28 Kiss Seafood
24 Pizzeria Delfina
   Bushi-tei
23 Maki
   Vivande Porta Via

RICHMOND

26 Aziza
   Richmond Rest.
   Chapeau!
   Kabuto
25 Pizzetta 211

SOMA

26 Ame
25 Yank Sing
   Sentinel
   Mochica
   Manora's Thai

SUNSET

25 Koo
24 Thanh Long
23 Ebisu
   San Tung
   Pomelo

Top Decor

29	Garden Court		Gitane
27	Farallon		BIX
	Ritz-Carlton Din. Rm.		Kokkari Estiatorio
	Gary Danko		Tonga Room
	Fleur de Lys		Seasons
26	Big 4		Ana Mandara
	Rotunda		Jardinière
	Waterbar	25	Boulevard
	Spruce		1300 on Fillmore
	Sutro's at Cliff Hse.		Silks

Top Service

29	Gary Danko		Boulevard
28	Ritz-Carlton Din. Rm.		Quince
27	Masa's	25	Ame
	La Folie		Albona Rist.
	Coi		Campton Place
	Acquerello		Jardinière
	Seasons		Aqua
	Fleur de Lys		Richmond Rest.
	Kiss Seafood		Kokkari Estiatorio
26	Michael Mina		Silks

Best Buys

In order of Bang for the Buck rating.

1. Saigon Sandwiches
2. In-N-Out
3. El Metate
4. Arinell Pizza
5. Blue Bottle
6. Rosamunde Grill
7. Sentinel
8. La Corneta
9. Taqueria Can-Cun
10. Papalote Mexican
11. La Taqueria
12. Cheese Steak Shop
13. Pancho Villa
14. Mixt Greens
15. Blue Barn Gourmet
16. Kasa Indian Eatery
17. Boogaloos
18. Truly Mediterranean
19. Nick's Crispy Tacos
20. Best-o-Burger

OTHER GOOD VALUES

A La Turca
Alice's
Angkor Borei
Asqew Grill
Brenda's
Delessio
Emmy's Spaghetti
Green Chile Kitchen
King of Thai
Little Star Pizza
Mijita
Out the Door
Tajine
Taylor's Automatic
Ti Couz
Tu Lan

City of San Francisco

Ⓩ **Absinthe** ●Ⓜ *French/Mediterranean* | 22 | 23 | 21 | $48 |

Hayes Valley | 398 Hayes St. (Gough St.) | 415-551-1590 | www.absinthe.com

"A place for both your mistress and your wife (not at the same time, however)", this "convivial" "art nouveau–style" brasserie "makes the heart grow fonder" with "*Top Chef* contestant" Jamie Lauren preparing "delicious" French-Med dishes (including "small plates galore" and "decadent" brunches) served with "grace"; it's a prime "midpriced pre-performance" option and attractive for a "clever" "nightcap" while "sitting outside on Hayes Street and watching the San Francisco night sail along."

🆕 **Academy Cafe** *Eclectic* | 21 | 16 | 16 | $19 |

Inner Richmond | California Academy of Sciences | 55 Music Concourse Dr. (bet. Fulton St. & Lincoln Way) | 415-876-6121 | www.academycafesf.com

On the main floor of the California Academy of Sciences, this new Eclectic "cafeteria" by Charles Phan (The Slanted Door) features "organically" geared grab-and-go stations dishing up everything from "made-to-order tacos" to "delectable" Vietnamese items; though it's "a bit expensive", the sleek dining room (lined with a massive aquarium) provides a "respite from the hubbub" and "usual fast food", and there's even an "outdoor courtyard" "for little ones to run around"; N.B. open to ticket-holders only.

Ace Wasabi's Rock-N-Roll Sushi *Japanese* | 21 | 15 | 18 | $35 |

Marina | 3339 Steiner St. (bet. Chestnut & Lombard Sts.) | 415-567-4903

This "energetic" Marina sushi bar (sister to Tokyo Go Go) "blasting Stones albums" was "fun in the '90s" and is still "bumping full" of "frat boys and drunk girls" "looking to impress" each other; even if the "affordable" fin fare "isn't authentic Japanese", "Ace is the place" for "playing bingo while you wait for your takeout" or "making it through a 750ml bottle of sake" before polishing off "adventurous rolls" during a "big night out."

Acme Chophouse ⓈⓂ *Steak* | 20 | 20 | 20 | $49 |

South Beach | AT&T Park | 24 Willie Mays Plaza (bet. King & 3rd Sts.) | 415-644-0240 | www.acmechophouse.com

Take that "stimulus check" and "make a night" of "juicy" steaks, "mean martinis" and a "Giants game" at this "sustainable" South Beacher by chef Traci Des Jardins "in the shadow of the ballpark"; the "clean, airy" interior is typically "swinging" with "baseball fans" who "eat and booze up" "before, during or after the game", though some guests grumble about a "hectic atmosphere" and grub that "doesn't justify the price"; N.B. hours vary depending on season schedule.

Ⓩ **Acquerello** ⓈⓂ *Italian* | 28 | 24 | 27 | $79 |

Polk Gulch | 1722 Sacramento St. (bet. Polk St. & Van Ness Ave.) | 415-567-5432 | www.acquerello.com

"When you long" for that "European-style" "quiet elegance" "that doesn't exist anymore", this "haute Italian" "tucked away" in a remodeled church in Polk Gulch "has no peer"; overseeing "outstanding" service, the "most gracious maitre d'" "carefully selects" and "decants"

	FOOD	DECOR	SERVICE	COST

vino to pair with the "exceptional", "luxurious" prix fixe menus, so while a few critics contend it's a bit "too stiff" and you may have to "borrow from your children to pay for it", most find it's just "the way you want it to be when you're out with your honey"; N.B. jacket suggested.

Alamo Square *French/Seafood*   `20` `16` `19` `$33`
Western Addition | 803 Fillmore St. (Grove St.) | 415-440-2828 | www.alamosquareseafoodgrill.com
"Have it your way" at this "simple" seafooder in the Western Addition where "you choose the fish, cooking method and sauce" and savor a "Parisian bistro feel" imparted by the "well-prepared" meals, "cozy" quarters and monsieur owner who's "quite the charmer"; *oui*, garçons are at times "stretched thin", but the nightly $15 prix fixe (till 7 PM) and "free corkage Wednesdays" are what "bargain"-hunters remember.

A La Turca *Turkish*   `21` `10` `17` `$18`
Tenderloin | 869 Geary St. (Larkin St.) | 415-345-1011 | www.alaturcasf.com
"A la tasty!" tout Tenderloin travelers about this Turkish "secret" turning out "large", "bang-for-the-buck" plates of "fresh" "Aegean treats" such as "delicious kebabs, "homemade pita" and "flaky" meat and vegetable pides; sure, it's a "no-thrills" "hole-in-the-wall", but "perfectly comfortable" and "authentic right down to the soccer on TV" and the "welcoming" young Turks who run the joint.

Albona Ristorante Istriano ⓈⓂ *Italian*   `24` `18` `25` `$43`
North Beach | 545 Francisco St. (bet. Mason & Taylor Sts.) | 415-441-1040 | www.albonarestaurant.com
"You may not know where Istria is beforehand, but you'll want to travel there after" sampling this "hidden" North Beach throwback beloved by "regulars" "at least as much for the owner's and staff's entertaining personalities" as for the "unique", "micro-regional" cuisine that's largely Venetian, yet with an "Eastern European slant"; while the "small" dining room is "dated", it's perfect when you're "tired of hitting the ultra-trendy places", and the "free valet parking is a plus."

Alegrias, Food From Spain *Spanish*   `21` `17` `21` `$36`
Marina | 2018 Lombard St. (Webster St.) | 415-929-8888
Fans fawn over this "family-run" Iberian "treasure" that despite being in a "blah location on busy Lombard Street" turns out "fantastic" paella, "delicious" sangria and "some of the best Spanish tapas in the city" for a "reasonable price"; the "homey", "slightly kitschy" digs, with a "large back room" for groups, are "quieter" than your typical Marina hangout but equally suitable for "bringing a date"; N.B. closed Tuesdays.

Alembic, The ● *Eclectic*   `22` `21` `20` `$34`
Haight-Ashbury | 1725 Haight St. (bet. Cole & Shrader Sts.) | 415-666-0822 | www.alembicbar.com
"Priding itself" on "compelling" cocktails whipped up by "serious" mixologists, this "refreshingly tie-dye-free" Haight-Ashbury gastropub with an "ambiance suitable for a *Deadwood* set" is "more of a bar than a restaurant" (with "very few tables"), but "hit it at the right time" (try "dusk" to avoid an "elbow in your back") and it's "perfect" for savoring equally "innovative", "brilliantly paired" Eclectic small plates; both are a "tad pricey", but where else can you get jerk-spiced duck hearts "to go with your bourbon"?

	FOOD	DECOR	SERVICE	COST

Alfred's Steakhouse ⌧Ⓜ *Steak* | 22 | 20 | 22 | $54 |

Downtown | 659 Merchant St. (bet. Kearny & Montgomery Sts.) | 415-781-7058 | www.alfredssteakhouse.com

"Round up the fellas", "sip a Manhattan and party like it's 1959" at this "ooold-school" Downtown steakhouse where the "delicious", "unadorned" cuts are "good-sized and so is the booze"; some doubters deem it merely "standard", but since little has changed, from the "ancient men's club" decor ("red leather booths", "meat display") to the "crusty", "formally dressed" waiters, traditionalists swear it leaves the big chains "in the dust"; P.S. "don't forget", a service charge is included in the bill.

Alice's *Chinese* | 19 | 15 | 18 | $20 |

Noe Valley | 1599 Sanchez St. (29th St.) | 415-282-8999 | www.alicesrestaurant.ypguides.net

"Cute, quick and affordable", this Noe Valley "fallback" comes through with "not greasy", "better-than-average" Chinese food served in a "tasteful" setting decorated with "orchids and art glass"; while the staff is "lovely" and lunch is a "bargain", some patrons pout it's "getting too predictable", with dishes that are "far too similar" and an ambiance that could be "warmer."

Alioto's *Italian* | 18 | 17 | 18 | $43 |

Fisherman's Wharf | 8 Fisherman's Wharf (Taylor St.) | 415-673-0183 | www.aliotos.com

"Locals love to avoid" this "landmark" right in the "heart of the tourist rip-off district", but nostalgics confess it's the "only place to take visitors to the Wharf" for "sourdough bread", "traditional" seafood and other "overpriced" "Sicilian specialties" served by "waiters wearing white"; while the decor is rather "tired", the view of the "Golden Gate Bridge", "fishing boats" and "sea lions" "makes up for a lot."

Amber India *Indian* | 24 | 20 | 20 | $36 |

SoMa | 25 Yerba Buena Ln. (bet. Market & Mission Sts.) | 415-777-0500 | www.amber-india.com

See review in South of San Francisco Directory.

☑ Ame *American* | 26 | 25 | 25 | $74 |

SoMa | St. Regis | 689 Mission St. (3rd St.) | 415-284-4040 | www.amerestaurant.com

"Stellar" New American dishes whose "clean", "intense" "East and West flavors" "explode on the tongue" attract "big foodies" and other "elite" eaters to this "sublime" SoMa sib of Hiro Sone and Lissa Doumani's Terra in St. Helena; providing a "gorgeous" backdrop, the "ultrachic" dining room and bar in the St. Regis is complemented by service in the "courtly tradition", so even those who aren't dining on a "corporate account" affirm that "every dollar is earned."

Americano *Californian* | 18 | 23 | 17 | $43 |

Embarcadero | Hotel Vitale | 8 Mission St. (The Embarcadero) | 415-278-3777 | www.americanorestaurant.com

The "perfect San Francisco setting with a view of the Bay Bridge" - and lots of "eye candy" - easily "overshadows" the "simple but tasty" Californian fare ("you can order food?") at this "hot" Embarcadero boîte in the Hotel Vitale; it's "all the rage" for "warm-weather" lunches

FOOD | DECOR | SERVICE | COST

Amici's East Coast Pizzeria *Pizza*

20 | 13 | 17 | $21

AT&T Park | 216 King St. (3rd St.) | 415-546-6666
Marina | 2200 Lombard St. (Steiner St.) | 415-885-4500
www.amicis.com

The "brick-oven char" and "hot oil dripping down your forearm" have the "same effect on NY transplants as Proust's madeleines" at this Bay Area "family pizzeria" chain that some call the "best on the Left Coast"; still, while California-fied options like "soy cheese" and "gluten-free crust" (at some locations) are a "bonus" for "allergy-prone" patrons, others gripe it's "getting very spendy" for a "large pie I can finish myself."

Ana Mandara *Vietnamese*

22 | 26 | 21 | $49

Fisherman's Wharf | Ghirardelli Sq. | 891 Beach St. (Polk St.) | 415-771-6800 | www.anamandara.com

"Ho Chi Minh City meets Ghirardelli" at this "wowing" Wharf "favorite" for "entertaining out-of-town guests" that serves "sumptuous", "marvelously presented" French-Vietnamese food amid "exotic" "stage-set" decor evoking a "colonial" "plantation" (or the "Pirates of the Caribbean" ride for some); if that doesn't "put you in a lusty mood", the "low lighting" and "potent specialty cocktails" in the "upper lounge", hosting "live jazz" on the weekends, surely will.

Anchor & Hope *Seafood*

21 | 21 | 20 | $46

SoMa | 83 Minna St. (2nd St.) | 415-501-9100 | www.anchorandhopesf.com

Offering "a taste of New England without the weather", this "upscale" SoMa "chowder house" (from the "Town Hall crew") "impresses" with "true lobster rolls", "gourmet fish 'n' chips" and "innovative" delicacies like "must-try" sea urchin "served in the shell"; customers in both "suits" and "jeans" are welcomed into the "refurbished" "old warehouse" by servers as "friendly as shipmates", though some critics claim it's a lot of clams "if you actually order enough to be full."

Anchor Oyster Bar *Seafood*

23 | 16 | 21 | $35

Castro | 579 Castro St. (bet. 18th & 19th Sts.) | 415-431-3990

A "Castro fixture" since 1977, this "unassuming", "postage stamp"–sized seafood bar decked with the requisite "nautical" knickknacks and loads of "local color" delivers "sweet succulent oysters", "fine chowder" and other "fresh daily" catches you can "wash down with an Anchor Steam"; just be ready for long "waits at peak periods" to "snag a seat at the counter" or precious few tables.

Andalu *Eclectic*

21 | 18 | 18 | $35

Mission | 3198 16th St. (Guerrero St.) | 415-621-2211 | www.andalusf.com

Missionites go wild for this "wizard of tapas" conjuring an Eclectic "confluence of flavors" (Coca-Cola ribs anyone?) and libations ("red and white sangria") to "mix and match" for a "decent" price; alas, the staff can resemble "hipsters working at a record stores" and the din of the "clubbing atmosphere" often "rises to dance-hall volume", so some favor it for "off-hour" dining and weekend brunch.

	FOOD	DECOR	SERVICE	COST

Angkor Borei *Cambodian*   23 | 15 | 22 | $20

Bernal Heights | 3471 Mission St. (Cortland Ave.) | 415-550-8417 | www.cambodiankitchen.com

"What's hot is the clay pot" among other "world-class" Cambodian dishes (including "winning" mock-meat options) at this "adorable family-run" Bernal Heights haven that's "unusual and unusually good for not a lot of cash"; the "ornate" room brightens up its "drab" block, while "motherly service" offers extra "warmth."

Antica Trattoria Ⓜ *Italian*   22 | 17 | 21 | $39

Russian Hill | 2400 Polk St. (Union St.) | 415-928-5797 | www.anticasf.com

"Loving attention and lovable pastas" by "passionate" chef-owner Ruggero Gadaldi combine to make "regulars" feel like they've "married into an Italian family" at this "simple", "charming" Russian Hill trattoria; so "never mind the noise" or the "crowds" with *bambini* in tow, the "excellent" vino and "moderate" tabs add up to a *molto bene* meal.

ANZU *European/Japanese*   22 | 20 | 22 | $52

Downtown | Hotel Nikko | 222 Mason St. (O'Farrell St.) | 415-394-1100 | www.restaurantanzu.com

A "regular stop on the pre-theater circuit" (including its own Rrazz Room downstairs), this Euro-Japanese fusion place "hidden on the second level" of Downtown's Hotel Nikko "graciously" serves "stylish, fragrant" cooked dishes as well as "excellent crudo and sake"; some critics complain of "cold", "'90s-glam" decor and "pricey" repasts, but many are appeased by the "tempting, plentiful" Sunday jazz brunch.

Aperto *Italian*   23 | 16 | 22 | $31

Potrero Hill | 1434 18th St. (bet. Connecticut & Missouri Sts.) | 415-252-1625 | www.apertosf.com

"Cozy" and "convivial", this "recession-busting" "neighborhood Italian" earns a Potrero Hill following with "honest", "well-crafted" meals (including a "nice brunch") featuring "terrific" specials; "solid", "family-friendly" service helps make up for "tightly packed tables" and a sometimes "annoying" wait, since reservations are only taken for six or more.

Ⓩ Aqua *Seafood*   26 | 25 | 25 | $79

Downtown | 252 California St. (bet. Battery & Front Sts.) | 415-956-9662 | www.aqua-sf.com

The "Le Bernardin of the Left Coast", this "five-star" Cal-French seafooder "still dazzles" Downtown's "glam" guests and "high rollers (a dwindling breed temporarily)" who "swim in" "after the market closes" for "masterful" meals served by a "splendid" staff; indeed, the "tasting menu with wine pairings" is as "extravagant" as the "over-the-top floral arrangements and huge mirrors", though "loud investment bankers" preclude any "whispers of romance"; N.B. the post-Survey departure of chef Laurent Manrique is not reflected in the Food score.

Ariake Japanese Ⓢ *Japanese*   ▽ 24 | 15 | 21 | $34

Outer Richmond | 5041 Geary Blvd. (bet. 14th & 15th Aves.) | 415-221-6210 | www.sfariake.com

Chef-owner Jin Kim prepares "superb house specialties" (highlighting "fish you won't find" elsewhere) and "takes care of everyone with good humor" at this "neighborhood sushi joint" in the Outer Richmond; it's "lower-key" than sibling Kabuto, but most feel "the food sells itself."

	FOOD	DECOR	SERVICE	COST

Arinell Pizza ∅ *Pizza* | 24 | 4 | 10 | $8

Mission | 509 Valencia St. (16th St.) | 415-255-1303
See review in East of San Francisco Directory.

Arlequin To Go Ⓢ *Mediterranean* | - | - | - | I

Hayes Valley | 384B Hayes St. (bet. Franklin & Gough Sts.) | 415-626-1211 |
www.arlequinwinemerchant.com
Part of the Absinthe and Arlequin Wine Merchant family that domi-
nates Hayes Valley's main drag, this casual, midpriced cafe serves
freshly made, Med-inspired breakfast and lunch fare, along with a
limited evening menu and housemade sorbets; space is tight and
plenty of customers opt for takeout, but insiders know to snag a table
on the sun-dappled secret backyard patio away from the hubbub;
N.B. closes at 8 PM.

Asia de Cuba *Asian/Cuban* | 20 | 24 | 20 | $58

Downtown | Clift Hotel | 495 Geary St. (Taylor St.) | 415-929-2300 |
www.chinagrillmanagement.com
"Dressing up is a must" when dropping into this "dark, chic" Philippe
Starck–designed Downtowner adjoining the "famous" Redwood Room
bar in the Clift Hotel, filled with "LA people", "Euros" and "twenty-
something bar-hoppers" sharing "huge", "tasty" Asian-Cuban fusion
plates for "out-of-control" costs; a bit of "waiter-actor-model attitude"
comes with the territory, riling reviewers who find the whole enterprise
"overexposed" and "passé."

AsiaSF Ⓜ *Asian/Californian* | 17 | 19 | 20 | $43

SoMa | 201 Ninth St. (Howard St.) | 415-255-2742 |
www.asiasf.com
"Take a walk on the wild side" at this "Bangkok-inspired" SoMa club
starring "really pretty" "waiter-esses" "lip-syncing to Madonna" in between "taking food and drink orders" for "bridal showers, girls' nights
out" and "unsuspecting visitors" in for a "San Francisco treat of another kind"; party-poopers pout "life's a drag already, why does dinner
have to be?", but the "overpriced" Cal-Asian small plates are "better
than expected" considering the "entertainment is worth the price of
admission"; N.B. prix fixe required Friday–Saturday, closed Monday–
Tuesday in the winter.

Ⓩ A16 *Italian* | 25 | 20 | 21 | $44

Marina | 2355 Chestnut St. (bet. Divisadero & Scott Sts.) | 415-771-2216 |
www.a16sf.com
"Like the Italian autostrada it's named for", this revved-up Marina
enoteca is a "guaranteed traffic jam" "loaded with impossibly good-
looking" *ragazzi* who "shout to be heard" over the "explosively noisy"
bar scene; "foodies" motor over to the "chef's bar to watch the *pizzaioli*
perform their magic", slinging "blistered thin-crust" pies, "sublime"
salumi and other Neapolitan specialties, matched by a "daunting" but
"dazzling" wine list that's "priced right"; N.B. a post-Survey chef
change is not reflected in the Food score.

Asqew Grill *Californian* | 16 | 11 | 14 | $16

Haight-Ashbury | 1607 Haight St. (Clayton St.) | 415-701-9301
Laurel Heights | 3415 California St. (bet. Laurel & Locust Sts.) |
415-386-5608

(continued)

Asqew Grill

Marina | 3348 Steiner St. (bet. Chestnut & Lombard Sts.) | 415-931-9201
www.asqewgrill.com

A "quick, easy" and "healthy alternative to fast food", this Californian chain skewers anything "you can imagine" into kebabs to "mix and match" with side dishes, attracting "meat-and-potato" eaters and "carb-shunners" alike; the grub is too "generic" for some, but it does the trick for "dependable takeout during the work week."

NEW Aurea *Californian*

| - | - | - | E |

Nob Hill | The Stanford Court | 905 California St. (bet. Pine & Stockton Sts.) | 415-989-1910 | www.aureasf.com

After a $325-million renovation, Nob Hill's historic Stanford Court hotel is courting foodies and tourists alike with a pricey Californian small-plates menu (from an ex-Quince chef) highlighting locally sourced fare; its lobby-level setting includes a glass-encased, floor-to-ceiling wine display, intimate 'cocktail cubbies' and an illuminated bar that doubles as a cafe by day.

Axum Cafe *Ethiopian*

| 20 | 8 | 17 | $18 |

Lower Haight | 698 Haight St. (Pierce St.) | 415-252-7912 | www.axumcafe.com

"Pleasantly spiced" meat and veggie stews and injera bread that you "eat with your hands and share with your friends" (or a "date") draw "students, political activists" and other Lower Haight habitués to this "modest little" Ethiopian; ok, it "isn't screaming ambiance" and the staff is "not in a hurry", but it's "hard to eat this well in SF for this price."

Z Aziza *Moroccan*

| 26 | 23 | 23 | $46 |

Outer Richmond | 5800 Geary Blvd. (22nd Ave.) | 415-752-2222 | www.aziza-sf.com

"*Iron Chef* winner" Mourad Lahlou crafts "phenomenal" Moroccan feasts that "show care from sourcing to plate" at this "nouveau" North African casbah whose "exceptional" cocktails, "personal" service and "beautiful tiled interior" that's "romantic as all get-out" "transport" you to Marrakesh "without the belly-dancing kitsch"; though it "seems misplaced" in the Outer Richmond, grateful guests feel the location "halves the price" of what it would be elsewhere; N.B. closed Tuesday.

NEW Baby Blues BBQ *BBQ/Southern*

| 21 | 15 | 17 | $25 |

Mission | 3149 Mission St. (Precita Ave.) | 415-896-4250 | www.babybluessf.com

The Mission's spankin'-new "sister to the original in LA" offers a big-tent approach to Southern BBQ, dishing out "fall-off-the-bone" Memphis- and Texas-style ribs and "delicious" North Carolina pulled pork sandwiches, plus sides like sautéed okra ("minus the slime!") and "addicting mac 'n' cheese" (aka "crack 'n' cheese"); even if service is "amateurish", the "old-drugstore" digs have an endearingly "funky" feel.

bacar *Californian/Mediterranean*

| 23 | 24 | 21 | $54 |

SoMa | 448 Brannan St. (bet. 3rd & 4th Sts.) | 415-904-4100 | www.bacarsf.com

An "impressive wall of wine" bolsters the "outstanding" by-the-glass selection – and "animated bar scene" – at this "lofty" SoMa Cal-Med

FOOD | DECOR | SERVICE | COST

serving up "lovely" fare and "live jazz" too; though it strikes some as "a little pricey" and "old hat", "happy-hour" deals (including $1 oysters on Fridays) and proximity to the "ballpark" are perks.

Bacco Ristorante *Italian*

23 | 19 | 21 | $42

Noe Valley | 737 Diamond St. (bet. Elizabeth & 24th Sts.) | 415-282-4969 | www.baccosf.com

"Expertly prepared" *cucina* "at better prices than most of its equals in the city" is the calling card of this "upscale trattoria" in Noe Valley that "feels and tastes like Italy"; there's no glitz, just "delightful" made-from-scratch risottos, pastas and gnocchi, a "homey" ambiance and a staff that's "happy to see you" and help you "navigate" the Boot-only wine list.

Baker Street Bistro Ⓜ *French*

21 | 16 | 20 | $35

Marina | 2953 Baker St. (bet. Greenwich & Lombard Sts.) | 415-931-1475

"High on charm", this Marina mainstay is "just as a bistro should" be, *avec* "crusty bread", "Paris sidewalk ambiance" and "sardine-can" seating that's "cozy" "in the fog"; it's a "favorite for brunch" on the "back patio", as well as "classic" Gallic meals like the "fantastic prix fixe dinner" that "you couldn't cook at home for less" (available nightly for $16.50, but only from 5:30–7 PM on Friday–Saturday); N.B. an off-shoot called 560 Central Park is slated to open in fall 2009.

Balboa Cafe *American*

19 | 17 | 18 | $35

Cow Hollow | 3199 Fillmore St. (Greenwich St.) | 415-921-3944 | www.plumpjack.com

It "always feels like hunting season" at this "old-timey", generation-spanning Cow Hollow pub (with a "crisp" new Mill Valley offshoot), which draws its share of "movers and shakers" for lunch, while later on the "new gentry's" young bucks "go for the burgers, the cougars" and the "hair-of-the-dog" brunch; despite the otherwise "plain" American grub, guests at the tables and the "sloppy Saturday night" bar all appreciate the "well-priced wine list."

Bambuddha Lounge Ⓢ Ⓜ *Pan-Asian*

17 | 19 | 15 | $36

Tenderloin | Phoenix Hotel | 601 Eddy St. (bet. Larkin & Polk Sts.) | 415-885-5088 | www.bambuddhalounge.com

"If you can nab a poolside seat", you might get into the groove of "after-work drinks" and "decent" (if "overpriced") Pan-Asian fusion plates at this "Miami"-like Tenderloiner plunked into the "cool" Phoenix hotel; otherwise "elders" protest the "snooty" staff and chant it's all "a bit much if you aren't in your 20s and able to wear low-slung jeans."

Bar Bambino Ⓜ *Italian*

23 | 21 | 21 | $41

Mission | 2931 16th St. (Mission St.) | 415-701-8466 | www.barbambino.com

"Reminiscent of a true Italian enoteca" despite its "gritty" locale in the Mission, this "hip" wine bar is "the bomb" swear nibblers who note its "amazing" house-cured salumi and cheeses, "homemade pastas" and other "carefully prepared" plates paired with "splendid" glasses by a staff that "really knows its stuff"; though the "communal tables" get "crowed and noisy" at night, the "covered courtyard" provides a "gorgeous" "oasis", even on a "drizzly February day."

	FOOD	DECOR	SERVICE	COST

Bar Crudo *Seafood* — 26 | - | 21 | $44

Western Addition | 655 Divisadero St. (Grove St.) | 415-409-0679 |
www.barcrudo.com

You better "be in the mood" for fish 'cause "that's all she wrote" (along
with "fantastic" Belgian ales) at this "beautiful-in-its-simplicity" raw
bar that relocated post-Survey from tight Downtown digs to this
roomier Western Addition perch; the brother-owners produce a
"top-quality" slate featuring "great oysters", "exquisite crudo" and the
"platonic ideal of clam chowder", though some warn the "bill adds up
if you're hungry."

Bar Jules Ⓜ *American* — 24 | 18 | 22 | $40

Hayes Valley | 609 Hayes St. (Laguna St.) | 415-621-5482 |
www.barjules.com

A "poor man's Chez Panisse", this "happening" Hayes Valley New
American offers an "ever changing", "brief but innovative" "blackboard" menu "featuring the day's fresh ingredients" in a colorful converted "coin-laundry" storefront, drawing "lines of hipsters and foodies
down the block"; it's a "chill" lunch or "pre-opera" stop (even if some
find it "steep"), "made all the better by fuss-free" waitresses wearing
"vintage aprons"; N.B. dinner-only Tuesdays, brunch-only Sundays.

Barney's Gourmet Hamburgers *Burgers* — 19 | 12 | 15 | $16

Marina | 3344 Steiner St. (bet. Chestnut & Lombard Sts.) | 415-563-0307
Noe Valley | 4138 24th St. (Castro St.) | 415-282-7770
www.barneyshamburgers.com

Bay Area "moms, dads and the next-generation of sustainable cheese-
burger addicts" are never "too far from one" of these "fab" "greasy
spoons" where the "juicy" meat and veggie burgers are capped off
with "abundant" toppings, "killer" curly fries and "crazy thick" milkshakes; despite "healthy" options, "forget dieting" here and don't expect tip-top service, but the patio offers a "pleasant" alternative to the
"nothing-special" digs.

Bar Tartine Ⓜ *Mediterranean* — 24 | 20 | 21 | $44

Mission | 561 Valencia St. (bet. 16th & 17th Sts.) | 415-487-1600 |
www.tartinebakery.com

"Adventurous", "locavore-friendly" Med dinners that start with that
"marvelous bread" and end with "sublime patisserie treats" "really up
the bar on Valencia Street" at this Mission hangout in a "rustic" old
printing shop, complete with a "gorgeous marble bar", "antler chandelier" and, "of course, the no-sign thing"; while the "whimsical" brunch
is pricier than at its bakery sib, the "moody, romantic setting" and "excellent" (if at times "too hip") service make it worth the extra dough;
N.B. a post-Survey chef change is not reflected in the Food score.

NEW **Basil Canteen** *Thai* — ▽ 21 | 21 | 19 | $26

SoMa | 1489 Folsom St. (11th St.) | 415-552-3963 | www.basilcanteen.com

"Flavorful", "contemporary" Bangkok street food for "fabulous"
prices, and "fun drinks" too, lure a "younger crowd" to this new SoMa
offshoot of Basil Thai, housed in a "hip brick-walled building" (formerly Public) that's "close to the clubs"; the "communal seating" isn't
for everyone, but since diners are still "discovering" the place, "it's not
much of a factor" yet.

	FOOD	DECOR	SERVICE	COST

Basil Thai Restaurant & Bar *Thai* | 22 | 18 | 20 | $28

SoMa | 1175 Folsom St. (bet. 7th & 8th Sts.) | 415-552-8999 | www.basilthai.com

"Like being in Chiang Mai" laud lovers of this "modern" Thai turning out "stunning", "authentic" and "affordable" eats (including "terrific curries") amid "chic" digs accommodating a "cross-section of the SoMa/Folsom crowd"; if you can't beat the "noon rush" for lunch, remember it's "super-fast for takeout."

Beach Chalet Brewery *American* | 15 | 21 | 15 | $31

Outer Sunset | 1000 Great Hwy. (bet. Fulton St. & Lincoln Way) | 415-386-8439 | www.beachchalet.com

"At the edge of Golden Gate Park", this Outer Sunset brewpub "overlooks the endless waterfront with a constant floorshow of windsurfers, dog-walkers and beach-goers", "never failing" to entertain "out-of-town guests" for "weekend brunch", "sunset dinner" or a "quick bite at the bar" with "all those microbrews"; the lobby's "historic Depression-era" murals and mosaics are "worth a visit" alone, but "locals sneer" the New American menu "needs an overhaul" and "service is MIA."

Belden Taverna ⊠ *Mediterranean* | 18 | 17 | 17 | $38

Downtown | 52 Belden Pl. (bet. Bush & Pine Sts.) | 415-986-8887 | www.belden-place.com

Despite the "interchangeable" feel of the sidewalk cafes on "quaint" Belden Place, this "low-key" New American–Med is a "pleasant" place to "nestle among the skyscrapers" and have a "leisurely outdoor meal"; still, some patrons are peeved by merely "passable" food and service, as well as "squished-in" seating.

Bella Trattoria *Italian* | ▽ 21 | 18 | 23 | $37

Inner Richmond | 3854 Geary Blvd. (3rd Ave.) | 415-221-0305 | www.bellatrattoriasf.com

"Regulars" "keep coming back" for the "homemade pastas" and other "dependable" Southern Italian specialties at this "excellent-value" Inner Richmond "hideaway" that's "sweetly, traditionally romantic to boot"; it's "by no means high-end gourmet, so don't go here to be surprised", but "golly do they try hard to please."

Beretta ● *Italian* | 23 | 19 | 20 | $36

Mission | 1199 Valencia St. (23rd St.) | 415-695-1199 | www.berettasf.com

"Top-end cocktails" and "amazing", "avant-garde" pizzas (plus "fabulous" small Italian plates) by Antica Trattoria's chef make a "thrilling combination" at this new Mission "must" whose "only problem is its own popularity"; amid "cool" though "deafening" digs, the "staff has to fight the crowds to get to your table" (communal or otherwise), "but hey", it's "heaven to have open so late" and for brunch too.

Best-o-Burger *Burgers* | 15 | 7 | 13 | $10

Downtown | 89 Belden Pl. (Pine St.) | 415-986-3808 | www.bestoburger.com

A bag o' "tasty", "greasy" Angus sliders downed with "delicious Strings and Ring-O's" will "leave you wanting a wet nap" confess FiDi workers who hit this Downtown take on "In-N-Out" (complete with its own 'secret menu'); still, some assess it's "not really the best-o-burgers", adding the "extras cost more than you'd like"; N.B. a recently added dining room and expanded menu are not reflected in the scores; closes at 4 PM most days, later on weekends.

Betelnut Pejiu Wu *Pan-Asian* | 22 | 21 | 19 | $39

Cow Hollow | 2030 Union St. (Buchanan St.) | 415-929-8855 | www.betelnutrestaurant.com

Sizzle-seekers say "skip Chinatown" and chow down on "innovative" Pan-Asian plates full of "explosive flavors" amid a "sultry" "Shanghai" beer-hall atmosphere at this Cow Hollow "scene", replete with "frilly drinks"; "service varies depending on the night", but "from the jumping bar to the warming fire in the back" to the inviting sidewalk tables, it's a "crowd-watching paradise."

B44 *Spanish* | 21 | 18 | 19 | $39

Downtown | 44 Belden Pl. (bet. Bush & Pine Sts.) | 415-986-6287 | www.b44sf.com

Serving "true-to-its-roots Catalan" tapas "long before the recent craze", this "loud", "well-priced" Downtown sidewalk cafe with an "amiable" staff is the "best way to get to Barcelona for the afternoon"; the "twinkling alley" is also "magical" at night, "especially after a bottle or three of Spanish red", though "blackened teeth is the price to pay for succulent squid ink paella" (one of 10 kinds offered).

☑ Big 4 *American* | 22 | 26 | 24 | $57

Nob Hill | Huntington Hotel | 1075 California St. (Taylor St.) | 415-771-1140 | www.big4restaurant.com

"Heads of state" and "bold-faced" regulars "party like it's 1899" at this Nob Hill "throwback to the robber baron age" whose "dark wood-paneled dining room", "fine", "hearty" New American fare and "exemplary" service "never lose their appeal"; it's always a boon for "getting business done", though things get a bit wilder during "game week" (showcasing "perfectly prepared" exotic eats) and in the "fabulous" piano bar whose "historic photos and railroad memorabilia" set the stage for martinis and a "tryst."

Bin 38 *Californian* | 19 | 19 | 17 | $39

Marina | 3232 Scott St. (Lombard St.) | 415-567-3838 | www.bin38.com

"Other than the bottleneck" of "twentysomethings" "when you first walk in", this "swanky" Marina boîte is a "charming" "place to mingle" over "bottles and bottles" of "wonderful" wines, especially by the "fire pit on the patio"; service could stand to be "improved", though, and while most call the Californian small plates "tasty", they can add up to "expensive" tabs.

Bistro Boudin *Californian* | 19 | 16 | 16 | $26

Fisherman's Wharf | 160 Jefferson St. (near Pier 43½) | 415-928-1849 | www.boudinbakery.com

Though it's a "total touristy cliché", this "home of the legendary" (and "much maligned") "sourdough bread bowl" "can't be beat" for a "more-than-chowder lunch" of Californian soups and salads along with "beautiful" Bay views from the second-floor terrace; it's "on the Wharf, so overpriced by definition", but after the meal it's still "fun to watch the bread-making" at the bakery downstairs and "pick up the obligatory" loaf.

	FOOD	DECOR	SERVICE	COST

Bistro Clovis ⑤ *French*

21	17	20	$40

Hayes Valley | 1596 Market St. (Franklin St.) | 415-864-0231 |
www.bistroclovis.com

"Ooh-la-la!", this Hayes Valley "secret" delights diners with its "well-priced, well-executed" French bistro dishes and wine flights served in a "low-key" atmosphere; while it's "a bit ho-hum" to some, many dub it a "favorite pre-opera spot" "without the waits and cost" of competitors; N.B. lunch-only on Mondays.

NEW Bistro St. Germain *French*

-	-	-	M

Lower Haight | 518 Haight St. (Fillmore St.) | 415-626-6262
Everything's coming up bistros in this economy, as evidenced by the arrival of this new Lower Haight French from the owners of Le P'tit Laurent; the casual storefront space is dressed up with a stylized mural of the Paris skyline, providing an apt backdrop for the menu of moderately priced crowd favorites such as moules, duck confit and tarte Tatin.

NEW Bistro 24 ●Ⓜ *American*
(fka City Grill)

-	-	-	M

Noe Valley | 4123 24th St. (Castro St.) | 415-285-2400
Located just a few blocks up from the main 24th Street drag, this new Noe Valley American bistro (a co-venture from the Lupa folks and former Contigo chef) offers a seasonally driven small-plates menu that runs the gamut from grilled calamari salad to mac 'n' cheese, along with a few larger offerings like family-style fried chicken; it's all served until midnight in an understated dining room filled with dark-wood booths and lively music; N.B. weekend brunch is in the works.

❷ BIX *American/French*

23	26	23	$55

Downtown | 56 Gold St. (bet. Montgomery & Sansome Sts.) | 415-433-6300 |
www.bixrestaurant.com

"Sam Spade would feel right at home" at this "sultry" Downtown supper club with a "Prohibition"-style "back-alley" entrance, "gorgeous" "deco interior" and "fine jazz" every night; it's a "throwback" to the days of "waiters in white tuxes", "big ol' martinis" and diners "dressed to the nines", but most feel the "delicious" "decadent" American-French menu has "kept up with the times"; N.B. lunch served Fridays only (Monday–Friday in December until Christmas).

Blowfish Sushi To Die For *Japanese*

20	19	17	$42

Mission | 2170 Bryant St. (20th St.) | 415-285-3848 | www.blowfishsushi.com
"Fugu is just a prop" at these "hyperactive" "post-dot-com-bubble scenes" in the Mission and San Jose where the "assault" of "anime on the walls" and "140-bpm house" makes you "feel like you've landed in a hip part of Tokyo"; despite "lovely" presentations, the "steeply priced" rolls might not "'blow' you away", but then again "you won't pick up a hot 28-year-old marketing chick at 'Sushi Express'" or get served saketinis by a "tattooed, pierced staff."

Blue Barn Gourmet *Californian*

22	16	17	$15

Marina | 2105 Chestnut St. (Steiner St.) | 415-441-3232 |
www.bluebarngourmet.com

"Organic, local veggies" (many from the owners' Oak Hill Farm) and other "fresh" ingredients go into the "fancy make-your-own-salads" and "addictive" sandwiches (like "terrific" grilled cheese) at this "cute" Marina spot; the counter service is "minimal" and there's "not too much seating", so "foodies" admonish "don't hang out and hog the tables!"

Blue Bottle Café *Californian/Coffeehouse* | 23 | 17 | 18 | $12 |

SoMa | Mint Plaza | 66 Mint St. (Jessie St.) | 415-495-3394 | www.bluebottlecoffee.net

Blue Bottle Kiosk *Californian/Coffeehouse*

NEW **Embarcadero** | 1 Ferry Bldg. (Embarcadero) | 510-653-3394

Hayes Valley | 315 Linden St. (Gough St.) | 415-252-7535 ⊘ www.bluebottlecoffee.net

**Rooftop Garden Blue Bottle
Coffee Bar** *Californian/Coffeehouse*

NEW **SoMa** | SFMOMA | 151 Third St. (bet. Howard & Mission Sts.) | 415-243-0455 | www.sfmoma.org/pages/coffee_bar

"It's true", the "small-batch coffees" at this "cult" roaster's SoMa sit-down outpost (and its newer satellites) are "amazing" affirm fans who wait in "ridiculous" lines to "savor" "phenomenally crafted" drinks along with "delectable" Californian breakfasts and lunches; some dub it "hipster hell" and knock the "nervy" prices, but factoring in the "tat-tooed-barista" wizardry behind the "mesmerizing siphon contrap-tion", "it's coffee and a show, really."

Blue Plate, The Ⓩ *American* | 24 | 18 | 21 | $37 |

Mission | 3218 Mission St. (bet. 29th & Valencia Sts.) | 415-282-6777 | www.blueplatesf.com

Dishing out "first-rate", "jazzed-up comfort food" "before everyone jumped on it", this "adorable" New American Mission joint exudes a "real homespun feel" despite its "party vibe" and post-ironic PBRs; still, "don't expect to just drop by", since a "loyal following" keeps the seats filled, whether "at the bar to watch the action" in the open kitchen, or out on the "garden patio."

Bocadillos Ⓩ *Spanish* | 22 | 19 | 19 | $34 |

North Beach | 710 Montgomery St. (bet. Jackson & Washington Sts.) | 415-982-2622 | www.bocasf.com

"Super Spanish mini-sandwiches" lend their name to this "stylish" North Beach boîte (by Piperade's Gerald Hirigoyen) that wows with "big-tasting" Basque small plates and "affordable" Spanish wines; it's worth "fighting" the "elbow-bumping" crowds for lunch or a "pre-party bite", but "roll in before 7 PM for the best seats" at the bar or communal table.

Bodega Bistro *Vietnamese* | 25 | 12 | 20 | $25 |

Tenderloin | 607 Larkin St. (Eddy St.) | 415-921-1218

"Quite possibly the best Vietnamese in Little Saigon", this "strangely named" eatery "looks like a total dive", but champions of its "shaking-beef-olicious" cooking commend it for "Slanted Door food at Tenderloin prices"; with "some swell French dishes" and "welcoming" service to boot, most "overlook the cheesy decor."

Boogaloos *Southwestern* | 20 | 14 | 19 | $15 |

Mission | 3296 22nd St. (Valencia St.) | 415-824-4088 | www.boogaloossf.com

For "cheap, abundant" and "wholesome" Southwestern "morning and midday" fare (including "vegan options") and "bottomless cups of

| | FOOD | DECOR | SERVICE | COST |

coffee", "boogie" to this colorful converted corner pharmacy where "Mission hipsters" blister "in the sun" enduring "epic" weekend waits; the staff is too "cool" for some, but game guests "have a blast" anyway.

Boulette's Larder American

| 25 | 18 | 19 | $38 |

Embarcadero | 1 Ferry Bldg. (Market St.) | 415-399-1155 | www.bouletteslarder.com

The Ferry Building's "own Phoenician trading station", brimming with "hard-to-find" ingredients for sale, is "not your standard place to eat" but a "foodie's delight" for "marvelous", "Slow Food–style" New American breakfasts and lunches; while "surly" service is a sore point, Sunday brunch (complete with "superb" beignets) remains "wildly popular" with crowds "spilling out" from the "communal table" onto the Embarcadero's patio; N.B. the dining room's open for weekday breakfast, lunch and Sunday brunch, as well as for private parties.

⊉ Boulevard American

| 27 | 25 | 26 | $68 |

Embarcadero | Audiffred Bldg. | 1 Mission St. (Steuart St.) | 415-543-6084 | www.boulevardrestaurant.com

A "San Francisco icon" that only "improves with age" (like its vaunted "wine vault"), chef/co-owner Nancy Oakes' "posh" "power-lunch" and "big-night-out" belle epoque brasserie facing the Embarcadero still "crams" 'em in and leaves 'em "smiling" with a trifecta of "outstanding" "French-inspired" New American food, "enchanting" Bay views and a staff that "treats you like royalty without the attitude"; it takes a lot of cash and patience to "get past" its "revolving doors", but those who've succeeded swoon "the memory still lingers."

Brandy Ho's Chinese

| 19 | 13 | 17 | $25 |

Castro | 4068 18th St. (bet. Castro & Hartford Sts.) | 415-252-8000
Chinatown | 217 Columbus Ave. (bet. Broadway St. & Pacific Ave.) | 415-788-7527 | www.brandyhos.com

Nicknamed "Brandy Hots", these "affordable" Hunan haunts are known for their "spicy" MSG-free "Chinese-American" eats – along with smoked meats "better than anything you could dig up in the deep South" – all "served within minutes of ordering"; the "hole-in-the-wall" Chinatown locale wows "tourists" with "flaming theatrics", while its "sleek" new Castro sib is "prettier", though some doubters dismiss both as just "Ho-hum."

Brazen Head, The ●⌀ American

| 20 | 20 | 20 | $38 |

Cow Hollow | 3166 Buchanan St. (Greenwich St.) | 415-921-7600 | www.brazenheadsf.com

It's "as if you need a secret password" to get into this "dark", "no-name" Cow Hollow "locals' joint" for catching up over "hearty cock-tails", "decent" steaks and other "high-end" American "pub food" "served till 1 AM"; the staff treats you "like a regular even if you're not", as you "brush up against" "trustafarians, bridge-workers" and off-work "chefs" all "jostling for a stool"; N.B. cash only.

Brenda's French Soul Food Creole/Southern

| 24 | 12 | 19 | $19 |

Civic Center | 652 Polk St. (bet. Eddy & Turk Sts.) | 415-345-8100 | www.frenchsoulfood.com

"Off-the-hook" Southern-Creole eats "straight from New Orleans" – from "buttery delicious biscuits" to "outstanding" grits to "proper

	FOOD	DECOR	SERVICE	COST

oyster po' boys" – lead daytime devotees to endure "Dostoyevsky-novel"-length waits for a table at this "small" Civic Center "gem"; the "watermelon iced tea and chicory coffee are always just right" and the krewe keeps everyone "content" "no matter how hectic" it gets – so now "how come it won't open for dinner?"; N.B. closed Tuesdays.

Brindisi Cucina di Mare ⊠ *Italian/Seafood*   ▽ 18 | 16 | 17 | $43

Downtown | 88 Belden Pl. (Pine St.) | 415-593-8000 |
www.brindisicucina.com
Set in one of Downtown's "cutest alleys", this "cozy" Southern Italian delivers a "European" feel, from its "chic/touristy" interior to the "happening" sidewalk scene; still, responses to the seafood-focused menu range from "all-around satisfactory" to "wildly inconsistent", and some cite "a lot of attitude" for such a "small, cramped place."

Brother's Korean Restaurant ● *Korean*   23 | 8 | 15 | $28

Inner Richmond | 4014 Geary Blvd. (bet. 4th & 5th Aves.) | 415-668-2028
Inner Richmond | 4128 Geary Blvd. (bet. 5th & 6th Aves.) | 415-387-7991
"Volcanic piles of charcoal" are the key to this "top-notch" "grill-your-own" Korean BBQ duo that's "so good it has two locations within blocks of each other" in the Inner Richmond; "affordable" tabs and frequent "on-the-house" extras help make up for "long waits", so "you'll leave full and happy" (despite your "smoky" clothes).

B Star Bar Ⓜ *Pan-Asian*   22 | 18 | 21 | $27

Inner Richmond | 127 Clement St. (bet. 2nd & 3rd Aves.) | 415-933-9900 |
www.bstarbar.com
"Burma Superstar's hipper, more experimental younger brother" "stands independently" with its own "creative" Pan-Asian fusion and "fresh drinks", luring Inner Richmonders to the "little covered patio" for a "fun brunch"; it also offers "many of the same dishes" as the original "without the long-ass wait" and "chaotic din", though a few curmudgeons with unwavering cravings say it still "can't hold a candle to its sister, the superstar."

Buca di Beppo *Italian*   14 | 16 | 16 | $27

SoMa | 855 Howard St. (bet. 4th & 5th Sts.) | 415-543-7673 |
www.bucadibeppo.com
See review in South of San Francisco Directory.

Burger Joint *Burgers*   18 | 11 | 15 | $14

AT&T Park | 242 King St. (bet. 3rd & 4th Sts.) | 415-371-1600
Lower Haight | 700 Haight St. (Pierce St.) | 415-864-3833
Mission | 807 Valencia St. (19th St.) | 415-824-3494 ⇗
www.burgerjointsf.com
"When you get the hankerin' for a juicy burger" and "thick fries" downed with "delicious shakes", this retro "diner-style" Bay Area chainlet offers a prime "patty fix" (at a slightly "upscale" price); "free-range chicken and Niman Ranch beef" translate into "guilt-free meals", but critics contend it's "only ok" and would like to see "more options" and "toppings" on the menu.

BurgerMeister ⇗ *Burgers*   19 | 11 | 14 | $15

Castro | 138 Church St. (Duboce Ave.) | 415-437-2874
Cole Valley | 86 Carl St. (Cole St.) | 415-566-1274

(continued)

(continued)

BurgerMeister

North Beach | 759 Columbus Ave. (Greenwich St.) | 415-296-9907
www.burgermeistersf.com

"The meister is the master" rave regulars of these "fine stops" flipping "killer" burgers with enough toppings and alternatives (including wings and things) "to make anyone happy"; portions "aren't small or cheap", but "you're paying for" organic beef, microbrews on tap and "real" Mitchell's ice cream in the milkshakes, all of which deliver "a month's worth of calories in 20 minutes, as they should"; N.B. cash only.

Burma Superstar *Burmese*   25 | 14 | 18 | $25

Inner Richmond | 309 Clement St. (4th Ave.) | 415-387-2147 |
www.burmasuperstar.com

For "a taste of Burma without the junta", head to this "wildly popular" Inner Richmond "hole-in-the-wall" (with new Alameda and Oakland offshoots) where the "refreshing" "mash-up of exotic textures and flavors" in specialties such as "addictive tea-leaf salad" and "rad" coconut rice helps "justify" the lines; so "leave your number on the waiting list" and "shop along the street" before you're called, or else opt for takeout.

Bursa Kebab *Mediterranean*   22 | 18 | 22 | $29

West Portal | 60 W. Portal Ave. (bet. Ulloa & Vicente Sts.) | 415-564-4006

This "out-of-the-way" Mediterranean sleeper impresses West Portal locals with its "succulent" Turkish kebabs and other Med "favorites" served with "hot housemade bread" in "prompt" fashion; more "posh" than the usual skewer joint, its newly decorated dark-blue interior is enlivened with "belly dancing on the weekends."

Bushi-tei *Asian Fusion/French*   24 | 24 | 24 | $63

Japantown | 1638 Post St. (bet. Laguna & Webster Sts.) | 415-440-4959 |
www.bushi-tei.com

NEW Bushi-tei Bistro *Asian Fusion/French*

Japantown | 1581 Webster St. (Post St.) | 415-409-4959

"Per Se meets Nobu, without the PR" at this "sublime" Asian fusion "find" showcasing chef Seiji Wakabayashi's "extraordinary", "delicate" French-Japanese fare in a "beautiful" "Zen" setting accented with "modern" touches and "traditional rough-hewn wood" in Japantown; despite "phenomenal" service, it's a tad "stiff" and steep for some, but "incredibly priced" lunches help keep it accessible; N.B. its more affordable bistro spin-off recently launched down the street.

Butler & The Chef Bistro, The Ⓜ *French*   20 | 19 | 18 | $21

SoMa | 155A South Park St. (bet. 2nd & 3rd Sts.) | 415-896-2075 |
www.thebutlerandthechefbistro.com

"Everything is fresh and French" at this "super-cute", green-certified daytime cafe on a "tree-lined street across from South Park" with service "spilling onto the sidewalk"; though the "food isn't surprising", customers coo over the "amazing" croque monsieur and "quiche of the day", as well as "delicious truffles that come with the check."

Butterfly Ⓜ *Asian/Californian*   20 | 22 | 19 | $44

Embarcadero | Pier 33 (Bay St.) | 415-864-8999 | www.butterflysf.com

Right "on the water at Pier 33" (and "slightly off the beaten Wharf"), this "cavernous" Embarcadero perch provides "picturesque Bay views"

	FOOD	DECOR	SERVICE	COST

and "better than anticipated", somewhat "expensive" Cal-Asian eats; it's best during daylight or "happy hour" to soak up the "wonderful waterfront atmosphere" and potent drinks, but on weekend nights, diners wish they'd "turn the volume down" and ramp the service up.

Cafe Bastille ☒ *French*

	18	15	16	$37

Downtown | 22 Belden Pl. (bet. Bush & Pine Sts.) | 415-986-5673 | www.cafebastille.com

Prime for "power lunches" and "the first place to begin on Bastille Day", this "cute" sidewalk bistro on Belden Place charms with "good French fare", "lots of noise" and decor that "transports us back to the Left Bank"; "don't get bothered by the barkers" and the "supercilious" staff advise *amis*, since the "lively" "street scene", "awesome jazz musicians on Friday nights" and "reasonable" tabs "will help you reclaim your cheer."

Café Claude *French*

	21	19	19	$38

Downtown | 7 Claude Ln. (Sutter St.) | 415-392-3515 | www.cafeclaude.com

"Squint your eyes" and "pretend" to be in the "City of Lights" at this "charming" "European-styled bistro" hidden in a Downtown alleyway, serving "delish", "affordable" French fare; service ranges from "competent" to "marginal", but when the "live jazz" gets "swinging" (Thursday–Saturday), it's "great for a date."

Café de la Presse *French*

	18	18	16	$34

Downtown | 352 Grant Ave. (bet. Bush & Sutter Sts.) | 415-249-0900 | www.aqua-sf.com/cdlp

"A mix of tourists and Euros" "enjoy" the bonhomie and "basic" but "pleasing" bistro cooking at this "busy" Downtown corner cafe that "says France all over it, down to the magazines on the shelf"; "well-located" "between Chinatown and Union Square", it's *très bien* for everything from a "mid-afternoon coffee" to a "pre-theater dinner", "as long as you're not in a hurry" – about the service, patrons pout *"vive la indifférence!"*

Café du Soleil *French*

	∇ 19	18	18	$21

Lower Haight | 200 Fillmore St. (Waller St.) | 415-934-8637

"Un café français" for any season, this sunny Lower Haight hangout near Duboce Park isn't fancy, but provides "fantastic French bread and pastries" (delivered throughout the day by La Boulange) as well as "good" sandwiches, salads and coffees; it also lures in locals with a "friendly" staff and free WiFi, though it tends to get crowded, so "good luck finding a table with an outlet for a computer plug."

Café Flore *American*

	15	15	12	$19

Castro | 2298 Market St. (Noe St.) | 415-621-8579 | www.cafeflore.com

This "quirky" classic corner sidewalk cafe is an "obligatory" stop in the Castro, "especially on weekend mornings when all the cute boys roll out of bed for coffee and brunch", or at night for a "glass of wine" "before hitting the clubs"; sure, it's more "about the people" and the "outrageous cruising" than the "ok" American eats, but there's no better place to "hang out at a sunny outdoor table" and "watch the world go by."

	FOOD	DECOR	SERVICE	COST

Café Gratitude *Vegan*

| 16 | 15 | 17 | $24 |

Mission | 2400 Harrison St. (20th St.) | 415-824-4652 |
www.cafegratitude.com

When "you're in a funk" or "need a good detox", these "New Age" cafes proffering "guilt-free" raw vegan dishes and "worthy" desserts named with "affirmations" (such as "I am Abundant" and "I am Cheerful") are a real "veggie hoot"; "hard-core" habitués are truly "grateful" for the grub, but critics find it "cultlike" and "cloying" ("I am annoyed") and prefer finding inner peace "without the high and mighty" prices.

Cafe Jacqueline Ⓜ *French*

| 25 | 18 | 19 | $46 |

North Beach | 1454 Grant Ave. (bet. Green & Union Sts.) | 415-981-5565

If "sharing a soufflé" with a "bottle of champagne" is your "idea of heaven", then plan for a "three-hour meal" at this "perfect date place" in North Beach; neither the "cholesterol" bump nor the "moody" garçons can deflate the "rewards" of "watching" the "queen" herself "whipping" up her "outstanding" sweet and savory specialties to "a loving puffiness" "in the back kitchen."

CAFÉ KATi Ⓢ Ⓜ *Asian Fusion*

| 21 | 15 | 19 | $47 |

Japantown | 1963 Sutter St. (bet. Fillmore & Webster Sts.) | 415-775-7313 |
www.cafekati.com

"Unique", "beautifully presented" dishes make an impression at this Asian fusion pioneer near Japantown that's a "great alternative to fancy restaurants", particularly "before going to the Kabuki theater"; still, many cite "inconsistent" cooking, "cramped" seating and service at a "snail's pace", though with the recent return of chef-owner Kirk Webber "back in good health", hopefuls predict it "should shine again."

Cafe Maritime ◗ *Seafood*

| 21 | 17 | 22 | $38 |

Marina | 2417 Lombard St. (Scott St.) | 415-885-2530 |
www.cafemaritimesf.com

Martha's Vineyard meets the Marina at this "upbeat" neighborhood seafooder swimming with an "under-the-sea atmosphere" and "attentive" service till the "wee hours" (1 AM); though some mateys say there are "no surprises", the fish is "well prepared" and a "wonderful value", and "late-night oysters on the half shell" are always a hit.

Café Tiramisu Ⓢ *Italian*

| 20 | 17 | 17 | $42 |

Downtown | 28 Belden Pl. (bet. Bush & Pine Sts.) | 415-421-7044 |
www.cafetiramisu.com

With its "fresco-lined walls" and "festive" atmosphere, this "noisy" cafe serving "wonderful" homemade pastas and other "traditional" Northern Italian dishes on Downtown's Belden Place feels like a true "Italian trattoria"; some cite "uneven" quality, but sidewalk scenesters are appeased since "outside heaters make the whole area warm, even on a chilly San Francisco night."

Caffe Delle Stelle *Italian*

| 16 | 15 | 17 | $34 |

Hayes Valley | 395 Hayes St. (Gough St.) | 415-252-1110

Show-goers stop for "pasta and Prosecco" served "pronto" at this "convivial" Hayes Valley trattoria delivering "old-fashioned Italian" meals in a "convenient location"; the food is "rarely better than decent" and the Tuscan decor is "nothing fancy" either, but at least it's "low-cost" "before you spend zillions on the opera or ballet", with "free bubbly water" to boot.

Caffè Macaroni 🅱️⇄ *Italian* | 20 | 12 | 18 | $31 |

North Beach | 59 Columbus Ave. (Jackson St.) | 415-956-9737 | www.caffemacaroni.com

About as "authentic as North Beach" gets these days, this "crowded" "postage stamp" of a trattoria "away from the noisy crowds" delivers a trifecta of "taste, value and charm"; "don't be deceived" by the decor (featuring real pasta glued to the "low ceilings") aver *amici* who insist that the staff's "colorful patter" and "people-watching on Columbus Avenue" ensure a "fun" time.

Caffè Museo *Italian/Mediterranean* | 18 | 14 | 10 | $22 |

SoMa | San Francisco Museum of Modern Art | 151 Third St. (bet. Howard & Mission Sts.) | 415-357-4500 | www.caffemuseo.com

"Artful surroundings" deserve "artful food" attest aficionados of this "minimalist" museum cafe in the SFMOMA serving "light", "simple" organic Italian-Med fare, along with "good coffee" and plenty of "sun"; it's a "nice respite" "before you return to the galleries" or nearby convention center, but critics find the scene too "hectic" and the menu "too lacking in variety for a full sit-down meal", though it's open for dinner on Thursdays; N.B. closed Wednesdays.

Cajun Pacific 🅱️Ⓜ️ *Cajun* | ▽ 20 | 14 | 19 | $29 |

Outer Sunset | 4542 Irving St. (47th Ave.) | 415-504-6652 | www.cajunpacific.com

Cajun cooking meets the Pacific Ocean (almost) at this "secret" Outer Sunset nook offering a "fantastic" seafood-focused menu that changes according to "what's fresh", served with "verve" and "N'Awlins" style; it's generally open Thursday–Saturday, but "cult" fans say it's "key to get on their e-mail list" to "stay in-the-know about special theme-dinners" and closures due to catering gigs; P.S. "BYO suggested."

Campton Place *Californian/Mediterranean* | 24 | 25 | 25 | $74 |

Downtown | Campton Place Hotel | 340 Stockton St. (bet. Post & Sutter Sts.) | 415-955-5555 | www.camptonplace.com

"Even though it's changed hands", this "expensive" hotel "hideaway" near Union Square is still a bastion of "civilized dining" where the "well-prepared" Cal-Med cuisine (with Indian accents) is presented by a "pampering" staff; it's "one of the few" places to wear "your fancy duds" and "enjoy your own conversation and not the next table's", so while there's "nothing radical about the menu" or the "staid" ambiance, "that's exactly how" the "discerning clientele" likes it.

Candybar Ⓜ️ *Dessert* | ▽ 17 | 18 | 17 | $23 |

Western Addition | 1335 Fulton St. (Divisadero St.) | 415-673-7078 | www.candybarsf.com

"Eat your meal before" swinging by this Western Addition dessert bar, or better yet, "skip dinner altogether" and dine on "decadent" sweets that are "small and expensive but so intense that a larger portion would probably make your mouth explode"; it has a "nice lounge feel" for playing a round of board games or nursing a "nightcap", but a scaled-back menu prompts cries for better "savory" bites and a "more inspired" wine list.

	FOOD	DECOR	SERVICE	COST

⛉ Canteen Ⓜ *Californian* — 27 | 15 | 22 | $45

Tenderloin | Commodore Hotel | 817 Sutter St. (Jones St.) | 415-928-8870 | www.sfcanteen.com

"Dennis Leary's labor of love is one-of-a-kind" declare "foodies" about the chef-owner's "delectable", "high-style" Californian dinners (and "awesome brunch") served in a Tenderloin "retro hotel diner" no bigger than a "clerk's office"; with three nightly shifts, it's a "get-in, get-fed, get-out", reservations-required deal (especially for Tuesday prix fixes), but the open kitchen, "personable service" and strong "value" add to its "must-try" cachet.

Capannina *Italian* — 24 | 20 | 24 | $43

Cow Hollow | 1809 Union St. (Octavia St.) | 415-409-8001 | www.capanninasf.com

"Italian through-and-through", this "homey" Cow Hollow ristorante serving up a taste of Capri and beyond "stands out among a crowded field" thanks to "solid" "regional" *cibo* and a "hospitable" padrone who's always there to "greet guests"; all in all, sober assessors say it's not quite special-occasion material, but "more than sufficient for date night" or the early-bird "deal."

Carnelian Room *Californian* — 18 | 25 | 20 | $69

Downtown | Bank of America Ctr. | 555 California St., 52nd fl. (bet. Kearny & Montgomery Sts.) | 415-433-7500 | www.carnelianroom.com

"Not just for gawking tourists", this "fancy" Downtown aerie at the "top of the BofA building" boasts "unrivaled panoramic views", making it a natural for "impressing a date" or "bringing the in-laws"; while critics call the "ok", "predictable" Californian food "overpriced and underflavored", some recommend Sunday brunch as "a bit more in line" with the tab.

Catch *Seafood* — 18 | 18 | 17 | $40

Castro | 2362 Market St. (bet. Castro & 16th Sts.) | 415-431-5000 | www.catchsf.com

The "A-list gay crowd" sips cocktails and dives into "deep-fried olives" at the "spiffy bar" and patio with a "roaring outdoor fire" at this Castro "people-watching" place; otherwise opinions vary over whether the fish is "delish" or "bland" and "overpriced", and some assess "when they have you in and out for a three-course dinner in under 50 minutes, it doesn't feel that special."

Cav Wine Bar & Kitchen Ⓢ *Mediterranean* — 20 | 19 | 20 | $40

Hayes Valley | 1666 Market St. (bet. Franklin & Gough Sts.) | 415-437-1770 | www.cavwinebar.com

A "limited menu and limitless wine selection" make this "long, narrow" Hayes Valley boîte handy for a "fast", "creative" Mediterranean bite "before a concert", but even "better for a glass of wine (or two or three)" "perfectly matched with sipping snacks"; reviewers report the "knowledgeable" bar staff is refreshingly "without snobbery" and the cost is "in step" with the times.

Cha Am Thai *Thai* — 19 | 14 | 17 | $22

SoMa | Museum Parc | 701 Folsom St. (3rd St.) | 415-546-9711 | www.chaamthaisf.com

Offering "consistent", "classic Thai food with a light touch", these separately owned eateries may "not be mind-blowing", but they're

	FOOD	DECOR	SERVICE	COST

nicer "than the usual mom-and-pop places"; the SoMa spot is sought out for "informal" meals "when at a conference at the Moscone Center", while the Berkeley longtimer, with a somewhat "dated" tree-house look, is a "student hangout" near the gourmet ghetto.

Cha Cha Cha *Caribbean*

| 20 | 16 | 16 | $27 |

Haight-Ashbury | 1801 Haight St. (Shrader St.) | 415-386-5758
Mission | 2327 Mission St. (bet. 19th & 20th Sts.) | 415-648-0504
www.cha3.com

Whipping up "tasty" Caribbean" tapas and a "party vibe", these Haight and Mission hot spots tricked out with "wall altars" and other "campy" decor are "mega-packed" with "twentysomethings" "getting tanked" and chowing down "for very little cha-cha-ching"; yeah, they're "noisy and crowded" and the waits are "hellish", but after "a pitcher or three" of "amazing" sangria, "it doesn't seem to bother much."

☑ Chapeau! Ⓜ *French*

| 26 | - | 24 | $51 |

Inner Richmond | 126 Clement St. (bet. 2nd & 3rd Aves.) | 415-750-9787 | www.chapeausf.com

Amis adore the "personal service" that really "does deserve an exclamation mark", making the "outstanding" country French fare "taste even better" at this Inner Richmond bistro that relocated post-Survey to owners Philippe and Ellen Gardelle's spiffier former Clémentine space; prix fixe "deals" and early-bird "steals" (Sunday–Thursday) are another plus.

Charanga ☒ Ⓜ *Pan-Latin*

| ▽ 21 | 16 | 19 | $31 |

Mission | 2351 Mission St. (bet. 19th & 20th Sts.) | 415-282-1813 | www.charangasf.com

"While everyone is waiting an hour" elsewhere for tapas, insiders "walk right" over to this Mission haunt cranking out "super-delicious", "(not-so) small" Pan-Latin plates and "Costa Rican specialties" to share with "fabulous drinks" in a "fun atmosphere"; service can lag when it's "packed", but overall it's a real "bargain,"

Chaya Brasserie *French/Japanese*

| 22 | 21 | 20 | $52 |

Embarcadero | 132 The Embarcadero (bet. Howard & Mission Sts.) | 415-777-8688 | www.thechaya.com

"Sexy" and "sophisticated", this Embarcadero expense-accounter proffering "carefully made" French-Japanese dishes (including sushi) has "all the trappings of its SoCal origins" – "flashy crowd", a "wonderful happy hour" and "atmosphere to the max"; still, it's "suited" to San Francisco with its "stunning views of the Bay Bridge", letting you "watch the ships go by" even if your ship doesn't come in at the bar.

Cha-Ya Vegetarian

| 22 | 12 | 17 | $23 |

Japanese Restaurant ⍗ *Japanese/Vegan*
Mission | 762 Valencia St. (bet. 18th & 19th Sts.) | 415-252-7825
See review in East of San Francisco Directory.

Cheesecake Factory *American*

| 16 | 17 | 16 | $29 |

Downtown | Macy's | 251 Geary St., 8th fl. (bet. Powell & Stockton Sts.) | 415-391-4444 | www.cheesecakefactory.com

The menu's "mammoth" – and "so are the crowds" – at this "family-pleasing" chain link in the Downtown Macy's where the "endless"

FOOD | DECOR | SERVICE | COST

American options arrive in equally "colossal" portions (ironically, "they give you so much there's no room" for their "heavenly" namesake desserts); despite an "ordinary" setting (apart from the Union Square view), this "well-oiled machine" stays so "busy" that it's best accessed "off-hours."

Cheese Steak Shop *Cheesesteaks*

23 | 6 | 14 | $11

Western Addition | 1716 Divisadero St. (bet. Bush & Sutter Sts.) | 415-346-3712 | www.cheesesteakshop.com

"Salty, cheesy and greasy – just as I remember them" wax "old Philadelphians" here in "coronary country", a chain of sandwich shops pumping out "the closest thing on the West Coast to East Coast cheesesteaks", along with "hoagies", "Tastykakes", "Amoroso rolls" and other Philly favorites; service varies and there's no ambiance to speak of, just "down 'n' dirty", "gooey" goodness.

Chenery Park Ⓜ *American*

21 | 19 | 22 | $39

Glen Park | 683 Chenery St. (Diamond St.) | 415-337-8537 | www.chenerypark.com

Proof positive that "fine dining and family-friendly" can coexist, this "tony" yet "intimate" "neighborhood restaurant" in "sleepy Glen Park" provides "consistent" New American–Cajun "comfort food" as well as the "latest gourmet specialty" (and "neat" drink list) with "zero attitude"; the "lovely" staff "truly welcomes" children, "especially for the Tuesday night kids' club" – but "avoid" those dinners "if you aren't bringing the tots"; N.B. a spin-off, Pi Bar, is set to open soon at 1432 Valencia Street.

Chez Maman *French*

22 | 14 | 20 | $27

Potrero Hill | 1453 18th St. (bet. Connecticut & Missouri Sts.) | 415-824-7166 | www.chezmamansf.com

"Jump up on a stool" at this "endearing" "Parisian" "luncheonette" on Potrero Hill plating up "unapologetically" Gallic "classics" along with "some French attitude, *oui*?"; there's not much seating (and a "nine-percent incline" on the sidewalk), but it's a "wonderful" alternative to sib Chez Papa that doesn't "break the bank."

Chez Papa Bistrot *French*

23 | 20 | 21 | $45

Potrero Hill | 1401 18th St. (Missouri St.) | 415-824-8210

Chez Papa Resto Ⓩ *French*

SoMa | 414 Jessie St. (bet. Market & Mission Sts.) | 415-546-4134 | www.chezpapasf.com

"Bring your own beret" to either location of these "real French bistros" where "handsome" garçons deliver "pleasing" Gallic classics and "easy" *vins de pays* with bonhomie; the "tiny", "lively" original keeps locals happy on "the Hill", while SoMa's new Provençal sib brings a "breath of fresh air" to Mint Plaza with "sexy surrounds" and a "large patio" for leisurely lunches.

Chez Spencer *French*

26 | 22 | 21 | $59

Mission | 82 14th St. (bet. Folsom & Harrison Sts.) | 415-864-2191 | www.chezspencer.net

"Ooh-la-la", this "out-of-the-way", "truly San Franciscan" haunt serves "exquisite" French dinners ("order the tasting menu with wine" and "die happy") to a "cool crowd" in a "slightly unfinished" Mission ware-

| | FOOD | DECOR | SERVICE | COST |

house that's "romantic without trying too hard"; its "hiddenness makes it super-special", as do the weekend piano music and heated patio, but some wish the service were more "attentive" given the price; N.B. the Spencer on the Go! truck can be tracked on Twitter.

Chloe's Cafe ⊉ American
23 | 14 | 20 | $19

Noe Valley | 1399 Church St. (26th St.) | 415-648-4116

Dubbed "the belle of Noe Valley", this "tiny" corner cafe "can't be beat" for "fluffy pancakes", "flavorful" scrambles and "better-than-home" Traditional American lunches, especially at the "coveted outdoor tables"; it's all served by such a "friendly" staff that "you'll want to linger for hours", though the "long lines" "will instill guilt for you to move on."

Chouchou French
22 | 18 | 22 | $38

Forest Hills | 400 Dewey Blvd. (Laguna Honda Blvd.) | 415-242-0960 | www.chouchousf.com

"If you can get over" the Forest Hills locale ("hardly the Champs-Elysées"), you might fall in "love" with this "bright" "little" French "favorite" where a "tremendous staff" serves up "scrumptious" country fare "just like Uncle Jacques would make"; the desserts are "killer", so "don't walk out without having a tart, or you'll be sorely missing out on heaven."

Chow American
21 | 16 | 19 | $26

Castro | 215 Church St. (bet. 15th & Market Sts.) | 415-552-2469

Park Chow American

Inner Sunset | 1240 Ninth Ave. (bet. Irving St. & Lincoln Way) | 415-665-9912 www.chowfoodbar.com

"Big flavors abound" at this "busy" "micro-chain" dishing up "eclectic", "organic" New American "comfort food–plus" that "ranks high with children" and chowhounds alike; it's "no foodie event place", just an "affordable" "fallback" that's "sure to please the pickiest of palates", with perks including "fast" service, "excellent" beer and "fresh homemade pies."

Circa American
18 | 18 | 16 | $36

Marina | 2001 Chestnut St. (Fillmore St.) | 415-351-0175 | www.circasf.com

"You won't be blown away by the food, but it is a fun place" assess surveyors of this "trendy" Marina "singles" spot with "inventive", "reasonable" New American small plates crafted by a *Top Chef* alum"; "lounge-lizard decor" and weekend DJs set the tone for a "hoppin'" scene, while brunch warrants a "woo-hoo" for its "bottomless mimosas."

Citizen Cake ⊠ Bakery/Californian
21 | 17 | 18 | $39

Hayes Valley | 399 Grove St. (Gough St.) | 415-861-2228 | www.citizencake.com

"Have your cake" with "wonderful", "wild" Californian meals and a cocktail too at Elizabeth Falkner's industrial-chic "pre-performance" brunch and dinner spot in Hayes Valley, "famous" for her "show-stealing" "deconstructed desserts"; some citizens protest paying "opera-crowd prices" for "ultrasmall portions" and head instead to the remodeled cafe/bakery for a "cup of joe", "killer pastries" and less "far-fetched" savories.

	FOOD	DECOR	SERVICE	COST

Citrus Club *Pan-Asian*

| 21 | 13 | 17 | $17 |

Haight-Ashbury | 1790 Haight St. (Shrader St.) | 415-387-6366

A "diamond" in the "rough" Upper Haight, this Pan-Asian "noodle house" ladles up "flavorful", "filling" soups and "heaping portions" of "one-dish" meals laced with copious amounts of fresh vegetables, citrus and garlic (see the "addictive edamame"); regulars say it sure "hits the spot on chilly nights" and for "cheap dates", though "long lines" and decor "one step away from folding chairs and card tables" can be drawbacks.

Cliff House Bistro *Californian*

| 18 | 24 | 19 | $42 |

Outer Richmond | 1090 Point Lobos Ave. (Balboa St.) | 415-386-3330 | www.cliffhouse.com

Perched above the Pacific Ocean with a "spectacular" "picture-window" view (including the "surfers and otters below"), this "resurrected" Outer Richmond "tourist attraction" is *the* place for weekend brunch" or sharing sunset "drinks and appetizers" with "out-of-town" guests; otherwise the Californian cuisine and "glorified coffee-shop" ambiance strike skeptical surveyors as "overpriced", but it's still a "cheaper" and easier table to "score" than the more formal Sutro's downstairs.

Coco500 ⊠ *Californian/Mediterranean*

| 22 | 19 | 21 | $45 |

SoMa | 500 Brannan St. (4th St.) | 415-543-2222 | www.coco500.com

"Loretta Keller and Co. keep playing their hits" (like "decadent" flatbreads) while adding "creative, seasonal" Cal-Mediterranean licks and "unique" cocktails at this "bustling" SoMa boîte that's still HQ for "VCs snuggling with unshaven dot-commers" and the "perfect start to a Giants game"; it's "modern" yet "cozy", though the din and the "dishes stack up, and so does the bill"; N.B. closed Sundays except on game days.

☑ Coi ⊠Ⓜ *Californian/French*

| 28 | 24 | 27 | $163 |

North Beach | 373 Broadway (Montgomery St.) | 415-393-9000 | www.coirestaurant.com

"Outstanding" chef-owner Daniel Patterson "leads the charge for molecular gastronomy" at this paean to "el Bulli", proffering a "stupendous" 11-course Cal-French "feast for the taste buds and the mind" amid a "minimalist" backdrop (set in a "dodgy" part of North Beach); the "scents-as-courses" and "too coy" presentations occasionally "provoke giggles from guests", but diehards assure that even in "hard-knock times", it's "worth saving your dollars to eat here"; N.B. dishes may be ordered à la carte in the lounge.

Colibrí Mexican Bistro *Mexican*

| 20 | 18 | 18 | $36 |

Downtown | 438 Geary St. (bet. Mason & Taylor Sts.) | 415-440-2737 | www.colibrimexicanbistro.com

"Nibble before a show or dine right after" at this "upscale" Downtown Mexican tapas and tequila bar slinging "solid" eats – including "tableside guacamole" and "standout" mole – and "don't-miss" margaritas delivered in a "party" atmosphere; some reviewers are ruffled by harried service and costly comida, but "what else do you expect" in "touristy Union Square"?

	FOOD	DECOR	SERVICE	COST

Conduit ⌧Ⓜ *American/French*   22 | 22 | 20 | $46

Mission | 280 Valencia St. (14th St.) | 415-552-5200

An "ultraconceptual", "industrial" design with lots of "exposed piping" (sort of like "my old New York basement") and an "off-the-hook" coed bathroom by starchitect Stanley Saitowitz sets apart this North Mission arrival that's "currently one of the trendiest places going"; judges josh that the "exciting", "well-crafted" New American–French cooking "isn't so bad either", plus the "mixologist does wonders" with seasonal cocktails at the bar, enhancing the "surprisingly attitude-free" service.

NEW Contigo *Spanish*   ▽ 19 | 22 | 17 | $49

Noe Valley | 1320 Castro St. (24th St.) | 415-285-0250 | www.contigosf.com

A "lively" atmosphere embraces eaters at this Noe Valley newcomer by chef/co-owner Brett Emerson, offering a "range of traditional (and slightly fanciful) takes on Catalan" and other Spanish dishes in a "welcoming" space bordered by salvaged redwood walls; while small plates like "pork belly sliders" and "Ibérico ham" are an early hit, some critics feel "let down" by the entrees, the "amateurish" service and the "prices"; N.B. reservations accepted for six or more.

NEW Corner, The ❶ *American/Italian*   - | - | - | M

Mission | 2199 Mission St. (18th St.) | 415-875-9258

Just a few storefronts away from sibling Weird Fish, this quirky corner cafe decorated with bird-stenciled walls and handmade wood tables offers Missionites yet another low-key WiFi and happy-hour haunt for nibbling on American-Italian small plates, washed down with wallet-friendly wines and brews till late; when the morning rolls around, habitués nurse their hangovers with daily brunch items like Dynamo doughnuts, waffles and pizzas.

Cosmopolitan, The ⌧ *American*   19 | 19 | 20 | $46

SoMa | Rincon Ctr. | 121 Spear St. (bet. Howard & Mission Sts.) | 415-543-4001 | www.thecosmopolitancafe.com

"Cosmopolitan in every sense", this SoMa "businessman's restaurant" with jazz-scene murals is a "winner after work" for "drink and dinner deals", and equally "reliable" for lunches of "refined" New American eats; some feel the "lively" bar outshines the food, but most are grateful for the "righteous" cocktails.

Côté Sud ⌧ *French*   19 | 16 | 18 | $42

Castro | 4238 18th St. (bet. Collingwood & Diamond Sts.) | 415-255-6565 | www.cotesudsf.com

Breathing a "little bit of southern France into the Castro", this "quaint" converted Victorian ("watch your step up the rickety stairs") offers a sunny "escape" enhanced by a "smiling" owner and a nightly prix fixe that "will fill your stomach" without emptying your wallet; there are "few surprises", but "live jazz" every other Thursday is an extra treat.

Crustacean *European/Vietnamese*   23 | 18 | 20 | $54

Polk Gulch | 1475 Polk St. (California St.) | 415-776-2722 | www.anfamily.com

"When you have a craving for crab", the "hot buttery" delicacy (with "secret-recipe" garlic noodles) is "so tasty you want to lick the sauce off the shell" at this "high-end" Euro-Vietnamese "Polk Street survivor" (and Than Long sib); amid updated Asian decor, the ambiance is "ebullient", though critics say cracking down on the "dress code" ("collared-shirts required, no shorts") seems "odd considering the plastic bibs."

Custom Burger/Lounge *Burgers* ▽ 19 | 13 | 17 | $16

SoMa | Best Western Americania | 121 Seventh St. (bet. Minna & Mission Sts.) | 415-252-2634

"Who knew picking a hamburger could be so challenging?" wonder novices at this upscale "have-it-your-way" patty purveyor offering an "amazing choice" of "custom condiments", sauces and meats (including Kobe and lamb); a few beef about the "pretty prime price" given the "dodgy" location in SoMa and merely "serviceable" retro diner surroundings, but most say it all stacks up with "recession-proof comfort food."

Delancey Street Ⓜ *Eclectic* 17 | 16 | 22 | $29

Embarcadero | 600 The Embarcadero (Brannan St.) | 415-512-5179 | www.delanceystreetfoundation.org

Staffed by "individuals who are making an effort to improve themselves", this "feel-good, taste-good spot on the Embarcadero" and its affordable Eclectic "comfort food" are "not perfect", but "regulars flock here" anyway for weekend brunch or a bite "before a Giants game" to support its "awesome" mission – "helping ex-convicts" and recovering addicts to "get back on their feet"; factor in the "views of the Bay and the bridge", and the "reasonable prices" are even more of a "bargain."

Delessio 21 | 12 | 16 | $19
Market & Bakery *Bakery*

Hayes Valley | 1695 Market St. (Gough St.) | 415-552-5559
Western Addition | Faletti's Plaza | 302 Broderick St. (Oak St.) | 415-552-8077
www.delessiomarket.com

"Grab a plate, pile on incredible food and pay by the pound" at these "delicious" if "a little pricey" self-serve bakeries that crank out "off-the-chart" croissants, an "ever-changing display" of organically sourced hot and cold "buffet-style entrees" and "splendiferous desserts"; the Hayes Valley branch offers "cafe-style" seating, while the primarily to-go Western Addition outpost boasts an expansive selection of "picnic items"; P.S. "they cater!"

Ⓩ Delfina *Italian* 26 | 19 | 23 | $47

Mission | 3621 18th St. (bet. Dolores & Guerrero Sts.) | 415-552-4055 | www.delfinasf.com

Some call it "my favorite Italian" or even a "religious experience", but *everyone* calls "well in advance" for reservations, because this "bustling" Mission "institution" just "keeps getting better – and more crowded" with devotees of Craig Stoll's "innovative" Tuscan cooking that's "fresh, simple" and "half the price of his peers"; the "impossible parking" and "deafening" din can be a drag, but a "cool neighborhood" atmosphere, "hip", "caring" staff and that "impossibly tasty" grub more than compensate; P.S. lucky "walk-ins" may "snag seats" at the "large bar."

	FOOD	DECOR	SERVICE	COST

Destino *Nuevo Latino* | 22 | 20 | 21 | $37 |

Castro | 1815 Market St. (bet. Guerrero St. & Octavia Blvd.) | 415-552-4451 | www.destinosf.com

As "warm and sexy as a Latin lover", this "lively" Nuevo Latino on the edge of the Castro is the "perfect place to gear up for a night out", starting with "flavorful, affordable" Peruvian-inflected tapas (including a "tasty ceviche sampler") followed by "delicious cocktails" at its Pisco Latin Lounge next door; if the "cramped" seating gets you down, the "smiling, hot waiters" and otherwise "nice surroundings" will pick you up.

District 🗷 *Eclectic* | 18 | 22 | 18 | $34 |

SoMa | 216 Townsend St. (bet. Ritch & 3rd Sts.) | 415-896-2120 | www.districtsf.com

"More of a wine bar than dinner establishment", this "airy, warehouselike space" becomes an "after-work" "pickup scene" once SoMa's "young professionals", "cougars-to-be" and other "eye candy" arrive en masse and start sipping vino "by the glass or in interesting flights" and nibbling "decent" Eclectic small plates; "beware": a few wallet-watchers warn it can be "pricey", so "come for the people-watching and drink slowly."

Domo Sushi *Japanese* | 23 | 18 | 20 | $35 |

Hayes Valley | 511 Laguna St. (Linden St.) | 415-861-8887 | www.domosf.com

From "creative" raw fin fare to "unique takes on Japanese-inspired salads", "everything is pretty delicious" at this "reasonably priced" "neighborhood sushi bar" in Hayes Valley; a "welcoming, appropriately attentive staff" oversees the simple, unfinished-wood interior, but it's a "tight squeeze" (only 20 seats), so "get there early."

Dosa *Indian* | 23 | 22 | 19 | $35 |

Mission | 995 Valencia St. (21st St.) | 415-642-3672
NEW **Upper Fillmore** | 1700 Fillmore St. (Post St.) | 415-441-3672
www.dosasf.com

"Fire lovers unite" at this "bustling" Bombay boîte in the Mission and its "stunning" new Upper Fillmore offshoot (with "fabulous chandeliers, vaulted ceilings, warm low lights"), where "spot-on" servers ply "high-energy crowds" with "upscale" South Indian cuisine that's "spicy but full of flavors" – including the "gut-busting" "namesake dosas" ("beware the mango habañero unless you have taste buds of steel"); expect "long waits" and a "rather high noise level", but "inventive cocktails" at the "happening bar" ease the pain.

Dottie's True Blue Cafe *Diner* | 25 | 13 | 19 | $18 |

Tenderloin | 522 Jones St. (bet. Geary & O'Farrell Sts.) | 415-885-2767

A "local treasure" with an "ambiance out of the '50s", this "cheap hole-in-the-wall diner" "unabashedly fires up the griddle and serves carb-laden pancakes", "delicious baked goods" and "strong coffee" that devotees describe as "da best"; just "go extra early" (or for lunch) to avoid waiting in a "Depression-era soup kitchen" line on a "sketchy" Tenderloin street known for scoring more than just "fantastic breakfasts that last all day"; N.B. closes at 3 PM.

	FOOD	DECOR	SERVICE	COST

Dragon Well *Chinese*
21 | 16 | 20 | $26

Marina | 2142 Chestnut St. (bet. Pierce & Steiner Sts.) | 415-474-6888 |
www.dragonwell.com

Its "menu has remained relatively unchanged", but "that's ok because
they're doin' it right" at this "informal" Marina Chinese whose
"friendly staff" dishes out "fresh", "always tasty and fairly healthy"
lunch and dinner eats; while a few critics contend its "California-ized"
chow won't "wow anyone", it remains a "safe choice" for those who
"don't want to spend a lot" to satisfy their weekly cravings, including
"families" who drag in their toddlers.

Ducca *Italian*
20 | 21 | 19 | $53

SoMa | Westin San Francisco | 50 Third St. (Market St.) | 415-977-0271 |
www.duccasf.com

"Not your typical Italian restaurant", this "beautiful Venetian"-
inspired venue in SoMa's Westin San Francisco lures "after-work"
Downtown customers and "convention crowds" alike with its
"inventive, satisfying" cuisine, including *cicchetti* (bar snacks), and
"attractive" seating in the "spacious" dining room and on the "fire
pit"-equipped terrace; still, an unimpressed minority mutters that
"service can be hit-or-miss" and that, overall, "something's missing at
these prices"; N.B. a post-Survey chef change is not reflected in
the Food score.

E&O Trading Company *SE Asian*
19 | 21 | 19 | $38

Downtown | 314 Sutter St. (bet. Grant Ave. & Stockton St.) | 415-693-0303 |
www.eotrading.com

Southeast Asian fusion meets "California fun" at this "over-the-top"
Bay Area chainlet, an "escape from the outside world" where "large
groups" imbibe "innovative cocktails" and share "tasty" small and
large plates from ex-Eos chef Arnold Eric Wong's revamped menu –
just "don't forget the corn fritters!"; surveyors are split on the tab
("reasonable" vs. "pricey"), though bargain-hunters hail the $19 prix
fixe lunch and "can't-go-wrong" happy hour.

E'Angelo Ⓜ *Italian*
21 | 12 | 21 | $31

Marina | 2234 Chestnut St. (bet. Pierce & Scott Sts.) |
415-567-6164

Delivering "the cheapest trip to Italy I've ever had", this "old-school"
Italian eatery in the Marina draws "mainly locals" for midpriced,
"family-style" portions of "homemade pastas" "served with a wink
and a nudge" by waiters who've "been here forever"; it's "hearty"
enough to "make you want to sing opera", but "go early to avoid the
mobs", as the "small" storefront doesn't take rezzies and is "always
crowded and loud."

Ebisu *Japanese*
23 | - | 18 | $37

Inner Sunset | 1283 Ninth Ave. (Irving St.) | 415-566-1770 |
www.ebisusushi.com

"Come to life again" after a million-dollar refurb, this "top-of-the-line"
Inner Sunset Japanese sporting a new sushi bar and robata dishes
draws an "in-the-know" crowd that likes its "fish so fresh it may still be
alive"; while "kids love the tatami room", "regulars" head to the counter
and "ask the chef to be creative" – just "go early or late to avoid the

	FOOD	DECOR	SERVICE	COST

wait" ("lunchtime is more sane"); N.B. in addition to SFO, a third branch is set to open on 336 Kearny Street.

Eiji Ⓜ *Japanese*

-	-	-	M

Castro | 317 Sanchez St. (bet. 16th & 17th Sts.) | 415-558-8149

This under-the-radar homestyle Japanese in the Castro showcases chef Eiji Onoda's housemade hot and cold tofu dishes, including an über-fresh, custardy *oboro* tofu, prepared tableside and served with an array of condiments; a chalkboard menu offers daily maki and sashimi as well, but there's no sleek sushi bar (or eye-catching rolls), just a handful of wooden tables and traditional bric-a-brac on display.

El Balazo *Mexican*

19	11	13	$15

Haight-Ashbury | 1654 Haight St. (Clayton St.) | 415-864-2140
NEW **Mission** | 2183 Mission St. (18th St.) | 415-522-0845
Potrero Hill | 2560 Marin St. (Bay Shore Blvd.) | 415-282-7130 🏠
www.elbalazo.net

"Bring a wheelbarrow for your servings" at this chain of colorful, "cafeteria-line" taquerias where an "efficient" counter crew cranks out "fresh", "reliable" Mexican fare with unusual ingredients (including nopales), plus "great agua fresca"; it's "cheap", "reliable" and *niño*-friendly, but even fans admonish "if you want character, go somewhere else."

Elite Cafe *American*

19	19	19	$41

Upper Fillmore | 2049 Fillmore St. (bet. California & Pine Sts.) | 415-673-5483 | www.theelitecafe.com

Exuding the feel of "old San Francisco with a little Cajun twist", this "lively", long-running American is "still going strong", drawing a "fun crowd" to its Upper Fillmore digs with "solid" (some say "expensive") "Southern comfort fare" and "service with a cool feel"; however, veterans who insist it "used to be better" advise "sticking to the raw bar" and "fabulous brunches" fueled by "beignets, biscuits and Bloody Marys."

Eliza's *Chinese*

21	16	16	$25

Pacific Heights | 2877 California St. (bet. Broderick & Divisadero Sts.) | 415-621-4819
Potrero Hill | 1457 18th St. (bet. Connecticut & Missouri Sts.) | 415-648-9999

These aren't "your typical Chinese restaurants" tout fans of the "always tasty", "California-style" Sino chow ("even the ostrich") at this "affordable" Pac Heights/Potrero Hill duo; "Wedgwood accessories" and "colorful glass-art surroundings" complete the picture, though some say "rushed, unfriendly" service ("it takes about a year before the staff warms up to you") can dampen an otherwise "addicting" experience.

Ella's *American*

22	14	19	$23

Presidio Heights | 500 Presidio Ave. (California St.) | 415-441-5669 | www.ellassanfrancisco.com

Your "low-carb diet doesn't stand a chance against the smell" of the "ethereal sticky buns", "excellent coffee", "mile-high biscuits" and "must-try" chicken hash at this "classic American brunch spot" in Presidio Heights proffering "high-fat goodness" with requisite "30–60 minute" weekend waits; fortunately, the vibe is surprisingly "mellow for such a crowded place"; N.B. no dinners.

	FOOD	DECOR	SERVICE	COST

El Metate *Mexican*

| | 23 | 16 | 18 | $10 |

Mission | 2406 Bryant St. (22nd St.) | 415-641-7209

"Cheap, fresh, tasty, authentic": that pretty much sums up this "friendly" Mission taqueria serving up "stellar" Baja-style fish tacos, chile verde and "delicious burritos" with "colorful" veggies; an "owner who treats everyone like family", an "expanded dining room that looks like an old Mexican patio" and "nice outdoor tables" add to the appeal.

El Raigón ⊠ *Argentinean*

| | 22 | 19 | 20 | $46 |

North Beach | 510 Union St. (Grant Ave.) | 415-291-0927 | www.elraigon.com

"It feels like home on the pampas" at this "authentic Argentinean" steakhouse in North Beach, where the "excellent beef" – some "brought in from South America" – is "cooked the way it's supposed to be": estancia-style, over wood and charcoal; "fantastic sides" ("the mashed potatoes are fluffy clouds"), a "relaxed" vibe and "charming service" further its rep as a "real winner."

Emmy's Spaghetti Shack *Italian*

| | 21 | 17 | 19 | $23 |

Bernal Heights | 18 Virginia Ave. (Mission St.) | 415-206-2086 | www.emmysspaghettishack.com

"Bring on the bowls of steaming spaghetti" and "monster meatballs" demand devotees who lose their noodle over this "cute", "rockin'" Bernal Heights "tradition" with "atmosphere oozing" from the walls; sure, it's "one funky joint", but "don't be fooled by the hipster vibe" or the "beyond loud" music: the "artisan cocktails" and "sizable portions" of Italian eats at "1950s prices" are "consistently good"; N.B. a new branch has opened in Sonoma.

Emporio Rulli *Dessert/Italian*

| | 22 | 21 | 17 | $24 |

Downtown | Union Square Pavilion | 225 Stockton St. (Post St.) | 415-433-1122
Marina | 2300 Chestnut St. (Scott St.) | 415-923-6464
www.rulli.com

See review in North of San Francisco Directory.

Enrico's Sidewalk Cafe *American/Mediterranean*

| | 16 | 21 | 16 | $34 |

North Beach | 504 Broadway (Kearny St.) | 415-982-6223 | www.enricossf.com

"Take off the tie and try something different" at this "revamped" "old San Francisco" "classic" featuring nightly "live jazz" ("without a cover charge") and "coveted" sidewalk seating "right in the middle of the Broadway smut parade"; it's a "fun place" for "North Beach people-watching" and knocking back a "killer mojito", but naysayers suggest that the "nostalgia is much better" than the merely "adequate" New American–Med cuisine; N.B. no longer serves lunch.

Eos Restaurant & Wine Bar *Asian Fusion/Californian*

| | 23 | 18 | 20 | $47 |

Cole Valley | 901 Cole St. (Carl St.) | 415-566-3063 | www.eossf.com

"After all these years", the "shiitake dumplings that appear in dreams" and other "creative" Cal-Asian "small plates" at this Cole Valley industrial-chic stalwart still have habitués "licking the plates" (though some hope the new owners will bring "new ideas" to the menu); some guests "stick" to the "clubby", "less sterile" salon for dessert and "flights of wine tastings" from the "awesome" cellar – provided, of course, they plan to "walk home" or hop the "streetcar outside."

EPIC Roasthouse *Steak*

20 | 25 | 20 | $67

Embarcadero | 369 The Embarcadero (bet. Folsom & Harrison Sts.) | 415-369-9955 | www.epicroasthousesf.com

Pat Kuleto's "aptly named" "swanky steakhouse" on the Embarcadero – boasting a "stunning" interior, "2-lb. chunks of meat" and "drop-dead views" for "watching the boats on the Bay" – is "paradise" for carnivores and the "dwindling expense-account crowd"; but considering the "gold bullion prices", a cadre of critics say "epic expectations" for chef/co-owner Jan Birnbaum's exhibition kitchen sometimes result in "disappointments", prompting suggestions to "go for lunch" "on the patio" to enjoy that "amazing ambiance" "without breaking the bank."

Eric's *Chinese*

22 | 15 | 18 | $22

Noe Valley | 1500 Church St. (27th St.) | 415-282-0919

Diners who claim they've "lost an affinity" for Chinese food change their tune at this "can't-go-wrong" Noe Valley "oasis" that's been wokking up "fresh", "innovative" Californian "takes on traditional" Asian chow since 1991; "reasonable prices" mean it's great "for those on a budget", but because the "small, minimally decorated" ground-floor Victorian is "almost always full", eager types "prefer taking it out to waiting forever."

Esperpento *Spanish*

19 | 13 | 16 | $28

Mission | 3295 22nd St. (Valencia St.) | 415-282-8867

For "tapas just like *mamita* made" and "delicious paella" serving "two times as many as it says", Missionistas craving an "affordable" "caz lunch" or "dinner with friends" "in the mood to party" head to this "festive", "loud" Spaniard; a few tender taste buds tell of "garlicky" grub ("don't plan on kissing anyone after eating here"), but then again, "anything will taste good after a carafe" of the "fantastic sangria."

Espetus Churrascaria *Brazilian*

22 | 17 | 21 | $65

Hayes Valley | 1686 Market St. (bet. Brady & Haight Sts.) | 415-552-8792 | www.espetus.com

"Carnivores unite", "gorge and drink sangria" at these "coma"-inducing Brazilian churrascarias in Hayes Valley and San Mateo where "gaucho-clad waiters" parade "swords" of "delicious" "grilled everything" through a "huge", "loud" dining room; the "plentiful salad bar with hot/cold items is included" in the "steep" all-you-can-eat price, but veterans advise "don't waste" "valuable stomach space" on it – "unless you need a breather."

Essencia Ⓩ *Peruvian*

∇ 19 | 17 | 19 | $39

Hayes Valley | 401 Gough St. (Hayes St.) | 415-552-8485 | www.essenciarestaurant.com

A welcome "change from the more Euro-centric restaurants" in Hayes Valley, this "tiny" "Peruvian treat" "near the symphony and opera" showcases "great ceviche" and other "completely unusual flavors" of Andean cuisine "with a Western twist"; service can be "slow" and pa-

	FOOD	DECOR	SERVICE	COST

trons are "packed together", but most say go anyway – "if you can snag a table", that is.

Eureka Restaurant & Lounge *American* | 20 | 19 | 22 | $44 |

Castro | 4063 18th St. (bet. Castro & Hartford Sts.) | 415-431-6000 | www.eurekarestaurant.com

A "worthy addition" to the Castro, this "well-appointed", "relaxed" sib of Chenery Park entices with "full-of-taste" "home cooking" like mac 'n' cheese that's "better than mama ever made", plus New American small plates; a "terrific", "responsive" staff adds to the appeal, while the "gentlemen's club atmosphere" extends to a "special upstairs lounge" proffering "super-sophisticated" libations; P.S. wallet-watchers who warn it's "expensive" may dig the recent pricing changes.

☒ Farallon *Seafood* | 24 | 27 | 24 | $67 |

Downtown | 450 Post St. (bet. Mason & Powell Sts.) | 415-956-6969 | www.farallonrestaurant.com

"Little Mermaid, eat your heart out" – this "fantastical" Union Square seafooder/raw bar is "still wowing" 'em with its "dreamlike" "Disney-on-a-buzz" decor ("can you beat glass squid floating above you?") and chef Mark Franz's "equally excellent" "just-off-the-boat" fin fare with a sustainable bent; "divine wine", "delicious desserts" and "downright telepathic service" are additional lures, though your bank account may also be "underwater" when the check comes.

Farina 🅼 *Italian* | 23 | 21 | 20 | $46 |

Mission | 3560 18th St. (bet. Guerrero & Valencia Sts.) | 415-565-0360 | www.farinafoods.com

It's "worth finding parking on this Mission block", because you'll think "you've landed in the middle of Genoa" after tasting the "unbelievable" Ligurian chow ("superb pastas" and "unbelievable" focaccia) at this "sleek", "open-style" trattoria with a "'Nighthawks'-style front window wall"; if nitpickers knock "high prices" and a "noisy" atmosphere, most maintain "SF needs more Italian places like this."

farmerbrown *Soul Food* | 21 | 18 | 18 | $33 |

Tenderloin | 25 Mason St. (bet. Eddy & Turk Sts.) | 415-409-3276 | www.farmerbrownsf.com

🆕 farmerbrown's little skillet ☒⊅ *Soul Food*

SoMa | 330 Ritch St. | 360 Ritch St. (bet. Brannan & Townsend Sts.) | 415-777-2777 | www.littleskilletsf.com

The "killer fried chicken" and other "upscale soul food" will "make you miss your grandma", while the "even better cocktails" will make you forget about her completely at this "industrial"-chic "hipster" haunt sowing good "vibes" with its "good cause" (sourcing sustainable ingredients from local and African-American farmers); "iffy" Tenderloin location aside, guests can't get enough of the jazz brunch and "hopping bar scene"; N.B. its new SoMa spin-off hawks chix 'n' waffles to go.

1550 Hyde Café & | 22 | 19 | 22 | $45 |
Wine Bar 🅼 *Californian/Mediterranean*

Russian Hill | 1550 Hyde St. (bet. Jackson St. & Pacific Ave.) | 415-775-1550 | www.1550hyde.com

"Run . . . don't hyde!" rave Russian Hill insiders about this "delightful", "off-the-beaten-track" "neighborhood bistro" where the "educated" staff and "dynamic" daily changing Cal-Med Slow Food menu are "down to earth" but the "wine flights soar"; its "simple" storefront space, replete with "recycled corks" on the ceiling and "cable cars whisking by", can feel "comfy or cramped", but "exceptional"-value vinos and $30 midweek prix fixe deals "make it a destination" bar none.

Fifth Floor ☒ American/French
| 25 | 23 | 24 | $86 |

SoMa | Hotel Palomar | 12 Fourth St., 5th fl. (Market St.) | 415-348-1555 | www.fifthfloorrestaurant.com

"Spot-on service" and a "wonderful" wine list ("thicker than Warren Buffett's will") complement "sparkling" fare (shifting from French to more affordable New American under a new toque) at this SoMa "celebration" place in the Hotel Palomar; if a few "sentimentalists" find the "refurbished" space too "formal", the "relaxing" front lounge beckons for "delicious quick plates and quenching martinis"; N.B. the post-Survey departure of chef Laurent Manrique is not reflected in the Food score.

NEW 54 Mint ☒ Italian
| - | - | - | M |

SoMa | 16 Mint Plaza (Mint St., off Mission St.) | 415-543-5100 | www.54mint.com

Lending some culinary heft to Mint Plaza's growing Restaurant Row, this SoMa Italian ristorante and wine bar (from New York's Il Buco founder Alberto Avalle) crafts rustic Italian lunches and dinners in a sleek room where sparkling white tiles and marble contrast with dark-wood tables and exposed brick; there's outdoor seating on the alley, plus an alimentari selling artisan food imports and European biodynamic wines.

Fior d'Italia Italian
| 18 | 16 | 19 | $44 |

North Beach | San Remo Hotel | 2237 Mason St. (Chestnut St.) | 415-986-1886 | www.fior.com

It's "America's oldest Italian restaurant", "and with good reason", declare devotees of this North Beach "classic" proffering "plentiful" portions of "reliable", "homestyle" Northern Boot fare; alas, nostalgists bray that it "ain't what it used to be" since its 2005 move to the San Remo Hotel, citing "mediocre" decor and tables "full of tourists."

Firefly Eclectic
| 25 | 20 | 24 | $43 |

Noe Valley | 4288 24th St. (Douglass St.) | 415-821-7652 | www.fireflyrestaurant.com

Noe Valleyites are "hesitant to sing the praises" of their "favorite neighborhood resto", because this "fine-dining secret" "is almost too good to share"; reservations are a must, though, because the "ever-changing", "vibrant" Eclectic "comfort food" served by a "down-to-earth" staff in "cozy" digs is "every bit as good as any" of its "name" competition – and "you won't pay as much", particularly during the Sunday–Thursday $35 prix fixe dinners.

Fish & Farm ☒ American/Seafood
| 20 | 16 | 20 | $47 |

Downtown | 339 Taylor St. (bet. Ellis & O'Farrell Sts.) | 415-474-3474 | www.fishandfarmsf.com

"If you can find the place", afishionados assure you'll "enjoy" this "inventive" New American next to the Hotel Twain – even if it means traipsing through a "beyond sketchy" area near the Tenderloin; it's a "locavore's paradise" with "sustainable", regionally sourced "land and sea fare", plus "wonderful cocktails", a "$5 corkage fee for Cal wines" and "gracious service"; still, some slam the "quirky ambiance" and say the overall experience "doesn't quite hit the mark"; N.B. the founding chef left post-Survey.

5A5 Steak Lounge 🖼 *Steak*

| - | - | - | E |

Downtown | 244 Jackson St. (bet. Battery & Front Sts.) | 415-989-2539 | www.5a5stk.com

Named for the highest grade of beef (A5 Wagyu), this swanky new self-billed 'steak lounge' is not your father's chophouse: the Downtown room sports the same disco circular-domed ceiling and Plexiglas partitions of its predecessor, Frisson, and DJs entertain during happy hour and weekends; the pricey menu ranges from traditional (22-oz. T-bone) to modern (hamachi shooters and lobster tempura), but the A1 offering is the World Wide Wagyu ($125), 4-oz. samples of steak from Japan, America and Australia.

🗵 Fleur de Lys 🖼 🅼 *Californian/French*

| 27 | 27 | 27 | $98 |

Downtown | 777 Sutter St. (bet. Jones & Taylor Sts.) | 415-673-7779 | www.fleurdelyssf.com

"Now I know how Napoleon felt" flutter Francophiles who delight in being treated "like the most important person in town" at this Downtown "institution" where Hubert Keller continues to "work his magic", composing "off-the-charts" "contemporary" Cal-French fare; the "fabric-lined" "Bedouin tent" setting is almost as "lush" as the "sublime" prix fixe dinners paired with "superb wines", and though you'll need to "dress up" and bring your "bailout money", it's "worth it" for an "ultra-romantic night out" "you'll never forget."

Florio *French/Italian*

| 21 | 20 | 21 | $41 |

Pacific Heights | 1915 Fillmore St. (bet. Bush & Pine Sts.) | 415-775-4300 | www.floriosf.com

A "real neighborhood" "standard", this "small, enticing" "Parisian"-style brasserie ("another in the BIX dynasty") pleases "Pac Heights thespians, society and business people alike" with its "hearty" French-Italian cuisine; "it's not the hippest joint" and "noise gets in the way", but when you want a "grown-up bar scene" coupled with "solid bistro fare", fans say "it's a lock"; N.B. a new 'Young Foodies' menu is geared toward *les enfants.*

NEW Flour + Water ● *Italian*

| - | - | - | E |

Mission | 2401 Harrison St. (20th St.) | 415-826-7000 | www.flourandwater.com

As the name suggests, hand-rolled pastas and wood-fired, thin-crust Neapolitan pies, complemented by an affordable, all-Italia wine list, are the main ingredients at this Mission arrival serving till midnight; the rustic room pays homage to the three Rs – refurbished, repurposed, reclaimed – with stained-glass wall dividers and a wood bar made from old cask barrels.

Fog City Diner *American*

| 19 | 19 | 19 | $35 |

Embarcadero | 1300 Battery St. (Greenwich St.) | 415-982-2000 | fogcitydiner.com

"Tourists turning up expecting meatloaf" are "surprised to find" that this "SF mainstay" "down the street from Pier 39" is "not a diner at all" but a "clever" New American restaurant and "oyster bar" "with prices to prove it"; sure, some sentimentalists sniff "it's not all that" since its "VISA commercial" days, but the "unique" setup in a converted "art deco" "trolley" remains an "enjoyable" backdrop for "decent", "basic" chow that can be "walked off along the Embarcadero."

Forbes Island ⓜ *American/Seafood* ▽ 19 | 24 | 21 | $52

Fisherman's Wharf | Pier 41 (The Embarcadero at Powell St.) | 415-951-4900 | www.forbesisland.com

It just may be SF's most "bizarre place for a meal": a "floating man-made island in the Bay" – replete with lighthouse, palm trees and white sand – where you can "eat with the fishes" in an "underwater dining room"; even admirers admit "you go here for the experience" and "outstanding views" and "not so much" for the "typical" American chow, and note "you're charged for the boat ride" from Fisherman's Wharf ("talk about getting you coming and going!"); N.B. dinners Wednesday–Sunday.

Foreign Cinema *Californian/Mediterranean* 23 | 25 | 22 | $47

Mission | 2534 Mission St. (bet. 21st & 22nd Sts.) | 415-648-7600 | www.foreigncinema.com

"There's no red carpet outside" this "upscale Mission surprise", but "just like going to a movie", the "unique" restaurant and its "funky front bar" filled with "trendy young moderns" "lets you step into another world"; "friendly" servers deliver a "bravo"-worthy double bill of "divine" Cal-Med dinners and an "amazing" "champagne brunch" ("one of the best in SF"), while the "roaring fireplace" inside and foreign "flicks" projected "drive-in" style on the "romantic" heated patio play their part to "distract from the bill."

Frascati *Californian/Mediterranean* 26 | 19 | 23 | $53

Russian Hill | 1901 Hyde St. (Green St.) | 415-928-1406 | www.frascatisf.com

"Take the cable car" that "rumbles past" this "neighborhood gem" set "high on Russian Hill" (where "parking is a bear") and also "high on the list for romantic dinners" with an "only-in-San Francisco flavor"; you can "watch the chefs prepare" the seasonal Cal-Med meals to "perfection" while "being well taken care of", or simply "drop in at the bar" and sample its "stupendous", "Pinot-focused" wine selection.

Fresca *Peruvian* 22 | 18 | 19 | $36

West Portal | 24 W. Portal Ave. (Ulloa St.) | 415-759-8087
Noe Valley | 3945 24th St. (bet. Noe & Sanchez Sts.) | 415-695-0549
Upper Fillmore | 2114 Fillmore St. (California St.) | 415-447-2668 | www.frescasf.com

"Refreshing" ceviche, "delicious" rotisserie chicken and "lomo saltado, baby!" "stand out" on an affordable Peruvian menu "packed with flavor" praise partisans of this "dynamic", "inviting" trio that delivers "amazing cocktails" too; as the typically "crowded" quarters result in "long waits", savvy guests say "get there off-hours" to beat the rush; N.B. an Inner Sunset branch is set to open at 737 Irving Street in fall 2009.

Fringale *Basque/French* 24 | 18 | 22 | $48

SoMa | 570 Fourth St. (bet. Brannan & Freelon Sts.) | 415-543-0573 | www.fringalesf.com

"Been there, done that, and loved every minute of it" enthuse fans of this "must-revisit" SoMa bistro, where the "new chef" continues to prepare a "beautifully thought-out menu" of "terrific" French-Basque

	FOOD	DECOR	SERVICE	COST

fare; with a "charismatic" staff and "reasonable prices", it's a welcome "escape" from the area's "overrated hot spots", but "be prepared to be friendly" with other diners, since the "understated" digs are "very tight."

Frjtz Fries *Belgian* | 18 | 14 | 14 | $17 |

Hayes Valley | 581 Hayes St. (Laguna St.) | 415-864-7654
Mission | 590 Valencia St. (17th St.) | 415-863-8272
www.frjtzfries.com

"Yep, you definitely want fries with that" at this Mission and Hayes Valley duo delivering "crisp", "authentic" Belgian frites with a cornucopia of "exotic dipping sauces", along with crêpes, Trappist brews and salads (to help you "feel a little better about yourself"); the "modern" "quasi cafeteria/lounge setting" isn't for everyone, but those with a "jones" call it a "cheap date with no complaints."

Frontera Fresco *Mexican* | ▽ 18 | 13 | 12 | $18 |

Downtown | Macy's | 170 O'Farrell St. (bet. Powell & Stockton Sts.) | 415-296-4349 | www.rickbayless.com

Boasting the imprimatur of Chicago-based chef Rick Bayless, this colorful, quick-service stop at Macy's showcases Mexican "street food" with a "gourmet" twist, making for an "affordable" "shopping break"; still, while it's "not bad for a department store", "disappointed" diners cite "bland" chow that doesn't hold a *candela* to his "real restaurants."

Front Porch, The *Caribbean/Southern* | 22 | 19 | 19 | $31 |

Bernal Heights | 65A 29th St. (bet. Mission St. & San Jose Ave.) | 415-695-7800 | www.thefrontporchsf.com

There's "no shame in eating a bucket of fried chicken anymore" proclaim Bernal Heights "hipsters" who hanker for the "serious" "soul food" served at this "super-cool" Caribbean-Southern "hangout"; from the "big cozy rocking chair out front" to the "great beer" and "music and chatter" inside, it's a real hootenanny, even if "epic waits" can be a "roadblock."

Gamine *French* | 22 | 14 | 20 | $27 |

Cow Hollow | 2223 Union St. (bet. Fillmore & Steiner Sts.) | 415-771-7771

Fans find some of the "best" French fare in SF "for the money" at this "fantastic" Cow Hollow bistro – a Chez Maman offshoot that was recently purchased by one of the partners and renamed; "great service" and an open kitchen add to the charm.

◪ Garden Court *Californian* | 20 | 29 | 22 | $58 |

Downtown | Palace Hotel | 2 New Montgomery St. (Market St.) | 415-546-5010 | www.gardencourt-restaurant.com

With its "lavish" "ballroom" setting "out of another time", this "quintessential old San Francisco" "beauty" inside Downtown's "historic Palace Hotel" is "a must for the ladies" or anyone wishing to "feel like royalty" at a "special-occasion" daytime buffet, Sunday "jazz brunch" or Saturday "tea service"; those who manage to "stop staring" at the ornate glass ceiling discover the pricey Californian fare is merely "standard", but it's "worth the price of admission" "just being" there.

Garibaldis *Californian/Mediterranean* | 22 | 20 | 21 | $47 |

Presidio Heights | 347 Presidio Ave. (bet. Clay & Sacramento Sts.) | 415-563-8841 | www.garibaldisrestaurant.com

Striking a "balance" of "neighborhoody but not too casual", this "patrician" Presidio Heights haunt and its larger, "more alive" Rockridge brother present a Cal-Med menu that "gets the taste buds moving"; they're "reliable" for a "civilized dinner" or "business lunch", and though they "seem pricier than they need to be" to some, the nightly "happy-hour" specials are a "screaming deal"; N.B. the bar is set to be converted into a new branch of the owner's Marzano.

⏣ Gary Danko *American*

29	27	29	$109

Fisherman's Wharf | 800 N. Point St. (Hyde St.) | 415-749-2060 | www.garydanko.com

Voted "numero uno" in Food and Service and once again Most Popular in this Survey, Gary Danko's "celebrated" "must-go" on the Wharf "transcends" the rest with its "exquisite", "create-your-own" New American tasting menus, enhanced by a "biblical" wine list and "astounding" "cheesemobile" and purveyed by an "exemplary" staff that "goes out of its way to make you feel comfortable and special" (even walk-ins "at the bar"); a "jewel box" setting pulls together the "whole package", making for a worthwhile "ultimate splurge."

Gaylord India *Indian*

18	17	19	$38

Downtown | 1 Embarcadero Ctr. | 333 Battery St. (Sacramento St.) | 415-397-7775 | www.gaylords1.com

"One of the few establishments with an authentic tandoor oven", this Downtown Indian (part of an international chain) curries favor for its "beautifully presented" dishes proffered in a "quiet", "formal" atmosphere; though naysayers knock it's "past its prime" and "nothing to write home to Delhi about", it remains a "practical choice" for a weekday lunch buffet or dinner "with colleagues."

Gialina *Pizza*

24	16	20	$27

Glen Park | 2842 Diamond St. (Kern St.) | 415-239-8500 | www.gialina.com

"Sensuous pizzas brimming with soul" and laced with "nettles and other rare toppings" (there's "even a dessert" iteration) are "worth the trip over and through the winding roads" to this "chic", "artisanal" Glen Park Italian where the "roasts of the day" and the salads also "follow the seasons"; the "lines can feel long during those foggy nights" and it's "quite cacophonous inside", but the "helpful" staff and "compelling" *cucina* "make up for it."

Giordano Bros. *Sandwiches*

▽ 22	18	19	$17

North Beach | 303 Columbus Ave. (B'way) | 415-397-2767

"Straight outta Pittsburgh", this late-night North Beach pit stop delivers a "sloppy, delicious" "kitchen-sink sandwich" (think "cheesesteak" "jammed with fries" and coleslaw), but with "fresh ingredients not available in the Iron City"; since it's a de facto "Steelers bar" too, "diehard fans" will "feel at home on Sundays."

Giorgio's Pizzeria *Pizza*

21	12	19	$19

Inner Richmond | 151 Clement St. (3rd Ave.) | 415-668-1266 | www.giorgiospizza.com

A "sentimental favorite" complete with "checkered tablecloths" and "plastic grapes", this Inner Richmond "family place" has been purveying pizza and calzones with a "glowing flavor" since 1972; it's often "packed on the weekends" but the staff "does a good job getting groups in and out", and boosts the "child-friendly" factor on Wednesdays (4–6 PM), when kids get to make their own pies.

	FOOD	DECOR	SERVICE	COST

ZⓃEW Gitane ●❶⍈Ⓜ *French/Spanish* | 22 | 26 | 22 | $46 |

Downtown | 6 Claude Ln. (bet. Bush & Sutter Sts.) | 415-788-6686 | www.gitanerestaurant.com

"Another hit from the Café Claude people", this new gypsy-inspired Downtown "date place" is "decked-to-the-nines", featuring an upstairs dining room whose "delightfully naughty bordello vibe" sets the mood for "aromatic", "exciting" dishes (starting with "stellar" bacon bonbons) from Spain, France and Morocco; downstairs, the bartenders "put on a show", mixing "artful" cocktails at the "painfully crowded bar."

Globe ● *Californian/Italian* | 20 | 17 | 20 | $42 |

Downtown | 290 Pacific Ave. (bet. Battery & Front Sts.) | 415-391-4132 | www.globerestaurant.com

Serving up a "showstopper steak for two" and "terrific" pastas "even after most are ready to go home", this "unpretentious", midpriced Cal-Ital with a "hidden old Barbary Coast" locale and "TriBeCa feel" is still a "haven for late-nighters" (including a following of "after-hours chefs"); day-trippers add that "business lunches" and "Sunday dinners fresh from the farmer's market" are "special" too.

Goat Hill Pizza *Pizza* | 18 | 10 | 16 | $18 |

Potrero Hill | 300 Connecticut St. (18th St.) | 415-641-1440
SoMa | 171 Stillman St. (bet. 3rd & 4th Sts.) | 415-974-1303
www.goathill.com

"Real San Francisco pizza" with a "sturdy sourdough crust" and "fresh toppings" wins over pie partisans at this "offbeat" Potrero Hill parlor (with a recently relocated SoMa branch); be sure to "get there early" (and "bring out the stretch pants") on "all-you-can-eat Mondays" when big "groups" "sample up a storm" and kids under five eat for free.

Godzila Sushi *Japanese* | 19 | 10 | 16 | $28 |

Pacific Heights | 1800 Divisadero St. (Bush St.) | 415-931-1773

Since the "small space" isn't exactly Godzilla-sized, "it can get pretty crowded fast" with patrons seeking sushi on the "cheap" at this Pac Heights Japanese; supporters say the wait is "worth it" for food that's "better than sex", while others opine it's only "passable", but the "hip" vibe and "cheerful" service are a plus for most.

Gold Mountain *Chinese* | 20 | 6 | 12 | $21 |

Chinatown | 644 Broadway (bet. Columbus Ave. & Stockton St.) | 415-296-7733

Fans "fill up on *har gow* and roll out a happier human" at this "dim sum delight" that's "brimming with authenticity" in Chinatown; while the "super-bright", "cafeteria"-like space is often "teeming with crowds", the "table turnover is quick" (it's "not a place to linger") and "you really get your money's worth."

Good Luck Dim Sum ⊅ *Chinese* | 22 | 5 | 11 | $12 |

Inner Richmond | 736 Clement St. (bet. 8th & 9th Aves.) | 415-386-3388

"Stuff yourself silly for less than $10" at this "dim sum dive" "in the heart of the new Chinatown" (i.e. the Inner Richmond's Clement Street) where the "price/quality ratio cannot be beat"; given the "dismal" digs and "brusque but quick" service (just "point to get what you want"), "lined-up" patrons feel lucky when they "take it to go"; N.B. closes at 6:30 PM.

	FOOD	DECOR	SERVICE	COST

Goood Frikin' Chicken *Mideastern* — 18 | 8 | 14 | $16

Mission | 10 29th St. (Mission St.) | 415-970-2428 | www.gfcsf.com

"You need that extra 'o' because" the "well-spiced chicken" ("rotis-serie or open-flame") is "soo moist and delicious" at this Middle Eastern near the Outer Mission purveying "value" kebabs and veggie plates too; foes cry fowl, claiming there's "no charm to the place", but most say it's "great for a take-out party."

Grand Cafe *French* — 19 | 25 | 20 | $47

Downtown | Hotel Monaco | 501 Geary St. (Taylor St.) | 415-292-0101 | www.grandcafe-sf.com

"Opulent" yet "playful", the "fin de siècle"–style dining room provides a "plush", "Parisian" atmosphere for "hearty" (if comparatively "ordi-nary") French bistro fare at this "dramatic" Downtowner attached to the Hotel Monaco; the location is "handy" "before or after" a show, and the "lovely" staff "gets you to the theater on time", though a few favor the bar and lounge areas for a "less expensive" bite.

Grandeho's Kamekyo *Japanese* — 23 | 14 | 20 | $36

Fisherman's Wharf | 2721 Hyde St. (bet. Beach & N. Point Sts.) | 415-673-6828

Cole Valley | 943 Cole St. (bet. Carl St. & Parnassus Ave.) | 415-759-8428

Frequented by "locals, tourists" and "Japan Airlines flight crews", this "top-notch" yet "affordable" sushi duo rolls up "nigiri so large it takes three bites to finish"; Wharf dwellers delight in the "high-quality sea-food" and "expanded Vietnamese" options, while parents prefer the "friendly" Cole Valley branch, which makes kids feel "welcome" too.

Grand Pu Bah *Thai* — 18 | 19 | 17 | $33

Potrero Hill | 88 Division St. (Townsend St.) | 415-255-8188 | www.grandpubahrestaurant.com

"Spicy" small plates, "fresh" raw bar bites and "amazing drinks" bring a "bustling" "happy-hour" crowd to this "trendy" Potrero Hill sopho-more specializing in Thai with a "twist"; despite the "vibrant scene", however, some surveyors cite "uneven" quality and "wish it weren't quite so expensive for what you get."

Great Eastern ● *Chinese* — 21 | 12 | 14 | $29

Chinatown | 649 Jackson St. (bet. Grant Ave. & Kearny St.) | 415-986-2500

"Excellent fresh seafood" (plucked straight "from the tank in front of you") stars at this "Chinatown favorite", an "authentic" option "amid a sea of tourist traps" that "fills up early with locals" for "dim sum dur-ing the day" ("ordered from the menu") and stays "open late"; with "typical drab" digs and "slow" service, though, it's merely "Good Eastern" to some.

Green Chile Kitchen & Market *Mexican* — 20 | 15 | 16 | $18

Western Addition | 601 Baker St. (Fulton St.) | 415-614-9411 | www.greenchilekitchen.com

"Takes me back to the homemade posole and green chile of Santa Fe" wax Southwestern transplants who frequent this "neighborhood sit-down or take-out" Western Addition Mexican also specializing in ro-tisserie chicken and the "best breakfast burritos"; it's "a little pricier" than the "typical" taqueria, but the "organic ingredients" are a "signif-icant step up" and there's even "curbside service."

FOOD | DECOR | SERVICE | COST

☑ Greens *Vegetarian* `24` `24` `22` `$45`

Marina | Fort Mason Ctr., Bldg. A | Marina Blvd. (Buchanan St.) | 415-771-6222 | www.greensrestaurant.com

"Still the standard-bearer when it comes to upscale vegetarian dining", this Marina "classic" continues to "surprise" and "satisfy" the "body and soul" under the "incredible command" of chef Annie Sommerville; the flavors are "bold", the "wine list is deep" and the "view of the Golden Gate" "glorious", so while a few feel it's "resting on its laurels", devotees defend this "queen of the green" for "making us all love our veggies."

Hamano Sushi *Japanese* `19` `14` `19` `$30`

Noe Valley | 1332 Castro St. (bet. Jersey & 24th Sts.) | 415-826-0825 | www.hamanosushi.com

Delivering "consistently fresh sushi, an outstanding selection of maki" and even its "own private label sake" with "no fanfare", this "down-home", affordable Noe Valley Japanese goes mano a mano with other contenders; the decor is "a bit flat", but the "friendly" staff makes it an appealing stop "if you're in the neighborhood."

Hard Knox Cafe *Southern* `19` `13` `17` `$19`

Outer Sunset | 2448 Clement St. (bet. 25th & 26th Aves.) | 415-752-3770
Potrero Hill | 2526 Third St. (bet. 22nd & 23rd Sts.) | 415-648-3770
www.hardknoxcafe.com

"As close as you're going to get to a 'meat-and-three'" on the West Coast, this Southern soul food duo in Potrero Hill and the Outer Sunset is the "real deal", whipping up "stick-to-your-ribs", "frigginlicious fried chicken" and "killer oxtails", served by a "friendly" staff in old-timey, "industrial" digs where space is "tight"; Texas-trained chef-owner Tony Hua may not be everyone's idea of "your typical 'Southern'" gent, but he "cranks out food like nobody's business" – and besides, "SF isn't typical."

Hard Rock Cafe *American* `12` `20` `14` `$29`

Fisherman's Wharf | Bldg. Q1 | Pier 39 (The Embarcadero at Beach St.) | 415-956-2013 | www.hardrock.com

An "iconic part of the tourist landscape", this guitar-shaped, rock 'n' roll–themed American chain link in Fisherman's Wharf was "cool in the '80s" but many feel it's "past its sell date", citing "mundane" grub, "haphazard" service and "way too loud" acoustics; despite a "surprisingly decent burger" and all that "fun music memorabilia", some opt to "buy the T-shirt" instead.

Harris' *Steak* `25` `22` `24` `$66`

Polk Gulch | 2100 Van Ness Ave. (Pacific Ave.) | 415-673-1888 | www.harrisrestaurant.com

"Satisfy the carnivore within" by "splurging" at this "grown-up" Polk Gulch steakhouse purveying "perfectly prepared" cuts of beef and "proper cocktails" fit for "Nick and Nora Charles"; no, "there's nothing trendy or nouvelle" about it, but the "army of servers" really "knows its stuff", and the "clubby wood paneling, cushy booths" and "soft lighting" set the mood for "quiet" conversation to the tune of "mellow" live jazz.

	FOOD	DECOR	SERVICE	COST

Hayes Street Grill *Seafood*   23 | 17 | 22 | $49

Hayes Valley | 320 Hayes St. (bet. Franklin & Gough Sts.) | 415-863-5545 | www.hayesstreetgrill.com

"Satisfying from start to finish", this "civilized" Hayes Valley "stalwart" specializes in "uniformly fresh", "simply prepared" sustainable seafood served to the "pre-performance" crowd "in plenty of time for the show"; though picky pescatarians would appreciate "a bit more innovation", the majority marvels it's "astonishing how good" it has been for years.

NEW Heaven's Dog *Chinese*   21 | 19 | 22 | $36

SoMa | SoMA Grand | 1148 Mission St. (bet. 7th & 8th Sts.) | 415-863-6008 | www.heavensdog.com

Charles Phan (The Slanted Door) "redefines Chinese food" at his stylish Sino small-plates restaurant, lounge and adjacent noodle bar in the SoMa Grand, which boosters dub "top dog" for its "deep flavors", "incredible wine list" and "accommodating" service; imbibers also applaud the bartender's "directional cocktails" (just start with "what spirit you like"), but some wallet-watchers wail the "pricing is way too high for dumplings and soup."

Helmand Palace *Afghani*   23 | 17 | 19 | $32

Russian Hill | 2424 Van Ness Ave. (bet. Green & Union Sts.) | 415-362-0641 | www.helmandpalace.com

"Kabul West" is what fans are calling this "quiet" Afghani "bang for the buck" in Russian Hill known for its "unfailingly polite staff" and "fantastic", "nuanced" cuisine ("must-tries" include "any lamb" or pumpkin dish); though the interior is "not glamorous", supporters are pleased that it "re-creates" the ambiance of the former North Beach location; N.B. valet parking Friday–Saturday.

Henry's Hunan *Chinese*   21 | 8 | 16 | $19

Downtown | 674 Sacramento St. (bet. Kearny & Montgomery Sts.) | 415-788-2234 🐧
NEW Noe Valley | 1708 Church St. (bet. Day & 29th Sts.) | 415-826-9189
SoMa | 1016 Bryant St. (bet. 8th & 9th Sts.) | 415-861-5808 🐧
SoMa | 110 Natoma St. (bet. New Montgomery & 2nd Sts.) | 415-546-4999 🐧
Hunan *Chinese*
Chinatown | 924 Sansome St. (Broadway St.) | 415-956-7727
www.henryshunanrestaurant.com

"Nobody else around here makes Hunan dishes like" this "low-cost" chain that "hits all the notes of Formica-table Chinese restaurant classics: spicy, salty, oily and piping hot"; "don't expect any ambiance", or anything more than "no-frills service", but it's "super-quick" and convenient for "workday lunches", even if some purists sniff "really, you can do better."

Herbivore *Vegan*   15 | 15 | 17 | $20

Mission | 983 Valencia St. (bet. 20th & 21st Sts.) | 415-826-5657
Western Addition | 531 Divisadero St. (bet. Fell & Hayes Sts.) | 415-885-7133
www.herbivorerestaurant.com

"Hearty" plates of "wholesome" vegan dishes with a "global" slant keep cost-conscious veggies "happy" at these "cafeteria"-like joints in the Mission, Western Addition and Berkeley, though critics claim it's "hit-or-miss", citing "uninspired", "unchanging" cuisine that "could easily be better"; service has improved but still tends to "vary", so just "don't be in a hurry, as the staff certainly isn't."

Hog Island
Oyster Co. & Bar *Seafood*

| 25 | 17 | 19 | $35 |

Embarcadero | 1 Ferry Bldg. (Market St.) | 415-391-7117 | www.hogislandoysters.com

Short of "driving to the farm" in Marshall where the eponymous bivalves are raised, this pair of oyster bars in the Embarcadero Ferry Building and Napa's Oxbow Market is the place for "slurpin'" "super-calishuckulous" shellfish and "gulping local brews", and those who don't like it "raw" are in "hog heaven" over chowder that fans swear is "better than Boston's"; "unbeatable happy hours" "save you some serious" clams, but "be prepared to battle it out" for seats and service.

Home ❶ *American*

| 18 | 15 | 17 | $29 |

Castro | 2100 Market St. (Church St.) | 415-503-0333 | www.home-sf.com

There's no place like Home for a "fix of meatloaf" and other "down-to-earth" American "classics" say Castro customers who throw back "sweet" "house specialty cocktails" before their "satisfying" mac 'n' cheese; the "friendly" staff and "casual" surroundings keep it "comfortable" (if you don't mind the "constant din"), and "daily early-bird specials" (5–6 PM) mean "you'll feel the impact" of a visit "on your waistline more than your wallet."

NEW Horatius *Mediterranean/Portuguese*

| - | - | - | M |

Potrero Hill | 350 Kansas St. (bet. 16th & 17th Sts.) | 415-252-3500 | www.horatius.com

A one-stop shop for foodies, this Potrero Hill mash-up is part specialty market gallery, part wine bar and part Med-Portuguese bistro all under one funky warehouse roof; it currently offers light breakfasts and seated lunch service, along with coffee drinks, wines and prepared foods to go until 8 PM, but is aiming to roll out dinner service by fall 2009.

Hotei *Japanese*

| 19 | 12 | 16 | $21 |

Inner Sunset | 1290 Ninth Ave. (Irving St.) | 415-753-6045 | www.hoteisf.com

"One of the few Japanese restaurants in the city offering more than just sushi and the usual teriyaki/tempura fare", this "divine" Inner Sunset "noodle house" "conveniently located next to Golden Gate Park and the museums" is the perfect "quick", "inexpensive" lunch stop for "excellent udon" and other "steaming, delicious bowls of soup"; some regulars grouse that "it's gotten more crowded" since finatics found out its raw fin fare is the "same as that served" at sibling Ebisu across the street.

☑ House, The *Asian Fusion*

| 27 | 15 | 21 | $42 |

North Beach | 1230 Grant Ave. (bet. Columbus Ave. & Vallejo St.) | 415-986-8612 | www.thehse.com

"Artful" Asian fusion fare full of "intense flavors and fresh ingredients" "blossoms in North Beach" at this "terrific-value", "easy-to-

FOOD | DECOR | SERVICE | COST

miss hideout" staffed by a "friendly" (if "rushed") crew; sure, the volume in the "cramped quarters" can reach "brain-damaging noise levels", but fans affirm "that's just because everyone there is having a good time."

House of Nanking Chinese

22 | 7 | 12 | $23

Chinatown | 919 Kearny St. (bet. Columbus Ave. & Jackson St.) | 415-421-1429

"Locals and tourists alike" form a "line out the door" of this Chinatown "dive", waiting to brave the famously "brusque" owner who "has no problem informing you of what to order"; if you "put yourself in his hands", the "frantic" experience "can be fun" declare devotees who say the often "spicy" food "shines in every respect" and "doesn't break the bank" either, though "if you want to be pampered", it's not for you; N.B. a soon-to-open spin-off called Fang (on 660 Howard Street) should help ease the crowds.

☑ House of Prime Rib American

24 | 19 | 22 | $51

Polk Gulch | 1906 Van Ness Ave. (Washington St.) | 415-885-4605 | www.houseofprimerib.net

"Welcome meat lovers!" to this "one-trick pony" in Polk Gulch, where "superior" prime rib "stars" on a "retro" American menu that recalls when "creamed spinach" was king, "salads were prepared tableside" and "great honkin' slabs" of beef were "rolled to your table on a silver cart"; most tout its tremendous "value", and while the impatient are irked by "long waits", others hit the bar to "indulge in a heavy-handed cocktail."

Hunan Home's Restaurant Chinese

22 | 12 | 18 | $25

Chinatown | 622 Jackson St. (bet. Grant Ave. & Kearny St.) | 415-982-2844

"Come hungry" since the "hot and spicy" Hunan dishes are "addictive" aver aficionados who are "just wild about" the "large menu" of "traditional" cuisine at this Chinatown-based chainlet; the food definitely "outshines" the "plain-Jane" decor, but "fine, fast" service and "cheap" tabs ensure it's "always crowded."

Hyde Street Bistro French

21 | 17 | 19 | $43

Russian Hill | 1521 Hyde St. (bet. Jackson St. & Pacific Ave.) | 415-292-4415 | www.hydestreetbistrosf.com

For a "real" "French bistro experience" that's "cheaper than a trip to Paris" – only the service is "friendly" and "you'll see the cable cars rolling by" – this "fabulous little find" on Russian Hill "can't be beat"; "parking is a bear" and *oui*, "they pack you in", "but that's half the battle" or "charm"; N.B. the post-Survey arrival of new Sancerre-native chef Mikal Audry and an imminent remodel (and possible name change) are not reflected in the scores.

NEW Il Cane Rosso Italian

- | - | - | I

Embarcadero | 1 Ferry Bldg. | Ferry Plaza (bet. Drumm & Spear Sts.) | 415-391-7599 | www.canerossosf.com

Pedigreed chefs Daniel Patterson (Coi) and Lauren Kiino (ex Delfina) are up to new tricks at this barking new quick-service stop in the Embarcadero's Ferry Building; the Italian-inspired, locally sourced menu provides breakfast fare and salads, but primarily revolves around a rotisserie that supplies the sandwiches and daily plates of roasted chicken and porchetta (with choice sides), served inside the rosso-colored room and on the bayside patio; N.B. closes at 8 PM.

Il Fornaio *Italian*

19 | 20 | 19 | $40

Downtown | Levi's Plaza | 1265 Battery St. (Greenwich St.) | 415-986-0100 | www.ilfornaio.com

The name translates as 'the baker', so naturally there's the "smell of fresh bread" in the air at this "higher end" Italian chain where the "authentic", "consistently tasty" offerings arrive in "elegantly casual" indoor/outdoor environs; "super weekly specials", "monthly regional menus" and a "solid wine selection" add to its "reliable" reputation and help explain the somewhat "upscale" price point.

Iluna Basque *Spanish*

21 | 19 | 18 | $39

North Beach | 701 Union St. (Powell St.) | 415-402-0011 | www.ilunabasque.com

Bring an "adventurous" attitude because the "fabulous chef" puts a "fresh", "unusual" "twist on Basque tapas" at this North Beach nook that invites mingling and "grazing to your heart's content" at its central communal table; while the ratings are all on the up-swing, a few contrarians quibble it's merely "ho-hum" and "pricey" for small plates.

Imperial Tea Court *Tearoom*

20 | 21 | 16 | $20

Embarcadero | 1 Ferry Bldg. (Market St.) | 415-544-9830 | www.imperialtea.com

Customers "come away feeling calmer and well-nourished" at these traditional Chinese tearooms where a "supreme" selection of leaves trumps the "light", "limited" menu; service can "be a little slow", but most savor the "relaxing", "Zen" environment, particularly in the "peaceful" garden of the Berkeley branch; N.B. the Embarcadero location closes at 6:30 PM most nights.

Incanto *Italian*

24 | 20 | 23 | $50

Noe Valley | 1550 Church St. (Duncan St.) | 415-641-4500 | www.incanto.biz

"Adventuresome" eaters find "gustatory nirvana" at this "joyful ode to all things meat" (i.e. "offal") by "irreverent" chef Chris Cosentino in a "beautiful", "out-of-the-way" Noe Valley setting, but "don't be scared" by the "nose-to-tail" "hype" counsel "squeamish" types, as there's "normal" "handcrafted" Northern Italian pasta and salumi too; what's more, the Boot-only "flights" are "sure to break any California wine rut"; N.B. now serving Sunday brunch.

Indian Oven *Indian*

23 | 15 | 18 | $29

Lower Haight | 233 Fillmore St. (bet. Haight & Waller Sts.) | 415-626-1628 | www.indianovensf.com

"Though you pay a bit more" than at some other Indian restaurants, it's well "worth the extra dough" for "fresh, light" cuisine that "rivals any you'll find in London or Mumbai" according to Lower Haight curry connoisseurs; the "intimate" environs "can get a bit cramped", but "polite", "efficient" servers help ease the crunch.

	FOOD	DECOR	SERVICE	COST

Indigo ☒ *American* | 19 | 18 | 21 | $47 |

Civic Center | 687 McAllister St. (Gough St.) | 415-673-9353 |
www.indigorestaurant.com

"Opera- and symphony-goers" enjoy a "pleasant start to the evening" – while grape nuts pour in "after the pre-theater push" for the "bargain" wine dinner – at this "low-key", "comfortable" Civic Center New American; though some note the food is "respectable but not life-changing", a "cordial" staff and "no-corkage" BYO option help keep customers "coming back."

☒ In-N-Out Burger ● *Burgers* | 22 | 10 | 18 | $8 |

Fisherman's Wharf | 333 Jefferson St. (bet. Jones & Leavenworth Sts.) |
800-786-1000 | www.in-n-out.com

"Quality ingredients make all the difference" in the "addictive" burgers, "real milkshakes" and fries "cut fresh each morning" at this "cheap and cheerful", "family-owned" chain ("SoCal's gift to NorCal") with a "cult" following; despite "limited" choices, you can "mix things up" by "learning the secret menu" ("get it 'animal-style'"), and though constant "crowds" mean "you're not always in 'n' out" in a jiffy, the "energetic" "kids" behind the counter are always "polite" and "efficient."

Isa ☒ *French* | 24 | 20 | 20 | $48 |

Marina | 3324 Steiner St. (bet. Chestnut & Lombard Sts.) | 415-567-9588 |
www.isarestaurant.com

"Delightful" "small plates" that are "easy to share" and served with "knockout, seldom seen wines" stand out at this "pricey" Marina French with a "bustling" interior and "quieter" "covered patio" that's "about as enchanting as you could possibly get"; on the downside, it's a gamble "if you like order in your life", as the "food comes at its own pace."

Isobune *Japanese* | 17 | 13 | 15 | $28 |

Japantown | Kintetsu Mall | 1737 Post St. (bet. Buchanan & Webster Sts.) |
415-563-1030 | www.isobuneburlingame.com

"Your boat always comes in" at this "entertaining" Japantown "conveyer-belt" Japanese (with a Burlingame sib) where you sit at a circular sushi bar and "grab" your catch as it "floats by in a canal"; it's "fairly inexpensive" and "kids love it", though detractors dub it a "gimmick" with "forgettable" fish that "goes around too many times" on "slow nights."

Izzy's Steaks & Chops *Steak* | 20 | 17 | 19 | $43 |

Marina | 3345 Steiner St. (bet. Chestnut & Lombard Sts.) | 415-563-0487 |
www.izzyssteaks.com

A "solid choice" for "dependable" steaks "without the pretense" of bigger chains, this "traditional" chophouse in the Marina (with three suburban sibs) is "one of the better bargains" around according to the "carnivore crowd", thanks in part to "included" sides like their "famous potatoes" ("cheesy, carby heaven"); no, it's "not fancy", but the "slightly dated" digs are still "comfortable", and the occasionally "crusty" servers are real "pros."

Jackson Fillmore Trattoria ☒ *Italian* | 21 | 12 | 16 | $40 |

Upper Fillmore | 2506 Fillmore St. (Jackson St.) | 415-346-5288 |
www.jacksonfillmoresf.com

The "huge" helpings of "homey", "garlicky" Italian fare are "just what you want from a small trattoria" say fans of this "no-frills" Upper

| | FOOD | DECOR | SERVICE | COST |

Fillmore "find"; just "go early" since it can get "horribly crowded" at peak times, and "have patience", because while "some servers are really good", others are infamously "surly."

Jai Yun *Chinese* ▽ 23 | 7 | 16 | $56

Chinatown | 680 Clay St. (bet. Kearny & Montgomery Sts.) | 415-981-7438 | www.menuscan.com/jaiyun

For "Chinese taken up a notch", Sino savants "reserve a day in advance", "pick a price per person", "then sit back and enjoy" at this relocated Chinatown dive as the chef crafts "artful", "customized" banquets from "what's he's purchased that day"; nevertheless some naysayers knock it as the "emperor's new clothes", citing "ugly" "storefront" digs, "difficult" communication and food that falls short of the "price" and the "hype."

Jake's Steaks *Cheesesteaks* ▽ 20 | 11 | 16 | $13

Marina | 3301 Buchanan St. (Lombard St.) | 415-922-2211 | www.jakessteaks.net

Homesick Philadelphians "hit" this "pretty authentic" cheesesteak shop and "Eagles bar" in the Marina for "Sunday football, cold beer" and a sandwich with "Whiz", giving shout-outs to their "fellow Philly fella" for supplying the "same rolls" as their hometown favorites and "quick delivery" too; just don't expect any "frills around the edges" (and "don't forget your Tastykakes" either).

Z Jardinière *Californian/French* 26 | 26 | 25 | $74

Civic Center | 300 Grove St. (Franklin St.) | 415-861-5555 | www.jardiniere.com

"The best thing to happen to *Tristan und Isolde* in many years" sing "cultured" customers who "float across the street post-opera or -symphony" to this Civic Center "celebration" place where Pat Kuleto's "glitzy" "supper-club" decor sets the stage for Traci Des Jardins' "exquisite" "artistry" with sustainable Cal-French cuisine, matched by "sublime" wines and "stellar" service; the "bar menu is perfect" for a "quick" nibble "without reservations", but many prefer to "stay for hours and savor an entire experience" as "rich as the price tag."

Jay's Cheesesteak *Cheesesteaks* 19 | 9 | 14 | $13

Mission | 3285 21st St. (bet. Lexington & Valencia Sts.) | 415-285-5200 ⊄
Western Addition | 553 Divisadero St. (bet. Fell & Hayes Sts.) | 415-771-5104

Maybe the cheesesteaks are "not so authentic, but who cares?" when they're so "rib-stickingly good" gush groupies who order "outrageously garlicky garlic fries" with their "sinful" Philly fare and "even better" burgers (they can even "do seitan for vegetarians") at this Mission and Western Addition duo; just "plan on getting your food to go" instead of eating in the "tiny" space (though on 21st Street you can "sit outside on a sunny day").

Joe DiMaggio's Italian Chophouse *Italian/Steak* 21 | 23 | 21 | $55

North Beach | 601 Union St. (Stockton St.) | 415-421-5633 | www.joedimaggiosrestaurant.com

"If you're a fan of Joltin' Joe or Ms. Monroe, you'll love" all the "snaps" adorning this "clubby", "nostalgic" North Beach Italian chophouse, where steaks "prepared exactly as one orders" and "hefty martinis" "make for a great night out" with your "buddies" or "business clients"; still, a frugal few fret that it's "overpriced" for fare that's only "decent."

Joe's Cable Car *Burgers*

| 21 | 15 | 17 | $18 |

Excelsior | 4320 Mission St. (bet. Silver Ave. & Tingley St.) | 415-334-6699 | www.joescablecar.com

Joe "grinds his own and is always good for a joke" at this "iconic" Excelsior "burger joint" offering "meaty-juicy goodness" "in each bite", accompanied by "good" fries and "thick malts"; the "kitschy" "cable-car" setup "suits the experience", but the "neighborhood is a bit rough around the edges" and detractors beef "I've never paid so much to eat off paper plates."

Joey & Eddie's *Italian*

| 14 | 16 | 16 | $40 |

North Beach | 1652 Stockton St. (bet. Filbert & Union Sts.) | 415-989-7800 | www.joeyandeddies.com

"Brash" and "busy", this North Beach Italian by 'Joey' Manzare (Globe, Zuppa) churns out groaning "family-style" plates of "garlic and oil"–laden "comfort food" like "Sunday gravy any day" that fit the bill "if you need to bulk up" or throw an "office party"; still, even the occasional "Rat Pack floor show" fails to distract "disappointed" diners, as most give it the Bronx cheer for "clueless service" and "substandard" grub.

Juban *Japanese*

| 19 | 14 | 16 | $33 |

Japantown | Kinokuniya Bldg. | 1581 Webster St. (Post St.) | 415-776-5822 | www.jubanrestaurant.com

See review in South of San Francisco Directory.

Kabuto Ⓜ *Japanese*

| 26 | 13 | 18 | $50 |

Outer Richmond | 5121 Geary Blvd. (bet. 15th & 16th Aves.) | 415-752-5652 | www.kabutosushi.com

"If you're tired of your same old, same old" Japanese, trek to this Outer Richmond "hole-in-the-wall" that "fills up quickly" for the "freshest" sushi presented in "intelligent", "inspired" combinations; afishiona-dos opt for a "deal" of a lunch or endure evening waits to "sit at the bar" and savor "specials" galore for a "phenomenal" feast.

Kan Zaman *Mideastern*

| 17 | 16 | 16 | $27 |

Haight-Ashbury | 1793 Haight St. (Shrader St.) | 415-751-9656

"You can always count on a good time" at this Haight-Ashbury hookah hangout, where savvy guests snag a "seat on the cushions next to the window" and "share" Middle Eastern meze, catch the "kitschy" belly dancers (Wednesday–Sunday) and smoke a pipe "at the bar" (or after dinnertime at the tables); some say they "expected more flavor" from the food, but others feel it's "hearty" for the "reasonable" price.

Kasa Indian Eatery *Indian*

| 20 | 15 | 15 | $14 |

Castro | 4001 18th St. (Noe St.) | 415-621-6940 | www.kasaindian.com

"Giving a whole new meaning to the idea of fast food", this "trendy" "assembly-line" subcontinental ("a cross between a taqueria and an Indian restaurant") in the Castro "draws large crowds" for its "limited" but "excellently spiced" renditions of "lamb, veggies and rice dishes", wrapped as kati rolls or served on metal Thali plates; it's a "bit pricey" for "self-service", but the "blend of convenience and taste" makes it "ideal before a night out"; N.B. a second branch in Cow Hollow is in the works.

	FOOD	DECOR	SERVICE	COST

Kate's Kitchen ⊄ *Southern*
▽ 22 | 14 | 18 | $14

Lower Haight | 471 Haight St. (bet. Fillmore & Webster Sts.) | 415-626-3984
"Nothing cures a hangover" like the "tummy-filling" Southern fare and endless mug of joe topped off by "attentive" servers at this daytime-only "mother of all breakfast joints" in the Lower Haight; the atmosphere is "humble" and even a "little funky", but that's all "part of the appeal" for regulars who recommend "arriving early" to beat the "deservedly long lines"; N.B. cash only.

Katia's Russian Tea Room Ⓜ *Russian*
▽ 23 | 17 | 20 | $31

Inner Richmond | 600 Fifth Ave. (Balboa St.) | 415-668-9292 | www.katias.com
"Welcoming" chef-owner Katia Troosh "puts her heart into her cooking" at this "little" Inner Richmond "jewel" where the "simple", "homey" Russian repasts "bring back memories of St. Petersburg"; admirers agree it's an "excellent value" all around – and the "accordion player" who squeezes out "Stairway to Heaven" on Saturday nights is just a "bonus."

Khan Toke Thai House *Thai*
22 | 24 | 21 | $30

Outer Richmond | 5937 Geary Blvd. (bet. 23rd & 24th Aves.) | 415-668-6654
Reviewers relish the "refined" Siamese dining "as it should be" proffered at this "funky, Thai-style house" replete with "ornate" "wall carvings", "cool sunken tables" and "lovely garden views" in the Outer Richmond; while it's "not for the mobility impaired", "somehow removing your shoes, sitting on the floor" and sharing "tasty", "well-priced" Bangkok bites is a "welcome bonding experience."

Kiji Sushi Bar & Cuisine Ⓜ *Japanese*
▽ 23 | 17 | 18 | $45

Mission | 1009 Guerrero St. (22nd St.) | 415-282-0400 | www.kijirestaurant.com
"Nontraditional maki and sashimi with some jalapeño kicks" come with "killer sake" at this "relatively undiscovered" "neighborhood sushi bar" in the Mission featuring mostly "organic", sustainable ingredients; housed in a low-lit, converted Victorian filled with electronica beats, it has a "private" feel and there's "never a wait."

King of Thai *Thai*
19 | 7 | 13 | $14

Downtown | 184 O'Farrell St. (bet. Powell & Stockton Sts.) | 415-677-9991 ◑⊄
Downtown | 420 Geary St. (bet. Mason & Taylor Sts.) | 415-346-3121 ◑⊄
Downtown | Hotel Milano | 55 5th St. (bet. Jessie & Mission Sts.) | 415-974-6285 ◑
Inner Richmond | 346 Clement St. (bet. 4th & 5th Aves.) | 415-831-9953 ◑⊄
Inner Richmond | 639 Clement St. (bet. 7th & 8th Aves.) | 415-752-5198 ◑⊄
North Beach | 1268 Grant Ave. (bet. Fresno & Vallejo Sts.) | 415-391-8219 | www.kingofthainoodlehouse.com ◑
Outer Sunset | 1507 Sloat Blvd. (bet. Everglade Dr. & Lakeshore Plaza) | 415-566-9921 ⊄
Outer Sunset | 1541 Taraval St. (bet. 25th & 26th Aves.) | 415-682-9958 ◑⊄
"It won't win any awards for decor", but this "cheap", "fast" and "divey" Thai octet knows "all about noodles" and other "satisfying", "spicy"

bites that will surely "make you sweat"; best of all, it's a "late-night" lifesaver, since most locations are open till at least 1 AM (the Sloat Boulevard branch closes earlier).

☑ Kiss Seafood ☒Ⓜ *Japanese*   28 | 19 | 27 | $76

Japantown | 1700 Laguna St. (Sutter St.) | 415-474-2866

"Each dish surpasses expectations" at this "swimmingly good" 12-seater hidden from the "Japantown action", so "buck up" and "put yourself in the hands" of the "true" sushi chef for a "sublime" seasonal culinary "adventure"; "warm", "family-run" service and "genuine Japanese ceramics" add to the "personal" touch, making "epicureans", "experts" and groupies in the "Kiss army" all the more willing to "rock all night long, so long as I can get a reservation."

Koh Samui & The Monkey *Thai*   21 | 19 | 18 | $29

SoMa | 415 Brannan St. (bet. 3rd & 4th Sts.) | 415-369-0007 | www.kohsamuiandthemonkey.com

Southeast Asia aficionados and SoMa suits "adore" this "lovely", antiques-adorned eatery delivering "refined", "tantalizing" Thai food complemented by "unique cocktails"; it fits the bill for weekday lunches (some of the "best values" around) as well as "first dates", even if some feel the menu and service could use a "revamp."

☑ Kokkari Estiatorio ☒ *Greek*   27 | 26 | 25 | $56

Downtown | 200 Jackson St. (Front St.) | 415-981-0983 | www.kokkari.com

It's like an "excursion to a Greek isle" at this "happening" Downtown Hellenic, "from the first smell" of meats "roasting in the fire" "to the last sip of coffee" in the "rustic room" that's suitable for "both romantic and business dinners"; the "perfectly prepared", "beautifully presented" fare is backed by a "large, diverse" wine list, while the "superb" staff provides "unparalleled" hospitality, and the "buzzing" bar accommodates scores of "young professionals."

Koo Ⓜ *Asian Fusion*   25 | 19 | 21 | $39

Inner Sunset | 408 Irving St. (bet. 5th & 6th Aves.) | 415-731-7077 | www.sushikoo.com

Inner Sunset sushi lovers find the "total package" – "screamingly fresh fish", a "great room and gracious service" "without spending too much money" – at this "busy little" "izakaya" presenting a "blend of traditional" Japanese and "modern" Asian fusion cuisine; for the full experience, "make sure to eat the Spoonfuls of Happiness (the best of everything they have)" or the "omakase at the bar" capped off by a "heavenly" dessert.

Kuleto's *Italian*   20 | 19 | 19 | $45

Downtown | Villa Florence Hotel | 221 Powell St. (bet. Geary & O'Farrell Sts.) | 415-397-7720 | www.kuletos.com

"Year after year", Pat Kuleto's Downtown "mainstay" in Union Square draws "throngs of tourists" who "shoe-horn" in "after shopping" or "before the theater" for "nothing fancy" but "reliable" Northern Italian and a "glass of wine"; the "old-world" dining room is appealing for "larger groups", while solo diners can "grab a spot" at the bar to eat, drink and "chat it up" with the "friendly staff"; N.B. Kuleto's Trattoria in Burlingame is separately owned.

	FOOD	DECOR	SERVICE	COST

Kyo-Ya ⊠ *Japanese* — 24 | 21 | 21 | $59

Downtown | Palace Hotel | 2 New Montgomery St. (Market St.) |
415-546-5090 | www.kyo-ya-restaurant.com

It's "hard to beat" the "excellent" sushi or the traditional kaiseki menu (which must be reserved 72 hours in advance) at this relatively "unknown" Japanese "hidden away" in Downtown's Palace Hotel; since it "tends not to be very crowded", connoisseurs say it's comfortable for a quiet "expense-account" lunch with colleagues from the "Tokyo office."

La Boulange *Bakery* — 22 | 17 | 17 | $16

Cow Hollow | 1909 Union St. (Laguna St.) | 415-440-4450
Cole Valley | 1000 Cole St. (Parnassus St.) | 415-242-2442
Hayes Valley | 500 Hayes St. (Octavia St.) | 415-863-3376
North Beach | 543 Columbus Ave. (bet. Powell & Stockton Sts.) |
415-399-0714
Pacific Heights | 2043 Fillmore St. (bet. California & Pine Sts.) |
415-928-1300
Russian Hill | 2310 Polk St. (Green St.) | 415-345-1107
NEW SoMa | 685 Market St. (bet. New Montgomery & 3rd Sts.) |
415-512-7610 ⊠
www.laboulangebakery.com

Self-professed "Francophiles" "thank god for Pascal Rigo" and his "wonderful" "breakfast/lunch cafes" serving "outrageous breads", "amazing pastries" and petite "baguette sandwiches" that "would make a Frenchman proud"; "you may have to wait" (and "don't trip over a stroller") and some could do without the Gallic "attitude", but whether "inside or outside", the ambiance and "people-watching" are "worth the time it takes to sip a latte" "served in a soup bowl."

La Ciccia ⊠ *Italian* — 24 | 16 | 24 | $42

Noe Valley | 291 30th St. (Church St.) | 415-550-8114 | www.laciccia.com

It's "definitely not your normal Italian restaurant", but this "mom-and-pop" "Sardinian wonderland" in Outer Noe has "captured the (tuna) hearts" of "adventurous eaters" and "neighborhood fans" who are "greeted like old friends" before tucking into "imaginative" seafood, pastas and "wines you've never heard of"; everything "seduces you" to "forget where you are", despite being "packed to the gills" in "very basic surroundings."

La Corneta *Mexican* — 22 | 13 | 15 | $11

Glen Park | 2834 Diamond St. (Kern St.) | 415-469-8757 ☏
Mission | 2731 Mission St. (bet. 23rd & 24th Sts.) | 415-643-7001
www.lacorneta.com

Whether you "go to the original Glen Park location" or its Mission or Burlingame offshoots, these "ultrafresh taquerias" help "keep Mexican cravings under control"; the "lines fold back on themselves at prime eating hours" and the counter service "lags", but the "tasty tacos" and "gigantic" "SF-style burritos" (along with 'baby' sizes) are an "incredible" deal for those on a "tight budget."

La Cumbre Taqueria *Mexican* — 19 | 7 | 12 | $12

Mission | 515 Valencia St. (bet. 16th & 17th Sts.) | 415-863-8205

Burritos ranging from "completely satisfactory" to "beyond tasty" put this "inexpensive" Mission mainstay (with a San Mateo sib) on the "top" list for Mex mavens who mention "don't be afraid of the hot

	FOOD	DECOR	SERVICE	COST

sauce" (it's "not so bad"); there's "not much in the way of decor", but that's all "part of the experience."

☑ La Folie ☒ French
28 | 24 | 27 | $99

Russian Hill | 2316 Polk St. (bet. Green & Union Sts.) | 415-776-5577 | www.lafolie.com

"Superlative", "artistically presented" tasting menus, "perfect" wine pairings and "extraordinary service" "rival anything in the City of Lights" aver *amis* of chef/co-owner Roland Passot's "luxuriously re-modeled" French "masterpiece" in Russian Hill; it's priced for "special occasions" ("like the day the Dow goes north of 10,000 again"), but "you really get what you pay for", and its clubby new lounge offers more accessible bites and bubbly.

Laïola *Spanish*
20 | 18 | 19 | $39

Marina | 2031 Chestnut St. (bet. Fillmore St. & Mallorca Way) | 415-346-5641 | www.laiola.com

What a "tapas bar" "is all about", this "cozy" Marina Iberian is a "fun place" to "go with a group" and "order everything off the menu" of "hearty, inventive" small plates and offerings from an "amazing Spanish wine selection" amid a "loud, energetic" atmosphere; recession specials also help assuage the "small portions/high price" conundrum, but a few feel it's become "more of a bar scene" and find the service "inconsistent"; N.B. the owners also run the Tacolicious stand at Thursday's Ferry Plaza Farmers Market.

NEW Lalola Bar de Tapas *Spanish*
▽ 21 | 18 | 24 | $38

Russian Hill | 1358 Mason St. (Pacific St.) | 415-981-5652 | www.lalolasf.com

For an "authentic Northern Spain tapas experience", amigos endorse this "cute" "little" newcomer on Russian Hill offering "solid" Spanish pintxos and slightly larger plates along with "excellent" Iberian wines by the glass and sangria by the pitcher; the staff is "well trained" and the "owner really elevates" the joint, "making everyone feel at home", but critics cry *caramba!* at the "expensive" and "ridiculously small" plates.

NEW La Mar Cebicheria Peruana *Peruvian*
23 | 23 | 20 | $49

Embarcadero | Pier 1.5 (Washington St.) | 415-397-8880 | www.lamarcebicheria.com

"One of the most exciting openings in 2008", this first "north-of-the-Equator" outpost by "star" chef Gastón Acurio "opens your taste-bud horizons" with a "big menu" of "bold, pure" Peruvian cuisine; the "fantastic" waterside location on the Embarcadero "puts you in a convivial mood before you have your first pisco sour" and while some find it "expensive and a little pretentious", for others the "amazing" "cocktails, ceviche and *causas*" savored at the "lively bar" or "on the patio" are "nirvana."

La Méditerranée *Mediterranean/Mideastern*
20 | 15 | 18 | $23

Castro | 288 Noe St. (Market St.) | 415-431-7210
Upper Fillmore | 2210 Fillmore St. (Sacramento St.) | 415-921-2956
www.cafelamed.com

Those "in the mood for a taste of the Mediterranean" and Middle East get their "fix" at this "tried-and-true" trio in the Castro, Upper Fillmore and Berkeley that boasts "winning" phyllo-dough specialties and "meze feasts" that "can't be beat for the variety"; even if the "casual" confines are a bit "snug", it's a "solid bet" that's always "easy on the budget."

	FOOD	DECOR	SERVICE	COST

La Provence *French*

▽ 20 | 17 | 20 | $39

Mission | 1001 Guerrero St. (22nd St.) | 415-643-4333 | www.laprovencesf.com

A "warm welcome" from the "friendly" chef-owner and "authentic" Provençal bistro dishes "transport you to the south of France" at this oft "overlooked" option offering a "delightful" diversion in the Mission; "comfortable" and "casual", it's a "nice place to go on a date" declare romantics, even though the less enamored mention it's less "memorable" than they'd like.

L'Ardoise ☒ Ⓜ *French*

24 | 21 | 24 | $44

Castro | 151 Noe St. (Henry St.) | 415-437-2600 | www.ardoisesf.com

"*Très charmant*", this "postage stamp" of a "neighborhood bistro" is "the best little restaurant that no one has heard about" (save devoted "Duboce Triangle locals"), in spite of the chef's Fringale pedigree; with "a French-accented staff that remembers your name" delivering "excellent", "reasonably priced" Gallic selections from a "chalkboard" (*ardoise*) menu in a "romantic" converted Victorian, converts call it a "real keeper" in the Castro.

Lark Creek Steak *Steak*

23 | 21 | 21 | $55

Downtown | Westfield San Francisco Ctr. | 845 Market St., 4th fl. (bet. 4th & 5th Sts.) | 415-593-4100 | www.larkcreeksteak.com

"Who would have thunk" you'd find a "fine restaurant at the mall", but Downtown's Westfield Centre houses this "soothing", "stylish" steakhouse where "high-quality" cuts and "out-of-this-world" sides are "guaranteed crowd-pleasers"; the "generous" portions provide "perfect fuel for an afternoon of shopping", but you better "save your money" at Bloomie's since it's rather "spendy."

La Scene Café & Bar *Californian/Mediterranean*

▽ 18 | 18 | 20 | $44

Downtown | Warwick Regis | 490 Geary St. (bet. Mason & Taylor Sts.) | 415-292-6430 | www.warwicksf.com

A "dependable" "choice for pre-theater dining" (right "across the street from A.C.T."), this "hidden" Cal-Med in Downtown's Warwick hotel cranks out "consistently good" if somewhat "ordinary" cuisine; though a few fret it's "lost its luster" lately, most are sold on the "value" and the "civilized" setting ("never overly crowded"), tended by servers who "understand you have places to go."

La Taqueria ⌷ *Mexican*

25 | 9 | 15 | $12

Mission | 2889 Mission St. (bet. 24th & 25th Sts.) | 415-285-7117

"Killer burritos" (with "no rice getting in the way" – "genius!") and "extraordinary" tacos "fill your tummy for the change in your pocket" at this Mission Mexican that's worth a "special trip" when you hunger for "heaven on a tortilla"; the "absolutely bare-bones" interior means it's generally "better for takeout", but "people-watching" patrons suggest "staying" for the "authentic" experience.

La Terrasse *French*

18 | 20 | 17 | $42

Presidio | 215 Lincoln Blvd. (bet. Graham St. & Keyes Ave.) | 415-922-3463 | www.laterrassepresidio.com

With a namesake terrace affording "one of the best views of the city", this little French bistro "tucked away in the historic Presidio" is a "delightful spot" for an "unhurried lunch" or "weekend brunch" "on a sunny afternoon", or an evening meal at the bar for "commuters before getting on the Golden Gate"; some critics, however, fume that "service leaves something to be desired" and "prices are a little on the high side."

La Trappe 🅢🅜 *Belgian* ▽ 18 | 24 | 20 | $31

North Beach | 800 Greenwich St. (Mason St.) | 415-440-8727 | www.latrappecafe.com

"In a neighborhood overrun with Italian restaurants", this Trappist bistro in North Beach is a "refreshing" option whose "highlight" is "great" Belgian brew and "plenty of it" (285 types), complemented by moules frites and other Flemish fare; some shrug the "simple" eats "will do", but most just come to "drink and run" in the "cool", "cave"-like downstairs bar where the staff "knows beer and can easily answer your questions."

Le Central Bistro 🅢 *French* 20 | 19 | 20 | $46

Downtown | 453 Bush St. (bet. Grant Ave. & Kearny St.) | 415-391-2233 | www.lecentralbistro.com

"A favorite watering hole" for "politicians", "journalists" and "city celebs" (Willie Brown is "still a regular"), this "classic French bistro" also attracts the hoi polloi with all the "old traditional" dishes and "crackling cold" martinis; the "laconic" staff can seem "standoffish" to "outsiders" who haven't been coming for "30-plus years", but Francophiles are just delighted to have "a bit of the Left Bank" Downtown.

Le Charm French Bistro 🅜 *French* 22 | 18 | 21 | $40

SoMa | 315 Fifth St. (bet. Folsom & Shipley Sts.) | 415-546-6128 | www.lecharm.com

On an "unlikely" industrial stretch of SoMa, this "darling" "oasis" attracts frugal Francophiles with its "soothing" bistro cooking and $30 prix fixe dinner deal that's "hard to beat"; though the "seats are rather close", it still has a "romantic aura" (see the "lovely back patio"), and servers who extend a "warm welcome" ensure you'll "leave in a good mood"; N.B. no lunch on the weekends.

Le Club 🅢🅜 *Californian/French* ▽ 15 | 20 | 16 | $59

Nob Hill | Clay-Jones | 1250 Jones St. (Clay St.) | 415-922-2582 | www.leclubsf.com

Tucked away in a swanky residential Nob Hill building, this revived legendary clubhouse attracts "mature" "society types" who come for an "evening out on the town" that includes "exotic hors d'oeuvres" and a "well-matched" nightcap, or even a game of "pool in the back"; "there's food there?" quip critics of the full, "high-priced" Cal-French fare, while others lambaste the service as "snooty, snooty, snooty"; N.B. the full dinner menu is served Wednesday–Sunday only.

Le Colonial *French/Vietnamese* 22 | 24 | 20 | $50

Downtown | 20 Cosmo Pl. (bet. Jones & Taylor Sts.) | 415-931-3600 | www.lecolonialsf.com

"Opulent" surroundings that "transport you to old Saigon" "set the stage for culinary drama" at this "gorgeous" French-Vietnamese destination that "always delivers on fresh flavors" and "sumptuous" meals; "tucked into" a Downtown alley, it offers "trendy", "spendy" colonialists "one-stop shopping" thanks to its "happening" upstairs bar, complete with live music and DJs, though a few huff it's "often too loud for a romantic meal."

	FOOD	DECOR	SERVICE	COST

Le P'tit Laurent *French*

| 22 | 19 | 22 | $40 |

Glen Park | 699 Chenery St. (Diamond St.) | 415-334-3235 | www.leptitlaurent.com

Walk or "BART to Glen Park" where this "small, crowded, lively" bistro offers "traditional" (read: "rich") French standards matched by wines "worthy of their accents" and "attentive" service with "no pomp nor ceremony"; "from the moment you are greeted by" Monsieur Laurent himself "to the last" digestif, it's like taking "a short weekend to Paris" "without the fuel surcharge" and a better exchange rate – especially Sunday–Thursday, when it offers an "incredible" prix fixe dinner deal.

Le Soleil *Vietnamese*

| ∇ 23 | 16 | 17 | $29 |

Inner Richmond | 133 Clement St. (bet. 2nd & 3rd Aves.) | 415-668-4848 | www.lesoleilusa.com

"Everything is so fresh!" say sunny surveyors who claim this "quality" Inner Richmonder cooks up some of the "best Vietnamese in the price range" in SF; it doesn't have "the biggest menu", but it's "worth the stop" for "imperial rolls to die for" and "well-prepared" crab.

NEW Let's Be Frank *Hot Dogs*

| - | - | - | I |

Marina | 3318 Steiner St. (bet. Chestnut & Lombard Sts.) | 415-674-6755 | www.letsbefrankdogs.com

Not much larger than a frankfurter cart (minus the wheels), this first brick-and-mortar outpost of a Bay Area haute wiener purveyor unleashes its dogs in the Marina, serving franks and brats made with sustainable ingredients, along with grass-fed-beef chili, ice-cream sandwiches from Bi-Rite Creamery and beer; its mustard-and-ketchup-red setting, designed by Cass Calder Smith (Restaurant LuLu), offers only limited counter seating plus a few sidewalk tables.

Level III *American*

| ∇ 18 | 20 | 19 | $36 |

Downtown | JW Marriott San Francisco | 500 Post St. (Mason St.) | 415-929-2087 | www.levelthreesf.com

A "pleasant surprise" on the third floor of Downtown's JW Marriott, this "underappreciated" New American offers a range of "innovative" fare, from breakfast till late, and "excellent" cocktails in a "lovely" setting; the "happy-hour menu is just right" after work, and by night it morphs into a "twentysomethings' pickup bar", but critics jeer that its "bright lights and dim service" make it "hard to pretend that you're not in" a hotel.

Le Zinc *French*

| 19 | 19 | 17 | $39 |

Noe Valley | 4063 24th St. (bet. Castro & Noe Sts.) | 415-647-9400 | www.lezinc.com

With its "transporting decor", "sidewalk tables" and "actual zinc" bar, this Gallic bistro brings a "little of Paris to Noe Valley", complete with "plenty of real French people on both sides of the counter"; a few foes find the fare "unremarkable" and the service "slow", but boosters insist it can't be beat "on sunny days" or "rare warm nights" when "you can sit with your dog in the garden and pretend you're in France."

Liberty Café, The Ⓜ *American*

| 22 | 17 | 21 | $30 |

Bernal Heights | 410 Cortland Ave. (bet. Bennington & Wool Sts.) | 415-695-8777 | www.thelibertycafe.com

Fans go flakey over the "wicked crust" on the "pot pies and banana cream pies" at this Bernal Heights American cafe and bakery, "driving

	FOOD	DECOR	SERVICE	COST

forever" from all points for its "killer comfort food" that's served in a "homey" setting made for "dates" or "visiting parents"; "no reservations" are a "bummer", but "the saloon next door" or the "wine bar out back" help "ease the wait"; N.B. new owners took over mid-Survey.

Lime ◐ *Eclectic*	17	20	18	$29

Castro | 2247 Market St. (bet. Noe & Sanchez Sts.) | 415-621-5256 | www.lime-sf.com
"Less a restaurant than a bar/club", this "super-trendy" spot is stuffed with "high-energy" "Castro kids" who down "creative cocktails" accompanied by a "satisfying nosh" of Eclectic small plates; "heavy techno music" means it's "no place to take your grandmother", but most maintain the "retro '60s" decor and "bottomless mimosas" during Sunday brunch offset the "over-the-top efforts to be hip."

Limón *Peruvian*	23	18	19	$33

Mission | 524 Valencia St. (16th St.) | 415-252-0918 | www.limon-sf.com

NEW **Limón Peruvian Rotisserie** *Peruvian*
Mission | 1001 S. Van Ness Ave. (21st St.) | 415-821-2134 | www.limonrotisserie.com
The casual Van Ness spin-off of the original Limón presents a "wonderful" "pared-down menu" of Peruvian faves – "the best ceviche this side of the Equator", "succulent rotisserie chicken" and "lomo saltado" – that can be "washed down with pitchers of sangria", and come at such "amazing" prices some think "the bill is a mistake"; downstairs, its new lounge (Thursday–Sunday) features South American wines and DJs spinning salsa and other tunes; N.B. after being shuttered following a fire, the Valencia Street location is set to reopen at press time.

Little Chihuahua *Mexican*	▽ 23	17	19	$15

Western Addition | 292 Divisadero St. (Page St.) | 415-255-8225 | www.thelittlechihuahua.com
"Awesome delicious Mexican using sustainable ingredients" "topped off with a $3 draft beer" and free trips to the "salsa bar" – "how can you beat that?" bark boosters of this "friendly" upscale taqueria in the Western Addition hawking "burritos the size of a small chihuahua" and a "perfect Sunday brunch" (mimosas and Mexican French toast, anyone?); just "get there early to avoid the hipster rush", because this "li'l" "place gets packed, especially before concerts at the Independent."

Little Nepal Ⓜ *Nepalese*	23	18	22	$25

Bernal Heights | 925 Cortland Ave. (bet. Folsom & Gates Sts.) | 415-643-3881 | www.littlenepalsf.com
Kathmandu connoisseurs counsel "taking a field trip to Bernal Heights" for the "special" cooking "with a kick" at this "family-run" "jewel" with a strong "native Nepali" following; while the "intimate" nook is "nothing to look at", the "good value" and "warm" service make it a "favorite."

Little Star Pizza Ⓜ *Pizza*	25	15	17	$22

Mission | 400 Valencia St. (15th St.) | 415-551-7827
Western Addition | 846 Divisadero St. (bet. Fulton & McAllister Sts.) | 415-441-1118 ♥
www.littlestarpizza.com
These Western Addition and Mission "meeting halls for Pizza Addicts Anonymous" are "accepting new members" quip pie-sani who can't

go long without a "fix" of the "amazing" deep-dish and "excellent" thin-crust varieties dished out by a "friendly" (if occasionally "brusque") staff at these "hipster pizzerias"; never mind the "marathon waits" or blaring "'80s tunes", most agree they're a "great value" and "deserving of every bit of praise"; N.B. Divisadero is cash-only.

Local Kitchen & Wine Merchant Ⓜ *Californian/Italian*

20 | 20 | 18 | $38

SoMa | 330 First St. (bet. Folsom & Harrison Sts.) | 415-777-4200 | www.sf-local.com

"Amazing" wood-fired pizza "set off with the perfect wine" selected by a "knowledgeable staff" makes this SoMa resto and wine bar a "cool" option for "after-work drinks" or a "light meal" of Cal-Ital cuisine (it also offers a "fabulous" Sunday brunch); oenophiles dig picking up a bottle at the "adjacent shop" then uncorking it with friends at the "communal table" in the "hyper-mod", "loftlike" space, though the setting leaves a few "cold."

Loló ⓏⓂ *Mediterranean/Pan-Latin*

▽ 22 | 19 | 19 | $34

Mission | 3230 22nd St. (bet. Bartlett & Mission Sts.) | 415-643-5656

"'Quirky' is the best way to describe" this "hip" Pan Latin–Mediterranean "hole-in-the-wall" in the Mission where the staff "helps you decipher" the "diverse" menu full of "unexpected delights" – "creative" small and large plates that add up to "some of the most unique dining in town"; the space boasts "recycled decor" that's "a little bit '50s, a little bit punk" with a "whole lot of character", and it's fairly "cheap" to boot.

L'Osteria del Forno ⱷ *Italian*

23 | 15 | 18 | $31

North Beach | 519 Columbus Ave. (bet. Green & Union Sts.) | 415-982-1124 | www.losteriadelforno.com

"Waiting on the street is a badge of good taste" boast boosters of this cash-only, no-rezzie North Beacher who go for the "excellent, cheap" Northern Italian cuisine and "reasonably priced" wines; "don't expect much in the way of service or ambiance" in digs that are "smaller than a bedroom", where the staff is "too quick", but most agree the "authentic" eats are "worth it."

Lovejoy's Tea Room Ⓜ *Tearoom*

21 | 22 | 23 | $24

Noe Valley | 1351 Church St. (Clipper St.) | 415-648-5895 | www.lovejoystearoom.com

"Leave your boyfriend at home" and "stick your pinky finger in the air" as you "enjoy" a "grown-up tea party" ("Village-style") with "prissy sandwiches" and "scrumptious scones" "served on mismatched porcelain" at this "cluttered" Noe tearoom; "it's like having tea at your great aunt Gertrude's" "with none of the pretension" of the "big hotels", but despite the laid-back bohemian vibe, insiders advise "reservations are a must."

Luce *Californian/Italian*

20 | 22 | 21 | $65

SoMa | InterContinental Hotel | 888 Howard St. (bet. 4th & 5th Sts.) | 415-616-6566 | www.lucewinerestaurant.com

"Who would guess you're in a hotel dining room – and this close to Moscone?" marvel fans of "artiste" chef Dominique Crenn's "first-class", "cutting-edge" Cal-Ital meals and tasting menus, served "with or without wine" by a "model" staff at this "sleeper" in SoMa's InterContinental; the "sleek" and "formal" yet "relaxing" room suits "business entertaining" or a "special occasion", but the recession-weary wince at the "high prices."

Luella *Californian/Mediterranean*　　22 | 19 | 22 | $44

Russian Hill | 1896 Hyde St. (Green St.) | 415-674-4343 | www.luellasf.com

A "wonderful neighborhood find" for "those who know of it" (including "local politicians" and "A-listers traveling through"), this "dark" Russian Hill hideaway offers "glorious peace and quiet" and "accommodating", "friendly" service along with a "short", "innovative" Cal-Med menu that "does not disappoint", though some say it "doesn't particularly dazzle", either; road warriors warn "it's a parking night-mare", but you can always hop "the cable car that goes grating by."

Luna Park *American/French*　　20 | 17 | 18 | $34

Mission | 694 Valencia St. (18th St.) | 415-553-8584 | www.lunaparksf.com

"Big portions" of "solid" French–New American grub ("who has a blue-plate special anymore?") and "fantastic desserts" deliver lots of "bang for your buck" at this Mission mainstay; it's "rocking at most hours" with a "hipster" crew crowding around the "popular" bar, so Luna-tics recommend "reserving one of the booths in the back" to "save yourself from going deaf."

Lupa Trattoria *Italian*　　22 | 18 | 22 | $35

Noe Valley | 4109 24th St. (bet. Castro & Diamond Sts.) | 415-282-5872 | www.lupatrattoria.com

It's "just like a trattoria in Rome" with the sounds of "Italian chatter all over the place" at this *famiglia*-"friendly" Noe Valley eatery run by "real" Romans who are "happy to fold up a stroller, bring you a glass of Chianti and set down a plate of "tasty, no-nonsense" "homemade pasta" with "fabulous lamb bolognese"; to those seeking a "nice change" from ubiquitous Northern cuisine at a "decent price", it's "perfecto."

Magnolia Gastropub & Brewery ◑ *American/Southern*　　18 | 16 | 17 | $26

Haight-Ashbury | 1398 Haight St. (Masonic Ave.) | 415-864-7468 | www.magnoliapub.com

"Not your run-of-the mill" brew house, this hopping "haunt in the Haight" offers "expertly crafted" beers and ales and "surprisingly tasty", "sustainably sourced" Southern-inspired American gastropub eats; there's "colorful people-watching" through the "picture win-dows" and the "communal table is a nice place to sit", though some advise that Joe Six-Packs "looking for simple munchies" may be put off by the "pretentious"-sounding menu.

Maki Ⓜ *Japanese*　　23 | 13 | 18 | $34

Japantown | Japan Ctr. | 1825 Post St., 2nd fl. (bet. Fillmore & Webster Sts.) | 415-921-5215

A "tiny" "haven" in the Japan Center with "limited" tables for the for-tunate few, this "cut-above" mom-and-pop operation is "worth seek-ing out" for "delicious" cooked Japanese dishes like *wappa meshi* (steamed rice, veggies and meat) as well as sushi; despite sometimes "long" lines, "cordial" service helps make the meal "a joy."

	FOOD	DECOR	SERVICE	COST

Mamacita *Mexican*
23 | **20** | **17** | **$37**

Marina | 2317 Chestnut St. (bet. Divisadero & Scott Sts.) | 415-346-8494 |
www.mamacitasf.com

This "yuppie" Marina Mex puts "a new spin on your *abuelita*'s cuisine", concocting "killer chilaquiles" and other "fresh, quality" plates with a "San Francisco twist"; some critics "can't handle" the "crowds", the "noise" or the "borderline" service, but many rely on the "strong" margaritas to help "dull the pain."

Mama's on Washington Square ☒⌖ *American*
25 | **14** | **18** | **$21**

North Beach | 1701 Stockton St. (Filbert St.) | 415-362-6421 |
www.mamas-sf.com

"Bring something to read" recommend those who've spent plenty of time "standing in line" outside this North Beacher that rewards patient patrons with "brilliant" banana-bread French toast, "unforgettable" eggs Benedict and "excellent" baked goods as well as American lunches in a "country-kitchen" setting; savvy souls remember to "take cash" too; N.B. closes at 3 PM.

Mandalay *Burmese*
22 | **15** | **21** | **$25**

Inner Richmond | 4348 California St. (bet. 5th & 6th Aves.) | 415-386-3895 |
www.mandalaysf.com

Diners "dream about" the "oddly addictive" tea leaf salad and other "refreshingly different" Burmese bites at this Inner Richmond roost where the "exotic" decor is "a kick"; it doesn't have the same "hype" (or "long lines") as some stars, but considering the "caring", "kid-friendly" staff and a bill that "won't bust your budget", allies assess it's "wildly underrated."

Mangarosa ☒ *Brazilian/Italian*
18 | **19** | **18** | **$45**

North Beach | 1548 Stockton St. (bet. Green & Union Sts.) | 415-956-3211 |
www.mangarosasf.com

Rio meets Rome at this "touristy" Italian-Brazilian mash-up where "melt-in-your-mouth" meat and fish dishes "compare very well" with "São Paolo" cuisine; the "air of excitement" means "it's hard not to have fun", especially on Thursdays "when the samba dancers arrive", but some critics beef that "better" fare "can be found for less" in North Beach.

Manora's Thai Cuisine *Thai*
25 | **16** | **18** | **$26**

SoMa | 1600 Folsom St. (12th St.) | 415-861-6224 |
www.manorathai.com

A "forever favorite" of SoMa Siamese connoisseurs, this "dependable", "easygoing" eatery dishes out "generous portions" of "top"-quality, "inexpensive" Thai fare; the location keeps it "popular with the business lunch crowd", while "accommodating" service, colorful cocktails and fresh flowers on the tables lend appeal for a "first date."

Mario's Bohemian Cigar Store Cafe *Italian*
18 | **17** | **15** | **$18**

North Beach | 566 Columbus Ave. (bet. Green & Union Sts.) | 415-362-0536

"For a taste of old North Beach", head to this "priceless" "postage stamp–size" Northern Italian cafe with "atmosphere aplenty" and a "view of Washington Square Park" across the street; the staff may seem "too cool for school", but it's "well worth chilling" for the "perfect" coffee and "hot meatball sandwich" that's "pure deliciousness."

	FOOD	DECOR	SERVICE	COST

MarketBar *Mediterranean*   16 | 19 | 17 | $38

Embarcadero | 1 Ferry Bldg. (Market St.) | 415-434-1100 |
www.marketbar.com

"On a sunny day", you can "catch some rays" on the Embarcadero and
"watch the world walk, run and roll by" at this "always busy" brasserie
in the Ferry Building; regarding the Med menu, what's "unpretentious"
to some is "uninspired" and "overpriced" to others, who say every aspect of the place "should be way more impressive" to live up to
the "prime location."

Marnee Thai *Thai*   23 | 13 | 17 | $24

Inner Sunset | 1243 Ninth Ave. (bet. Irving St. & Lincoln Way) |
415-731-9999

Outer Sunset | 2225 Irving St. (bet. 23rd & 24th Aves.) | 415-665-9500

"Venture into uncharted waters", ordering "dishes you haven't had before", or just let the staff "choose your menu" at this "no-frills" Sunset
duo where the "above-average", "attractively priced" Thai cooking
"will excite your taste buds"; proprietress Marnee may "boss you
around" and "ham it up", but most consider it "additional entertainment" while they eat.

⚡ Masa's ⊠Ⓜ *French*   28 | 24 | 27 | $117

Downtown | Hotel Vintage Ct. | 648 Bush St. (bet. Powell & Stockton Sts.) |
415-989-7154 | www.masasrestaurant.com

"Decadent" diners "plan a trip around" this "haute" Downtown "classic"
that "still shines" thanks to chef Gregory Short's "outstanding" New
French cuisine; most agree each bite "will blow you away", whether
you "go all out with the nine-course menu" with "spot-on wine pairings"
or take advantage of the three-course recession special (available
upon request), and though critics say the prices "border on ridiculous"
and the room is "so hushed you feel like you're eating at the Vatican",
the staff will always "make you feel special."

Massawa *African*   ▽ 19 | 9 | 17 | $22

Haight-Ashbury | 1538 Haight St. (bet. Ashbury & Clayton Sts.) |
415-621-4129

"Hipster Haighters" head to this Eritrean eatery for "excellent" dishes
(similar to "Ethiopian") scooped up with "spongy bread"; the barebones setting strikes some as "kind of bleak", but the service is "helpful", there's "good" African beer and wine and the "price is right."

Matterhorn Swiss Restaurant Ⓜ *Swiss*   23 | 22 | 21 | $43

Russian Hill | 2323 Van Ness Ave. (bet. Green & Vallejo Sts.) | 415-885-6116

"I had forgotten that fondue was so much fun" yodel Alpine aficionados who "don't tell their cardiologists" about visiting this "wonderfully
cheesy – in more ways than one" – "wood-paneled" ersatz mountain
chalet in Russian Hill; the "nice" staff "runs a highly efficient ship",
serving 12 different types of somewhat "expensive" "dip-and-eat"
dinners as well as other "classic Swiss cuisine" and wines "to match."

Maverick *American*   24 | 20 | 23 | $42

Mission | 3316 17th St. (bet. Mission & Valencia Sts.) | 415-863-3061 |
www.sfmaverick.com

For regional American "comfort food kicked up a notch or two", fans
head to this "small, dark" Mission storefront that "makes you feel

warm and fuzzy inside" with its "foodie vibe" and "amazing, fresh" fare made with "high-quality" sustainable ingredients and served by a "knowledgeable" staff; though "weekend brunch get all the press" ("and by golly it does live up to it"), many insist "dinners are the real hidden star", especially on Monday wine nights when you can "buy the most expensive bottle without the guilt"; P.S. "make a reservation."

Max's *Deli*

17 | 14 | 17 | $27

Downtown | Hotel Frank | 398 Geary St. (Mason St.) | 415-646-8600
Downtown | Bank of America Ctr. | 555 California St., concourse level (Montgomery St.) | 415-788-6297 Ⓢ
Civic Center | Opera Plaza | 601 Van Ness Ave. (Golden Gate Ave.) | 415-771-7301
www.maxsworld.com

East Coast expats "crave" the sandwiches "piled high" with pastrami ("worth its weight in gold") and "mammoth portions" of other "old-fashioned" deli fare at this "family-friendly" Bay Area chain whose "extensive menu" offers "something for everyone"; it's "easy on the budget", and the "live piano" and singing are "a plus" at some locations, but kvetchers who want "quality, not quantity", complain it'll "disappoint any NY native."

Maya *Mexican*

21 | 18 | 18 | $39

SoMa | 303 Second St. (bet. Folsom & Harrison Sts.) | 415-543-2928 | www.mayasf.com

Not your typical "tacos-and-burritos place", this "haute Mexican" hacienda in SoMa, recently redone with dark walnut walls and a marble bar, dishes out "fresh, bright and beautiful" south-of-the-border fare "gussied up for a fine dining experience"; it's a "little pricey" and the service sometimes "lacks the personal touch", but most wonder "why is this place still a secret?"

Mayflower *Chinese*

22 | 11 | 14 | $29

Outer Richmond | 6255 Geary Blvd. (bet. 26th & 27th Aves.) | 415-387-8338
When they want to "dodge the tourists" and avoid the "attitude" at its better-known competitors, "locals go" to this "bargain" Hong Kong hangout in the Outer Richmond that must have "about one hundred ways" to cook seafood; it "helps if you can read Cantonese", but neither the "spotty" service nor "shabby" decor can keep folks away from the "original dim sum" delicacies.

Maykadeh *Persian*

▽ 26 | 18 | 22 | $34

North Beach | 470 Green St. (Grant Ave.) | 415-362-8286 | www.maykadehrestaurant.com
Seek out this "elegant" eatery in North Beach and "your taste buds will thank you" proclaim Persian partisans who "can't get enough" of the "authentic" fare, such as "superb kebabs", "tender lamb" and "other favorite Iranian dishes"; "solicitous" servers who "remember" the regulars add to its appeal for a "special night out."

McCormick & Kuleto's *Seafood*

20 | 22 | 20 | $47

Fisherman's Wharf | Ghirardelli Sq. | 900 N. Point St. (Larkin St.) | 415-929-1730 | www.mccormickandkuletos.com
"Lucky" guests "get a table by the window" to soak in the "amazing" "sunset over the Golden Gate Bridge" while chowing down on "bountiful"

plates of "reliable" seafood at this Fisherman's Wharf chain link; as some critics carp about the "touristy" clientele, "marginal" cooking and "average" service, it's not quite a catch if you "really want to impress."

Medjool *Mediterranean*

| 18 | 20 | 16 | $41 |

Mission | 2522 Mission St. (bet. 21st & 22nd Sts.) | 415-550-9055 | www.medjoolsf.com

A real "date" destination for "drinks, dinner and dancing", this "super-stylish" multitasker in the Mission has it all: a "fabulous rooftop lounge" with a "panoramic view", and a "high-energy" Med restaurant that "transforms" into a "cool" club "after dark"; "you'll feel like one of the beautiful people" "sprawling on the couches and sampling a wonderful variety of small dishes", though a few fret about "mediocre" morsels with a side of "attitude."

Mel's Drive-In ☻ *Diner*

| 14 | 15 | 15 | $18 |

Civic Center | 1050 Van Ness Ave. (bet. Geary & Myrtle Sts.) | 415-292-6358
Inner Richmond | 3355 Geary Blvd. (bet. Beaumont & Parker Aves.) | 415-387-2255
Marina | 2165 Lombard St. (bet. Fillmore & Steiner Sts.) | 415-921-2867
SoMa | 801 Mission St. (4th St.) | 415-227-0793
www.melsdrive-in.com

Looking "like the set of *Happy Days*", this "nostalgic" mini-chain is a "throwback to the 1950s", serving "good" and "greasy" burgers, "blue-plate specials" and "thick" milkshakes; no, it's "not terribly gourmet" – mel-contents muse "eh, I could take or leave it" – but it's "oh-so-helpful" when you have "kids in tow" or want a "late-night snack."

Memphis Minnie's BBQ Joint Ⓜ *BBQ*

| 20 | 11 | 14 | $18 |

Lower Haight | 576 Haight St. (bet. Fillmore & Steiner Sts.) | 415-864-7675 | www.memphisminnies.com

Loyalists say "a lot of love" goes into the BBQ at this "down-home" Lower Haight meat mecca where "melt-in-your-mouth" brisket and "righteous" ribs come with "sides you dream about"; "cafeteria-style" ordering and "limited" seating mean it's not a place to linger – and a few 'cue connoisseurs comment it "doesn't touch the real deal" – but the service is "quick" and "the price is right too."

Mescolanza *Italian*

| ▽ 21 | 17 | 22 | $33 |

Outer Richmond | 2221 Clement St. (bet. 23rd & 24th Aves.) | 415-668-2221 | www.mescolanza.net

"You just cannot go wrong with anything you order here" enthuse Outer Richmond residents who call this "intimate" Northern Italian their "favorite neighborhood" haunt; though the menu is fairly "standard", it delivers "excellent value for the money", plus the "homey atmosphere" makes it a "nice place to linger."

🆕 Metro Café Ⓢ Ⓜ *Californian*

| - | - | - | M |

(fka Metro Kathmandu)

Western Addition | 311 Divisadero St. (Page St.) | 415-552-0903 | www.metrocafe311.com

Harkening back to its more mainstream roots and former name, this latest reincarnation of the Western Addition Metro Kathmandu jettisons its Nepalese menu (with the exception of its signature momos, which remain) for a slate of easy-on-the-wallet Californian comfort

	FOOD	DECOR	SERVICE	COST

food with a Mediterranean twist, including burgers, pasta, tagines and moules with homemade kennebec fries; the red-brick interior has been enlivened with new murals, while a 35-seat back patio opens up for weekend brunch.

Mexico DF *Mexican*
20 | 18 | 18 | $36

Embarcadero | 139 Steuart St. (bet. Howard & Mission Sts.) | 415-808-1048 | www.mex-df.com

Margaritas "heighten" the pleasure of "top-quality" meals ("don't miss out on the carnitas") at this "trendy" cantina bringing "high-end Mexican" to the Embarcadero; while it's more "gorgeous" than "your typical" taqueria, enemigos insist it's "a little expensive" and "too crowded" for comfort.

☑ Michael Mina ⑤Ⓜ *American*
27 | 25 | 26 | $137

Downtown | Westin St. Francis | 335 Powell St. (bet. Geary & Post Sts.) | 415-397-9222 | www.michaelmina.net

"Wow, wow, wow" exclaim Downtown diners who shell out "a large amount of economic stimulus" at Michael Mina's "storied" Westin St. Francis "flagship" where the "three-of-everything" New American prix fixes and "dedicated" "wine wizardry" deliver a "plethora of palate pleasure"; the "professional" staff manages to be both "invisible and omnipresent", and "giant columns" add to the "grandiose" "vibe" of the dining room, which can get "loud with the hotel traffic"; P.S. for a "good buy", try the à la carte and pre-theater menus at the bar.

NEW Midi ⑤ *American/French*
- | - | - | M

Downtown | Galleria Park Hotel | 185 Sutter St. (Kearny St.) | 415-835-6400 | www.midisanfrancisco.com

Appealing to everyone from power suits to power-shoppers, this swank yet convivial Downtown arrival in the Galleria Park Hotel showcases a midpriced French–New American brasserie menu crafted by rising chef Michelle Mah (ex Ponzu and Grand Cafe); guests can sup downstairs in the street-level lounge or upstairs in the modern dining room dominated by a giant Gauguin-esque mural.

Mifune *Japanese*
17 | 11 | 15 | $19

Japantown | Kinetsu Mall | 1737 Post St. (bet. Laguna & Webster Sts.) | 415-922-0337 | www.mifune.com

Japantown's "go-to place for udon", as well as "simple" soba dishes that "delight the palate", this "busy" noodle nirvana "captures" the "hustle-and-bustle" atmosphere of its Tokyo kin; the interior is "barebones" – and "don't expect the servers to be extraordinarily warm and fuzzy" (just "quick" and "courteous") – but it's still a "solid choice" delivering the "best value for the yen."

Mijita *Mexican*
20 | 12 | 13 | $17

Embarcadero | 1 Ferry Bldg. (Market St.) | 415-399-0814 | www.mijitasf.com

Traci Des Jardins (Jardinière) "nails the perfect taco" and other "terrific Mexican basics" made from "local, sustainable ingredients" at her "upscale" taqueria in the Ferry Building, where the "amazing" *comida* is "worth waiting in line for (even cutting a few tourists)"; "it's impossible to get a seat on weekend" market days, but since there's "no atmosphere" inside anyway, amigos advise taking it "outside to soak in the sunshine and views of the Bay."

	FOOD	DECOR	SERVICE	COST

Millennium *Vegan*

| 25 | 21 | 23 | $48 |

Downtown | Hotel California | 580 Geary St. (Jones St.) | 415-345-3900 |
www.millenniumrestaurant.com

Chef/co-owner Eric Tucker "pushes the envelope", inventing "visually stunning" vegan vittles that "even hard-core meat lovers" adore at this "sophisticated" Downtown "haven" in the Hotel California; boasting "biodynamic wines", "superb" cocktails and "rocking" desserts, it all adds up to a "full-on upscale" feast, but "come prepared to spend" for the "sensual experience."

Miller's East Coast West Delicatessen *Deli/Jewish*

| 22 | 10 | 16 | $19 |

Polk Gulch | 1725 Polk St. (Clay St.) | 415-563-3542 |
www.millersdelisf.com

"Transplanted NYers" kvell over nosh "just like nana used to make" at this Polk Gulch Jewish deli that "feels like it belongs in Times Square", and while it's "not Katz's", to many it's still the "best place in SF" to get a "piled-high" Reuben or "matzo ball soup when you're sick" (and don't forget the "amazing pickles"); but, oy, it's "cramped" and "service is not the best", so it's often "better for picking up" than a "sit-down meal."

Mission Beach Café *Californian*

| 21 | 17 | 18 | $33 |

Mission | 198 Guerrero St. (14th St.) | 415-861-0198 |
www.missionbeachcafesf.com

This "hot brunch spot" and "afternoon cafe" in the Mission pleases with "excellent" pastries and other baked goods "beyond compare", as well as "reasonably priced" "seasonal" Californian eats; the staff dishes out "much less attitude than other places" in the neighborhood, but some say the service can be "scattered", while cynics sniff the "iron tech"–meets–"coffee shop" decor and serially "changing" chefs "make it hard to take dinner seriously."

Mixt Greens ⌧ *Health Food*

| 22 | 12 | 17 | $14 |

Downtown | Adam Grant | 120 Sansome St. (bet. Bush & Pine Sts.) |
415-433-6498
Downtown | 475 Sansome St. (Commercial St.) | 415-296-9292
Downtown | JP Morgan Chase | 560 Mission St. (bet. 1st & 2nd Sts.) |
415-543-2505
www.mixtgreens.com

Bowls of lettuce have "never known" such "greatness before" declare devotees of this "bright, airy" Downtown lunch trio where the "almost bewildering variety" of "made-to-order salads and sandwiches" are so "wonderfully fresh" and "healthy" it's "like eating at the farmer's market"; sure, it's "expensive" (thanks to "sustainably farmed" ingredients) and the lines are "ridiculous", but the "upbeat", "efficient" staff keeps them "moving quickly."

Mochica *Peruvian*

| 25 | 20 | 21 | $34 |

SoMa | 937 Harrison St. (bet. 5th & 6th Sts.) | 415-278-0480 |
www.mochicasf.com

"Lima" comes to SoMa at this "beautiful" "little jewel" where the "must-order" ceviche and other "outstanding" eats achieve "Peruvian perfection"; despite the "out-of-the-way" locale, reviewers relish the "change of pace", whether "for a date" or an affordable feast with a "group of friends."

	FOOD	DECOR	SERVICE	COST

Moishe's Pippic 🏮 Deli/Jewish
| 18 | 7 | 16 | $15 |

Hayes Valley | 425A Hayes St. (Gough St.) | 415-431-2440
"A great solution" when you're craving a "Chicago dog", "corned beef sandwich" or "excellent brisket" like your *bubbe* made, this "kosher-style" Hayes Valley noshery with a Windy City theme is as "authentic as it gets on the Left Coast"; a "sweet" staff helps soften the "work-manlike" atmosphere, but some critics cry "eh", "we need a better Jewish deli in San Francisco"; N.B. closes at 4 PM.

Moki's Sushi & Pacific Grill Japanese
| 22 | 16 | 18 | $32 |

Bernal Heights | 615 Cortland Ave. (bet. Anderson & Moultrie Sts.) | 415-970-9336 | www.mokisushi.com
"Melt-in-your-mouth masterpieces" like "rock-star modern sushi rolls" and other "island-influenced" fare lure finatics to this Japanese "go-to" with South Pacific style; despite getting lightly knocked as "another little piece of Bernal hipsterism", the "quality, value" and "friendly" (if "sometimes slow") service add up to "good times."

MoMo's American
| 17 | 18 | 17 | $38 |

South Beach | 760 Second St. (King St.) | 415-227-8660 | www.sfmomos.com
"Electric" on game days, this "boisterous" South Beacher "packs in" Giants fans for "drinks, apps" and "hanging out" before they "cross the street to the ballpark"; go in the off-season for a "fair shake of the place" say supporters of the "straightforward" New American eats, but opponents protest it's "overpriced", sighing "if only the food matched the very loud buzz."

Monk's Kettle ● Californian
| 18 | 17 | 17 | $27 |

Mission | 3141 16th St. (Albion St.) | 415-865-9523 | www.monkskettle.com
Lagerheads laud this "swanky" late-night gastropub for its "insane range of beers" and Californian "pub food taken to a higher degree" to "soak up the 8% brews"; despite a soupçon of "Mission attitude", not to mention "horrendous" weekend waits, there's plenty of "good cheer" in the air, thanks in no small part to barkeeps who "value" the suds selection as "seriously as a sommelier takes his wine list" and strive to ensure you "always walk away with a new favorite"; N.B. open till 1 AM.

Morton's The Steakhouse Steak
| 24 | 21 | 24 | $73 |

Downtown | 400 Post St. (bet. Mason & Powell Sts.) | 415-986-5830 | www.mortons.com
"Consistency abounds" at these "can't-go-wrong" steakhouse chain links (Downtown and in San Jose) pairing "well-prepared" chops that "hang off the plate" with "seriously powerful martinis"; "arm-and-a-leg" prices come with the territory, along with a "Saran-wrapped presentation" of raw meats (accompanied by an instructional "recitation" by the waiter) – so despite "terrific" service, some are "tired" of the "shtick."

Mo's American
| ▽ 20 | 9 | 15 | $18 |

North Beach | 1322 Grant Ave. (bet. Green & Vallejo Sts.) | 415-788-3779
SoMa | Yerba Buena Gdns. | 772 Folsom St. (bet. 3rd & 4th Sts.) | 415-957-3779
www.mosgrill.com
"Juicy" burgers, "hand-cut" fries and "fantastic" malts keep customers coming to this "gourmet" "diner-food" duo that does "lots of takeout"; the SoMa outpost is convenient "if you're at the convention center",

	FOOD	DECOR	SERVICE	COST

but many are mo' enamored of the North Beach original, where you can watch the patties take a spin on the "charbroil carousel."

NEW Moss Room *Californian/Mediterranean* 21 | 24 | 21 | $53

Inner Richmond | California Academy of Sciences | 55 Music Concourse Dr. (bet. Fulton St. & Lincoln Way) | 415-876-6121 | www.themossroom.com

"Where else can you dine subterranean and subtyrannosaurus?" quip cronies of this dino-mite downstairs "oasis" by Loretta Keller (Coco500) in the California Academy of Sciences that's accessible via a staircase passing a two-story-tall living wall of moss; by day, the "excellent", "environmentally sustained" and pricey Cal-Med surf 'n' turf is available to museum-goers only on a walk-in basis, but at dinner it stirs up a "happening" "sexy" scene that includes "inventive drinks", "pampering" service and "enough candles to evoke a prayer."

Muracci's Japanese ▽ 21 | 7 | 15 | $12
Curry & Grill Ⓢ *Japanese*

Downtown | 307 Kearny St. (Bush St.) | 415-773-1101 | www.muraccis.com

"Go for the curry, but don't be in a hurry" at this "always packed" Downtown lunch-only "hole-in-the-wall" where the "wonderful" eponymous bowls are "cooked to order", resulting in "long lines" but are "worth the wait", especially "on a cold day"; "darn tasty" "bargain" Japanese eats such as "crunchy, delicious" tonkatsu and "homemade pickles" also make it a popular option among FiDi workers; N.B. open weekdays only.

My Tofu House *Korean* 22 | 8 | 15 | $18

Inner Richmond | 4627 Geary Blvd. (bet. 10th & 11th Aves.) | 415-750-1818

"Only those who miss mom's own kimchi would claim" they can find better Korean food elsewhere declare devotees of this "bargain" Inner Richmonder delivering "extraordinary" "steaming hot pots of spicy tofu" as well as "lovingly" prepared BBQ and a "mean" bibimbop; otherwise the "vibe is a bit cold and sparse", so go for "takeout" or simply "stop looking around and eat."

Naan 'n Curry *Indian/Pakistani* 17 | 7 | 10 | $15

Downtown | 336 O'Farrell St. (bet. Mason & Taylor Sts.) | 415-346-1443 ☾
Inner Sunset | 642 Irving St. (bet. 7th & 8th Aves.) | 415-664-7225
North Beach | 533 Jackson St. (Columbus Ave.) | 415-693-0499 Ⓢ
Polk Gulch | 690 Van Ness Ave. (Turk St.) | 415-775-1349
www.naancurry.com

"Budget-conscious" folks "jonesing" for "fiery", "filling" Indian-Pakistani fare "crowd" in for the "namesake menu items" at this "cheap, cheap" mini-chain in SF and Berkeley, unfazed by its "spartan surroundings" ("like a grade-school cafeteria") and "lack of service"; still, pickier patrons grouse about "greasy" grub, saying "you get what you pay for."

Namu *Californian/Korean* - | - | - | M

Inner Richmond | 439 Balboa St. (6th Ave.) | 415-386-8332 | www.namusf.com

Contemporary Californian meets Seoul food at this Inner Richmond arrival that incorporates Korean and Japanese techniques into the preparation of its small plates, grilled entrees, hot pots and other specialties with a local, seasonal bent; the smoke-free, minimalist dining room is enlivened by late-night DJs (Wednesday–Saturday), weekend brunch and midweek happy hours at the reclaimed cypress bar, offering over 30 kinds of sake by the glass.

Nectar Wine Lounge *Californian*

18 | 20 | 18 | $38

Marina | 3330 Steiner St. (bet. Chestnut & Lombard Sts.) | 415-345-1377 | www.nectarwinelounge.com

"Beautiful young" Marina "professionals" (aka "eye candy") "crowd" inside for a "drop-in drink" and "fine nibbles" at this "plush", somewhat "pricey" Californian enoteca; if you "don't know" what to order from the "eclectic", "cleverly described" wine list, "ask for advice" or "try the tastes" with a flight; N.B. the Burlingame branch has a more extensive menu.

NEW Nettie's Crab Shack *Seafood*

20 | 19 | 19 | $38

Cow Hollow | 2032 Union St. (bet. Buchanan & Webster Sts.) | 415-409-0300 | www.nettiescrabshack.com

With its "airy" "Cape Cod"–style interior and "patio for people-watching", this "straightforward" seafood shack in Cow Hollow "hooks" afishionados with "true-to-its-roots" fare, including "perfect lobster rolls" and "real-deal po' boys", all served "with a smile"; affordable "house wines" and "free filtered water" can save you some clams, and the Sunday night DIY "crab feeds" are "messy fun", but a few critics carp that it's "not all it's cracked up to be."

Nick's Crispy Tacos ⊄ *Mexican*

22 | 11 | 14 | $13

Russian Hill | 1500 Broadway (Polk St.) | 415-409-8226

Russian Hill habitués "craving" a "supreme" "crispy-taco" fix line up at this "fantastically bizarre" Mexican that takes over the "kitschy" nightclub Rouge (think "red velvet booths and chandeliers") till 10 PM; "it's a rookie move to go for the burritos" insist those in-the-know, who advise sticking with the "cheap" signature dish (ordered "Nick's Way for the full effect") and "fierce margaritas."

Nihon 🖪🅜 *Japanese*

20 | 22 | 19 | $40

Mission | 1779 Folsom St. (14th St.) | 415-552-4400 | www.nihon-sf.com

"Pre-Mission partying" begins at this "out-of-the-way" "urban-chic" izakaya serving "inventive sashimi" and Japanese small plates (at "larger-than-life prices"), which complement an "absurdly large" whiskey selection that makes some "wish dad were with me"; the ground floor is "always packed during happy hour", so if you want to avoid "jostling elbows with everyone", head upstairs where "romantics" canoodle and "wealthy" regulars "keep their own bottles."

Nob Hill Café *Italian*

21 | 16 | 20 | $34

Nob Hill | 1152 Taylor St. (bet. Clay & Pleasant Sts.) | 415-776-6500 | www.nobhillcafe.com

Nob Hill neighbors sitting "elbow-to-elbow" enjoy "excellent" Northern Italian eats at this "quaint", "homey" cafe, a "perennial favorite" that "satisfies every time"; "pleasant" service and a "good value" mean it's the sort of place "you could actually go every night", but – "bummer" – you better "be prepared to wait" 'cause "they don't take reservations."

	FOOD	DECOR	SERVICE	COST

nopa ◑ *Californian*

25 **21** **22** **$45**

Western Addition | 560 Divisadero St. (Hayes St.) | 415-864-8643 | www.nopasf.com

At this "late-night" Western Addition Californian, chef/co-owner Laurence Jossel "nails the local/sustainable" construct in his "astounding", "creative" "comfort food" (complemented by a "seasonal drinks menu") that's "so good you forget to be sanctimonious"; despite "impossible parking" and the challenge of "beating through the crowds" (including a large contingent of off-duty "restaurant workers") to "wrestle a spot at the communal table", most agree the "stellar" dining experience is "worth every bit of hassle."

NEW Nopalito *Mexican*

23 **16** **21** **$27**

Western Addition | Falletti's Plaza | 306 Broderick St. (Oak St.) | 415-437-0303 | www.nopalitosf.com

Nopa's new fresh-Mex spin-off in a Western Addition "strip mall" churns out "carnitas as good as anything in the city" and other "amazing" "slow-cooked" *comida* made with "well-sourced local" ingredients that "elicits oohs and aahs"; the "small portions" and relatively large "bill can be a shocker" to some, but the eco "see-and-be-seen" environs, "super-friendly" servers and "late hours" make it a no-brainer for many; P.S. "no reservations, but you can call ahead to get your name on the list."

North Beach Pizza *Pizza*

20 **10** **15** **$18**

Excelsior | 4787 Mission St. (bet. Persia & Russia Aves.) | 415-586-1400
Fisherman's Wharf | Pier 39 (The Embarcadero at Beach St.) | 415-433-0400
Haight-Ashbury | 3054 Taraval St. (41st Ave.) | 415-242-9100
Haight-Ashbury | 800 Stanyan St. (Haight St.) | 415-751-2300
North Beach | 1462 Grant Ave. (Union St.) | 415-433-2444 ◑
www.northbeachpizza.net

"Who needs a fancy place when the pie is right?" ask fans of this "always crowded" pizza chain whose "consistent" quality comes through for "family outings" and a "slice on the run"; pickier patrons call it merely "passable" and "overly cheesed", but still dial up (or order online) for "predictable" delivery.

North Beach Restaurant ◑ *Italian*

22 **19** **20** **$49**

North Beach | 1512 Stockton St. (bet. Green & Union Sts.) | 415-392-1700 | www.northbeachrestaurant.com

Amid a "sea of tourist eateries" in North Beach, this upscale, "old-school" Tuscan draws the "power elite" with its "wonderful", "home-cooked" dishes and "interesting wine selections" served in a "warm", "convivial" atmosphere; though a few cite "snooty" treatment, most maintain the "polished professionalism" of the "bow-tied" waiters "enhances the experience."

O Izakaya Lounge *Japanese*

17 **16** **17** **$37**

Japantown | Hotel Kabuki | 1625 Post St. (Laguna St.) | 415-614-5431 | www.jdvhotels.com

It's "not a traditional izakaya", but this "modern", "high-end" late-night "Japanese sports bar" – think baseball-themed wall paper – is a "fun place" for the "younger generation" in Japantown to sip sake cocktails and "share" "tasty" "country"-style "finger food" ("don't come looking for sushi"); the service is "friendly enough", but critics

| | FOOD | DECOR | SERVICE | COST |

complain that the "coziness quotient is too low" in a sensory O-verload setting, with "video screens all over the place", and the fare is merely "average."

Old Jerusalem *Mediterannean/Mideastern* ∇ 20 | 9 | 17 | $18

Mission | 2976 Mission St. (bet. 25th & 26th Sts.) | 415-642-5958 | www.oldjerusalemsf.com

Falafel fans are "so happy to find" this Mediterranean hole-in-the-wall in the Mission serving "big plates of freshly prepared", "totally authentic" Middle Eastern eats, including some of "the best hummus west of Jerusalem"; despite the "cold interior", many recommend it as an option when "you get a little tired of Latin food", but take note it "does not serve alcohol or allow it to be brought in."

One Market Ⓢ *American* 22 | 21 | 21 | $58

Embarcadero | 1 Market St. (Steuart St.) | 415-777-5577 | www.onemarket.com

Bradley Ogden's "biz-class" "staple" on the Embarcadero "doesn't rely on gimmicks" to lure "all of the power brokers of SF" for "working lunches and dinners", just "reliable", "seasonal" American cuisine and an "extensive list" of "big wines", plus foodies can enjoy a "unique" dining experience at the kitchen's "chef's table"; service has a "personal" touch, but some report "the staff cannot" always "keep up with the large" dining room or "overcrowded bar."

Oola Restaurant & Bar ◑ *Californian* 20 | 18 | 18 | $43

SoMa | 860 Folsom St. (bet. 4th & 5th Sts.) | 415-995-2061 | www.oola-sf.com

Cool customers say you "can't beat the babyback ribs and cocktails" at this "sexy, modern" SoMa Californian with a "hip", "dark" loft setting that's "open late" (till midnight or 1 AM nightly); though it's "nothing spectacular" to some, others mention you might "meet the foodie you'll marry here."

Oriental Pearl *Chinese* 22 | 14 | 18 | $32

Chinatown | 760 Clay St. (Walter U. Lum Pl.) | 415-433-1817 | www.orientalpearlsf.com

Sinophiles seeking a "serene" meal head to this two-floor "oasis of calm" in clangorous Chinatown, a "reasonably priced" choice delivering "excellent" dim sum as well as both "Americanized" eats and specialties that seem "fresh from Hong Kong"; service "with a smile" and tables that are often "available with no wait" (a "puzzlement") ensure it's an easy "go-to."

Orson ⓈⓂ *Californian* 18 | 20 | 18 | $54

SoMa | 508 Fourth St. (Bryant St.) | 415-777-1508 | www.orsonsf.com

If you're "seeking a scene" in SoMa, you can "walk on the wild side" at Elizabeth Falkner's "wall-to-wall happy-hour" place presenting "innovative" yet "recently toned-down" Californian bistro dishes ("exploding balls of Caesar salad dressing is a hoot!") and "fantastic desserts" in an "edgy", "post-industrial interior" highlighted by an illuminated catwalk; some "high-end stunts" "miss the mark", but it's still "worth a visit" for intrepid foodies who wonder "why can't more places do a little experimenting?"; N.B. now serving lunch Tuesday–Friday.

Osha Thai *Thai*

| | 21 | 19 | 17 | $26 |

Cow Hollow | 2033 Union St. (Webster St.) | 415-567-6742 ◐
Downtown | 4 Embarcadero Ctr. (Drumm St.) | 415-788-6742
NEW **Glen Park** | 2922 Diamond St. (Bosworth St.) | 415-586-6742
Mission | 819 Valencia St. (19th St.) | 415-826-7738 ◐
SoMa | 149 Second St. (bet. Howard & Mission Sts.) | 415-278-9991
Tenderloin | 696 Geary St. (Leavenworth St.) | 415-673-2368 ◐
www.oshathai.com

You may want to dress like a "clubber" to "fit in" at these "upscale" Thai "resto-clubs" "multiplying like rabbits" across the city, "each with its own decor, menu and atmosphere" (from the "cheaper" "late-night" Tenderloin vet to the "too-chic" Glen Park newcomer); all feature "fresh" fare "with a kick", "fast, if not friendly service" and "lines out the door", and a few wonder with such "affordable prices, how can they afford all the designer furniture?"

Ottimista Enoteca-Café Ⓜ *Italian/Mediterranean*

| | 19 | 19 | 20 | $33 |

Cow Hollow | 1838 Union St. (Octavia St.) | 415-674-8400 |
www.ottimistasf.com

A "bit of heaven on Union Street", this "rustic", "intimate" Cow Hollow enoteca is a "favorite stop" among ottimistic oenophiles who order wines in a "wide range of prices" to match "terrific" Med-Italian "small bites"; with some of "San Francisco's most beautiful all around you" and servers who "take the time to educate" imbibers, it's a "fun" "date" destination, especially if you can score a seat on the heated patio.

Out the Door *Vietnamese*

| | 22 | 14 | 16 | $23 |

Downtown | Westfield San Francisco Ctr. | 845 Market St. (bet. 4th & 5th Sts.) | 415-541-9913
Embarcadero | Ferry Plaza | 1 Ferry Bldg. (Market St.) | 415-321-3740 Ⓢ
www.outthedoors.com

For "the best of Slanted Door without the crowds, wait or attitude", the "lunch and shopping" set is glad to "take a table now and skip the pretty views" at these "Phan-tastic" "second label" venues that "elevate humble" Vietnamese street food, both at the "'to-go' counter inside the Ferry Building" and at Downtown's Westfield Centre, where signature Austrian wines are also served; while it's "cheaper" than the "mothership", some find it "expensive" for the "fast-food" setting; N.B. a Pac Heights sit-down sib is slated to open soon at 2232 Bush Street.

Oyaji Ⓜ *Japanese*

| | 23 | 13 | 16 | $36 |

Outer Richmond | 3123 Clement St. (bet. 32nd & 33rd Aves.) | 415-379-3604

"One of the most authentic izakayas in SF", this "hidden find" in the Outer Richmond brims with a "comfortable atmosphere", "grilling fish smells" and a gregarious owner who "takes good care of you" with "affordable", "traditional" cooked Japanese small plates "you wouldn't find" elsewhere and "lots" of sake; while he's "entertaining" to many, his "personality" and off-color "jokes" can be a "turnoff" to others.

Ozumo *Japanese*

| | 24 | 23 | 20 | $56 |

Embarcadero | 161 Steuart St. (bet. Howard & Mission Sts.) | 415-882-1333 |
www.ozumo.com

The "beautiful", "sophisticated" dining room and "hopping" bar "have the feel of Tokyo down pat" at this "vibrant" Embarcadero Japanese and its "newly opened Oakland" offshoot, providing "outstanding", "delicate" sushi and "marvelous" robata, complemented by "impeccable" sakes; just be prepared to fork over a "fortune" – or save it for when "someone else is paying."

Pacific Café *Seafood* | 23 | 17 | 23 | $34 |

Outer Richmond | 7000 Geary Blvd. (34th Ave.) | 415-387-7091
"Fantastic, fresh seafood served simply" and "affordably" draws diners to "schlep" to this "renowned" "neighborhood gem" in the Outer Richmond; the "retro" digs (dating back to 1974) are "nothing fancy", but that's fine with the "convivial crowd" that quaffs "complimentary wine" while "waiting for a table."

Pacific Catch *Seafood* | 20 | 15 | 18 | $24 |

Inner Sunset | 1200 Ninth Ave. (Lincoln Way) | 415-504-6905
Marina | 2027 Chestnut St. (bet. Fillmore & Steiner Sts.) | 415-440-1950
www.pacificcatch.com
"Tempting" sustainable seafood with a Pacific Rim "twist" hooks fans at this "family-friendly" trio offering "unusual" combos like wasabi rice bowls to "dream about", as well as "fabulous" tacos and "delicious" drinks; "you'll be packed in like sardines" at the "small" Marina original (which is why "takeaway" is tops there), but at least the prices "won't leave you high and dry"; P.S. the "airy" Corte Madera and Inner Sunset outposts are far more "spacious."

Pagan Ⓜ *Burmese* | - | - | - | I |

NEW **Inner Richmond** | 731 Clement St. (bet. 8th & 9th Aves.) |
415-221-3888
Outer Richmond | 3199 Clement St. (33rd Ave.) | 415-751-2598
www.pagansf.com
Named after an ancient city in Burma (and pronounced 'bagan'), this Southeast Asian duo in the Inner and Outer Richmond draws adventurous diners with its unique culinary mash-up of flavors from tea leaf salads to samusa soup, without the epic waits of its competitors; the 3199 Clement branch serves Thai food as well.

Pakwan *Pakistani* | 22 | 6 | 11 | $15 |

Mission | 3180-3182 16th St. (bet. Guerrero & Valencia Sts.) |
415-255-2440 ⓟ
Tenderloin | 501 O'Farrell St. (Jones St.) | 415-776-0160
www.pakwanrestaurant.com
There are "no frills" at this pack of Pakistanis with "DIY" "cafeteria-style" service and "sparsely decorated" digs featuring "limited seating" and "long lines", but that's because the "focus is 100% on feeding you" "superior" "cheap eats"; while "takeout" is a must for some, tipplers are tickled you can "BYO."

Palio d'Asti Ⓢ *Italian* | 20 | 19 | 20 | $42 |

Downtown | 640 Sacramento St. (bet. Kearny & Montgomery Sts.) |
415-395-9800 | www.paliodasti.com
"Rock solid" for "quick business lunches" and a "killer happy hour" ("buy two drinks" and get a "free" "thin-crust pizza"), this "comfortable" Downtowner dishes out "old-style" Italian fare updated with "modern ingredients"; "cheerful" service is another plus, though critics claim the whole package feels a bit "clichéd."

	FOOD	DECOR	SERVICE	COST

Pancho Villa Taqueria ● *Mexican*

| 22 | 9 | 15 | $12 |

Mission | 3071 16th St. (bet. Mission & Valencia Sts.) | 415-864-8840 | www.panchovillasf.com

"Humongous", "flavorful" burritos are "heaven in a foil wrapper" at this "well-lit" (some say "antiseptic") taqueria twosome in the Mission and San Mateo; amigos aver "you can't get any better" "inexpensive" Mexican eats – just make sure you "know what you want" before joining the "factory-style queue", because the "fast" servers "won't slow down for you."

Pane e Vino *Italian*

| 22 | 18 | 22 | $41 |

Cow Hollow | 1715 Union St. (Gough St.) | 415-346-2111 | www.paneevinotrattoria.com

The staff "welcomes you like family" at this "quintessential" Northern Italian trattoria offering "lovingly prepared" "thin-crust pizzas" and a "variety" of "fresh" pastas for "moderate prices" in Cow Hollow; it's "so simple" yet "so good" maintain most, though a few find it's "not especially enjoyable" during "loud" peak hours.

Papalote Mexican Grill *Mexican*

| 22 | 11 | 15 | $12 |

Mission | 3409 24th St. (Valencia St.) | 415-970-8815
Western Addition | 1777 Fulton St. (Masonic Ave.) | 415-776-0106
www.papalote-sf.com

"I want to be buried in their salsa" sigh "chip-dipping" supporters of these "hip" Mission and Western Addition taquerias whose "fresh ingredients" and "plentiful veggie options" ("like soyrizo") make for Mexican fare that's a "notch above"; just "go to devour, not to linger", or else "order ahead" and get it "to go."

Park Chalet
Garden Restaurant *Californian*

| 16 | 22 | 15 | $28 |

Outer Sunset | 1000 Great Hwy. (bet. Fulton St. & Lincoln Way) | 415-386-8439 | www.beachchalet.com

"What would Sundays be?" without this "open-air" cafe adjoining Beach Chalet at the "foot of Golden Gate Park" ask admirers who love to "sit outside on the lawn" with their "kids and dog", "enjoying live music", even if the New American–Californian "brewpub" grub is merely "mediocre" and the service only "so-so"; there's no ocean view, but that means "fewer tourists" too; N.B. a recent chef change is not reflected in the Food score.

Patxi's Chicago Pizza Ⓜ *Pizza*

| 22 | 13 | 17 | $21 |

Hayes Valley | 511 Hayes St. (bet. Laguna & Octavia Sts.) | 415-558-9991 | www.patxischicagopizza.com
See review in South of San Francisco Directory.

Pauline's Pizza Ⓢ Ⓜ *Pizza*

| 23 | 14 | 18 | $24 |

Mission | 260 Valencia St. (bet. Duboce Ave. & 14th St.) | 415-552-2050 | www.paulinespizza.com

The "quality of the ingredients" "could not be better" than at this Mission "standby" whose "delicious thin-crust pizzas" – including a "superb" pesto pie among other "brilliant" combos – and "creative" salads often incorporate "veggies from the owners' own organic farm"; it's "great for groups", but "prepare to wait" otherwise (no rezzies are taken for parties of fewer than eight).

	FOOD	DECOR	SERVICE	COST

Paul K Ⓜ *Mediterranean* **21** | **17** | **21** | **$46**

Hayes Valley | 199 Gough St. (Oak St.) | 415-552-7132 |
www.paulkrestaurant.com

A slightly "offbeat" "alternative" to the usual "pre-performance" options
in Hayes Valley, this "arty" Med entices opera-goers with an "inventive"
menu, wines "enjoyable for every taste" and "great cocktails" (as well as
a "tasty" weekend brunch); service is "colorful" and "helpful", despite
a "crowded, noisy" atmosphere amid "closely packed tables", but a
fretful few are "underwhelmed", calling it "nothing special, just nice."

Pazzia Ⓧ *Italian* **23** | **12** | **19** | **$32**

SoMa | 337 Third St. (bet. Folsom & Harrison Sts.) | 415-512-1693

"Thin, thin, thin-crust pizza" wins over *amici* of this "authentic" SoMa
Italian where "you won't regret" going with either the "value"-priced
pies or the "rich pasta dishes"; true, the "tiny" interior is "crammed"
("outside tables are the best"), but since the "charming" owner "makes
everyone feel at home", customers "keep coming back for more."

Ⓩ Perbacco Ⓧ *Italian* **25** | **22** | **23** | **$53**

Downtown | 230 California St. (bet. Battery & Front Sts.) | 415-955-0663 |
www.perbaccosf.com

Popular for "power lunches", a "night on the town" or just "primi at the
bar", this Downtown Italian offers "fantastico" Piedmontese "housemade" salumi, pastas, crudos and "regional wines", delivered by
"servers who really care"; while some "head upstairs to escape the
ear-splitting noise levels" below, others "don't let the din stop them
from enjoying" "serious cuisine" "without the price or attitude."

Pesce *Italian/Seafood* **24** | **17** | **20** | **$43**

Russian Hill | 2227 Polk St. (bet. Green & Vallejo Sts.) | 415-928-8025 |
www.pescesf.com

"Are we in Italy?" marvel fans of this "excellent" Russian Hill seafooder
from Ruggero Gadaldi (Antica Trattoria, Beretta), providing "fabulous
Venetian"-style tapas prepared with sustainable catches, as well as
oysters and "well-made cocktails", served by a "prompt, efficient"
staff; "local regulars" are often sardine-packed into the "bare", "noisy"
room, but "with food this good, no one seems to mind."

NEW Phat Philly *Cheesesteaks* ▽ **20** | **10** | **18** | **$12**

Mission | 3388 24th St. (bet. Mission & Valencia Sts.) | 415-550-7428

Phanatics are phlocking to this "kitschy" newcomer in the Mission for
"real-deal" cheesesteaks made with "the right peppers", Cheez Whiz
and Amoroso's "rolls flown in from Philly", along with "nontraditional"
veggie hoagies; a few critics complain the staff "needs to turn the
lights down" in the chrome-filled setting, but diehards "wear shades
just to get a bite of that roll-onion-cheese-and-beefy goodness."

Picaro *Spanish* ▽ **17** | **15** | **16** | **$25**

Mission | 3120 16th St. (bet. Guerrero & Valencia Sts.) | 415-431-4089 |
www.picarotapasrestaurant.com

"Big groups" who "just want some nibbles" and "fruity, delicious sangria"
find their way to this "cheap" Spaniard in a "hip" location "right on 16th
and Valencia" in the Mission; those who "like garlic" and "don't expect" too much are "happy", but sober sorts say the "subpar tapas
don't come close to making up for the bachelorette-party atmosphere."

Piccino Ⓜ *Californian/Italian* ▽ 24 | 16 | 20 | $26

Dogpatch | 801 22nd St. (Tennessee St.) | 415-824-4224 |
www.piccinocafe.com

"Fabulous" "thin-crust pizzas", "tasty salads" and other "light" Cal-
Italian locavore dishes are "the stuff of dreams" at this "little (and I mean
little)" Dogpatch sidewalk cafe where "everything is made to order,
slowly"; since indoor seating is limited, some like to "go on a nice day and
sit outside", while others swing by its "coffee stand" (relocated a few
doors down) for "great baked goods", Blue Bottle drinks and sandwiches.

NEW **Pickles** Ⓢ *American* - | - | - | M
(fka Clown Alley)

Downtown | 42 Columbus Ave. (Jackson St.) | 415-421-2540

Downtown's long-running kitschy hamburger shack, formerly known as
Clown Alley, is back and spiffier than ever with wood paneling, skylights
and a revamped American menu; along with burgers, hot dogs and the
signature pot of pickles (plus frozen custard for dessert), a former
Zinnia chef has added hand-cut pasta and wild seafood to the mix.

Piperade Ⓢ *Spanish* 25 | 21 | 22 | $52

Downtown | 1015 Battery St. (Green St.) | 415-391-2555 |
www.piperade.com

If you want to "eat outside the box", regulars recommend Gerald
Hirigoyen's "elevated Basque" in an "off-the-beaten-path" Downtown
location, where his "soulful", "consistently superb" fare is backed by a
wine list that "celebrates offbeat Spanish" and "little-known" regional
wines; the "table-hopping chef-owner" enlivens the "beautiful setting
that's formal enough for a business" lunch, "yet intimate enough" for
a night out, and the prices are a "relative bargain."

Piqueo's *Peruvian* ▽ 24 | 20 | 20 | $41

Bernal Heights | 830 Cortland Ave. (Gates St.) | 415-282-8812 |
www.piqueos.com

A "favorite" (and "sadly, no longer a secret") in Bernal Heights, this
Peruvian showcases such a "variety" of "phenomenal" South American tapas with "unusual flavors and outstanding sauces" that "it'll take
you about 20 minutes just to read the menu" (the "amazing" chickpea
apps served make it harder to concentrate); "welcoming service" and
"excellent, well-priced" sangria add to the "social experience."

NEW **Pizza Nostra** *Pizza* - | - | - | M

Potrero Hill | 300 De Haro St. (16th St.) | 415-558-9493 |
www.pizzanostrasf.com

Restaurateur Jocelyn Bulow (Chez Papa) offers Potrero Hillites this casual new outpost for enjoying authentic antipasti, pastas and Neapolitan
thin-crust pies, plus imported gelato and vino; its snug, warm environs
offer booths, a bar overlooking an exhibition kitchen and a gas-fired
oven, plus outdoor seating; N.B. no reservations.

Pizza Place on Noriega *Pizza* - | - | - | I

Outer Sunset | 3901 Noriega Ave. (46th Ave.) | 415-759-5752 |
www.pizzaplacesf.com

Dude, this aptly named "local" pizza place just blocks from the beach
in the Outer Sunset "gets it right", exuding a "perfect" California
"surfer vibe" but baking up "straight New York–style" pies cut into "big

FOOD · DECOR · SERVICE · COST

floppy slices" that drip with "that beautiful orange grease"; just "save room" for sides like hot wings and roasted cauliflower too, and wash it all down with an "inexpensive" pint; N.B. closed Tuesdays.

Pizzeria Delfina *Pizza*

| 24 | 15 | 19 | $27 |

Mission | 3611 18th St. (Guerrero St.) | 415-437-6800 | www.delfinasf.com
NEW Pacific Heights | 2406 California St. (bet. Fillmore & Steiner Sts.) | 415-440-1189 | www.pizzeriadelfina.com

Craig Stoll's "pizza-nirvana" pair in the Mission and Pac Heights is arguably "more popular than its upscale sibling" (Delfina) and "certainly as delicious", with antipasti "revelations" and "charred", "blistered" pies straight out of "Rome" – but "better with California ingredients"; so go during "off-hours", get "takeout" or "write your name on the chalkboard list and wait", since it's "worth the crush of customers" and a bit of extra dough.

Pizzetta 211 ⊘ *Pizza*

| 25 | 14 | 15 | $24 |

Outer Richmond | 211 23rd Ave. (California St.) | 415-379-9880 | www.pizzetta211.com

"To know" the "scrumptious" "artisanal" "thin-crust pizzas" – topped with the "best of the bounty" weekly – "is to crave them" proclaim pie partisans who squeeze into this "microscopic" joint way "out of the way" in the Outer Richmond; still, a handful huff that it would be "more inviting" if the staff "lost the attitude"; P.S. "go early" since the "wait can be terrible" and "once the pizza dough runs out, that's it!"

Plant Cafe Organic, The *Health Food*
(fka Lettus: Cafe Organic)

| 20 | 16 | 15 | $21 |

NEW Embarcadero | Pier 3 (Washington St.) | 415-984-1973
Marina | 3352 Steiner St. (bet. Chestnut & Lombard Sts.) | 415-931-2777
www.theplantcafe.com

A "casual" health-food haven that's neither "pretentious" nor "too granola", this "welcome" Marina venue offers an "extensive menu" of "well-prepared", "veggie-friendly" options, including an uncommonly "tasty" garden burger; yes, it's a "yuppie" "meeting spot for baby carriages", but "reasonable" tabs mean both your "belly and your wallet" will be "pleasantly full"; N.B. a new branch planted itself along the Embarcadero post-Survey.

Plouf ☒ *French*

| 22 | 16 | 19 | $42 |

Downtown | 40 Belden Pl. (bet. Bush & Pine Sts.) | 415-986-6491 | www.ploufsf.com

Mussels "cooked in so many luscious ways" and "mouthwatering" pommes frites are the raison d'être of this "bustling" French bistro with "close-together" tables, "right smack Downtown" on a "cute" pedestrian alley ("*bienvenue à Paris*" on "balmy nights"); "charming" Gallic waiters are a plus, though some guests still feel the excursion is "overpriced."

Pluto's Fresh Food
for a Hungry Universe *American*

| 19 | 12 | 14 | $14 |

Inner Sunset | 627 Irving St. (bet. 7th & 8th Aves.) | 415-753-8867
Marina | 3258 Scott St. (bet. Chestnut & Lombard Sts.) | 415-775-8867
www.plutosfreshfood.com

"Satisfying" salads ("tossed to order" with "plenty of toppings to choose from"), sandwiches and "huge portions" of "home cooking"

	FOOD	DECOR	SERVICE	COST

come at "recession" prices at this cluster of "healthy" American eateries in San Francisco and the South Bay; the "confusing" ordering system contributes to the "chaos", and the "noise can be daunting", which is why some suggest "take it to go" and bypass the "battle for seats."

Poesia *Italian* ▽ 20 | 15 | 20 | $41

Castro | 4072 18th St. (bet. Castro & Hartford Sts.) | 415-252-9325 | www.poesiasf.com

"After many short-lived restaurants" in the space, this "adorably cozy" Calabresi osteria "tucked away" in a Castro Victorian walk-up is a "keeper" cooking up "surprisingly good" specialties ("for the gay Wharf at least"); vintage Italian "films on the wall" coupled with "warm" service lend it a "romantic" feel, and though some label it "a little over-priced", it's "reliably pleasant" for most.

Poleng Lounge Ⓜ *Pan-Asian* 19 | 17 | 16 | $35

Western Addition | 1751 Fulton St. (bet. Central & Masonic Aves.) | 415-441-1751 | www.polenglounge.com

Tearoom by day, "eclectic" Pan-Asian eatery in the evening and a club at night, this Western Addition multitasker delivers an "education" in "ambitious" "fusion" flavors, like "out-of-this-world" garlic crab noodles; sure, "service can be slow", but tea-totalers tout the "great" selection of loose-leaf brews, and the "hip" Balinese-inspired lounge inspires lingering for "a night on the town."

Pomelo *Eclectic* 23 | 15 | 19 | $26

Inner Sunset | 92 Judah St. (6th Ave.) | 415-731-6175
Noe Valley | 1793 Church St. (30th St.) | 415-285-2257
www.pomelosf.com

"Loyal" locals "love to get a front-row seat" and watch the "action" in the "itty-bitty kitchen" at this Inner Sunset Eclectic (its "yuppie-serving counterpart in Noe Valley" is a little larger) where "global" grains and "cosmopolitan" noodle dishes provide "something for everyone's palate"; considering the "fair" cost, most aren't miffed by the "cramped" confines and "nondescript" decor.

Pomodoro *Italian* 17 | 13 | 17 | $22

Cow Hollow | 1875 Union St. (Laguna St.) | 415-771-7900
Laurel Heights | 3611 California St. (Spruce St.) | 415-831-0900
Noe Valley | 4000 24th St. (Noe St.) | 415-920-9904
North Beach | 655 Union St. (Columbus Ave.) | 415-399-0300
www.pastapomodoro.com

"The price is right" at these Italian eateries, a "safe bet" for "generous portions" of "decent" dishes; "relatively quick" service and "lots of menu options" mean it's "about as kid-friendly as it gets" gush boosters with *bambini*, but the less impressed note "nothing pops" at this "IHOP for pasta", pouting it's "pedestrian" at best.

Ponzu *Pan-Asian* 20 | 19 | 20 | $46

Downtown | Serrano Hotel | 401 Taylor St. (bet. Geary & O'Farrell Sts.) | 415-775-7979 | www.ponzurestaurant.com

"Excellent" servers who "get you out in time" for your show make this Pan-Asian in Union Square's Serrano Hotel a "pre-theater" natural; its "major appeal" is the "dark" dining room and "fun upscale lounge" setting – some say it's "more about the atmosphere" than the

Pork Store Café *American*   22 | 11 | 18 | $17

Haight-Ashbury | 1451 Haight St. (bet. Ashbury St. & Masonic Ave.) | 415-864-6981
Mission | 3122 16th St. (bet. Guerrero & Valencia Sts.) | 415-626-5523

An "eclectic crowd including hungover partyers" and "people on fixies" pigs out on "large" plates of "real, greasy" "American diner" eats at this "good-value" daytime duo; picky porkers prefer the "funky" Upper Haight "original" to the larger Mission digs, but "be prepared to wait" at either, especially for the "delicious" Sunday brunch; N.B. the 16th Street branch is also open for a nighttime shift, 7 PM-3 AM, Thursday–Saturday.

Pot de Pho *Vietnamese*   ∇ 18 | 17 | 19 | $21

Inner Richmond | 3300 Geary Blvd. (Parker Ave.) | 415-668-0826 | www.potdepho.com

If you "want a little ambiance to go with your pho", among other "upscale Vietnamese" specialties, this "modern" Ana Mandara-offshoot in the Inner Richmond presents its "fresh, organic" cuisine in an "East-meets-West" setting that's "a bit fancy" but still a "comforting" place to "hang out with friends"; on the downside, pot-stirrers protest that the somewhat "overpriced" portions lack the "flavor" of more "authentic" eateries.

Presidio Social Club *American*   18 | 20 | 19 | $43

Presidio | 563 Ruger St. (Lombard St.) | 415-885-1888 | www.presidiosocialclub.com

Stirring up "dangerous" cocktails inside "cool" "'40s-style barracks", this modern-day mess hall in the Presidio rounds up "nearby worker bees" and Pac Heights socialites with its "solid", "homestyle" New American comfort food and "grown-up" retro "charms"; though some cite merely "ok" cooking, "mediocre" service and a "meat-market" vibe, fans are tickled to "feel like an old army officer is about to tap you on the shoulder."

Puccini & Pinetti *Italian*   18 | 17 | 17 | $33

Downtown | 129 Ellis St. (Cyril Magnin St.) | 415-392-5500 | www.pucciniandpinetti.com

"Casual" and "kid-friendly", this "convenient" Downtown ristorante also pulls in a "pre-theater" clientele that's content with its "good", "reasonably priced" Italian plates; some say the "staff makes you feel at home", but others are "disappointed", citing merely "average" cooking; N.B. a recent chef change may not be fully reflected in the above Food score.

Puerto Alegre *Mexican*   18 | 12 | 16 | $19

Mission | 546 Valencia St. (bet. 16th & 17th Sts.) | 415-255-8201

"Hipsters and highchairs coexist peacefully" at this "down-home" Mission Mexican known for its "pitchers" of "killer" margaritas ("leave your keys at the door") and "price-efficient", "traditional" plates; while the cooking is "basic" and "you'll have to be patient" when "waiting for a table", lots of fans still "love" it.

	FOOD	DECOR	SERVICE	COST

Q *American* — 19 | 16 | 18 | $25

Inner Richmond | 225 Clement St. (bet. 3rd & 4th Aves.) | 415-752-2298 | www.qrestaurant.com

A "down-home oasis", this "value" American fills with "USF students and Inner Richmond families" "chowing" on "comfort food like your mama makes" and "very good BBQ" that "puts the 'amen' in stick-to-your-ribs"; the setting is "funky at best", but "sometimes you just really need their mac 'n' cheese and meatloaf" (not to mention those "excellent" beers) to "chase the blues away."

Z Quince *French/Italian* — 27 | - | 26 | $84

Downtown | 470 Pacific Ave. (bet. Montgomery St. & Osgood Pl.) | 415-775-8500 | www.quincerestaurant.com

Showcasing daily changing "splendid" meals "handcrafted" with "care" that "will have even a seasoned foodie Googling unfamiliar ingredients", this New French-Italian "splurge" spot delivers a "fine, fine, fine"-dining experience "approaching perfection"; frugal gourmets fret about "forced prix fixe" menus and a wine list that "hasn't noticed the collapse of the economy", but a relocation at press time from Pac Heights to more spacious Downtown digs should make it less "stuffy" and "easier to get reservations"; N.B. a more casual spin-off, Cotogna, is slated to open at 490 Pacific Avenue in fall 2009.

Ramblas *Spanish* — 20 | 18 | 19 | $31

Mission | 557 Valencia St. (bet. 16th & 17th Sts.) | 415-565-0207 | www.ramblastapas.com

"Go with a group so you can try it all" recommend regulars who "share a carafe of sangria" and sup on "delightful" Spanish tapas (many made with "organic ingredients") at this affordable Mission "hang" offering a bit of "Barcelona by the Bay", with its "active bar scene" and "energetic" vibe; "friendly, flirtatious" servers lend it an extra kick.

R & G Lounge *Chinese* — 23 | 12 | 15 | $32

Chinatown | 631 Kearny St. (bet. Clay & Sacramento Sts.) | 415-982-7877 | www.rnglounge.com

"When the menu isn't in English, you know you've found the right spot" cluck customers who crash this Cantonese seafood place that's "a bit pricier" than other Chinatown dives but "worth the extra money", "next-to-impossible weekend lines" and "brusque" service for the "best salt-and-pepper crab in town"; the upstairs dining room offers "fancy" "banquet" service, but "locals" cram downstairs for "everyday meals."

Range *American* — 26 | 20 | 23 | $51

Mission | 842 Valencia St. (bet. 19th & 20th Sts.) | 415-282-8283 | www.rangesf.com

"Impress your date and your palate without depressing your wallet" at this "winning" "Mission hideaway" where the "stellar" "one-page" New American menu and "cool cocktails" (both with a "seasonal slant") are served by a "top-notch" staff in "unpretentious" deco-accented digs providing "that special San Francisco style"; romantics beat a trail to the "back room" with a "mellow vibe", but it's "easier to get a seat without reservations" at the "noisy" bar; P.S. "parking is tough so arrive early."

	FOOD	DECOR	SERVICE	COST

Red's Java House *Burgers*

16 | 12 | 14 | $12

Embarcadero | Pier 30 (Bryant St.) | 415-777-5626

"Feed your inner longshoreman" at this "cheap" "blue-collar shack", a "divey-looking joint" "right on the Bay"; the food "is what it is" – mostly "basic burgers", "dynamite double cheese dogs" and "cold beer" – but the "salty atmosphere can't be beat" and even the "grudging" service is "part of the charm"; P.S. it's "busy during baseball season", when it stays open past its usual 3 PM closing.

Regalito Rosticeria Ⓜ *Mexican*

▽ 21 | 18 | 21 | $26

Mission | 3481 18th St. (Valencia St.) | 415-503-0650 | www.regalitosf.com

"Pork – that is all" declare carnita-vores about this little Missionite preparing "well-executed", "inexpensive" Mexican rotisserie dishes using sustainably produced meats; though a few bemoan "bland" preparations, some are appeased by sidewalk seating (a "bonus") on sunny days.

Restaurant Cassis Ⓜ *French*

▽ 22 | 21 | 23 | $43

Pacific Heights | 2101 Sutter St. (Steiner St.) | 415-440-4500 | www.restaurantcassis.com

"You can't help but say *merci beaucoup*" at this "tasteful" neighborhood bistro in Pac Heights where the "mostly French staff" "welcomes neighbors effusively"; the niçoise menu might be a bit "confusing with all the Italian dishes", but it's "delicious" whether you "dine elegantly", "stop in for a pizza and glass of wine" at the bar or enjoy Sunday brunch.

Restaurant LuLu *French/Mediterranean*

21 | 19 | 20 | $41

SoMa | 816 Folsom St. (bet. 4th & 5th Sts.) | 415-495-5775

LuLu Petite *Sandwiches*

Embarcadero | 1 Ferry Bldg. (Market St.) | 415-362-7019 www.restaurantlulu.com

Even though "it's no longer the hot new thing", this "pleasurable", "midrange" SoMa "standby" is "still going strong", serving up "hearty" French-Med fare – "anything from the wood-fired oven is worth a try" – matched by a "deep" wine selection; cautious customers warn that it does get "noisy" and you may "smell like a campfire" when you leave; P.S. the Ferry Building storefront specializes in "tasty sandwiches" and other "satisfying" takeout.

Richmond Restaurant & Wine Bar Ⓢ *Californian*

26 | 20 | 25 | $46

Inner Richmond | 615 Balboa St. (bet. 7th & 8th Aves.) | 415-379-8988 | www.therichmondsf.com

"The whole menu sings" at this "casual but elegant" "treasure" croon "in-the-know" connoisseurs who "can't figure out" how it manages to serve such "delectable", "inventive" Californian dinners for "such a small price"; maybe it's thanks to the "unassuming", "under-the-radar" location "tucked away" in the Inner Richmond, run by "gracious" chef-owners who "care about creating accessible food."

Rigolo *French*

▽ 16 | 12 | 12 | $19

Presidio Heights | Laurel Village Shopping Ctr. | 3465 California St. (Laurel St.) | 415-876-7777 | www.rigolocafe.com

Pascal Rigo's "casual" "sandwich/pizza place" feels like it's been in Presidio Heights "forever", offering "great baked goods" and a "something-for-everyone" French menu that works for "simple dinners", a "quick breakfast" or "mid-afternoon snack after shopping in Laurel Village"; it's "kid-friendly" for sure, but some say there's "not anything interesting" about the whole rigmarole.

Ristorante Ideale *Italian*

| 23 | 15 | 21 | $41 |

North Beach | 1309 Grant Ave. (Vallejo St.) | 415-391-4129 | www.idealerestaurant.com

The "name says it all" at this "charming", "non-touristy" North Beach trattoria that's "ideale" for "refreshingly authentic", "classic Roman" *cucina*, like "superb" thin-crust pizzas and "delicious" pastas; despite its "packed" layout, the "irreverent" servers seem to "thoroughly enjoy their work", making a pit stop here a "pleasure"; N.B. reservations suggested on the weekends.

Ristorante Milano *Italian*

| 22 | 15 | 21 | $41 |

Russian Hill | 1448 Pacific Ave. (bet. Hyde & Larkin Sts.) | 415-673-2961 | www.milanosf.com

"Why waste time in North Beach?" wonder Russian Hill habitués who prefer this "cozy" neighborhood nook where "authentic", "good-value" Northern Italian eats – from "unbelievably light" homemade pasta to desserts "rich enough to kill a man" – "warm the soul", as does "caring" chef/co-owner Aldo Blasi; if you're packed in "cheek-by-jowl", most maintain it would be "worth sitting in your neighbor's lap" for the "wonderful" experience.

Ristorante Parma ⊠ *Italian*

| ▽ 23 | 16 | 22 | $35 |

Marina | 3314 Steiner St. (bet. Chestnut & Lombard Sts.) | 415-567-0500

"Lots of garlic" and other "fresh ingredients" go into the "fantastic pastas" and other "consistent" Italian dishes at this "tiny" dinner place in the Marina that's as comfortable as a "warm, cozy sweater"; "sweet" service is another draw, and economizers enthuse that it's "not expensive" either.

Ristorante Umbria ⊠ *Italian*

| 21 | 17 | 18 | $36 |

SoMa | 198 Second St. (Howard St.) | 415-546-6985 | www.ristoranteumbria.com

This "quaint" Northern Italian trattoria, a "warm, friendly" "neighborhood" place that "just happens to be" in the thick of things near Market Street, offers "very fine" Umbrian fare for "fair" tabs; it can get "extremely crowded" with SoMa suits at lunchtime, but evenings it's easier to appreciate the "attentive" servers who "make you feel glad that you came."

⛉ Ritz-Carlton Dining Room ⊠Ⓜ *French*

| 27 | 27 | 28 | $103 |

Nob Hill | Ritz-Carlton Hotel | 600 Stockton St. (bet. California & Pine Sts.) | 415-773-6198 | www.ritzcarltondiningroom.com

"A tried-and-true pick" of "ladies and gentlemen" who "dress for dinner", this Nob Hill hotel haunt "puts the 'fine' in fine dining" while "exhilarating the taste buds" with "genius" chef Ron Siegel's "brilliant", "cutting-edge" New French prix fixes, boasting his "very *Iron Chef*" Japanese details; the "hush, hush" atmosphere and "fabulous", "seamless" service complete the picture, though it feels a "tad stuffy"

	FOOD	DECOR	SERVICE	COST

for some; P.S. those sans "expense accounts" can now order small bites or à la carte at the bar.

rnm restaurant 🅂🅼 American/French

| 23 | 21 | 22 | $43 |

Lower Haight | 598 Haight St. (Steiner St.) | 415-551-7900 | www.rnmrestaurant.com

"Inventive" yet "approachable" New American–French small plates and "superb" cocktails served at this "shiny, modern" crib in the "gritty" Lower Haight add up to a "potent combination" for either a "neighborhood dinner" or "celebratory" night; the "posh" bi-level space, accented with chain-mail curtains, gets "louder than most bars", but the service is "great" and the menu practically "underpriced" for the quality.

NEW RN74 French

| - | - | - | E |

SoMa | Millennium Tower | 301 Mission St. (Beale St.) | 415-543-7474 | www.rn74.com

Named after the main road running through Burgundy's vineyards, this Michael Mina wine bar in SoMa's Millennium Tower offers New French lunch, dinner and light bites from a French Laundry alum along with an expansive wine selection (with 50 glasses dispensed by Enomatic) steered by sommelier Rajat Parr; in keeping with the transportation theme, the room is designed to resemble a railroad station, with daily vintages displayed on a train-schedule board.

Roadside BBQ BBQ

| ∇ 17 | 9 | 13 | $17 |

Inner Richmond | 3751 Geary Blvd. (2nd Ave.) | 415-221-7427 | www.roadsidebbq.com

BBQ buffs find a "bargain for fall-off-the-bone ribs" and brisket at this "order-at-the-counter" Inner Richmond pit stop complete with "real Southern (sweetened) tea", as well as a nod to SF with "actual healthy veggies" on the side; some are put off by merely "passable" grub, but others are already "hooked" for eat-in or "takeout"; N.B. a San Rafael branch is in the works for early 2010.

Rosamunde Sausage Grill ⌀ German

| 25 | 6 | 16 | $10 |

Lower Haight | 545 Haight St. (bet. Fillmore & Steiner Sts.) | 415-437-6851

It's "hard to beat the links" at this German "sausage heaven", a Lower Haight "hole-in-the-wall" that "does only one thing" (two, if you count off-the-menu Tuesday burgers) "and does it extremely well"; "grilled to order" and topped with "mustards and condiments" by an "entertaining" staff, the specialty will "satisfy any foodie cravings" – but just "don't eat there", have it "delivered to your barstool" at the adjacent Toronado bar.

Rose Pistola Italian

| 22 | 20 | 20 | $45 |

North Beach | 532 Columbus Ave. (bet. Green & Union Sts.) | 415-399-0499 | www.rosepistolasf.com

This "Ligurian trattoria captures the wonderful vibes of North Beach" with its "wood-oven pizzas" as well as other "flavorful" specialties served in a "big, busy" room offering "top-notch people-watching" and weekend jazz; "plenty of tourists" can be a downside, though, and some feel it's "overpriced" for somewhat "uninspired" cooking and "mixed" service.

	FOOD	DECOR	SERVICE	COST

Rose's Cafe *Italian*

	22	17	19	$33

Cow Hollow | 2298 Union St. (Steiner St.) | 415-775-2200 |
www.rosescafesf.com

"Breakfast pizza rocks the weekend brunch" at this "smart", "family-friendly" Northern Italian "favorite" in Cow Hollow that serves "killer" pastas too; "it can be crowded, and sometimes loud", but the "staff tries hard to please", and if you snag an outdoor table, you can "people-watch on Union Street with your pooch."

Roti Indian Bistro *Indian*

	22	17	19	$33

West Portal | 53 W. Portal Ave. (bet. Ulloa & Vicente Sts.) | 415-665-7684 |
www.rotibistro.com

See review in South of San Francisco Directory.

◪ Rotunda *American*

	19	26	21	$38

Downtown | Neiman Marcus | 150 Stockton St. (bet. Geary & O'Farrell Sts.) |
415-362-4777 | www.neimanmarcus.com

It's "worth wading through the ladies who lunch" to "indulge" in an "exquisite lobster club" and "unbelievable popovers with strawberry butter" while "reveling in the nostalgia" and service that "makes you feel like a queen" at this "magnificent" "top-of-Neiman's" aerie; some unsold surveyors feel the New American meals are otherwise "mundane" for "sky-high prices", but other customers are contented by "staring" at the stained-glass dome and "views of Union Square"; N.B. closes at 5 PM.

Roy's *Hawaiian*

	23	22	21	$51

SoMa | 575 Mission St. (bet. 1st & 2nd Sts.) | 415-777-0277 |
www.roysrestaurant.com

The "next best thing to being oceanside in Maui", this "haute Hawaiian" SoMa chain link via celeb chef Roy Yamaguchi offers a "top-shelf" fusion menu that's as "eye-pleasing as it is palate-pleasing"; "wonderful" service and an "upscale casual" atmosphere add to its luster, though given the "upmarket pricing", it does "taste better when someone else is paying."

Ruth's Chris Steak House *Steak*

	23	20	22	$65

Polk Gulch | 1601 Van Ness Ave. (California St.) | 415-673-0557 |
www.ruthschris.com

"Nothing beats a steak sizzling in butter" at these "special-occasion" chain links in Polk Gulch and Walnut Creek where the "melt-in-your-mouth" chops are "cooked to perfection" and presented on "hot plates"; while the "classic" surroundings are "nothing creative or fancy", the service is "attentive" and the "off-the-charts" pricing manageable "so long as your boss doesn't care how much you spend."

Ryoko's ☻ *Japanese*

	▽ 22	14	17	$34

Downtown | 619 Taylor St. (bet. Post & Sutter Sts.) | 415-775-1028

A "find for late-night dining", this "underground" (literally) Japanese "lounge" near Union Square with "'70s basement decor" gets packed "full of locals" who come as much for the "scene" – often set to a "soundtrack of trance or house music" – as for the "fresh", "experimental" sushi served till 1:30 AM; the neighborhood is off-putting and the service quality "varies", but at least the "welcoming" owners keep the "good sake" flowing.

	FOOD	DECOR	SERVICE	COST

Saha Arabic Fusion *Mideastern* — 25 | 23 | 23 | $39

Tenderloin | Carlton Hotel | 1075 Sutter St. (bet. Hyde & Larkin Sts.) | 415-345-9547 | www.sahasf.com

Diners are delighted by the "wonderful delicacies" – such as "succulent" lamb, "incredibly inventive" veggie options and "out-of-this-world" desserts – prepared at this Arabic fusion "sleeper" in the Tenderloin; the "intimate", "exotic" dining room is tended by a "pleasant" staff, so it's fitting for a "first date" over a "satisfying prix fixe" menu.

Saigon Sandwiches ⊄ *Sandwiches/Vietnamese* — 25 | 1 | 12 | $5

Tenderloin | 560 Larkin St. (Turk St.) | 415-474-5698

The "hard-working" women who "run the operation" wrap up the "best *banh mi* in town" – "fabulous Vietnamese pork sandwiches" on "crisp" baguettes – at this Tenderloin take-out "hole-in-the-wall", voted the Survey's top Bang for the Buck; while "waiting in line" could likely eat up a whole lunch hour, most agree it delivers "all you could hope for" and more for a few bucks; N.B. closes at 6 PM.

Sai Jai Thai *Thai* — ∇ 25 | 13 | 18 | $16

Tenderloin | 771 O'Farrell St. (Larkin St.) | 415-673-5774

"Get the BBQ pork shoulder – you won't regret it" say Siamese seekers who "eat up a storm" (and still have "leftovers for lunch the next day") at this "excellent" orange-striped nook in the Tenderloin that's "one of the few places" around providing "authentic, 'roast-your-keister' spicy" Thai–Southeast Asian dishes; it's a real "deal", plus "BYO helps keep the check low", though cautious types say "be careful" in the neighborhood.

NEW Saison ⓜ *American* — - | - | - | VE

Mission | 2124 Folsom St. (17th St.) | 415-828-7990 | www.saisonsf.com

Positioning itself as the ultimate maverick restaurant, this stealth, saisonally driven, farm-to-table New American housed in a onetime Mission stable proffers a single $60 prix fixe dinner that begins with a meet-and-greet with chef Joshua Skenes (ex Chez TJ and Stonehill Tavern) in the kitchen, and features optional biodynamic wine pairings by sommelier Mark Bright (ex Michael Mina); it currently offers just two seatings on Sunday nights only, but expanded service is in the works.

Salt House *American* — 21 | 20 | 19 | $48

SoMa | 545 Mission St. (bet. 2nd St. & Shaw Alley) | 415-543-8900 | www.salthousesf.com

"Every bit the scene" as its sister, Town Hall, this SoMa "power-lunch" and "after-work date spot" is a "hot commodity" replete with "offbeat decor", pulsating "atmo" and "inspired" New American dishes with "flavors that pop"; some knock that it's "objectionably noisy", "overpriced" and rezzies are "hard to get", but "walk-ins" recommend the "family-style tables at the bar", known for its "great drinks" and "attractive crowd"; N.B. eat-in and take-out breakfast is now served weekdays.

Samovar Tea Lounge *Tearoom* — 20 | 23 | 20 | $23

Castro | 498 Sanchez St. (18th St.) | 415-626-4700
NEW Hayes Valley | 297 Page St. (Laguna St.) | 415-861-0303
SoMa | 730 Howard St. (bet. 3rd & 4th Sts.) | 415-227-9400
www.samovarlife.com

A "tranquil" trio of "urban oases" in the Castro, Hayes Valley and SoMa (the latter location "overlooks the Yerba Buena gardens"), these

	FOOD	DECOR	SERVICE	COST

"elegant" teahouses pour "delightful" "little pots of tea" "from around the world", complemented by "pretty", "surprisingly good" plates with Asian, British and Russian accents; while they're largely ideal for "lounging with friends on a lazy day", a few are tea-ed off by "portions that could be a little larger" for the price.

Sam's Grill & Seafood Restaurant Ⓔ *Seafood*

22	19	20	$42

Downtown | 374 Bush St. (bet. Kearny & Montgomery Sts.) | 415-421-0594
"The only thing older than the decor" is the "crusty" but "efficient" staff in "tuxes" at this "classic" Downtown seafooder where "power-lunchers" sip martinis in the "private booths"; most assure you "can't go wrong" with the "fresh" (if "not innovative") fare, and the "superb" "sand dabs are not to be missed" when they're on the menu; N.B. lunch reservations accepted for six or more only.

Sanraku *Japanese*

24	16	21	$39

SoMa | Sony Metreon Ctr. | 101 Fourth St. (Mission St.) | 415-369-6166
Sanraku Four Seasons *Japanese*
Downtown | 704 Sutter St. (Taylor St.) | 415-771-0803
www.sanraku.com
It "may not be the fanciest" Japanese in town, but "spectacular quality fish" at a "price that doesn't break the bank" makes this "convenient" piscatory pair Downtown and in SoMa's Metreon a "treasure"; the many "inventive" rolls are complemented by "solid land-food too", and since the staff is "super-welcoming", it's an "exceptional" option "in a city bursting with sushi bars."

San Tung *Chinese/Korean*

23	8	13	$20

Inner Sunset | 1031 Irving St. (bet. 11th & 12th Aves.) | 415-242-0828
"It's all about" the "addictive" dry fried chicken wings – "sweet, savory and spicy" – at this "no-frills" "madhouse" in the Inner Sunset, but you can also "gorge yourself" on "awesome" noodles and other "cheap" Chinese and Korean fare; "service can be surly at times" but it's "worth it" insist wing nuts, who "go early" to avoid the "line out the door."

Sauce Ⓓ *American*

19	16	20	$42

Hayes Valley | 131 Gough St. (Oak St.) | 415-252-1369 | www.saucesf.com
"Comfort and creativity" are "masterfully intertwined" in dishes like "bacon-wrapped meatloaf" at this "eclectic", semi-"upscale" young American "on the fringes of Hayes Valley", making for a "very pleas-ant" meal "before the show" or after getting sauced elsewhere (it's open till 2 AM); some say the gussied-up grub "falls short of promise" and also cite "slapped-together" decor, but "interesting drinks" at the redwood bar are a plus.

Savor *Mediterranean*

18	16	19	$23

Noe Valley | 3913 24th St. (bet. Noe & Sanchez Sts.) | 415-282-0344
This Noe Valley Med generates "long waits" at brunch for its "awe-some omelets and crêpes" that are "stuffed with tons of fresh ingredi-ents" and served for a "good value"; the staff "knows your name (or at least recognizes your children)" and there's a "wonderful" back patio, so while it's "nothing fancy, it will do the trick, especially if you have strollers or dogs joining you."

	FOOD	DECOR	SERVICE	COST

Scala's Bistro ● *French* — 21 | 21 | 21 | $46

Downtown | Sir Francis Drake Hotel | 432 Powell St. (bet. Post & Sutter Sts.) | 415-395-8555 | www.scalasbistro.com

"Perfect after a day of shopping or before a show", this Downtown "staple" presents a "satisfying" French bistro menu as well as "excellent" pastas that show a "definite Italian touch"; the "beautiful interior with stunning murals" and a "lively bar" often gets "jammed" with "wall-to-wall tourists", and the service can be "rushed" at times, but night owls appreciate that it's "one of the few places near Union Square" that's open till midnight.

NEW Schmidt's ☒Ⓜ⇗ *German* — - | - | - | I

Mission | 2400 Folsom St. (20th St.) | 415-401-0200

A chip off the old bloc, this Walzwerk deli/bierhaus spin-off in the Mission is winning over new customers with more than eight kinds of sausages, along with schnitzel, spaetzle and other German-inspired specialties; unlike its kitschy sibling, the storefront space has a minimalist atmosphere, with bare wood tables for knocking back a stein or three, which are also for sale, along with pickles, mustards and other imported products.

Scoma's *Seafood* — 22 | 18 | 21 | $47

Fisherman's Wharf | Pier 47 | 1 Al Scoma Way (bet. Jefferson & Jones Sts.) | 415-771-4383 | www.scomas.com

"Enormous" portions of "fresh-off-the-boat seafood" "attract locals and tourists" alike to this "sure bet" at Fisherman's Wharf and its Sausalito sib; there may "never be a culinary revolution launched" from these locations, and the "dated" digs are "a bit rough around the edges", but both offer "fabulous views of the Bay" ("the smell of the salty air" just adds to the experience), and the "agile" staff ensures a "wonderful time"; N.B. prix fixe menus are a "reasonable" option for lunch and dinner.

Sears Fine Food *Diner* — 19 | 13 | 18 | $22

Downtown | 439 Powell St. (Sutter St.) | 415-986-0700 | www.searsfinefood.com

"In a world where nothing is certain", the "fluffy" "little Swedish pancakes are unchanging" at this "old-time" Downtown diner where "locals rub elbows with business travelers and tourists" in the "long line", then sit down to "humongous", "solid" breakfasts served by waitresses who "remind you of Flo"; though some say "forget the other meals", the American lunches and dinners are "ok for an after-shopping meal near Union Square."

Z Seasons *Seafood/Steak* — 26 | 26 | 27 | $69

Downtown | Four Seasons Hotel | 757 Market St., 5th fl. (bet. 3rd & 4th Sts.) | 415-633-3838 | www.fourseasons.com

For "first-class cosseting and cuisine", seasoned Downtown diners celebrating "special events" elect this "refined" yet "gratifying" hotel destination; of course it's "expensive", but it delivers "pretty much what you would expect from the Four Seasons", from "outstanding", "stylishly prepared" steak and seafood dishes to "beautiful surroundings" to "superb" service that "makes you want to move in"; N.B. the bar menu is served till midnight.

	FOOD	DECOR	SERVICE	COST

Sebo ⓜ *Japanese* — 25 | 18 | 19 | $57

Hayes Valley | 517 Hayes St. (bet. Laguna & Octavia Sts.) | 415-864-2122 | www.sebosf.com

This "minimalist" Hayes Valley's Japanese is a cult favorite for fans who "insist on sitting at the bar" and letting the guys behind it (some of the "whitest sushi chefs" around) decide what they'll have; there's "not a rainbow roll in sight", just "sublime" fish flown in daily (largely from Japan), "special rice" and drinks from True Sake, all fit for a "fat wallet"; P.S. the "Sunday night izakaya", offering cooked dishes instead of sushi, is also a treat.

Sens Restaurant ⓩ *Mediterranean/Turkish* — 20 | 22 | 21 | $41

Downtown | 4 Embarcadero Ctr. (Drumm St.) | 415-362-0645 | www.sens-sf.com

It's "wonderful if you get a seat at the window" suggest surveyors besotted with the sensational "view of the Ferry Building" from this stone-walled, Kuleto-designed Embarcadero Center perch; by day it "caters to the Downtown office crowd" with a "rare-to-find" (albeit somewhat "uneven") "Turkish-inspired" Med menu, "attentive" service and "validated parking", but it really gets smoking during weekday Hookah Happy Hours (3-7:30 PM) when peeps hit the patio for pipes and meze.

Sentinel, The ⓩ *Sandwiches* — 25 | 12 | 20 | $12

SoMa | 37 New Montgomery St. (bet. Market & Mission Sts.) | 415-284-9960 | www.thesentinelsf.com

Devotees "dare you" to do better on your "lunch hour" than this "high-end" "take-out" SoMa stop set in an "old cigar shop", where chef-owner Dennis Leary (Canteen) "does for the sandwich what Blue Bottle did for coffee - elevating it to an art with fresh-baked rolls topped with juicy savory goodness"; "hot-out-of-the-oven morning muffins and coffee cake" are "another reason to swing in before" the FiDi "crowd queues up", and while there's no seating, service is "fast" and "you can call ahead"; N.B. open weekdays only, 7 AM-2:30 PM.

Serpentine *American* — 21 | 20 | 20 | $38

Dogpatch | 2495 Third St. (22nd St.) | 415-252-2000 | www.serpentinesf.com

"A great addition to the developing Third Street corridor", this "Slow Club spin-off" offers Dogpatch denizens an easy place to go for "farm-fresh" New American fare and "creative cocktails" amid "industrial" digs with "just a touch of warmth to make you want to linger"; in an area "lacking breakfast offerings", it's a "hidden brunch gem", though some say it's "not different enough for the hike out to the 'patch."

Shabu-Sen *Japanese* — ∇ 19 | 13 | 18 | $29

Japantown | 1726 Buchanan St. (bet. Post & Sutter Sts.) | 415-440-0466

A "fun" "date spot" to "dip and cook your food", this "DIY Japanese" "in the middle of J-town" provides "great", plentiful shabu-shabu and sukiyaki with a "variety of meat options" at a "low cost" (with an "all-you-can-eat" option Sunday–Thursday); the cauldron cuisine is "not in the same class as what you can get in Tokyo", but it's "about as good as you are going to get in SF" and the staff is "helpful" too.

	FOOD	DECOR	SERVICE	COST

Shalimar ▷ *Indian/Pakistani* | 23 | 3 | 10 | $16 |

Polk Gulch | 1409 Polk St. (Pine St.) | 415-776-4642
Tenderloin | 532 Jones St. (Geary St.) | 415-928-0333 ☽
www.shalimarsf.com

The "ferociously delicious", "fiery" fare at "fantastically cheap" prices delivers serious "bang for your buck" at these Indian-Pakistani "dives" that "still rule" among "lots of competition"; regulars recommend "ignoring" the surroundings or getting "takeout" from the "hurried" counter servers to avoid the "intense smell permeating your clothes."

Shanghai Dumpling King *Chinese* | 23 | 4 | 11 | $16 |

Outer Richmond | 3319 Balboa St. (34th Ave.) | 415-387-2088

"Everyone speaks Chinese" at this "divine" "dumpling dive" in the Outer Richmond, but neophytes need only "order what your neighbor is eating and slurp away"; "stick to" the "large steamers" of "juicy" *"xiao long bao"* ("supreme" soup-filled dumplings) and the "sugary egg-puff dessert" that'll "have you licking your fingers" and "you'll be thrilled" – just "don't expect fancy" since this tiny "linoleum-clad" "go-to" is better for to-go.

Shanghai 1930 ⑤ *Chinese* | 20 | 21 | 19 | $45 |

Embarcadero | 133 Steuart St. (bet. Howard & Mission Sts.) | 415-896-5600 | www.shanghai1930.com

Surveyors savor this "subterranean" "Chinese speakeasy" on the Embarcadero whose "tasty", "high-end" Shanghai-style fare (including dim sum "done right") and "glamorous" "period" decor "really do evoke the Paris of the East"; it's relatively "pricey" (you could even "spend four figures splurging on wine"), but for some posh patrons the nightly "live jazz" makes it "the joint."

🆕 Showdogs ⑤ *Hot Dogs* | - | - | - | I |

Downtown | 1020 Market St. (6th St.) | 415-558-9560

Spotlighting the best of the wurst – from Fatted Calf, Let's Be Frank and other all-natural top dog vendors – elevated with housemade condiments and artisanal buns, this affordable Downtown gourmet frank and sausage emporium from the Foreign Cinema folks, tricked out with 200-year-old church pew banquettes, caters to worker bees and showgoers en route to the Golden Gate Theater; sides of onion rings and fries, and seven local brews on tap, all play their supporting roles.

Silks *Californian* | 24 | 25 | 25 | $79 |

Downtown | Mandarin Oriental Hotel | 222 Sansome St., 2nd fl.
(bet. California & Pine Sts.) | 415-986-2020 | www.mandarinoriental.com

"Magnificent" French- and Asian-inflected Californian dishes live up to the "sophisticated" setting at this "sleeper" "hidden" amid the office buildings Downtown; the "quiet", "luxurious space" and "superb service" satisfy suitors who want to "impress a date", but don't forget the "pricing is commensurate with its host hotel", the Mandarin Oriental.

⭐ Slanted Door, The *Vietnamese* | 26 | 22 | 21 | $49 |

Embarcadero | 1 Ferry Bldg. (Market St.) | 415-861-8032 | www.slanteddoor.com

Charles Phan's "justly famous" Ferry Plaza "juggernaut" "dazzles" with "remarkable", "high-end" Vietnamese ("the shaking beef still shakes me to the core") and "off-the-main-path" wines served in a "minimalist" "glassed-in" waterfront setting with "gorgeous" views; since it's a "tough reservation", customers "congratulate themselves for even getting a seat" in the "roaring" room, tended by a "ruthlessly efficient and competent" staff.

Slow Club *American*
22 | 18 | 19 | $32

Mission | 2501 Mariposa St. (Hampshire St.) | 415-241-9390 | www.slowclub.com

"The plain concrete exterior hides a trendy" "gem" at this "out-of-the-way" Mission drink kitchen that "in-the-know" types frequent for a "mean Bloody Mary" and the "best burger and fries" among other New American comfort food; "it's still hip after so many years", with just the "perfect amount of popularity", though some say it's "not worth the hype" or the "noise"; N.B. no reservations taken.

Sociale 🗷 *Italian*
24 | 21 | 23 | $48

Presidio Heights | 3665 Sacramento St. (bet. Locust & Spruce Sts.) | 415-921-3200 | www.caffesociale.com

"Dining alfresco" in the "darling little" courtyard of this "hidden" haunt is "like taking a mini-holiday to Europe" insist Presidio Heights patrons who prefer the "heated patio" to the "cozy" (and sometimes "noisy") interior; either way, the upscale Northern Italian eats are "simply delicious" – "inventive without being too fussy" – and the "informed" staff proffers "generous pours" of vino.

South Food + Wine Bar 🗷 *Australian*
21 | 17 | 20 | $44

South Beach | 330 Townsend St. (4th St.) | 415-974-5599 | www.southfwb.com

"Inventive" Australian and Kiwi cuisine, "well-chosen wines and a lot of in-jokes" come with the territory at this "laid-back" South Beach "gem" by Sydney's celeb chef Luke Mangan, whose "sometimes crazy"-sounding "modern Oz" menu is "good on ya, mate"; the "loud", "trendy" den is "nice enough for a date", though so "small" you might have to squeeze into the "communal table" or wine bar.

South Park Cafe 🗷 *French*
23 | 19 | 22 | $39

SoMa | 108 South Park St. (bet. 2nd & 3rd Sts.) | 415-495-7275 | www.southparkcafesf.com

The dot-com neighborhood "keeps going through changes", but this "timeless" French bistro across from South Park "never wavers", offering the same "charming" ambiance and steak frites that "will make you forget you're thousands of miles from Paris"; those who "work nearby" "arrive before 11:30 AM to beat the lines" for "fast" sandwiches and salads, while "in-the-know" eaters come around in the evening for "delicious bargain" prix fixes and "house wines."

Sozai Restaurant & Sake Lounge 🅼 *Japanese*
∇ 18 | 12 | 17 | $33

Inner Sunset | 1500 Irving St. (16th Ave.) | 415-681-7150 | www.sozaisf.com

This edamame-sized Inner Sunset "neighborhood hangout" provides "flavorful" Japanese izakaya cuisine and a "generous sake selection" to suit a "light meal or a large dinner", but unsold surveyors say the "humble portions" mean "you don't get a bang for your buck" (except during $1 oyster happy hours), and all areas "need some work to get up to par."

	FOOD	DECOR	SERVICE	COST

Spork *American* | 21 | 18 | 21 | $39 |

Mission | 1058 Valencia St. (bet. 21st & 22nd Sts.) | 415-643-5000 | www.sporksf.com

"Fully modernized and hipster-ified", this "novel" redo of an "old KFC" (complete with "kitschy" decor "remnants") provides a "funky" Mission setting for "well-crafted" New American "comfort food", including a "delicious" "deconstructed" burger, served by a "spunky" staff; some naysayers knock, though, that the "transformation" of the space is "more creative than the food", and harrumph about "too much hype."

SPQR *Italian* | 23 | 17 | 20 | $41 |

Pacific Heights | 1911 Fillmore St. (bet. Bush & Pine Sts.) | 415-771-7779 | www.spqrsf.com

"When in Rome, eat like they do at SPQR", this "hip" Pac Heights osteria and wine bar "from the A16 crew" offering "incredible", "sumptuous" Southern Italian plates with a "daring" edge; the "no-reservations policy and long waits are frustrating", but many forget all about it once they "land a seat" at the marble bar and "watch them turn out fabulous dish after dish"; N.B. a post-Survey chef change is not reflected in the Food score.

☑ Spruce *American* | 25 | 26 | 24 | $68 |

Presidio Heights | 3640 Sacramento St. (bet. Locust & Spruce Sts.) | 415-931-5100 | www.sprucesf.com

"Quite the chic place", this "opulent", "ultracosmopolitan" New American in Presidio Heights is where the "bling-bling crowd of this tony zip code" goes for "celebrations", "serious dates" and "power" meals over "refined" yet "robust" fare (including "excellent" burgers) matched by "amazing" wines; since it's "on the pricey side", less flush "foodies" "pop into" the bar for the "same white-glove treatment" in a "more laid-back" atmosphere.

Stacks *American* | 18 | 13 | 17 | $19 |

Hayes Valley | 501 Hayes St. (Octavia St.) | 415-241-9011 | www.stacksrestaurant.com

See review in South of San Francisco Directory.

St. Francis Fountain *Diner* | 19 | 20 | 17 | $18 |

Mission | 2801 24th St. (York St.) | 415-826-4200

This "classic" (circa 1918) Mission diner is "just like it used to be", only "adjusted for inflation" and "instead of the boy-next-door, the soda jerk is pierced and tattooed"; it's crammed at brunch with "skinny jean"-clad customers "slurping awesome shakes" to wash down "fried delights" and "indulging in their childhood whims" (buying "Garbage Pail Kids cards"), and while there's often a "wait", you're "treated pretty well" once you sit down.

Straits Restaurant *Singaporean* | 19 | 19 | 17 | $39 |

Downtown | Westfield San Francisco Ctr. | 845 Market St., 4th fl. (bet. 4th & 5th Sts.) | 415-668-1783 | www.straitsrestaurants.com

"Playful" Pan-Asian plates and "out-of-this-world" cocktails "take you away from the woes of the day" at this "beautiful" chainlet of "vaguely Singaporean" sisters in Downtown's Westfield Centre and south of SF; the "small dishes" can "add up", and sometimes it seems the "modellike"

	FOOD	DECOR	SERVICE	COST

waitresses "weren't hired for their talent", but "young" "hipsters" who aren't fazed by the "pounding music" and "clubbing atmosphere" "keep going back for more"; N.B. the Palo Alto branch is separately owned.

Street Restaurant ⓜ *American*   ▽ 21 | 18 | 19 | $32

Russian Hill | 2141 Polk St. (bet. B'way & Vallejo St.) | 415-775-1055 | www.streetrestaurant.com

The word on this street is "this place rocks" when you want to "pull up to the bar" for "great" infused vodkas and "one of the best burgers in town"; the New American "comfort food" is "geared toward the red-meat aficionado", but all sorts of Russian Hill regulars can appreciate the "homey atmosphere", as well as the "good prices" and "nice staff."

Suppenküche *German*   22 | 16 | 18 | $30

Hayes Valley | 601 Hayes St. (Laguana St.) | 415-252-9289 | www.suppenkuche.com

"*Ja*", this "always crowded Hayes Valley hot spot" is "just like the beer halls back in München", where "heaping helpings" of "homestyle" fare "satisfy your hankering for *güt* German soul food"; just don't come expecting a peaceful dinner" – everyone "shares a communal table" with others "vying to be heard" above the din – but after downing some "fantastic" suds during the "long wait", your "inner Bavarian" will have a "ton of fun."

supperclub ⓜ *Eclectic*   15 | 25 | 17 | $76

SoMa | 657 Harrison St. (bet. 2nd & 3rd Sts.) | 415-348-0900 | www.supperclub.com

You "never know what to expect" at this SoMa supper club where your prix fixe dinner might be "delivered on roller skates" while "acrobatic eye candy" and other "wild" spectacles "tantalize" as you "eat in bed"; "all combined" it makes for a "memorable evening", but picky patrons are "underwhelmed" by the "expensive" Eclectic fare and grouse the experience is "gimmicky."

Suriya Thai ⓜ⊅ *Thai*   ▽ 20 | - | 18 | $25

SoMa | 1532 Howard St. (11th St.) | 415-355-9999

Beloved restaurateur Khun Suriya "and his wonderful food" are back on the scene since relocating post-Survey from his Mission locale to this new, more compact, cash-only SoMa outpost; the Thai menu's been updated, but still showcases his signature 'money bags' appetizer (deep-fried rice-paper bundles of prawn and chicken) along with the "famous pumpkin curry", served by the same "humble staff without the attitude" in a traditionally decorated room replete with carved wooden elephant; N.B. the red exterior is currently unmarked.

Sushi Groove *Japanese*   21 | 18 | 17 | $38

Russian Hill | 1916 Hyde St. (bet. Green & Union Sts.) | 415-440-1905

SoMa | 1516 Folsom St. (bet. 11th & 12th Sts.) | 415-503-1950 Ⓢ

With their "trendy" rolls and "urban decor", these Japanese sibs are "not your typical neighborhood sushi shacks"; both offer appealing "sake cocktails" and "pricey", "melt-in-your-mouth" fin fare, but the Russian Hill outpost on the "Hyde Street cable-car line" is groovy for "special occasions", while the "deafeningly noisy" SoMa branch is more of a "scene" with "a good DJ always on hand."

	FOOD	DECOR	SERVICE	COST

Sushi Zone ⚏✎ *Japanese*   26 | 11 | 17 | $28

Castro | 1815 Market St. (Pearl St.) | 415-621-1114

"Good things come if you wait" remind "die-hard sushi fans" who "say a little prayer" or "whip out the camping chair" outside this "itty-bitty" Castro hole-in-the-wall that's "worth every second of the rather substantial wait" for "high-quality" fish "that seems straight out of Tsukiji"; it's "definitely not fancy" but if you zone out the "dingy" decor, "put your name down and have a drink" nearby, you'll feast for a "crazy-low" price.

🅉 Sutro's at the Cliff House *Californian*   21 | 26 | 20 | $52

Outer Richmond | 1090 Point Lobos Ave. (Great Hwy.) | 415-386-3330 | www.cliffhouse.com

"The Cliff House is back" salute fans since George Morrone (Aqua, Fifth Floor) "took over" the kitchen of this "attractively remodeled", "historic" Outer Richmonder "suspended on the cliffs"; the "sweeping ocean views" are still the main draw, but most say "you can't go wrong with the service, wine" or the "lovely", seafood-focused Cal-American cuisine, so go ahead and "join the tourists"; N.B. a less expensive bistro is upstairs.

Swan Oyster Depot ⚏✎ *Seafood*   26 | 12 | 22 | $31

Polk Gulch | 1517 Polk St. (bet. California & Sacramento Sts.) | 415-673-1101

Fans find "incomparable", "simply prepared" seafood that's "so fresh it's nearly flopping" at this "iconic" oyster bar and fish market in Polk Gulch that's "full of character"; expect "excruciating lines" unless you "go early or late", but "when you finally snag a seat" on one of the 20 "rickety" stools, the "amazingly proficient and entertaining crew behind the counter" will "make you feel like part of the family"; N.B. closes at 5:30 PM.

🅉 Tadich Grill ⚏ *Seafood*   23 | 20 | 21 | $45

Downtown | 240 California St. (bet. Battery & Front Sts.) | 415-391-1849

The "ancient mariner of SF seafood joints" (around since 1849), this "blast from the past" is "jammed with tourists" and Downtown businessfolk who cotton to its "clubby atmosphere", "excellent martinis" and "the freshest fish" dishes served with a "hunk of sourdough on the table"; "chic it's not", and the "crusty old waiters" are "equal parts efficiency and curmudgeon", but if you "stick to the simplest preparations" (or the "spectacular cioppino"), it "never fails to satisfy."

Tajine Ⓜ *Moroccan*   - | - | - | I

Pacific Heights | 2080 Van Ness Ave. (Pacific Ave.) | 415-440-1718 | www.tajinerestaurant.com

Following a brief closure in 2009, Mohammed Ghaled has taken his "super-authentic" Moroccan "home cooking" to new digs on the Van Ness corridor; low brass tables and pillows lend it a leisurely feel, while belly dancers on weekend nights complete the picture; N.B. Friday–Saturday after 10 PM it turns into the Heights Lounge.

Takara *Japanese*   21 | 12 | 19 | $29

Japantown | 22 Peace Plaza (bet. Laguna & Webster Sts.) | 415-921-2000

"Off the beaten path from the rest" of Japantown, this "Zen"-like "favorite" doles out "excellent sushi" and "consistently good" "Japanese

	FOOD	DECOR	SERVICE	COST

home cooking", including "iron pot rice dishes" and a "silky smooth egg custard" that "comes with every dinner"; surveyors split on service ("polite" vs. "standoffish"), but most agree you'll be rewarded with "quality food at modest prices" – "especially the daily lunch special."

Taqueria Can-Cun ● *Mexican*

23	8	14	$10

Downtown | 1003 Market St. (6th St.) | 415-864-6773
Mission | 2288 Mission St. (19th St.) | 415-252-9560
Mission | 3211 Mission St. (Valencia St.) | 415-550-1414

They're "not much to look at", but these "no-frills", "longtime winners" answer the call when you're itching for an "excellent monster burrito" or "tasty", "spicy" "homemade salsa" ("the free chips aren't bad either"); night owls note they're "open late" and the "terrific jukebox" "might be playing a Mexican love song" while you "devour" "top-notch food that won't stretch your wallet"; N.B. no alcohol at the Downtown venue.

⊠ Tartine Bakery *Bakery*

27	14	15	$16

Mission | 600 Guerrero St. (18th St.) | 415-487-2600 |
www.tartinebakery.com

With its "lines out the door" and "insane waits", "you'll want to hate" this "hipster"-packed Mission patisserie with "no obvious sign (just follow the smell of butter)" and "cramped seating", but nothing "can trump" its "mind-blowing pastries", "eponymous open-faced treats" and "bread that comes out of the oven exactly at 5 PM"; sure, a slew slam "lackadaisical" service, but no matter: most just "keep going back."

NEW Taverna Aventine ⊠ *Californian/Italian*

–	–	–	M

Downtown | 582 Washington St. (Montgomery St.) | 415-981-1500 |
www.aventinesf.com

San Francisco's Barbary Coast comes back to life at this Downtown restaurant and bar (run by the Umami and Mamacita folks), where FiDi workers soak up the Gold Rush ambiance while tucking into moderately priced Cal-Italian fare; two full bars serve retro cocktails while a brick-walled parlor downstairs offers patrons a chance to rent private liquor lockers; N.B. lunch served weekdays, dinner and bar menu Saturdays.

Taylor's Automatic Refresher *Diner*

22	13	15	$18

Embarcadero | 1 Ferry Bldg. (Market St.) | 866-328-3663 |
www.taylorsrefresher.com

See review in North of San Francisco Directory.

Ten-Ichi *Japanese*

20	13	19	$31

Upper Fillmore | 2235 Fillmore St. (bet. Clay & Sacramento Sts.) |
415-346-3477 | www.tenichisf.com

A "long-standing" favorite of Upper Fillmore fin fans, this "reliable" Japanese reels 'em in with "extremely fresh" sashimi, "terrific" cooked dishes and "cold" sake that all "hit the spot"; the "casual" setting may not shine, but the "ever-welcoming" staff and "reasonable" prices keep it a "great choice after all these years"; N.B. no lunch on the weekends.

Terzo *Mediterranean*

23	22	22	$48

Cow Hollow | 3011 Steiner St. (Union St.) | 415-441-3200 |
www.terzosf.com

Cow Hollowers "enjoy being away from the crowds" and "lingering over" seasonal Mediterranean "small bites" and entrees, matched by

	FOOD	DECOR	SERVICE	COST

"many intriguing sips available by the glass" at this "warm but modern" "neighborhood place" (with a "fireplace for cold winter nights"); "service hits just the right notes" and "makes it run like a clock", but some peckish patrons feel it delivers "too little for too much."

Thai House Express *Thai*

	23	12	16	$21

Castro | 599 Castro St. (19th St.) | 415-864-5000
Tenderloin | 901 Larkin St. (Geary St.) | 415-441-2248 ◗
www.thhexpress.com

For some of the "best" "spicy, authentic" cuisine "this side of the Pacific", fans "always default" to these "busy-for-a-good-reason" Thai twins; the "open-late" Tenderloin dive "allows for some unique people-watching", while its Castro brother is "sleek and minimal", but "what really wins people over" is the "tasty, low-cost" chow.

Thanh Long Ⓜ *Vietnamese*

	24	15	18	$47

Outer Sunset | 4101 Judah St. (46th Ave.) | 415-665-1146 |
www.anfamily.com

"Impress your date at Crustacean, then take her" to its Outer Sunset Vietnamese sib "without the high-end atmosphere" "once you know she's a keeper" crack cads who "wear a bib" and "use their fingers" to devour "pricey" Dungeness crab and "frighteningly addictive" garlic noodles like "most customers" (ok, all) and "leave happy as a clam"; the "other offerings are dull", but valet parking and "flavored vodkas made in-house" are pluses.

Thep Phanom Thai Cuisine *Thai*

	24	17	18	$29

Lower Haight | 400 Waller St. (Fillmore St.) | 415-431-2526 |
www.thepphanom.com

The "flavorful", "amazing" Thai food "thankfully has not gone too sweet to cater to Americans" at this standout Siamese with "ridiculously low" prices "for the quantity and quality" offered; despite the "nice remodel", impatient types often opt for takeout to "avoid the long wait" and the Lower Haight's "seven levels of parking hell."

1300 on Fillmore *Soul/Southern*

	22	25	22	$46

Western Addition | 1300 Fillmore St. (Eddy St.) | 415-771-7100 |
www.1300fillmore.com

"Soul'd!" declare devotees of this "energetic" "speakeasy" with a "Harlem of the West" vibe in the Western Addition's "revitalized" Fillmore jazz district where an "attentive staff" doles out Southern "hospitality" along with "fabulous" "upscale" New American riffs on "down-home" food; it's a "sleek", versatile venue, be it for "dinner before Yoshi's", the monthly "gospel brunch" or drinks in the "living room–like" lounge (with an "impressive photo wall" of musical greats) that showcases live jazz on Sunday nights.

Three Seasons *Vietnamese*

	21	20	18	$40

Marina | 3317 Steiner St. (bet. Chestnut & Lombard Sts.) | 415-567-9989 |
www.threeseasonsrestaurant.com

An "innovative" menu of "excellent" "nouveau" Vietnamese vittles sets apart this "hip" duo with an "upscale" vibe; the "trendy" Marina branch draws a "fun-loving crowd" and the "beautiful" Palo Alto location boasts "outdoor seating for warmer nights", making both of them "lively", "date-friendly" destinations.

Ti Couz *French* | 23 | 15 | 16 | $22 |

Mission | 3108 16th St. (bet. Guerrero & Valencia Sts.) | 415-252-7373
"Nobody beats" this Mission crêperie for the "combo of flavor, value and European style" laud lovers of its "fabulous" "buckwheat"-wrapped delicacies and "enormous salads"; despite the "mob" scene, if you "top off" the meal with some cider (and "leave room to share a sweet") "at the bar" or "outside on a sunny day", "you'll swear you're on the Breton coast."

NEW Tipsy Pig *American* | ▽ 21 | 22 | 19 | $33 |

Marina | 2231 Chestnut St. (bet. Pierce & Scott Sts.) | 415-292-2300 | www.thetipsypigsf.com
The "Marina glitterati are out in force", getting tipsy on "tasty" cocktails and pigging out on "high-end bar food" (as well as weekend brunch) at this "happening" American upstart (from the Mamacita folks) that "feels like a proper pub"; some complain about "way-too-crowded" digs and "lines everywhere", but those who get past the "wait" agree the garden patio is "lovely."

Toast *American* | 17 | 14 | 16 | $19 |

Noe Valley | 1748 Church St. (Day St.) | 415-282-4328
Noe Valley | 3991 24th St. (Noe St.) | 415-642-6328
www.toasteatery.com
"Neighborhood brunching" all day long keeps these "cheap" "American diners" the "toast of Noe Valley" for avid fans who chow down on "gigantic" plates of "comfort food", including both "healthy and unhealthy" options; while critics call it "bland", it remains popular (especially in the early evenings) among "families with young kids" – "good or bad, depending who you are."

Tokyo Go Go *Japanese* | 21 | 17 | 18 | $35 |

Mission | 3174 16th St. (bet. Guerrero & Valencia Sts.) | 415-864-2288 | www.tokyogogo.com
"Surrounded by hipster bars" on 16th Street in the Mission, this jumping Japanese joint is always "crowded" with the "cool" kids, who come for "quality hand-rolls and cocktails" served with a side of "blaring techno"; most maintain the sushi is "surprisingly good" considering the "neon atmosphere" and recommend "going during happy hour" for the best deals, but a minority mutters it has more "style" than "substance."

Tommaso's Ⓜ *Italian* | 25 | 15 | 19 | $30 |

North Beach | 1042 Kearny St. (bet. B'way & Pacific Ave.) | 415-398-9696 | www.tommasosnorthbeach.com
The "wood-fired" pizza ("the closest you'll get to Noo Yawk") is "justifiably famous" at this "venerable" North Beach "den of red sauce" delivering "strictly old-school" Neapolitan eats; since "no reservations" are taken, its "cult following" is always "crowding the door" to the "no-nonsense" basement digs, but the "family" "takes exceptional care of you" with "a glass of wine while you wait."

Tommy Toy's Cuisine Chinoise *Chinese* | 23 | 25 | 24 | $65 |

Downtown | 655 Montgomery St. (bet. Clay & Washington Sts.) | 415-397-4888 | www.tommytoys.com
"Tommy's spirit is alive and well" at this "glitzy" "fine-dining" Downtowner dishing up "stylish" Chinese food with "French over-

tones", and still sporting the same "magnificent" "Ming Dynasty" decor and waiters in "tuxes" who give you the "royal treatment"; since the "high-priced" banquet menus "never change" either, some feel it's "fun for first-time visitors", but "can get old" otherwise.

Z Tonga Room M *Pacific Rim/Pan-Asian* | 13 | 26 | 17 | $40 |

Nob Hill | Fairmont Hotel | 950 Mason St. (bet. California & Sacramento Sts.) | 415-772-5278 | www.fairmont.com

"Cross your fingers that developers don't drain the pool and sink all the fun" at this "landmark" "faux Polynesian" tiki bar "complete with floating lounge band and indoor rain storm" ("every half-hour") that's been "a hoot" for generations in Nob Hill; the "overpriced" Pan-Asian-Pacific Rim "pupus" are only "so-so" and the service often "surly", but locals intend to get "lei'd" and "soak up" the "tropical" "drink bowls" and "all-you-can-eat happy hours" (Thursday–Friday) "before it vanishes"; N.B. currently closed Monday–Tuesday.

Ton Kiang *Chinese* | 24 | 13 | 16 | $30 |

Outer Richmond | 5821 Geary Blvd. (bet. 22nd & 23rd Aves.) | 415-387-8273 | www.tonkiang.net

Weekend crowds "mob" this Outer Richmond "dim sum palace" that "keeps those carts" of an "astonishing variety" of small plates "rolling along" "straight through dinner" (when "Hakka" delicacies are added to the mix); while some dis the "outdated decor" and service, for most the "white-linens", "fresh veggies" and lack of "mystery meat" are worth it – just "be careful how much you grab" lest you and your wallet "burst."

NEW Tony's Pizza Napoletana M *Italian* | - | - | - | M |

North Beach | 1570 Stockton St. (Union St.) | 415-835-9888 | www.tonyspizzanapoletana.com

Nine-time world-champion pizzaiolo Tony Gemignani struts his stuff at this North Beach newcomer, hand-throwing over 26 specialty pies categorized by region (such as American, Neapolitan and Sicilian) and oven (wood-burning, electric brick and gas brick), which are served along with antipasti and pastas till midnight on the weekends; it also houses the International School of Pizza, the state's first branch of Italy's oldest pizza *scuola*, which offers certification classes for chefs and laypeople on Monday–Tuesday, when the restaurant is closed.

Town Hall *American* | 24 | 20 | 21 | $51 |

SoMa | 342 Howard St. (Fremont St.) | 415-908-3900 | www.townhallsf.com

"More people would be in politics if town hall meetings were held here" crack constituents of this "high-energy", "NoLa-comes-to-SoMa" New American dishing out "fantastic" "comfort food" with "Cajun flair" and equally "rich" desserts in a "turn-of-the-century" warehouse; it's "well-suited for" "power lunches", "first dates" and "all occasions (except a quiet chat)", and though service can be "hurried" at times, "happy crowds" still have "fun sitting at the bar or communal tables."

Town's End Restaurant & | 20 | 15 | 19 | $28 |
Bakery M *American/Bakery*

Embarcadero | South Beach Marina Apts. | 2 Townsend St. (The Embarcadero) | 415-512-0749 | www.townsendrb.com

Although this New American cafe and bakery is "better known for breakfast" (including "divine" "complimentary mini-muffins"), aficionados aver you also "can't go wrong" with "down-home" prix fixe dinners that offer "exceptional" value; the setting is "pretty" "indoors and out", with "great views" from the patio overlooking the Embarcadero, but descriptions of the service range from "delightful" to "aloof."

NEW Trademark Grill 🗷 *American* | - | - | - | M |

Downtown | 56 Belden Pl. (bet. Bush & Pine Sts.) | 415-397-8800 | www.trademarksf.com

The lone New American on an otherwise European pedestrian alley of Belden Place, this new Downtown bar and grill from the Elite Cafe folks aims to lure FiDi workers with its traditional weekday Yankee lunch fare, 'closing bell' happy hours and affordable comfort dinners; its rich interior, decorated with cork walls and tin ceilings, is complemented by the requisite streetside seating area.

Trattoria Contadina *Italian* | 22 | 16 | 21 | $38 |

North Beach | 1800 Mason St. (Union St.) | 415-982-5728 | www.trattoriacontadina.com

"Step around the corner from the glitz of Columbus Avenue" to find this "old-style", "reasonably priced" North Beach "red-saucer" where the "wonderful" food tastes like "mama's cooking"; since it's a "slice of local lore" that "more people have begun to discover", the "cozy" confines are "always packed" and "a bit noisy" – but it's "so charming, who cares after a glass of wine?"

Tres Agaves *Mexican* | 15 | 17 | 15 | $33 |

South Beach | 130 Townsend St. (bet. 2nd & 3rd Sts.) | 415-227-0500 | www.tresagaves.com

"*Una fiesta fantástica*" can be found at this South Beach Mexican featuring "must-have" margaritas made with "top-shelf" tequilas and "sturdy" cuisine that's a "welcome departure" from your average taqueria's; detractors, though, dismiss the eats as "mediocre" offerings "just there to soak up the booze", and bewail the "ear-splitting noise" and "frat-house atmosphere", especially "before a Giants game."

Troya *Turkish* | ▽ 21 | 16 | 22 | $33 |

Inner Richmond | 349 Clement St. (5th Ave.) | 415-379-6000 | www.troyasf.com

This "totally under-the-radar" *taverna* in the Inner Richmond is a "reasonably priced" option for "perfectly executed", "homespun" Turkish treats such as "delicious" "meat kebabs" and lamb manti (ravioli) that's "not to be missed"; the setting may be "casual" and the "simple" menu "fairly small", but the "original" flavors and "friendly service" make it a "real find."

Truly Mediterranean *Mediterranean* | 23 | 6 | 16 | $13 |

Mission | 3109 16th St. (Valencia St.) | 415-252-7482 | www.trulymedsf.com

Fans are shawarming to this "tiny" Mission Mediterranean-Middle Eastern "hole-in-the-wall" dishing out "shawarma to-die-for", "fantastic lavosh wraps" and "excellent veggie plates" from "lunchtime" to "late-night"; when "you need a break from a burrito", the "cheap eats" washed down with a "great garlic mint yogurt drink" can hit the spot, but many recommend it strictly for "takeout", as "there's very little seating."

	FOOD	DECOR	SERVICE	COST

Tsar Nicoulai Caviar Café *Caviar/Seafood* | 23 | 13 | 20 | $50 |

Embarcadero | 1 Ferry Bldg. (Market St.) | 415-288-8630 |
www.tsarnicoulai.com

If you "want to feel like a decadent tsar despite the current economic
crisis", you can "live it up" with some "outstanding farm-raised caviar"
with blini and a "glass of bubbly" at this "casual" combination roe bar and
retail shop in the Embarcadero's Ferry Building, where you'll always
"learn something new" from the "knowledgeable", "friendly" staff; it's
a "fun splurge" for many, but a few revolt over the "ridiculous" prices.

Tsunami Sushi & Sake Bar Ⓢ *Japanese* | 22 | 20 | 17 | $40 |

NEW South Beach | 301 King St. (4th St.) | 415-284-0111
Western Addition | 1306 Fulton St. (Divisadero St.) | 415-567-7664 ◗
www.nihon-sf.com

"Fresh-as-can-be" fish, including some "unusual" selections, an "extensive sake list" and "great cocktails" are the hallmarks of this
"sceney" Western Addition sushi joint that "feels like a lounge in Hong
Kong"; there's "always a new flavor combination to try" from among
the selection of "creative", "modern" rolls, which helps excuse what
some describe as "spotty" service; N.B. a new outpost recently
opened in South Beach.

Tu Lan Ⓢ⊬ *Vietnamese* | 22 | 3 | 10 | $14 |

SoMa | 8 Sixth St. (Market St.) | 415-626-0927

"Serious noodles" and "imperial rolls" are sought out at this "superb
Vietnamese dive" (once frequented by "Julia Child") where the "cheap
eats" are "amazing" but "the rest is just dang scary" given the "grease-
pit" digs in a "dodgy" section of SoMa; even if you're the type who's "just
about the food", vets advise "dress in your worst and go for lunch."

TWO Ⓢ *Californian* | 19 | 19 | 20 | $46 |

SoMa | 22 Hawthorne St. (bet. Folsom & Howard Sts.) | 415-777-9779 |
www.two-sf.com

"While many miss" the "hip opulence of the old Hawthorne Lane", this
second coming of David Gingrass' "hidden" SoMa haunt (and take-out
lunch spot) is "good for the times"; while not all are down with the
"minimalist" redo, the staff does a "reasonable job" and the "down-
sized" Cal-New American menu is "surprisingly good", plus the
"happy-hour specials" "are a gift to all"; P.S. those who are "not part of
the singles scene" can "skip the noisy bar and head to the back room."

2223 Restaurant *Californian* | 23 | 19 | 21 | $41 |

Castro | 2223 Market St. (bet. Noe & Sanchez Sts.) | 415-431-0692 |
www.2223restaurant.com

A "longtime stronghold in the Castro", this "guppy" "go-to" brightened
by large windows and a "happening bar" (complete with "oversized"
martinis) "still delivers" when it comes to Cal-New American "comfort
food done right"; it's "gay brunch central" on sparkling Sunday after-
noons when the "handsome" staff is "equally sunny", but the "hip" dining
room is "welcoming to all" – especially on "12-buck Tuesday" nights.

Udupi Palace ⊬ *Indian/Vegetarian* | 21 | 10 | 16 | $17 |

Mission | 1007 Valencia St. (21st St.) | 415-970-8000 |
www.udupipalaceca.com
See review in East of San Francisco Directory.

Umami ☒ *Japanese*　　22　22　19　$43

Cow Hollow | 2909 Webster St. (Union St.) | 415-346-3431 |
www.umamisf.com

"Creative cocktails invite all the pretty people" to this "loud", "dark"
and "trendy" Cow Hollow izakaya delivering "excellent" sushi and
Japanese small plates that are "large enough to share"; though some
sniff at the "totally Marina" "striped-shirt crowd" dining on "over-
styled" dishes, many are "pleasantly surprised" by the "tasty treats"
and "comfortable", two-floor setting.

Underdog Hot Dog & Sausage ☒ *Hot Dogs*　▽ 20　12　21　$10

Inner Sunset | 1634 Irving St. (bet. 17th & 18th Aves.) | 415-665-8881
"Healthy hot dogs? I want to believe" utter frank fans of this "politi-
cally correct" Inner Sunset "joint" whose "organic-everything" menu
includes "juicy" grass-fed beef dogs, vegan sausages and "yummy"
baked 'potato-tots'; "super-friendly service" and smart, compostable
packaging help make up for the "funky", "cramped" space with limited
seating; N.B. BYO only.

Unicorn Pan Asian Cuisine ☒ *Pan-Asian*　23　19　20　$37

Downtown | 191 Pine St. (Battery St.) | 415-982-9828 |
www.unicorndining.com

As "unique" as the mythical creature itself, this "bustling lunch" spot
presents a horn of plenty of "spectacular" yet "reasonably priced"
Pan-Asian "noodles, meats" and vegetarian dishes that are "far above
the usual Downtown fare"; a "sleek atmosphere" (with "blown glass
fixtures") and "soju cocktails" add to the "'let's get out of the office
and go now' excitement"; P.S. it's open until 10 PM – "a lifesaver"
in these parts.

Universal Cafe ☒ *American*　　23　17　19　$34

Mission | 2814 19th St. (bet. Bryant & Florida Sts.) | 415-821-4608 |
www.universalcafe.net

Daily changing New American menus offer "seasonal food that's
fresh, exciting and on par" with more "expensive" places at this "perennial" Mission "favorite" with a "warm, local" indoor/outdoor atmosphere; sure, there "can be a long wait" for the "fantastic" weekend
brunch, but flatbread fans say "who doesn't love getting away with
eating pizza for breakfast?"; N.B. dinner-only on Tuesday.

NEW Urban Tavern *American*　　17　19　17　$46

Downtown | Hilton | 333 O'Farrell St. (bet. Mason & Taylor Sts.) |
415-923-4400 | www.urbantavernsf.com

This all-day gastropub in the Hilton San Francisco pleases Downtowners
with New American fare "well served" in an "attractive" setting with lots
of "green" details such as the "long" reclaimed wood communal table, as
well as sustainable wines poured at the marble-topped bar; however,
after much "turnover", including post-Survey changes in chef and cuisine (not reflected in the Food score), it's "still a work in process."

Uva Enoteca *Italian*　　20　20　19　$38

Lower Haight | 568 Haight St. (bet. Fillmore & Steiner Sts.) | 415-829-2024 |
www.uvaenoteca.com

For an "urbane" "enoteca experience" in a "beer-oriented neighborhood", oenophiles (and the *Sex and the City* crowd") head to this

"small", late-night Lower Haight vino venue where Italian wines can be "well matched" with "tasty small plates" such as "cured meats" and "rare cheeses"; cognoscenti caution it's not for "intimate" conversation or "if you're hungry", for "as the night goes on, the decibels start climbing" and "service gets slower."

Venticello   *Italian*

| 23 | 22 | 22 | $48 |

Nob Hill | 1257 Taylor St. (Washington St.) | 415-922-2545 | www.venticello.com

"Celebrate that very special evening" at this "ultimate romantic neighborhood restaurant" perched on Nob Hill with "cable cars clanging outside"; the "upscale" Northern Italian menu is "full of interesting choices" that have "just enough of a modern bent to the preparations", while the "intimate" setting with an "old San Francisco feeling" is bolstered by a staff that "treats you right"; P.S. some tables offer a "peek of a view of the Bay."

Vitrine   *American*

| ▽ 23 | 23 | 25 | $43 |

SoMa | St. Regis | 125 Third St., 4th fl. (Mission St.) | 415-284-4049 | www.stregis.com/sanfrancisco

"One of the best little vacations to be had near Moscone", this "delightfully serene" SoMa hideaway on the fourth floor of the St. Regis hotel caters to conventioneers, museum-goers and hotel guests, proffering "sophisticated twists" on New American breakfasts and lunches, including "fresh fish flown in" daily from Japan; the "modern", light-filled dining room is open till 2 PM; N.B. a post-Survey chef change is not reflected in the Food score.

Vivande Porta Via   *Italian*

| 23 | 16 | 19 | $41 |

Pacific Heights | 2125 Fillmore St. (bet. California & Sacramento Sts.) | 415-346-4430 | www.vivande.com

You'll "think the Pope is in town" when you pop into this Sicilian trattoria and deli in Pac Heights that "still gets it right after all these years"; just order "whatever" chef/co-owner "Carlo recommends" ("anything with pasta is a winner"), but be prepared for "rock-hard seats" and "tables so close you can smell the other person's aftershave."

Walzwerk   *German*

| 21 | 18 | 19 | $28 |

Mission | 381 S. Van Ness Ave. (bet. 14th & 15th Sts.) | 415-551-7181 | www.walzwerk.com

"Memorabilia" from the "Eastern Bloc" "transports you to some blue-collar neighborhood outside of Berlin" at this "campy" Mission eatery serving "stick-to-your-ribs" East German fare, including "awesome" schnitzel (and a "veggie" version too); beer "from the old country", a "festive" atmosphere and "reasonable" tabs all add to the "*liebe.*"

Warming Hut
Café & Bookstore   *Sandwiches*

| 15 | 14 | 12 | $15 |

Presidio | Crissy Field, Bldg. 983 | Marine Dr. (Mason St.) | 415-561-3040 | www.crissyfield.org

Boasting a "billion-dollar view" of the Golden Gate Bridge, this otherwise humble "little" Presidio cafe/bookstore offers "organic", "simply prepared" soups, sandwiches and "snacks" that satisfy "after a stroll along the shore at Crissy Field" in the "brisk Bay air"; just be prepared to "wait in line" on "weekends" when it's "overcrowded" and "understaffed."

	FOOD	DECOR	SERVICE	COST

Washington Square Bar & Grill *American* — | — | — | M

North Beach | 1707 Powell St. (bet. Columbus Ave. & Union St.) | 415-982-8123 | www.washingtonsquarebarandgrill.com

The ghost of Herb Caen suffuses the atmosphere at this resurrected North Beach bar and grill, dubbed 'The Washbag' by the late columnist; if its midpriced New American–Italian menu of fried calamari, Caesar salad, steak and burgers offers few surprises, the history-rich, memorabilia-lined walls – and the return of legendary bartender Michael McCourt – more than make up for it.

☑ Waterbar *Seafood* 20 | 26 | 20 | $62

Embarcadero | 399 The Embarcadero (Folsom St.) | 415-284-9922 | www.waterbarsf.com

The "ambiance is fantastic" at Pat Kuleto's "hip, high-end seafooder on the Embarcadero" boasting "stunning Bay vistas" from the waterfront patio, as well as a "beautiful", "entertaining" interior complete with "floor-to-ceiling aquariums"; "inventive" (and "pricey") fin fare is served by a "knowledgeable" staff, and while some demur at the "touristy" scene, many recommend it when you want to "impress" a "client, date" or "out-of-towner" – especially if "someone else is paying."

Waterfront Restaurant *Californian/Seafood* 18 | 22 | 18 | $53

Embarcadero | Pier 7 (B'way) | 415-391-2696 | www.waterfrontsf.com

"It's all about the view" at this "pricey" Embarcadero institution that attracts "locals" and "out-of-town" visitors alike with "gorgeous" vistas of the Bay Bridge and "outdoor seating" that's "perfect" for "people-watching" during the day; opinions are split over the seafood-centric Californian fare ("well-prepared" vs. "average") and service ("efficient" vs. "spotty"), but all agree the scenery's "amazing."

Weird Fish *Seafood* 21 | 16 | 20 | $28

Mission | 2193 Mission St. (18th St.) | 415-863-4744 | www.weirdfishsf.com

You know this "itsy-bitsy", "eco-friendly" Mission seafooder (and "veggie-friendly brunch spot") is "going to be weird" when you see "'suspicious fish dish'", "yo-yos (beer-battered fried pickles)" and 'buffalo trannies' on the menu; still, aficionados insist "even a confirmed carnivore would love" the "out-of-this-world" vegan fish 'n' chips and other "delectable" options, so those undeterred by the "sketchy neighborhood" and "ridiculous long waits" keep "going back for more."

NEW Wexler's ☒ *BBQ* — | — | — | M

Downtown | 568 Sacramento St. (Montgomery St.) | 415-983-0102 | www.wexlerssf.com

FiDi folks tuck in their ties before diving into short ribs, lamb sliders and mac 'n' cheese at this high-concept BBQ arrival where the midpriced menu also includes creative cocktails and American microbrews; evoking a plume of smoke, a black wood canopy snakes across the ceiling in the white, contemporary dining room.

'wichcraft *Sandwiches* 18 | 14 | 14 | $16

Downtown | Westfield San Francisco Ctr. | 868 Mission St., ground fl. (bet. 4th & 5th Sts.) | 866-942-4272 | www.wichcraftsf.com

"Tom Colicchio gives good sandwich" say bewitched boosters of this Downtown "self-serve" NYC import who take a break from the Westfield mall scene to refuel with "inventive" eats and "satisfying" soups; others, unmoved by the *Top Chef* star's crafty spell, grumble that the sandwiches are "overpriced" and "don't taste as good as they sound", and dub the digs "too industrial" (though "you can order online and they'll have it waiting").

Woodhouse Fish Company *Seafood* | 21 | 14 | 19 | $26 |

Castro | 2073 Market St. (14th St.) | 415-437-2722
NEW **Pacific Heights** | 1914 Fillmore St. (bet. Bush & Pine Sts.) | 415-437-2722
www.woodhousefish.com

Bringing a "touch of New England" to the Castro – and now Pacific Heights – this piscatory pair is a "stunning replica of a Massachusetts chowder house" dishing out "large portions" of "no-frills seafood" in "bare-bone surroundings" with "cute nautical decor"; while it's "no bargain" (except for "$1 oyster Tuesdays"), most agree it "hits the spot" for "a beer and bowl of cioppino" or "Dungeness crab away from the pier mayhem."

Woodward's Garden 🚫Ⓜ *American/Californian* | 25 | 16 | 21 | $52 |

Mission | 1700 Mission St. (Duboce St.) | 415-621-7122 | www.woodwardsgarden.com

At this "fabulous little find" in the Mission, the Californian–New American cuisine is so "impressive" and "well prepared", followers affirm it "will make you forget" the "uninviting" location in the shadows of a "looming freeway overpass"; the service is "always competent", if a bit "terse" at times, while the interior is "charming" and "romantic", and if the address causes some people to "stay away", that's just "fine" with devotees.

XYZ *American/Californian* | 19 | 22 | 20 | $48 |

SoMa | W Hotel | 181 Third St. (Howard St.) | 415-817-7836 | www.xyz-sf.com

The "S&M (stand and model) crowd" flocks "to be seen" at this "spendy" SoMa spot at the W Hotel, whose "hip" dining room boasts "comfy booths" and marble tables, and a "sophisticated" Cal–New American menu; a few claim the food can't compare to the "people-watching" and the "bar scene", but others argue it's "not your typical hotel restaurant", advising "get to XYZ – PDQ!"

Yabbies Coastal Kitchen *Seafood* | 21 | 18 | 20 | $47 |

Russian Hill | 2237 Polk St. (bet. Green & Vallejo Sts.) | 415-474-4088 | www.yabbiesrestaurant.com

"Ignore the name and go for the seafood" at this slightly "pricey" neighborhood "keeper" in Russian Hill, where customers are "blown away by the flavors" of the "delicious" fish; it's "not fancy", but it's "pleasant" for a "meal with friends", and "eating fresh oysters at the bar" is always a treat.

Yamo 🚫🍴 *Burmese* | ▽ 23 | 5 | 15 | $10 |

Mission | 3406 18th St. (Mission St.) | 415-553-8911

"All that greets you when you walk into" this "little hole-in-the-wall" in the Mission is a small counter and the "ladies busting their tails in the kitchen", churning out "great Burmese food at super-cheap prices"; it's so "popular" there's often a "line", but most will happily wait to eat in or "take out" the "best $5 meal that's not a burrito."

	FOOD	DECOR	SERVICE	COST

☑ Yank Sing *Chinese*

25 | 18 | 19 | $37

SoMa | Rincon Ctr. | 101 Spear St. (Mission St.) | 415-957-9300
SoMa | 49 Stevenson St. (bet. 1st & 2nd Sts.) | 415-541-4949
www.yanksing.com

"Overeating is mandatory in order to sample" the "huge variety" of "exceptional", "inventive" dumplings and "banquet dishes" "wheeled around" at these "ritzy" SoMa "dim sum houses" "catering to the financial suits" and "Chinatown-phobic"; "you pay a pretty penny", but "there's no Formica or fluorescent lighting in sight" and the "English-speaking" "trolley dollies" who keep "piling on food" and refilling "lovely tea" "justify the price."

Yoshi's San Francisco *Japanese*

22 | 24 | 19 | $50

Western Addition | Fillmore Heritage Ctr. | 1330 Fillmore St. (Eddy St.) | 415-655-5600 | www.yoshis.com

You "almost expect Miles Davis to walk in" to this "gorgeous" Western Addition outpost of the "original Oakland" supper club; the restaurant is a "nice start" before "enjoying a show next door", but also a "class act" in itself whose "see-and-be-seen crowd" savors Sho Kamio's "serious sushi", robata and other "artistic" Japanese dishes that "rival the incredible music"; still, some warn you might "run out of money" and patience before "feeling full"; N.B. the nightclub also serves a separate menu on-site.

Yuet Lee ◐ *Chinese*

21 | 5 | 13 | $23

Chinatown | 1300 Stockton St. (B'way) | 415-982-6020

"Wear sunglasses because you'll be sitting under blinding fluorescent lights" at this Chinatown "dive" dishing up "authentic", "down-home" and "cheap" "Cantonese seafood", to "cops", "chefs" and other "late-night" chowhounds; "vying for the meanest waiter is part of the charm", so "be brave and go for it" – the "salt and pepper squid" is worthy of a "last meal"; N.B. now closes at midnight Sunday–Thursday, 3 AM Friday–Saturday; closed Tuesday.

Yumma's *Mideastern*

▽ 21 | 9 | 18 | $12

Inner Sunset | 721 Irving St. (bet. 8th & 9th Aves.) | 415-682-0762

Diners drop into this "tiny, order-at-the-counter" shop for "inexpensive", "filling" "Middle Eastern comfort food", including "excellent" shawarma and kebabs made with organic meats; sure, there's "no atmosphere", but the "outdoor patio" and nearby Golden Gate Park are pleasant options.

Zadin Ⓜ *Vietnamese*

▽ 22 | 20 | 21 | $30

Castro | 4039 18th St. (Hartford St.) | 415-626-2260 | www.zadinsf.com

"Incredibly tasty" "homemade recipes", including "excellent gluten-free" dishes, make this Castro Vietnamese a "great find" for "lucky" locals; add in an "elegant" setting and "personable", "professional" service, and you may "wonder if you're getting away with something when your bill arrives."

Zante Pizza & Indian Cuisine *Indian/Pizza*

20 | 7 | 14 | $20

Bernal Heights | 3489 Mission St. (Cortland St.) | 415-821-3949 | www.zantespizza.com

Say *namaste* to "amazingly different", "richly spiced" Indian pizzas that are like "naan with tandoori chicken and other delicious toppings" at this "inexpensive" Bernal Heights mash-up; "the rest of the menu is so-so", but lots of customers stay loyal since "they deliver anywhere in the city for free"; N.B. vegan versions available.

NEW Zaré at
Fly Trap ⧄ *Californian/Mediterranean*

| 22 | 21 | 23 | $47 |

SoMa | 606 Folsom St. (Second St.) | 415-243-0580 | www.zareflytrap.com
"San Francisco's finest host", chef-owner Hoss Zaré, "is back", having purchased this SoMa "treasure" and "kicked up the menu a notch", preparing "delicious" Cal-Med cuisine with "Persian flavors" and "flair"; the "brightened" space, which still has some of the "old magic", draws "well-heeled office types" for lunch, while the bar stays "hopping" till midnight with regulars downing "late-night food" and "incredible" martinis.

Zarzuela ⧄Ⓜ *Spanish*

| 25 | 18 | 22 | $39 |

Russian Hill | 2000 Hyde St. (Union St.) | 415-346-0800
"Come with a group of friends" to "share paella, sangria" and "magnificent" "traditional" Spanish tapas at this "lively" "longtime favorite" in a "charming" Russian Hill locale fitted out with "bullfighting posters" and other "Sevillean" stylings; the "humorous" staff is "accommodating" and "knowledgeable", and it's an "incredible value" to boot; P.S. "no reservations."

Zazie *French*

| 22 | 18 | 20 | $27 |

Cole Valley | 941 Cole St. (bet. Carl St. & Parnassus Ave.) | 415-564-5332 | www.zaziesf.com
"Paris bistros don't do it any better" sigh Francophiles who have no regrets "waiting their turn" for a "wonderful" *petit déjeuner* or "well-prepared" steak frites at this "breezy European cafe" with a "relaxed San Francisco vibe" in Cole Valley; the back garden is "lovely" (and has "ample heat lamps" for cold days), though many avoid the "brutal" brunch lines and seek out the appealing "value and ambiance for dinner"; P.S. Monday is "dog night" on the patio.

Zazil Coastal Mexico Cuisine *Mexican*

| 18 | 20 | 18 | $35 |

Downtown | Westfield San Francisco Ctr. | 845 Market St., 4th fl. (bet. 4th & 5th Sts.) | 415-495-6379 | www.zazilrestaurant.com
It's not "your average mall-Mexican food" at this "upscale", surprisingly "intimate" cantina (and Colibrí cousin) in Downtown's Westfield San Francisco Centre, where guacamole "prepared tableside" and "standout" seafood dishes lend it a "refreshing" touch; just "don't expect taqueria prices", though "happy hour is a bargain" and the "great tequilas" (more than 280 of them) are a plus.

Zeitgeist ●⧄ *BBQ*

| 15 | 14 | 11 | $14 |

Mission | 199 Valencia St. (Duboce Ave.) | 415-255-7505
"Don't go for the food" advise frequenters of this "German beer garden crossed with a Hell's Angels biker bar" in the Mission, citing "big pitchers of beer on the cheap" and "amazing Bloody Marys" as the main reason to "hit the patio" "on a sunny afternoon"; still, some recommend the "huge, smoky" burgers "straight off the BBQ" – or treats from the "celebrated tamale lady" who drops by – if you can stand the "rowdy" hipster-grunge crowd and service "so bad that it's somehow good."

	FOOD	DECOR	SERVICE	COST

NEW Zinnia ⑤ⓜ *American*   `23` `21` `20` `$57`

Downtown | 500 Jackson St. (bet. Columbus Ave. & Montgomery St.) | 415-956-7300 | www.zinniasf.com

Sean O'Brien's "mythic return" to Downtown's Jackson Square is "off to a good start", thanks to a "well-executed", "modestly priced" "2.0-version" New American menu, boasting "some favorites, some new dishes" and many in "half-portions", with "wines to match"; while some feel the two-tiered room "isn't as cool" as his former venue, a "quiet elegance" and "professional" service "permeates" nonetheless, prompting fans to predict it'll "become a hot spot" and "overcome this bad-luck location."

☲ Zuni Café ⓜ *Mediterranean*   `25` `20` `21` `$51`

Hayes Valley | 1658 Market St. (bet. Franklin & Gough Sts.) | 415-552-2522 | www.zunicafe.com

"After 30 years", "grande dame" Judy Rodgers' "iconic" Hayes Valley Mediterranean "still feels up-to-the-minute" to "tourists and locals" who come "early or late" for the "ultimate trifecta" of "oysters, Caesar salad" and the "justifiably famous" "one-hour chicken" (plus burgers at lunch or after 10 PM); there are "lots of nooks" for "people-watching", while "massive martinis" from the copper bar further fuel the "buzz", despite gripes about "pretentious" airs and "sky-high prices."

Zuppa *Italian*   `19` `17` `17` `$39`

SoMa | 564 Fourth St. (bet. Brannan & Bryant Sts.) | 415-777-5900 | www.zuppa-sf.com

"Great for groups and salumi lovers" this SoMa Italian (and Globe sib) pleases with "delicious" *affettati*, "creative, well-executed" pizzas and "just the right mix of classics and modern interpretations"; *amici* "love the industrial feel", but critics call it "cold" and "surprisingly pricey", and claim the "so-so" staff "adds no warmth to the decor."

Zushi Puzzle ⑤ *Japanese*   `26` `9` `18` `$45`

Marina | 1910 Lombard St. (Buchanan St.) | 415-931-9319 | www.zushipuzzle.com

Gung-ho guests take an "amazing journey into the world of sushi" under the guidance of "fish god" Roger Chong at this Marina nook purveying a "fabulous selection" of "exotic" morsels, like "live scallops" and "some of the craziest rolls anywhere"; while some suggest the "staff could take a friendly pill" and "you have to wait forever" to get into the "dark and dingy" (yet "pricey") room, most agree the "food makes up for" it.

EAST OF SAN FRANCISCO

Top Food Ratings

Excludes places with low votes.

28 Erna's Elderberry | *Cal./French*
Chez Panisse | *Cal./Med.*

27 Chez Panisse Café | *Cal./Med.*
Wolfdale's | *Californian*
Rivoli | *Cal./Med.*

26 Cheese Board | *Bakery/Pizza*
Lalime's | *Cal./Med.*

25 Kirala | *Japanese*
BayWolf | *Cal./Med.*
Pizzaiolo | *Pizza*

Ajanta | *Indian*
Moody's Bistro | *American*
Tratt. La Siciliana | *Italian*
Wood Tavern | *Californian*
Oliveto Restaurant | *Italian*
Dopo | *Italian*
Burma Superstar | *Burmese*

24 Zachary's Pizza | *Pizza*
Oliveto Cafe | *Italian*
Corso Trattoria | *Italian*

BY CUISINE

AMERICAN
25 Moody's Bistro
23 Flora
21 Lark Creek
Rick & Ann's
Chow/Park Chow

CALIFORNIAN
28 Erna's Elderberry
Chez Panisse
27 Chez Panisse Café
Wolfdale's
Rivoli

CHINESE
23 Great China
Koi Garden
22 Shen Hua
20 Rest. Peony
Imperial/Berkeley Tea

FRENCH
28 Erna's Elderberry
24 Soizic
À Côté
23 Citron
Café Fanny

INDIAN
25 Ajanta
24 Vik's Chaat Corner
23 Shalimar
21 Udupi Palace
19 Breads of India

ITALIAN
25 Pizzaiolo
Tratt. La Siciliana
Oliveto Restaurant
Dopo
24 Oliveto Cafe

JAPANESE
25 Kirala
24 O Chamé
Ozumo
22 Cha-Ya Vegetarian
20 Yoshi's

MEDITERRANEAN
28 Chez Panisse
27 Chez Panisse Café
Rivoli
26 Lalime's
25 BayWolf

MEXICAN/PAN-LATIN
24 Tamarindo Antojeria
Tacubaya
23 Fonda Solana
Doña Tomás
21 Picante Cocina

SOUTHEAST ASIAN
23 Soi4
22 Pho 84
21 Le Cheval
19 Cha Am Thai

Menus, photos, voting and more – free at ZAGAT.com

BY SPECIAL FEATURE

BREAKFAST/BRUNCH
23 Café Fanny
Bette's Oceanview
Venus
21 La Note
Rick & Ann's

CHILD-FRIENDLY
24 Zachary's Pizza
23 Great China
Bellanico
Bette's Oceanview
22 Lo Coco's

MEET FOR A DRINK
25 Moody's Bistro
Wood Tavern
24 Oliveto Cafe
Ozumo
Prima

OPEN LATE
23 Fonda Solana
22 In-N-Out
20 Home of Chicken/Waffles
Luka's Taproom
18 Caspers Hot Dogs

OUTDOOR SEATING
25 Dopo
24 Oliveto Cafe
O Chamé
À Côté
Prima

PEOPLE-WATCHING
27 Chez Panisse Café
25 Moody's Bistro

Wood Tavern
24 Oliveto Cafe
À Côté

ROMANCE
28 Erna's Elderberry
Chez Panisse
27 Wolfdale's
26 Lalime's
24 Soizic

SMALL PLATES
24 À Côté
23 Va de Vi
22 César
20 Mezze

TRENDY
27 Chez Panisse Café
25 Wood Tavern
24 Corso Trattoria
À Côté
Ozumo

VIEWS
28 Erna's Elderberry
27 Wolfdale's
Rivoli
24 Christy Hill
23 Wente Vineyards

WINNING WINE LISTS
28 Erna's Elderberry
Chez Panisse
27 Chez Panisse Café
Rivoli
25 BayWolf

BY LOCATION

BERKELEY
28 Chez Panisse
27 Chez Panisse Café
Rivoli
26 Cheese Board Collective
Lalime's

LAKE TAHOE AREA
27 Wolfdale's
25 Moody's Bistro

24 Christy Hill
22 Dragonfly
18 Sunnyside Resort

OAKLAND
25 BayWolf
Pizzaiolo
Wood Tavern
Oliveto Restaurant
Dopo

Top Decor

28 Ahwahnee Din. Rm.	Sunnyside Resort
27 Erna's Elderberry	Bridges
	Chez Panisse Café
24 Wente Vineyards	Vic Stewart's
Postino	Blackhawk Grille
Bing Crosby's	Rivoli
Christy Hill	Camino
23 Chez Panisse	Oliveto Restaurant
Ozumo	Esin
Wolfdale's	Amber Bistro
22 Gar Woods Grill	

Top Service

27 Erna's Elderberry	Soizic
Chez Panisse	22 Ajanta
26 Wolfdale's	Wood Tavern
25 Rivoli	PlumpJack Cafe
BayWolf	Ruth's Chris
Chez Panisse Café	Esin
24 Christy Hill	Prima
Lalime's	Peasant & Pear
23 Wente Vineyards	Postino
Oliveto Restaurant	Vic Stewart's

Best Buys

In order of Bang for the Buck rating.

1. In-N-Out	11. Imperial/Berkeley Tea
2. Arinell Pizza	12. Picante Cocina
3. Caspers Hot Dogs	13. BurgerMeister
4. Cheese Board Collective	14. El Balazo
5. Gioia Pizzeria	15. Vik's Chaat Corner
6. Cheese Steak Shop	16. Fentons Creamery
7. Cactus Taqueria	17. Barney's
8. Mama's Royal Cafe	18. Café Fanny
9. Tacubaya	19. Udupi Palace
10. Bette's Oceanview	20. Lanesplitter

OTHER GOOD VALUES

Ajanta	Jimmy Bean's
Amici's Pizzeria	Juan's Place
Asqew Grill	Le Cheval
Bo's Barbecue	Naan 'n Curry
Chow/Park Chow	Pho 84
FatApple's	Rick & Ann's
Home of Chicken/Waffles	Saul's Rest./Deli

East of San Francisco

À Côté *French/Mediterranean*   24 | 21 | 21 | $41
Oakland | 5478 College Ave. (Taft Ave.) | 510-655-6469 |
www.acoterestaurant.com

Others may have ridden its coattails, but this "bustling" tapas bar is
"still rocking" Rockridge "after all these years" thanks to a "rotating"
roster of "scrumptious small plates" with a French-Med bent, "old-
world wines" and "artisanal cocktails" mixed by "black-belt bartenders";
while there are "eternal waits" to "rendezvous" on the "covered terrace",
"walk-ins" can also "party like a grown-up" at the bar or "squeeze in"
at one of the "long communal tables."

Adagia Restaurant ⌧ *Californian*   18 | 21 | 18 | $37
Berkeley | Westminster House | 2700 Bancroft Way (College Ave.) |
510-647-2300 | www.adagiarestaurant.com

"It's like eating in the dining hall at Hogwarts" at this "collegiate" Cal-
Med decked out with "lots of wood and stone", "big table seating" and
a "wonderful" fireplace; though the "very Berkeley-esque", "local, sustainable" fare is "not quite up to the decor" and the staff could be more
schooled, it's "the obvious (perhaps only) place for an elegant lunch
or dinner near campus", and the patio is "enjoyable in good weather."

NEW Adesso ◑⌧ *Italian*   - | - | - | M
Oakland | 4395 Piedmont Ave. (Pleasant Valley Ave.) | 510-601-0305
Dopo's little Italian-centric wine bar and salumeria offshoot lures
Oaklanders into its tiny lair with cocktails, antipasti and over 30 types
of cured meats and pâtés on display, served from early evening to late
night (1 AM Thursday–Saturday); the minimalist storefront, replete
with foosball table, is more aperitivo bar than sit-down dinner joint,
but gratis happy-hour bar bites (served from 5–7 PM and 10:30 PM–
midnight) affirm that good things come in small packages.

⌧ Ahwahnee
Dining Room, The *American/Californian*   19 | 28 | 20 | $54
Yosemite | Ahwahnee Hotel | 1 Ahwahnee Rd. | Yosemite National Park |
209-372-1489 | www.yosemitepark.com

Yosemite campers clean up to savor the "magnificent views", "spectacular architecture" and "fabulous" wines at this "remarkable" "historic inn" that calls for your "best bib and tucker"; while service is
"highly variable" and the Cal-American meals merely "adequate"
("they need to quit milking the environment and improve the food"),
"Sunday brunch is quite a spread", "especially after you've been eating at a campsite all week."

Ajanta *Indian*   25 | 21 | 22 | $30
Berkeley | 1888 Solano Ave. (bet. The Alameda & Fresno Ave.) |
510-526-4373 | www.ajantarestaurant.com

"Take an epicurean journey through India" and reach "spice nirvana" at
this "beautiful" "Berkeley classic" that's a "big cut above the usual"
Bombay buffet houses, thanks in part to "monthly regional specialties"
that "take advantage of seasonal" produce; "UC alumni" and other "loyal
patrons" appreciate the "warm" owner and servers, who "help put well-
rounded meals together" with "carefully chosen, fairly priced wines."

	FOOD	DECOR	SERVICE	COST

Amanda's *Californian/Health Food*   ▽ 18 | 14 | 18 | $15

Berkeley | 2122 Shattuck Ave. (Center St.) | 510-548-2122 |
www.amandas.com

"You won't miss the cholesterol" swoons the *Super Size Me* set over the "healthy" "baked fries" and "non-greasy" burgers at this cafe and take-out joint offering "enlightened fast food" for "Downtown Berkeleyans on the run"; the operation is sustainable down to the "massive" reclaimed-wood "picnic table" and compostable containers, though a few skeptics sniff "I think they cut the calories by serving small portions."

Amber Bistro ⑤ *Californian*   22 | 22 | 20 | $44

Danville | 500 Hartz Ave. (Church St.) | 925-552-5238 |
www.amberbistro.com

"One of the better options in Danville", this "worthwhile local spot" specializes in "carefully prepared" Cal cuisine with an "inventive" Southeast Asian streak, served in a "gorgeous" room suffused with an amber glow; the "casual" atmosphere is a further draw, though with a fortysomething bar scene "spilling into the dining area", it gets "so loud you need to know American Sign Language to have a conversation."

Amici's East Coast Pizzeria *Pizza*   20 | 13 | 17 | $21

Danville | Rose Garden Ctr. | 720 Camino Ramon (Sycamore Valley Rd.) |
925-837-9800
Dublin | 4640 Tassajara Rd. (bet. Central Pkwy. & Dublin Blvd.) |
925-875-1600
www.amicis.com
See review in City of San Francisco Directory.

Arinell Pizza ⴲ *Pizza*   24 | 4 | 10 | $8

Berkeley | 2119 Shattuck Ave. (Addison St.) | 510-841-4035
Fans "fold up" "a big slice of NYC, right in the Mish" and Berkeley at these "grungy" "stand-up pizzerias" where "rad", "cheap and greasy" thin-crust 'za is slung by a "rough", "copiously tattooed" staff with "awful attitudes"; the digs "feel like a crack house", so unless you love "screeching" "death metal" and "watching yourself eating drunk in the enormous mirrors", get your "fix" to go.

NEW Artisan Bistro Ⓜ *Californian/French*   - | - | - | M

Lafayette | 1005 Brown Ave. (Mt. Diablo Blvd.) | 925-962-0882 |
www.artisanlafayette.com

Though the chef at this new Californian-French bistro in Lafayette clocked time at rarefied establishments like Coi, the French Laundry and Per Se, the artisanal menu's prices are surprisingly recession-friendly; its casual, converted-cottage setting is equally accessible, replete with high windows, a stone fireplace and a large brick patio.

Asqew Grill *Californian*   16 | 11 | 14 | $16

Emeryville | Bay Street Mall | 5614 Bay St. (Shellmound St.) | 510-595-7471 |
www.asqewgrill.com
See review in City of San Francisco Directory.

NEW Barlata *Spanish*   - | - | - | M

Oakland | 4901 Telegraph Ave. (49th St.) | 510-450-0678 | www.barlata.com
Catalan native Daniel Olivella (SF's B44) and professional cyclist Chechu Rubiera are behind this convivial, no-reservations Spanish tapas arrival

in Oakland's up-and-coming Temescal neighborhood; an all-Iberian wine list complements the midpriced small plates – many served in *latas* (tin cans) – plus a handful of paellas, while seating options include a long communal table and marble-topped bar.

Barney's Gourmet Hamburgers *Burgers* | 19 | 12 | 15 | $16 |

Berkeley | 1591 Solano Ave. (Ordway St.) | 510-526-8185
Berkeley | 1600 Shattuck Ave. (Cedar St.) | 510-849-2827
Oakland | 4162 Piedmont Ave. (Linda Ave.) | 510-655-7180
Oakland | 5819 College Ave. (Chabot Rd.) | 510-601-0444
www.barneyshamburgers.com
See review in City of San Francisco Directory.

BayWolf Ⓜ *Californian/Mediterranean* | 25 | 21 | 25 | $50 |

Oakland | 3853 Piedmont Ave. (Rio Vista Ave.) | 510-655-6004 |
www.baywolf.com
Michael Wild's "grand old dame" of Oakland "never goes out of style", turning out monthly "regional menus" of "sublime" "sustainable" Cal-Med fare ("any duck dish" will do ya) that's "comfort food for foodies"; boasting "impressive wines", "fair prices" and "professional", "pampering" service in a "quiet, houselike setting", it's HQ for "special occasions" and "open-air lunches" on the deck.

Bellanico *Italian* | 23 | 19 | 21 | $38 |

Oakland | 4238 Park Blvd. (Wellington St.) | 510-336-1180 |
www.bellanico.net
Importing "San Francisco quality and style to Oaktown", this "tiny" Aperto spin-off attracts Glenview residents and "diners from far beyond" with its locally sourced menu of "exceptional" pastas and "fresh, creative" *cicchetti* (Venetian tapas) for a "reasonable" cost; though the "long waits" for "tight tables" are "a drag" (rezzies are only accepted for six or more), you can "eat at the bar" and enjoy "interesting flights of wine."

Berkeley Teahouse *Tearoom* | 20 | 21 | 16 | $20 |

Berkeley | Epicurious Gdn. | 1511 Shattuck Ave. (bet. Cedar & Vine Sts.) | 510-540-8888 | www.imperialtea.com
Customers "come away feeling calmer and well-nourished" at these traditional Chinese tearooms where a "supreme" selection of leaves trumps the "light", "limited" menu; service can "be a little slow", but most savor the "relaxing", "Zen" environment, particularly in the "peaceful" garden of the Berkeley branch; N.B. the Embarcadero location closes at 6:30 PM most nights.

Bette's Oceanview Diner *Diner* | 23 | 17 | 19 | $19 |

Berkeley | 1807 Fourth St. (bet. Hearst Ave. & Virginia St.) | 510-644-3230 | www.bettesdiner.com
There's "no bette-r place" for "brekkie" ("if you don't mind waiting until mid-afternoon") than this "iconic" Berkeley diner where an "efficient staff of characters" sets down "legendary" pancakes, "soft scrambled eggs", "scrapple" and American lunches to the tune of a "vintage jukebox"; just remember there are "no dinners", "no ocean view" and no rezzies, but for anyone averse to the "abysmally long lines" of "baby boomers", its adjacent shop offers "takeout as a second resort."

	FOOD	DECOR	SERVICE	COST

Bing Crosby's *American*

| | 19 | 24 | 20 | $53 |

Walnut Creek | 1342 Broadway Plaza (S. Main St.) | 925-939-2464 | www.bingcrosbysrestaurant.com

"Nostalgia abounds" at this "sumptuous", "memorabilia"-decked supper club in Walnut Creek, where the "over-40" "meat market" and "loud music" from the "popular" piano bar are a "turn-on for some and a turnoff for others"; while the New American cuisine strikes most as "well prepared" but "not gourmet", and some decry "SF prices in suburbia", at least "you know you are going out when you go here."

Bistro Liaison *French*

| | 22 | 18 | 21 | $38 |

Berkeley | 1849 Shattuck Ave. (bet. Delaware St. & Hearst Ave.) | 510-849-2155 | www.liaisonbistro.com

This "convivial" Berkeley bistro near campus cranks out "well-prepared", "traditional" French dishes set down by a "pleasant, efficient" staff amid all the "hustle-bustle of a well-loved Parisian cafe"; it's a "civilized place for lunch" or "pre-theater" dining, and though critics cite "oppressive" noise at "peak times", the "great recession prix fixes will make you forget your woes."

Blackberry Bistro *Southern*

| | 19 | 13 | 14 | $20 |

Oakland | 4240 Park Blvd. (Wellington St.) | 510-336-1088

Delivering "all the basics of a good breakfast", this daytime cafe in "up-and-coming Glenview" elevates its "omelets and French toast" with "memorable" "Southern twists"; though prickly patrons protest that the "service and food break down when it's crowded", it remains "incredibly popular" on the weekends, so "expect the usual brunch waits."

Blackhawk Grille *Californian*

| | 19 | 22 | 19 | $48 |

Danville | The Shops at Blackhawk | 3540 Blackhawk Plaza Circle (Camino Tassajara) | 925-736-4295 | www.blackhawkgrille.com

Boasting a "snazzy" setting that "sizzles in the summer" next to the man-made pond and waterfall, this "precious" après-shopping and "business-dining" locale in an "upscale" Danville mall is "pleasant" for Californian "basics done well" should you "find yourself out in that neck of the woods"; hawks, however, suggest it's rather "tired" (suffering from too much "chef turnover") and "living on its reputation."

Bo's Barbecue Ⓜ⇄ *BBQ*

| | 23 | 11 | 14 | $23 |

Lafayette | 3422 Mt. Diablo Blvd. (Brown Ave.) | 925-283-7133

"It's all about the smoke" coaxed "low and slow" at "Bo McSwine's" "iconic" "Southern-style BBQ" joint in Lafayette 'cueing up "awesome ribs and brisket" (from "Niman Ranch") that make regulars "whimper for more"; some take issue with "monastic" decor and "pricey" tabs, but most forgive any flaws due to "excellent" weekend-night jazz and blues and "refrigerator-coolers packed full" of "independent foreign beers."

Breads of India & Gourmet Curries *Indian*

| | 19 | 12 | 16 | $23 |

Berkeley | 2448 Sacramento St. (Dwight Way) | 510-848-7684
Oakland | 948 Clay St. (bet. 9th & 10th Sts.) | 510-834-7684 🗷
Walnut Creek | 1358 N. Main St. (bet. Cypress & Duncan Sts.) | 925-256-7684 Ⓜ
www.breadsofindia.com

Paratha pals "match the special breads with the special food" at this trio of "gentrified" East Bay Indians offering a "limited menu" of daily changing, "uniquely flavored" dishes that are "prepared with care and feature free-range meats"; despite its "popularity", however, some naan-believers dub it "mysteriously crowded" for food they "wish were tastier, or cheaper."

Bridges Restaurant *Asian/Californian*

22 | 22 | 21 | $52

Danville | 44 Church St. (Hartz Ave.) | 925-820-7200 | www.bridgesdanville.com

"Largely past the movie-fan aura that ruined it" (*Mrs. Doubtfire* was filmed here), this "gorgeous" Downtown Danville destination "has been reborn" with "innovative" Cal-Asian cuisine that's especially pleasant on the vine-covered patio "during warmer weather"; many save it for "special occasions" and "semi-private" parties, considering it "too pricey for everyday", but "reduced" costs on the new bar menu make it more accessible.

Bridgetender Tavern *Pub Food*

▽ 19 | 14 | 17 | $21

Tahoe City | 65 W. Lake Blvd. (Rte. 89) | 530-583-3342

"Relax and enjoy" the "fantastic burgers", "good selection" of brews and "woodsy" surroundings "overlooking the Truckee River" at this "Tahoe City classic" that "always hits the spot" with "comforting" pub grub "after a day of skiing or rafting"; barstool buddies say the "service is friendly, if unrushed – but why rush? you're on vacation."

Bucci's Ⓢ *Californian/Italian*

21 | 18 | 19 | $33

Emeryville | 6121 Hollis St. (bet. 59th & 61st Sts.) | 510-547-4725 | www.buccis.com

"Still swingin' after all these years", this "unpretentious" Emeryville "oasis" overseen by "mamma Bucci" is "always a pleasure to return to" for "well-prepared", "robustly flavored" Cal-Italian fare that's a "solid value"; brightened by "big windows", rotating "local art" and a "nice" patio, the "warehouse" space pulls in an "office" "mob scene" at lunch, but is more "comfortable" for dinner.

BurgerMeister *Burgers*

19 | 11 | 14 | $15

NEW **Alameda** | 2319 Central Ave. (bet. Oak & Park Sts.) | 510-865-3032 | www.burgermeistersf.com

See review in City of San Francisco Directory.

Burma Superstar Ⓜ *Burmese*

25 | 14 | 18 | $25

NEW **Alameda** | 1345 Park St. (Central Ave.) | 510-522-6200
NEW **Oakland** | 4721 Telegraph Ave. (47th St.) | 510-652-2900
www.burmasuperstar.com

See review in City of San Francisco Directory.

Cactus Taqueria *Mexican*

21 | 11 | 14 | $13

Berkeley | 1881 Solano Ave. (bet. The Alameda & Fresno Ave.) | 510-528-1881
Oakland | 5642 College Ave. (bet. Keith Ave. & Ocean View Dr.) | 510-658-6180
www.cactustaqueria.com

Cranking out "quick, fresh and cheap" Cal-Mex with "free-range meats" and other ingredients that "food snobs prefer", these taquerias are a "lifesaver" for "Oaklanders coming off of BART" and Berkeley families "on a budget"; the "tasty crispy chicken tacos", "fresh salsas" and "great agua fresca" are a "big step up" from the

FOOD | DECOR | SERVICE | COST

chains but the atmosphere is not, so "takeout is a must" to "avoid the mayhem" of "children acting up."

Café Fanny *French*
23 | 12 | 15 | $18

Berkeley | 1603 San Pablo Ave. (Cedar St.) | 510-524-5447 | www.cafefanny.com

"Gourmet ghetto heaven on a budget" awaits at Alice Waters' "tiny", "so Berkeley" French stand-up bar (with some "parking-lot" tables), serving "Chez Panisse–style" breakfasts and lunches, replete with "cloudlike" eggs, "dreamy, creamy lattes" and "granola taken to another level"; expect to "pay through the nose" for the pleasure and to "wait" awhile (the "pretentious" staff "adds a new dimension to 'Slow Food'"), but fans agree "this little nothing place is something."

Café Fiore *Italian*
∇ 25 | 18 | 24 | $49

South Lake Tahoe | 1169 Ski Run Blvd. (Tamarack Ave.) | 530-541-2908 | www.cafefiore.com

Perhaps "the only gem" in South Lake Tahoe, this "pricey" Northern Italian set in a "charming" cabin provides "creative" pastas and other "well-executed" dishes capped off by white chocolate ice cream that "will make your forget your troubles"; though the "tiny" space can be a "squeeze", it's a welcome alternative to dining at the casinos, with plenty of half bottles to ensure you drive back to the hotel safely.

Café Gratitude *Vegan*
16 | 15 | 17 | $24

Berkeley | 1730 Shattuck Ave. (bet. Francisco & Virginia Sts.) | 415-824-4652 | www.cafegratitude.com

See review in City of San Francisco Directory.

Café Rouge *French/Mediterranean*
22 | 19 | 20 | $41

Berkeley | Market Plaza | 1782 Fourth St. (bet. Hearst Ave. & Virginia St.) | 510-525-1440 | www.caferouge.net

"From burgers to steak frites", this French-Med "carnivore" mecca (with "on-site butcher shop") specializing in "sustainable" meats, "top-notch" charcuterie and an "imaginative" Sunday brunch is the "place to get your organs stuffed" in Berkeley; service has its "ups and downs", but "when the sun lights up" the room and the patio, there's no better place to "people-watch" and "call it a day"; P.S. check out the "dynamite" oyster bar too.

Caffè Verbena ☒ *Californian/Italian*
∇ 17 | 17 | 17 | $41

Oakland | Walter Shorenstein Bldg. | 1111 Broadway (bet. 11th & 12th Sts.) | 510-465-9300 | www.caffeverbena.com

"See and be seen by the office-building elite" at this Downtown Oakland haunt that's "one of the best options" in the area for a "business lunch" (especially considering the "lack of competition" nearby); the "tasty but uninteresting", largely organically sourced Cal-Italian eats are enhanced by "great cocktails" and an "atrium looking out at the sculpture garden"; N.B. closed weekends.

Camino *Californian/Mediterranean*
22 | 22 | 21 | $47

Oakland | 3917 Grand Ave. (Sunny Slope Ave.) | 510-547-5035 | www.caminorestaurant.com

"Be prepared to be wowed" at this "handsome", "high-concept" Oakland "destination" where "Alice Waters protégé" Russell Moore "lovingly prepares" "exceptional" Cal-Med dinners and brunches in a "giant wood-burning oven" and "open hearth", while the "creative bar" highlights small batches from "local distilleries"; though the "extremely limited menu" isn't for everyone, "if you can live with just a few entree choices" and "monastic" seating at communal tables, "you'll be rewarded" in spades; N.B. closed Tuesdays.

Casa Orinda *Italian/Steak*   18 | 19 | 19 | $38

Orinda | 20 Bryant Way (Moraga Way) | 925-254-2981 | www.casaorinda.net
"The Old West comes alive" at this "time-warp" Orinda "watering hole" that's filled with "Contra Costa ranching" "memorabilia" and "antique rifles mounted on the wall", and staffed by hands who are "a hoot"; it "still serves the same old" Italian steakhouse menu at "updated prices", and while the "knockout" fried chicken is "reputable with good reason", it's best to "ignore anything fancy" on the menu; P.S. "make reservations" – "blue hairs" "love this place."

Caspers Hot Dogs ⊅ *Hot Dogs*   18 | 5 | 13 | $8

Albany | 545 San Pablo Ave. (bet. Brighton Ave. & Garfield St.) | 510-527-6611
Dublin | 6998 Village Pkwy. (Dublin Blvd.) | 925-828-2224
Hayward | 21670 Foothill Blvd. (Grove Way) | 510-581-9064 ◑
Hayward | 951 C St. (bet. Main St. & Mission Blvd.) | 510-537-7300
Oakland | 5440 Telegraph Ave. (55th St.) | 510-652-1668
Pleasant Hill | 6 Vivian Dr. (Contra Costa Blvd.) | 925-687-6030 ◑
Richmond | 2530 MacDonald Ave. (Civic Center St.) | 510-235-6492
Walnut Creek | 1280 Newell Hill Pl. (bet. Newell Ave. & San Miguel Dr.) | 925-930-9154
www.caspershotdogs.com
"If you're in the mood for a snappy", "greasy" dog with "lots" of toppings, hit these East Bay "time-warp" frank stands furnished with "pink and orange barstools" and run by "ladies in hairnets"; they sure "bring back memories" even if they're "lowbrow to the max", so some recommend you take these pups "and run."

César ◐ *Spanish*   22 | 19 | 19 | $37

Berkeley | 1515 Shattuck Ave. (bet. Cedar & Vine Sts.) | 510-883-0222
Oakland | 4039 Piedmont Ave. (bet. 40th & 41st Sts.) | 510-883-0222
www.barcesar.com
"Squint and you could be in Barcelona" at either one of these "bustling" tapas bars in Berkeley and Oakland, where the "communal tables" and outdoor seats are crammed with "eclectic citizenry" "drinking, socializing" and sharing "terrific" small plates (that "do add up"); mornings are calmer on Piedmont Avenue, where "Spanish breakfasts" are served.

Cha Am Thai *Thai*   19 | 14 | 17 | $22

Berkeley | 1543 Shattuck Ave. (Cedar St.) | 510-848-9664
See review in City of San Francisco Directory.

Cha-Ya Vegetarian   22 | 12 | 17 | $23
Japanese Restaurant *Japanese/Vegan*

Berkeley | 1686 Shattuck Ave. (bet. Cedar & Virginia Sts.) | 510-981-1213
"Beautifully crafted", "satisfying" vegan Japanese food (such as "incredible" rolls) from the *shojin ryori* tradition "transcends meat" and draws long "lines" to these Mission and Berkeley nooks; they're not everyone's cup of "barley tea", due to "spartan" looks and "cafeteria"

lighting, but they're priced "just right for Depression-era dining"; N.B. closed for lunch Monday–Tuesday.

☒ Cheese Board Collective ⊠Ⓜ Ⓥ *Bakery/Pizza*

26 | 12 | 18 | $13

Berkeley | 1512 Shattuck Ave. (bet. Cedar & Vine Sts.) | 510-549-3055 | www.cheeseboardcollective.coop

"Addictive pizza, one type daily, always veggie" "captures the heart of Berkeley and its food scene" at this "legendary", collectively owned locale with a side of "left-wing politics" and "live jazz"; customers line up in "droves" for the delicacy, so plan to "sit on the grassy median like everyone else" or get it "half-baked" "to go" before loading up on "exquisite" cheeses, pastries and breads next door.

Cheese Steak Shop *Cheesesteaks*

23 | 6 | 14 | $11

Alameda | 2671 Blanding Ave. (Tilden Way) | 510-522-5555
Berkeley | 1054 University Ave. (bet. San Pablo Ave. & 10th St.) | 510-845-8689
NEW Lafayette | 3455 Mount Diablo Blvd. (2nd St.) | 925-283-1234
Oakland | 3308 Lakeshore Ave. (bet. Lake Park Ave. & Mandana Blvd.) | 510-832-6717
Pleasanton | Gateway Sq. Shopping Ctr. | 4825 Hopyard Rd. (Stoneridge Dr.) | 925-734-0293
Walnut Creek | 1626 Cypress St. (bet. California Blvd. & Locust St.) | 925-934-7017
www.cheesesteakshop.com
See review in City of San Francisco Directory.

NEW Chevalier Ⓜ *French*

- | - | - | E

Lafayette | 960 Moraga Rd. (Moraga Blvd.) | 925-385-0793 | www.chevalierrestaurant.com

This petite Lafayette newcomer, decorated in a modern yet earthy style with a cherrywood bar, clay-tile floors and white tablecloths, is a portal to the south of France where guests bid adieu to 'strip-mall-ville' and, on sunny days, can dine in a garden graced with roses, grapevines and lavender; chef Philippe Chevalier (ex Chez Papa) completes the fantasy, preparing classic, high-end French fare with modern twists.

☒ Chez Panisse ⊠ *Californian/Mediterranean*

28 | 23 | 27 | $85

Berkeley | 1517 Shattuck Ave. (bet. Cedar & Vine Sts.) | 510-548-5525 | www.chezpanisse.com

"Still 'keeping it fresh' after lo these many years", "Alice and her crew" continue to "enchant" "foodies" who "come to worship" at her Berkeley "altar", where the "ultimate" Cal-Med prix fixe dinners are prepared with "unadorned" ingredients "right off the boat and garden"; "not everyone loves the Craftsman decor" or "being locked into the menu of the day", but most are "thrilled" to "walk through the kitchen" "where it all started" – "a philosophy and a movement, and it tastes so damn good" too; P.S. "reserve ahead."

☒ Chez Panisse Café ⊠ *Californian/Mediterranean*

27 | 22 | 25 | $52

Berkeley | 1517 Shattuck Ave. (bet. Cedar & Vine Sts.) | 510-548-5049 | www.chezpanisse.com

"Experience the legend like a local" wink Berkeleyites who "show up in jeans" and treat themselves to "what lunch" (and dinner) "ought to be" at Alice Waters' "more accessible" à la carte Cal-Med bistro, a "low-key" "Arts and Crafts"–style space located above her "shrine"; the "to-die-for" pizzas, "composed salads" and "impeccable" service reflect the same "superior" standards as downstairs, but they come "without the religious intensity" or dowry-required price tags.

Chow *American*

| 21 | 16 | 19 | $26 |

NEW **Danville** | 445 Railroad Ave. (San Ramon Valley Blvd.) | 925-838-4510 | www.chowfoodbar.com
Lafayette | La Fiesta Sq. | 53 Lafayette Circle (Mt. Diablo Blvd.) | 925-962-2469 | www.chowrestaurant.com
See review in City of San Francisco Directory.

Christy Hill Ⓜ *Californian*

| 24 | 24 | 24 | $54 |

Tahoe City | 115 Grove St. (Rte. 28) | 530-583-8551 | www.christyhill.com
The Californian food is as "fantastic as the lakefront setting" at this "off-the-beaten-path" Tahoe City "surprise" perched 100 feet above the shoreline; though it's "expensive", "personal" service and a "wonderful deck" for "eating outdoors in the summer" "only add to the enjoyment."

Citron *Californian/French*

| 23 | 20 | 22 | $51 |

Oakland | 5484 College Ave. (bet. Lawton & Taft Aves.) | 510-653-5484 | www.citronrestaurant.biz
"Definitely fit for foodies", this "lovely" Cal-French Rockridger presents "splendid" meals with "fine wine" in a "sedate, sophisticated" setting; some are enticed by the "new recession menu" for dinner, while others go for "breakfast on the weekends", since you can "reserve a table and avoid the hour-plus waits elsewhere"; N.B. no lunch on Mondays.

NEW Commis Ⓜ *American*

| - | - | - | VE |

Oakland | 3859 Piedmont Ave. (W. MacArthur Blvd.) | 510-653-3902 | www.commisrestaurant.com
Fine dining without the pomp and circumstance is the conceit behind this Oakland newcomer (in the former JoJo space) from chef James Syhabout (ex Manresa), whose nightly ingredient-driven, build-your-own New American prix fixe menu with French accents reflects both traditional and more contemporary cooking techniques; the sleek 31-seat room, including a small counter overlooking the kitchen, gives off an intimate dinner-party vibe.

Corso Trattoria *Italian*

| 24 | 18 | 22 | $39 |

Berkeley | 1788 Shattuck Ave. (Delaware St.) | 510-704-8004 | www.trattoriacorso.com
"It didn't take long for the crowds to discover" this "exciting" new Berkeley "gem" from the Rivoli team, where the "real", "world-class" Florentine fare (including weekend brunch) and "reasonable carafes" "transport you to Italy with every taste"; the "cacophony" and "Mussolini-era" decor, with "Fellini movies" projected by the bar, is a "far cry from the quiet sophistication of its older sibling", but "fantastic cocktails" help "smooth out the edges."

Cottonwood *Eclectic*

| ∇ 21 | 19 | 22 | $41 |

Truckee | Brockway Rd./Old Hwy. 267 (Old Brockway Rd.) | 530-587-5711 | www.cottonwoodrestaurant.com
Customers cotton to the "splendid view" overlooking "old Truckee" at this "rustic" eatery whose historic site holds artifacts of the "early

FOOD | DECOR | SERVICE | COST

"1900s ski area" surrounding it; "fine" Eclectic dinners, a "decent" wine list and weekend entertainment on the patio in the summer keep it a year-round "favorite."

Digs Bistro *American/Mediterranean* ▽ 25 | 21 | 25 | $43

Berkeley | 1453 Dwight Way (Sacramento St.) | 510-548-2322 | www.digsbistro.com

"Everything is as it should be" at this "coool" Berkeley "incarnation" of a once-clandestine Oakland dinner club proffering a "limited menu" of "exceptional", locally sourced New American–Med meals; it's a "tiny living room of a place" ("we need more digs"), but "exquisite" service and a "warm" atmosphere have romantics vying for a table by the "curl-up-and-stay" fireplace and families flocking to the "child-friendly" Parents' Night Out; N.B. closed Tuesday–Wednesday.

Doña Tomás ⑤Ⓜ *Mexican* 23 | 18 | 19 | $36

Oakland | 5004 Telegraph Ave. (bet. 49th & 51st Sts.) | 510-450-0522 | www.donatomas.com

Though this "hip, high-end" cantina in Oakland's "up-and-coming" Temescal district "may come off like a fun place to grab some guacamole" or a "mean margarita", just beneath the "festive" facade is some of the "finest", most "creative" "regional Mexican" chow "north of the border" (including "don't-miss" carnitas); happily, if the "frenetic" bar and "noise level" prove irksome, quiet types can head to the "pleasant" patio that's "perfect for warm evenings."

Dopo ⑤ *Italian* 25 | 17 | 21 | $36

Oakland | 4293 Piedmont Ave. (Echo Ave.) | 510-652-3676

"There are no pretenses" at this neighborhood Italian "hot spot", just a whole "lot of carbohydrates" and "devoted" Oaklanders fawning over "exquisite thin-crust pizza" ("passes the no-droop test"), "housemade pastas" and "inventive" salumi while sipping "interesting" "wines you've never heard of"; "it doesn't take reservations", so the "expanded" surroundings remain" "jam-packed", but because "everyone is trying to make sure you're happy", the "long waits" go down easily.

downtown Ⓜ *Californian/Mediterranean* 19 | 20 | 19 | $43

Berkeley | 2102 Shattuck Ave. (Addison St.) | 510-649-3810 | www.downtownrestaurant.com

For "well-executed" but "not overly foo-foo" Californian-Mediterranean small plates in Downtown Berkeley, theatergoers and "foodies" flock to this "convenient" "grown-up restaurant" with a "big-city bar" and "friendly service"; it's become a "reliable" go-to for "special-occasion dinners" or to "catch a bite before or after" shows at Berkeley Rep or the Aurora, though a few fret about paying "high prices for what you get."

Dragonfly *Asian/Californian* 22 | 18 | 21 | $40

Truckee | Porter Simon Bldg. | 10118 Donner Pass Rd. (Spring St.) | 530-587-0557 | www.dragonflycuisine.com

"Lunch or dinner, sun or snow", this second-story walk-up with a "cute view of Downtown Truckee" presents "fabulous" Cal-Asian flavors "that actually work together" (from "wonderful noodle bowls" to dim sum and then some), along with a "sushi chef who knows his way around a knife";

	FOOD	DECOR	SERVICE	COST

if a few fume it's on the "expensive side" and "noisy", regular happy hours and "timely" service make it a "recommended destination."

Duck Club, The *American* | 19 | 20 | 20 | $50 |

Lafayette | Lafayette Park Hotel & Spa | 3287 Mt. Diablo Blvd. (Pleasant Hill Rd.) | 925-283-3700 | www.lafayetteparkhotel.com
See review in South of San Francisco Directory.

El Balazo *Mexican* | 19 | 11 | 13 | $15 |

Concord | 785 Oak Grove (Treat Blvd.) | 925-969-9978
Danville | 480 San Ramon Valley Blvd. (Hartz Way) | 925-838-6421
Lafayette | 3518 Mt. Diablo Blvd. (bet. 1st St. & Moraga Rd.) | 925-284-8700
Pleasanton | 4515 Rosewood Dr. (Owens Dr.) | 925-734-8226
Pleasanton | 5331 Hopyard Rd. (Owens Dr.) | 925-737-1300
San Ramon | 2005 Crow Canyon Pl. (Fostoria Way) | 925-543-0000
San Ramon | 250 Market Pl. (Alcosta Blvd.) | 925-328-0510
www.elbalazo.net
See review in City of San Francisco Directory.

⊠ Erna's | 28 | 27 | 27 | $97 |
Elderberry House *Californian/French*

Oakhurst | Château du Sureau | 48688 Victoria Ln. (Hwy. 41) | 559-683-6800 | www.elderberryhouse.com

"You'll feel like you've died and gone to heaven" at this "tweet"-worthy "European elixir among the Sierras" that displays "remarkable attention to sauces, presentation and service" and pairs "top flights of wine" with some of the "finest" Californian–New French prix fixe meals around; the "super-cute, super-expensive" Oakhurst "château inn" is also a super "long drive from the city", but "if you're heading to Yosemite, it's worth stopping in", and high-fliers not you can "park the jet in Fresno" and hop over from there.

Esin Restaurant & | 24 | 22 | 22 | $47 |
Bar *American/Mediterranean*
(fka Cafe Esin)

Danville | Rose Garden Ctr. | 750 Camino Ramon (Sycamore Valley Rd.) | 925-314-0974 | www.esinrestaurant.com

Whatever you do, "save room for the desserts" (including "amazing bread pudding") at this "never disappointing" American–Med bistro, whose recent move to "prettier" "urban-chic" digs in an "upscale" Danville "strip mall" is a "definite improvement" over its old San Ramon haunt; locals "crowd in night after night" for "quality, fresh" fare, "great cocktails" and "warm service" from the "husband-and-wife" team that runs the place.

Evan's American | ▽ 28 | 23 | 27 | $59 |
Gourmet Cafe *American*

South Lake Tahoe | 536 Emerald Bay Rd. (Lukins Way) | 530-542-1990 | www.evanstahoe.com

For two decades, this "jewel by the Lake" has been a "favorite" for "special dinners" in the Tahoe Basin, proffering "creative, consistent" seafood-centric New American cuisine (with Pan-Asian influences), a bounty of bourbons and West Coast wines, and a "gracious" feel that's more akin to "eating in a private home"; "reservations are a must in high season" counsel converts, because this "intimate" woodsy cabin serves some of "the only real food" on the South Shore and seats only 40.

Everett & Jones Barbeque *BBQ*

| 20 | 10 | 13 | $21 |

Berkeley | 1955 San Pablo Ave. (University Ave) | 510-548-8261
Hayward | 296 A St. (Filbert St.) | 510-581-3222
Oakland | Jack London Sq. | 126 Broadway (bet. The Embarcadero & 2nd St.) | 510-663-2350
Oakland | 2676 Fruitvale Ave. (bet. Davis & E. 27th Sts.) | 510-533-0900
www.eandjbbq.com

Resistance is futile when "you get a whiff" of the "finger-licking good" smokehouse wares "slathered with sauce" – "hot" being "an 'I dare you' eating event" – at these "mostly take-out", family-run BBQ "shacks" (a fancier Jack London sib offers music Friday–Saturday); "don't let the dicey locations" or "funky" atmosphere "dissuade you", or you'll miss out on "no-frills" fare "delivered with soul" and Sistah Ale, though some 'cue-nivores carp about "inconsistent quality" and perhaps the "slowest service in Oakland."

FatApple's *Diner*

| 18 | 12 | 16 | $19 |

Berkeley | 1346 Martin Luther King Jr. Way (bet. Berryman & Rose Sts.) | 510-526-2260
El Cerrito | 7525 Fairmount Ave. (bet. Carmel & Ramona Aves.) | 510-528-3433

"It's all about the comfort food" at this "homey", "value-oriented" Berkeley diner and its "less cramped" El Cerrito sidekick where "happy servers" satisfy "lots of old-time regulars" and "families" with "excellent pancake breakfasts", "first-rate burgers" and "blue-plate dinners (i.e. meatloaf, roast turkey)"; but "save room" for the "fantastic bakery items", because sweet tooths insist the other grub "is there just so you can eat the pie afterward."

Fentons Creamery *Ice Cream*

| 19 | 13 | 14 | $16 |

Oakland | 4226 Piedmont Ave. (bet. Entrada & Glenwood Aves.) | 510-658-7000
Oakland | Oakland Int'l Airport | Terminal 2 (Doolittle Dr.)🅂🅼
www.fentonscreamery.com

"Rich in butterfat" and "nostalgia", this "Oakland landmark" – an "Archie and Veronica ice cream fountain with lunch counter menu" – has catered to "four generations of crab sandwich lovers" and the "eternal kid in us all" who screams for the "best milkshakes" and "legendary" "monster" sundaes "dripping with homemade caramel"; service can be "unpredictable", but the "gargantuan concoctions" (also scooped up at Oakland International) "still rock the house", so "expect a wait."

NEW Five *American/Californian*

| - | - | - | E |

Berkeley | Hotel Shattuck Plaza | 2086 Allston Way (Shattuck Ave.) | 510-845-7300 | www.five-berkeley.com

Downtown Berkeleyites take five at Five, a modern New American-Californian bistro in the newly renovated Hotel Shattuck Plaza, where chef Scott Howard offers familiar classics with quirky twists – think mac 'n' cheese with orzo, goat cheese and braised morels – along with biodynamic wines and updated retro cocktails; the dramatic dining room is blinged out with a 100-year-old chandelier, smooth white columns and soaring arched windows.

Flora 🅂Ⓜ *American*   23 | 21 | 20 | $45

Oakland | 1900 Telegraph Ave. (19th St.) | 510-286-0100 | www.floraoakland.com

"Tables are already hard to come by" at this "snazzy" Uptown Oaklander "set in an old flower mart", but now that the renovated "Fox Theater is in full swing", supporters sigh it'll be "that much harder"; sib to Doña Tomás and Tacubaya, it purveys "punched up", midpriced New American cuisine and "some pretty wild cocktails" in a "happening" setting "right out of a Raymond Chandler novel", the only noir spot being what some call "lackluster" service.

Fonda Solana ❶ *Pan-Latin*   23 | 19 | 20 | $39

Albany | 1501A Solano Ave. (Curtis St.) | 510-559-9006 | www.fondasolana.com

"Part of the Lalime empire", this "upscale Pan-Latin" that "makes Albany feel hipper than it is" hawks "imaginative tapas" and "unusual cocktails" in a "two-story" converted repair shop with a "large", "lively bar" and "polished service"; even folks fonda the "four-alarm-loud" digs ("upstairs is more relaxed") admit prices for the "teensy" portions "can add up", but they find solace in the "all-day recession specials" – "now that's a stimulus package!"

Forbes Mill Steakhouse *Steak*   22 | 20 | 21 | $64

Danville | 200 Sycamore Valley Rd. W. (San Ramon Valley Blvd.) | 925-552-0505 | www.forbesmillsteakhouse.com
See review in South of San Francisco Directory.

Garibaldis *Californian/Mediterranean*   22 | 20 | 21 | $47

Oakland | 5356 College Ave. (bet. Bryant & Manila Aves.) | 510-595-4000 | www.garibaldisrestaurant.com
See review in City of San Francisco Directory.

Gar Woods   17 | 22 | 17 | $39

Grill & Pier *American/Mediterranean*

Carnelian Bay | Carnelian Bay | 5000 N. Lake Blvd. (Center St.) | 530-546-3366 | www.garwoods.com

There's no more "perfect Tahoe experience" than "sitting out on the deck" ("in summer or winter") at this Carnelian Bay "clubhouse" "right on the water" (with a "pier for docking your boat"); the "scenery is spectacular", the drinks "good" and even the "fair" New American-Med food "gets better" with every Wet Woody downed – plus "who goes to the Lake to eat" anyway?

Gioia Pizzeria 🅂 *Pizza*   23 | 9 | 16 | $12

Berkeley | 1586 Hopkins St. (bet. McGee & Monterey Aves.) | 510-528-4692 | www.gioiapizzeria.com

"Brooklyn" meets Berkeley at this prized pizzeria where the "blow-your-mind blistered-crust pies" come with "sophisticated", "California-fresh" toppings; it's "way too" small "to enjoy anything but takeout" (and hours are "limited" too), but pick up "whatever's special that day" and you'll have a meal "of the gods."

	FOOD	DECOR	SERVICE	COST

Great China *Chinese*
| 23 | 8 | 11 | $25 |

Berkeley | 2115 Kittredge St. (bet. Oxford St. & Shattuck Ave.) |
510-843-7996 | www.greatchinaberkeley.com

Reviewers rave the "superb Peking duck" "rivals what you can get in Beijing" at this "bargain" Berkeleyite where the "traditional" Chinese cuisine is matched by a surprisingly "excellent" by-the-bottle wine list ("who knew?"); even with a "long wait", "squished" seating and "surly" service, many feel it's ideal for a "group dinner."

grégoire *French*
| 22 | 9 | 17 | $22 |

Berkeley | 2109 Cedar St. (Shattuck Ave.) | 510-883-1893
Oakland | 4001B Piedmont Ave. (40th St.) | 510-547-3444
www.gregoirerestaurant.com

"Berkeley faculty" and Oaklanders who "don't mind paying sit-down prices for takeout" head to these "French fast food" "shacks" doling out "hella fattening" but "well-crafted" meals to go; if the aroma of the "world-famous" potato puffs that complement the "monthly changing" menu "gets to you", you can always cop a squat at one of the few "picnic tables" outside; P.S. "order ahead" to avoid "long waits."

Herbivore *Vegan*
| 15 | 15 | 17 | $20 |

Berkeley | 2451 Shattuck Ave. (Haste St.) | 510-665-1675 |
www.herbivorerestaurant.com
See review in City of San Francisco Directory.

Home of Chicken and Waffles ● *Southern*
| 20 | 11 | 16 | $20 |

Oakland | 444 Embarcadero W. (B'way) | 510-836-4446

While some "wouldn't think that chicken and waffles" "smothered in gravy" go together, "ohmigod, do they" cluck boosters of this "ultimate soul- and comfort-food joint" in Oakland's Jack London Square that "rivals SoCal's Roscoe's"; "folksy, painted menus on murals" and "great music" (Motown, gospel) "set the mood", plus a new "full bar" lures the "post-club" crowds, but "who needs atmosphere" anyway when you can get a "1,200-calorie" breakfast served until 4 AM on the weekends?

Il Fornaio *Italian*
| 19 | 20 | 19 | $40 |

Walnut Creek | 1430 Mt. Diablo Blvd. (B'way) | 925-296-0100 |
www.ilfornaio.com
See review in City of San Francisco Directory.

☑ In-N-Out Burger *Burgers*
| 22 | 10 | 18 | $8 |

Oakland | 8300 Oakport St. (bet. Edgewater Dr. & Roland Way) |
800-786-1000 | www.in-n-out.com
See review in City of San Francisco Directory.

Izzy's Steaks & Chops *Steak*
| 20 | 17 | 19 | $43 |

San Ramon | 200 Montgomery St. (bet. Alcosta Blvd. & Market Pl.) |
925-830-8620 | www.izzyssteaks.com
See review in City of San Francisco Directory.

Jake's on the Lake *Californian*
| 16 | 20 | 16 | $40 |

Tahoe City | Boatworks Mall | 780 N. Lake Blvd. (Jackpine St.) |
530-583-0188 | www.jakestahoe.com

"Sun"-seeking Sierrans say there's "no better place for a hamburger with a view" than this "summer" standby in Tahoe with a "stunning" lakeside location; like the "dated" decor, the "average, high-priced"

Californian menu just "doesn't seem to change" and the service is "iffy", but "no one cares", especially during "happy hour" on the deck, or weekend nights when a band strikes up in the bar; N.B. dinner-only in the off-season.

Jimmy Bean's *Diner*

| 19 | 10 | 15 | $18 |

Berkeley | 1290 Sixth St. (Gilman St.) | 510-528-3435 | www.jimmybeans.com

Though it's "open for all three meals", this "casual", certified-green Berkeley diner "really does breakfast best", dishing up "delicious scrambles" and "fluffy silver-dollar pancakes" all day long; the "nondescript", order-at-the-counter digs are "totally mobbed" during "weekend brunch", but more accommodating (with table service) for Californian "comfort food" at dinner – a real "value" considering the "high-quality ingredients" and $12 prix fixe option (including wine).

Jordan's *Californian/French*

| 17 | 21 | 19 | $53 |

Berkeley | Claremont Resort & Spa | 41 Tunnel Rd. (Domingo Ave.) | 510-549-8510 | www.claremontresort.com

"Be sure to ask for a window table", the better to "take in" the "breathtaking view" "of the entire Bay" at this "expensive" Cal-French in Berkeley's Claremont Resort that's a natural for "impressing out-of-town relatives"; still, a number of diners are "disappointed", noting both the menu and "staid" room "feel more institutional than romantic."

Juan's Place *Mexican*

| 16 | 11 | 17 | $20 |

Berkeley | 941 Carleton St. (9th St.) | 510-845-6904

"Rollicking" *rancheros* get "stuffed" on "big bowls" of tortilla chips and "down-home" Mexican dishes at this "festive", "family-run" Berkeley "dive"; though skeptics "suspect most come for the quantity, not the quality", the "super-nice" staff and "vibrant" vibe keep it a "favorite" for "quenching south-of-the-border cravings."

Kirala *Japanese*

| 25 | 16 | 18 | $38 |

Berkeley | 2100 Ward St. (Shattuck Ave.) | 510-549-3486

Kirala 2 *Japanese*

Berkeley | Epicurious Gdn. | 1511 Shattuck Ave. (bet. Cedar & Vine Sts.) | 510-649-1384
www.kiralaberkeley.com

"Top-quality" sushi meets "rocking" robata "under one roof" at this "Berkeley mainstay" whose "local fans" are willing to "queue up 30 minutes before doors open" and tolerate "earsplitting noise" to boot; those who won't (or who get a "craving" between lunch and dinner service) "hit up" its spin-off at Epicurious Garden, which stocks "most everything the resto has but in the to-go variety."

Koi Garden *Chinese*

| 23 | 16 | 13 | $34 |

Dublin | Ulferts Ctr. | 4288 Dublin Blvd. (bet. Glynnis Rose Dr. & John Monego Ct.) | 925-833-9090 | www.koipalace.com
See Koi Palace review in South of San Francisco Directory.

Koryo Wooden Charcoal BBQ ● *Korean*

| ∇ 23 | 10 | 13 | $26 |

Oakland | 4390 Telegraph Ave. (44th St.) | 510-652-6007

"Savory" Seoul food – such as "heavenly" Korean BBQ and "fantastic soups with a gazillion condiments" – inspires enthusiasts to endure the "dive" decor and "brusque" service at this budget-friendly Oaklander; occasionally you'll "wait awhile", but "it's a small sacrifice" for the experience.

NEW Lake Chalet *Californian*

| - | - | - | M |

Oakland | Lake Merritt Boathouse | 1520 Lakeside Dr. (bet. 14th & 17th Sts.) | 510-208-5253 | www.thelakechalet.com

This forthcoming waterside bar and grill (slated to open in August '09) in Oakland's newly restored, century-old Lake Merritt Boathouse takes the lead of SF siblings the Beach Chalet Brewery and Park Chalet, reviving a vintage setting and rolling out Cal cuisine and brewpub beers; the midpriced menu will showcase seasonal seafood along with burgers and other simple eats, though the true lure should be the BBQ and weekend brunch, served outside on the 100-seat lakeside patio and bar area.

Lalime's *Californian/Mediterranean*

| 26 | 21 | 24 | $52 |

Berkeley | 1329 Gilman St. (bet. Neilson St. & Peralta Ave.) | 510-527-9838 | www.lalimes.com

Serving "superb" dinners "made from the highest-quality ingredients", this Sea Salt sib in Berkeley will "leave you hungry – for a return visit" effuse fans who call the Cal-Med "seasonal specialties" an "ever-changing adventure of flavor"; with a "homey" setting and "fantastic" service, it all adds up to a "first-class" option "without having to cross the bridge."

La Méditerranée *Mediterranean/Mideastern*

| 20 | 15 | 18 | $23 |

Berkeley | 2936 College Ave. (Ashby Ave.) | 510-540-7773 | www.cafelamed.com

See review in City of San Francisco Directory.

Lanesplitter Pub & Pizza *Pizza*

| 17 | 11 | 15 | $16 |

Berkeley | 1051 San Pablo Ave. (Monroe St.) | 510-527-8375
Berkeley | 2033 San Pablo Ave. (University Ave.) | 510-845-1652 ☽
Oakland | 4799 Telegraph Ave. (48th St.) | 510-653-5350 ☽
www.lanesplitterpizza.com

"For a few bones" you can get "two slices and a beer" at these East Bay "biker bar"–pizzerias that attract "grubby hipsters" as well as "families" with "decent", "massive" "old-school NY" pies (thin or thick) and salads; critics gripe "you have to shout to be heard" by the "inky staff", but most agree it's a "nice alternative to the hegemony of California- and Chicago-style" parlors; N.B. the branch near San Pablo and Monroe is takeout and delivery only.

La Note *French*

| 21 | 19 | 17 | $28 |

Berkeley | 2377 Shattuck Ave. (bet. Channing Way & Durant Ave.) | 510-843-1535 | www.lanoterestaurant.com

"French country food warms your soul" at this Berkeley bistro where dinner (Thursday–Saturday) is "excellent", but the "killer" "breakfast is even better", boasting "huge bowls" of café au lait and "incredible" eats that attract "crazy" crowds; some tut about "tight" tables and "spotty" service, but the "lovely patio" is a perk on "sunny mornings."

Lark Creek *American*

| 21 | 19 | 20 | $46 |

Walnut Creek | 1360 Locust St. (bet. Cypress St. & Mt. Diablo Blvd.) | 925-256-1234 | www.larkcreek.com

A "tried-and-true" homage to the red, white and blue, this "upmarket" American in a "see-and-be seen" Downtown Walnut Creek setting serves "darn good" "comfort food like pot roast" and "butterscotch pudding", as well as "seasonal offerings" with an emphasis on organic ingredients; cynics sniff it's "nothing to write home about, or even text", but when suburbanites "need a nice evening out" or a "trustworthy" lunch spot "to take business clients", it "always comes through"; P.S. in July the entire wine list is "50% off."

Le Cheval *Vietnamese*   21 | 15 | 18 | $26
Oakland | 1007 Clay St. (10th St.) | 510-763-8495
Walnut Creek | 1375 N. Broadway (bet. Cypress & Duncan Sts.) | 925-938-2288 Ⓜ

Le Petit Cheval Ⓩ⇱ *Vietnamese*
Berkeley | 2600 Bancroft Way (Bowditch St.) | 510-704-7018
www.lecheval.com

Customers "crave" the "fantastic" Vietnamese fare, from "homestyle rice and noodle" noshes to "sophisticated seafood dishes", at these "popular" pit stops – the "cavernous" Oakland original and its smaller, more "pleasant" Walnut Creek and "university"-oriented Berkeley branches – purveying a "steal of a meal"; while the staff keeps the "tables turning", on-the-go guests appreciate the service "in record time."

Levende East Ⓩ *Eclectic*   19 | 20 | 17 | $40
Oakland | 827 Washington St. (bet. 8th & 9th Sts.) | 510-835-5585 | www.levendeeast.com

"Luscious libations" lubricate Oakland's "beautiful people", who also indulge in "interesting" Eclectic plates for a "reasonable" price at this "loungey" locale that's "so hip it hurts", especially once DJs start spinning on weekend nights; service has its ups and downs, with some diners deeming it "dicey"; N.B. a late-night menu is served Friday–Saturday till 1 AM.

Lo Coco's Restaurant & Pizzeria Ⓜ *Italian*   22 | 14 | 20 | $29
Berkeley | 1400 Shattuck Ave. (Rose St.) | 510-843-3745
Oakland | 4270 Piedmont Ave. (Echo Ave.) | 510-652-6222 ⇱
www.lococospizzeria.com

The "enthusiastic" crew "makes you feel like family" at these "fabulous" *fratelli* in Berkeley and Oakland, two "hole-in-the-wall" Sicilian "sleepers" serving "homestyle" pastas and "awesome" pizzas; just try to "arrive early or be prepared to wait", since they're "always crowded."

Luka's Taproom & Lounge ❶ *Californian/French*   20 | 15 | 16 | $29
Oakland | 2221 Broadway (W. Grand Ave.) | 510-451-4677 | www.lukasoakland.com

A "favorite after-work stop", this Cal-French brasserie attracts an "eclectic" Oakland crowd with its "comfort-food standouts" (such as "juicy burgers") and "Belgian brews"; it's "easy" for "shooting a round of pool" too, but some are deterred by the "deafening" volume and "long" waits; P.S. "half-priced" bottles on Sunday and "$1 oysters on Monday" are additional draws.

Mama's Royal Cafe ⇱ *American*   21 | 15 | 17 | $17
Oakland | 4012 Broadway (40th St.) | 510-547-7600 | www.mamasroyalcafeoakland.com

"Providing an entire menu's worth of reasons" not to skip the "most important meal of the day", this "quirky" longtimer still whips up the "most happening breakfast" in Oakland (as well as American lunches, served till 3 PM); "funky" decor (including entrants from the "annual napkin art contest") and "arty" servers who "look like they just rolled in from a night out" ensure its appeal for "meeting up with everyone else who has a hangover."

Marica *Seafood*   ▽ 23 | 17 | 21 | $44

Oakland | 5301 College Ave. (B'way) | 510-985-8388

Despite the "plain-Jane decor", with lots of wood and exposed-brick walls, this "casual" Oakland seafooder offering an "interesting changing menu" "deserves more attention" according to afishionados who say you "can't go wrong with any fish entree" or the "exquisite" lobster; "respectful service" and "reasonable prices" are other reasons it "satisfies", even if a few piscatarians pout the plates "can be uneven."

NEW Marzano *Italian/Pizza*   23 | 19 | 21 | $35

Oakland | 4214 Park Blvd. (Glenfield Ave.) | 510-531-4500 | www.marzanorestaurant.com

It "feels more like NYC than Oakland" at this new "jam-packed" "addition to Glenview's food ghetto" from the "Garibaldis folks", where "servers skinny between tables" ferrying "phenomenal pizzas" from a "wood-fired oven" and other Southern Italian "delicacies", while "bartenders put on a great show"; while some report that service and ambiance can "suffer on busy nights", with its "stimulus pricing" and weekend brunch, it's a "haven" for "local families" who "no longer need to drive to Rockridge for good eats"; N.B. a new branch is slated to open adjacent to Garibaldis.

Max's *Deli*   17 | 14 | 17 | $27

Oakland | Oakland City Ctr. | 500 12th St. (bet. B'way & Clay St.) | 510-451-6297 ☒

San Ramon | 2015 Crow Canyon Pl. (Crow Canyon Rd.) | 925-277-9300 www.maxsworld.com

See review in City of San Francisco Directory.

Metro *Californian/French*   - | - | - | M

Lafayette | 3524 Mt. Diablo Blvd. (bet. 1st St. & Moraga Rd.) | 925-284-4422 | www.metrolafayette.com

Looking as if it were plucked from trendy LA, this minimalist-chic Lafayette hangout poses as a haven for beautiful people, yet the crowd is a cross-section, as is chef Jason Low's Cal-French menu ranging from spring rolls to pasta to croque monsieur; the 140-seat, umbrella-shaded patio is embraced by an austere, L-shaped dining room with black tile floors and persimmon-colored upholstery, which also features a stainless-steel bar that's a magnet for the cocktail crowd.

Mezze *Californian/Mediterranean*   20 | 20 | 20 | $42

Oakland | 3407 Lakeshore Ave. (bet. Mandana Blvd. & Trestle Glen Rd.) | 510-663-2500 | www.mezze.com

"Beautifully presented", "inventive" Mediterranean dishes with a "California sensibility" tend to please at this "popular", "family-run" "sleeper" in Oakland; most deem it a "neighborhood treasure" for an "upscale", "leisurely dinner" or a bite at the bar, but a minority maintains that it "misses" the mark too often with "spotty" service and "inconsistent" cuisine.

NEW Miss Pearl's Jam House *Caribbean* 17 | 18 | 17 | $42

Oakland | Waterfront Plaza Hotel | 1 Broadway (Embarcadero W.) |
510-444-7171 | www.misspearlsjamhouse.com

Joey Altman's Oakland "reincarnation" of his '80s island-themed spot
is one of the "most interesting options in Jack London Square", cranking out "jerk chicken that rocks" and other "tasty" Caribbean eats;
while some grouse that "his food was much better on TV" and the
plantation-style dining room lacks the "edge" of the original, the "outdoor patio" with "wonderful" water views and live bands on weekends
"make for a festive atmosphere", and optimists forecast "given a little
time for polish", this pearl could "be a star again."

Moody's Bistro & Lounge *American* 25 | 20 | 22 | $51

Truckee | Truckee Hotel | 10007 Bridge St. (Donner Pass Rd.) | 530-587-8688 |
www.moodysbistro.com

Après-skiers seeking "San Francisco sophistication in Tahoe" schuss
on over to the Truckee Hotel to indulge in "inventive" yet "comforting"
New American fare in a retro dining room; though it's a bit "pricey",
"excellent" service and frequent "live jazz" lend a "welcoming" feel.

Naan 'n Curry *Indian/Pakistani* 17 | 7 | 10 | $15

Berkeley | 2366 Telegraph Ave. (bet. Channing Way & Durant Ave.) |
510-841-6226 | www.naancurry.com

See review in City of San Francisco Directory.

Naked Fish, The *Japanese* ▽ 21 | 14 | 18 | $34

South Lake Tahoe | 3940 Lake Tahoe Blvd. (Hwy. 50 & Pioneer Trail) |
530-541-3474 | www.thenakedfish.com

While it's "hard to believe that you can get good sushi" in South Lake
Tahoe, many commend the "high-quality sashimi" and "creative"
rolls by "attentive" chefs at this "terrific" Japanese; it's "low-
key" rather than lavish, with simple nautical decor, but happy hour
from 5-6:30 PM adds to the "treat."

Nan Yang Rockridge Ⓜ *Burmese* 20 | 15 | 19 | $25

Oakland | 6048 College Ave. (Claremont Ave.) | 510-655-3298

"Aromatic", "well-balanced" Burmese dishes "burst with flavor" at
this "distinctive" Oaklander whose "wonderful Rockridge location"
presents a "peaceful" "alternative to the usual suspects"; since the
"ample portions" offer "great value" to boot, "nan fans" say it "should
be more than a neighborhood secret."

Nizza La Bella *French/Italian* ▽ 20 | 15 | 18 | $36

Albany | 825 San Pablo Ave. (bet. Solano & Washington Aves.) |
510-526-2552 | www.nizzalabella.com

"What a treat!" exclaim enthusiasts of this "lovely little" Albany bistro
where the "high-end pizzas", wood-fired French dishes and "interesting cocktails" are "a surprise, given the casual atmosphere" and "reasonable" tabs; still, while it's "pleasant" enough, less impressed
eaters note it's really a "neighborhood spot, not a destination."

North Beach Pizza *Pizza* 20 | 10 | 15 | $18

Berkeley | 1598 University Ave. (California St.) | 510-849-9800 |
www.northbeachpizza.net

See review in City of San Francisco Directory.

	FOOD	DECOR	SERVICE	COST

O Chamé *Japanese*
| | 24 | 21 | 21 | $36 |

Berkeley | 1830 Fourth St. (bet. Hearst Ave. & Virginia St.) | 510-841-8783

"Superb soba" and "intensely flavorful" udon noodle soups are "perfection in a bowl" attest acolytes of this "divine" Berkeley Japanese where the "beautifully arranged" fare "just makes you feel good"; its "tasteful" environs and service "soothe" the soul too, so most don't mind the "limited" menu (no sushi) and somewhat "pricey" tabs.

Oliveto Cafe *Italian*
| | 24 | 20 | 21 | $40 |

Oakland | 5655 College Ave. (Shafter Ave.) | 510-547-5356 | www.oliveto.com

Offering the same "great food" as the "restaurant upstairs" at "much more reasonable prices", this 'beautiful" "newly remodeled" "seat-yourself" "sidewalk cafe" in Oakland is the "perfect drop-in" spot for what caf-fiends call the "best cup of espresso this side of Rome" and "breakfast pizza with egg on top" or "midday" panini at the bar; you're "almost climbing over each other" inside, but alfresco dinners while "watching the Rockridge crowds go by" is la dolce vita.

Oliveto Restaurant *Italian*
| | 25 | 22 | 23 | $60 |

Oakland | 5655 College Ave. (Shafter Ave.) | 510-547-5356 | www.oliveto.com

"For more than 20 years", this super Tuscan in Oakland's Market Hall has "set the standard" for Italian with "authentically, caringly prepared" cuisine, served by a "knowledgeable" staff in a "romantic" second-floor setting; the "seasonal themed dinners aren't to be missed", while the "housemade salumi and pastas" and "anything from the rotisserie" make it a "foodie's" "destination worthy" of "paying Euro prices", but the "pretentious" vibe and "small portions" "just don't cut it" for a few.

Ozumo Ⓢ *Japanese*
| | 24 | 23 | 20 | $56 |

NEW **Oakland** | 2251 Broadway (Grand Ave.) | 510-286-9866 | www.ozumo.com

See review in City of San Francisco Directory.

Pakwan ⊘ *Pakistani*
| | 22 | 6 | 11 | $15 |

Fremont | 41068 Fremont Blvd. (Irvington Ave.) | 510-226-6234 Ⓜ
Hayward | 25168 Mission Blvd. (Central Ave.) | 510-538-2401
www.pakwanrestaurant.com

See review in City of San Francisco Directory.

Pappo Ⓜ *Californian/Mediterranean*
| | ▽ 24 | 19 | 21 | $41 |

Alameda | 2320 Central Ave. (bet. Oak & Park Sts.) | 510-337-9100 | www.papporestaurant.com

Alameda diners feel "lucky" to have this "quality" Cal-Med purveying a "small" but "surprising" menu of largely organic fare that gives them a "reason to eat" locally; an "intimate" "bistro" atmosphere, "professional" service and a location across from a "historic" movie theater are pluses, even if a few find it "pricey"; N.B. closed Monday–Tuesday.

Peasant & the Pear, The Ⓜ *Mediterranean*
| | 22 | 20 | 22 | $38 |

Danville | 267 Hartz Ave. (Diablo Blvd.) | 925-820-6611 | www.thepeasantandthepear.com

"Salads and sandwiches shine" at this Danville Mediterranean with a "quiet outdoor patio" and "fancily decorated" dining room where the "budding" chef "visits each table"; "it can get a little loud", "especially around the bar", but fans say the "excellent" "food and service make up for it."

NEW Penelope ⑤ *Californian* — — — M

Oakland | 555 12th St. (Clay St.) | 510-834-0404

Named after, but bearing no relation to, Penelope Cruz, this sharp new Oakland gastropub serves up midpriced panini, salads and other Californian lunch fare, along with heartier evening plates like mac 'n' cheese and bangers 'n' mash to soak up the true stars – potent infused vodka cocktails and local brews; lots of wood, a concrete countertop and a plethora of sunny sidewalk seating lend style to its Downtown office-building locale.

Pho 84 *Vietnamese* 22 13 17 $21

Oakland | 354 17th St. (Franklin St.) | 510-832-1338

"Lines at lunchtime attest" to the popularity of the "phantastic pho" ("rich and full-flavored") and other "cheap" but "gorgeous Vietnamese" fare at this Oakland "favorite"; regulars always feel "well taken care of" by the "friendly" staff, and since the space has recently been redone in "warm" tones, it's not quite the "hole-in-the-wall it once was."

Pianeta *Italian* ∇ 23 21 20 $46

Truckee | 10096 Donner Pass Rd. (Brockway Rd.) | 530-587-4694 | www.pianetarestaurant.com

Housemade pastas and other Northern Italian eats "continue to satisfy" at this "lovely" Italian that's among the "best" in Truckee; "cozy in winter" ("ask for a booth downstairs") with "attentive" service, it "pleasantly surprises" sporty surveyors who say "just because you're skiing doesn't mean your food has to suffer."

Piatti *Italian* 18 18 18 $40

Danville | 100 Sycamore Valley Rd. W. (San Ramon Valley Blvd.) | 925-838-2082 | www.piatti.com

"Not too formal, not too casual", this "busy" Bay Area chainlet is a "go-to" for "quick lunches" and "festive", "family-friendly" dinners of pizza, "delicious" pastas and other Boot bites; proponents praise their "great patios", but pickier patrons say the quality "varies by location" and lament that "nothing will wow you" "if you want Italian made with love."

NEW Picán *Southern* — — — E

Oakland | 2295 Broadway (23rd St.) | 510-834-1000 | www.picanrestaurant.com

Bringing a little Southern hospitality to the East Bay, a chef from Atlanta's South City Kitchen gives New Orleans–inspired comfort food a Californian spin at this high-end arrival in Oakland's up-and-coming Uptown neighborhood; the sumptuously appointed dining room exudes a plantation vibe, while the bar stocks what's claimed to be the largest collection of handmade single-batch bourbons west of the Mississippi.

Picante Cocina Mexicana *Mexican* 21 12 16 $17

Berkeley | 1328 Sixth St. (bet. Camelia & Gilman Sts.) | 510-525-3121 | www.picante.biz

"Still doing it right" since 1982, this "cafeteria-style" *cocina* cooks up Mexican fare "made Berkeley-style, with fresh ingredients and tons of flavor"; the menu "goes beyond the usual enchiladas, burritos and tacos", tallying up "a hundred ways to knock your socks off", but it can get "chaotic" with lots of kids, so non-breeders "brave the long line for to-go orders" or take the edge off with "terrific margaritas"; P.S. there's "nice outdoor seating in the summer."

Pizza Antica *Pizza*
21 | 16 | 17 | $28

Lafayette | 3600 Mt. Diablo Blvd. (Dewing Ave.) | 925-299-0500 | www.pizzaantica.com
See review in South of San Francisco Directory.

Pizzaiolo ⊠ *Pizza*
25 | 18 | 20 | $35

Oakland | 5008 Telegraph Ave. (51st St.) | 510-652-4888 | www.pizzaiolooakland.com
"Pizza is his thing" but Charlie Hallowell's "diamond" in the Temescal rough also crafts "Chez Panisse–quality" handmade pastas and "wood-roasted" Southern Italian specialties with a touch of "Oakland hipster attitude"; a few critics grouse that the "music is sometimes too loud" and "service is a bit slow", while others are elated that it now takes reservations, so "you don't have to wait a lifetime" to dine here on a "school night"; N.B. a spin-off is slated to open at 3306 Grand Avenue.

Pizza Rustica *Pizza*
18 | 12 | 16 | $22

Oakland | 5422 College Ave. (bet. Kales & Manila Aves.) | 510-654-1601
Oakland | 6106 La Salle Ave. (Mountain Ave.) | 510-339-7878
www.caferustica.com
"Gourmet" pizzas and "different versions of rotisserie chicken" elevate this pie parlor pair "above the usual" insist optimistic Oaklanders who note the "nice neighborhoody feel"; still, more particular patrons pout it's only "passable", touting "takeaway" to avoid the "unremarkable surroundings" and maintaining its main "claim to fame" is it "delivers."

Plearn Thai Cuisine *Thai*
∇ 21 | 14 | 19 | $24

Berkeley | 1923 University Ave. (bet. Bonita St. & Martin Luther King Ln.) | 510-549-9999

Plearn Thai Kitchen *Thai*
Berkeley | 2283 Shattuck Ave. (Bancroft St.) | 510-704-1442

Plearn Thai Palace *Thai*
Walnut Creek | 1510 N. Main St. (Lincoln Ave.) | 925-937-7999 | www.plearnthaipalace.com
A "staple" in Berkeley and Walnut Creek, these three Siamese sisters serve up "generous portions" of "excellent basic Thai food" that "won't break the bank"; the original eatery (on University Avenue) has moved to a "new location" half a block down the street, but is staffed by the same "accommodating" servers who "will help if you are unsure of what to order, or how hot to order it."

PlumpJack Cafe *Californian/Mediterranean*
23 | 21 | 22 | $56

Olympic Valley | PlumpJack Squaw Valley Inn | 1920 Squaw Valley Rd. (Hwy. 89) | 530-583-1576 | www.plumpjackcafe.com
"Fantastic" Cal-Med food in a "refined", "unobtrusive" setting makes this "surviving PlumpJack enterprise at Tahoe" a "delightful and indul-gent repast after a day of exercise on the mountain"; while some say the cooking "goes up and down depending on the season", the "excep-tional" "well-priced wine list" (at near "retail prices") is "always amaz-

ing", and staffers are "friendly and very competent"; P.S. San Francisco's original Cow Hollow branch is slated to reopen as a new concept in 2010.

Pomodoro *Italian*
17 | 13 | 17 | $22

Emeryville | Bay Street Mall | 5614 Bay St. (Shellmound St.) | 510-923-1173
Oakland | 5500 College Ave. (Lawton Ave.) | 510-923-0900
www.pastapomodoro.com

See review in City of San Francisco Directory.

Postino *Italian*
23 | 24 | 22 | $52

Lafayette | 3565 Mt. Diablo Blvd. (Oak Hill Rd.) | 925-299-8700 | www.postinorestaurant.com

"Sophisticated without being fussy", this "winner" in a former Lafayette post office delivers "delicious" Italian fare, including "whimsical specials" that supplement the "great staples"; even if it's "getting to be too traditional" for some, "gorgeous" touches like slate floors and "big fireplaces" make it extra "inviting", plus the "bar scene is a blast."

Prima *Italian*
24 | 20 | 22 | $58

Walnut Creek | 1522 N. Main St. (bet. Bonanza St. & Lincoln Ave.) | 925-935-7780 | www.primaristorante.com

"Fabulous" Northern Italian eats are matched by an "impressive" wine list of "exceptional breadth" (the owners also run a "first-rate" retail shop next door) at this "reliable favorite" in Walnut Creek; with a touch of "old-fashioned" appeal, it's "like visiting your friend's mother's house for dinner", with the sole exception that it's "a little on the pricey side for the portions."

Red Hut Café *Diner*
▽ 23 | 13 | 18 | $15

South Lake Tahoe | 2749 Lake Tahoe Blvd. (Al Tahoe Blvd.) | 530-541-9024 ⊘
NEW **South Lake Tahoe** | Ski Run Ctr. | 3668 Lake Tahoe Blvd. (Hwy. 50) | 530-544-1595
www.redhutcafe.com

This "classic" diner in South Lake Tahoe (with a new spin-off at the Ski Run Center) is exactly "what a hometown cafe is supposed to be", serving "great pancakes and waffles" as well as the "must-have" "'usual' (biscuits and gravy, eggs and hash browns)"; since many consider it the "only place for a locals' breakfast", the only downside is "you may have to wait"; N.B. closes at 2 PM; a third hut is just over the border in Stateline, Nevada.

Restaurant Peony *Chinese*
20 | 12 | 13 | $27

Oakland | Pacific Renaissance Plaza | 388 Ninth St. (bet. Franklin & Webster Sts.) | 510-286-8866 | www.restaurantpeony.com

At lunchtime, "come with a large group" to best "enjoy the variety" of "excellent" dim sum dishes declare devotees of this "reasonably priced" Oaklander, who also return in the evening for "fresh seafood", Peking duck "to die for" and other Hong Kong–style specialties for "a steal"; just be "prepared to wait" (especially on weekends) for a seat in the "huge" and "pretty impersonal" dining room.

Rick & Ann's *American*
21 | 13 | 18 | $23

Berkeley | 2922 Domingo Ave. (bet. Ashby & Claremont Aves.) | 510-649-8538 | www.rickandanns.com

The "original" breakfasts are the "perfect way to start the weekend" praise patrons of this Berkeley brunch "staple" whose "down-home"

FOOD | DECOR | SERVICE | COST

"American comfort-food" dinners are "made with love" too; it gets "crammed" in the AM (when a "long line" forms outside), but evenings are much more "relaxed."

River Ranch Lodge & Restaurant *Californian*

▽ 15 | 21 | 16 | $36

Tahoe City | 2285 River Rd. (Alpine Meadows Rd.) | 530-583-4264 | www.riverranchlodge.com

Offering a "priceless" setting right over the "rushing" Truckee River, this "fun" Tahoe City Californian is "the perfect place" to "idle away an afternoon as you watch rafters climb out" of the water; the "hearty" grilled fare is humble and the bar gets "overrun with wet and wild revelers", but with a fireplace inside, it's "cozy" in any season.

☑ Rivoli *Californian/Mediterranean*

27 | 22 | 25 | $52

Berkeley | 1539 Solano Ave. (bet. Neilson St. & Peralta Ave.) | 510-526-2542 | www.rivolirestaurant.com

One of the "best" in Berkeley "for the money", Corso's "understated" big sister still "dazzles" after 15 years, combining "magnificent" "seasonal" Cal-Med dishes, an "appealing" wine list (plus classic cocktails) and "outstanding" service "without the pretentiousness" elsewhere; the view of the "lit-up" garden is "lovely", and a summer 2009 remodel (not reflected in the Decor score) has transformed the space into a ranch house with Japanese influences.

Ruth's Chris Steak House *Steak*

23 | 20 | 22 | $65

Walnut Creek | 1553 Olympic Blvd. (bet. Locust & Main Sts.) | 925-977-3477 | www.ruthschris.com

See review in City of San Francisco Directory.

Salute Marina Bay *Italian*

▽ 18 | 23 | 20 | $34

Richmond | Marina Bay | 1900 Esplanade Dr. (Melville Sq.) | 510-215-0803 | www.salutemarinabay.com

"Gorgeous" bay views, "excellent" service and homemade pastas "are the trademarks" of this historic Victorian Cape Cod–style dinner house "overlooking the Richmond Marina", an affordable East Bay "favorite" for impressing "out-of-town guests"; some feel the food is merely "basic", but saluting surveyors say it's simply "wonderful" all around.

Saul's Restaurant & Delicatessen *Deli*

19 | 14 | 17 | $22

Berkeley | 1475 Shattuck Ave. (bet. Rose & Vine Sts.) | 510-848-3354 | www.saulsdeli.com

"Carnegie Deli meets Berkeley" at this "nurturing" noshery that calls to "expat Easterners" "jonesing" for "piles of pastrami", "matzo ball soup" and other "irresistible" "Jewish basics"; the servers are a whole lot more respectful, though less fun" than their Manhattan counterparts – and you really know "you're not in New York anymore" when the kitchen offers "free-range meats" and at least "five choices of bread" – but "transplants" full of "nostalgia" "take what we can get."

Scott's Seafood *Seafood*

18 | 18 | 19 | $42

Oakland | 2 Broadway (Water St.) | 510-444-3456
Walnut Creek | 1333 N. California Blvd. (Mt. Diablo Blvd.) | 925-934-1300
www.scottsrestaurants.com

An "oldie but a goodie", this "comfy" American mini-chain provides "surprisingly" fine fin fare in a "fun" atmosphere – especially with occasional "jazz" at some branches – plus you can "watch the yachts go by" from the "nautical and nice" Oakland locale; still, crabbier critics call it "stodgy", sighing "you'll feel like you've been here before" – "two decades ago"; N.B. the Palo Alto and San Jose pair is separately owned.

Sea Salt *Seafood* | 22 | 18 | 20 | $38 |

Berkeley | 2512 San Pablo Ave. (Dwight Way) | 510-883-1720 | www.seasaltrestaurant.com

"Any fish dish will please the palate" at this Berkeley "success" "from the Lalime's folks", known for its "well-prepared" catches, "delish lobster rolls" and "daily dollar oyster" happy hour (3-6 PM), as well as "imaginative bar food" and "inventive" cocktails; the expanded space's skylight, picnic tables and "beautiful cobalt tiles" make it an extra "unexpected pleasure on San Pablo Avenue."

Shalimar ⊐ *Indian/Pakistani* | 23 | 3 | 10 | $16 |

Fremont | 3325 Walnut Ave. (Paseo Padre Pkwy.) | 510-494-1919 | www.shalimarsf.com

See review in City of San Francisco Directory.

Shen Hua *Chinese* | 22 | 17 | 19 | $27 |

Berkeley | 2914 College Ave. (bet. Ashby Ave. & Russell St.) | 510-883-1777

"Addicts" "can't stay away" from the "distinctive" Sichuan cuisine, including many "items not found elsewhere", at this "big", "busy" Berkeley Chinese; most are willing to "pay a bit more" than elsewhere, saying it's "worth dealing with the arena-level volume" and "semi-snooty" service to enjoy the "fresh" eats.

NEW Sidebar 🅱 *Californian* | ▽ 20 | 23 | 22 | $33 |

Oakland | 542 Grand Ave. (Euclid Ave.) | 510-452-9500 | www.sidebar-oakland.com

That "clever Zax Tavern team is back in town" at this new Oakland gastropub, and fans are happy to see it "continue the tradition" of "nicely done", "fancified" Cal-Med "bar food" "more reasonably priced than previously"; a 20-ft., copper-topped "cocktail bar" in the middle of the room adds to the "action", and while it's "still feeling its way", most agree it makes a "great addition to the neighborhood."

Soi4 *Thai* | 23 | 19 | 20 | $34 |

Oakland | 5421 College Ave. (bet. Kales & Manila Aves.) | 510-655-0889 | www.soifour.com

"Not your everyday" Thai, this "fab" Oaklander with a "Bangkok" bent boasts a "different take" on the cuisine that "goes beyond the traditional plates"; "slightly less expensive" than its Rockridge neighbors, it's still a "sleek" (if "noisy") setting for an "unpretentious" night out, and you can even Thai one on with "well-selected" wines and cocktails too.

Soizic 🅱 *Californian/French* | 24 | 20 | 23 | $43 |

Oakland | 300 Broadway (3rd St.) | 510-251-8100 | www.soizicbistro.com

"Don't be fooled" by the "drab exterior" of this "warehouse" near Oakland's Jack London Square, because inside is a "beautiful" if "offbeat" bi-level loft where romantics on "first dates" can nestle into corner banquettes and dine on "mouthwatering", "delightfully unusual" Cal-French fare; a "well-chosen, reasonable" wine list and "attentive" service only add to the "relaxed" atmosphere.

Somerset *American*

▽ 17 | 18 | 15 | $36

Oakland | 5912 College Ave. (Chabot Rd.) | 510-428-1823 |
www.somersetrestaurant.com

A Rockridge "favorite for lunch" and "fabulous brunches", particularly
"when the weather's warm", this "romantic Craftsman" with a "beautiful, vine-covered patio" "rewards" diners with "down-home" American
food and "killer" sweets; still, some are "disappointed" by "derivative"
dinners and "amateurish" service, and stick to daytime meals.

Soule Domain *American*

▽ 22 | 23 | 23 | $47

Kings Beach | 9983 Cove Ave. (Stateline Rd.) | 530-546-7529 |
www.souledomain.com

Reviewers stumble on a "rustic and real" "old log cabin" "near the
Lake" serving "excellent", "upscale" New American fare at this Kings
Beach place to "take someone special"; though the food is too "retro"
for some, most praise it as a "change of pace from the usual Tahoe
scene" and a "much better value than nearby casino tables."

Sunnyside Resort *Seafood/Steak*

18 | 22 | 18 | $37

Tahoe City | 1850 W. Lake Blvd. (bet. Pineland Dr. & Tahoe Park Ave.) |
530-583-7200 | www.sunnysideresort.com

"With the Lake as its backdrop", this surf 'n' turfer is "great any time
of year" to "end a day in Tahoe", be it to "watch the snow fall" by the
fireplace in winter or "arrive by boat" in the summer and "sit on the deck
at sunset"; the food is "satisfying but not stellar" and "service can be
spotty", but for many it's the "most fun place to dine on the West Shore."

Tacubaya *Mexican*

24 | 13 | 14 | $16

Berkeley | 1788 Fourth St. (bet. Hearst Ave. & Virginia St.) | 510-525-5160 |
www.tacubaya.net

"Definitely not your run-of-the-mill" Mexican, this "bustling little
gourmet taqueria" (kin to "fancier cousin Doña Tomás") dishes out
"fantastic" fare with "fresh flavors" that feel "like a mariachi band in your
mouth"; "smallish portions" put off ravenous reviewers, and the counter
staff, though "quick", can be "indifferent"; still, the "casual" (if
"crowded") room and "pleasant" patio are *numero uno* with taco mavens
"in the middle of shopping madness" on Berkeley's Fourth Street.

Tamarindo Antojeria Mexicana 🖾 *Mexican*

24 | 18 | 19 | $34

Oakland | 468 Eighth St. (bet. B'way & Washington St.) | 510-444-1944 |
www.tamarindoantojeria.com

The "extensive" menu of "authentic" *antojitos* ("think south-of-the-
border tapas") and "delicious homemade salsas" will "widen your
concept of Mexican food" at this "upscale" cafe "tucked away in
Downtown Oakland"; the "small space" means it's "perennially
packed" (if only it would "start taking reservations"), but amigos
agree that coupled with "creative, tasty" margaritas and "hard-to-find
craft beers", the "fantastic, fresh" fare "consistently delivers."

Thai Buddhist Temple
Mongkolratanaram 🖾🗐 *Thai*

▽ 19 | 13 | 15 | $13

Berkeley | 1911 Russell St. (bet. Martin Luther King Jr. Way & Otis St.) |
510-849-3419

Like going to church, this "unique", "Sunday-only" "outdoor" Thai
"food court" "served by monks and temple volunteers" at a Buddhist

monastery in Berkeley is a weekly "cultural" rite for devout bargain-hunters; "don't expect much" – just queue up, then "pull up a spot at a picnic table or plop onto the lawn" to enjoy the "enormous" servings of "good", "hearty" home cooking, served 10 AM–1 PM.

Townhouse Bar & Grill ☒ *Californian*

| 21 | 18 | 20 | $37 |

Emeryville | 5862 Doyle St. (bet. 59th & Powell Sts.) | 510-652-6151 | www.townhousebarandgrill.com

Tucked away "on a side street in Emeryville", this Californian is a locals' "favorite spot for team lunches" or "sliders at the bar" that you can wash down with "memorable Cosmos"; though some find it a "bit spendy for what it is", the "well-prepared" fare, "pleasant" service and "comfy" setting with a patio boasting a "water fountain and a big tree in the middle" are enough to keep many "coming back"; N.B. live jazz Wednesdays and Thursdays.

Trader Vic's *Polynesian*

| 17 | 21 | 19 | $48 |

Emeryville | 9 Anchor Dr. (Powell St.) | 510-653-3400 | www.tradervics.com

The "rum-loaded cocktails" "will get you tipsy before you realize it" at these "amusingly retro" "tacky" tiki temples ("home of the mai tai") that "bring back memories" (albeit foggy ones) for many; the original Emeryville outpost has "fantastic views over the water", while Palo Alto sports a "very pleasant" veranda, and even if foes find the South Seas–themed menu "mediocre" and "way overpriced", it's "still fun" for fans of "kitsch."

Trattoria La Siciliana ⌿ *Italian*

| 25 | 14 | 17 | $32 |

Berkeley | 2993 College Ave. (bet. Ashby Ave. & Webster St.) | 510-704-1474 | www.trattorialasiciliana.com

"There's always a line out the door" at this "loud! crowded! fantastico!" Berkeley bastion of Sicilian cuisine, where the "affordable" "family-style" dishes – including some "hard-to-find" specialties – are "made with warmth and quality" (plus plenty of "garlic") by the D'Alo family; service is fairly "random" and it's "cash only", yet "everyone still loves it."

T Rex Barbecue *BBQ*

| 18 | 18 | 17 | $29 |

Berkeley | 1300 10th St. (Gilman St.) | 510-527-0099 | www.t-rex-bbq.com

'Cue-noisseurs counsel "better wear your stretch pants" to this "trendy BBQ joint" in Berkeley, a "temple of meat" smoking "free-range" "finger-licking" "humongous ribs" (reminiscent of the "opening credits of the *Flintstones*") that are served up "with even better sides" in a "modern", "split-level" loft; "more trendy than quality" sniff purists who also pan the service as "uneven", but it remains a "popular" choice of many for a "wonderful" "beignet brunch" or "happy hour."

Udupi Palace ⌿ *Indian/Vegetarian*

| 21 | 10 | 16 | $17 |

Berkeley | 1901-1903 University Ave. (Martin Luther King Jr. Way) | 510-843-6600 | www.udupipalaceca.com

Even "die-hard meat lovers" could "turn vegetarian" once they taste the "delicately spiced", "classic South Indian food", including "humongous" dosas and uttapams, for a "fantastic value" at this Berkeley eatery (with Mission and Sunnyvale sibs); while the surroundings are "less than palatial", they still take you on "a little trip to Bangalore, including the noise."

	FOOD	DECOR	SERVICE	COST

Uzen 🗷 *Japanese* — ▽ 24 | 15 | 19 | $33

Oakland | 5415 College Ave. (bet. Kales & Manila Aves.) | 510-654-7753

"Simple" yet "amazing" nigiri "rewards" reviewers at this "tiny", modestly priced Oakland Japanese where the "toothsome" noodles and specials are also "a hit"; since it's a "step up from your typical neighborhood sushi place", most don't mind the "sparse" surroundings or variable service.

Va de Vi *Eclectic* — 23 | 20 | 19 | $47

Walnut Creek | 1511 Mt. Diablo Blvd. (Main St.) | 925-979-0100 | www.vadevibistro.com

"Savory" Eclectic tapas "perfect for sharing" and pairing with "winning wine flights" "tempt" plenty of Walnut Creek "trendies" at this tightly packed "hot spot" where the best seats are at the "chef's counter" or outside "under the massive oak tree"; "top-notch" servers are "helpful in explaining the menu" – maybe too helpful, some warn, since those "small plates add up fast."

Venezia *Italian* — 18 | 21 | 19 | $35

Berkeley | 1799 University Ave. (Grant St.) | 510-849-4681 | www.caffevenezia.com

A "faux" piazza embellished with "murals" and even "laundry on a clothesline" creates a "festive" atmosphere at this longtime eatery that "feels like Italy, not Berkeley"; though the "service and decor outshine" the "straightforward, American-style" *cibo*, groups make it a "gathering place" since the "good-value" plates tend to "please all."

Venus *Californian* — 23 | 16 | 20 | $31

Berkeley | 2327 Shattuck Ave. (bet. Bancroft Way & Durant Ave.) | 510-540-5950 | www.venusrestaurant.net

"Take that hot grad student you want to impress but not overawe" to this Berkeley "sleeper" where "local, sustainable" Californian cuisine "pleases the palate", particularly during the "fabulous" weekend brunch; the "pre-theater" rush "can overwhelm the small kitchen" and "too-close tables" invite "eavesdropping", but loyal diners "love the warmth of the service" and the "laid-back" vibe.

Vic Stewart's 🅼 *Steak* — 21 | 22 | 22 | $61

Walnut Creek | 850 S. Broadway (bet. Mt. Diablo Blvd. & Newell Ave.) | 925-943-5666 | www.vicstewarts.com

Supping inside a 1909 Pullman dining car "makes for a romantic escape from the ordinary" (though the "other room lacks cachet") at this "classic" former Walnut Creek train depot turning out "tender, delicious" steaks; an older clientele commends the "great service" from a "handsome" staff, and while few complain it's "overpriced" for the quality, most agree it's "up to snuff."

Vik's Chaat Corner 🅼 *Indian* — 24 | 5 | 10 | $13

Berkeley | 724 Allston Way (bet. 4th & 5th Sts.) | 510-644-4412 | www.vikschaatcorner.com

"You'd swear you were in Bombay" not Berkeley at this "cheap", "barebones" and "mind-blowingly good" "street-food" lunch outpost where the "5,000,000 people who like this place" come to "chaat and chew" "the best dosa" and "bhatura cholle" (aka "the poofy thing") "this side of Madras"; the "plastic utensils" aren't likely to change, but look for "new digs" when it moves to a roomier warehouse space at 2390 Fourth Street in fall 2009; N.B. closes at 6 PM weekdays, 8 PM Saturday–Sunday.

Wente Vineyards, The Restaurant at *Californian/Mediterranean*

| 23 | 24 | 23 | $57 |

Livermore | 5050 Arroyo Rd. (Wetmore Rd.) | 925-456-2450 | www.wentevineyards.com

For a "celebration" or "finale to a day in Livermore Valley", it's worth "driving through the country" to this winery retreat "set among the vineyards" for "well-prepared", "seasonal" Cal-Med dinners (and "lovely" Sunday brunch); "terrific" service, a "world-class" wine list and summer "concert series" on the grounds "complete the package", so despite the "expensive" menu, "as the evening wears on, it's hard to leave."

☑ Wolfdale's *Californian*

| 27 | 23 | 26 | $58 |

Tahoe City | 640 N. Lake Blvd. (Grove St.) | 530-583-5700 | www.wolfdales.com

Chef Douglas Dale creates "innovative" Californian cuisine "with an Asian influence" (including "wonderful fish options") at this "must-stop on any trip to Tahoe", where dishes "beautifully presented" on "handmade pottery" are matched by what many consider "the best wine list on the Lake"; the staff is "friendly and knowledgeable", the ambiance is "dressy" and, yes, it's "expensive", but it's good to "reward yourself after a hard day of skiing"; N.B. closed Tuesdays from September–June.

Wood Tavern *Californian*

| 25 | 20 | 22 | $45 |

Oakland | 6317 College Ave. (bet. Alcatraz Ave. & 63rd St.) | 510-654-6607 | www.woodtavern.net

"More fine bistro" than "neighborhood" "tavern" – but with "no pretenses" – this "happening spot" "above the fray of College Avenue" in Oakland really "knows how to win you over" with Californian "comfort food", "super-friendly" service and bartenders who can "mix a mean cocktail", putting "higher-falutin' places to shame"; when it's "overrun by foodies", the "compact" space can get "unbelievably loud", though insiders advise it's a "bit more sane at lunch."

Xyclo *Vietnamese*

| ▽ 22 | 19 | 19 | $31 |

Oakland | 4218 Piedmont Ave. (bet. Entrada & Ridgeway Aves.) | 510-654-2681 | www.xyclorestaurant.com

"Modern Vietnamese cuisine with American sensibilities" keeps "locals" "coming back" to this "chic" eatery on Oakland's "restaurant-choked Piedmont Avenue" that's "not your" typical "joint"; a few sniff it's "ethnic food for the less adventurous", but most praise the affordable menu of "generous", "well-prepared" dishes with "creative twists."

Yankee Pier *New England/Seafood*

| 17 | 15 | 17 | $37 |

Lafayette | Lafayette Mercantile Bldg. | 3593 Mt. Diablo Blvd. (bet. Dewing Ave. & Lafayette Circle) | 925-283-4100 | www.yankeepier.com

See review in North of San Francisco Directory.

Yoshi's at Jack London Square *Japanese*

| 20 | 21 | 19 | $44 |

Oakland | Jack London Sq. | 510 Embarcadero W. (bet. Clay & Washington Sts.) | 510-238-9200 | www.yoshis.com

"Even if there weren't a jazz show to see, the food stands on its own" at this Zen dining room adjacent to Oakland's "world-class" nightclub, sporting chef Shotaro Kamio's "pricey" Japanese menu that "now goes far beyond" "beautifully prepared" sushi to include "cedar-planked fish" and other "pleasing" eats; the service can be "rushed", but since the staff can "reserve your seats before the rest of the audience gets in" for the show, it's "great for a date."

Z Zachary's Chicago Pizza *Pizza*   24 | 12 | 16 | $20
Berkeley | 1853 Solano Ave. (The Alameda) | 510-525-5950
Oakland | 5801 College Ave. (Oak Grove Ave.) | 510-655-6385
San Ramon | 3110 Crow Canyon Pl. (Crow Canyon Rd.) | 925-244-1222
www.zacharys.com
"If God were to order a pizza" it would be one of the "zantastic" pies at this East Bay "legend" claim converts who call the trio's deep-dish "gut-busters" a "religious experience" thanks to the "buttery, rich crust", "wonderful chunky-tomato sauce" and "fresh" toppings "heaped high"; since it's "always mobbed", mere mortals may want to "call ahead for takeout" or "pick up a half-baked" pie.

Zatar 🗷🗷🏳 *Mediterranean*   ▽ 22 | 17 | 18 | $38
Berkeley | 1981 Shattuck Ave. (University Ave.) | 510-841-1981 |
www.zatarrestaurant.com
Customers give kudos to the "exceptional owners" of this "intimate" Berkeley Med for their "creatively presented" dishes made with "organic fresh produce" and complemented by "appealing" nonalcoholic drinks (as well as beer and wine); most find it "satisfying", but a few dissenters dub it "a bit pricey" and are peeved by the policy of "no reservations for parties smaller than six"; N.B. open for dinner Wednesday–Saturday, lunch on Friday.

NORTH OF SAN FRANCISCO

Top Food Ratings

Excludes places with low votes, unless indicated by a ∇.

<u>29</u> Cyrus | *French*
French Laundry | *Amer./French*
<u>28</u> Sushi Ran | *Japanese*
<u>27</u> Terra | *American*
Applewood Inn | *Cal.*
Redd | *Californian*
<u>26</u> Étoile | *Californian*
La Toque | *French*
Farmhouse Inn/Rest. | *Cal.*
Ubuntu | *Californian/Vegan*

Cafe La Haye | *Amer./Cal.*
Madrona Manor | *Amer./Fr.*
El Paseo | *French*
Willi's Wine Bar | *Eclectic*
Auberge du Soleil | *Cal./French*
Picco | *Italian*
Mirepoix | *French*
Bouchon | *French*
ad hoc | *American*
Meadowood Rest.| *Cal.*

BY CUISINE

AMERICAN
<u>29</u> French Laundry
<u>27</u> Terra
<u>26</u> Cafe La Haye
Madrona Manor
ad hoc

CALIFORNIAN
<u>27</u> Applewood Inn
Redd
<u>26</u> Étoile
Farmhouse Inn/Rest.
Ubuntu

ECLECTIC
<u>26</u> Willi's Wine Bar
<u>25</u> Avatar's
<u>24</u> Willow Wood Mkt.
Celadon
<u>22</u> Go Fish

FRENCH
<u>29</u> Cyrus
<u>26</u> La Toque
El Paseo
Mirepoix
Bouchon

ITALIAN
<u>26</u> Picco
<u>25</u> Santi
zazu
Bottega
Cook St. Helena

JAPANESE
<u>28</u> Sushi Ran
<u>24</u> Hana Japanese
<u>23</u> Osake/Sake 'O∇
<u>21</u> Robata Grill∇

MEDITERRANEAN
<u>25</u> Insalata's
<u>24</u> Willow Wood Mkt.
Central Market
Underwood Bar
El Dorado Kitchen

SEAFOOD/STEAK
<u>25</u> Hog Island Oyster
<u>24</u> Willi's Seafood
Cole's Chop House
<u>23</u> Fish
Press

BY SPECIAL FEATURE

BREAKFAST/BRUNCH
<u>26</u> Auberge du Soleil
<u>25</u> Downtown Bakery
<u>24</u> Willow Wood Mkt.
<u>22</u> Alexis Baking Co.
<u>19</u> Dipsea Cafe

CHILD-FRIENDLY
<u>23</u> Fish
<u>22</u> Taylor's Automatic
Azzurro Pizzeria
<u>21</u> Pizzeria Tra Vigne
Pizza Antica

OUTDOOR SEATING

26 Étoile
Madrona Manor
Auberge du Soleil
Martini House
24 Tra Vigne

PEOPLE-WATCHING

26 Bouchon
Martini House
25 Bottega
Mustards Grill
23 Bistro Don Giovanni

ROMANCE

29 Cyrus
27 Terra
26 Étoile
Madrona Manor
El Paseo

SMALL PLATES

26 Willi's Wine Bar
Picco

24 Willi's Seafood
Underwood Bar
21 Monti's Rotisserie

TASTING MENUS

27 French Laundry
Redd
26 Étoile
La Toque
Meadowood Rest.

WINE BARS

26 Étoile
La Toque
Willi's Wine Bar
Martini House
19 Bounty Hunter

WINNING WINE LISTS

29 Cyrus
French Laundry
27 Terra
26 Meadowood Rest.
Martini House

BY LOCATION

MARIN COUNTY

28 Sushi Ran
26 El Paseo
Picco
25 Marché aux Fleurs
Avatar's

MENDOCINO COUNTY

25 Cafe Beaujolais
Albion River Inn
24 Mendo Bistro
Moosse Café
23 955 Ukiah

NAPA COUNTY

29 French Laundry
27 Terra
Redd
26 Étoile
La Toque

SONOMA COUNTY

29 Cyrus
26 Farmhouse Inn/Rest.
Cafe La Haye
Madrona Manor
Willi's Wine Bar

Top Decor

28	Auberge du Soleil
27	Cyrus
	French Laundry
	Madrona Manor
26	Farm
	Bottega
	Étoile
	El Paseo
25	Meadowood Rest.
	Press

Murray Circle
Dry Creek Kitchen
Martini House
Tra Vigne
John Ash & Co.
Albion River Inn

24	Poggio
	Terra
	Farmhouse Inn/Rest.
	Brix

Top Service

28	Cyrus
	French Laundry
26	Meadowood Rest.
	La Toque
	Madrona Manor
	El Paseo
	Étoile
	Auberge du Soleil
25	Farmhouse Inn/Rest.
	Applewood Inn

LaSalette
Albion River Inn

24	Marché aux Fleurs
	Syrah
	Terra
	Cafe La Haye
	ad hoc
	Redd
	Bottega
	Press

Best Buys

In order of Bang for the Buck rating.

1. In-N-Out
2. Cheese Steak Shop
3. La Boulange
4. Downtown Bakery
5. Jimtown Store
6. Sol Food
7. Avatar's
8. Joe's Taco
9. Taylor's Automatic
10. Barney's
11. Model Bakery
12. Alexis Baking Co.
13. Emporio Rulli
14. Emmy's Spaghetti
15. Asqew Grill
16. Amici's Pizzeria
17. Bovolo
18. Della Fattoria
19. Pizzeria Picco
20. Dipsea Cafe

OTHER GOOD VALUES

Azzuro Pizzeria
Betty's Fish & Chips
Bovolo
Café Citti
Fish
Hopmonk Tavern

Las Camelias
Pacific Catch
Pizza Antica
Pizzeria Tra Vigne
Table Café
Willow Wood Mkt.

North of San Francisco

Z ad hoc *American* | 26 | 20 | 24 | $57 |

Yountville | 6476 Washington St. (bet. Mission & Oak Circle) | 707-944-2487 | www.adhocrestaurant.com

"All hail" this "not-so-poor man's French Laundry" in a former Yountville diner where Thomas Keller "lets his hair down" and channels his "Midwestern roots" into a "family-style" prix fixe; the game of "menu roulette pays off in spades" as the "bottomless plates" of American classics ("sublime fried chicken on alternating Mondays") reflect the "same genius", "out-of-this-world ingredients" and "impeccable service (albeit in khakis, not black pants)" as at its siblings; thankfully, it's now as "'temporary' as income tax", and has "added Sunday brunch" to boot; N.B. closed Tuesday–Wednesday.

NEW AKA Bistro **M** *American* | ▽ 21 | 18 | 20 | $44 |

St. Helena | 1320 Main St. (Hunt Ave.) | 707-967-8111 | www.akabistro.com

LA's Robert Simon "takes his Bistro 45 magic to St. Helena" at this "up-Valley" upstart where the "artistic" yet "solid" New American menu is complemented by the "remade" surroundings of the old Keller Brothers Meats shop, complete with restored pressed-tin ceilings and a 'Wall of Wine' housing the "world-class" selection; despite its "thoughtful" touches, though, a few find it "too expensive" to work as a "neighborhood place."

Albion River Inn *Californian* | 25 | 25 | 25 | $51 |

Albion | 3790 N. Hwy. 1 (Spring Grove Rd.) | 707-937-1919 | www.albionriverinn.com

"Million-dollar views", a "fireplace and piano music" make for "magical evenings" at this Californian "refuge" "overlooking the misty cliffs" of Albion, where the "superior" food and "unrushed" service also delight diners who "time dinner with the sunset" and "stroll the lawn afterwards"; be sure to take full advantage of the other "star" – "the bar" – stocked with "reasonably priced" "Mendocino wines" and "one of the best single-malt scotch selections this side of Scotland."

Alexis Baking Company *Bakery* | 22 | 11 | 15 | $19 |
(aka ABC)

Napa | 1517 Third St. (bet. Church & School Sts.) | 707-258-1827 | www.alexisbakingcompany.com

The place for "early breakfast with the farmers" in Napa, this "funky" "little bake shop" and daytime cafe is a real "locals' hangout", plating up "mouthwatering eggs" ("amazing" huevos rancheros) and "down-home" lunches; their pastries "will make your eyes roll to the back of your head", but so does the sometimes "clueless service", so "take-out" is often the best bet.

All Seasons Bistro **M** *Californian* | ▽ 20 | 15 | 20 | $43 |

Calistoga | 1400 Lincoln Ave. (Washington St.) | 707-942-9111 | www.allseasonsnapavalley.net

"Tucked into the top end of Napa Valley", this "easygoing" Calistogan offers "deft", "seasonal" Californian cooking that's "presented without pretense" and "surpasses" the "simple" decor; sippers say the owner's "three decades of wine service" show in the "creative list" and adjoining retail space, from which any bottle can be uncorked for only $15 extra.

Amici's East Coast Pizzeria *Pizza*

| 20 | 13 | 17 | $21 |

San Rafael | 1242 Fourth St. (bet. B & C Sts.) | 415-455-9777 | www.amicis.com
See review in City of San Francisco Directory.

Angèle *French*

| 22 | 22 | 21 | $49 |

Napa | 540 Main St. (3rd St.) | 707-252-8115 | www.angelerestaurant.com
"There's no better way to start off a wine-country weekend" than an "alfresco lunch" or dinner at this "rustic" French bistro affirm fans of its "terrific" terrace overlooking the Napa River (providing "it's warm and high tide"), "spot-on" country cooking and "killer" house wines; a few cite "haughty" treatment, but most enjoy "bumping elbows" with winemakers in the "boisterous" boathouse bar.

Annalien ⑤Ⓜ *Vietnamese*

▽ | 23 | 18 | 20 | $34 |

Napa | 1142 Main St. (bet. 1st & Pearl Sts.) | 707-224-8319
"Thank God for this Vietnamese heaven in 'Californian cuisine' country" praise patrons of this Downtown Napa "jewel", set inside "comfortable", French colonial–style surroundings; prices are "high" for the genre, but they're backed up by "efficient" service and hearty "hospitality", as "Annalien herself could not be sweeter."

ⓩ Applewood Inn & Restaurant ⑤Ⓜ *Californian*

| 27 | 23 | 25 | $44 |

Guerneville | 13555 Hwy. 116 (River Rd.) | 707-869-9093 | www.applewoodinn.com
The Gravenstein apple doesn't fall far from the tree at this "serene" Guerneville "getaway" showcasing "delicious", "imaginative" locally sourced Cal dishes matched by a "strong Russian River Valley wine list" and "attentive" service; its "country-club atmosphere" – "especially by the fire in the cool evenings" – sets the stage for a "perfect, upscale evening" "in the woods"; N.B. no relation to the South Bay pizzeria.

Asqew Grill *Californian*

| 16 | 11 | 14 | $16 |

NEW **Mill Valley** | Strawberry Vill. | 800 Redwood Hwy. (Belvedere Dr.) | 415-383-9011 | www.asqewgrill.com
See review in City of San Francisco Directory.

ⓩ Auberge du Soleil *Californian/French*

| 26 | 28 | 26 | $80 |

Rutherford | Auberge du Soleil | 180 Rutherford Hill Rd. (Silverado Trail) | 707-967-3111 | www.aubergedusoleil.com
"Unforgettable" views "overlooking the vineyards in Rutherford" are "only the beginning" at this "boutique resort nestled in the hills", where a "superb" staff serves "sensational" Cal-French cuisine complemented by "fabulous" wines in a "dreamy", fireplace-warmed dining room; if the tabs "seem so pre-Lehman", consider a "leisurely lunch" or apps at the "terrific bar", offering "all the ambiance but half the price."

AVA ⑤Ⓜ *American*

| 22 | 20 | 22 | $44 |

San Anselmo | 636 San Anselmo Ave. (Magnolia Ave.) | 415-453-3407 | www.avamarin.com
Deeming it a "worthy sibling to Marché aux Fleurs", diners praise this San Anselmo "youngster" for its "high-quality" "locally farmed" New

American food that can be savored with "sustainable" (if "obscure") wines in the "cozy" interior or "under the stars"; "knowledgeable" service and "sensible" midweek menus add extra appeal.

Avatar's ☒ Eclectic

| 25 | 12 | 23 | $20 |

Sausalito | 2656 Bridgeway (Coloma St.) | 415-332-8083

Avatar's Punjabi Burritos ⭑ Eclectic

Mill Valley | 15 Madrona St. (bet. Lovell & Throckmorton Aves.) | 415-381-8293

"Away from the throngs of sight-seers", this Sausalito "Marindian" and its Mill Valley spin-off (with just a few tables) provide "outstanding" "Punjabi burritos" "wrapped in naan" and other "original", "inexpensive" Eclectic eats; plus, "if you have a yen for a particular combination of ingredients", the "fast", "enthusiastic" staff will happily oblige.

Azzurro Pizzeria & Enoteca Pizza

| 22 | 18 | 18 | $26 |

Napa | 1260 Main St. (Clinton St.) | 707-255-5552 | www.azzurropizzeria.com

Let 'em eat pie – individual "crisp", "thin-crust wood-fired pizza", that is – along with "incredible" pastas, salads and "soft-serve" ice cream at this "unfussy" local Italian joint that's settled into its "sleek new setting" on Napa's "burgeoning Main Street"; though it gets "noisy as heck" at peak times, when it's "jammed with tourists" and locals "who get louder" as they down "big pours" of California wine, "that just makes it more festive."

Balboa Cafe American

| 19 | 17 | 18 | $35 |

NEW **Mill Valley** | 38 Miller Ave. (Presidio Ave.) | 415-381-7321 | www.plumpjack.com

See review in City of San Francisco Directory.

BarBersQ BBQ

| 22 | 17 | 20 | $33 |

Napa | Bel Aire Plaza | 3900 Bel Aire Plaza (Redwood Rd.) | 707-224-6600 | www.barbersq.com

"When you're tired of the fancy-shmancy places" in Napa, "bring the kids", "'q' up" and "get good and messy" at this "friendly" "strip-mall" barbecue joint presenting "flavorful" pulled pork, ribs and American "comfort food" laced with "local, organic" ingredients; a few blow smoke about "fine-dining" tabs for a "parking-lot-side location", but most are appeased by the "great wine list."

NEW Bardessono American

| ▽ 23 | 24 | 21 | $57 |

Yountville | Bardessono Hotel & Spa | 6526 Yount St. (bet. Finnell Rd. & Washington St.) | 707-204-6030 | www.bardessono.com

Chef Sean O'Toole's "amazing background" (Michael Mina, Mix) comes through in the "imaginative" garden-to-table New American fare served at this "subdued" Yountville arrival set in a "strikingly modern" eco-conscious luxury resort; organic spirits and natural elements such as a reclaimed cypress communal table follow the theme, and even the somewhat 'green' staff "seems to be getting its act together."

Barndiva ☒ American

| 19 | 22 | 17 | $44 |

Healdsburg | 231 Center St. (Matheson St.) | 707-431-0100 | www.barndiva.com

"MySpace meets" wide open space at this "trendy", "beautiful old barn only steps" from Healdsburg Plaza, where the "rock-your-world" "cocktails are shaken with as much love" as goes into the "creative" sustainable American eats; plenty of "twentysomethings" are taken with the atmosphere – bucolic on the patio and "pure coolness" at the bar – though "intermittent attitude" from the staff can be a buzzkill.

Barney's Gourmet Hamburgers *Burgers*   19 | 12 | 15 | $16

San Rafael | 1020 Court St. (4th St.) | 415-454-4594 | www.barneyshamburgers.com

See review in City of San Francisco Directory.

Betty's Fish & Chips 🅼 *Seafood*   ▽ 21 | 11 | 17 | $19

Santa Rosa | 4046 Sonoma Hwy. (bet. Bush Creek Rd. & Mission Blvd.) | 707-539-0899

Pond-hoppers proclaim this longtime Santa Rosa "strip-maller" "rivals the English's best" for "huge portions" of "crispy fish 'n' chips" and "heavenly" pies; the family-run shop is "not fancy nor publike", but new booths and nautical decor lend it a "casual" "coffee-shop" feel.

Bistro des Copains *French*   ▽ 25 | 19 | 24 | $42

Occidental | 3782 Bohemian Hwy. (bet. Coleman Valley & Graton Rds.) | 707-874-2436 | www.bistrodescopains.com

It's "worth the detour down dark forest roads" to this "small, quaint" bistro that dares to present "superb" wood-fired country French fare "in the shadows of the Occidental Italian behemoths"; along with its "quirkiness, character" and a "welcoming staff" that "enhances the experience", it also wins over guests with its "good-value prix fixes" and "wine bargains" such as free corkage for "Sonoma bottles" on Tuesdays.

Bistro Don Giovanni *Italian*   23 | 21 | 21 | $47

Napa | 4110 Howard Ln. (bet. Oak Knoll & Salvador Aves.) | 707-224-3300 | www.bistrodongiovanni.com

"Packed to the gun walls every night" with "winemakers" and "tourists" "enjoying themselves", this "not-so-secret" Napa stop offers "excellent" Italian cooking surrounded by an "idyllic" "vineyard setting"; many savor "blissful" meals out on the terrace, though a few soured surveyors gripe about the "noise of the rabble trying to get the attention of the servers", and cite "rosé colored glasses" for boosting its rep.

🆉 Bistro Jeanty *French*   25 | 22 | 23 | $51

Yountville | 6510 Washington St. (Mulberry St.) | 707-944-0103 | www.bistrojeanty.com

Guests go gaga for this "Gallic treasure" in Yountville where the "robust" "culinary flair" of chef-owner Philippe Jeanty always "resonates" (the "tomato soup is legendary") and the "rustic" surroundings, including a "communal table" and "pleasant" patio, benefit from "warm" service (all the way to "the *au revoir* when you depart"); fortunately it's "free of the pretension and cost" of other "Washington Street" stars and, heck, "sometimes you only need three courses."

Bistro Ralph 🅂 *Californian/French*   23 | 19 | 23 | $45

Healdsburg | 109 Plaza St. (Healdsburg Ave.) | 707-433-1380 | www.bistroralph.com

"You can always find Ralph in the kitchen" or serving the "biggest, baddest martinis in town" at his "quality" "Healdsburg institution" that's been "doin'" the Cal-French bistro thing since the early '90s, with some "refreshing" new turns of late; for a "lively" repast, "sit at the bar" and chat up "winemakers" and the "colorful" longtime staff, or head outside for lunch "overlooking the town square."

Boca *Argentinean/Steak* 22 | 22 | 21 | $43

Novato | 340 Ignacio Blvd. (Rte. 101) | 415-883-0901 | www.bocasteak.com
"One of the few restaurants in Novato that doesn't feel like Novato", George Morrone's "carnivore heaven" sets a "metropolitan" mood for "top-notch" Argentinean steaks - complemented by "excellent empanadas" and "duck-fat fries" - that call to customers "when I can afford both the cholesterol and the prices"; some cite "inconsistency" all around, but the "half-price" happy hour eats help keep it an "excellent value for the buck."

Boon Fly Café *Californian* 22 | 20 | 20 | $32

Napa | Carneros Inn | 4048 Sonoma Hwy. (Los Carneros Ave.) | 707-299-4900 | www.thecarnerosinn.com
A "terrific" "take-out or take-in" stop on the Southern Napa trail, this "funky" "red barn on the grounds of the Carneros Inn" proffers "killer" Californian "comfort food" ("breakfast thru dinner") and local vino "without any wine-country hype"; service can get "strained" by the brunch crowds, but both the wait and the "doughnut holes served hot out of the fryer" are "worth the years they take off your life."

Boonville Hotel *Californian* 22 | 19 | 21 | $42

Boonville | Boonville Hotel | 14050 Hwy. 128 (Lambert Ln.) | 707-895-2210 | www.boonvillehotel.com
Rising like a mirage off Highway 128, this Boonville hotel restaurant in a lovingly restored 1864 building rewards weekenders "on the way to the Mendocino Coast" with "simple" but "memorable" Californian dishes and "awesome local wines"; the "congenial" staff operates on "hippie time" - it's "the boonies" after all - but the "cozy" Shaker-style room and "lovely garden" allow for leisurely dinners; N.B. closed Tuesday–Wednesday; hours change seasonally, so call ahead.

Z NEW Bottega *Italian* 25 | 26 | 24 | $53

Yountville | V Mktpl. | 6525 Washington St. (Yount St.) | 707-945-1050 | www.botteganapavalley.com
"Spirited" TV personality Michael Chiarello "does it again" at his latest off-air venture, set in a vintage Yountville winery, crafting "sublime", "rustic" Italian chow and "workin'" the "beautiful" room; service is "on the ball", prices are "unbelievably reasonable" and the "buzz" is building, so "make reservations" or plan on cooling your jets on the "rockin'" covered terrazzo tricked out with two wood-burning fireplaces.

Z Bouchon ❂ *French* 26 | 23 | 23 | $56

Yountville | 6534 Washington St. (Yount St.) | 707-944-8037 | www.bouchonbistro.com
Guests "get the 'Keller experience'" at more "approachable" prices via this "exquisite alternative" to the French Laundry in Yountville, providing "delectable" French fare amid "boisterous" surroundings that "nail the look and feel" of a "Paris bistro", complete with a "wonderful zinc oyster bar" and newly opened patio for dinner; a "hard-working" staff and "real treats" from the bakery next door help keep it "packed to the brim" from lunch to "late-night."

	FOOD	DECOR	SERVICE	COST

Bounty Hunter *BBQ*
19 18 19 $31

Napa | 975 First St. (Main St.) | 707-226-3976 | www.bountyhunterwine.com
"Wine is definitely the focus" at this "Wild West-like" Napa option where diners fill up on fairly "standard" barbecue (including specialties like "tender beer-can chicken") matched with vintages from the "fab", 400-strong list by "bottle jockeys" who "know" their *terroir*; still, many feel the service "isn't stellar" and the room could be more "comfortable", but those hankering for a "hangout" say it has a "nice vibe."

Bovolo *Italian*
24 13 16 $23

Healdsburg | Copperfield's Bookstore | 106 Matheson St. (Healdsburg Ave.) | 707-431-2962 | www.bovolorestaurant.com
"Pork lovers are in hog heaven" at zazu's "informal" "little sister" (more of a "lunch-stand sorta thing") in the "back of Copperfield's Bookstore" in Healdsburg, where you can "get your pig on" over "astounding" "bacon-laden breakfasts", "flavorful" pizzas and "housemade salumi" for "very little money"; some snort about "spaced-out counter service" and "zero" ambiance inside, but contented customers give props to the "wonderful" back patio; N.B. closes at 6 PM Monday–Thursday (often later in the summer) and 8 PM Friday–Sunday.

Brannan's Grill *American/French*
20 22 19 $40

Calistoga | 1374 Lincoln Ave. (Washington St.) | 707-942-2233 | www.brannansgrill.com
"Elegant but with a casual attitude", this "old boys' club" Calistogan is "frequented by winemakers" who wash down the "basic" meaty American-French fare ("great once it arrives!") with California trophy vino; some like to "grab a window table and watch the world go by", while others prefer the "happening bar and live music scene" on weekends.

Brix *Californian/Mediterranean*
22 24 21 $50

(fka 25º Brix Restaurant & Gardens)
Napa | 7377 St. Helena Hwy. (Yount Mill Rd.) | 707-944-2749 | www.25degreesbrix.com
"Amazing" "vineyard views" delight at this "revived" Napa standby where chef Anne Gingrass-Paik creates "colorful" Cal-Med meals from "backyard"-grown ingredients; some critics cite "average" service and food that "costs more than it should", but others purr the "wine list is beyond compare" since the adjacent shop lets you drink at "retail prices."

☑ Buckeye Roadhouse *American/BBQ*
23 23 22 $46

Mill Valley | 15 Shoreline Hwy. (Hwy. 101) | 415-331-2600 | www.buckeyeroadhouse.com
"One of *the* icons of Marin's fabled history", this "inviting" Mill Valley roadhouse with a "mountain-lodge" feel "keeps on truckin'" thanks to house-smoked "down 'n' dirty" BBQ ribs and other "spot-on" New American eats with an "upscale twist"; you'll feel welcome in "hiking boots or a tux", and though rezzies are a "hard ticket" on the weekends, it's worth a stop if only for "oysters Bingo" at the "hopping bar."

Bungalow 44 *American*
21 18 19 $45

Mill Valley | 44 E. Blithedale Ave. (Sunnyside Ave.) | 415-381-2500 | www.bungalow44.com
Run by the "same peeps as the Buckeye", this Mill Valley "meeting place" has the formula "down", serving "solid" New American eats "just

slightly lighter than comfort fare" in an Arts and Crafts bungalow exuding "old-school style" and a "definite buzz"; the "wild bar scene" (attracting "beautiful 40-year-old women who look 30") amps up the "decibels", but there's "more quiet and ambiance" out on the "convertible patio with a fireplace."

Cacti Grill *Southwestern* ▽ 19 | 18 | 19 | $32

Novato | 1200 Grant Ave. (2nd St.) | 415-898-2234 | www.cactigrill.com
"Hearty", "reasonable" Southwestern food and margaritas served in a former "Spanish colonial church" appeal to plenty of "groups" at this "longtime favorite" in Novato; while advocates say "attentive service" and a "nice bar" make it "elegant enough for date night", others assert it's "old and tired" but "seems to just roll along."

Cafe Beaujolais *Californian/French* 25 | 21 | 22 | $54

Mendocino | 961 Ukiah St. (School St.) | 707-937-5614 |
www.cafebeaujolais.com
"Despite a number of ownership changes since Margaret Fox held court here", this "Mendocino must" "carries on the tradition", presenting "innovative", "super-flavorful" Cal-French cuisine, "wonderful homemade breads" and "fine wines" in an "old Victorian" home staffed by "caring" servers; diehards declare "it's nothing like it was", but now enhanced with an outdoor patio and regular lunch service, it remains a "winner" among "locals and visitors."

Cafe Citti *Italian* 22 | 13 | 19 | $27

Kenwood | 9049 Sonoma Hwy./Hwy. 12 (Shaw Ave.) | 707-833-2690
"Right off the Sonoma Highway", this "low-key" "roadhouse in rural Kenwood" is a "bargain" for "picnic foods" or a "spontaneous" meal of "phenomenal roast chicken and Caesar" among other "garlicky" Tuscan eats, particularly if you "BYO from one of the nearby wineries"; there's "not much ambiance inside" the "deli-style" digs ("you pick it", they "bring it"), but there's a "cute garden with tables in the back."

Café Gratitude *Vegan* 16 | 15 | 17 | $24

San Rafael | 2200 Fourth St. (bet. Alexander Ave. & Santa Margarita Dr.) |
415-824-4652 | www.cafegratitude.com
See review in City of San Francisco Directory.

Cafe La Haye 🅢🅜 *American/Californian* 26 | 19 | 24 | $51

Sonoma | 140 E. Napa St. (bet. E. 1st & 2nd Sts.) | 707-935-5994 |
www.cafelahaye.com
"Sure as sunshine in California", this "treasure" "off the main square" that "doubles as a gallery" "churns out" arguably "the best" Cal-New American in Sonoma – "and that ain't hay"; the "chalkboard menu", "choreographed" staff and "unreal" bottles for "fair prices" make it "worthy of its wine-country cred", so if you wonder "how they can accomplish this with 35 seats" and a "postage stamp–size" open kitchen, make rezzies and "watch the magic as it's performed."

Cafe Saint Rose 🅜 *Californian/Mediterranean* ▽ 23 | 15 | 20 | $40

Sebastopol | 9890 Bodega Hwy. (Montgomery Rd.) | 707-829-5898 |
www.cafesaintrose.com
Despite a "remote location", this "quirky" "roadside dive" "west of Sebastopol" (relocated from Santa Rosa), with LPs on the "record

player" and "old movies projected on the wall", lures locals and "even a celeb or two" with its "astonishingly sophisticated", "farmer's market-sourced" Cal-Med dinners; service is on the "laid-back" side, and since half of the seating is "on the patio out back", it's "best to go when the weather is good"; N.B. closed Monday–Tuesday.

Caprice, The Ⓜ *American* — ▽ 21 | 25 | 23 | $61

Tiburon | 2000 Paradise Dr. (Mar W. St.) | 415-435-3400 | www.thecaprice.com

For an "incredible view of the Golden Gate Bridge" accompanied by "well-prepared" (if "pricey") food, "you can't go wrong" at this "gracious" Tiburon New American with an "amazing location right on the water"; it's been HQ for "quiet, romantic dinners" since 1964, but some insist "if you haven't been here in the past few years, you need to revisit it"; N.B. under a new chef/co-owner, the restaurant is set to close for a remodel in October and reopen with a less expensive seafood-oriented menu.

Carneros Bistro & Wine Bar *Californian* — ▽ 23 | 21 | 22 | $50

Sonoma | The Lodge at Sonoma | 1325 Broadway (bet. Clay St. & Leveroni Rd.) | 707-931-2042 | www.thelodgeatsonoma.com

"Inspired" chef Janine Falvo "pulls food from the adjacent garden" to prepare her "whimsical", "upscale" breakfasts, lunches and "porkalicious" dinners, matched by a "great" local wine list, at this "delightful" Lodge at Sonoma Californian that's a "big step up from the typical hotel" restaurant; a few find the dining room "a bit corporate", but others revel in enjoying "fine service" while "wearing jeans."

Celadon *American/Eclectic* — 24 | 21 | 23 | $49

Napa | The Historic Napa Mill | 500 Main St. (5th St.) | 707-254-9690 | www.celadonnapa.com

A Downtown pioneer, Greg Cole's "treasure" in the historic Napa Mill complex still delivers "innovative", "high-quality" New American-Eclectic "comfort food" and "excellent" service at relatively "reasonable" "wine-country prices"; whether you savor "handcrafted cocktails at the bar", dinner in the "modern" dining room or a weekday lunch by the outdoor fireplace ("when the weather cooperates"), it's a "favorite" that will likely "improve" when the construction by the nearby river walk is finished.

Central Market *Californian/Mediterranean* — 24 | 19 | 22 | $43

Petaluma | 42 Petaluma Blvd. N. (Western Ave.) | 707-778-9900 | www.centralmarketpetaluma.com

The evening's "commute traffic is bearable knowing that a dinner here is the reward" attest Petaluma patrons who brake for this "homespun temple" of Cal-Med Slow Food, where "anything from the wood-fired oven" or otherwise "conjured" in the open kitchen is bound to please; the atmosphere of the "old" brick building "hums with good vibes", enhanced by "friendly" service and an "eclectic", "well-priced" selection of "local" wines.

Chapter & Moon Ⓜ *American* — ▽ 22 | 15 | 18 | $31

Fort Bragg | 32150 N. Harbor Dr. (S. Main St.) | 707-962-1643

"You'd never guess it from the looks of this place", "hidden among the trailers at the butt-end of the wharf", but this "easygoing" all-day Fort

Bragg cafe serving a limited menu of "hearty", "seafood-oriented chow", "simple American breakfasts" and "fresh-baked" bread "right on the bay" offers the "best value in the Mendocino area"; nobody's mooning over the "funky" decor, but it "clearly survives on the quality of the food."

Charcuterie *French*

22 | 17 | 21 | $37

Healdsburg | Healdsburg Plaza | 335 Healdsburg Ave. (Plaza St.) | 707-431-7213

A "sleeper" in Healdsburg, this little piggy goes to town serving "terrific" French bistro "classics" ("starring a huge charcuterie plate" that's "perfect to pack up"), "good local wines" and "incredible desserts"; it may "seem about one server short", but offers lots of "value" when you want to "line your stomach before" or after "wine tasting."

Cheese Steak Shop *Cheesesteaks*

23 | 6 | 14 | $11

NEW **Santa Rosa** | 750 Stony Point Rd. (bet. Hwy. 12 & Sebastopol Rd.) | 707-527-9877 | www.cheesesteakshop.com

See review in City of San Francisco Directory.

Cindy's Backstreet Kitchen *American/Californian*

24 | 20 | 23 | $45

St. Helena | 1327 Railroad Ave. (bet. Adams St. & Hunt Ave.) | 707-963-1200 | www.cindysbackstreetkitchen.com

Customers "can't say enough" about this "outstanding" Cal-New American in St. Helena where chef-owner Cindy Pawlcyn (Go Fish, Mustards Grill) creates "comfort food" "at its finest" in a "breezy", "down-home setting"; "guest bartenders" and "gentle markups" ensure a "winemaker" following, but "tourists who wander in" are amazed to discover one of the "most relaxing" and least pretentious perches in Napa.

Cole's Chop House *Steak*

24 | 21 | 23 | $65

Napa | 1122 Main St. (bet. 1st & Pearl Sts.) | 707-224-6328 | www.coleschophouse.com

This "big-city steakhouse in the country" by co-owner Greg Cole (Celadon) delivers "top-notch" aged cuts as well as "fantastic hash browns" and "martinis to die for" in a "high-energy", "beautiful old stone building" overlooking Downtown's Napa Creek; with "wonderful" service too, it's a fine place to "bring those beefy reds you've been drinking all day", or take a crack at the "incredible", if "pricey", wine list.

Cook St. Helena *Italian*

25 | 16 | 22 | $39

St. Helena | 1310 Main St. (Hunt Ave.) | 707-963-7088

"Watch St. Helena go by" while "surrounded by winemakers and locals" who fill every seat at this "tiny" but "big-hearted" "find" for "honest" Northern Italian food "like grandma made" and vino that "won't break the bank"; despite somewhat "cramped" tables, it's prized as an "unpretentious" "alternative to the big, splashy restaurants in the valley"; N.B. Sundays are dinner-only.

Cottage Eatery 🅼 *Californian*

▽ 23 | 14 | 21 | $41

Tiburon | 114 Main St. (Tiburon Blvd.) | 415-789-5636 | www.thecottageeatery.com

Tucked away at the end of Tiburon's Ark Row in a "converted houseboat", this "plain" but "cozy" cookery is helmed by a "delightful" cou-

	FOOD	DECOR	SERVICE	COST

ple whose Med-influenced, "market-fresh" Californian fare is "sophisticated and earthy at the same time"; while some feel the "focused" menu means "limited appeal", most consider it a "bargain find" for some of the "best food in Southern Marin"; N.B. now serving lunch Tuesday–Saturday.

Cucina Paradiso ⊠ *Italian* | 24 | 18 | 23 | $38 |

Petaluma | 114 Petaluma Blvd. N. (Western Ave.) | 707-782-1130 | www.cucinaparadisopetaluma.com
"The dons are quivering" (or ought to be) since this formerly "unknown" Petaluma trattoria worked up the "swagger" to move into "bigger", more "beautiful" digs on the main drag that better complement its "feather-light", "housemade pastas" among other "outstanding" Southern Italian dishes "done right"; add in a "helpful" staff and "kind-to-the-wallet" cost, and it's "one of the best deals near the wine country."

Cucina Restaurant & Wine Bar Ⓜ *Italian* | 23 | 16 | 21 | $38 |

San Anselmo | 510 San Anselmo Ave. (Tunstead Ave.) | 415-454-2942 | www.cucinarestaurantandwinebar.com
Exuding an "urban cafe feel in suburban Marin", this "popular" mid-priced trattoria and wine bar in San Anselmo (an offshoot of SF's Jackson Fillmore) can be counted on for "reliable", "wood-oven" Southern Italian "basics" and "charming Jack K. around to talk you into a good bottle of wine"; despite "lacking" decor, some fans would go there for the "warm, foamy zabaglione" alone.

Cuvée *American* | 21 | 21 | 21 | $45 |

Napa | 1650 Soscol Ave. (Vallejo St.) | 707-224-2330 | www.cuveenapa.com
"Wrapped around a fabulous courtyard", this budding Napa American is a "pleasant surprise" for both "locals" and nearby "hotel guests", delivering "delicious" dishes in a "chic", "Zen" atmosphere; service is "chipper" and the "bar is always hopping", offering "nice specials" and local wines on tap, plus live music on Thursdays in season.

ⓩ Cyrus *French* | 29 | 27 | 28 | $133 |

Healdsburg | 29 North St. (Healdsburg Ave.) | 707-433-3311 | www.cyrusrestaurant.com
"Champagne wishes and caviar dreams" really "do come true" (and on carts) at this "luscious" Healdsburg "palace of gastronomy" where chef/co-owner Douglas Keane ushers forth "transcendental" New French prix fixes and "grand tastings" laced with "unique Asian-fusion flavors", "exceptionally" served with tableside "theatrics" in an "ornate" dining room "worthy of Paris"; abandon "all thoughts of sticking to a budget", but it's "a steal" considering you're getting "dinner and a show" that "should be called 'Sigh-rus'!"; P.S. à la carte dishes and "splendid drinks" are available at the bar.

Della Fattoria | 24 | 16 | 17 | $25 |
Downtown Café Ⓜ *Bakery/Eclectic*

Petaluma | 141 Petaluma Blvd. N. (bet. Washington St. & Western Ave.) | 707-763-0161 | www.dellafattoria.com
"The closest thing to a European cafe" in Petaluma, this "family-owned" bakery sates its "huge cult following" with "destination-worthy" artisan breads and "otherworldly" desserts; it's also an "excellent" choice for breakfast or a self-serve lunch, with an Eclectic menu of "delicious"

soups, salads and "lattes served in a bowl" that may seem "expensive compared with standard deli fare – but it's in a different league entirely"; N.B. stays open for dinner on Fridays.

Della Santina's *Italian* | 21 | 19 | 20 | $38 |

Sonoma | 133 E. Napa St. (1st St.) | 707-935-0576 | www.dellasantinas.com
"When the Italian spirit moves you, there's no better place for handmade pasta" paired with "wonderful wine" than this "comfortable" Tuscan trattoria off Sonoma Plaza "specializing in rotisserie meats" and "gnocchi better than nonna's"; true, there may be "nothing extraordinary" about the "simply prepared" Lucca-style chow, but enjoying a midpriced "summer lunch or dinner" on the "delightful" vine-covered courtyard, overseen by a "lovely" owner exuding "old-style friendliness", feels "like being on vacation."

Diavola Pizzeria & Salumeria *Italian* | ▽ 24 | 18 | 22 | $32 |

Geyserville | 21021 Geyserville Ave. (Hwy. 128) | 707-814-0111 | www.diavolapizzeria.com
Chef/co-owner "Dino Bugica and his wood oven will blow your mind" "ooh and aah" Italophiles about this "casual" Geyserville pizza joint that produces "perfect crusts", "even better antipasto" and "incredible salumi" you'd "swear was flown in from Florence"; conceived as a midpriced "spin-off of Santi" (soon to relocate to Santa Rosa), it's been "discovered by tourists" and locals alike who aren't "embarrassed to drink its jug wine in the heart of wine country."

Dipsea Cafe, The *American* | 19 | 15 | 17 | $22 |

Mill Valley | 200 Shoreline Hwy./Hwy. 1 (Tennessee Valley Rd.) | 415-381-0298 | www.dipseacafe.com
For a "reliable" "carbo-load" "on your way to the beach" or before a "trek up Mt. Tam", "you can't beat" this "quintessential breakfast place" in Mill Valley where "all of Marin comes" to feast on "fluffy pancakes", "eggs Benedict and fresh OJ" as well as "homey, filling" American dinners; "expect a lot of kids" and "long waits on weekends", though "views of the river and passing bicycle racers" help pass the time.

Downtown Bakery & Creamery ⊄ *Bakery* | 25 | 13 | 17 | $17 |

Healdsburg | 308A Center St. (Matheson St.) | 707-431-2719 | www.downtownbakery.net
"Sugar-aholics" "can't pass by" this "old-fashioned" "little bakery" that's "deservedly famous" for its "phenomenal" pastries – including "some of the stickiest sticky buns" – and "artisanal" breads fashioned from "local ingredients"; there's "no atmosphere" and "limited" seating, but affordable prices and some of Healdsburg's "best breakfasts" and "light lunches" (including "wonderful to-go sandwiches for picnics") more than compensate; N.B. not open for dinner.

Drake's Beach Café ⓜ *Californian* | ▽ 21 | 14 | 17 | $27 |

Inverness | Point Reyes National Seashore | 1 Drake's Beach Rd. (Sir Francis Drake Blvd.) | 415-669-1297
Surf-seekers say "hats off to the creative staffers" transforming this "funky", weather-beaten National Park Service cafe "by the seashore" into much "more than a beach shack"; the "fresh, organic" Californian lunches are a "cut above usual snack bar" fare, but what's really "worth the trip" to the Inverness coast are the affordable Friday-

	FOOD	DECOR	SERVICE	COST

Saturday prix fixe dinners (reservations required) that "seem extra comforting when the fog rolls in."

NEW Dreamfarm *American*   - | - | - | M
(fka Fork)

San Anselmo | 198 Sir Francis Drake Blvd. (bet. Bank St. & Tunstead Ave.) | 415-453-9898 | www.dreamfarmmarin.com

The latest attempt to keep the dream behind the now-shuttered Fork alive, this casual San Anselmo redux of the cozy, two-room storefront offers an à la carte menu of New American comfort food (think spaghetti and meatballs and chicken and dumplings) sourced from the same local farms, dairies and fisheries, but with prices that better reflect these recession-minded times (topping out at $20), complemented by a dialed-down, small-producer wine list.

Dry Creek Kitchen *American*   24 | 25 | 23 | $69

Healdsburg | Hotel Healdsburg | 317 Healdsburg Ave. (Matheson St.) | 707-431-0330 | www.charliepalmer.com

In a town teeming with "choice restaurants", Charlie Palmer's "high-end" New American in "beautiful" Healdsburg "stands out" with its "imaginative", "exceptional tasting menus" (and à la carte dishes) prepared with "fresh local ingredients", as well as "attentive service" and an "enchanting courtyard" overlooking the Plaza; "free corkage" on Sonoma bottles "helps keep the bill tolerable", and if a few feel you're "up a creek" if the "famous chef" isn't around, most agree this is a "top-class" "California dining experience."

Duck Club, The *American*   19 | 20 | 20 | $50

Bodega Bay | Bodega Bay Lodge & Spa | 103 S. Hwy. 1 (Doran Park Rd.) | 707-875-3525 | www.bodegabaylodge.com

See review in South of San Francisco Directory.

E&O Trading Company *SE Asian*   19 | 21 | 19 | $38

Larkspur | 2231 Larkspur Landing Circle (Sir Francis Drake Blvd.) | 415-925-0303 | www.eotrading.com

See review in City of San Francisco Directory.

El Dorado Kitchen *Californian/Mediterranean*   24 | 23 | 22 | $47

Sonoma | El Dorado Hotel | 405 First St. W. (Spain St.) | 707-996-3030 | www.eldoradosonoma.com

There's culinary "gold in them thar hills" – or at least "on the square" in Sonoma's El Dorado Hotel – report regulars of this "friendly" "favorite" where the "amazing truffle fries" elicit swoons ("did I tell you that they're heaven?"); "creative, ever-changing" Cal-Med meals and an "outstanding" "wine list that takes advantage of the local vineyards" can be enjoyed in the "cool, modern" dining room or on the "exquisite patio" "under the shade of a fig tree", while the "new" adjacent cafe "features live music" and picnic fixin's.

NEW Elements Restaurant &   ▽ 22 | 20 | 21 | $43
Enoteca *Californian/Mediterranean*

Napa | 1400 Second St. (Franklin St.) | 707-224-4518 | www.elementsnapa.com

Elements of California and the Mediterranean inspire the "quite good and imaginative" (sometimes "too creative") "small plates" at this

FOOD | DECOR | SERVICE | COST

"new" Downtown Napa enoteca and wine shop stocking more than 60 international wines "by the glass" or for retail; "you can really run up the tab if you're not careful" and a few quibble that "service needs improvement", but the modern storefront (formerly Pizza Azzurro) already gets as "crowded" and "noisy" as a "college cafeteria before a big game."

⚡ El Paseo Ⓜ French
26 | 26 | 26 | $77

Mill Valley | 17 Throckmorton Ave. (Blithedale Ave.) | 415-388-0741 | www.elpaseorestaurant.com

"Romance is in the air" at this "lovely" "prix fixe gem" hidden down a Mill Valley "brick alley", where the "amazing" French fare with a "contemporary Japanese" flair is matched only by a wine list "deeper than the ocean" and a staff that really "rocks the service"; a few scoff at "Tokyo prices" and call it "pretentious (with a capital P)", but most agree it's "still tops"; N.B. closed Monday–Tuesday.

Emmy's Spaghetti Shack Italian
21 | 17 | 19 | $23

NEW **Sonoma** | 691 Broadway (Andrieux St.) | 707-933-3823 | www.emmysspaghettishack.com

See review in City of San Francisco Directory.

Emporio Rulli Dessert/Italian
22 | 21 | 17 | $24

Larkspur | 464 Magnolia Ave. (bet. Cane & Ward Sts.) | 415-924-7478 | www.rulli.com

"Until the person next to you says something like 'awesome, dude'", "you truly feel you're in Rome" at this "real-deal" (and "reasonably priced") Italian bakery/cafe – particularly while "sipping espresso" and nibbling "amazing" cookies; while Larkspur's "gleaming counters" spotlight "sinfully delicious" pastries and panini and the Union Square enoteca is a "people-watching" mecca, the Marina outlet ups the ante with "sublime" guest-chef dinners served under "gorgeous" frescoed ceilings; and though cynics suggest "service needs work", no matter: this is "pure decadence."

NEW Estate Californian/Italian
▽ 20 | 26 | 24 | $52

Sonoma | 400 W. Spain St. (W. 4th St.) | 707-933-3663 | www.estate-sonoma.com

La dolce vita is alive and well at this Downtown Sonoma newcomer from Sondra Bernstein (of the girl & the fig), which lures wine-country diners with an "attentive staff" and "terrific", midpriced Cal-Italian antipasti, pizzas and cocktails; while a few feel it "hasn't found its stride", the "beautifully revamped" Victorian farmhouse setting (formerly the General's Daughter) wins kudos for its oversized photos of Italian cinema icons, "intimate tables" and wraparound porch perfect for warm-weather dinners and brunch.

⚡ Étoile Californian
26 | 26 | 26 | $79

Yountville | Domaine Chandon Winery | 1 California Dr. (Solano Ave.) | 707-944-2892 | www.chandon.com

For a "wow experience in the heart of wine country", "foodies" flock to this Domaine Chandon Winery "winner" and revel in the "total package": "wonderful" Californian à la carte and tasting menus with "intelligent pairings", "spot-on service", a "romantic, intimate dining room" and a "beautiful" terrace with "fabulous views" for lunch and "bubbly"; somehow, it's often "overlooked", which is "not a bad thing" say

	FOOD	DECOR	SERVICE	COST

Yountville "locals" who dodge "pricey" tabs with deals like the '$29 on HWY 29' two-course lunch; N.B. jackets recommended in the evening.

⚡ Farm *American*

	24	26	23	$62

Napa | Carneros Inn | 4048 Sonoma Hwy. (Los Carneros Ave.) | 707-299-4882 | www.thecarnerosinn.com

"From cocktails outside in front of the fire to the perfect dinner menu", this "idyllic" "gem" in the Carneros Inn manages to be "elegant and casual at the same time"; enthusiasts "enjoy the Napa ambiance" while indulging in "terrific", "locally sourced" New American fare and "half bottles" of area vintages, generally shrugging off "pricey" tabs since, after all, this is what "wine country chic should be."

⚡ Farmhouse Inn & Restaurant *Californian*

	26	24	25	$72

Forestville | Farmhouse Inn | 7871 River Rd. (bet. Trenton & Wohler Rds.) | 707-887-3300 | www.farmhouseinn.com

For one of the "finest restaurants in Sonoma" with the least "pretension", "city folks" follow the long and "windy road" through the "rural Russian River Valley" to dine at this "romantic", "stately manor house" in Forestville; the "pricey but fabulous" Californian dinners (including "rabbit three ways – and all of them should worry Bugs") are "exquisite" down to the "outstanding" "cheese cart" and "wine pairings", plus "you couldn't ask for better service"; N.B. closed Tuesday–Wednesday.

fig cafe & winebar *French*

	24	20	23	$38

Glen Ellen | 13690 Arnold Dr. (bet. Carmel Ave. & Odonnell Ln.) | 707-938-2130 | www.thefigcafe.com

A rare "hot spot" in "quaint Glen Ellen", this "always busy" cafe "with a focus on affordability" is "every bit the delight as big sister" girl & the fig (and "less touristy"); the "no corkage policy" keeps it packed with diners digging into "reliably terrific" French fare while sipping "something they picked up" or from "their own vineyards", while the "wonderful" staff and "down-home" decor provide the "perfect ambiance" for brunch; N.B. no reservations.

Fish ⌀ *Seafood*

	23	13	14	$31

Sausalito | 350 Harbor Dr. (Clipper Yacht Harbor) | 415-331-3474 | www.331fish.com

"Go fish takes on new meaning" when "sittin' on a dock in the Bay" "feasting" on "über-generous portions" of "fresh-off-the-boat" seafood at this "sustainably focused" Sausalito "crab shack"; some resent the "long lines" and "sit-down prices for take-out service" at "picnic tables in the wind", but the "lovely" deck with "magnificent views" and "damn good" chow make most "forget the wait and the price."

Flavor *Californian/Eclectic*

	19	16	18	$30

Santa Rosa | 96 Old Courthouse Sq. (bet. 3rd & 4th Sts.) | 707-573-9600 | www.flavorbistro.com

A "mélange of styles" and serving sizes, along with "three- and six-ounce" samples of local vintages "for mixing and matching", makes this "high-energy" all-day bistro in "boring ol'" Downtown Santa Rosa a "no-brainer" when you want to "savor the flavor" of "delicious" Cal-Eclectic meals; it's "extremely popular", so it's "extremely noisy", but "attentive service", a "well-diversified wine list" and "bargain prices" win out over the din.

Folio Enoteca & Winery *Californian/Mediterranean*

▽ 16 | 14 | 16 | $28

Napa | Oxbow Public Mkt. | 610 First St. (bet. Silverado Trail & Soscol Ave.) | 707-256-3700 | www.foliowine.com

The "wine is the draw" at this petite enoteca, cafe and micro-winery owned by Michael Mondavi offering selections from his enological portfolio, as well as custom blends made on-site; a "limited menu" of Cal-Med nibbles makes it "serviceable" for "tasting" and "grazing" when shopping at Napa's Oxbow Public Market; N.B. kitchen closes at 6:45 PM.

Frantoio *Italian*

21 | 21 | 20 | $46

Mill Valley | 152 Shoreline Hwy. (Hwy. 101) | 415-289-5777 | www.frantoio.com

"After hiking on Mt. Tam", customers carbo-load on Northern Italian "gnocchi-to-die-for" and "paper-thin pastas" at this Mill Valley "hide-away", a "hip-for-Marin" "hangout" with a "beautiful" interior and "pleasant" service; it's "especially lively" "when the olive press is running" (October–December) and "you can watch the huge crush stone turn" from the dining room, and sample the "great" e-v-o-o.

⚡ French Laundry, The *American/French*

29 | 27 | 28 | $264

Yountville | 6640 Washington St. (Creek St.) | 707-944-2380 | www.frenchlaundry.com

Thomas Keller "still kills" at his "legendary" Yountville "mothership" in an "old stone" cottage, where "gastronauts" embark on "tour de force" French–New American tasting menus that blast off with a "glass of champagne in the garden", soar though nine "sublime" courses with "unbelievable" service and "end with sighs"; "in these economic times", it's a "once-in-a-lifetime-experience", and that's all you're likely to "snag reservations" for "anyway", unless you "try for lunch" (Friday–Sunday).

Fumé Bistro & Bar *American*

22 | 18 | 21 | $39

Napa | 4050 Byway E. (Avalon Ct.) | 707-257-1999 | www.fumebistro.com

One of "the last restaurants locals can depend on without mortgaging their houses", this "solid performer" is a true "Napa hangout" where "waiters who welcome you back" ferry "awesome" wood-fired pizzas and other "high-quality" New American eats in a "down-to-earth" atmosphere (with "outdoor tables" for lunch and brunch); it suffers from a "not-so-good location just off the highway", but "satisfies" nonetheless.

Gary Chu's Ⓜ *Chinese*

20 | 18 | 19 | $31

Santa Rosa | 611 Fifth St. (bet. D St. & Mendocino Ave.) | 707-526-5840 | www.garychus.com

"If there is a better Chinese restaurant north of the bridge, please tell me" insist admirers of this Santa Rosa "flagship" providing "gourmet" Mandarin and Sichuan "delights" by chef about town Gary Chu (Osake); still, some guests "don't get" the hype, suggesting it's "getting a little dated and in need of an infusion of creativity."

girl & the fig, the *French*

24 | 21 | 22 | $45

Sonoma | Sonoma Hotel | 110 W. Spain St. (1st St.) | 707-938-3634 | www.thegirlandthefig.com

"A slice" of the "real wine country, from the clientele" to the staff that "makes you feel like a local", this "convivial" art-filled cafe off the

Sonoma Plaza offers "remarkable, farm-fresh" "French countryside" dishes, "wonderful" cheeses and "unusual" Rhône varietals, plus a "lovely back garden" for savoring it all; since it's "a must" for many, consider "going midweek to avoid the crowds and resulting slow service."

Go Fish *Eclectic/Seafood*   22 | 21 | 20 | $51

St. Helena | 641 Main St. (bet. Charter Oak Ave. & Mills Ln.) | 707-963-0700 | www.gofishrestaurant.net

"Another big splash" from Cindy Pawlcyn (Mustards Grill, Cindy's Backstreet Kitchen), this "packed"-to-the-gills, all-day Eclectic seafood "nirvana" showcasing "fish in all its glory" – from "fantastic" sushi to "shrimp mac 'n' cheese" – is a "fun, friendly alternative" to fancier St. Helena options; the "big bar area" and "idyllic" patio invite visitors to "unwind", though "pricey" plates and "stretched" service leave some anglers "unimpressed."

Guaymas *Mexican*   16 | 20 | 17 | $36

Tiburon | 5 Main St. (Tiburon Blvd.) | 415-435-6300 | www.guaymasrestaurant.com

Tiburon tequila-lovers sing the praises of "sipping margaritas in the sunshine" and catching the "captivating view of San Francisco" from "across the Bay" at this Mexican seafooder "right by the ferry"; though many lament the "lackluster" service and "mediocre" menu that "would be better at half the price", bright-siders reason that if the cooking improved, "you'd never be able to get in."

Hana Japanese Restaurant *Japanese*   24 | 16 | 21 | $44

Rohnert Park | 101 Golf Course Dr. (Roberts Lake Rd.) | 707-586-0270 | www.hanajapanese.com

"An oasis in the desert of a Rohnert Park" strip mall, this "spectacular Japanese" run by chef-owner "Ken [Tominaga]-san" "rocks the raw fish" and other "unique" fare like "sake-braised pork belly", as well as standard lunch and bento box specials; there are "no fancy flourishes", but "for true bliss", devotees say "drinking sake from square wooden cups" at the sushi bar and ordering omakase is "like having Picasso paint just for you."

Harmony Restaurant *Chinese*   22 | 20 | 21 | $34

Mill Valley | Strawberry Vill. | 800 Redwood Hwy. (Belvedere Dr.) | 415-381-5300 | www.harmonyrestaurantgroup.com

For "fabulous" dumplings and other "upscale Chinese" fare "minus the MSG", this thoroughly modern Mill Valley Sino (with a brisk "take-out" arm) hits all the right notes, steaming up the "best dim sum on the beat" (not surprising given its "Yank Sing roots") in a "pretty" setting; some grouse that "portions tend to be small for the price", but many "appreciate the attention given to high-quality, organic ingredients", adding the staff "couldn't be nicer"; N.B. carts only during weekend lunch.

Harvest Moon Café *Californian/Mediterranean*   ▽ 24 | 17 | 20 | $47

Sonoma | 487 First St. W. (W. Napa St.) | 707-933-8160 | www.harvestmooncafesonoma.com

Run by a husband-and-wife team (ex Chez Panisse and La Toque, respectively), this "laid-back" bistro on the "Sonoma Plaza" is one of "the best" in town according to loyal "locals" who laud the "first-class home-cooked" Cal-Med fare featuring the "freshest of local meats, poultry, seafood and produce", backed by "excellent wines"; though a few feel the service "misses the mark" at times, most agree that whether you sit at the chef's table or "under the stars" in "the back garden", it's an experience "you won't soon forget."

Healdsburg Bar & Grill *American*

| 19 | 16 | 18 | $32 |

Healdsburg | 245 Healdsburg Ave. (bet. Matheson & Mill Sts.) | 707-433-3333 | www.healdsburgbarandgrill.com

"When you want something better than Applebee's but not" "over the top", this "no-frills" pub "spiffed up" by the "Cyrus folks" is a great "quick" "wine route lunch" or dinner stop for "killer" "burgers and brews" or "adult mac 'n' cheese", and "no corkage fee" encourages "local" "tasting room" purchases; regulars say the space "can get loud", and recommend "sitting on the patio" and "watching the scene" on the Healdsburg Plaza; N.B. there's live music on the weekends.

Hog Island Oyster Co. & Bar Ⓜ *Seafood*

| 25 | 17 | 19 | $35 |

NEW Napa | Oxbow Public Mkt. | 610 First St. (bet. Silverado Trail & Soscol Ave.) | 707-251-8113 | www.hogislandoysters.com

See review in City of San Francisco Directory.

Hopmonk Tavern *Eclectic*

| 17 | 18 | 17 | $27 |

Sebastopol | 230 Petaluma Ave. (Sebastopol Ave.) | 707-829-7300 | www.hopmonk.com

Reviving an old "Sebastopol microbrewery", this rustic gastropub, "music venue" and "beer garden" from Dean Biersch (of Gordon Biersch fame) is a "hoppening place" that draws a mostly "younger crowd" with what many call "the best beer selection north of the Golden Gate"; the Eclectic, "Sonoma"-accented "pub fare" works for a "pre-concert dinner" before hitting the adjacent "Hopmonk Abbey", and cronies are confident the "anxious-to-please" staff "will surely improve" in time.

Hurley's Restaurant & Bar *Californian/Mediterranean*

| 21 | 20 | 22 | $47 |

Yountville | 6518 Washington St. (Yount St.) | 707-944-2345 | www.hurleysrestaurant.com

"Halfway up the wine trail", this "welcoming" Californian serving "beautiful" Med-accented dishes lures "locals" to "sit out on the patio" (by the new fire pit) for a "vintner's lunch" or dinner, or dine till midnight at the bar; though loyalists lament it's "underrated", naysayers note it's "not a standout" considering the "stiff competition" down the street.

Il Davide Ⓜ *Italian*

| 21 | 18 | 21 | $40 |

San Rafael | 901 A St. (bet. 3rd & 4th Sts.) | 415-454-8080 | www.ildavide.net

"Excellent" "housemade pastas" and other "steady" Tuscan dishes star at this San Rafael "favorite" where the "outside seating is a special treat in nice weather"; recently redecorated with creamy beige and burgundy tones, the interior gets "crowded with regulars" who relish the "affordable" lunch specials and "family-friendly atmosphere."

Il Fornaio *Italian*

| 19 | 20 | 19 | $40 |

Corte Madera | Town Center Corte Madera | 223 Corte Madera Town Ctr. (Madera Blvd.) | 415-927-4400 | www.ilfornaio.com

See review in City of San Francisco Directory.

	FOOD	DECOR	SERVICE	COST

⚡ In-N-Out Burger ☻ *Burgers* — 22 | 10 | 18 | $8

Mill Valley | 798 Redwood Hwy. (Belvedere Dr.) | 800-786-1000
Napa | 820 Imola Ave./Hwy. 121 (Napa Valley Hwy.) | 800-786-1000
www.in-n-out.com
See review in City of San Francisco Directory.

Insalata's *Mediterranean* — 25 | 22 | 23 | $45

San Anselmo | 120 Sir Francis Drake Blvd. (Barber Ave.) | 415-457-7700 |
www.insalatas.com
The "marvelous Mediterranean" cooking and "winning wine list" really "sing" at this San Anselmo "star" where the "satisfying", locally sourced fare is served in "presentations" as "lovely" as the "open, airy room" with "original artwork everywhere"; service is "professional and pleasant", and there's an "excellent to-go counter" too.

Izzy's Steaks & Chops *Steak* — 20 | 17 | 19 | $43

Corte Madera | 55 Tamal Vista Blvd. (Sandpiper Circle) | 415-924-3366 |
www.izzysrestaurant.com
See review in City of San Francisco Directory.

Jimtown Store *Deli* — 18 | 18 | 18 | $18

Healdsburg | 6706 Hwy. 128 (Chaffee Rd.) | 707-433-1212 |
www.jimtown.com
"Charmed" by its vintage "country-store" facade, "bike riders" and motorists en route from Healdsburg "just can't pass by" this "Alexander Valley pit stop" to fuel up on "lovingly prepared" breakfasts "on the patio" or "tasty" deli "box lunches" for a "winery picnic"; "service isn't always 'snap-to'", but it's "fun" to browse the shop's "quirky wares" and "toys from the '50s" "while you wait."

Joe's Taco Lounge & Salsaria *Mexican* — 20 | 15 | 17 | $18

Mill Valley | 382 Miller Ave. (bet. Evergreen & Montford Aves.) |
415-383-8164
"It's all *bueno*" at this "bargain" Mill Valley Mexican, from fish tacos that "will make a convert out of any carnivore" to the "best chipotle salsa ever" aver amigos; sure, the "colorful", "kitschy", "kid"-friendly cantina "can get a little crazy", but it's "worth the chaos" for a "quick pick-me-up."

John Ash & Co. *Californian* — 24 | 25 | 23 | $59

Santa Rosa | 4330 Barnes Rd. (River Rd.) | 707-527-7687 |
www.vintnersinn.com
"Plunked down in the middle of its own vineyard" and gardens, this "expensive" Santa Rosa "classic" that's "captivated Sonoma County folk for years" has lately been "reinvigorated" by a "new chef" crafting a "creative" farm-to-table Californian menu to match the "fabulous" wines; with "accommodating" service and a "lovely" ambiance on the patio or "inside by the fireplace", it's a "real treat" all around.

JoLe Ⓜ *American* — ▽ 26 | 16 | 20 | $48

Calistoga | Mount View Hotel | 1457 Lincoln Ave. (bet. Fair Way & Washington St.) | 707-942-5938 | www.jolerestaurant.com
Not nearly as overexposed as the other Jolie, this "relatively new" entry opened by a "friendly couple" on Calistoga's main drag serves "creative", "well-executed" New American small plates that allow for

"plenty of variety without feeling stuffed"; despite dubbing the dark-wood decor "a bit bleak", customers conclude that "like a fine wine, it should continue to excel and develop its strengths in time."

K&L Bistro 🏛 French
25 | 18 | 23 | $47

Sebastopol | 119 S. Main St. (Bodega Ave.) | 707-823-6614
"A Francophile's dream in hippie heaven", this "cozy" bistro is "without a doubt the culinary gem" of "sleepy" "little Sebastopol"; "delicious blackboard specials" spice up the menu of "refined" French "classics" delivered by a "seasoned staff", though it's a bit "too intimate" for critics who carp about "being sardined in the tiny space."

Kenwood 🅼 American/French
23 | 21 | 22 | $45

Kenwood | 9900 Sonoma Hwy./Hwy. 12 (Warm Springs Rd.) | 707-833-6326 | www.kenwoodrestaurant.com
"One of the last places in Sonoma that's not pretentious", this Kenwood "roadhouse" on Highway 12 beckons "locals and tourists" alike with its "straightforward", sometimes "swoon"-worthy New American–French fare and regional wines served all day on a "gorgeous" patio overlooking "vineyards" and a sculpture garden; though a few complain the menu "hasn't changed" in years, the "experienced" staff keeps it a "treasure."

La Boulange Bakery
22 | 17 | 17 | $16

Mill Valley | Strawberry Vill. | 800 Redwood Hwy. (Belvedere Dr.) | 415-381-1260
NEW Novato | Hamilton Mktpl. | 5800 Nave Dr. (bet. Hamilton Pkwy. & Roblar Dr.) | 415-382-8594
www.laboulangebakery.com
See review in City of San Francisco Directory.

La Gare 🅼 French
▽ 19 | 15 | 21 | $41

Santa Rosa | 208 Wilson St. (3rd St.) | 707-528-4355 | www.lagarerestaurant.com
Since 1979, this "quaint", "family-run" French in Old Railroad Square has been delivering "Châteaubriand to-die-for" and other "comfort European food", a "great wine list" and the "most courteous service"; while some cynics scoff it "used to be the best place in town – in 1985", it remains a "reliable" "mainstay" for stalwarts, for whom it evokes "memories" of "old Santa Rosa."

La Ginestra 🅼 Italian
▽ 21 | 14 | 23 | $32

Mill Valley | 127 Throckmorton Ave. (bet. Madrona St. & Miller Ave.) | 415-388-0224
The "traditional" Southern Italian fare "tastes like my grandma made it" maintain Mill Valley *mangiatori* who hanker for the "house-special ravioli", "handmade pastas" and "crisp, thin pizzas" at this "old-school" Marinite; no, it's "not trendy" and the digs are "rather plain", but it's good for "groups" with a "quick" staff that "keeps the wine coming."

LaSalette Portuguese
25 | 21 | 25 | $47

Sonoma | Mercado Ctr. | 452 First St. E. (bet. Napa & Spain Sts.) | 707-938-1927 | www.lasalette-restaurant.com
"Tucked off" the Sonoma Plaza, this "welcoming", "family-run" favorite "always satisfies", serving "distinctive", slightly high-end "Portuguese

FOOD DECOR SERVICE COST

food with wine-country notes"; both the wood-fired bread and "fresh seafood" stand out, but surveyors say save "some space for dessert" (especially the rice pudding reminiscent of "grandmother's kitchen").

Las Camelias *Mexican* ▽ 18 | 15 | 19 | $27

San Rafael | 912 Lincoln Ave. (bet. 3rd & 4th Sts.) | 415-453-5850 | www.lascameliasrestaurant.com

"Addicting" chips and salsa and "unique house specialties" served with "savory sauces" "satisfy cravings" at this "gracious" San Rafaelite that's "a cut above the usual Mexican restaurant"; "beautiful artwork on display" and windows "thrown open on sunny days" are a plus, though lack of a hard liquor license means no "real margaritas."

Z La Toque *French* 26 | 23 | 26 | $102

Napa | Westin Verasa | 1314 McKinstry St. (Soscol Ave.) | 707-257-5157 | www.latoque.com

"The best thing to happen to Napa in ages", Ken Frank's "stunning" relocated "high-end" French in the Westin Verasa is a "sophisticated", "special dining experience" featuring "unbelievable" "food and wine" pairings, thanks to "phenomenal" wine director Scott Tracy and sommelier Yoon Ha, and "impeccable service"; a few say it "lost" some "rustic charm in the move" from Rutherford, but many others feel it "gained" even more, namely, a more "flexible" "tasting format" and its "baby", the casual Bank Cafe and Bar.

Ledford House M *Californian/Mediterranean* ▽ 25 | 26 | 24 | $46

Albion | 3000 N. Hwy. 1 (Spring Grove Rd.) | 707-937-0282 | www.ledfordhouse.com

For more than three decades, this "inviting" family-run bistro perched on a bluff on the Mendocino Coast with "180-degree ocean views" has been the go-to place in Albion for "special occasions, romantic evenings or just a drink at the bar" to watch the "splendid sunsets"; with "superb", "well-priced" Cal-Med fare by chef Lisa Geer, "great guidance" on "regional wines" "from her husband", Tony, and live jazz nightly – "what more could one ask for?"

Left Bank *French* 18 | 19 | 18 | $41

Larkspur | Blue Rock Inn | 507 Magnolia Ave. (Ward St.) | 415-927-3331 | www.leftbank.com

There's "no need to fly" to the Left Bank "for your fix of steak frites" with this moderately priced French trio "for the Cheesecake Factory set" situated around the Bay; because "it's a chain", service "varies" by location, but *amis* insist "for the price, you'd be hard-pressed to find a better combination of food and decor" – a classic brasserie "reproduction" complete with a "plenty noisy" bar and sidewalk seating for watching *le monde* "go by."

Little River Inn *Californian/Seafood* 21 | 22 | 22 | $45

Little River | Little River Inn | 7901 N. Hwy. 1 (Little River Airport Rd.) | 707-937-5942 | www.littleriverinn.com

"Start the day out right" with "famous Ole's" Swedish hotcakes before "a hike in Van Damme State Park" or end it with a "romantic dinner" of "solid" Californian seafood after a "day at the beach" at this Little River Inn "throwback" that's "recently joined the very best of coastal dining"; the atmosphere is "intoxicating" in the "beautiful" dining room with garden views, and you can take in the "most beautiful" ocean sunsets over "banter, drinks" and "fish 'n' chips" at the bar.

Lotus Cuisine of India *Indian*
∇ 25 | 20 | 23 | $30

San Rafael | 704 Fourth St. (Tamalpais Ave.) | 415-456-5808 | www.lotusrestaurant.com

NEW Anokha Cuisine of India *Indian*
Novato | 811 Grant Ave. (Reichert Ave.) | 415-892-3440 | www.anokharestaurant.com

Café Lotus *Indian*
Fairfax | 1912 Sir Francis Drake Blvd. (Claus Dr.) | 415-457-7836 | www.cafelotusfairfax.com

Lotus eaters lavish praise on the "savory" "Indian food at its finest" served by a "welcoming" staff at this "beautiful", art-adorned San Rafaelite; the Monday–Saturday lunch buffet is a "real bargain", but alfresco fans prefer to go on a "warm night when the roof is pulled back"; N.B. new branches have opened in Fairfax and Novato.

MacCallum House *Californian*
21 | 22 | 21 | $54

Mendocino | MacCallum House Inn | 45020 Albion St. (bet. Hesser & Kasten Sts.) | 707-937-5763 | www.maccallumhouse.com

"Big fireplaces warm you up" at this "romantic getaway" presenting "great views" of the Mendocino coast coupled with "imaginative" "twists" on Californian cuisine; "breakfasts to die for" delight as much as the "delicious" dinners, and if a few fret about "high" tabs, "dining in the Gray Whale Bar" is a "lower-cost, less formal alternative."

☑ Madrona Manor Ⓜ *American/French*
26 | 27 | 26 | $81

Healdsburg | Madrona Manor | 1001 Westside Rd. (W. Dry Creek Rd.) | 707-433-4231 | www.madronamanor.com

"Gorgeous" dining rooms and a "delightful veranda" create a "memorable" (even "magical") backdrop for "world-class" French–New American meals at this "luxurious" Healdsburg "Victorian mansion" tended by a "gracious" staff; "book a room and make a weekend of it" urge the amorous, who are carried away by the "super-romantic" ambiance.

Manzanita Ⓜ *Californian/Mediterranean*
∇ 19 | 17 | 18 | $46

Healdsburg | 336 Healdsburg Ave. (bet. Plaza & W. North Sts.) | 707-433-8111 | www.manzanita336.com

For a "casual" dinner or weekend brunch without breaking the bank, fans tout this low-key "wine country restaurant" "near the Healdsburg Plaza" for its "great pizzas" from a "wood-burning oven" and other Cal-Med fare (with "choices for kids and teens"), backed by an "extensive wine list"; the service is "always friendly", but cynics shrug that it "lacks excitement" and a clear "identity."

Marché aux Fleurs ☒Ⓜ *French*
25 | 22 | 24 | $49

Ross | 23 Ross Common (Lagunitas Rd.) | 415-925-9200 | www.marcheauxfleursrestaurant.com

"You'll forget you're in Downtown Ross" at this "beautiful retreat" whose "outstanding" New French fare, "superlative" wine list and "charming cottage setting" with outdoor tables would be at home on a "cobblestone street in Paris"; admirers also appreciate the "attention to detail" by "hands-on" owners Holly and Dan Baker, which "shows" in the "pleasant", "professional" service and enriches the "real value."

NEW Marinitas ● *Pan-Latin*

▽ 21 | 24 | 20 | $33

San Anselmo | 218 Sir Francis Drake Blvd. (Bank St.) | 415-454-8900 | www.marinitas.net

"Holy guacamole" exclaim San Anselmites, "Insalata's baby sister" "has taken off with a bang", serving up "flavorful", "SF-caliber" Pan-Latin and Mexican "shared plates" and "amazing margaritas" "in sleepy Marin"; the "primo", "eccentric" room has a rustic Latin American feel and the "awesome" bar is a "much needed venue for the mature party-ers", but critics report the staff has some "kinks to work out."

Market *American*

22 | 19 | 21 | $38

St. Helena | 1347 Main St. (bet. Adams St. & Hunt Ave.) | 707-963-3799 | www.marketsthelena.com

For a break from the airs and "high prices of other Valley restaurants", fans endorse this "friendly" American in Downtown St. Helena cranking out "not fancy, but flavorful" "comfort food" (including "great desserts") and local vinos "with minimal markups" all day long; "prix fixe lunch specials" and no corkage make it the "perfect" "midday winery touring gem", with a full bar for those who are "over the wine scene."

Martini House *American*

26 | 25 | 23 | $64

St. Helena | 1245 Spring St. (bet. Main St. & Oak Ave.) | 707-963-2233 | www.martinihouse.com

"Just say yes to the 'shrooms" (in the soup and tasting menus) on fungi "specialist" Todd Humphries' New American menu at this St. Helena haunt where the "exceptional" cuisine is backed by "extensive wine and liquor lists" and served in a Pat Kuleto–designed "lodge" setting with a "garden patio" and "magical vibe"; you can also "hang out" in the Prohibition-era "downstairs bar" for a recession-friendly snack or "kick-ass" "Kobe beef burger", which is also served at lunch Friday–Sunday.

Max's *Deli*

17 | 14 | 17 | $27

Corte Madera | 60 Madera Blvd. (Hwy. 101) | 415-924-6297 | www.maxsworld.com

See review in City of San Francisco Directory.

Meadowood, The Grill *Californian*
(aka The Grill at Meadowood)

22 | 21 | 23 | $52

St. Helena | Meadowood Napa Valley | 900 Meadowood Ln. (Silverado Trail) | 707-963-3646 | www.meadowood.com

"Well-prepared" and "reasonably priced" Californian fare is served by an "accommodating" staff at this all-day grill set in the "beautiful" "gated Meadowood resort" in St. Helena; fresh-air fans enjoy "wining and dining casually" "on the patio" while "smelling the pine trees" and taking in "the pristine golf course and hills", while others prefer the "quiet", "odd-shaped room" where you can "hear your conversation."

☒ Meadowood, The Restaurant ☒ *Californian*
(aka The Restaurant at Meadowood)

26 | 25 | 26 | $96

St. Helena | Meadowood Napa Valley | 900 Meadowood Ln. (Silverado Trail) | 707-967-1205 | www.meadowood.com

"After years of dormancy", the flagship restaurant at the Meadowood in St. Helena "has returned with a vengeance" and now presents a "hidden challenge" to "the best in the Napa Valley"; "there are no duds" on

FOOD | DECOR | SERVICE | COST

chef Christopher Kostow's "creative", "elegant" seasonal Californian prix fixe menus, complemented by "top-of-the-line" service and a "gorgeous", "bucolic" setting; for some "extra bucks", you can order the "vintner's menu and vintage matches", which oenophiles swear is an experience "you'll never forget."

Mendo Bistro *American*

| 24 | 19 | 22 | $36 |

Fort Bragg | The Company Store | 301 N. Main St., 2nd fl. (Redwood St.) | 707-964-4974 | www.mendobistro.com

"Tourists rub elbows with the locals" and can "learn a thing or two not in the guidebooks" at this Fort Bragg New American, a "no-brainer for big events" or a "leisurely" midweek dinner of Nicholas Petti's "outstanding" fare, highlighted by his "creative use of local ingredients"; from the "great views of the town from the second floor" of the "historic" Arts and Crafts–style building to "service that goes that extra mile", it's a "purely Mendo experience" at "about half what you would pay" in the Mendocino village.

Mendocino Hotel *Californian*

| 18 | 21 | 18 | $45 |

Mendocino | Mendocino Hotel | 45080 Main St. (bet. Kasten & Lansing Sts.) | 707-937-0511 | www.mendocinohotel.com

"It's like stepping back in time" at this "old Victorian" hotel in Mendocino where the "ornate wooden bar" and "ghostly ambiance" "set the scene" for "the local 'in' crowd entertaining tourists"; while "sitting by the fireplace on a cold, rainy night" or lunch in the "sunny garden room" "are worth the price", critics "skip" the "formal dining room", grousing that the Californian dinners and service "aren't up to Bay Area standards."

Meritage Martini
Oyster Bar & Grille *Italian*

| ▽ 20 | 17 | 21 | $49 |

Sonoma | 165 W. Napa St. (bet. 1st & 2nd Sts. W.) | 707-938-9430 | www.sonomameritage.com

"Homemade" Northern Italian pasta dishes, a "nice selection of seafood apps" (served in chilled combo platters for groups) and "terrific martinis" make this slightly "clubby" Sonoman a "locals' favorite"; the "friendly" atmosphere is a further draw for most, even if some feel "underwhelmed" by the meal; N.B. closed Tuesday.

Mirepoix Ⓜ *French*

| 26 | 19 | 24 | $47 |

Windsor | 275 Windsor River Rd. (bet. Honsa Ave. & Windsor Rd.) | 707-838-0162 | www.restaurantmirepoix.com

"*C'est magnifique*" agree guests of this "gem" in "sleepy little" Windsor, where "fresh local ingredients" and an "interesting" list of largely local wines give a Sonoma spin to the "very French" bistro menu; while the "small" size can make it a "tough reservation", the "lovely" patio expands your options on "warm nights", and the "charming" owners always "treat you like guests in their own home."

Model Bakery *Bakery*

| 20 | 11 | 16 | $17 |

Napa | Oxbow Public Mkt. | 644 First St. (bet. Silverado Trail & Soscol Ave.) | 707-963-8192

St. Helena | 1357 Main St. (bet. Adams St. & Hunt Ave.) | 707-963-8192 | www.themodelbakery.com

"Wonderful, wonderful" bread, sandwiches and brick-oven pizzas make this "neighborhood bakery" in St. Helena and its newer offshoot in

Napa's Oxbow Market popular stops for a "pastry-and-a-coffee breakfast" or "quick" lunch; the "baked treats" are what "locals and tourists" "come for", rather than the "casual" art deco digs of the original, which look to some as if they haven't been "refreshed" "in decades."

Monti's Rotisserie &
Bar *American/Mediterranean*

21 | 20 | 20 | $35

Santa Rosa | Montgomery Village Shopping Ctr. | 714 Village Ct. (Farmers Ln.) | 707-568-4404 | www.montisroti.net

An "unexpected" "oasis" "in the Village", this "reliable" Santa Rosa rotisserie and "raw-bar" specialist gets kudos for "coziness", with a "raging fire" contributing to the "comfortable setting"; supporters "keep going back" for the "varied", "well-prepared" New American-Med plates and "excellent" "wines by the glass", though a few suggest it's "fine as a shopping break" rather than a "destination."

Moosse Café *Californian*

24 | 19 | 22 | $45

Mendocino | The Blue Heron Inn | 390 Kasten St. (Albion St.) | 707-937-4323 | www.themoosse.com

The "spectacular garden view" makes for "delightful" dining among both Mendo "locals" and weekenders at this "comfy" Californian serving "lively" specials to top off a "pleasing" seasonal menu; though the tables are a bit "close", "no one seems to mind" since the staff ensures you "feel well taken care of"; N.B. closed Tuesday–Wednesday in winter.

Mosaic Restaurant &
Wine Lounge *Californian*

▽ 26 | 22 | 23 | $45

Forestville | 6675 Front St. (off Mirabel Rd.) | 707-887-7503 | www.mosaiceats.com

"Is this Forestville or Xanadu?" wonder fans enchanted by this "phenomenal hidden gem", a garden of eatin' "in the middle of nowhere" whose "outstanding", locally leaning Californian fare, "excellent" selection of boutique bottles and "wonderful" service make it one of "the best in West Sonoma County"; it "looks so plain" at first, but "lovely once you get inside", and there's a "beautiful backyard patio" with fire pits and an outdoor grill.

Murray Circle *Californian*

24 | 25 | 22 | $66

Sausalito | Cavallo Point Resort in Fort Baker | 602 Murray Circle (Sausalito Lateral Rd.) | 415-339-4750 | www.murraycircle.com

Aficionados attest it's "worth the drive" down "windy roads" to find this "special-occasion" Californian nestled in the forts of Sausalito, where the "magical setting" and "views of the Golden Gate" are "a bit of heaven", and Joseph Humphrey's "clever" tasting dinners are a "real treat"; some cynics snort that the "expensive" "diet portions" are "spoof"-worthy, however, and wallet-watchers recommend dining at the adjacent Farley Bar, which boasts an "inviting" ambiance and "better prices."

ⓩ Mustards Grill *American/Californian*

25 | 19 | 23 | $48

Yountville | 7399 St. Helena Hwy./Hwy. 29 (bet. Oakville Grade Rd. & Washington St.) | 707-944-2424 | www.mustardsgrill.com

"If this is truck-stop food then get me a truck!" exclaim fans of Cindy Pawlcyn's "irreverent" Yountville "roadhouse" on the wine trail where "the only thing serious is the appetite you have to bring with you"; "after 25 years", it "still wows" with "just the right mix" of Cal–New American "home-cookin' Napa style" and "top-notch service in an informal setting", and it "won't cost an arm and a leg" – though maybe "a few fingers, with its high-end wine selection."

Napa General Store *Californian/Eclectic*   20 | 15 | 17 | $24

Napa | 540 Main St. (5th St.) | 707-259-0762 | www.napageneralstore.com
For lunch "on the move" or as a "complement to getting sloshed on good wine", this "informal" cafe inside a general store in the historic Napa Mill is a "solid" choice with its "limited" Cal-Eclectic menu of "great sandwiches, pizza and soups"; there's a "gorgeous outside deck overlooking the Napa River" and a new promenade, but "not enough people to help with the maddening crowds" according to critics; N.B. closes at 3 PM.

Napa Valley Grille *Californian*   21 | 19 | 21 | $45

Yountville | Washington Sq. | 6795 Washington St. (off Hwy. 29) | 707-944-8686 | www.napavalleygrille.com
Wayfarers on "winery tours" "love" this "perfect lunch stop" "right in the heart of Yountville" for its "consistent" Cal cuisine that's a "commendable" "alternative to the more expensive" options in the area; a few naysayers note that it's "not so special", but "relaxing" "under an umbrella" on the patio is "heaven" to some.

Napa Valley Wine Train *Californian*   16 | 23 | 20 | $67

Napa | 1275 McKinstry St. (bet. 1st St. & Soscol Ave.) | 707-253-2111 | www.winetrain.com
"Go for the experience" recommend rail-riders about this "rolling restaurant traveling through the bucolic Napa Valley" that lends itself to "leisurely" (if "touristy") meals on its "well-restored" vintage cars, especially if you go "first-class"; others opine "only if you really must", as the Cal menu is "pedestrian" and "expensive", and the route misses much of the region's "fine beauty."

Nick's Cove *Californian*   21 | 24 | 20 | $46

Marshall | Nick's Cove & Cottages | 23240 Hwy. 1 (4 mi. north of Marshall-Petaluma Rd.) | 415-723-1071 | www.nickscove.com
Pat Kuleto and Mark Franz "have done it again" with this "seriously popular" "reconstructed shoreside roadhouse" in Marshall, whose "wonderful" Californian cuisine features "local products" (including "oysters fresh from Tomales Bay") matched by "delightful" wines; it's "not as cheap" or laid-back "as before", but the "spectacular views" - complete with "harbor seals and otters swimming by" - keep it a "worthy destination."

955 Ukiah Ⓜ *American/French*   23 | 18 | 22 | $47

Mendocino | 955 Ukiah St. (School St.) | 707-937-1955 | www.955restaurant.com
"Locals know" it's "worth seeking out" this "mom-and-pop operation" "located down a garden path in the village of Mendocino", where a "limited" menu of "superior" New American–French fare and a "charming" staff await; while the "rustic" interior "could use a post-early-'90's update" and a few feel it's "overpriced", the selection of "affordable" North Coast wines helps "ease the pain"; N.B. open for dinner only Thursday–Sunday.

Olema Inn *Californian* 22 | 23 | 21 | $47

Olema | Olema Inn | 10000 Sir Francis Drake Blvd. (off Hwy. 101) |
415-663-9559 | www.theolemainn.com

Not far from the "Point Reyes lighthouse and beaches", this restored
1876 country inn "in the middle of nowhere" in Olema is a "wonderful
retreat for fabulous" Cal dinners and weekend lunches of "designer
comfort food" appealing to "locavores", served by a "friendly" staff in a
"simple", "old-fashioned" dining room "steeped in the history of the
West"; though it's "nothing too fancy", it is "elegant" (and "expensive").

Osake Ⓢ *Californian/Japanese* 23 | 18 | 22 | $38

Santa Rosa | 2446 Patio Ct. (Farmers Ln.) | 707-542-8282 |
www.garychus.com

Sake 'O Ⓜ *Californian/Japanese*

Healdsburg | 505 Healdsburg Ave. (Piper St.) | 707-433-2669
Sonomans desperately seeking sushi "love" these Santa Rosa and
Healdsburg "forays" by "emperor of inventive" Asian eats Gary Chu;
you're "not going for decor", but rather "fresh fish to die for", as well
as "must-get" Cal-Japanese plates such as "martini prawns"; and "if
you sit at the bar" to sample the "great sake", "you'll quickly realize
that he's a great showman too."

NEW **Osteria Stellina** *Italian* – | – | – | M

Point Reyes Station | 11285 Hwy. 1 (bet. 2nd & 3rd Sts.) | 415-663-9988 |
www.osteriastellina.com

A bright light on the barren Point Reyes Station dining scene, this new
West Marin osteria is winning over locals and day-trippers alike with
its one-page menu of rustic, sustainably sourced Italian specialties
prepared by chef-owner Christian Caiazzo (ex Postrio and more recently the nearby Toby's Coffee Bar); the simple, homey dining room
camouflages the big-city sophistication of the food, while prices are
comfortably middle-of-the-road; N.B. closed Tuesdays.

Oxbow Wine ▽ 22 | 18 | 20 | $26
Merchant *Californian/Mediterranean*

Napa | Oxbow Public Mkt. | 610 First St. (bet. Silverado Trail & Soscol Ave.) |
707-257-5200 | www.oxbowwinemerchant.com

This "new kid on the block" in Napa's Oxbow Market with "a wine
shop on one side and a cheese monger on the other" turns out "no-
fuss meals" of "tasty" Cal-Med small plates expertly paired with
"good vino" in a "casual environment"; many take "delight" in "whiling
away a weekend afternoon" here, be it at the circular oak bar or "taking in the view of the river" from the patio; N.B. anything in stock can
be uncorked for only $6.

Pacific Catch *Seafood* 20 | 15 | 18 | $24

Corte Madera | Town Center Corte Madera | 133 Corte Madera Town Ctr.
(off Hwy. 101) | 415-927-3474 | www.pacificcatch.com
See review in City of San Francisco Directory.

Pearl ⓈⓂ *Californian* ▽ 23 | 18 | 20 | $38

Napa | 1339 Pearl St. (bet. Franklin & Polk Sts.) | 707-224-9161 |
www.therestaurantpearl.com

Locals "hate to expose this Napa gem of a pearl", an "unpretentious"
"little" Cal bistro owned by a "warm, friendly" couple, but still glow

FOOD DECOR SERVICE COST

about the "marvelous" oysters, "superb" specials and well-chosen wines for a "reasonable price"; while the industrial office-building location is fairly "unimpressive", most overlook it in light of the "great value."

Peter Lowell's *Italian*

▽ 22 | 19 | 16 | $27

Sebastopol | 7385 Healdsburg Ave. (Florence Ave.) | 707-829-1077 | www.peterlowells.com

"Cheers to the trailblazers" who run this low-on-the-radar Italian "gourmet haven just north of Sebastopol" and show "concern for the environment" while turning out "terrific breakfasts", some of "the best thin-crust pizzas in Sonoma County", "healthful" veggie lunch bowls and "fairly priced" dinners "prepared with local farm products"; a recycled paper-stone wine bar stocking biodynamic pressings highlights the "ultramodern" "green setting."

Piatti *Italian*

18 | 18 | 18 | $40

Mill Valley | 625 Redwood Hwy. (Hwy. 101) | 415-380-2525 | www.piatti.com
See review in East of San Francisco Directory.

Piazza D'Angelo *Italian*

20 | 18 | 20 | $39

Mill Valley | 22 Miller Ave. (bet. Sunnyside & Throckmorton Aves.) | 415-388-2000 | www.piazzadangelo.com

"A solid Italian soldier" serving "reliable" grub at "fair prices", this Mill Valley "standby" is "good for groups" out to "celebrate" over "decent" "wood-fired" pies and pastas; true, the "singles bar scene for Marin divorcees" is "too much" for some, so sedate types advise "go in nice weather and sit outside" if you expect to "hear your date."

Pica Pica Maize Kitchen *Venezuelan*

▽ 25 | 13 | 18 | $14

Napa | Oxbow Public Mkt. | 610 First St. (bet. Silverado Trail & Soscol Ave.) | 707-251-3757 | www.picapicakitchen.com

You'll "learn lots about different ways to eat corn" at this amaizing Venezuelan in Napa's Oxbow Market, which is "turning heads and bringing in crowds" with its "addictive", "delectable" arepas and grilled maize sandwiches (and "don't forget the yuca fries") going for "bargain-basement" prices; though the limited seating may send you out to sit in the food court, most agree it's still an "excellent" "change from ordinary fast food."

Picco *Italian*

26 | 20 | 22 | $50

Larkspur | 320 Magnolia Ave. (King St.) | 415-924-0300 | www.restaurantpicco.com

With a "hip, busy bar", "beautiful clientele" and "inviting patio" for "watching the Marinites go by", chef-owner Bruce Hill's "see-and-be-seen" small-plates shop is a "welcome departure from the traditional restaurants" in sleepy Larkspur; with "fantastic", "eclectic" Cal-Italian offerings (from sliders to "risotto from scratch served every half hour") that are made "for sharing", most agree it's "worth every penny, even in a recession."

Pine Cone Diner ⌂ *Diner*

▽ 20 | 14 | 16 | $25

Point Reyes Station | 60 Fourth St. (bet. 3rd & 5th Sts.) | 415-663-1536 | www.thepineconediner.com

"Off the beaten track" in Point Reyes Station, this "kitschy" New American daytime diner is a "cult foodie find" whose "homespun" "comfort food" and "retro" decor "hit all the right notes" for "throw-back" buffs; just prepare to be patient, since the "snarling" servers "will get to you when they're good and ready."

Pizza Antica *Pizza*

21 | 16 | 17 | $28

Mill Valley | Strawberry Vill. | 800 Redwood Hwy. (Belvedere Dr.) | 415-383-0600 | www.pizzaantica.com
See review in South of San Francisco Directory.

🆕 Pizzavino 707 Ⓜ *Pizza*
(fka West County Grill)

- | - | - | I

Sebastopol | 6948 Sebastopol Ave. (bet. Main St. & Petaluma Ave.) | 707-829-9500 | www.pizzavino707.com
Restaurateur Stephen Singer and Foreign Cinema chef-owners Gayle Pirie and John Clark have transformed the shuttered West County Grill space, with a plum bi-level perch on the Sebastopol plaza, into a casual haunt offering wood-fired pies topped with ingredients from local Sonoma vendors, as well as daily entree specials, wallet-friendly wines and specialty cocktails crafted at the long bar; starting hours are dinner Wednesday–Saturday, but expanded service, live music and an adjacent retail shop selling bottles from the 707 are forthcoming.

Pizzeria Picco *Pizza*

25 | 15 | 19 | $26

Larkspur | 316 Magnolia Ave. (King St.) | 415-945-8900 | www.pizzeriapicco.com
Picco's Southern Italian sidekick serving "adventurous", "hard-to-beat" "wood-fired" pizzas, "outstanding" salads and "amazing soft-serve" ("try the olive oil and salt" combo) is a "fun place with no pretense" for enjoying a Larkspur evening or "sunny" weekend lunch; "the only problem is when it's too cold to sit outside and too crowded at the counter", but the "pre-baked frozen" take-out option is a "stroke of genius."

Pizzeria Tra Vigne *Pizza*

21 | 15 | 17 | $27

St. Helena | Inn at Southbridge | 1016 Main St. (Pope St.) | 707-967-9999 | www.pizzeriatravigne.com
Pleasing both grown-ups and "kids who are fed up with all the fancy stuff" in St. Helena, this "everyday" pizzeria (and Tra Vigne spin-off) serves "dependably delicious" Neapolitan pies, pastas and salads that are a "wonderful value"; the room is "comfortable" with a big-screen TV and a "pool table", plus the "outdoor dining is great on a summer day."

Poggio *Italian*

22 | 24 | 21 | $48

Sausalito | Casa Madrona | 777 Bridgeway (Bay St.) | 415-332-7771 | www.poggiotrattoria.com
It's "worth climbing over the tourists" of Sausalito to enjoy the "rustic meats" "cooked in the fireplace" and "delicately sauced" "homemade pastas" at this "reasonably priced" Il Fornaio sib that's a "cut above" the chain; run by a "lively" staff, the sprawling setting is as "warm as Tuscany itself" for an "alfresco lunch" or a bit of "enjoyable hubbub at night."

Press *American/Steak*

23 | 25 | 24 | $72

St. Helena | 587 St. Helena Hwy. (White Ln.) | 707-967-0550 | www.pressthelena.com
The "beautiful" dining room – an "arty" modern farmhouse with greenhouse windows all around – is a "memorable" setting for "melt-

in-your-mouth" steaks and sides that "excel" at this American chop-house in St. Helena; a "convivial crowd" and "friendly" servers make the space "seem intimate", but a few fret that the prices are "up there" while the quality doesn't always "follow along"; P.S. "blue-plate specials" are served at the bar Sunday, Wednesday and Thursday.

Ravenous Cafe M *Californian/Eclectic*   22 | 17 | 19 | $43

Healdsburg | 420 Center St. (North St.) | 707-431-1302

"Go on a warm summer night and sit outside" (or take in the "tangerine walls" inside that "somehow work") at this "cute little" Healdsburg "winemaker hangout" that's "appealing" for a "burger and glass of local Pinot", among other "excellent-value" Cal-Eclectic eats and "fine regional" wines; most forgive service that's on the "slow" side, saying "relax and enjoy the wait"; N.B. closed Monday–Tuesday.

Ravens Restaurant, The *Vegan*   ▽ 22 | 20 | 20 | $45

Mendocino | Stanford Inn & Spa | 44850 Comptche Ukiah Rd. (Hwy. 1) | 707-937-5615 | www.stanfordinn.com

"Haute vegan" dinners and "hard-to-beat" breakfasts show guests "how great a meatless meal can be" at this "down-to-earth" Mendocino stop where "much of the food is grown in the gardens" of the inn; "gorgeous views" are a plus, though a few disappointed diners feel the meals get a bit "tiresome."

Z Redd Restaurant *Californian*   27 | 22 | 24 | $71

Yountville | 6480 Washington St. (bet. California Dr. & Oak Circle) | 707-944-2222 | www.reddnapavalley.com

Chef-owner Richard Reddington's "ingenious" dishes "combine flavors beautifully" at this "confident" Californian that "succeeds" in "foodies' paradise" (aka Yountville) with "simply superb" tasting menus "at a cost compatible with what you receive"; the "minimalist" dining room feels a touch "cold" to some (though the "patio is a dream"), but the "focus is on the food and wine", proffered "without too much pretension" by a "delightful" staff.

Rendezvous Inn &   ▽ 25 | 20 | 22 | $53
Restaurant M *French*

Fort Bragg | 647 N. Main St. (bet. Bush & Fir Sts.) | 707-964-8142 | www.rendezvousinn.com

"If Mendocino tourists trekked to Fort Bragg, they'd be pleasantly surprised" by this "special-occasion" French in a Craftsman B&B whose chef-owner, Kim Badenhop, "knows how to fix an excellent repast" "from the amuse-bouche to those wonderful soufflés"; he selects "exemplary" wine pairings and enhances the "personable" service too, "always making a point to visit every table" in the "cozy" room.

Restaurant, The *American/Eclectic*   ▽ 23 | 20 | 24 | $45

Fort Bragg | 418 N. Main St. (Laurel St.) | 707-964-9800 | www.therestaurantfortbragg.com

"Loved by locals for many, many years", this Fort Bragg "classic" provides "first-rate" New American–Eclectic dinners by chef/co-owner James Larsen, served amid a "funky" interior featuring "odd" artwork by Olaf Palm; some regulars "remember when it was the only choice for a nice meal out", adding it's still a "special place" with servers who treat you "like family"; N.B. closed Tuesday–Wednesday.

FOOD | DECOR | SERVICE | COST

Restaurant at Stevenswood, The *American*   ▽ 26 | 26 | 26 | $70

Little River | Stevenswood Lodge | 8211 Shoreline Hwy./N. Hwy. 1 (1 mi. south of Mendocino) | 707-937-2810 | www.stevenswood.com

One of the "best-kept secrets" in the region, this Little River "gem" offers "fresh, innovative" New American cooking (for "blow-the-wallet" prices) in a "romantic", "intimate setting" with a "crackling fire" and "beautiful views" of surrounding redwoods; though a cadre of country mice call the cuisine too "big-city", most praise its "impeccable" quality and commend the "professional" staff too.

NEW Restaurant Eloise *French/Mediterranean*   - | - | - | E

Sebastopol | 2295 Gravenstein Hwy. S. (Bloomfield Rd.) | 707-823-6300 | www.restauranteloise.com

Bringing their Big Apple pedigree to Sebastopol's apple country, married chef-owners Ginevra Iverson and Eric Korsh (both ex NYC's Prune) have opened this Med-French bistro, providing rustic yet sophisticated dishes based on local ingredients (some from their on-site garden) in a big-windowed, white-tablecloth dining room; housemade pasta and charcuterie head up the high-end lunch and dinner menus, while weekend brunch and a Wednesday night $35 three-course prix fixe (with no corkage fee) lend additional appeal.

Risibisi *Italian*   ▽ 25 | 20 | 21 | $46

Petaluma | 154 Petaluma Blvd. N. (Washington St.) | 707-766-7600 | www.risibisirestaurant.com

"Honest Italian food" (including "reasonable" options) and an "inviting" atmosphere make this "Petaluma gem" serving Venetian-inspired, Sonoma-sourced meals "right on the boulevard" a "real find"; accented with exposed brick, the contemporary dining room is "a bit crowded, but worth it" for the namesake risi e bisi – "daily risottos" that are "rich and full of flavor" – and piccolo wine bar pouring *vini* and Bellinis.

Robata Grill & Sushi *Japanese*   ▽ 21 | 15 | 17 | $38

Mill Valley | 591 Redwood Hwy. (Seminary Dr.) | 415-381-8400 | www.robatagrill.com

"Beautiful sushi combos", "tempura and noodle dishes", and "delicious" grilled meat, fish and veggies from the robata bar draw eclectic eaters to this Mill Valley Japanese that's offered a "great variety" since 1984; some deem it no more than "decent", but the lunch specials prove tempting "time and time again."

Rocker Oysterfellers Ⓜ *American*   ▽ 21 | 17 | 21 | $37

Valley Ford | Valley Ford Hotel | 14415 Hwy. 1 (School St.) | 707-876-1983 | www.rockeroysterfellers.com

Oysters are "number one" at this "lively" hang in the restored Valley Ford Hotel, a "fun" dinner depot "on the way to Bodega Bay" serving Sunday brunch to boot; there's American "comfort food" "for those who don't eat" bivalves, "but for those who do", don't miss Thursday's 5-7 PM "happy hour" when the local Drakes Bay beauts are only $1 each.

Rosso Pizzeria & Wine Bar *Italian/Pizza*   25 | 17 | 22 | $29

Santa Rosa | Creekside Ctr. | 53 Montgomery Dr. (bet. 2nd & Sotoyome Sts.) | 707-544-3221 | www.rossopizzeria.com

Devotees "dream" of the "exceptional" wood-fired pies and salad-topped piadines at this "sports-bar-meets-trattoria" run by Tra Vigne vets who show dedication to "locally farmed", "unexpectedly fine" fare; a "carefully selected", "reasonable" wine list, "spot-on" service and weekly Slow Food specials like "oven-roasted Dungeness crab" (in season) and "suckling pig on Sundays" ("eat your heart out, Tony Bourdain") secures its status on the "Santa Rosa foodie scene."

Rôtisario *Chicken*

- | - | - | I

Napa | Oxbow Public Mkt. | 610 First St. (bet. Silverado Trail & Soscol Ave.) | 707-226-7700 | www.roliroti.com

RoliRoti rotisseur's "excellent Oxbow Market lunch place" – the first stationary outpost of the mobile fleet – offers "one of the best values in Napa" cluck plucky patrons who flock here for rotisserie chicken and other sustainable meats served with roasted potatoes or in sandwiches, along with Italian-style porchetta plates (Tuesday, Friday and Saturday only); there's only an eight-seat counter, so most fly the coop and dine alfresco on the riverfront patio.

Royal Thai *Thai*

▽ 23 | 17 | 20 | $26

San Rafael | 610 Third St. (Irwin St.) | 415-485-1074 | www.royalthaisanrafael.com

Thai lovers will "travel miles" to this converted house in San Rafael for "terrific", "balanced" dishes including "several items that are quite unique"; the "attentive but not intrusive" staff "takes direction on spice level well" ("you want hot, you can get it here!"), and the "affordable" menu delivers lots of Bangkok for the buck.

Rutherford Grill *American*

24 | 21 | 21 | $41

Rutherford | 1180 Rutherford Rd. (Hwy. 29) | 707-963-1792 | www.rutherfordgrill.com

A "boisterous crowd" feasts on "craveable" wood-fired American "comfort food" with a "Napa touch" – including "incredible" ribs and cornbread that "should be a controlled substance" – at this "reasonable" Rutherford "hangout"; "sure, it's a chain" (a sibling to Houston's), but "comfortable booths" and a "happening" patio ensure you "feel at home", and the "free-corkage" policy is a plus; N.B. no reservations taken.

Sabor of Spain ⓜ *Spanish*

19 | 17 | 19 | $38

San Rafael | 1301 Fourth St. (C St.) | 415-457-8466 | www.saborofspain.com

This San Rafael vinoteca presenting "savory" Spanish tapas and entrees is an "enjoyable" place for a bite while sampling *tintos* from the "first-rate" wine list, enhanced by "welcoming" service and weekend flamenco guitar; still, some are unsatisfied by the "pricey", "small portions" and would like a little more "action" in the ambiance; N.B. new owners have redone the retail space next door to double as a private dining room.

Santé *Californian/French*

▽ 25 | 24 | 26 | $68

Sonoma | Fairmont Sonoma Mission Inn & Spa | 100 Boyes Blvd. (Sonoma Hwy.) | 707-939-2415 | www.fairmont.com

"Worthy of wine country" "without the pompous attitude", this Cal-French in the Fairmont Sonoma Mission Inn "does a nice job of high-end dining", providing "expertly prepared" Cal-French dinners, tasting menus and Sunday brunch featuring "local, seasonal ingredients" complemented by "wines from the surrounding vineyards"; a "well-trained" staff and "inviting" setting with "windows looking out at the swimming pool" "round out" the package.

Santi *Italian*

| 25 | 20 | 22 | $52 |

Geyserville | 21047 Geyserville Ave. (Hwy. 128) | 707-857-1790 | www.tavernasanti.com

This "top wine-country" "find" in Geyserville "transports you" with "superb" handcrafted pastas, salumi and other "rustic" Northern Italian *cibo* matched by a "nice" slate of Cal-Ital bottles; diners will still be able to "sit at the bar" or "dine under the stars" when it moves to a more contemporary venue in Santa Rosa's Fountaingrove Village in fall 2009.

Scoma's *Seafood*

| 22 | 18 | 21 | $47 |

Sausalito | 588 Bridgeway (Princess St.) | 415-332-9551 | www.scomassausalito.com

See review in City of San Francisco Directory.

NEW Scopa M *Italian*

| ▽ 24 | 20 | 22 | $45 |

Healdsburg | 109A Plaza St. (bet. Center St. & Healdsburg Ave.) | 707-433-5282 | www.scopahealdsburg.com

A "young, hopping" "alternative to more expensive digs in Healdsburg", this "tiny" new "locals' haunt wedged into the Plaza" "pulls off" "incredible" dinners of antipasti, pizza and pasta in a "cozy" setup run by a "cool" couple; many call it a "must for foodies" "post-wine tasting", but "those over 40 who complain about how loud it is" vie for the few outdoor seats "away from the bustle."

Sol Food *Puerto Rican*

| 23 | 16 | 17 | $18 |

San Rafael | 732 Fourth St. (Lincoln Ave.) | 415-451-4765
San Rafael | 901 Lincoln Ave. (3rd St.) | 415-451-4765
www.solfoodrestaurant.com

"Take a vacation to Puerto Rico without leaving Marin" at these San Rafael Sol sisters, both the original "big green thing" and its late-night, predominantly "take-out" Fourth Street spin-off serving "amazing", "healthy Californian-style" "Caribbean food" for "cheap"; the "quirky", "tropical" settings quench a thirst for "that island ambiance" as well as fruity iced tea (you can't buy or bring anything stiffer), and the "chili sauce alone is worth the price of admission."

Starlight Wine Bar & Restaurant M *Southern*

| ▽ 22 | 24 | 24 | $37 |

Sebastopol | 6167 Sebastopol Ave. (bet. Morris St. & Petaluma Ave.) | 707-823-1943 | www.starlightwinebar.com

Regulars "never tire of the standards" served at this Sebastopol New American-Creole, complemented by small-producer wines in a restored railroad car with a "great retro feel"; though some opine it's "overpriced", the "welcoming" owners and "friendliness of the other diners" make it easy to "join in the fun."

Station House Cafe *Californian*

| 20 | 15 | 18 | $33 |

Point Reyes Station | 11180 State Rte. 1 (2nd St.) | 415-663-1515 | www.stationhousecafe.com

Enthusiasts say "there's no better end" to a "day of hiking" in West Marin than this "casual" Point Reyes Station stop where the "generous", "consistent" Cal "comfort" dishes are created with "lots of local ingredients"; "when the weather's right" there's a "buzz" in the "pretty" garden (the "highlight" of a visit here), though a minority mutters it's "nothing special" and the "staff has a definite attitude problem."

St. Orres *Californian*

∇ 22 | 26 | 22 | $60

Gualala | St. Orres Hotel | 36601 S. Hwy. 1 (Seaside School Rd.) | 707-884-3303 | www.saintorres.com

Escapists "enjoy the wild food" foraged along the North Coast at this "offbeat" Gualala Californian, whose "unique" domed, Russian-style architecture and "beautiful scenery" makes for an "incredible experience"; though critics complain the kitchen "hasn't kept up with any foodie trends in the last 30 years", it's still praised as "one of the prettiest spaces you'll ever eat in."

☑ Sushi Ran *Japanese*

28 | 20 | 22 | $56

Sausalito | 107 Caledonia St. (bet. Pine & Turney Sts.) | 415-332-3620 | www.sushiran.com

"A gift from the Japanese gods", this "paragon of sushi" in Sausalito "soars" with "pristine" "fish flown in from Tsukiji market" and "perfect" cooked dishes served in an "inviting" setting; it's "expensive" and "tough to get a table" (less so at its next-door "sister wine bar" stocking a "gold-medal sake list"), but "sashimi lovers" and others happily "head over the bridge" for the "phenomenal" "experience."

Syrah *Californian/French*

25 | 19 | 24 | $50

Santa Rosa | 205 Fifth St. (Davis St.) | 707-568-4002 | www.syrahbistro.com

"Que syrah, syrah!", chef/co-owner Josh Silvers "nails it every time", "surprising and delighting" diners with "sensuous", "seasonal" Cal-French fare that's "picture-perfect in its presentation" at this "industrial"-style "favorite" in Santa Rosa; the wine pairings "hit a home run" too, since "boy", do the "efficient" servers "know their list", making it a top pick for "date night" or a "special-occasion splurge"; N.B. lunch is served Tuesday–Saturday.

Table Café ☑Ⓜ *Californian*

- | - | - | M

Larkspur | 1167 Magnolia Ave. (Estelle Ave.) | 415-461-6787 | www.table-cafe.com

Marinites march to this Larkspur "hole-in-the-wall" for its "mostly take-out" Californian cafe fare "with an Indian twist"; it's "just an easy place to eat", and while some "would love to see it move to a nicer space", "it's still worth going" to for its "nicely prepared" dosas, sandwiches and homemade ice cream; N.B. closes at 7 PM, 3:30 PM on Saturday.

NEW Tavern at Lark Creek *American*

- | - | - | M

Larkspur | 234 Magnolia Ave. (Madrone Ave.) | 415-924-7766 | www.tavernatlarkcreek.com

This dialed-down reincarnation of Larkspur's Lark Creek Inn has swung open its Victorian doors with a recession-friendly, farm-to-table New American menu served in an airy dining room with an atrium ceiling; even its beverage program is value-oriented, offering affordable artisan cocktails and cask-drawn house wines.

Taylor's Automatic Refresher *Diner*

22 | 13 | 15 | $18

Napa | Oxbow Public Mkt. | 644 First St. (bet. Silverado Trail & Soscol Ave.) | 707-224-6900

(continued)

(continued)

Taylor's Automatic Refresher

St. Helena | 933 Main St. (bet. Charter Oak Ave. & Pope St.) | 707-963-3486
www.taylorsrefresher.com

"Don't be fooled by the picnic tables" and "drive-in" service, this "idealized version of a roadside burger stand" with a "foodie-approved menu" is the "perfect" "wine country–style" "fast-food" pit stop in St. Helena (with sit-down spin-offs in Napa and the SF Ferry Building); it's "a bit pricey", but "rich" milkshakes and "affordable glasses of the Valley's best" are an automatic upgrade – just "stay away when the tour buses drop anchor."

Tea Room Café ⊠ *American*　　　∇ 24 | 18 | 18 | $25

Petaluma | 316 Western Ave. (Liberty St.) | 707-765-0199 |
www.tearoomcafe.com

"Small and cute and always filled with locals", this bohemian Petaluma cafe is a "wonderful" daytime stop serving "fresh" American breakfast fare, sandwiches and "superlative baked goods", along with "delicious teas" and "gigantic lattes"; the only downside is "ordering at the counter and fending off the hordes for a table"; N.B. closes at 3 PM (2 PM Saturday–Sunday).

⨀ Terra *American*　　　27 | 24 | 24 | $72

St. Helena | 1345 Railroad Ave. (bet. Adams St. & Hunt Ave.) |
707-963-8931 | www.terrarestaurant.com

"As reliable as the sunset", this St. Helena "haute" spot in a "romantic" "historic stone building" continues to be a "gastronomic paradise" where chef-owners Hiro Sone and Lissa Doumani (SF's Ame) "meld European and Asian influences" into "exquisite" New American dishes complemented by an "exceptional" wine list and "excellent" desserts; the "refined" service can be "haughty" at times, but most find the experience "magnificent" all around.

Toast *American*　　　- | - | - | M

Mill Valley | 31 Sunnyside Ave. (Blithedale Ave.) | 415-388-2500 |
www.toastmillvalley.com
NEW **Novato** | Hamilton Mktpl. | 5800 Nave Dr. (Bel Marin Keys Blvd.) |
415-382-1144 | www.toastnovato.com

There's more than toast at Marin County's dual breakfast meccas, which are filled to the brim with mountain bikers and Lexus-wielding families looking for morning joe, carb-loading brunches and hearty dinners of midpriced American comfort food; the original in Mill Valley sports a diner vibe, while the larger Novato location (offering brick-oven pizza too) is turning heads with an ultramodern design by architect Stanley Saitowitz.

Tra Vigne *Italian*　　　24 | 25 | 23 | $56

St. Helena | 1050 Charter Oak Ave. (Main St.) | 707-963-4444 |
www.travignerestaurant.com

St. Helena's legendary "wine country hangout" "remains a bastion" of "outstanding" Northern Italian cuisine, backed by a "wine list befitting a bistro in the middle of the vineyards"; while some sniff that the staff can be "a bit full of itself", most are too smitten by the "dreamy Napa Valley atmosphere" of the "Tuscan villa" dining room and the "hard-to-score" "gorgeous courtyard" to notice ("no corkage" helps too).

⨄ Ubuntu *Californian/Vegan* | 26 | 23 | 23 | $52 |

Napa | 1140 Main St. (Pearl St.) | 707-251-5656 | www.ubuntunapa.com
If you "get past the hippie vibe", proponents promise you'll find "love at first bite" at this "soaring, woodsy" "fine-dining" spot in Downtown Napa where chef Jeremy Fox "pushes the envelope" with "highly original", "rich" Cal-vegan fare made with produce from the restaurant's own "biodynamic garden"; the "well-versed staff" provides "wonderful explanations", and the "green atmosphere makes you feel healthy", though some find the upstairs yoga studio "a little distracting"; N.B. there's a wine bar and retail annex next door.

Underwood Bar & Bistro Ⓜ *Mediterranean* | 24 | 22 | 22 | $42 |

Graton | 9113 Graton Rd. (Edison St.) | 707-823-7023 | www.underwoodgraton.com
Though it's "off-the-beaten-path" in the "one-horse town" of Graton, this "West Country hangout" is "never empty"; rather, the "loud, crowded" scene "feels like you're in the big city", and "locals" who "squeeze into the beautiful mahogany bar for a well-poured cocktail" or a "full meal" of Mediterranean tapas "wouldn't have it any other way"; the service is "impressive" and "lunch on the patio" is "wonderful" to "cap off a day" of "wine tasting."

Uva Trattoria & Bar Ⓜ *Italian* | ▽ 23 | 19 | 21 | $37 |

Napa | 1040 Clinton St. (bet. Brown & Main Sts.) | 707-255-6646 | www.uvatrattoria.com
"Wonderful selections of wine", "delicious" Italian food and "divine" live jazz Wednesday–Sunday fuel a "locals' love affair" with this "lively" Napa "hangout" where the staff "makes you feel at home"; "reasonable" prices are a plus, and there's no corkage fee on the first BYO bottle.

Vin Antico Ⓜ *Italian* | ▽ 23 | 21 | 22 | $37 |

San Rafael | 881 Fourth St. (Cijos St. & Lootens Pl.) | 415-454-4492 | www.vinantico.com
With its "Continental atmosphere" and "nice bar scene", this "hip-looking" Fourth Street sidewalk trattoria and enoteca is "the kind of gem you'd expect to find tucked away in SoHo" rather than San Rafael; nibblers note the "creative", "ever-changing" Italian plates and "unique" wine list "work well before or after the movie", and say the "fantastic" Wednesday prix fixe is a bonus.

Volpi's Ristorante & Bar Ⓜ *Italian* | ▽ 19 | 18 | 19 | $35 |

Petaluma | 24 Washington St. (bet. Kentucky St. & Petaluma Blvd.) | 707-762-2371
Petaluma *paisani* appreciate this "family-friendly" "old-schooler" delivering "substantial" Italian dishes for "quite a bargain"; the atmosphere is right out of "*Lady and the Tramp*", plus the "Prohibition-era" back bar is worth "checking out" too; N.B. closed Monday-Tuesday.

Water Street Bistro ⊅ *French* | ▽ 23 | 21 | 21 | $26 |

Petaluma | 100 Petaluma Blvd. N. (Western Ave.) | 707-763-9563
"Sitting outside right on the waterfront" is a "treat" at this "no-frills" bistro overlooking the Petaluma River, where the "true foodie" chef-owner "caringly" presents a chalkboard menu of "authentic French" homemade soups, salads and specials from a farm-"fresh" Sonoma

larder; regulars "love the breakfast, lunch" and "monthly dinners", calling it an experience that "cannot be beat."

Willi's Seafood & Raw Bar *Seafood*
24 | 21 | 21 | $45

Healdsburg | 403 Healdsburg Ave. (North St.) | 707-433-9191 | www.willisseafood.net

The "flavors are bold and playful" in the "creative small plates" of "terrific seafood" "both raw and cooked" at this "local hangout" in Healdsburg, where the staff provides "attentive" service amid a "bustling" scene; you can snuggle in an "intimate" booth, "people-watch" at the "hoppin' bar" or relax on the "beautiful patio", just keep in mind that those "little plates will add up."

Willi's Wine Bar *Eclectic*
26 | 20 | 23 | $47

Santa Rosa | Orchard Inn | 4404 Old Redwood Hwy. (Ursuline Rd.) | 707-526-3096 | www.williswinebar.net

This "secret roadhouse" in Santa Rosa is a "wine country jewel" offering a "constantly" changing menu of Eclectic "small plates" "loaded with flavor" and "global inspiration", served by a "cordial" staff that's "knowlegeable about pairings"; a "mix" of "locals and tourists" dines "alfresco" in the "garden" or "sits at the bar" – but cognoscenti caution "the bill can add up."

Willow Wood
Market Cafe *Eclectic/Mediterranean*
24 | 18 | 20 | $28

Graton | 9020 Graton Rd. (Edison St.) | 707-823-0233 | www.willowwoodgraton.com

There's "lots of heart and soul" at this "charming country cafe" in Graton that dishes up "amazingly good breakfasts" (try the "excellent polenta") and "perfect lunches" of "fresh" Eclectic-Med eats, served by a "caring staff"; you can "relax" and enjoy the "patio" or "funky" interior during a "stop on a wine-tasting day in Sonoma" or when you're trying to "get over your hangover", and while some gripe that "service can be slow", others insist the "food is worth the wait."

Wine Spectator Greystone *Californian*
22 | 23 | 22 | $60

St. Helena | Culinary Institute of America | 2555 Main St. (Deer Park Rd.) | 707-967-1010 | www.ciachef.edu

For foodies it's a "culinary dream" come true to "watch the kitchen live in action" at this "impressive" winery-cum-restaurant located on the Culinary Institute of America's St. Helena campus, where "well-prepared" Cal-Eclectic fare and an "outstanding wine list" are served in an "impressive" dining room with "great stone walls"; a staff of professionals and students provides "attentive" service and the terrace offers "fantastic views" of the vineyards, but some cynics sneer "Hyde Park it's not."

Yankee Pier *New England/Seafood*
17 | 15 | 17 | $37

Larkspur | 286 Magnolia Ave. (bet. King St. & William Ave.) | 415-924-7676 | www.yankeepier.com

"Bradley Ogden's tribute to a New England clambake" with a sustainable West Coast slant "satisfies cravings for lobster rolls" and "good chowder" at this mini-chain "in the 'burbs" (and SFO); still, "disappointed" diners (especially "Eastern seaboard" transplants) say they've "had better", noting the "catch of the day is your wallet."

	FOOD	DECOR	SERVICE	COST

zazu Ⓜ *American/Italian* — 25 | 20 | 23 | $46

Santa Rosa | 3535 Guerneville Rd. (Willowside Rd.) | 707-523-4814 | www.zazurestaurant.com

"Woweekazowee!" exclaim fans of this "funky", "out-of-the-way" Santa Rosa "roadhouse" where the small but "marvelous" New American–Northern Italian menu "reflects the passion" of chef-owners Duskie Estes and John Stewart, with flavors that "shout out to you from the plate"; "as local as local gets", since "much of the produce comes from the garden out back" (and the "spectacular" salumi is housemade), it also boasts an "awesome" wine list and "relaxed" atmosphere, all adding up to "quirky Sonoma hospitality at its finest."

Zin *American* — 23 | 19 | 22 | $43

Healdsburg | 344 Center St. (North St.) | 707-473-0946 | www.zinrestaurant.com

"Industry" folks banter about the "wine biz" at this bustling "Southern-inspired" New American where chef/co-owner Jeff Mall "makes everything he can from scratch" and even "grows a good part of his own vegetables", creating "killer comfort food" (including "cult favorites" like "phenomenal" beer-battered green beans) complemented by "extraordinary" wines; with its "unpretentious vibe" and servers who "genuinely care", visitors vouch for it as the "best value in Healdsburg."

Zinsvalley Ⓩ *American* — ▽ 19 | 16 | 20 | $39

Napa | Browns Valley Shopping Ctr. | 3253 Browns Valley Rd. (Austin Way) | 707-224-0695 | www.zinsvalley.com

Locals "love to take out-of-town friends and family" to this "welcoming" "neighborhood treasure" serving "down-to-earth", reasonably priced New American fare in the Browns Valley area of Napa; two fireplaces and a "lovely" creekside patio make it a "cozy" "hangout", particularly for enjoying "happy-hour deals" and midweek specials; P.S. "no corkage fee" on your first two bottles.

ZuZu *Spanish* — 23 | 18 | 22 | $41

Napa | 829 Main St. (bet. 2nd & 3rd Sts.) | 707-224-8555 | www.zuzunapa.com

Small Spanish bites "packed with flavor" (such as "buttery bacalao") make this "find in Downtown Napa" "tops in tapas" as well as "wonderful" wines; the "eclectic" candlelit space is filled with "lots of lively folks", and while a few caution the plates "add up in a hurry", others holler "keep 'em coming!"; P.S. "no reservations."

SOUTH OF SAN FRANCISCO

Top Food Ratings

Excludes places with low votes.

28 Kaygetsu | *Japanese*

27 Marinus | *French*
Manresa | *American*
Le Papillon | *French*
Cafe Gibraltar | *Mediterranean*
Sierra Mar | *Cal./Eclectic*

26 Passionfish | *Cal./Seafood*
La Forêt | *Continental/French*
Evvia | *Greek*
Village Pub | *American*

Tamarine | *Vietnamese*
Sent Sovi | *Californian*

25 Marché | *French*
Plumed Horse* | *Californian*
Aubergine | *Cal.*
Dio Deka | *Greek*
Roy's | *Hawaiian*
Alexander's | *Japanese/Steak*
Fresh Cream | *French*
Gayle's Bakery | *Bakery*

BY CUISINE

AMERICAN
27 Manresa
26 Village Pub
25 Flea St. Café
Pacific's Edge
24 Navio

ASIAN
26 Tamarine
24 Flying Fish Grill
23 Xanh
21 Three Seasons
20 Krung Thai

CALIFORNIAN
27 Sierra Mar
26 Passionfish
Sent Sovi
25 Plumed Horse
Aubergine

CHINESE
24 O'mei
23 Tai Pan
Koi Palace
22 Fook Yuen Seafood
Hunan Home/Garden

CONTINENTAL
26 La Forêt
23 Anton & Michel
Ecco
19 Bella Vista

FRENCH
27 Marinus
Le Papillon

25 Marché
Fresh Cream
24 Citronelle

INDIAN
24 Amber India
23 Shalimar
Junnoon
22 Roti Indian Bistro
21 Udupi Palace

ITALIAN
23 Pasta Moon
Chantilly
Osteria
Casanova
Cantinetta Luca

JAPANESE
28 Kaygetsu
25 Alexander's Steak
23 Ebisu
GoChi.
22 Fuki Sushi

MED./GREEK
27 Cafe Gibraltar
26 Evvia
25 Dio Deka
23 Fandango
22 71 Saint Peter

SEAFOOD
26 Passionfish
24 Flying Fish Grill
23 Koi Palace
22 Fook Yuen Seafood
Old Port Lobster

---

* Indicates a tie with restaurant above

Menus, photos, voting and more – free at ZAGAT.com

BY SPECIAL FEATURE

BREAKFAST/BRUNCH

26 La Forêt
Gayle's Bakery
24 Navio
23 Koi Palace
St. Michael's

OUTDOOR SEATING

27 Sierra Mar
25 Roy's
23 Casanova
Anton & Michel
20 Sam's Chowder Hse.

PEOPLE-WATCHING

26 Evvia
Village Pub
Tamarine
Dio Deka
18 Joya Restaurant

ROMANCE

27 Marinus
Sierra Mar
26 La Forêt
25 Pacific's Edge
23 Casanova

SINGLES SCENES

23 Xanh
Junnoon
20 Cascal
19 E&O Trading Co.
Sino

SMALL PLATES

26 Tamarine
Three Seasons
20 Cascal
Lavanda
19 Zibibbo

TASTING MENUS

28 Kaygetsu
27 Marinus
Manresa
25 Aubergine
23 Chez TJ

WINNING WINE LISTS

27 Marinus
Manresa
Le Papillon
Sierra Mar
26 Passionfish

BY LOCATION

CARMEL/MONTEREY

27 Marinus
25 Aubergine
Fresh Cream
Pacific's Edge
24 Grasing's Coastal

HALF MOON BAY/COAST

27 Cafe Gibraltar
24 Navio
23 Pasta Moon
22 Flying Fish Grill
21 Mezza Luna

PALO ALTO/MENLO PK

28 Kaygetsu
26 Evvia
Tamarine
25 Marché
Flea St. Café

PENINSULA

26 Village Pub
25 John Bentley's
23 Koi Palace
Viognier
22 231 Ellsworth

SANTA CRUZ/ CAPITOLA

25 Gayle's Bakery
24 O'mei
23 Gabriella Café
18 Shadowbrook

SILICON VALLEY

27 Manresa
Le Papillon
26 La Forêt
25 Dio Deka
Alexander's Steak

Top Decor

29	Sierra Mar		Tai Pan
28	Pacific's Edge		Shadowbrook
27	Navio		Village Pub
	Marinus		Quattro Restaurant
26	Plumed Horse		Aubergine
	Roy's	23	Dio Deka
25	Casanova		Marché
24	Nepenthe		Fresh Cream
	Anton & Michel		Joya Restaurant
	Manresa		Evvia

Top Service

27	Manresa		Aubergine
	Le Papillon		Plumed Horse
26	Marinus		Passionfish
	Sierra Mar	24	Anton & Michel
	Chantilly		Roy's
	Sent Sovi		Navio
25	La Forêt		Pacific's Edge
	Kaygetsu		Tai Pan
	Fresh Cream		Flea St. Café
	Village Pub		John Bentley's

Best Buys

In order of Bang for the Buck rating.

1. In-N-Out
2. La Corneta
3. Cheese Steak Shop
4. Pancho Villa
5. Pluto's Fresh Food
6. La Cumbre Taqueria
7. Burger Joint
8. Gayle's Bakery
9. BurgerMeister
10. Udupi Palace
11. Stacks
12. Patxi's Chicago Pizza
13. Don Pico's
14. North Beach Pizza
15. Flying Fish Grill
16. Amici's Pizzeria
17. Hotaru
18. Shalimar
19. Dish Dash
20. Pomodoro

OTHER GOOD VALUES

Amber India
Barbara's Fish Trap
Basque Cultural Center
Big Sur Bakery
Bucca di Beppo
Calafia
Cool Café

Fishwife
Happy Café
Hunan Home/Garden
Kabul Afghan
Krung Thai
Original Joe's
Ristorante Avanti

South of San Francisco

	FOOD	DECOR	SERVICE	COST

Alexander's Steakhouse *Japanese/Steak* | 25 | 23 | 24 | $75 |

Cupertino | Cupertino Sq. | 10330 N. Wolfe Rd. (bet. Rte. 280 & Stevens Creek Blvd.) | 408-446-2222 | www.alexanderssteakhouse.com
"Magnificent cuts of meat on display" tempt connoisseurs to go "full-tilt Kobe beef" at this Japanese steakhouse in Cupertino whose "exquisite" delicacies, "impeccable" decor and "grown-up service" make it "stand out in the cattle field"; "if you have the scratch", "splurge on the Wagyu" (and throw in some "hamachi shots") purr Silicon Valley "fat cats", but "save room for the flavored cotton candy they bring with the check."

Amber Café *Indian* | 24 | 20 | 20 | $36 |

Mountain View | 600 W. El Camino Real (View St.) | 650-968-1751

Amber India *Indian*

Mountain View | Olive Tree Shopping Ctr. | 2290 W. El Camino Real (bet. Ortega & S. Rengstorff Aves.) | 650-968-7511
San Jose | 377 Santana Row (Olin Ave.) | 408-248-5400
www.amber-india.com
"Even after expanding" from its "white-tablecloth" Mountain View strip-mall location to "snazzier" digs in SoMa and San Jose, complete with "top-notch bar service", this "incredible" Indian is "still the king" for "unbeatable lunch buffets" frequented by the "business crowd", as well as "distinctively flavored", "delightful dinners"; by comparison, the cafeteria-style Café branch sells "chaat" for cheap.

Amici's East Coast Pizzeria *Pizza* | 20 | 13 | 17 | $21 |

NEW Cupertino | 10310 S. De Anza Blvd. (Rodrigues Ave.) | 408-252-3333
Mountain View | 790 Castro St. (Yosemite Ave.) | 650-961-6666
Redwood Shores | 226 Redwood Shores Pkwy. (Twin Dolphin Dr.) | 650-654-3333
San Jose | 225 W. Santa Clara St. (bet. N. Almaden Ave. & Notre Dame St.) | 408-289-9000
San Mateo | 69 Third Ave. (San Mateo Dr.) | 650-342-9392
www.amicis.com
See review in City of San Francisco Directory.

Anton & Michel Restaurant *Continental* | 23 | 24 | 24 | $59 |

Carmel | Mission St. (bet. Ocean & 7th Aves.) | 831-624-2406 | www.antonandmichel.com
Embodying a "vision of Carmel", this 1980-founded "hideaway" proffers "classic Continental cuisine" ("flambéed desserts!") matched by a "comprehensive wine list" in a fireplace-lit setting with a "glassed-in" solarium and "fountain" views; though the experience is "relaxing" for most, a few find it a bit too "fussy" and "formal."

NEW Aquarius *American* | - | - | - | M |

Santa Cruz | Santa Cruz Dream Inn | 175 W. Cliff Dr. (Bay St.) | 831-460-5012 | www.aquariussantacruz.com
Reflecting a new dawn in Santa Cruz dining, this beachfront arrival in the completely remodeled Dream Inn showcases a midpriced New American menu of sustainable seafood along with the other epicurean and viticultural bounty of the Central Coast; wraparound glass windows offer panoramic views of the Pacific, while those who want to actually

FOOD | DECOR | SERVICE | COST

get their toes wet can dine poolside at the Aquarius bar; N.B. open daily for breakfast, dinner and cocktails, with lunch served weekends only.

Arcadia *American* — 21 | 21 | 19 | $58

San Jose | San Jose Marriott | 100 W. San Carlos St. (Market St.) | 408-278-4555 | www.michaelmina.net

"Michael Mina's food without the push to get in" makes this swanky New American steakhouse with "sumptuous" "modern" decor and "well-clad servers" a "San Jose favorite by a mile"; regulars who "enjoy the beef and cognac later" don't mind that it's "not as amazing" as his eponymous SF flagship or even its "former glorious self" (before the menu redux) – they just "wish it weren't in the Marriott."

Aubergine *Californian* — 25 | 24 | 25 | $94
(fka L'Auberge Carmel)

Carmel | L'Auberge Carmel | Monte Verde St. (7th Ave.) | 831-624-8578 | www.laubergecarmel.com

With a new name that reflects chef Christophe Grosjean's dedication to fresh vegetables, this "luxurious" 12-table establishment in the "exclusive" L'Auberge inn remains one of the "best in Carmel", thanks to "out-of-this-world" "nouveau" Cal-French dinners served by a "spot-on" staff; the portion police quip "don't forget your magnifying glass", while others warn "if you have to ask how much it costs, don't bother", but most agree it's "perfect" for a "grown-up special occasion."

Barbara's Fish Trap ⊘ *Seafood* — 20 | 13 | 16 | $24

Princeton by the Sea | 281 Capistrano Rd. (Hwy. 1) | 650-728-7049

"Any closer to the water and you'd be on a boat" josh fans of this "kitschy" "little wooden-frame" "fish shack" right on the Princeton pier, serving up "super-fresh, super-fried goodness" (as well as some "healthier" options); with aquatic-themed "plastic tablecloths" and "fishing nets hanging from the ceiling", it ain't "four-star", but hits the spot "when you want a day-at-the-beach feeling", particularly if you take it to go with a brew at a picnic table.

Basin, The *American* — ▽ 21 | 19 | 23 | $44

Saratoga | 14572 Big Basin Way (5th St.) | 408-867-1906 | www.thebasin.com

It's "not a destination", mind you, but locals insist this easygoing Saratogan known for its "simple", "consistent" seasonal New American fare (with Spanish and Italian accents), stiff drinks and "affable" host who "greets and seats you personally" is a "great place to end up"; the martini bar "fills with activity on the weekends", while the patio (beneath the canopy of a giant ancient oak tree) is "romantic on a warm night."

Basque Cultural Center Ⓜ *Spanish* — 22 | 15 | 21 | $30

South San Francisco | 599 Railroad Ave. (bet. Orange & Spruce Aves.) | 650-583-8091 | www.basqueculturalcenter.com

"Honest" Basque dishes and "table wines" among the "best north of Bakersfield" are worth the "GPS" required for feasting at this "old-timey ethnic club" in South San Francisco; the "huge" prix fixe dinners ($19.95) served family-style at communal tables are a "hell of a deal", and if you're lucky, you can "hear old-world stories" or "watch the young bucks play hotly contested *pilota* on the indoor court" after lunch.

	FOOD	DECOR	SERVICE	COST

Bella Vista 🎫Ⓜ *Continental*   19 | 22 | 23 | $62

Woodside | 13451 Skyline Blvd. (5 mi. south of Rte. 92) | 650-851-1229 | www.bvrestaurant.com

"Old-school Continental" cuisine like "steak Diane with the spectacle of a flambé presentation" by tuxedoed waiters "rewards the hair-raising drive into the mountains" at this Woodside "institution" with a 500-bottle cellar", though many consider the food "overdone" and "overpriced", the location "nestled in the woods" "overlooking the Bay" and Silicon Valley ("ask to be seated by the window") is what makes it a destination "where dreams come true."

Big Sur Bakery &   21 | 17 | 19 | $29
Restaurant *American/Bakery*

Big Sur | Hwy. 1 (½ mi. south of Pfeiffer State Pk.) | 831-667-0520 | www.bigsurbakery.com

Both "locals" and road-trippers embarking on their "Big Sur adventure" are "enamored" of this "quaint" "pit stop" in an old ranch house "surrounded by nature's cathedral of trees and bird songs"; its "excellent", "home-cooked" American eats and wood-fired pizzas are joined by a "limited supply" of "delicious breads and pastries" that pull in a "steep premium"; N.B. only the bakery is open Mondays.

Bistro Elan 🎫Ⓜ *Californian/French*   24 | 18 | 21 | $51

Palo Alto | 448 S. California Ave. (bet. Birch St. & El Camino Real) | 650-327-0284

"European sensibilities" and "seasonal produce" combine to create "continually satisfying" Cal-French meals at this "see-and-be-seen" Palo Alto bistro that's "aged well"; though the "superior" service strikes some as "supercilious", and others balk at "sardine-style" seating, it remains "madly popular" with "affluent" Silicon Valley-ites for "business lunches" and "romantic" summertime dinners in the "spectacular" back garden.

Bistro Moulin 🎫 *European*   - | - | - | E

Monterey | 867 Wave St. (bet. David & Irving Aves.) | 831-333-1200 | www.bistromoulin.com

Just up the street from the Monterey Bay Aquarium, this unapologetically European bistro run by a 25-year veteran of Carmel's Casanova proffers Gallic classics like moules frites and boeuf bourguignon for a slightly upscale lunch and dinner in a convivial, intimate storefront; occasional Moulin Rouge–themed events and an adjacent retail shop selling imported ceramics and private label oils, vinegars and wines further the Francophile fantasy.

Bistro Vida *French*   18 | 19 | 18 | $38

Menlo Park | 641 Santa Cruz Ave. (bet. Curtis St. & El Camino Real) | 650-462-1686 | www.bistrovidamp.com

"Charming" with "French cafe" decor and sidewalk seating, this "agreeable" Menlo Park haunt leads diners to differ over whether it "holds its own" against the neighboring competition, or "doesn't measure up" to the "Parisian bistro it hopes to be" ("everything could be better with a little effort"); some say "stick with brunch" since the "good pastries and espresso will save the day for the adults, and an ice cream crêpe will thrill the kids."

	FOOD	DECOR	SERVICE	COST

Blowfish Sushi To Die For *Japanese* | 20 | 19 | 17 | $42 |

San Jose | 335 Santana Row (bet. Moorpark Ave. & Stevens Creek Blvd.) |
408-345-3848 | www.blowfishsushi.com
See review in City of San Francisco Directory.

Buca di Beppo *Italian* | 14 | 16 | 16 | $27 |

Campbell | Pruneyard Shopping Ctr. | 1875 S. Bascom Ave. (Campbell Ave.) |
408-377-7722
Palo Alto | 643 Emerson St. (bet. Forest & Hamilton Aves.) | 650-329-0665
San Jose | Oakridge Mall | 925 Blossom Hill Rd. (bet. Santa Teresa &
Winfield Blvds.) | 408-226-1444
www.bucadibeppo.com
An "ode to excess", this "campy" chain draws "noisy families" and
"birthday" celebrants with a "1950s Italian" menu served in "feed-an-
army", family-style portions; "memorabilia"-laden settings and "cheap"
tabs ratchet up the "boisterous" goings-on, though "more-is-less"
proponents say "food quality is not its strong suit."

Burger Joint *Burgers* | 18 | 11 | 15 | $14 |

South San Francisco | San Francisco Int'l Airport | Int'l Terminal,
Boarding Area A (San Bruno Ave.) | 650-821-0582 | www.burgerjointsf.com
See review in City of San Francisco Directory.

BurgerMeister *Burgers* | 19 | 11 | 14 | $15 |

Daly City | 507 Westlake Ctr. (John Daly Blvd.) | 650-755-1941 |
www.burgermeistersf.com
See review in City of San Francisco Directory.

Café Brioche *Californian/French* | 22 | 17 | 19 | $32 |

Palo Alto | 445 S. California Ave. (bet. Ash St. & El Camino Real) |
650-326-8640 | www.cafebriochepaloalto.com
Palo Altans give props to this "unpretentious" "French treat" where
there's "no need to dress up to be spoiled" by a staff delivering "wonderful sandwiches and salads" and "high-quality" Cal-Provençal
"blackboard specials" for a "good value"; it's "intimate", so "space is
at a premium", particularly on "weekend nights" and at the "popular"
brunch; N.B. the owner and chef changed post-Survey.

☑ Cafe Gibraltar Ⓜ *Mediterranean* | 27 | 20 | 23 | $43 |

El Granada | 425 Avenue Alhambra (Palma St.) | 650-560-9039 |
www.cafegibraltar.com
El Granada–goers are "enthralled and enticed" by the "exceptional",
"boldly flavored" dishes "creating sensory overload" at this
Mediterranean "jewel" that's "romantic" with an "ocean view" and
North African touches like low-slung tables; several vegetarian
choices, an "exemplary, reasonably priced wine list" and "cheerful"
service add to the appeal.

Café Rustica Ⓜ *Californian* | 23 | 20 | 21 | $37 |

Carmel Valley | 10 Del Fino Pl. (Carmel Valley Rd.) | 831-659-4444 |
www.caferusticacarmelvalley.com
"Off the beaten track", this "country gem" in Carmel Valley is "popular" for its "to-die-for" wood-fired pizzas, salads and other Californian
fare at "half the cost" of fancier haunts; visitors venture it's "worth the
30-minute drive from Downtown" if only to "enjoy all the deliciousness"
in a "picturesque setting" with "views of the mountains."

	FOOD	DECOR	SERVICE	COST

NEW Calafia *Californian* — 21 | 19 | 18 | $31

Palo Alto | Town & Country Vill. | 855 El Camino Real (Embarcadero Rd.) | 650-322-9200 | www.calafiapaloalto.com

"Named after fabled queen Calafia, the namesake of the Golden State", this "enticing" Eclectic and "very Californian" new cafe from former Google chef Charlie Ayers lures Palo Altans in search of "imaginative", "healthy locavore" Slow Food served fast for a "reasonable price"; the "novel", "industrial-chic" setting, tricked out with handheld ordering devices and reclaimed wooden tables, is on the "noisy" side, but the adjacent "market-a-go-go" offers an easy take-out option.

Cantankerous Fish, The *Seafood* — 18 | 17 | 17 | $41

Mountain View | 420 Castro St. (bet. California & Mercy Sts.) | 650-966-8124 | www.thecantankerousfish.com

"A fish out of water on suburban Castro Street in Mountain View", this "less formal" spin-off of Scott's Seafood is a "reliable" choice for "business lunches" or "pre-theater" dinners of "fresh", "simple" fin fare with a bit of a "scene"; still, it's "not terrifically memorable", causing the cantankerous to complain "the food is plain dull and so is the overall experience."

Cantinetta Luca *Italian* — 23 | 21 | 21 | $49

Carmel | Dolores St. (bet. Ocean & 7th Aves.) | 831-625-6500 | www.cantinettaluca.com

"A must for salumi lovers", this "busy, noisy" Italian by David Fink on "one of the cutest streets in Carmel" cranks out "authentic" pizza and other plates along with "terrific" wines in a "visually arresting" space showcasing a "glassed-in" room for "curing meats"; service is generally "accommodating", though some critics bemoan "Beverly Hills prices"; N.B. no lunch served Monday–Thursday in the off-season.

Casanova *French/Italian* — 23 | 25 | 24 | $53

Carmel | Fifth Ave. (bet. Mission & San Carlos Sts.) | 831-625-0501 | www.casanovarestaurant.com

Like something "out of a fairy tale", this "romantic", "relaxing" Carmel "cottage" with an "amazing" wine cellar presents "fabulous" "country" French–Northern Italian dishes in "beautiful copper pots" for meals reminiscent of "Tuscany or Provence"; whether "inside by the fireplace" or out on the "dog-friendly" patio, "tourists", "weekenders" and others who have "been going for 30 years" declare it "always delights."

Cascal *Pan-Latin* — 20 | 20 | 19 | $37

Mountain View | 400 Castro St. (California St.) | 650-940-9500 | www.cascalrestaurant.com

"Multiculti", "flavorful" small plates and sangria are "always a hit" at this "colorful" Pan-Latin tapas place where "Silicon Valley types" and Mountain View minglers come to "celebrate anything", "dance" to the "live music" on weekends and "leave happy"; it's "relatively reasonable", but "be prepared for the din" and "slow" service during peak hours.

Cetrella Ⓜ *Mediterranean* — 20 | 21 | 17 | $54

Half Moon Bay | 845 Main St. (Monte Vista Ln.) | 650-726-4090 | www.cetrella.com

Reopened after a winter hiatus, this "beautiful", sprawling Half Moon Bay haunt, warmed by stone fireplaces and an open kitchen, offers a "winning combination of top-flight jazz" (Thursday–Saturday) and "delicious, hearty" Mediterranean meals; despite its assets, though, some locals fret it's too "expensive for the coast"; N.B. the post-Survey arrival of new chef Sylvain Montassier, who brings more French techniques, is not reflected in the Food score.

✷ Chantilly ⌧ *French/Italian*   23 | 23 | 26 | $65

Redwood City | 3001 El Camino Real (Selby Ln.) | 650-321-4080 | www.chantillyrestaurant.com

"*L'ancien régime*" lives on at this "classy", "well-appointed" grande dame in Redwood City where Peninsula patrons are pleased by the "exquisite", "traditional" French–Northern Italian cuisine provided with "excellent" service; though *très cher* and a touch "snooty", it's the ideal "quiet" place "to take your mom" or "splurge" for dinner when you "value your companions' conversation as well as the food."

Cheesecake Factory   *American*   16 | 17 | 16 | $29

San Jose | 925 Blossom Hill Rd. (bet. Oakridge Mall & Winfield Blvd.) | 408-225-6948

Santa Clara | Westfield Shoppingtown Valley Fair | 3041 Stevens Creek Blvd. (N. Winchester Blvd.) | 408-246-0092
www.cheesecakefactory.com

See review in City of San Francisco Directory.

Cheese Steak Shop   *Cheesesteaks*   23 | 6 | 14 | $11

San Jose | Monterey Plaza | 5524 Monterey Rd. (bet. Blossom Hill & Ford Rds.) | 408-972-0271

NEW **Sunnyvale** | 832 W. El Camino Real (Hollenbeck Ave.) | 408-530-8159
www.cheesesteakshop.com

See review in City of San Francisco Directory.

Chef Chu's   *Chinese*   22 | 14 | 20 | $28

Los Altos | 1067 N. San Antonio Rd. (El Camino Real) | 650-948-2696 | www.chefchu.com

"Consummate host" and "celebrity chef" "Lawrence Chu (and now his son, Larry Jr.)" continues to attract a "cult following" to this "Los Altos institution" serving "Chinese-American favorites" as well as more "authentic" Mandarin meals and "high-end banquets in a "hectic" yet "happy" setup; since the decor is "dated" and service sometimes suffers from the "crowds begging for entry", many simply opt to "take out."

Chez Shea   *Eclectic*   ▽ 23 | 14 | 16 | $24

Half Moon Bay | 408 Main St. (Mill St.) | 650-560-9234 | www.chez-shea.com

Dubbed "Cafe Gibraltar light", this "kid-friendly" Half Moon Bay storefront cafe offers an inexpensive, "global-inspired" Eclectic menu for the "best lunch in town" or a "quiet dinner" on the "charming, European" back patio; unfortunately, there's "not much room inside" and "not unlike the weather", the food and service can be "unpredictable" (plan on "waiting awhile after ordering"); N.B. no dinner on Mondays.

Chez TJ ⌧Ⓜ *French*   23 | 21 | 21 | $111

Mountain View | 938 Villa St. (bet. Castro St. & Shoreline Blvd.) | 650-964-7466 | www.cheztj.com

Peninsulans seeking a big "night out" head to this "fancy French" "old favorite" in a Mountain View "Victorian home", serving "superb" prix fixes that "pack a lot of intensity in small packages", with "matched wines" and "whimsical desserts"; the interior is "romantic" ("if creaky"), but some fret there's "no wow factor" and say the "inconsistent" service falls short of the steep tariff.

Cin-Cin Wine Bar & Restaurant ⓂEclectic

▽ 23 | 21 | 23 | $42

Los Gatos | 368 Village Ln. (Saratoga Los Gatos Rd.) | 408-354-8006 | www.cincinwinebar.com

"The best thing to happen to Los Gatos in a long time" cheer "happy-hour" pals about this new boîte (replacing Café Marcella) serving "well-priced, occasionally inspired" American and global "grazings" along with "creative cocktails" and biodynamic wines in an eco-chic space decorated with bamboo floors and recycled wood and glass; as at its "sister restaurant", Cascal, service is "friendly" and the scene is "lively to some" but "loud to me."

Citronelle ⓈⓂ Californian/French

24 | 23 | 22 | $75

Carmel | Carmel Valley Ranch | 1 Old Ranch Rd. (Carmel Valley Rd.) | 831-626-2599 | www.carmelvalleyranch.com

A "solid addition to top Carmel restaurants", this West Coast spin-off of Michel Richard's DC flagship "hits all the right notes", presenting "innovative, refined" French cuisine with a "fresh" Californian twist in a "gorgeous room" befitting a "special meal"; its "happening" hotel setting generates the "best bar buzz in the area", though a few who cite "inconsistency" maintain that monsieur "should visit more often."

Club XIX ⓈⓂ Californian/French

▽ 23 | 29 | 23 | $89

Pebble Beach | The Lodge at Pebble Beach | 1700 17-Mile Dr. (Cypress Dr.) | 831-625-8519 | www.pebblebeach.com

"Put your putter away and pull out your wallet" for this "sophisticated", "well-decorated" dinner destination at the Lodge at Pebble Beach, serving "good" Cal-French cuisine and showing "attention to detail" all around; even if the prices deter "locals", wowed wayfarers say it's "worth a trip" just for the location overlooking the 18th hole and Pacific, not to mention the extensive selection of cognacs and cigars.

Cool Café Californian

- | - | - | I

NEW Menlo Park | 1525 O'Brien Dr. (University Ave.) | 650-325-3665 Ⓢ

Palo Alto | Stanford Univ. Cantor Arts Ctr. | 128 Lomita Dr. (Museum Way) | 650-725-4758 Ⓜ

www.cooleatz.com

Chef Jesse Cool (Flea St. Café) has long been pleasing "socially conscious foodies" and Cantor Art Center exhibit-goers with salads, sandwiches and other local, organic Californian fare at her counter-service Stanford campus lunch cafe, where patrons can opt for the patio and "ruminate over the Rodins" in the adjacent sculpture garden; it's closed Monday-Tuesday and serves dinner on Thursday only; N.B. a new Menlo Park branch is opening soon.

Dasaprakash Indian

▽ 19 | 18 | 21 | $22

Santa Clara | 2636 Homestead Rd. (bet. Kiely Blvd. & San Tomas Expwy.) | 408-246-8292 | www.dasaprakash.com

While it's a "SoCal transplant", satisfied surveyors insist it's really "South India" that made the leap to this Downtown Santa Clara sub-

| | FOOD | DECOR | SERVICE | COST |

continental proffering "solid", "authentic" vegetarian dosas, pakoras and Thali plates that "bring back memories of Madras"; "good service" adds to the appeal, while all-day weekend dining is a boon for lassi-and-lentil-lovin' late-risers.

Deetjen's Big Sur Restaurant *Californian* 22 | 22 | 22 | $41

Big Sur | Deetjen's Big Sur Inn | 48865 Hwy. 1 (30 mi. south of Carmel) | 831-667-2377 | www.deetjens.com

"One of the most romantic pit stops" on PCH, this "rustic", "Hobbit-esque" "favorite" in a "historic" inn "across from the Pacific" is "deservedly legendary" for its "fantastic breakfasts", though its "wonderful" Cal dinners – "prepared from local fish, game and vegetables" and complemented by "vintages you'll be surprised to see here" – are also "worth the trip"; yes, the "hippie-ish vibe" may be "too funky for some", but acolytes aver "this is where to eat in Big Sur"; N.B. no lunch.

Dio Deka *Greek* 25 | 23 | 23 | $57

Los Gatos | Hotel Los Gatos | 210 E. Main St. (High School Ct.) | 408-354-7700 | www.diodeka.com

"Satisfied patrons" pack this "let's-try-something-different" Los Gatos estiatorio for a "dining experience fit for the gods" – assuming they'd enjoy a "delightfully prepared" Greek–Med menu, "spectacular wine list" and quintet of "hands-on" owners who ensure "top-flight service"; even if it's "noisy" and "a bit pricey", no matter: many insist you'll find "some of the best food in the South Bay" here; P.S. its name (210 in Greek) refers to "both the address" and the area code "for Athens."

Dish Dash ⑤ *Mideastern* 23 | 16 | 19 | $27

Sunnyvale | 190 S. Murphy Ave. (Washington Ave.) | 408-774-1889 | www.dishdash.net

"Several steps above your average falafel joint", this "family-owned" Middle Eastern on "Sunnyvale's Restaurant Row" cranks out some of the Peninsula's "most economical", "interesting" chow, including "heavenly hummus", *mansaf* (lamb stew) and "wonderful vegetarian selections"; just try hitting it in the evening or before "the lunch rush", because despite "doubling in size", it's "always packed" – though "once in, the food comes fast."

NEW Donato Enoteca *Italian* - | - | - | M

Redwood City | 1041 Middlefield Rd. (Jefferson Ave.) | 650-701-1000 | www.donatoenoteca.com

Bergamo native chef Donato Scotti struts his stuff in the open kitchen of his sprawling eponymous Redwood City ristorante, preparing mid-priced handmade pastas, wood-fired pizzas and weekly changing Northern Italian secondi; in addition to the rustic dining room with exposed wood beams, there's a piazza-style patio and an enoteca room serving boutique Boot vinos by the glass, quartino and mezzo.

Don Pico's Original
Mexican Bistro ⑤Ⓜ *Mexican* 23 | 15 | 19 | $23

San Bruno | 461 El Camino Real (Jenevein Ave.) | 650-589-1163 | www.donpicosbistro.com

"*Dios mio!*" cry converts of this "bustling" San Bruno bistro boasting "lively" "crowds enjoying gigantic margaritas" and an equally huge 96-item menu of "downright tasty" Mexican (and occasionally Spanish)

"home cooking", including "intriguing daily specials" and "to-die-for skirt steak"; *sí*, the "atmosphere is noisy", but "reasonable prices", "eclectic decor" (red booths, crystal chandeliers, vintage sombreros) and nightly music raise it "two steps above your standard" taqueria.

Duarte's Tavern *American*

| 21 | 14 | 19 | $29 |

Pescadero | 202 Stage Rd. (Pescadero Creek Rd.) | 650-879-0464 | www.duartestavern.com

This "100-plus-year-old" "former stage stop" in Pescadero is a "kick in the pants" for "Wild West" wonks, and its "reasonably priced" American "comfort food" "ain't bad" either; sure, it's a "tourist madhouse on weekends" (just try squeezing in with the "ol' timers" at the "vintage bar"), but the Duarte family "treats you well", and the "no-frills fresh fish", "famous" artichoke soup and "pies worthy of my dear grandmother" make it a "must-do" on any "coastal junket."

Duck Club, The *American*

| 19 | 20 | 20 | $50 |

Menlo Park | Stanford Park Hotel | 100 El Camino Real (Sand Hill Rd.) | 650-330-2790 | www.stanfordparkhotel.com

Duck Club Grill *American*

Monterey | Monterey Plaza Hotel & Spa | 400 Cannery Row (Wave St.) | 831-646-1700 | www.woodsidehotels.com

"Cozy and genteel", this flock of "upscale" New Americans proffers "well-prepared" meals (particularly the "signature duck") and "professional" service in "elegant" settings that "lend themselves" to "real conversations" and "cozy nightcaps"; while other pluses include "excellent Sunday brunches" and "breathtaking" water views at some branches, a few quibblers quack that "mediocre" food and "stuffy" decor means it's "time for a revamp."

E&O Trading Company *SE Asian*

| 19 | 21 | 19 | $38 |

San Jose | 96 S. First St. (San Fernando St.) | 408-938-4100 | www.eotrading.com

See review in City of San Francisco Directory.

Ebisu *Japanese*

| 23 | - | 18 | $37 |

South San Francisco | San Francisco Int'l Airport | Int'l Terminal, Main Hall, N. Food Court | 650-588-2549 | www.ebisusushi.com

See review in City of San Francisco Directory.

Ecco Restaurant ⓩ *Californian/Continental*

| 23 | 20 | 22 | $49 |

Burlingame | 322 Lorton Ave. (Burlingame Ave.) | 650-342-7355 | www.eccorestaurant.com

"What a find" purr Peninsulans who happen upon this Burlingame "hidden gem", arguably the best "special-occasion" restaurant "no one knows about"; the "chef-owner prepares each dish with an artistic flair", including Continental-Californian classics like rack of lamb that are complemented by an "excellent wine list"; if a fraction find fault with erratic service that can "make the experience frustrating", the "elegant" setting and overall "attention to detail" soothe most.

Emile's ⓩ Ⓜ *French/Swiss*

| ▽ 22 | 19 | 21 | $64 |

San Jose | 545 S. Second St. (bet. E. Reed & William Sts.) | 408-289-1960 | www.emilesrestaurant.com

Despite "worries about the future" of this "expensive" "longtime standard for San Jose dining" after its founder left, its "traditional, elegant"

Franco-Swiss à la carte and tasting menus, paired with "fantastic" wines, remain "a notch above many"; still, some feel the food "lacks creativity" and the "decor needs some work" to "keep up with the times."

Espetus Churrascaria *Brazilian* | 22 | 17 | 21 | $56 |

NEW **San Mateo** | 710 S. B St. (7th Ave.) | 650-342-8700 | www.espetus.com

See review in City of San Francisco Directory.

Estéban *Spanish* | - | - | - | M |

Monterey | Casa Munras Hotel | 700 Munras Ave. (Fremont St.) | 831-375-0176 | www.estebanrestaurant.com

Named for the last Spanish diplomat to California, this new tapas place next to the recently remodeled Casa Munras hotel in Downtown Monterey offers an array of Spanish small plates and wines by the glass, along with sandwiches and entrees; wood beams and a glass wall lend the interior an airy feel, while the outdoor patio is enlivened with a fire pit and flamenco guitar on weekends.

Eulipia Restaurant & Bar ⓂAmerican | ▽ 24 | 20 | 23 | $41 |

San Jose | 374 S. First St. (bet. E. San Carlos & San Salvador Sts.) | 408-280-6161 | www.eulipia.com

For three decades, this "grand old lady of San Jose" has been a Downtown "oasis" for the "opera and theater"–bound, thanks to "reliable" New American fare, "friendly service" and a bar stocked with "good wine" and spirits; if a few say "her star isn't shining as brightly as it did", the "comfortable" brick room gets a standing O from those who like "private conversations."

Ⓩ Evvia *Greek* | 26 | 23 | 24 | $51 |

Palo Alto | 420 Emerson St. (bet. Lytton & University Aves.) | 650-326-0983 | www.evvia.net

It may arguably have the "best Greek dishes this side of Athens", including "fantastic" "fish and lamb", but add in one "heck of a Palo Alto scene", "warm" service and "beautiful, rustic" digs, and this "always hopping" Hellenic haunt (and sib to SF's Kokkari) becomes a "transporting" "taverna experience" – except "nobody is tossing empty ouzo glasses into the wood-fired oven"; its "prices are a bit steep" and it can get "godawful noisy", but "for the love" of Zeus, it's "totally worth it."

Fandango *Mediterranean* | 23 | 22 | 23 | $51 |

Pacific Grove | 223 17th St. (bet. Laurel & Lighthouse Aves.) | 831-372-3456 | www.fandangorestaurant.com

Although this Pacific Grove "gem" is "much enlarged from its original cozy house", its "warm" French country setting and "dynamite service" still "make you feel as if you're dining in a private home"; sure, some scoff it's "seen better times", with food and an interior that "could use refreshing", but most hearts flutter over "romantic dinners" of "consistently good" Med fare like paella or its "famous" rack of lamb, plus "brunches worth an apology to your cardiologist."

Fishwife at Asilomar Beach *Californian/Seafood* | 20 | 15 | 19 | $32 |

Pacific Grove | 1996½ Sunset Dr. (Asilomar Ave.) | 831-375-7107 | www.fishwife.com

"Don't let the cheap motel next door or its appearance scare you" – this "laid-back", "family-friendly" seafooder serving a "full plate" of simple Californian fin fare "with a slight Caribbean slant" (and side of black beans) reels in "tourists and locals" alike for "quick fish fixes"; sure, it's "old school", but "fair prices" and a "delightful" hostess make it "plenty a-lure-ing" in "high-priced" Pacific Grove; N.B. also operates two Turtle Bay Taquerias nearby.

Flea St. Café Ⓜ *American* | 25 | 21 | 24 | $52 |

Menlo Park | 3607 Alameda de las Pulgas (Avy Ave.) | 650-854-1226 | www.cooleatz.com

"The Peninsula's counterpart to Chez Panisse", Jesse Ziff Cool's "Menlo Park hideaway" continues to "set itself apart" with its "dedication to seasonal, organic ingredients" that are "cooked with love", resulting in "innovative" Cal–New American "food that rivals the best in the city"; the "charming" "small rooms" and updated "modern" decor in the bar make it "better than ever" (and appropriate for "special occasions" or "business lunches"), while "sophisticated staffers" add to the "romantic" vibe and help allay woes about "pricey" tabs.

Flying Fish Grill *Californian/Seafood* | 24 | 19 | 23 | $42 |

Carmel | Carmel Plaza | Mission St. (bet. Ocean & 7th Aves.) | 831-625-1962

"Seafood salvation" – that's what you'll find at Kenny and Tina Fukumoto's "mecca" for Cal-Asian chow, where the "good vibrations" and "lovely space in a basement (you have to go there to understand)" "make you feel relaxed and happy"; expect "outstanding" dishes made from the "freshest fish and local organic produce", "service with care" and "reasonable prices"; all in all, it's a "great way to end the day in Carmel."

Flying Fish Grill *Californian/Seafood* | 22 | 14 | 19 | $23 |

Half Moon Bay | 99 San Mateo Rd. (bet. Main St. & Rte. 92) | 650-712-1125 | www.flyingfishgrill.net

"Blink and you'll miss" this "bargain" Californian seafood "shack" in Half Moon Bay dishing up "incredible fish tacos (get them with the works)", "fish 'n' chips", "out-of-this-world fried sweet potatoes" and "crabby cheesy bread"; it's got a "funky" tropical vibe but only "a few tables", "so get there early or prepare to wait" – or do takeout and picnic on the beach.

Fook Yuen Seafood *Chinese/Seafood* | 22 | 11 | 15 | $29 |

Millbrae | 195 El Camino Real (Victoria Ave.) | 650-692-8600

"Juveniles loves to giggle when they say the name", but smitten Peninsulans insist the "flavorful", "right-from-the-tank" fin fare and "top-rate dim sum" at this midpriced Hong Kong–style banquet house in Millbrae is no laughing matter; "if you don't mind" "horrendous waits" on weekends, "nonexistent decor" and inconsistent service, Sinophiles will find the "real deal" here: "just point at what you want" from "passing trays" or "order a few items from the menu."

Forbes Mill Steakhouse *Steak* | 22 | 20 | 21 | $64 |

Los Gatos | 206 N. Santa Cruz Ave. (Royce St.) | 408-395-6434 | www.forbesmillsteakhouse.com

For slabs of beef "with all the bells and whistles", carnivores stampede to these "solid" "suburban" chophouses in Danville and Los Gatos with the requisite "dark decor", myriad "meat choices" and "bars comfy enough to go on your own and still feel at home"; still, the un-

FOOD | DECOR | SERVICE | COST

impressed bristle at "inconsistent", "too expensive" food and service, concluding there's "not enough reason to cheat" on their big-name competitors; N.B. Danville also serves lunch midweek.

Forge in the Forest *Pub Food*

18 | 19 | 18 | $34

Carmel | Junipero Ave. (bet. 5th & 6th Aves.) | 831-624-2233 | www.forgeintheforest.com

"All is fine in the forest" at this "rustic" converted "old forge" with "outdoor fireplaces" offering "pure Carmel" ambiance (without any "pretentiousness") that's just right for "apps and drinks"; "canine companions" love that "they let the patio 'go to the dogs'" (with a "pooch menu"), though some suggest to "forage in the forest" would improve upon the "ordinary" American pub grub.

Fresh Cream *French*

25 | 23 | 25 | $66

Monterey | Heritage Harbor | 99 Pacific St. (Scott St.) | 831-375-9798 | www.freshcream.com

A "GPS system comes in handy" for finding this veteran "formal" French in Monterey, but most agree it's "worth the adventure" for "excellent", traditional cooking matched with "wonderful" wines; a crème de la crème staff in "starched white uniforms" makes guests "feel like a queen", while the "window tables" ensure "beautiful" harbor views.

Fuki Sushi *Japanese*

22 | 18 | 19 | $43

Palo Alto | 4119 El Camino Real (bet. Arastradero & Page Mill Rds.) | 650-494-9383 | www.fukisushi.com

"It's super to watch five sushi chefs at work" at the bar, or to "relax" in a "secluded tatami room", at this Palo Alto pioneer that presents "beautifully prepared" fish and "turns out entrees to perfection"; "pleasant" servers in "kimonos" add to the "Japanese experience", though some take issue with "Tokyo prices" for "competent but standard" fare.

Gabriella Café Ⓜ *Californian/Italian*

23 | 18 | 21 | $44

Santa Cruz | 910 Cedar St. (bet. Church & Locust Sts.) | 831-457-1677 | www.gabriellacafe.com

A "sensational" menu "tailored to seasonal, organic produce" is the hallmark of this midrange Cal-Italian ("part of the farmer's market trend" for years) that continues to provide "superior" quality for the price; the candlelit room "oozes Santa Cruz charm", though a few critics are less taken by the "crowded-together" tables.

Gayle's Bakery & Rosticceria *Bakery*

25 | 13 | 18 | $18

Capitola | 504 Bay Ave. (Capitola Ave.) | 831-462-1200 | www.gaylesbakery.com

"Definitely the place to have your cake and eat it" too, this "destination bakery" in Capitola is "take-out heaven" for indulging in "1,000-calorie breakfasts" of "flaky, buttery" pastries, as well as "super sandwiches", excellent "blue-plate" dinners and "awesome" desserts; you'll need to "save up your patience" and pennies, but the "huge crowds say it all"; P.S. angle for a table "on the patio" or "take a picnic to the beach."

GoCHi. Japanese Fusion Tapas Ⓩ *Japanese*

23 | 16 | 14 | $38

Cupertino | 19980 E. Homestead Rd. (bet. Blarney & Heron Aves.) | 408-725-0542 | www.gochifusiontapas.com

"Not your parents' Japanese" restaurant, this "tucked-away" fusion tapas place in Cupertino offers "innovative", "tasty" small plates and sashimi for dinner, as well as "stick-to-your-ribs rice bowls" and udon dishes that are a "deal" for lunch; the option of low-slung tables appeals to traditionally minded diners, though some are put off by "snooty" service and find it "too expensive for what's really bar food in Japan."

Grasing's Coastal Cuisine *Californian*   24 | 21 | 23 | $53

Carmel | Jordan Ctr. | Sixth Ave. (Mission St.) | 831-624-6562 | www.grasings.com

Boasting a "cozy" cottage setting (including a pet-friendly patio for al-fresco mimosa brunches) and "excellent" service, this "quintessential Carmel" Californian by chef/co-owner Kurt Grasing (Kurt's Carmel Chop House) presents "wonderful" coastal cuisine coupled with a vast selection of wine-country bottles; despite some "pretty pricey" plates, midweek dinner prix fixes (with sommelier-selected pairings) are a welcome stimulus package.

Half Moon Bay Brewing Company *Pub Food/Seafood*   16 | 16 | 16 | $29

Half Moon Bay | 390 Capistrano Rd. (bet. Cabrillo Hwy. N. & Prospect Way) | 650-728-2739 | www.hmbbrewingco.com

"It's all about the harbor views, sunsets", "live music" and "beer brewed on-site" at this "party place" in Half Moon Bay, where "great outdoor fire pits" "combat the cool ocean air"; while the pub grub with a "coastal twist" strikes many as "just so-so", most agree it's "enjoy-able" on the whole when you want to "get away from it all."

Happy Cafe Restaurant Ⓜ♿ *Chinese*   ∇ 21 | 2 | 9 | $16

San Mateo | 250 S. B St. (bet. 2nd & 3rd Aves.) | 650-340-7138

Regulars accustomed to "30-minute waits on the weekend" for "simply amazing" dim sum are "ever so happy" this "authentic Shanghainese" "hole-in-the-wall" in San Mateo has "expanded the menu and hours" (now serving lunch Wednesdays–Sundays, with beefed-up dinner of-ferings Wednesdays, Fridays and Saturdays); critics grouse that the service remains "minimal", but it's still the source for some of the "best *xiao long bao* (steamed pork dumpling) within a 100-mile radius of the Bay Area."

Hotaru *Japanese*   21 | 12 | 16 | $22

San Mateo | 33 E. Third Ave. (bet. S. El Camino Real & S. San Mateo Dr.) | 650-343-1152 | www.hotarurestaurant.com

"Bang-up bento boxes" at "bargain prices" and "large portions" of "fresh sushi" mean "nothing beats" this San Mateo Japanese when you want "lots of grub for not too much dough"; the surroundings are "no-frills" and there's usually a "long wait" for a table, but most main-tain it's "well worth every minute" in line; P.S. it's "open 365 days a year to boot."

Hunan Garden *Chinese*   22 | 12 | 18 | $25

Palo Alto | 3345 El Camino Real (bet. Fernando & Lambert Aves.) | 650-565-8868

Hunan Home's Restaurant *Chinese*

Los Altos | 4880 El Camino Real (Jordan Ave.) | 650-965-8888 | www.hunanhomes.com

See review in City of San Francisco Directory.

	FOOD	DECOR	SERVICE	COST

Iberia *Spanish* — 21 | 20 | 18 | $45

Menlo Park | 1026 Alma St. (Ravenswood Ave.) | 650-325-8981
"Delicious" tapas delight surveyors who sip sangria that "really packs a punch" in the "cozy" bar or patio, or retire to the dining room for Spanish entrees like "authentic paella" at this Menlo Park perch; still, the "mandatory tip" chafes critics who say service is "slow" and declare the fare "just misses."

Il Fornaio *Italian* — 19 | 20 | 19 | $40

Burlingame | 327 Lorton Ave. (Donnelly Ave.) | 650-375-8000
Carmel | The Pine Inn | Ocean Ave. (Monte Verde St.) | 831-622-5100
Palo Alto | Garden Court Hotel | 520 Cowper St. (bet. Hamilton & University Aves.) | 650-853-3888
San Jose | Sainte Claire | 302 S. Market St. (San Carlos St.) | 408-271-3366
www.ilfornaio.com
See review in City of San Francisco Directory.

Il Postale *Italian* — 20 | 17 | 20 | $35

Sunnyvale | 127 W. Washington Ave. (Sunnyvale Ave.) | 408-733-9600 | www.ilpostale.com
The "staff treats you like family (the side that likes you)" at this "cheerful" "little" Sunnyvaler, delivering "unpretentious" Italian cooking accompanied by a "reasonable, well-selected" wine list; customers content with the "cozy" "old post-office" setting "always leave relaxed and satisfied", but those who find the "tables too close for conversation" advise "try to sit outside"; N.B reservations accepted for five or more.

Z In-N-Out Burger ● *Burgers* — 22 | 10 | 18 | $8

Millbrae | 11 Rollins Rd. (bet. Adrian Rd. & E. Millbrae Ave.) | 800-786-1000
Mountain View | 1159 N. Rengstorff Ave. (Amphitheatre Pkwy.) | 800-786-1000
Mountain View | 53 W. El Camino Real (bet. Bay St. & Grant Rd.) | 800-786-1000
San Jose | 5611 Santa Teresa Blvd. (Blossom Hill Rd.) | 800-786-1000
www.in-n-out.com
See review in City of San Francisco Directory.

Isobune *Japanese* — 17 | 13 | 15 | $28

Burlingame | 1451 Burlingame Ave. (bet. El Camino Real & Primrose Rd.) | 650-344-8433 | www.isobuneburlingame.com
See review in City of San Francisco Directory.

Izzy's Steaks & Chops *Steak* — 20 | 17 | 19 | $43

San Carlos | 525 Skyway Rd. (Hwy. 101) | 650-654-2822 | www.izzyssteaks.com
See review in City of San Francisco Directory.

Jin Sho ⊠ *Japanese* — ▽ 24 | 16 | 17 | $46

Palo Alto | 454 S. California Ave. (bet. El Camino Real & Mimosa Ln.) | 650-321-3454 | www.jinshorestaurant.com
Alums of New York's Nobu present a "new kind of Japanese" dining with a Latin "twist" at this "stylish" Palo Alto newcomer offering both "classic sushi" and "inventive", "carefully prepared" dishes laced with "zippy" sauces; as it has "low noise and distraction", focused foodies dub it a "nice splurge place."

	FOOD	DECOR	SERVICE	COST

John Bentley's Ⓢ *Californian* | 25 | 21 | 24 | $58 |

Redwood City | 2915 El Camino Real (Selby Ln.) | 650-365-7777
Woodside | 2991 Woodside Rd. (bet. Cañada & Whiskey Hill Rds.) |
650-851-4988 Ⓜ
www.johnbentleys.com

Amid a "sea of mediocre" dining, suburbanites consider themselves
"lucky to have" these "Silicon Valley casual" "gems" serving "wonderfully prepared" Californian fare that's both "innovative" and "unpretentious"; the "business-y" Redwood City branch with a "hopping" full
bar "lacks the offbeat architectural charm" of the "tiny" Woodside
original, but both are as "consistent as tapioca", if a bit "pricey."

NEW Joya Restaurant *Nuevo Latino* | 18 | 23 | 18 | $42 |

Palo Alto | 339 University Ave. (Florence St.) | 650-853-9800 |
www.joyarestaurant.com

"The hippest place to hit Palo Alto" "since Spago moved out", this
"chic" open-air newcomer offering a "zippy" Nuevo Latino menu attracts both "hipsters and suits" to "commingle" over "clever" tapas
and caipirinhas, or enjoy "Cuban sandwiches" at lunch while "scoping
out passersby on University Avenue"; since the less impressed cite
"stingy portions" of "bland" fare, some just "come for the scene."

Juban *Japanese* | 19 | 14 | 16 | $33 |

Burlingame | 1204 Broadway (Laguna Ave.) | 650-347-2300
Menlo Park | 712 Santa Cruz Ave. (El Camino Real) | 650-473-6458
www.jubanrestaurant.com

Servers set down "fresh ingredients and flavorful marinades" before
you "pitch in" and "cook the food yourself" over "in-table" grills at
these "fun", "interactive" yakiniku joints in Japantown, Burlingame
and Menlo Park; it's a "novel" experience for newbies, who note "you
can only blame or praise yourself" for the results, but detractors who
aren't the "DIY" type deride tabs that are "too high" "for what it is."

Junnoon *Indian* | 23 | 22 | 20 | $44 |

Palo Alto | 150 University Ave. (High St.) | 650-329-9644 |
www.junnoon.com

Putting a "modern spin on classic Indian dishes", this "upscale" Palo
Altan is "a nice change of pace", serving up "stylish" subcontinental
sustenance and "innovative" cocktails in a "sexy, nightclubby" space;
of course "you pay for all that fabulousness", and a minority mentions
it's "hit-or-miss", but most maintain the "delicate creations" are a
"wonderful excursion from the ordinary."

Kabul Afghan Cuisine *Afghan* | 22 | 16 | 19 | $31 |

NEW Burlingame | 1101 Burlingame Ave. (California Dr.) |
650-343-2075
San Carlos | San Carlos Plaza | 135 El Camino Real (bet. Hull Dr. & Oak St.) |
650-594-2840
www.kabulcuisine.com

When they're "in the mood for a quick trip" to Kabul, "nothing else will
do" declare kebab buffs who are "blown away" by the "superb" skewers and other "amazing" Afghan eats at this San Carlos "secret"; even
if the "unpretentious" strip-mall digs are less than impressive, the "extraordinary" hospitality makes you "feel like a member of the ex-
tended family"; N.B. a new Burlingame branch opened post-Survey.

	FOOD	DECOR	SERVICE	COST

Kanpai ⓈL *Japanese* ▽ 22 | 18 | 18 | $40

Palo Alto | 330 Lytton Ave. (bet. Bryant & Florence Sts.) |
650-325-2696

It's "omakase all the way, baby" at this "sophisticated, intimate"
Downtown Palo Alto outpost of the "famous (to the Peninsula) sushi
chef from Naomi" whose specials showcasing "sparkling" fish are an
"inventive" alternative to "standard Japanese fare"; on the downside,
critics say service is "super uneven" and the food has its "hit-or-
miss" moments too.

ⓏL Kaygetsu Ⓜ *Japanese* 28 | 19 | 25 | $93

Menlo Park | Sharon Heights Shopping Ctr. | 325 Sharon Park Dr.
(Sand Hill Rd.) | 650-234-1084 | www.kaygetsu.com

"Don't be surprised to see Steve Jobs having tuna rolls with Larry
Ellison" at this Menlo Park "strip-mall" standout known for "pristine" sushi and "elaborate", "work-of-art" kaiseki dinners providing the "most sublime experience this side of Kyoto"; while it's
"splurge territory" indeed, "gracious" service and "lots of great
sakes help you forget about the cost", plus weekday set lunches
and à la carte menus on Tuesday and Sunday nights help lower the
price of admission.

Koi Palace *Chinese* 23 | 16 | 13 | $34

Daly City | Serramonte Plaza | 365 Gellert Blvd. (bet. Hickey &
Serramonte Blvds.) | 650-992-9000 | www.koipalace.com

"If you're willing to brave crowds thicker than a Hong Kong subway
in rush hour on Chinese New Year", head to this "stadium-size"
Daly City seafood "palace" to "flag down" "dim sum carts" loaded
with "dumpling deliciousness"; "fat-walleted aficionados" return
for "pricey" dinner delicacies right out of the "fish tank", but caution "the staff can be completely unhelpful" "even if you speak
Cantonese"; P.S. the new Dublin branch "has the same food
without the wait."

Krung Thai *Thai* 20 | 13 | 15 | $25

Mountain View | San Antonio Shopping Ctr. | 590 Showers Dr.
(bet. California & Latham Sts.) | 650-559-0366
San Jose | 642 S. Winchester Blvd. (bet. Moorpark Ave. & Riddle Rd.) |
408-260-8224 | www.newkrungthai.com

"Fresh" noodle dishes and "spicy curries" keep customers returning
"again and again" to these "reliable" Thai twins in Mountain View and
San Jose; the somewhat "shabby", "noisy" surroundings and servers
who "hover to clear your table" explain why they tend to be "popular
for takeout", but even put-off patrons admit they "will do in a pinch if
you're pinching pennies."

Kuleto's Trattoria *Italian* 20 | 19 | 19 | $45

Burlingame | 1095 Rollins Rd. (B'way) | 650-342-4922 |
www.kuletostrattoria.com

"Warm and inviting", this Northern Italian in Burlingame "consistently" delivers "good food and wine" in a Tuscan-inspired setting
that's "great for family gatherings"; though some critics "expect more
for the price", others consider it the "best place to eat near the airport"; N.B. not affiliated with the Kuleto's in San Francisco.

Kurt's Carmel Chop House *Steak*

▽ 23 | 20 | 19 | $60

Carmel | Fifth Ave. (San Carlos St.) | 831-625-1199 | www.carmelchophouse.com

After all those cutesy Carmel cafes, carnivores stake their claim at this gentlemen's steakhouse where local chef Kurt Grasing (Grasing's) presents "delectable" cuts and the usual sides in an "inviting", "quiet room"; an "attentive staff" and a 500-bottle cellar of California wines, including many half-bottles and magnums, adds to the "memorable" (if "pricey") evening.

La Corneta *Mexican*

22 | 13 | 15 | $11

Burlingame | 1123 Burlingame Ave. (bet. Hatch Ln. & Lorton Ave.) | 650-340-1300 | www.lacorneta.com

See review in City of San Francisco Directory.

La Cumbre Taqueria *Mexican*

19 | 7 | 12 | $12

San Mateo | 28 N. B St. (bet. Baldwin & Tilton Aves.) | 650-344-8989

See review in City of San Francisco Directory.

⚡ La Forêt Ⓜ *Continental/French*

26 | 22 | 25 | $72

San Jose | 21747 Bertram Rd. (Almaden Rd.) | 408-997-3458 | www.laforetrestaurant.com

"Way out of the way" on the "rural" outskirts of San Jose, this "charming" "special-occasion place" "exceeds expectations" for ambiance with its "rustic", "historic" dining room "overlooking a slow-running creek"; add in "exquisite" Continental-French fare and "very gracious" service, and guests agree it's "well worth the trip" and the "splurge."

La Strada *Italian*

21 | 19 | 19 | $43

Palo Alto | 335 University Ave. (bet. Bryant & Florence Sts.) | 650-324-8300 | www.lastradapaloalto.com

Paisani "ooh and aah over the pizzas", "aromatic" pastas and "changing" prix fixes that "transport you to the coastal towns of bella Italia" at this "appealing" Palo Altan with a "doting" staff and "attractive streetside seating" on the main *strada* – the perfect perch for "people-watching" when the "loud" interior just won't do; N.B. a recent chef change may not be reflected in the Food score.

Lavanda *Mediterranean*

20 | 19 | 20 | $51

Palo Alto | 185 University Ave. (bet. Emerson & High Sts.) | 650-321-3514 | www.lavandarestaurant.com

The "intriguing" Mediterranean menu (including "seasonal" small plates) keeps fans "coming back for more" at this "top pick" in Palo Alto for "lunchtime business meetings" or a "hot date"; the "outstanding" wine list is a virtue for vino lovers, who also applaud the staff's "helpful, honest" recommendations, but a few fuss it seems "slightly overpriced" for "variable" results.

La Victoria Taqueria *Mexican*

▽ 20 | 9 | 14 | $11

San Jose | 131 W. Santa Clara St. (bet. Market & San Pedro Sts.) | 408-993-8230 ☽

San Jose | 140 E. San Carlos St. (bet. 3rd & 4th Sts.) | 408-298-5335 ☽

NEW **San Jose** | 5015 Almaden Expwy. (Rte. 85) | 408-978-7666

"Broke college kids" and thrifty "teens" are "addicted to the mysterious orange sauce" – "liquid fun" that enlivens the "cheap" burritos and other "oh-so-good" Mexican items at this San Jose trio; the setting is beyond "basic", and there's "not much room" to accommodate the crowds, but "you can't get any better food for the price" – plus the San Carlos and Santa Clara Street locations are open till at least 2 AM nightly.

NEW LB Steak Steak
-｜-｜-｜M

San Jose | Santana Row | 334 Santana Row (Stevens Creek Blvd.) | 408-244-1180 | www.lbsteak.com
This new Santana Row venture from Roland Passot (La Folie), located in the former Tanglewood space, takes its culinary inspiration (and initials) from the Left Bank, presenting a classic steakhouse menu with Gallic additions like escargots in Pernod garlic butter, plus treats from a glass-encased pastry cart that's wheeled tableside; the setting is decked out with the requisite dark wood and leather booths, and there's also sidewalk seating.

Left Bank French
18｜19｜18｜$41

Menlo Park | 635 Santa Cruz Ave. (Doyle St.) | 650-473-6543
San Jose | Santana Row | 377 Santana Row (Olin Ave.) | 408-984-3500
www.leftbank.com
See review in North of San Francisco Directory.

Z Le Papillon French
27｜23｜27｜$74

San Jose | 410 Saratoga Ave. (Kiely Blvd.) | 408-296-3730 | www.lepapillon.com
"Outstanding" French fare, down to the "heavenly" soufflé for dessert, "will knock your socks off" at this San Jose "tradition" offering an "elegant, civilized setting" (despite the surrounding "strip mall") for "Silicon Valley dining"; true, it "costs a ransom", but "top-class" service enhances the "blissful experience."

Lion & Compass Z American
∇ 20｜18｜20｜$43

Sunnyvale | 1023 N. Fair Oaks Ave. (E. Weddell Dr.) | 408-745-1260 | www.lionandcompass.com
The "onetime center of deal-making in the high-tech world", this "off-the-beaten-path" Sunnyvale New American is "still" a popular venue for "business lunches", "working dinners" and office banquets with its "hopping bar" and "pleasant" colonial Caribbean indoor/outdoor setting; it offers a "large menu" of "consistent" fare that a few find "unexceptional", but most agree it's "worth a visit, if historic Silicon Valley is your thing" or "somebody else is paying."

Lure ZM Seafood
∇ 20｜18｜18｜$62

San Mateo | 204A Second Ave. (S. Ellsworth Ave.) | 650-340-9040 | www.lurerestaurant.com
It "feels like San Francisco in the 'burbs", at this San Mateo seafooder offering "inventive" (some say "complicated") Californian preparations of oceanic eats (plus "amazing" desserts); many find the "modern" decor the "most interesting on the Peninsula", though that doesn't keep critics from carping about "pricey" tabs.

MacArthur Park American
16｜18｜17｜$42

Palo Alto | 27 University Ave. (El Camino Real) | 650-321-9990 | www.macarthurparkpaloalto.com
The "perennial parents' place for Stanford students", this Traditional American in a "magnificent Julia Morgan building" is a "safe" bet for

the signature ribs and other "decent" BBQ items according to Palo Alto partisans who say there's "something for almost every mood"; nay-sayers note, however, it "needs a shot of adrenaline" to revive the "in-attentive" staff and "mediocre" menu with "rising prices."

NEW Madera *American* | - | - | - | E |

Menlo Park | Rosewood Sand Hill | 2825 Sand Hill Rd. (Hwy. 280) | 650-561-1500 | www.maderasandhill.com

Boasting a wood-fired grill, this all-day New American newcomer in Menlo Park's Rosewood Sand Hill luxury hotel and spa offers a high-end menu of rustic, locally sourced classics from chef Peter Rudolph (ex Campton Place and Navio); it has a rustic, ranch-style interior with vaulted ceilings and a terrace with two outdoor fireplaces.

Mandaloun *Californian/Mediterranean* | 20 | 19 | 18 | $38 |

Redwood City | 2021 Broadway (bet. Jefferson Ave. & Main St.) | 650-367-7974 | www.mandaloun.biz

Hungry "movie"-goers and happy-hour habitués make a beeline for the Cal-Med menu, including "delicious" small plates, pizzas and wood-grilled steaks, at this "hip" haunt, a "real find" in Redwood City; the "open", "light"-filled space "can get noisy" at times, but the patio with fountains is "pleasant in the summer", and supporters say the "staff couldn't be nicer."

☑ Manresa Ⓜ *American/French* | 27 | 24 | 27 | $124 |

Los Gatos | 320 Village Ln. (bet. N. Santa Cruz & University Aves.) | 408-354-4330 | www.manresarestaurant.com

"Spoil yourself" at David Kinch's "gem in Los Gatos" where "foodies" and the "tech crowd" "swoon" over "idiosyncratic" New American–French "five-hour meals" featuring produce "sourced from its own" biody-namic farm and enhanced by "astonishing wine pairings" and "choreo-graphed" service; the setting is "lovely" and there's "no sense of being in 'the 'burbs'", so most agree this "culinary adventure" (culminating in a "kitchen tour") is one "you'll remember forever."

Mantra *Californian/Indian* | 20 | 20 | 19 | $50 |

Palo Alto | 632-636 Emerson St. (bet. Forest & Hamilton Aves.) | 650-322-3500 | www.mantrapaloalto.com

This upscale Palo Alto haunt "manages to be funky and fancy at the same time", offering "innovative" Cal-Indian fusion fare and "fine" "wine pairings" in a "plush" interior graced with contemporary art-work from India and pulsing with "loud bhangra" music; while critics find the prices "too high" for food and service that occasionally "fall flat", the lounge offers early and late-night "happy-hour specials" that are "unbelievable bargains."

Marché ⓈⓂ *French* | 25 | 23 | 24 | $78 |

Menlo Park | 898 Santa Cruz Ave. (University Dr.) | 650-324-9092 | www.restaurantmarche.com

"Fabulous" New French fare with an "organic emphasis" is matched by a "strong" wine list at this "stylish" Menlo Park "asset" where the "best seats in the house" offer a view of the kitchen through glass windows; most agree it's an "elegant" meal from "beginning to end", though some "belt-tightening" patrons are peeved by the "expense-account" tabs; N.B. a post-Survey chef change may affect the Food score.

	FOOD	DECOR	SERVICE	COST

☑ Marinus *Californian/French*
27 | 27 | 26 | $97

Carmel Valley | Bernardus Lodge | 415 Carmel Valley Rd. (Laureles Grade Rd.) |
831-658-3500 | www.bernardus.com

Foodies make the "drive" to Carmel Valley's Bernardus Lodge for
"four-hour-long" prix fixe dinners showcasing chef Cal Stamenov's
"exquisite" Californian-French "creations" and "superb wine
pairings" of local pressings (including coveted Bernardus bottlings) by
a "knowledgeable" sommelier; the staff "coddles diners" in a
"gorgeous", "inviting" space dominated by a "massive" fireplace that
creates a memorably "romantic atmosphere."

NEW Martins West ☑ *British*
- | - | - | M

Redwood City | 831 Main St. (bet. Broadway & Stambaugh Sts.) |
650-366-4366 | www.martinswestgp.com

Redwood City meets the West End at this new gastropub housed in a
110-year-old former saloon, where British-inspired eats like fish 'n'
chips and black pudding are updated with seasonal, sustainable
Californian sensibilities; the booze-centric venue serves a wide
selection of wines, cask ales and scotches to Silicon Valley swells at its
long redwood-plank bar or at tables in the Prohibition-era brick-
lined dining room.

Max's *Deli*
17 | 14 | 17 | $27

Burlingame | 1250 Old Bayshore Hwy. (B'way) | 650-342-6297
Palo Alto | Stanford Shopping Ctr. | 711 Stanford Shopping Ctr.
(Sand Hill Rd.) | 650-323-6297
Redwood City | Sequoia Station | 1001 El Camino Real (James Ave.) |
650-365-6297
www.maxsworld.com
See review in City of San Francisco Directory.

NEW Mayfield
19 | 20 | 19 | $36

Bakery & Café *Bakery/Californian*

Palo Alto | Town & Country Vill. | 855 El Camino Real (Embarcadero Rd.) |
650-853-9200 | www.mayfieldbakery.com

"OMG good" Californian fare is served in a setting "straight out of
Napa" at this "spanking new" cafe that converts call "the place to go
in Palo Alto" for brunch on the patio or "dinner in a booth", even though
some report service is "still ironing out the kinks"; be sure to swing by
the "adjacent bakery" purveying "buttery pastries" and the "amazing"
"fresh baked breads that come with your meal."

Mayflower *Chinese*
22 | 11 | 14 | $29

Millbrae | 51 Millbrae Ave. (bet. Broadway & El Camino Real) | 650-692-6666
Milpitas | 428 Barber Ln. (Bellew Dr.) | 408-922-2700
See review in City of San Francisco Directory.

Mezza Luna *Italian*
21 | 17 | 21 | $36

Princeton by the Sea | 459 Prospect Way (Capistrano Rd.) |
650-728-8108 | www.mezzalunabythesea.com

"Locals and visitors alike" are over the moon about this "peaceful"
trattoria in Princeton by the Sea, where the servers "seem proud" of
the Southern Italian dishes – such as "simply prepared" seafood and
carefully "crafted" pastas – "and they should be"; given the "romantic"
ambiance and "reasonable" cost, it's an inviting option "any time of

the week"; P.S. its new cafe offshoot at 240 Capistrano Road provides panini as well as "great espresso and pastries."

Mistral ⧄ French/Italian   18 | 18 | 17 | $38

Redwood Shores | 370-6 Bridge Pkwy. (Marine Pkwy.) | 650-802-9222 | www.mistraldining.com

A "frequent haunt" of Silicon Valley execs for "business lunches and dinners", this "comfortable" bistro is a "dependable" "go-to" for "tasty" French-Italian fare; the "lovely location" on Redwood Shores' lagoon is enhanced by a "pleasant patio" with a "romantic" fireplace, but "it won't knock your socks off" say some, who claim "nothing (aside from the wine list, perhaps) is particularly noteworthy."

Montrio Bistro Californian   ▽ 21 | 19 | 21 | $48

Monterey | 414 Calle Principal (Franklin St.) | 648-8880 | www.montrio.com

"Popular" and "packed" at peak times, this Monterey "favorite" in a landmark converted firehouse serves an "eclectic" menu of "tasty" Californian cuisine along with "great" cocktails and "nicely priced" wines; some savor the bistro "bustle", but others suggest "go for lunch" to "avoid the boisterous evening crowd"; P.S. try it Sunday-Thursday for the "eat-and-go-to-a-movie package."

Morton's The Steakhouse Steak   24 | 21 | 24 | $73

San Jose | 177 Park Ave. (bet. S. Almaden Blvd. & S. Market St.) | 408-947-7000 | www.mortons.com
See review in City of San Francisco Directory.

Naomi Sushi Ⓜ Japanese   ▽ 21 | 11 | 17 | $41

Menlo Park | 1328 El Camino Real (bet. Glenwood & Oak Grove Aves.) | 650-321-6902 | www.naomisushi.com

"Sit at the sushi bar and chat up the chefs" or "sign up for the sake tasting dinners" for the full experience recommend "regulars" of this "reliable" Menlo Park Japanese where "everything is top-shelf" from the "creative rolls" to the "old standards"; the "simple", "family"-friendly setting is "nothing fancy", but lends itself to a "satisfying" meal.

⧄ Navio American   24 | 27 | 24 | $80

Half Moon Bay | Ritz-Carlton Half Moon Bay | 1 Miramontes Point Rd. (Hwy. 1) | 650-712-7000 | www.ritzcarlton.com

"Treat yourself" to "gorgeous views of the Pacific" from this "gem" in the Ritz-Carlton Half Moon Bay, where "sightseers will salivate over the seaside setting" and "foodies will flip" for the New American fare; sure, you may "have to save your pennies" to partake of the "legendary", "over-the-top" Sunday brunch, but most say it's "worth it", especially since the service "makes you feel like you're the only one there."

Nectar Wine Lounge Californian   18 | 20 | 18 | $38

Burlingame | 270 Lorton Ave. (bet. Burlingame & Howard Aves.) | 650-558-9200 | www.nectarwinelounge.com
See review in City of San Francisco Directory.

Nepenthe American   17 | 24 | 17 | $36

Big Sur | 48510 Hwy. 1 (¼ mi. south of Ventana Inn & Spa) | 831-667-2345 | www.nepenthebigsur.com

"Eating outside" with "your feet dangling over the Pacific" has a "magical" mystique at this Big Sur "treasure" where the "views of the coastline" "amaze" and the "funky" "wood-hewn" digs take you "back in time to the hippie era"; while the American grub (apart from the "tasty" burger) and potentially "poky" service are an "afterthought", soaking in the "unsurpassed" vista with a "bottle of wine" is a "recipe for ecstasy" nonetheless.

Nick's on Main 🄢 🄼 *American* ▽ 25 | 19 | 22 | $45

Los Gatos | 35 E. Main St. (College Ave.) | 408-399-6457 | www.nicksonmainst.com

Chef Nick Difu (of the late Cafe Marcella fame) "rocks it" at his "impressive" Los Gatos bistro, a "local fave" where "he greets each table" before laying out "nothing fancy" yet "wonderful" New American comfort food and Santa Cruz Mountain wines in such a "tiny" space you feel like you're in "a friend's home"; you're practically "sitting on top of your neighbors", so "go early to beat the crowds to better enjoy it."

North Beach Pizza *Pizza* 20 | 10 | 15 | $18

San Mateo | 240 E. Third Ave. (B St.) | 650-344-5000 | www.northbeachpizza.net

See review in City of San Francisco Directory.

Old Port Lobster Shack *Seafood* 22 | 13 | 15 | $29

Redwood City | 851 Veteran's Blvd. (bet. Jefferson Ave. & Middlefield Rd.) | 650-366-2400 | www.oplobster.com

For "real-deal" "New England–style seafood" – "lobstah rolls, chowdah" and "steamers" – complemented by "good beers on tap", finatics head to this "no-frills" port of call in a Redwood City "strip mall"; the atmosphere is "welcoming", "even to families with unruly children", and though it's definitely "not fine dining" (think "casual picnic bench seating" and "kitschy" decor, complete with "gulls and buoys" restrooms), critics complain it's "pricey for what you get."

O'mei 🄼 *Chinese* 24 | 14 | 16 | $33

Santa Cruz | 2316 Mission St. (King St.) | 831-425-8458

Its "terrific", "creative" Chinese cuisine is "by far the best for miles around" say surveyors of this "gourmet" Sichuan that's "worth finding" in a Santa Cruz "strip mall"; while picky patrons often "prefer to do takeout", citing "questionable" decor, "slow" service and a "weird mandatory tipping policy", most feel the food makes up for any "shortcomings."

Original Joe's ➊ *American/Italian* 20 | 16 | 19 | $31
(aka Joe's, OJ's)

San Jose | 301 S. First St. (San Carlos St.) | 408-292-7030 | www.originaljoes.com

"The Rat Pack lives on" at this "recently spruced up" "San Jose staple" where "crusty" "waiters in tuxedos" make you feel like you're in a "mobster movie"; "sit at the counter and watch the master grillmen", or sink into an "overstuffed" booth to "indulge" in "ample", "meat-centric" Italian-American dishes that are "good, not gourmet", but a "bargain" nonetheless.

Osteria 🄢 *Italian* 23 | 16 | 21 | $36

Palo Alto | 247 Hamilton Ave. (Ramona St.) | 650-328-5700

"Fresh homemade pastas" trigger "nostalgia" for the Old Country at this "popular", "family-run" Palo Alto Italian whose "loyal" patrons endure a "line out the door" and "tight" tables to feast on "consistently satisfying", fairly "inexpensive" eats; it's "cheery enough" for most, though some newcomers say unless the staff "knows you by name, it's just not fun"; P.S. reserve "in advance" or "come early."

☑ Pacific's Edge *American/French*   25 | 28 | 24 | $78

Carmel | Hyatt Highlands Inn | 120 Highlands Dr. (Hwy. 1) | 831-620-1234 | www.pacificsedge.com

"Spectacular sunsets" draw "romantics" to this pop-the-question "perch on the cliffs of Carmel highlands", where "magnificent" French–New American fare, "rustic" decor and "elegant" service complete the picture; it's a bit too "pretentious" and "pricey" for some, though frugal gourmets "save big bucks" by "grazing in the cocktail lounge that has the same fantastic view."

Pampas *Brazilian*   21 | 22 | 21 | $56

Palo Alto | 529 Alma St. (Hamilton Ave.) | 650-327-1323 | www.pampaspaloalto.com.

"Roving waiters" "run around with swords stacked with" seemingly "anything that walks, flies or swims", sating "carnivorous gauchos" who opt for the "delicious" "all-you-can-eat" Brazilian "meatfest" and "endless" bar of "tasty salads, veggies and extras" at this "expensive" Palo Alto churrascaria (with an à la carte option too); jazz bands add to the "lively ambiance" Thursday–Saturday.

Pancho Villa Taqueria *Mexican*   22 | 9 | 15 | $12

San Mateo | 365 S. B St. (bet. 3rd & 4th Aves.) | 650-343-4123 | www.panchovillasm.ypguides.net

The "humongous", "flavorful" burritos are "heaven in a foil wrapper" at this "well-lit" (some say "antiseptic") taqueria twosome in the Mission and San Mateo; amigos aver "you can't get any better" "inexpensive" Mexican eats – just make sure you "know what you want" before joining the "factory-style queue", because the "fast" servers "won't slow down for you."

Parcel 104 *Californian*   23 | 19 | 20 | $62

Santa Clara | Santa Clara Marriott | 2700 Mission College Blvd. (Great America Pkwy.) | 408-970-6104 | www.parcel104.com

"Reliable for a business meal", this high-end Californian "tucked away" in the Santa Clara Marriott earns kudos for its "thoughtful", "flavorful" preparations of "local ingredients" served amid "spacious" surroundings that afford plenty of "privacy"; nevertheless, doubters declare the "hotel setting" "lacks soul", with uneven service and a wine list geared toward "expense-account" dining; N.B. weekends are breakfast-only.

Passage to India *Indian*   ∇ 18 | 11 | 15 | $25

Mountain View | 1991 W. El Camino Real (Clark Ave.) | 650-969-9990 | www.passagetoindia.net

"Offering something for everyone", the weekday lunch and Friday–Sunday dinner buffet at this Mountain View option boasts "more variety than most", presenting "hot and spicy" Northern Indian eats that'll "wake you up" along with milder Desi Chinese dishes; the "worn" digs, however, "need updating", and some critics call the fare only "average" for the area; N.B. à la carte is available too.

	FOOD	DECOR	SERVICE	COST

☑ Passionfish *Californian/Seafood* `26` `19` `25` `$47`

Pacific Grove | 701 Lighthouse Ave. (Congress Ave.) | 831-655-3311 |
www.passionfish.net

"Impeccable", "imaginative", "right-off-the-dock" seafood attracts
Pacific Grove guests to this "seasonal, sustainable" Californian whose
"excellent" staff handles the "simple", "crowded" dining room "very
well"; with a "wonderful" wine selection priced "just a few dollars
above retail", it's a "blissful" "bargain" all around.

Pasta Moon *Italian* `23` `20` `22` `$42`

Half Moon Bay | 315 Main St. (Kelly St.) | 650-726-5125 |
www.pastamoon.com

"Passionately prepared", "fresh homemade" pastas "imbued with a
bit of California inspiration" (and lots of "local" ingredients) are the
claim to fame of this "unassuming" but "excellent" Italian in Half
Moon Bay, whose "thoughtful" wine list is dedicated entirely to Boot
bottles; fans find the "relaxed yet sophisticated" setting just "lovely",
but even more mention "proprietress Kim Levin", who "pampers every
diner" in sight.

Patxi's Chicago Pizza Ⓜ *Pizza* `22` `13` `17` `$21`

Palo Alto | 441 Emerson St. (bet. Lytton & University Aves.) | 650-473-9999 |
www.patxischicagopizza.com

Windy City "natives" longing to "feel right back in sweet home
Chicago" head to these Hayes Valley and Palo Alto pizzerias for a
"real-deal" deep-dish pie to "dream about" (though "you know it's in
California when you can get a whole-wheat crust"); service is "ok" but
it's "cramped" inside, so rather than "wait forever and a day" some
"call ahead for a half-baked" pizza to go; N.B. a larger Marina branch
is slated to open on 3318 Fillmore Street in fall 2009.

Piatti *Italian* `18` `18` `18` `$40`

Carmel | Sixth Ave. (Junipero Ave.) | 831-625-1766
Santa Clara | 3905 Rivermark Plaza (Montague Expwy.) | 408-330-9212
www.piatti.com

See review in East of San Francisco Directory.

Pizza Antica *Pizza* `21` `16` `17` `$28`

San Jose | 334 Santana Row (Stevens Creek Blvd.) | 408-557-8373 |
www.pizzaantica.com

When the urge for "cracker-crisp" "artisan" pies, "the best salads in
town" and a "well-priced carafe of wine" strikes, "well-heeled" suburbanites head to one of these "legendary Neapolitan-style" pizzerias
"with a California twist"; cynics find it "awfully expensive" considering
"long waits" (and "loads of kids") are to be expected, while cognoscenti counsel "go later" or "sit outside under the heat lamps" "if you
want a quieter meal."

☑ Plumed Horse Ⓢ *Californian* `25` `26` `25` `$85`

Saratoga | 14555 Big Basin Way (4th St.) | 408-867-4711 |
www.plumedhorse.com

High rollers are betting on this "magnificent" reincarnated Saratoga
thoroughbred that went from staid to "stunning" with a "kicking" piano bar (on the weekends), "unbelievable" double-decker "glass-floor
wine room" and "elegant", "unique" Californian food that outpaces

the original by a long shot; odds are good you'll "impress a date" or a business client here, but a few critics are miffed by "minuscule plates" for "top-dollar" tabs.

Pluto's Fresh Food for a Hungry Universe *American*

| 19 | 12 | 14 | $14 |

Palo Alto | 482 University Ave. (Cowper St.) | 650-853-1556
San Jose | 3055 Olin Ave. (S. Winchester Blvd.) | 408-247-9120
www.plutosfreshfood.com
See review in City of San Francisco Directory.

Pomodoro *Italian*

| 17 | 13 | 17 | $22 |

San Jose | Evergreen Mkt. | 4898 San Felipe Rd. (Yerba Buena Blvd.) | 408-532-0271 | www.pastapomodoro.com
See review in City of San Francisco Directory.

Quattro Restaurant & Bar *Italian*

| 21 | 24 | 22 | $64 |

East Palo Alto | Four Seasons Hotel | 2050 University Ave. (Woodland Ave.) | 650-470-2889

"Hotel guests" and "Silicon Valley types" populate this "opulent" Italian in East Palo Alto's Four Seasons, a "stunning" setting for meeting over "more than respectable" dishes and "after-dinner drinks"; service is "solicitous" as you'd expect, but those who feel they're the "only person not on an expense account" pout it's "overpriced" considering the "ambiance outshines the food."

Red Lantern *SE Asian*

| 19 | 22 | 19 | $39 |

Redwood City | 808 Winslow St. (B'way St.) | 650-369-5483 | www.redlanternrwc.com

"Hipsters" who hang at this "beautifully decorated" "jewel" in Redwood City "love" the "dark, moody" interior, a "sophisticated" setting for "imaginative" Pan-Southeast Asian plates, "terrific" wines by the glass and "exciting" cocktails; you can "eat in the bar" or settle into the dining room's "comfortable seats", though some find the experience marred by "uneven" service.

Rio Grill *Californian*

| 21 | 19 | 21 | $42 |

Carmel | Crossroads Shopping Ctr. | 101 Crossroads Blvd. (Rio Rd.) | 831-625-5436 | www.riogrill.com

"A perfect ending to a day hiking around Carmel", this "boisterous" "old-time favorite" "fits comfortably as an old cowboy boot" say boosters, who come for the "hearty" Californian eats and suggest saving "room for dessert"; the "efficient", "upbeat" staff "does a great job of making you feel important", and it's "good for families" too (you can even "color the table covering while you wait"), so "don't let the shopping-center location" put you off.

Ristorante Avanti *Californian*

| – | – | – | M |

Santa Cruz | Palm Shopping Ctr. | 1711 Mission St. (Bay St.) | 831-427-0135 | www.ristoranteavanti.com

"One of the best-kept secrets on the Central Coast", holed up in a Santa Cruz "strip-mall" space that "does not do justice to the food", this pioneering Cal-Ital locavore bistro has been going strong for more than 20 years; "foodies appreciate" the affordable, "well-made" dishes prepared with "high-quality" ingredients, along with the bar's selection of old-world vintages.

	FOOD	DECOR	SERVICE	COST

Ristorante Capellini *Italian* — 20 | 19 | 19 | $39

San Mateo | 310 Baldwin Ave. (B St.) | 650-348-2296 | www.capellinis.com
"It's nice to know that some things never change" affirm customers who "count on" this "popular", "long-standing" San Mateo Italian for "hearty", "old-school" cuisine and "friendly" service, whether in the "comfortable" main dining room or "romantic" upstairs of the Pat Kuleto–designed space; true, it may not be "the best meal you've ever had, but it's always good" nonetheless.

Roti Indian Bistro *Indian* — 22 | 17 | 19 | $33

Burlingame | 209 Park Rd. (bet. Burlingame & Howard Aves.) | 650-340-7684 | www.rotibistro.com
"Sensational" subcontinental specialties "highlighting fresh ingredients" pull in the "crowds" at this West Portal and Burlingame Indian pair that makes for a "nice change from the all-you-can-eat" curry couriers elsewhere; though it's a bit more "expensive" too, most eaters are willing to shell out extra for the "elegant bistro" atmosphere.

☑ Roy's at Pebble Beach *Hawaiian* — 25 | 26 | 24 | $59

Pebble Beach | The Inn at Spanish Bay | 2700 17 Mile Dr. (Congress Rd.) | 831-647-7423 | www.roysrestaurant.com
"Roy's famous" surf-inspired "Hawaiian fusion" fare "plays to" the "breathtaking" ocean-cliff golf-course setting at this "special" chain link at the Inn at Spanish Bay, staffed by an "efficient, jovial" crew; delighted duffers time their "sunset" dinners to catch "the bagpiper on the patio bar" before tucking into dishes like "awesome" seafood and "excellent" chocolate soufflé, all of which help ease the pinch of "Pebble Beach prices."

NEW Sakoon *Indian* — - | - | - | M

Mountain View | 357 Castro St. (California St.) | 650-965-2000 | www.sakoonrestaurant.com
This swanky Indian newcomer in Mountain View lures in Google-aires and Silicon Valley expats alike with its playful juxtaposition of contemporary and traditional tastes; chef Sachin Chopra (ex Mantra and NYC's Spice Grill) puts a local spin on lunch buffet and dinner classics, while the interior, decked out with carved Buddha panels and a fiber optic chandelier, offers daily happy hours featuring half-priced bites chased by cocktails like the Guru and the Kamasutra.

Sam's Chowder House *Seafood* — 20 | 21 | 18 | $37

Half Moon Bay | 4210 N. Cabrillo Hwy. (Capistrano Rd.) | 650-712-0245 | www.samschowderhouse.com
"Magnificent" "ocean views" lure customers to this "hip" cliffhanger serving chowder "worthy of the name" and "greatly improved" upscale "beach fare" (like the "famous" lobster roll) with "prices to match"; though some say it fails to top "Boston or Maine", it's still a "pearl" for savoring a "glorious red sunset or foggy Half Moon Bay day"; N.B. the whereabouts of Sam's roving ChowderMobile can be tracked on Twitter.

Sardine Factory *American/Seafood* — 21 | 21 | 22 | $59

Monterey | 701 Wave St. (Prescott Ave.) | 831-373-3775 | www.sardinefactory.com
"Old-fashioned" sustainable American seafood, "amiable" "waiters who've been there for years" and a "fun" piano bar (Tuesday-

Saturday) draw guests to this expensive Cannery Row "legend" in Monterey; patrons praise the "beautiful" conservatory as well as the "smaller private rooms", though critics call it "too touristy" and "over-the-top", saying it's "seen better days."

Scott's of Palo Alto *Seafood*
18 | 18 | 19 | $42

Palo Alto | Town & Country Vill. | 855 El Camino Real (Embarcadero Rd.) | 650-323-1555

Scott's of San Jose *Seafood*
San Jose | 185 Park Ave. (Almaden Blvd.) | 408-971-1700
See Scott's Seafood review in East of San Francisco Directory.

☒ Sent Sovi Ⓜ *Californian*
26 | 22 | 26 | $73

Saratoga | 14583 Big Basin Way (5th St.) | 408-867-3110 | www.sentsovi.com

This Downtown Saratoga "celebration" destination showcases "innovative", French-influenced Californian food prepared with "ultra-modern techniques" and matched with "fabulous wines" in a "romantic" setting with a garden patio; "though not inexpensive", the "customized tasting menus" are "worth every cent", bolstered by "effusive" owners who "greet everyone like family"; P.S. "locals in-the-know never miss the BYO wine dinners."

7 Restaurant & Lounge Ⓢ *American/French*
▽ 21 | 17 | 17 | $45

San Jose | 754 The Alameda (Bush St.) | 408-280-1644 | www.7restaurant.com

Part resto, part lounge, this "modern" industrial-chic hangout in San Jose attracts groups for "after-work drinks" as well as "fine", "flavor-ful" New American-French meals and bar bites prepared by the twin chef-owners; though a few find it "lacking" for the price, it's "near enough to the Shark Tank" for grabbing a "good meal" "before a hockey game."

71 Saint Peter Ⓢ *Californian/Mediterranean*
22 | 18 | 21 | $43

San Jose | San Pedro Sq. | 71 N. San Pedro St. (bet. W. Santa Clara & W. St. John Sts.) | 408-971-8523 | www.71saintpeter.com

"A bit more exotic than the other San Pedro Square restaurants", this Cal-Mediterranean grill specializing in "amazing" "bargain" tasting menus of "seasonal" fare with wine pairings is a "little gem in Downtown San Jose" that's rightly "popular at lunch with lawyers and judges, and at night with Sharks fans"; the "charming" exposed-brick interior with a "quaint" outdoor patio is "small enough to feel like you're getting that desirable personal attention", even if "tables are a bit close."

Shadowbrook *American/Californian*
18 | 24 | 20 | $49

Capitola | 1750 Wharf Rd. (Capitola Rd.) | 831-475-1511 | www.shadowbrook-capitola.com

With its "fairy tale-like surroundings" and "stunning view of a Capitola creek", this hideaway is the "ultimate fantasy restaurant" for dinner with "your honey" or entertaining "out-of-town guests"; most concede "you pay for" the location, calling the Californian-New American fare fairly "unmemorable", and recommend "eating in the bar" if you're out with friends; P.S. "walk down, but take the tram up" for the full experience.

	FOOD	DECOR	SERVICE	COST

Shalimar ⊅ *Indian/Pakistani* — 23 | 3 | 10 | $16
Sunnyvale | 1146 W. El Camino Real (bet. Bernardo & Grape Aves.) | 408-530-0300 | www.shalimarsf.com
See review in City of San Francisco Directory.

Shokolaat ⊠ *Californian* — 19 | 18 | 18 | $48
Palo Alto | 516 University Ave. (Cowper St.) | 650-289-0719 | www.shokolaat.com
Shoko-holics enthuse over the "exquisite" chocolates and pastries at this Palo Altan that also purveys "deftly" concocted, European-influenced Cal cuisine ("each dish is a little jewel") prepared in the "open kitchen" of the "sleek", "modern" space; still, a few mutter about "mini-dishes for maxi-prices" and "pretentious" airs, with some proposing "skip the entrees and go straight for dessert."

Ƶ Sierra Mar *Californian/Eclectic* — 27 | 29 | 26 | $89
Big Sur | Post Ranch Inn | Hwy. 1 (30 mi. south of Carmel) | 831-667-2800 | www.postranchinn.com
The "otherworldly" "views from the tables" "overlooking the breath-taking Big Sur seascape" "overwhelm the senses" at this "magical" destination in the Post Ranch Inn, voted No. 1 for Decor in the Bay Area; meanwhile, the "serious" Cal-Eclectic fare and "marvelous" wines elicit "swooning" too, and the "staff is in 'total yes' mode", making it "well worth the tab" and "45-minute drive from civilization", whether for lunch or dinner at "sunset."

Sino *Chinese* — 19 | 21 | 15 | $40
San Jose | Santana Row | 377 Santana Row (Olin Ave.) | 408-247-8880 | www.sinorestaurant.com
With a "touch of dark opium den" about it, this "sleek" Santana Row option is a "real treat" for the "trendy" San Jose crowd that savors its "vibrant bar scene" as well as the "fresh, delicious" Chinese food; most fans don't mind "going a bit wild in the budget" for it, but purists pout it's "less exciting" than some more "authentic" choices; N.B. dim sum is served 11 AM–4 PM daily.

Stacks *American* — 18 | 13 | 17 | $19
Burlingame | 361 California Dr. (Lorton Ave.) | 650-579-1384
Menlo Park | 600 Santa Cruz Ave. (El Camino Real) | 650-838-0066 www.stacksrestaurant.com
The "name says it all" for flapjack fans who order "satisfying" "pancakes the size of their head" at these "family-friendly" (if somewhat "generic") breakfast and lunch "joints" in Burlingame, Menlo Park and Hayes Valley, though the "extensive" American menu actually offers "something for everyone"; weekend lines are "so long you may think they're dishing out pure gold", leaving some doubters "not sure it's worth the wait."

St. Michael's Alley ⊠Ⓜ *Californian* — 23 | 20 | 22 | $38
Palo Alto | 140 Homer Ave. (High St.) | 650-326-2530 | www.stmikes.com
Recently relocated, this "new version" of the "Palo Alto staple" "may be the best yet", offering the same "excellent", "reasonably priced" Cal cuisine and "caring" service in an "expanded, more attractive space" that's "easier to get into"; even if it's "not hip", it's a "comforting" retreat for "Stanford post-grads and high-tech thirtysomethings",

and weekend brunch is "worth waking up" for – though it's still served at the "original" 806 Emerson Street location; N.B. the mid-Survey move is not fully reflected in the Decor score.

Stokes Restaurant & Bar *Californian/Mediterranean*

▽ 21 | 22 | 21 | $49

Monterey | 500 Hartnell St. (Madison St.) | 831-373-1110 | www.stokesrestaurant.com

A "maze of rooms" in a "historic adobe house" (circa 1883) provides a "comfortable" setting for "imaginatively prepared", "satisfying" Cal-Med dishes and "local" wines at this "longtime favorite" of Montereyans; supporters are stoked about the "freshest of the fresh" ingredients that go into the large and small plates, even if some have yet to sample it since a recent chef change (not fully reflected in the Food score).

Straits Cafe *Singaporean*

19 | 19 | 17 | $39

Palo Alto | 3295 El Camino Real (Lambert Ave.) | 650-494-7168

Straits Restaurant *Singaporean*

Burlingame | 1100 Burlingame Ave. (California Dr.) | 650-373-7883
San Jose | 333 Santana Row (bet. Alyssum & Tatum Lns.) | 408-246-6320
www.straitsrestaurants.com

See review in City of San Francisco Directory.

Tai Pan *Chinese*

23 | 24 | 24 | $36

Palo Alto | 560 Waverley St. (bet. Hamilton & University Aves.) | 650-329-9168 | www.taipanpaloalto.com

It's the "Chinese food they serve in heaven" exult enthusiasts of the Hong Kong–style Cantonese "morsels cooked by a seasoned hand" at this "elegant" Palo Alto Sino, where "made-to-order dim sum" and "elegantly presented" main courses like clay pot chicken are "served with finesse" in a "lovely" dining room; true, it's "not cheap", but it's "quiet even when full", so "take your relatives here when they come to town."

Tamarine *Vietnamese*

26 | 23 | 22 | $51

Palo Alto | 546 University Ave. (bet. Cowper & Webster Sts.) | 650-325-8500 | www.tamarinerestaurant.com

"Sweet memories" are made at this "sleek-in-every-way" Vietnamese whose combo of "arty decor", "gracious service" and "brilliant" Southeast Asian small plates "intended for sharing" adds up to "one of Palo Alto's best places to eat"; "young Silicon Valley professionals" like to happy-hour at the "long", "lively" bar, and while budgeteers bemoan it's "best when you aren't footing the bill", that's the cost of "sophistication with a heart" – and besides, "you get cooler just eating here."

Taqueria 3 Amigos *Mexican*

▽ 19 | 9 | 14 | $14

Half Moon Bay | 270 S. Cabrillo Hwy. (Kelly Ave.) | 650-726-6080
San Mateo | 243 S. B St. (bet. 2nd & E. 3rd Aves.) | 650-347-4513 ●

"Super" burritos that "will satisfy the hungriest" paired with "homemade salsa and chips" make this "basic" taqueria twosome an "absolute favorite" in Half Moon Bay ("close to the beach") and San Mateo; the setting is "nondescript" and the service cafeteria-style, but the "frugal can find many items for less than $5", making it one of the "best bargains" around.

	FOOD	DECOR	SERVICE	COST

Taqueria Tlaquepaque *Mexican*   ▽ 25 | 10 | 15 | $18

San Jose | 2222 Lincoln Ave. (bet. Curtner & Franquette Aves.) | 408-978-3665

San Jose | 699 Curtner Ave. (Canoas Garden Ave.) | 408-448-1230 🗷

San Jose | 721 Willow St. (Delmas Ave.) | 408-287-9777

"Cheap, delicious" eats like "shrimp al diablo that will set your mouth on fire" explain why this "homestyle" Mexican trio in San Jose is "always busy" – even if "service is not a strong point"; in addition, tipplers "love the sangria" and signature "Super Chavela" (beer, lemon juice and a shot of tequila), which "beats any mixologist's concoction."

Tarpy's Roadhouse *American*   20 | 20 | 20 | $41

Monterey | 2999 Monterey-Salinas Hwy. (Canyon Del Rey Blvd.) | 831-647-1444 | www.tarpys.com

The "historic" 1917 stone house and garden provide a "lovely" setting for "big plates" of Traditional American "comfort food" at this "casual", "bustling" roadhouse; "pleasantly" removed from the "mob scene" of Downtown Monterey, it's "fun for the family" (and "affordably priced" to boot), but "bring your earplugs" since "it's in the airport flight path."

Thea Mediterranean   20 | 21 | 18 | $41
Cuisine *Greek/Mediterranean*

San Jose | Santana Row | 3090 Olsen Dr. (S. Winchester Blvd.) | 408-260-1444 | www.thearestaurant.com

"Delightful spices and seasonings" energize the "eclectic" menu combining "classic" and "innovative" dishes at this somewhat "spendy" Greek-Med *taverna* on Santana Row; it gets "a little noisy" on the weekends, when belly dancing shakes things up, but otherwise it's "cozy and romantic", and in warm weather you can "eat on the patio."

Three Seasons *Vietnamese*   21 | 20 | 18 | $40

Palo Alto | 518 Bryant St. (University Ave.) | 650-838-0353 | www.threeseasonsrestaurant.com

See review in City of San Francisco Directory.

Trader Vic's *Polynesian*   17 | 21 | 19 | $48

Palo Alto | Dina's Garden Hotel | 4269 El Camino Real (bet. Charleston & San Antonio Rds.) | 650-849-9800 | www.tradervicspaloalto.com

See review in East of San Francisco Directory.

Trevese Ⓜ *American*   23 | 23 | 21 | $68

Los Gatos | 115 N. Santa Cruz Ave. (bet. Bean & Nicholson Aves.) | 408-354-5551 | www.trevese.com

At this New American set in an "old Victorian house" in Los Gatos, there are "no crowds, no noise and no glare" – just "ambitious", "delish" à la carte and tasting menus served in a "beautiful", "super-sexy" setting with a "quiet bar area for a nice glass of wine"; the servers are "eager to make a good impression" and "most of the time they deliver", but critics grouse "at these prices, they should do better."

Turmeric *Indian*   ▽ 19 | 15 | 17 | $30

Sunnyvale | 141 S. Murphy St. (bet. Evelyn & Washington Aves.) | 408-617-9100 | www.turmericrestaurant.com

Look for "a lot of unique dishes you won't find elsewhere" at this economical Sunnyvale staple that "tries to be a bit more inventive than the

	FOOD	DECOR	SERVICE	COST

average Indian restaurant", and "a touch nicer" when it comes to decor too; while it's most "popular" among Silicon Valley workers for the lunch buffet, there's also an à la carte dinner option (with a buffet offered Friday–Sunday nights), served by a "friendly, responsive" staff.

TusCA Ristorante *Californian/Italian*

| – | – | – | E |

Monterey | Hyatt Regency Monterey | 1 Old Golf Course Rd. (Mark Thomas Dr.) | 831-657-6675 | www.hyatt.com/gallery/tusca
With its "pleasant views" overlooking the golf course, "well-timed service" and sleek open dining room with exhibition kitchen, this flagship restaurant at the Hyatt Regency Monterey appeals for hotel breakfasts, "rotary club lunches" and "leisurely" dinners of "surprisingly good" Californian-meets-Tuscany offerings by celebrity chef Mark Ayers (of Pacific's Edge in Carmel); a light menu is served in the Fireplace Lounge, featuring live jazz Friday–Saturday.

Twist Bistro 🆂🅼 *American/French*

| ▽ 22 | 17 | 21 | $38 |

Campbell | 245 E. Campbell Ave. (bet. 1st & 2nd Sts.) | 408-370-2467 | www.twist-bistro.com

Twist Café 🅼 *American/French*

Campbell | 247 E. Campbell Ave. (bet. 1st & 2nd Sts.) | 408-374-8982 | www.twist-cafe.com
Francophiles can "save the airfare" and head to this "unpretentious" "gem" of a bistro in Campbell that's "very French", right down to the "hot Parisian bread bag set on the table" and "charming" Provençal ambiance; the "seasonal" American dinners with a Gallic "twist" are "served with panache" by the chef-owner who "treats you like guests in his home"; P.S. the adjacent cafe is "great for lunch" or breakfast.

231 Ellsworth 🆂 *American*

| 22 | 20 | 23 | $61 |

San Mateo | 231 S. Ellsworth Ave. (bet. 2nd & 3rd Aves.) | 650-347-7231 | www.231ellsworth.com
Yes, Virginia, "there is fine dining in San Mateo" as this "white-tablecloth" "stalwart" proffering "fancy-pants" New American tasting menus and "phenomenal wine pairings" attests; fans insist the new chef's "creative" touch and "accommodating" service make it "one of the best choices in the South Bay" for "client entertainment" or a "splashy occasion", but critics bemoan the "bland" dining room as "lacking big-city verve."

Udupi Palace *Indian/Vegetarian*

| 21 | 10 | 16 | $17 |

Sunnyvale | 976 E. El Camino Real (Poplar Ave.) | 408-830-9600 | www.udupipalaceca.com
See review in East of San Francisco Directory.

Uncle Frank's at Francesca's 🆂🅼 *BBQ*

| ▽ 20 | 4 | 12 | $20 |

Mountain View | 2135 Old Middlefield Way (Rengstorff Ave.) | 650-964-4476 | www.unclefranksbbq.com
"You'll be too full to move once Frank is done with you" at this "sassy southern BBQ joint" "smack in the middle of Mountain View"; there's "plenty of soul" in the "slow-smoked" meats and sides ("get there early before they run out"), but "don't go expecting decor or service" – it's "the very definition of a dive", tucked behind a "raunchy bar" ("kids can't eat inside") with "grouchy old men doing the cooking"; N.B. open Mondays in the summer.

Village Pub, The *American* 26 | 24 | 25 | $64

Woodside | 2967 Woodside Rd. (Whiskey Hill Rd.) | 650-851-9888 |
www.thevillagepub.net

It takes a village of "ritzy Woodside locals" to sustain this "legendary venture capitalist haunt" that, despite its name, is a "high-end restaurant" offering "memorable" New American "foodie" fare and a "gratifying" but "expensive" wine selection; "everything is fabulous" from the staff to the "dressed-down" "who's who" inhabiting the "clubby", "fireplace"-warmed dining room, while the bar's "pub menu" and "perfect cocktails go a long way" toward making even non-"survivors of the D-process" "happy."

Viognier *Californian/French* 23 | 20 | 23 | $56

San Mateo | Draeger's Mktpl. | 222 E. Fourth Ave. (bet. B St. & Ellswoth Ave.) | 650-685-3727 | www.viognierrestaurant.com

A "dandy" Cal-French menu, "sophisticated" ambiance and service with "panache" overcome the "odd" location above Draeger's Marketplace at this "pricey" San Mateo option; many call it a "sure thing" for a "satisfying meal", though a few fret that it's "going through some bumps" in "changing chefs" and closing for lunch.

Will's Fargo Dining
House & Saloon *Seafood/Steak* ▽ 22 | 19 | 21 | $48

Carmel Valley | Carmel Valley Vill. | 16 W. Carmel Valley Rd.
(El Caminito Way) | 831-659-2774 | www.bernardus.com

"Good steak and cheer" are the draw at this Carmel Valley "hitching post" offering "well-prepared" surf 'n' turf dinners, an "extensive local wine list" and "first-class cocktails", all served by a "pleasant staff"; a "garden" patio and on-site butcher shop enhance the space that a few find "kitschy", while most agree this 50-year-old "landmark" is a "great value" that's "worth the drive up the valley."

Xanh *Vietnamese* 23 | 22 | 20 | $40

Mountain View | 110 Castro St. (Evelyn Ave.) | 650-964-1888 |
www.xanhrestaurant.com

"Elegant eaters" enjoy the "delectable, delicate fish" and other "impressive", "shareable" Vietnamese fare served in a "slinky" setting at this "stylish" Mountain View "hot spot", complete with "DJs" on the weekends; though some sniff it's "too cool for its own good", most applaud the "fantastic presentation", "intriguing drinks" and "gracious service" as "tasteful" all around.

Yankee Pier *New England/Seafood* 17 | 15 | 17 | $37

San Jose | 378 Santana Row (S. Winchester Ave.) | 408-244-1244
South San Francisco | San Francisco Int'l Airport |
United Domestic Departure Terminal 3 | 650-821-8938
www.yankeepier.com

See review in North of San Francisco Directory.

Zibibbo *Mediterranean* 19 | 19 | 19 | $45

Palo Alto | 430 Kipling St. (bet. Lytton & University Aves.) | 650-328-6722 |
www.zibibborestaurant.com

"Comforting" Mediterranean fare, featuring "tasty" rotisserie specials, satisfies appetites at this "upscale" "hangout" in a "stately Palo Alto home" complete with a "captivating garden patio" and "popular" "bar for sophisticates"; there are "lots of good small plates to share", while the "family-style meals" are "fun for big groups" – though some shout it's "too noisy" and others hint it's time for "a bit of a face-lift."

Zitune *Moroccan*

25 | 20 | 22 | $49

Los Altos | 325 Main St. (2nd St.) | 650-947-0247 | www.zitune.com

"Could I be in Marrakesh?" a caravan-load of customers asks about this "upscale", "modern" Moroccan that's "waking up sleepy Downtown Los Altos" with "beautiful", "fascinating" dishes by chef Chafik Larobi, presented in a "sophisticated" setting with arched ceilings; "excellent" service completes the picture, though a few fuss it's become "too expensive"; N.B. free corkage on Sunday.

Zucca Ristorante *Mediterranean*

18 | 15 | 17 | $37

Mountain View | 186 Castro St. (bet. Evelyn Ave. & Villa St.) | 650-864-9940 | www.zuccaristorante.com

"Simple", "well-made" large and small Med plates for a "reasonable price" keep this "neighborhood place" in Mountain View "popular for lunch" (when "awesome" grilled wraps are served), happy-hour drinks and "lively" dinners; low-key types like to escape the "crowded, noisy" interior to "dine outside" on the patio, particularly Thursday–Saturday when a guitarist entertains.

INDEXES

LOCATION MAPS

All places are in San Francisco unless otherwise noted (East of San Francisco=E; North of San Francisco=N; South of San Francisco=S).

Cuisines

Includes restaurant names, locations and Food ratings.

AFGHAN

Helmand Palace	**Russian Hill**	23
Kabul Afghan	**multi.**	22

AMERICAN (NEW)

NEW AKA Bistro	**St. Helena/N**	21
Z Ame	**SoMa**	26
NEW Aquarius	**Santa Cruz/S**	-
Arcadia	**San Jose/S**	21
AVA	**San Anselmo/N**	22
NEW Bardessono	**Yountville/N**	23
Bar Jules	**Hayes Valley**	24
Basin	**Saratoga/S**	21
Beach Chalet	**Outer Sunset**	15
Belden Taverna	**Downtown**	18
Z Big 4	**Nob Hill**	22
Bing Crosby's	**Walnut Creek/E**	19
Blue Plate	**Mission**	24
Boulette's Larder	**Embarcadero**	25
Z Boulevard	**Embarcadero**	27
Z Buckeye Rdhse.	**Mill Valley/N**	23
Bungalow 44	**Mill Valley/N**	21
Cafe La Haye	**Sonoma/N**	26
Caprice	**Tiburon/N**	21
Celadon	**Napa/N**	24
Chenery Park	**Glen Pk**	21
Chow/Park Chow	**multi.**	21
Cindy's	**St. Helena/N**	24
Circa	**Marina**	18
NEW Commis	**Oakland/E**	-
Conduit	**Mission**	22
Cosmopolitan	**SoMa**	19
Digs Bistro	**Berkeley/E**	25
NEW Dreamfarm	**San Anselmo/N**	-
Dry Creek	**Healdsburg/N**	24
Duck Club	**multi.**	19
Enrico's	**N Beach**	16
Esin Rest.	**Danville/E**	24
Eulipia	**San Jose/S**	24
Eureka	**Castro**	20
Evan's	**S Lake Tahoe/E**	28
Z Farm	**Napa/N**	24

Fifth Floor	**SoMa**	25
Fish & Farm	**Downtown**	20
NEW Five	**Berkeley/E**	-
Flea St. Café	**Menlo Pk/S**	25
Flora	**Oakland/E**	23
Fog City Diner	**Embarcadero**	19
Z French Laundry	**Yountville/N**	29
Fumé Bistro	**Napa/N**	22
Gar Woods	**Carnelian Bay/E**	17
Z Gary Danko	**Fish. Wharf**	29
Indigo	**Civic Ctr**	19
JoLe	**Calistoga/N**	26
Kenwood	**Kenwood/N**	23
Level III	**Downtown**	18
Lion & Compass	**Sunnyvale/S**	20
Luna Park	**Mission**	20
NEW Madera	**Menlo Pk/S**	-
Z Madrona	**Healdsburg/N**	26
Z Manresa	**Los Gatos/S**	27
Martini House	**St. Helena/N**	26
Mendo Bistro	**Ft Bragg/N**	24
Z Michael Mina	**Downtown**	27
NEW Midi	**Downtown**	-
MoMo's	**S Beach**	17
Monti's	**Santa Rosa/N**	21
Moody's Bistro	**Truckee/E**	25
Z Mustards	**Yountville/N**	25
Z Navio	**Half Moon Bay/S**	24
Nick's on Main	**Los Gatos/S**	25
955 Ukiah	**Mendocino/N**	23
One Market	**Embarcadero**	22
Z Pacific's Edge	**Carmel/S**	25
Park Chalet	**Outer Sunset**	16
NEW Penelope	**Oakland/E**	-
Pine Cone Diner	**Pt Reyes/N**	20
Presidio Social	**Presidio**	18
Range	**Mission**	26
Restaurant	**Ft Bragg/N**	23
Rest. at Stevenswood	**Little River/N**	26
rnm rest.	**Lower Haight**	23
Z Rotunda	**Downtown**	19
NEW Saison	**Mission**	-

Menus, photos, voting and more - free at ZAGAT.com

Salt House	**SoMa**	21
Serpentine	**Dogpatch**	21
7 Restaurant	**San Jose/S**	21
Shadowbrook	**Capitola/S**	18
Slow Club	**Mission**	22
Soule Domain	**Kings Bch/E**	22
Spork	**Mission**	21
⊿ Spruce	**Presidio Hts**	25
Starlight	**Sebastopol/N**	22
Street	**Russian Hill**	21
NEW Tavern at Lark Creek	**Larkspur/N**	-
⊿ Terra	**St. Helena/N**	27
1300/Fillmore	**W Addition**	22
NEW Tipsy Pig	**Marina**	21
Town Hall	**SoMa**	24
Town's End	**Embarcadero**	20
NEW Trademark Grill	**Downtown**	-
Trevese	**Los Gatos/S**	23
Twist	**Campbell/S**	22
TWO	**SoMa**	19
231 Ellsworth	**San Mateo/S**	22
2223	**Castro**	23
Universal Cafe	**Mission**	23
NEW Urban Tavern	**Downtown**	17
Village Pub	**Woodside/S**	26
Vitrine	**SoMa**	23
Warming Hut	**Presidio**	15
Washington Sq. B&G	**N Beach**	-
Woodward's Gdn.	**Mission**	25
XYZ	**SoMa**	19
zazu	**Santa Rosa/N**	25
Zin	**Healdsburg/N**	23
NEW Zinnia	**Downtown**	23
Zinsvalley	**Napa/N**	19

AMERICAN (TRADITIONAL)

⊿ ad hoc	**Yountville/N**	26
⊿ Ahwahnee	**Yosemite/E**	19
Balboa Cafe	**multi.**	19
Barndiva	**Healdsburg/N**	19
Big Sur	**Big Sur/S**	21
NEW Bistro 24	**Noe Valley**	-
⊿ BIX	**Downtown**	23
Brannan's Grill	**Calistoga/N**	20

Brazen Head	**Cow Hollow**	20
Café Flore	**Castro**	15
Chapter & Moon	**Ft Bragg/N**	22
Cheesecake	**multi.**	16
Chloe's Cafe	**Noe Valley**	23
NEW Corner	**Mission**	-
Cuvée	**Napa/N**	21
Dipsea Cafe	**Mill Valley/N**	19
Duarte's Tavern	**Pescadero/S**	21
Elite Cafe	**Upper Fillmore**	19
Ella's	**Presidio Hts**	22
Forbes Island	**Fish. Wharf**	19
Hard Rock	**Fish. Wharf**	12
Healdsburg B&G	**Healdsburg/N**	19
Home	**Castro**	18
⊿ House of Prime	**Polk Gulch**	24
⊿ In-N-Out	**multi.**	22
Lark Creek	**Walnut Creek/E**	21
Liberty Café	**Bernal Hts**	22
MacArthur Pk.	**Palo Alto/S**	16
Magnolia	**Haight-Ashbury**	18
Mama's on Wash.	**N Beach**	25
Mama's Royal	**Oakland/E**	21
Market	**St. Helena/N**	22
Maverick	**Mission**	24
Mo's	**multi.**	20
Nepenthe	**Big Sur/S**	17
Original Joe's	**San Jose/S**	20
NEW Pickles	**Downtown**	-
Pluto's	**multi.**	19
Pork Store	**multi.**	22
Press	**St. Helena/N**	23
Q	**Inner Rich**	19
Red Hut	**S Lake Tahoe/E**	23
Rick & Ann's	**Berkeley/E**	21
Rocker Oysterfellers	**Valley Ford/Nt**	21
Rutherford Grill	**Rutherford/N**	24
Sardine Factory	**Monterey/S**	21
Sauce	**Hayes Valley**	19
Scott's	**multi.**	18
Sears Fine Food	**Downtown**	19
Somerset	**Oakland/E**	17
Stacks	**multi.**	18
Tarpy's	**Monterey/S**	20
Taylor's Auto	**multi.**	22

Tea Room Café | **Petaluma/N**	24
Toast | **Noe Valley**	17
Toast | **multi.**	-

ARGENTINEAN

Boca | **Novato/N**	22
El Raigón | **N Beach**	22

ASIAN

AsiaSF | **SoMa**	17
Bridges | **Danville/E**	22
Butterfly | **Embarcadero**	20
Dragonfly | **Truckee/E**	22
Flying Fish | **Carmel/S**	24

ASIAN FUSION

Asia de Cuba | **Downtown**	20
Bushi-tei | **Japantown**	24
CAFÉ KATi | **Japantown**	21
Eos Rest. | **Cole Valley**	23
Flying Fish | **Half Moon Bay/S**	22
Z House | **N Beach**	27
Koo | **Inner Sunset**	25

AUSTRALIAN

South Food/Wine | **S Beach**	21

BAKERIES

Alexis Baking | **Napa/N**	22
Big Sur | **Big Sur/S**	21
Z Cheese Board | **Berkeley/E**	26
Citizen Cake | **Hayes Valley**	21
Delessio Market | **multi.**	21
Della Fattoria | **Petaluma/N**	24
Downtown Bakery | **Healdsburg/N**	25
Emporio Rulli | **multi.**	22
Gayle's Bakery | **Capitola/S**	25
La Boulange | **multi.**	22
Liberty Café | **Bernal Hts**	22
Mama's on Wash. | **N Beach**	25
NEW Mayfield | **Palo Alto/S**	19
Model Bakery | **multi.**	20
Z Tartine | **Mission**	27
Town's End | **Embarcadero**	20

BARBECUE

NEW Baby Blues BBQ | **Mission**	21
BarBersQ | **Napa/N**	22
Bo's Barbecue | **Lafayette/E**	23

Bounty Hunter | **Napa/N**	19
Z Buckeye Rdhse. | **Mill Valley/N**	23
Everett & Jones | **multi.**	20
Memphis Minnie | **Lower Haight**	20
Q | **Inner Rich**	19
Roadside BBQ | **Inner Rich**	17
T Rex BBQ | **Berkeley/E**	18
Uncle Frank's | **Mtn View/S**	20
NEW Wexler's | **Downtown**	-
Zeitgeist | **Mission**	15

BELGIAN

Frjtz Fries | **multi.**	18
La Trappe | **N Beach**	18

BRAZILIAN

Espetus | **multi.**	22
Mangarosa | **N Beach**	18
Pampas | **Palo Alto/S**	21

BRITISH

Betty's Fish | **Santa Rosa/N**	21
Lovejoy's Tea | **Noe Valley**	21
NEW Martins West | **Redwood City/S**	-

BURGERS

Balboa Cafe | **Cow Hollow**	19
Barney's | **multi.**	19
Best-o-Burger | **Downtown**	15
Burger Joint | **multi.**	18
BurgerMeister | **multi.**	19
Custom Burger | **SoMa**	19
FatApple's | **multi.**	18
Healdsburg B&G | **Healdsburg/N**	19
Z In-N-Out | **multi.**	22
Joe's Cable Car | **Excelsior**	21
Mel's Drive-In | **multi.**	14
Mo's | **multi.**	20
NEW Pickles | **Downtown**	-
Red's Java | **Embarcadero**	16
Taylor's Auto | **multi.**	22

BURMESE

Burma Superstar | **multi.**	25
Mandalay | **Inner Rich**	22
Nan Yang | **Oakland/E**	20

Pagan	**multi.**	–
Yamo	**Mission**	23

CAJUN

Cajun Pacific	**Outer Sunset**	20
Chenery Park	**Glen Pk**	21
Elite Cafe	**Upper Fillmore**	19

CALIFORNIAN

Adagia	**Berkeley/E**	18
☑ Ahwahnee	**Yosemite/E**	19
Albion River Inn	**Albion/N**	25
All Seasons	**Calistoga/N**	20
Amanda's	**Berkeley/E**	18
Amber Bistro	**Danville/E**	22
Americano	**Embarcadero**	18
☑ Applewood Inn	**Guerneville/N**	27
☑ Aqua	**Downtown**	26
NEW Artisan Bistro	**Lafayette/E**	–
AsiaSF	**SoMa**	17
Asqew Grill	**multi.**	16
☑ Auberge du Sol.	**Rutherford/N**	26
Aubergine	**Carmel/S**	25
NEW Aurea	**Nob Hill**	–
bacar	**SoMa**	23
BayWolf	**Oakland/E**	25
Bin 38	**Marina**	19
Bistro Boudin	**Fish. Wharf**	19
Bistro Elan	**Palo Alto/S**	24
Bistro Ralph	**Healdsburg/N**	23
Blackhawk Grille	**Danville/E**	19
Blue Barn Gourmet	**Marina**	22
Blue Bottle	**multi.**	23
Boon Fly Café	**Napa/N**	22
Boonville Hotel	**Boonville/N**	22
Bridges	**Danville/E**	22
Brix	**Napa/N**	22
Bucci's	**Emeryville/E**	21
Butterfly	**Embarcadero**	20
Cactus Taqueria	**multi.**	21
Cafe Beaujolais	**Mendocino/N**	25
Café Brioche	**Palo Alto/S**	22
Cafe La Haye	**Sonoma/N**	26
Café Rustica	**Carmel Valley/S**	23
Cafe Saint Rose	**Sebastopol/N**	23

Caffè Verbena	**Oakland/E**	17
NEW Calafia	**Palo Alto/S**	21
Camino	**Oakland/E**	22
Campton Place	**Downtown**	24
☑ Canteen	**Tenderloin**	27
Carnelian Room	**Downtown**	18
Carneros Bistro	**Sonoma/N**	23
Central Market	**Petaluma/N**	24
☑ Chez Panisse	**Berkeley/E**	28
☑ Chez Panisse Café	**Berkeley/E**	27
Christy Hill	**Tahoe City/E**	24
Cindy's	**St. Helena/N**	24
Citizen Cake	**Hayes Valley**	21
Citron	**Oakland/E**	23
Citronelle	**Carmel/S**	24
Cliff House	**Outer Rich**	18
Club XIX	**Pebble Bch/S**	23
Coco500	**SoMa**	22
☑ Coi	**N Beach**	28
Cool Café	**multi.**	–
Cottage Eatery	**Tiburon/N**	23
Deetjen's	**Big Sur/S**	22
downtown	**Berkeley/E**	19
Dragonfly	**Truckee/E**	22
Drake's	**Inverness/N**	21
Ecco	**Burlingame/S**	23
El Dorado	**Sonoma/N**	24
NEW Elements	**Napa/N**	22
Eos Rest.	**Cole Valley**	23
☑ Erna's Elderberry	**Oakhurst/E**	28
NEW Estate	**Sonoma/N**	20
☑ Étoile	**Yountville/N**	26
☑ Farmhouse Inn	**Forestville/N**	26
1550 Hyde	**Russian Hill**	22
Fishwife	**Pacific Grove/S**	20
NEW Five	**Berkeley/E**	–
Flavor	**Santa Rosa/N**	19
Flea St. Café	**Menlo Pk/S**	25
☑ Fleur de Lys	**Downtown**	27
Flying Fish	**Carmel/S**	24
Flying Fish	**Half Moon Bay/S**	22
Folio Enoteca	**Napa/N**	16
Foreign Cinema	**Mission**	23
Frascati	**Russian Hill**	26
Gabriella Café	**Santa Cruz/S**	23
☑ Garden Court	**Downtown**	20

Garibaldis	multi.	22
Globe	Downtown	20
Grasing's Coastal	Carmel/S	24
Harvest Moon	Sonoma/N	24
Hurley's	Yountville/N	21
Jake's/Lake	Tahoe City/E	16
Z Jardinière	Civic Ctr	26
Jimmy Bean's	Berkeley/E	19
John Ash	Santa Rosa/N	24
John Bentley's	multi.	25
Jordan's	Berkeley/E	17
NEW Lake Chalet	Oakland/E	–
Lalime's	Berkeley/E	26
La Scene	Downtown	18
Le Club	Nob Hill	15
Ledford Hse.	Albion/N	25
Little River Inn	Little River/N	21
Local Kitchen	SoMa	20
Luce	SoMa	20
Luella	Russian Hill	22
Luka's Taproom	Oakland/E	20
Lure	San Mateo/S	20
MacCallum Hse.	Mendocino/N	21
Mandaloun	Redwood City/S	20
Mantra	Palo Alto/S	20
Manzanita	Healdsburg/N	19
NEW Mayfield	Palo Alto/S	19
Meadowood Grill	St. Helena/N	22
Z Meadowood Rest.	St. Helena/N	26
Mendocino Hotel	Mendocino/N	18
Metro	Lafayette/E	–
NEW Metro Café	W Addition	–
Mezze	Oakland/E	20
Mission Bch. Café	Mission	21
Monk's Kettle	Mission	18
Montrio Bistro	Monterey/S	21
Moosse Café	Mendocino/N	24
Mosaic	Forestville/N	26
NEW Moss Room	Inner Rich	21
Murray Circle	Sausalito/N	24
Z Mustards	Yountville/N	25
Namu	Inner Rich	–
Napa General	Napa/N	20
Napa Valley Grille	Yountville/N	21
Napa Wine Train	Napa/N	16
Nectar Wine	multi.	18
Nick's Cove	Marshall/N	21
nopa	W Addition	25
Olema Inn	Olema/N	22
Oola	SoMa	20
Orson	SoMa	18
Osake/Sake 'O	Santa Rosa/N	23
Oxbow Wine	Napa/N	22
Pappo	Alameda/E	24
Parcel 104	Santa Clara/S	23
Park Chalet	Outer Sunset	16
Z Passionfish	Pacific Grove/S	26
Pearl	Napa/N	23
Piccino	Dogpatch	24
Picco	Larkspur/N	26
NEW Pizzavino	Sebastopol/N	–
Z Plumed Horse	Saratoga/S	25
PlumpJack	Olympic Valley/E	23
Ravenous Cafe	Healdsburg/N	22
Z Redd	Yountville/N	27
Richmond Rest.	Inner Rich	26
Rio Grill	Carmel/S	21
Rist. Avanti	Santa Cruz/S	–
River Ranch	Tahoe City/E	15
Z Rivoli	Berkeley/E	27
Santé	Sonoma/N	25
Z Sent Sovi	Saratoga/S	26
71 Saint Peter	San Jose/S	22
Shadowbrook	Capitola/S	18
Shokolaat	Palo Alto/S	19
NEW Sidebar	Oakland/E	20
Z Sierra Mar	Big Sur/S	27
Silks	Downtown	24
Soizic	Oakland/E	24
Station House	Pt Reyes/N	20
St. Michael's	Palo Alto/S	23
Stokes	Monterey/S	21
St. Orres	Gualala/N	22
Z Sutro's	Outer Rich	21
Syrah	Santa Rosa/N	25
Table Café	Larkspur/N	–
NEW Taverna Aventine	Downtown	–
Townhouse B&G	Emeryville/E	21
TusCA	Monterey/S	–
TWO	SoMa	19

2223 | **Castro**	23
Z Ubuntu | **Napa/N**	26
Venus | **Berkeley/E**	23
Viognier | **San Mateo/S**	23
Waterfront | **Embarcadero**	18
Wente Vineyards | **Livermore/E**	23
Wine Spectator | **St. Helena/N**	22
Z Wolfdale's | **Tahoe City/E**	27
Woodhse. | **multi.**	21
Wood Tavern | **Oakland/E**	25
Woodward's Gdn. | **Mission**	25
XYZ | **SoMa**	19
NEW Zaré/Fly Trap | **SoMa**	22

CAMBODIAN

Angkor Borei | **Bernal Hts**	23

CARIBBEAN

Cha Cha Cha | **multi.**	20
Fishwife | **Pacific Grove/S**	20
Front Porch | **Bernal Hts**	22
NEW Miss Pearl's | **Oakland/E**	17

CAVIAR

Tsar Nicoulai | **Embarcadero**	23

CHEESESTEAKS

Cheese Steak Shop | **multi.**	23
Jake's Steaks | **Marina**	20
Jay's | **multi.**	19
NEW Phat Philly | **Mission**	20

CHICKEN

Goood Frikin' Chicken | **Mission**	18
Green Chile | **W Addition**	20
Home of Chicken | **Oakland/E**	20
NEW Il Cane Rosso | **Embarcadero**	-
Rôtisario | **Napa/N**	-

CHINESE

(* dim sum specialist)

Alice's | **Noe Valley**	19
Imperial/Berkeley | **multi.**	20
Brandy Ho's | **multi.**	19
Chef Chu's | **Los Altos/S**	22
Dragon Well | **Marina**	21
Eliza's | **multi.**	21

Eric's | **Noe Valley**	22
Fook Yuen* | **Millbrae/S**	22
Gary Chu's | **Santa Rosa/N**	20
Gold Mountain* | **Chinatown**	20
Good Luck* | **Inner Rich**	22
Great China | **Berkeley/E**	23
Great Eastern* | **Chinatown**	21
Happy Cafe* | **San Mateo/S**	21
Harmony Rest.* | **Mill Valley/N**	22
NEW Heaven's Dog | **SoMa**	21
Henry's Hunan | **multi.**	21
House of Nanking | **Chinatown**	22
Hunan | **multi.**	22
Jai Yun | **Chinatown**	23
Koi* | **multi.**	23
Mayflower* | **multi.**	22
O'mei | **Santa Cruz/S**	24
Oriental Pearl | **Chinatown**	22
R & G Lounge | **Chinatown**	23
Rest. Peony* | **Oakland/E**	20
San Tung | **Inner Sunset**	23
Shanghai Dumpling | **Outer Rich**	23
Shanghai 1930* | **Embarcadero**	20
Shen Hua | **Berkeley/E**	22
Sino* | **San Jose/S**	19
Tai Pan | **Palo Alto/S**	23
Tommy Toy's | **Downtown**	23
Ton Kiang* | **Outer Rich**	24
Z Yank Sing* | **SoMa**	25
Yuet Lee | **Chinatown**	21

COFFEEHOUSES

Blue Bottle | **multi.**	23

COFFEE SHOPS/DINERS

Bette's Oceanview | **Berkeley/E**	23
Dottie's | **Tenderloin**	25
FatApple's | **multi.**	18
Jimmy Bean's | **Berkeley/E**	19
Mel's Drive-In | **multi.**	14
Pine Cone Diner | **Pt Reyes/N**	20
Red Hut | **S Lake Tahoe/E**	23
Sears Fine Food | **Downtown**	19
St. Francis | **Mission**	19
Taylor's Auto | **multi.**	22

CONTINENTAL

Anton & Michel	**Carmel/S**	23
Bella Vista	**Woodside/S**	19
Ecco	**Burlingame/S**	23
☑ La Forêt	**San Jose/S**	26

CREOLE

Brenda's	**Civic Ctr**	24
Starlight	**Sebastopol/N**	22

CUBAN

Asia de Cuba	**Downtown**	20

DELIS

Jimtown Store	**Healdsburg/N**	18
Max's	**multi.**	17
Miller's/Deli	**Polk Gulch**	22
Moishe's Pippic	**Hayes Valley**	18
Saul's Rest./Deli	**Berkeley/E**	19
NEW Schmidt's	**Mission**	–

DESSERT

Cafe Jacqueline	**N Beach**	25
Candybar	**W Addition**	17
Cheesecake	**multi.**	16
Delessio Market	**multi.**	21
Downtown Bakery	**Healdsburg/N**	25
Emporio Rulli	**multi.**	22
☑ Farallon	**Downtown**	24
Gayle's Bakery	**Capitola/S**	25
La Boulange	**multi.**	22
NEW Mayfield	**Palo Alto/S**	19
Model Bakery	**multi.**	20
Orson	**SoMa**	18
Shokolaat	**Palo Alto/S**	19
☑ Tartine	**Mission**	27
Town Hall	**SoMa**	24

ECLECTIC

NEW Academy Cafe	**Inner Rich**	21
Alembic	**Haight-Ashbury**	22
Andalu	**Mission**	21
Avatar's	**multi.**	25
Celadon	**Napa/N**	24
Chez Shea	**Half Moon Bay/S**	23
Cin-Cin Wine	**Los Gatos/S**	23
Cottonwood	**Truckee/E**	21

Delancey St.	**Embarcadero**	17
Della Fattoria	**Petaluma/N**	24
District	**SoMa**	18
Firefly	**Noe Valley**	25
Flavor	**Santa Rosa/N**	19
Go Fish	**St. Helena/N**	22
Hopmonk Tav.	**Sebastopol/N**	17
Levende	**Oakland/E**	19
Lime	**Castro**	17
Napa General	**Napa/N**	20
Pomelo	**multi.**	23
Ravenous Cafe	**Healdsburg/N**	22
Restaurant	**Ft Bragg/N**	23
☑ Sierra Mar	**Big Sur/S**	27
supperclub	**SoMa**	15
Va de Vi	**Walnut Creek/E**	23
Willi's Wine	**Santa Rosa/N**	26
Willow Wood	**Graton/N**	24
Wine Spectator	**St. Helena/N**	22

ERITREAN

Massawa	**Haight-Ashbury**	19

ETHIOPIAN

Axum Cafe	**Lower Haight**	20

EUROPEAN

ANZU	**Downtown**	22
Bistro Moulin	**Monterey/S**	–
Crustacean	**Polk Gulch**	23
Shokolaat	**Palo Alto/S**	19

FRENCH

À Côté	**Oakland/E**	24
Ana Mandara	**Fish. Wharf**	22
Angèle	**Napa/N**	22
☑ Aqua	**Downtown**	26
☑ Auberge du Sol.	**Rutherford/N**	26
Aubergine	**Carmel/S**	25
Bistro/Copains	**Occidental/N**	25
☑ BIX	**Downtown**	23
Brannan's Grill	**Calistoga/N**	20
Bushi-tei	**Japantown**	24
Cafe Beaujolais	**Mendocino/N**	25
Café du Soleil	**Lower Haight**	19
Café Fanny	**Berkeley/E**	23
Cafe Jacqueline	**N Beach**	25

Casanova | **Carmel/S**	23
☑ Chantilly | **Redwood City/S**	23
Chaya | **Embarcadero**	22
NEW Chevalier | **Lafayette/E**	-
Chez Spencer | **Mission**	26
Chez TJ | **Mtn View/S**	23
Citron | **Oakland/E**	23
Citronelle | **Carmel/S**	24
Club XIX | **Pebble Bch/S**	23
☑ Coi | **N Beach**	28
Conduit | **Mission**	22
☑ Cyrus | **Healdsburg/N**	29
☑ El Paseo | **Mill Valley/N**	26
Emile's | **San Jose/S**	22
☑ Erna's Elderberry | **Oakhurst/E**	28
Fifth Floor | **SoMa**	25
fig cafe | **Glen Ellen/N**	24
☑ Fleur de Lys | **Downtown**	27
☑ French Laundry | **Yountville/N**	29
Fresh Cream | **Monterey/S**	25
☑**NEW** Gitane | **Downtown**	22
grégoire | **multi.**	22
Isa | **Marina**	24
☑ Jardinière | **Civic Ctr**	26
Jordan's | **Berkeley/E**	17
Kenwood | **Kenwood/N**	23
La Boulange | **multi.**	22
☑ La Folie | **Russian Hill**	28
☑ La Forêt | **San Jose/S**	26
La Gare | **Santa Rosa/N**	19
☑ La Toque | **Napa/N**	26
Le Club | **Nob Hill**	15
Le Colonial | **Downtown**	22
☑ Le Papillon | **San Jose/S**	27
Luna Park | **Mission**	20
☑ Madrona | **Healdsburg/N**	26
Marché | **Menlo Pk/S**	25
Marché aux Fleurs | **Ross/N**	25
☑ Marinus | **Carmel Valley/S**	27
☑ Masa's | **Downtown**	28
Metro | **Lafayette/E**	-
Mistral | **Redwood Shores/S**	18
955 Ukiah | **Mendocino/N**	23
Nizza La Bella | **Albany/E**	20
☑ Pacific's Edge | **Carmel/S**	25
☑ Quince | **Downtown**	27
Rendezvous Inn | **Ft Bragg/N**	25
NEW Restaurant Eloise | **Sebastopol/N**	-
Rest. LuLu/Petite | **SoMa**	21
Rigolo | **Presidio Hts**	16
☑ Ritz-Carlton Din. Rm. | **Nob Hill**	27
rnm rest. | **Lower Haight**	23
NEW RN74 | **SoMa**	-
Santé | **Sonoma/N**	25
7 Restaurant | **San Jose/S**	21
Soizic | **Oakland/E**	24
Twist | **Campbell/S**	22
Viognier | **San Mateo/S**	23

FRENCH (BISTRO)

Alamo Sq. | **W Addition**	20
NEW Artisan Bistro | **Lafayette/E**	-
Baker St. Bistro | **Marina**	21
Bistro Clovis | **Hayes Valley**	21
Bistro Elan | **Palo Alto/S**	24
☑ Bistro Jeanty | **Yountville/N**	25
Bistro Liaison | **Berkeley/E**	22
Bistro Ralph | **Healdsburg/N**	23
NEW Bistro St. Germain | **Lower Haight**	-
Bistro Vida | **Menlo Pk/S**	18
☑ Bouchon | **Yountville/N**	26
Butler & Chef | **SoMa**	20
Cafe Bastille | **Downtown**	18
Café Brioche | **Palo Alto/S**	22
Café Claude | **Downtown**	21
Café de la Presse | **Downtown**	18
Café Rouge | **Berkeley/E**	22
☑ Chapeau! | **Outer Rich**	26
Charcuterie | **Healdsburg/N**	22
Chez Maman | **Potrero Hill**	22
Chez Papa | **multi.**	23
Chouchou | **Forest Hills**	22
Côté Sud | **Castro**	19
Florio | **Pacific Hts**	21
Fringale | **SoMa**	24
Gamine | **Cow Hollow**	22
girl & the fig | **Sonoma/N**	24
Grand Cafe | **Downtown**	19
Hyde St. Bistro | **Russian Hill**	21
K&L Bistro | **Sebastopol/N**	25
La Note | **Berkeley/E**	21

La Provence | **Mission**	20
L'Ardoise | **Castro**	24
La Terrasse | **Presidio**	18
Le Central Bistro | **Downtown**	20
Le Charm Bistro | **SoMa**	22
Le P'tit Laurent | **Glen Pk**	22
Le Zinc | **Noe Valley**	19
Mirepoix | **Windsor/N**	26
Plouf | **Downtown**	22
Rest. Cassis | **Pacific Hts**	22
Scala's Bistro | **Downtown**	21
South Park | **SoMa**	23
Syrah | **Santa Rosa/N**	25
Ti Couz | **Mission**	23
Water St. Bistro | **Petaluma/N**	23
Zazie | **Cole Valley**	22

FRENCH (BRASSERIE)

☑ Absinthe | **Hayes Valley**	22
Left Bank | **multi.**	18
Luka's Taproom | **Oakland/E**	20
NEW Midi | **Downtown**	–

GASTROPUB

Alembic | Eclectic | **Haight-Ashbury**	22
Destino | Nuevo Latino | **Castro**	22
Hopmonk Tav. | Eclectic | **Sebastopol/N**	17
La Trappe | Belgian | **N Beach**	18
Magnolia | Amer. | **Haight-Ashbury**	18
NEW Martins West | Brit. | **Redwood City/S**	–
Monk's Kettle | Cal. | **Mission**	18
NEW Penelope | Amer. | **Oakland/E**	–
Salt House | Amer. | **SoMa**	21
NEW Sidebar | Cal. | **Oakland/E**	20
NEW Tipsy Pig | Amer. | **Marina**	21
NEW Urban Tavern | Amer. | **Downtown**	17

GERMAN

Rosamunde Grill | **Lower Haight**	25
NEW Schmidt's | **Mission**	–
Suppenküche | **Hayes Valley**	22
Walzwerk | **Mission**	21

GREEK

Dio Deka | **Los Gatos/S**	25
☑ Evvia | **Palo Alto/S**	26
☑ Kokkari | **Downtown**	27
Thea Med. | **San Jose/S**	20

HAWAIIAN

Roy's | **SoMa**	23
☑ Roy's | **Pebble Bch/S**	25

HEALTH FOOD

(See also Vegetarian)	
Amanda's | **Berkeley/E**	18
Mixt Greens | **Downtown**	22
Plant Cafe | **multi.**	20

HOT DOGS

Caspers Hot Dogs | **multi.**	18
NEW Let's Be Frank | **Marina**	–
NEW Pickles | **Downtown**	–
NEW Showdogs | **Downtown**	–
Underdog | **Inner Sunset**	20

ICE CREAM PARLORS

Fentons Creamery | **Oakland/E**	19

INDIAN

Ajanta | **Berkeley/E**	25
Amber | **multi.**	24
Breads of India | **multi.**	19
Dasaprakash | **Santa Clara/S**	19
Dosa | **multi.**	23
Gaylord India | **Downtown**	18
Indian Oven | **Lower Haight**	23
Junnoon | **Palo Alto/S**	23
Kasa Indian | **Castro**	20
Lotus/Anokha | **multi.**	25
Mantra | **Palo Alto/S**	20
Naan/Curry | **multi.**	17
Passage to India | **Mtn View/S**	18
Roti Indian | **multi.**	22
NEW Sakoon | **Mtn View/S**	–
Shalimar | **multi.**	23
Turmeric | **Sunnyvale/S**	19
Udupi Palace | **multi.**	21
Vik's Chaat | **Berkeley/E**	24
Zante | **Bernal Hts**	20

ITALIAN

(N=Northern; S=Southern)

Z Acquerello | Polk Gulch — 28

NEW Adesso | Oakland/E — -

Albona Rist. | N | N Beach — 24

Alioto's | S | Fish. Wharf — 18

Antica Trattoria | Russian Hill — 22

Aperto | Potrero Hill — 23

Z A16 | S | Marina — 25

Azzurro Pizzeria | Napa/N — 22

Bacco Ristorante | Noe Valley — 23

Bar Bambino | Mission — 23

Bellanico | Oakland/E — 23

Bella Trattoria | S | Inner Rich — 21

Beretta | Mission — 23

Bistro Don Giovanni | Napa/N — 23

Z NEW Bottega | Yountville/N — 25

Bovolo | Healdsburg/N — 24

Brindisi | S | Downtown — 18

Buca di Beppo | multi. — 14

Bucci's | Emeryville/E — 21

Cafe Citti | N | Kenwood/N — 22

Café Fiore | N | S Lake Tahoe/E — 25

Café Tiramisu | N | Downtown — 20

Caffe Delle Stelle | N | Hayes Valley — 16

Caffè Macaroni | S | N Beach — 20

Caffè Museo | SoMa — 18

Caffè Verbena | Oakland/E — 17

Cantinetta Luca | Carmel/S — 23

Capannina | Cow Hollow — 24

Casanova | N | Carmel/S — 23

Casa Orinda | Orinda/E — 18

Z Chantilly | N | Redwood City/S — 23

Cook St. Helena | N | St. Helena/N — 25

NEW Corner | Mission — -

Corso | N | Berkeley/E — 24

Cucina Paradiso | S | Petaluma/N — 24

Cucina Rest. | San Anselmo/N — 23

Z Delfina | N | Mission — 26

Della Santina's | N | Sonoma/N — 21

Diavola | Geyserville/N — 24

NEW Donato | N | Redwood City/S — -

Dopo | Oakland/E — 25

Ducca | N | SoMa — 20

E'Angelo | Marina — 21

Emmy's Spaghetti | multi. — 21

Emporio Rulli | multi. — 22

NEW Estate | Sonoma/N — 20

Farina | Mission — 23

NEW 54 Mint | SoMa — -

Fior d'Italia | N | N Beach — 18

Florio | Pacific Hts — 21

NEW Flour + Water | Mission — -

Frantoio | N | Mill Valley/N — 21

Gabriella Café | Santa Cruz/S — 23

Gialina | Glen Pk — 24

Globe | Downtown — 20

NEW Il Cane Rosso | Embarcadero — -

Il Davide | N | San Rafael/N — 21

Il Fornaio | multi. — 19

Il Postale | Sunnyvale/S — 20

Incanto | N | Noe Valley — 24

Jackson Fillmore | Upper Fillmore — 21

Joe DiMaggio's | N Beach — 21

Joey & Eddie's | N Beach — 14

Kuleto's | N | Downtown — 20

Kuleto's | N | Burlingame/S — 20

La Ciccia | Noe Valley — 24

La Ginestra | S | Mill Valley/N — 21

La Strada | Palo Alto/S — 21

Local Kitchen | SoMa — 20

Lo Coco's | S | multi. — 22

L'Osteria | N | N Beach — 23

Luce | SoMa — 20

Lupa Trattoria | Noe Valley — 22

Mangarosa | N Beach — 18

Mario's Bohemian | N | N Beach — 18

NEW Marzano | S | Oakland/E — 23

Meritage Martini | N | Sonoma/N — 20

Mescolanza | N | Outer Rich — 21

Mezza Luna | S | Princeton Sea/S — 21

Mistral | Redwood Shores/S — 18

Nizza La Bella | Albany/E — 20

Nob Hill Café | N | Nob Hill — 21

North Beach Rest. | N | N Beach — 22

Oliveto Cafe | Oakland/E — 24

Oliveto Restaurant | Oakland/E — 25

Original Joe's | San Jose/S — 20

Osteria | Palo Alto/S — 23

CUISINES

NEW Osteria Stellina | Pt Reyes/N	-
Ottimista | Cow Hollow	19
Palio d'Asti | Downtown	20
Pane e Vino | N | Cow Hollow	22
Pasta Moon | Half Moon Bay/S	23
Pazzia | SoMa	23
☑ Perbacco | Downtown	25
Pesce | N | Russian Hill	24
Peter Lowell's | Sebastopol/N	22
Pianeta | N | Truckee/E	23
Piatti | multi.	18
Piazza D'Angelo | Mill Valley/N	20
Piccino | Dogpatch	24
Picco | Larkspur/N	26
Pizza Antica | multi.	21
Pizzaiolo | S | Oakland/E	25
Pizzeria Delfina | Pacific Hts	24
Pizzeria Picco | S | Larkspur/N	25
Pizzeria Tra Vigne | St. Helena/N	21
Poesia | S | Castro	20
Poggio | N | Sausalito/N	22
Pomodoro | multi.	17
Postino | Lafayette/E	23
Prima | N | Walnut Creek/E	24
Puccini & Pinetti | Downtown	18
Quattro | E Palo Alto/S	21
☑ Quince | Downtown	27
Risibisi | N | Petaluma/N	25
Rist. Avanti | Santa Cruz/S	-
Rist. Capellini | San Mateo/S	20
Rist. Ideale | S | N Beach	23
Rist. Milano | N | Russian Hill	22
Ristorante Parma | Marina	23
Rist. Umbria | N | SoMa	21
Rose Pistola | N | N Beach	22
Rose's Cafe | N | Cow Hollow	22
Rosso Pizzeria | Santa Rosa/N	25
Salute Marina | Richmond/E	18
Santi | N | Geyserville/N	25
NEW Scopa | Healdsburg/N	24
Sociale | N | Presidio Hts	24
SPQR | S | Pacific Hts	23
NEW Taverna Aventine | Downtown	-
Tommaso's | S | N Beach	25

NEW Tony's Pizza | N Beach	-
Tratt. Contadina | N Beach	22
Tratt. La Siciliana | S | Berkeley/E	25
Tra Vigne | N | St. Helena/N	24
TusCA | N | Monterey/S	-
Uva Enoteca | Lower Haight	20
Uva Trattoria | Napa/N	23
Venezia | Berkeley/E	18
Venticello | N | Nob Hill	23
Vin Antico | San Rafael/N	23
Vivande | S | Pacific Hts	23
Volpi's Rist. | Petaluma/N	19
Washington Sq. B&G | N Beach	-
zazu | N | Santa Rosa/N	25
Zuppa | S | SoMa	19

JAPANESE

(* sushi specialist)

Ace Wasabi's* | Marina	21
Alexander's | Cupertino/S	25
ANZU* | Downtown	22
Ariake* | Outer Rich	24
Blowfish Sushi* | multi.	20
Bushi-tei | Japantown	24
Chaya | Embarcadero	22
Cha-Ya Veg.* | multi.	22
Domo Sushi* | Hayes Valley	23
Ebisu* | multi.	23
Eiji* | Castro	-
Fuki Sushi* | Palo Alto/S	22
GochI | Cupertino/S	23
Godzila Sushi* | Pacific Hts	19
Grandeho Kamekyo* | multi.	23
Hamano Sushi* | Noe Valley	19
Hana Japanese* | Rohnert Pk/N	24
Hotaru* | San Mateo/S	21
Hotei* | Inner Sunset	19
Isobune* | multi.	17
Jin Sho* | Palo Alto/S	24
Juban | multi.	19
Kabuto* | Outer Rich	26
Kanpai* | Palo Alto/S	22
☑ Kaygetsu* | Menlo Pk/S	28
Kiji Sushi Bar* | Mission	23
Kirala* | Berkeley/E	25
☑ Kiss Seafood* | Japantown	28
Koo* | Inner Sunset	25

Kyo-Ya* | **Downtown**	24
Maki | **Japantown**	23
Mifune | **Japantown**	17
Moki's Sushi* | **Bernal Hts**	22
Muracci's | **Downtown**	21
Naked Fish* | **S Lake Tahoe/E**	21
Naomi Sushi* | **Menlo Pk/S**	21
Nihon | **Mission**	20
O Chamé | **Berkeley/E**	24
O Izakaya | **Japantown**	17
Osake/Sake 'O' | **multi.**	23
Oyaji* | **Outer Rich**	23
Ozumo* | **multi.**	24
Robata Grill* | **Mill Valley/N**	21
Ryoko's* | **Downtown**	22
Sanraku* | **multi.**	24
Sebo* | **Hayes Valley**	25
Shabu-Sen | **Japantown**	19
Sozai Rest. | **Inner Sunset**	18
Sushi Groove* | **multi.**	21
☑ Sushi Ran* | **Sausalito/N**	28
Sushi Zone* | **Castro**	26
Takara* | **Japantown**	21
Ten-Ichi* | **Upper Fillmore**	20
Tokyo Go Go* | **Mission**	21
Tsunami* | **multi.**	22
Umami* | **Cow Hollow**	22
Uzen* | **Oakland/E**	24
Yoshi's* | **Oakland/E**	20
Yoshi's SF | **W Addition**	22
Zushi Puzzle* | **Marina**	26

JEWISH

Miller's/Deli | **Polk Gulch**	22
Moishe's Pippic | **Hayes Valley**	18
Saul's Rest./Deli | **Berkeley/E**	19

KOREAN

(* barbecue specialist)

Brother's Korean* | **Inner Rich**	23
Koryo BBQ* | **Oakland/E**	23
My Tofu* | **Inner Rich**	22
Namu | **Inner Rich**	-
San Tung | **Inner Sunset**	23

MEDITERRANEAN

☑ Absinthe | **Hayes Valley**	22
À Côté | **Oakland/E**	24

Adagia | **Berkeley/E**	18
Arlequin | **Hayes Valley**	-
bacar | **SoMa**	23
Bar Tartine | **Mission**	24
BayWolf | **Oakland/E**	25
Belden Taverna | **Downtown**	18
Brix | **Napa/N**	22
Bursa Kebab | **W Portal**	22
☑ Cafe Gibraltar | **El Granada/S**	27
Café Rouge | **Berkeley/E**	22
Cafe Saint Rose | **Sebastopol/N**	23
Caffè Museo | **SoMa**	18
Camino | **Oakland/E**	22
Campton Place | **Downtown**	24
Cav Wine Bar | **Hayes Valley**	20
Central Market | **Petaluma/N**	24
Cetrella | **Half Moon Bay/S**	20
☑ Chez Panisse | **Berkeley/E**	28
☑ Chez Panisse Café | **Berkeley/E**	27
Coco500 | **SoMa**	22
Digs Bistro | **Berkeley/E**	25
Dio Deka | **Los Gatos/S**	25
downtown | **Berkeley/E**	19
El Dorado | **Sonoma/N**	24
NEW Elements | **Napa/N**	22
Enrico's | **N Beach**	16
Esin Rest. | **Danville/E**	24
Fandango | **Pacific Grove/S**	23
1550 Hyde | **Russian Hill**	22
Folio Enoteca | **Napa/N**	16
Foreign Cinema | **Mission**	23
Frascati | **Russian Hill**	26
Garibaldis | **multi.**	22
Gar Woods | **Carnelian Bay/E**	17
Harvest Moon | **Sonoma/N**	24
NEW Horatius | **Potrero Hill**	-
Hurley's | **Yountville/N**	21
Insalata's | **San Anselmo/N**	25
Lalime's | **Berkeley/E**	26
La Méditerranée | **multi.**	20
La Scene | **Downtown**	18
Lavanda | **Palo Alto/S**	20
Ledford Hse. | **Albion/N**	25
Loló | **Mission**	22
Luella | **Russian Hill**	22
Mandaloun | **Redwood City/S**	20

Manzanita | **Healdsburg/N**	19
MarketBar | **Embarcadero**	16
Medjool | **Mission**	18
NEW Metro Café | **W Addition**	–
Mezze | **Oakland/E**	20
Monti's | **Santa Rosa/N**	21
NEW Moss Room | **Inner Rich**	21
Old Jerusalem | **Mission**	20
Ottimista | **Cow Hollow**	19
Oxbow Wine | **Napa/N**	22
Pappo | **Alameda/E**	24
Paul K | **Hayes Valley**	21
Peasant & Pear | **Danville/E**	22
PlumpJack | **Olympic Valley/E**	23
NEW Restaurant Eloise | **Sebastopol/N**	–
Rest. LuLu/Petite | **SoMa**	21
Z Rivoli | **Berkeley/E**	27
Savor | **Noe Valley**	18
Sens Rest. | **Downtown**	20
71 Saint Peter | **San Jose/S**	22
NEW Sidebar | **Oakland/E**	20
Stokes | **Monterey/S**	21
Terzo | **Cow Hollow**	23
Thea Med. | **San Jose/S**	20
Truly Med. | **Mission**	23
Underwood Bar | **Graton/N**	24
Wente Vineyards | **Livermore/E**	23
Willow Wood | **Graton/N**	24
NEW Zaré/Fly Trap | **SoMa**	22
Zatar | **Berkeley/E**	22
Zibibbo | **Palo Alto/S**	19
Zucca | **Mtn View/S**	18
Z Zuni Café | **Hayes Valley**	25

MEXICAN

Cactus Taqueria | **multi.**	21
Colibrí Mexican | **Downtown**	20
Doña Tomás | **Oakland/E**	23
Don Pico's | **San Bruno/S**	23
El Balazo | **multi.**	19
El Metate | **Mission**	23
Frontera Fresco | **Downtown**	18
Green Chile | **W Addition**	20
Guaymas | **Tiburon/N**	16
Joe's Taco | **Mill Valley/N**	20
Juan's | **Berkeley/E**	16

La Corneta | **multi.**	22
La Cumbre | **multi.**	19
Las Camelias | **San Rafael/N**	18
La Taqueria | **Mission**	25
La Victoria | **San Jose/S**	20
Little Chihuahua | **W Addition**	23
Mamacita | **Marina**	23
NEW Marinitas | **San Anselmo/N**	21
Maya | **SoMa**	21
Mexico DF | **Embarcadero**	20
Mijita | **Embarcadero**	20
Nick's Tacos | **Russian Hill**	22
NEW Nopalito | **W Addition**	23
Pancho Villa | **multi.**	22
Papalote | **multi.**	22
Picante Cocina | **Berkeley/E**	21
Puerto Alegre | **Mission**	18
Regalito Rosticeria | **Mission**	21
Tacubaya | **Berkeley/E**	24
Tamarindo | **Oakland/E**	24
Taqueria Can-Cun | **multi.**	23
Taqueria 3 Amigos | **multi.**	19
Taqueria Tlaquepaque | **San Jose/S**	25
Tres Agaves | **S Beach**	15
Zazil Coastal | **Downtown**	18

MIDDLE EASTERN

Dish Dash | **Sunnyvale/S**	23
Goood Frikin' Chicken | **Mission**	18
Kan Zaman | **Haight-Ashbury**	17
La Méditerranée | **multi.**	20
Old Jerusalem | **Mission**	20
Saha | **Tenderloin**	25
Truly Med. | **Mission**	23
Yumma's | **Inner Sunset**	21

MOROCCAN

Z Aziza | **Outer Rich**	26
Tajine | **Pacific Hts**	–
Zitune | **Los Altos/S**	25

NEPALESE

Little Nepal | **Bernal Hts**	23

NEW ENGLAND

Old Port Lobster | **Redwood City/S**	22
Yankee Pier | **multi.**	17

NEW ZEALAND

South Food/Wine | S Beach — 21

NOODLE SHOPS

Citrus Club	Haight-Ashbury	21
Hotei	Inner Sunset	19
Mifune	Japantown	17
Osha Thai	multi.	21
San Tung	Inner Sunset	23

NUEVO LATINO

Destino	Castro	22
NEW Joya	Palo Alto/S	18

PACIFIC RIM

Pacific Catch	multi.	20
Z Tonga	Nob Hill	13

PAKISTANI

Naan/Curry	multi.	17
Pakwan	multi.	22
Shalimar	multi.	23

PAN-ASIAN

Bambuddha	Tenderloin	17
Betelnut Pejiu	Cow Hollow	22
B Star Bar	Inner Rich	22
Citrus Club	Haight-Ashbury	21
Poleng	W Addition	19
Ponzu	Downtown	20
Red Lantern	Redwood City/S	19
Straits	multi.	19
Z Tonga	Nob Hill	13
Unicorn Pan Asian	Downtown	23

PAN-LATIN

Cascal	Mtn View/S	20
Charanga	Mission	21
Fonda Solana	Albany/E	23
Loló	Mission	22
NEW Marinitas	San Anselmo/N	21

PERSIAN

Maykadeh | N Beach — 26

PERUVIAN

Destino	Castro	22
Essencia	Hayes Valley	19
Fresca	multi.	22

NEW La Mar	Embarcadero	23
Limón	Mission	23
Mochica	SoMa	25
Piqueo's	Bernal Hts	24

PIZZA

Amici's	multi.	20
Arinell Pizza	multi.	24
Azzurro Pizzeria	Napa/N	22
Beretta	Mission	23
Z Cheese Board	Berkeley/E	26
Diavola	Geyserville/N	24
NEW Flour + Water	Mission	-
Gialina	Glen Pk	24
Gioia Pizzeria	Berkeley/E	23
Giorgio's Pizzeria	Inner Rich	21
Goat Hill Pizza	multi.	18
La Ginestra	Mill Valley/N	21
Lanesplitter Pub	multi.	17
Little Star Pizza	multi.	25
Local Kitchen	SoMa	20
Lo Coco's	multi.	22
NEW Marzano	Oakland/E	23
North Beach Pizza	multi.	20
Palio d'Asti	Downtown	20
Patxi's Pizza	multi.	22
Pauline's Pizza	Mission	23
Pizza Antica	multi.	21
Pizzaiolo	Oakland/E	25
NEW Pizza Nostra	Potrero Hill	-
Pizza Place on Noriega	Outer Sunset	-
Pizza Rustica	Oakland/E	18
NEW Pizzavino	Sebastopol/N	-
Pizzeria Delfina	multi.	24
Pizzeria Picco	Larkspur/N	25
Pizzeria Tra Vigne	St. Helena/N	21
Pizzetta 211	Outer Rich	25
Rigolo	Presidio Hts	16
Rosso Pizzeria	Santa Rosa/N	25
Tommaso's	N Beach	25
NEW Tony's Pizza	N Beach	-
Z Zachary's Pizza	multi.	24
Zante	Bernal Hts	20

POLYNESIAN

Trader Vic's | multi. — 17

PORTUGUESE

NEW Horatius | **Potrero Hill**	–
LaSalette | **Sonoma/N**	25

PUB FOOD

Bridgetender | **Tahoe City/E**	19
Forge in Forest | **Carmel/S**	18
Half Moon Brew | **Half Moon Bay/S**	16

PUERTO RICAN

Sol Food | **San Rafael/N**	23

RUSSIAN

Katia's Tea | **Inner Rich**	23

SANDWICHES

Cheese Steak Shop | **multi.**	23
Downtown Bakery | **Healdsburg/N**	25
Gayle's Bakery | **Capitola/S**	25
Giordano | **N Beach**	22
NEW Il Cane Rosso | **Embarcadero**	–
Jimtown Store | **Healdsburg/N**	18
Mario's Bohemian | **N Beach**	18
Max's | **multi.**	17
Model Bakery | **multi.**	20
Plant Cafe | **multi.**	20
Pluto's | **multi.**	19
Rest. LuLu/Petite | **Embarcadero**	21
Saigon Sandwiches | **Tenderloin**	25
Sentinel | **SoMa**	25
Warming Hut | **Presidio**	15
'wichcraft | **Downtown**	18

SEAFOOD

Alamo Sq. | **W Addition**	20
Alioto's | **Fish. Wharf**	18
Anchor & Hope | **SoMa**	21
Anchor Oyster | **Castro**	23
Z Aqua | **Downtown**	26
NEW Aquarius | **Santa Cruz/S**	–
Barbara's Fish Trap | **Princeton Sea/S**	20
Bar Crudo | **W Addition**	26
Brindisi | **Downtown**	18
Cafe Maritime/East | **Marina**	21
Cajun Pacific | **Outer Sunset**	20
Cantankerous | **Mtn View/S**	18

Catch | **Castro**	18
Z Farallon | **Downtown**	24
Fish | **Sausalito/N**	23
Fish & Farm | **Downtown**	20
Flying Fish | **Carmel/S**	24
Flying Fish | **Half Moon Bay/S**	22
Fook Yuen | **Millbrae/S**	22
Forbes Island | **Fish. Wharf**	19
Go Fish | **St. Helena/N**	22
Great Eastern | **Chinatown**	21
Guaymas | **Tiburon/N**	16
Half Moon Brew | **Half Moon Bay/S**	16
Hayes St. Grill | **Hayes Valley**	23
Hog Island Oyster | **multi.**	25
Koi | **Daly City/S**	23
NEW Lake Chalet | **Oakland/E**	–
Little River Inn | **Little River/N**	21
Lure | **San Mateo/S**	20
Marica | **Oakland/E**	23
Mayflower | **Outer Rich**	22
McCormick | **Fish. Wharf**	20
Meritage Martini | **Sonoma/N**	20
NEW Nettie's | **Cow Hollow**	20
Old Port Lobster | **Redwood City/S**	22
Pacific Café | **Outer Rich**	23
Pacific Catch | **multi.**	20
Z Passionfish | **Pacific Grove/S**	26
Pesce | **Russian Hill**	24
Sam's Chowder | **Half Moon Bay/S**	20
Sam's Grill | **Downtown**	22
Sardine Factory | **Monterey/S**	21
Scoma's | **multi.**	22
Scott's | **multi.**	18
Sea Salt | **Berkeley/E**	22
Z Seasons | **Downtown**	26
Sunnyside | **Tahoe City/E**	18
Swan Oyster | **Polk Gulch**	26
Z Tadich Grill | **Downtown**	23
Tsar Nicoulai | **Embarcadero**	23
Z Waterbar | **Embarcadero**	20
Waterfront | **Embarcadero**	18
Weird Fish | **Mission**	21
Willi's Seafood | **Healdsburg/N**	24

Will's Fargo | **Carmel Valley/S** 22

Z Wolfdale's | **Tahoe City/E** 27

Woodhse. | **multi.** 21

Yabbies Coastal | **Russian Hill** 21

Yankee Pier | **multi.** 17

Zazil Coastal | **Downtown** 18

SINGAPOREAN

Straits | **multi.** 19

SMALL PLATES

(See also Spanish tapas specialist)

Z Absinthe | French/Med. | 22
Hayes Valley

À Côté | French/Med. | 24
Oakland/E

NEW Adesso | Italian | –
Oakland/E

Alembic | Eclectic | 22
Haight-Ashbury

Andalu | Eclectic | **Mission** 21

AsiaSF | Asian/Cal. | **SoMa** 17

NEW Aurea | Cal. | **Nob Hill** –

Bin 38 | Cal. | **Marina** 19

NEW Bistro 24 | Amer. | –
Noe Valley

Cascal | Pan-Latin | **Mtn View/S** 20

Cha Cha Cha | Carib. | **multi.** 20

Charanga | Pan-Latin | **Mission** 21

Circa | Amer. | **Marina** 18

District | Eclectic | **SoMa** 18

downtown | Cal./Med. | 19
Berkeley/E

E&O Trading | SE Asian | 19
Downtown

NEW Elements | Cal./Med. | 22
Napa/N

Eos Rest. | Asian/Cal. | **Cole Valley** 23

Grand Pu Bah | Thai | **Potrero Hill** 18

Isa | French | **Marina** 24

JoLe | Amer. | **Calistoga/N** 26

Lavanda | Med. | **Palo Alto/S** 20

Lime | Eclectic | **Castro** 17

Medjool | Med. | **Mission** 18

Mezze | Cal./Med. | **Oakland/E** 20

Monti's | Med. | **Santa Rosa/N** 21

Nectar Wine | Cal. | **Marina** 18

Nihon | Japanese | **Mission** 20

Orson | Cal. | **SoMa** 18

Ottimista | Italian/Med. | 19
Cow Hollow

Oxbow Wine | Amer. | **Napa/N** 22

Oyaji | Japanese | **Outer Rich** 23

Park Chalet | Amer. | **Outer Sunset** 16

Pesce | Italian/Seafood | 24
Russian Hill

Picco | Italian | **Larkspur/N** 26

Piqueo's | Peruvian | **Bernal Hts** 24

Poleng | Pan-Asian | **W Addition** 19

Ponzu | Pan-Asian | **Downtown** 20

rnm rest. | Amer./French | 23
Lower Haight

Stokes | Cal./Med. | **Monterey/S** 21

Straits | Singapor. | **multi.** 19

Tamarine | Viet. | **Palo Alto/S** 26

Terzo | Med. | **Cow Hollow** 23

Three Seasons | Viet. | **multi.** 21

Underwood Bar | Med. | **Graton/N** 24

Va de Vi | Eclectic | 23
Walnut Creek/E

Willi's Seafood | Seafood | 24
Healdsburg/N

Willi's Wine | Eclectic | 26
Santa Rosa/N

Zibibbo | Med. | **Palo Alto/S** 19

Zucca | Med. | **Mtn View/S** 18

SOUL FOOD

Brenda's | **Civic Ctr** 24

Elite Cafe | **Upper Fillmore** 19

farmerbrown/skillet | **multi.** 21

Hard Knox | **multi.** 19

Home of Chicken | **Oakland/E** 20

Starlight | **Sebastopol/N** 22

1300/Fillmore | **W Addition** 22

SOUTHEAST ASIAN

E&O Trading | **multi.** 19

Red Lantern | **Redwood City/S** 19

Sai Jai Thai | **Tenderloin** 25

Tamarine | **Palo Alto/S** 26

SOUTHERN

NEW Baby Blues BBQ | **Mission** 21

Blackberry Bistro | **Oakland/E** 19

Brenda's | **Civic Ctr** 24

Everett & Jones | **multi.** 20

CUISINES

Front Porch	**Bernal Hts**	22
Hard Knox	**multi.**	19
Home of Chicken	**Oakland/E**	20
Kate's Kitchen	**Lower Haight**	22
Magnolia	**Haight-Ashbury**	18
NEW Picán	**Oakland/E**	-
1300/Fillmore	**W Addition**	22

SOUTHWESTERN

Boogaloos	**Mission**	20
Cacti Grill	**Novato/N**	19

SPANISH

(* tapas specialist)

Alegrias*	**Marina**	21
NEW Barlata*	**Oakland/E**	-
Basque Cultural	**S San Francisco/S**	22
B44	**Downtown**	21
Bocadillos*	**N Beach**	22
César*	**multi.**	22
NEW Contigo*	**Noe Valley**	19
Esperpento*	**Mission**	19
Estéban*	**Monterey/S**	-
Fonda Solana*	**Albany/E**	23
Z NEW Gitane	**Downtown**	22
Iberia*	**Menlo Pk/S**	21
Iluna Basque*	**N Beach**	21
Laïola*	**Marina**	20
NEW Lalola Bar*	**Russian Hill**	21
Picaro*	**Mission**	17
Piperade	**Downtown**	25
Ramblas*	**Mission**	20
Sabor of Spain*	**San Rafael/N**	19
Zarzuela*	**Russian Hill**	25
ZuZu*	**Napa/N**	23

STEAKHOUSES

Acme Chophse.	**S Beach**	20
Alexander's	**Cupertino/S**	25
Alfred's Steak	**Downtown**	22
Arcadia	**San Jose/S**	21
Boca	**Novato/N**	22
Casa Orinda	**Orinda/E**	18
Cole's Chop Hse.	**Napa/N**	24
El Raigón	**N Beach**	22
EPIC	**Embarcadero**	20

Espetus	**multi.**	22
5A5 Steak Lounge	**Downtown**	-
Forbes Mill Steak	**multi.**	22
Harris'	**Polk Gulch**	25
Z House of Prime	**Polk Gulch**	24
Izzy's Steak	**multi.**	20
Joe DiMaggio's	**N Beach**	21
Kurt's Carmel	**Carmel/S**	23
Lark Creek Steak	**Downtown**	23
Morton's	**multi.**	24
Press	**St. Helena/N**	23
Ruth's Chris	**multi.**	23
Z Seasons	**Downtown**	26
Sunnyside	**Tahoe City/E**	18
Vic Stewart's	**Walnut Creek/E**	21
Will's Fargo	**Carmel Valley/S**	22

SWISS

Emile's	**San Jose/S**	22
Matterhorn Swiss	**Russian Hill**	23

TEAROOMS

Imperial/Berkeley	**multi.**	20
Lovejoy's Tea	**Noe Valley**	21
Poleng	**W Addition**	19
Samovar Tea Lounge	**multi.**	20

THAI

NEW Basil Canteen	**SoMa**	21
Basil Thai	**SoMa**	22
Cha Am Thai	**multi.**	19
Grand Pu Bah	**Potrero Hill**	18
Khan Toke	**Outer Rich**	22
King of Thai	**multi.**	19
Koh Samui	**SoMa**	21
Krung Thai	**multi.**	20
Manora's Thai	**SoMa**	25
Marnee Thai	**multi.**	23
Osha Thai	**multi.**	21
Plearn Thai	**multi.**	21
Royal Thai	**San Rafael/N**	23
Sai Jai Thai	**Tenderloin**	25
Soi4	**Oakland/E**	23
Suriya Thai	**SoMa**	20
Thai Buddhist	**Berkeley/E**	19
Thai House	**multi.**	23
Thep Phanom	**Lower Haight**	24

TURKISH

A La Turca | **Tenderloin**	21
Bursa Kebab | **W Portal**	22
Sens Rest. | **Downtown**	20
Troya | **Inner Rich**	21

VEGETARIAN

(* vegan)

Café Gratitude* | **multi.**	16
Cha-Ya Veg.* | **multi.**	22
☑ Greens | **Marina**	24
Herbivore* | **multi.**	15
Millennium* | **Downtown**	25
Ravens Rest.* | **Mendocino/N**	22
☑ Ubuntu* | **Napa/N**	26
Udupi Palace | **multi.**	21

VENEZUELAN

Pica Pica Maize | **Napa/N**	25

VIETNAMESE

Ana Mandara | **Fish. Wharf**	22
Annalien | **Napa/N**	23
Bodega Bistro | **Tenderloin**	25
Crustacean | **Polk Gulch**	23
Le Cheval | **multi.**	21
Le Colonial | **Downtown**	22
Le Soleil | **Inner Rich**	23
Out the Door | **multi.**	22
Pho 84 | **Oakland/E**	22
Pot de Pho | **Inner Rich**	18
Saigon Sandwiches | **Tenderloin**	25
☑ Slanted Door | **Embarcadero**	26
Tamarine | **Palo Alto/S**	26
Thanh Long | **Outer Sunset**	24
Three Seasons | **multi.**	21
Tu Lan | **SoMa**	22
Xanh | **Mtn View/S**	23
Xyclo | **Oakland/E**	22
Zadin | **Castro**	22

CUISINES

Locations

Includes restaurant names, cuisines, Food ratings and, for locations that are mapped, top list with map coordinates.

City of San Francisco

AT&T PARK/ SOUTH BEACH
(See map on page 283)

TOP FOOD
Tsunami | Japanese | **G5**   22
South Food/Wine | Australian | **F5**   21
Acme Chophse. | Steak | **H5**   20

LISTING
Acme Chophse. | Steak   20
Amici's | Pizza   20
Burger Joint | Burgers   18
MoMo's | Amer.   17
South Food/Wine | Australian   21
Tres Agaves | Mex.   15
Tsunami | Japanese   22

BERNAL HEIGHTS
Angkor Borei | Cambodian   23
Emmy's Spaghetti | Italian   21
Front Porch | Carib./Southern   22
Liberty Café | Amer.   22
Little Nepal | Nepalese   23
Moki's Sushi | Japanese   22
Piqueo's | Peruvian   24
Zante | Indian/Pizza   20

CASTRO
(See map on page 284)

TOP FOOD
Sushi Zone | Japanese | **A6**   26
L'Ardoise | French | **C3**   24
Anchor Oyster | Seafood | **E3**   23
Thai House | Thai | **E3**   23
2223 | Cal. | **C4**   23

LISTING
Anchor Oyster | Seafood   23
Brandy Ho's | Chinese   19
BurgerMeister | Burgers   19
Café Flore | Amer.   15

Catch | Seafood   18
Chow/Park Chow | Amer.   21
Côté Sud | French   19
Destino | Nuevo Latino   22
Eiji | Japanese   -
Eureka | Amer.   20
Home | Amer.   18
Kasa Indian | Indian   20
La Méditerranée | Med./Mideast.   20
L'Ardoise | French   24
Lime | Eclectic   17
Poesia | Italian   20
Samovar Tea Lounge | Tea   20
Sushi Zone | Japanese   26
Thai House | Thai   23
2223 | Cal.   23
Woodhse. | Seafood   21
Zadin | Viet.   22

CHINA BASIN/ DOGPATCH
Piccino | Cal./Italian   24
Serpentine | Amer.   21

CHINATOWN
(See map on page 280)

TOP FOOD
R & G Lounge | Chinese | **G7**   23
Hunan | Chinese | **F6**   22
Oriental Pearl | Chinese | **G6**   22

LISTING
Brandy Ho's | Chinese   19
Gold Mountain | Chinese   20
Great Eastern | Chinese   21
House of Nanking | Chinese   22
Henry's Hunan | Chinese   21
Hunan | Chinese   22
Jai Yun | Chinese   23
Oriental Pearl | Chinese   22
R & G Lounge | Chinese   23
Yuet Lee | Chinese   21

Menus, photos, voting and more – free at ZAGAT.com

COW HOLLOW

(See map on page 282)

TOP FOOD

Capannina | *Italian* | **H5** | 24
Terzo | *Med.* | **F5** | 23
Pane e Vino | *Italian* | **H5** | 22
Betelnut Pejiu | *Pan-Asian* | **G5** | 22
Gamine | *French* | **F5** | 22

LISTING

Balboa Cafe | *Amer.* | 19
Betelnut Pejiu | *Pan-Asian* | 22
Brazen Head | *Amer.* | 20
Capannina | *Italian* | 24
Gamine | *French* | 22
La Boulange | *Bakery* | 22
NEW Nettie's | *Seafood* | 20
Osha Thai | *Thai* | 21
Ottimista | *Italian/Med.* | 19
Pane e Vino | *Italian* | 22
Pomodoro | *Italian* | 17
Rose's Cafe | *Italian* | 22
Terzo | *Med.* | 23
Umami | *Japanese* | 22

DOWNTOWN

(See map on page 280)

TOP FOOD

Masa's | *French* | **I5** | 28
Fleur de Lys | *Cal./French* | **I4** | 27
Michael Mina | *Amer.* | **J5** | 27
Quince | *French/Italian* | **F7** | 27
Kokkari | *Greek* | **F8** | 27

LISTING

Alfred's Steak | *Steak* | 22
ANZU | *Euro./Japanese* | 22
Z Aqua | *Seafood* | 26
Asia de Cuba | *Asian/Cuban* | 20
Belden Taverna | *Med.* | 18
Best-o-Burger | *Burgers* | 15
B44 | *Spanish* | 21
Z BIX | *Amer./French* | 23
Brindisi | *Italian/Seafood* | 18
Cafe Bastille | *French* | 18
Café Claude | *French* | 21
Café de la Presse | *French* | 18

Café Tiramisu | *Italian* | 20
Campton Place | *Cal./Med.* | 24
Carnelian Room | *Cal.* | 18
Cheesecake | *Amer.* | 16
Colibrí Mexican | *Mex.* | 20
E&O Trading | *SE Asian* | 19
Emporio Rulli | *Dessert/Italian* | 22
Z Farallon | *Seafood* | 24
Fish & Farm | *Amer./Seafood* | 20
5A5 Steak Lounge | *Steak* | -
Z Fleur de Lys | *Cal./French* | 27
Frontera Fresco | *Mex.* | 18
Z Garden Court | *Cal.* | 20
Gaylord India | *Indian* | 18
Z NEW Gitane | *French/Spanish* | 22
Globe | *Cal./Italian* | 20
Grand Cafe | *French* | 19
Henry's Hunan | *Chinese* | 21
Il Fornaio | *Italian* | 19
King of Thai | *Thai* | 19
Z Kokkari | *Greek* | 27
Kuleto's | *Italian* | 20
Kyo-Ya | *Japanese* | 24
Lark Creek Steak | *Steak* | 23
La Scene | *Cal./Med.* | 18
Le Central Bistro | *French* | 20
Le Colonial | *French/Viet.* | 22
Level III | *Amer.* | 18
Z Masa's | *French* | 28
Max's | *Deli* | 17
Z Michael Mina | *Amer.* | 27
NEW Midi | *Amer./French* | -
Millennium | *Vegan* | 25
Mixt Greens | *Health* | 22
Morton's | *Steak* | 24
Muracci's | *Japanese* | 21
Naan/Curry | *Indian/Pakistani* | 17
Osha Thai | *Thai* | 21
Out the Door | *Viet.* | 22
Palio d'Asti | *Italian* | 20
Z Perbacco | *Italian* | 25
NEW Pickles | *Amer.* | -
Piperade | *Spanish* | 25
Plouf | *French* | 22
Ponzu | *Pan-Asian* | 20
Puccini & Pinetti | *Italian* | 18

Z Quince	*French/Italian*	27	Red's Java	*Burgers*	16
Z Rotunda	*Amer.*	19	Rest. LuLu/Petite	*Sandwiches*	21
Ryoko's	*Japanese*	22	Shanghai 1930	*Chinese*	20
Sam's Grill	*Seafood*	22	**Z** Slanted Door	*Viet.*	26
Sanraku	*Japanese*	24	Taylor's Auto	*Diner*	22
Scala's Bistro	*French*	21	Town's End	*Amer./Bakery*	20
Sears Fine Food	*Diner*	19	Tsar Nicoulai	*Caviar/Seafood*	23
Z Seasons	*Seafood/Steak*	26	**Z** Waterbar	*Seafood*	20
Sens Rest.	*Med./Turkish*	20	Waterfront	*Cal./Seafood*	18

NEW Showdogs | *Hot Dogs* —

Silks | *Cal.* — 24

Straits | *Singapor.* — 19

Z Tadich Grill | *Seafood* — 23

Taqueria Can-Cun | *Mex.* — 23

NEW Taverna Aventine | *Cal./Italian* — —

Tommy Toy's | *Chinese* — 23

NEW Trademark Grill | *Amer.* — —

Unicorn Pan Asian | *Pan-Asian* — 23

NEW Urban Tavern | *Amer.* — 17

NEW Wexler's | *BBQ* — —

'wichcraft | *Sandwiches* — 18

Zazil Coastal | *Mex.* — 18

NEW Zinnia | *Amer.* — 23

EMBARCADERO

Americano | *Cal.* — 18

Blue Bottle | *Cal./Coffee* — 23

Boulette's Larder | *Amer.* — 25

Z Boulevard | *Amer.* — 27

Butterfly | *Asian/Cal.* — 20

Chaya | *French/Japanese* — 22

Delancey St. | *Eclectic* — 17

EPIC | *Steak* — 20

Fog City Diner | *Amer.* — 19

Hog Island Oyster | *Seafood* — 25

NEW Il Cane Rosso | *Italian* — —

Imperial/Berkeley | *Tea* — 20

NEW La Mar | *Peruvian* — 23

MarketBar | *Med.* — 16

Mexico DF | *Mex.* — 20

Mijita | *Mex.* — 20

One Market | *Amer.* — 22

Out the Door | *Viet.* — 22

Ozumo | *Japanese* — 24

Plant Cafe | *Health* — 20

EXCELSIOR

Joe's Cable Car | *Burgers* — 21

North Beach Pizza | *Pizza* — 20

FISHERMAN'S WHARF

(See map on page 280)

TOP FOOD

Gary Danko | *Amer.* | **B3** — 29

Grandeho Kamekyo | *Japanese* | **B3** — 23

Scoma's | *Seafood* | **A4** — 22

LISTING

Alioto's | *Italian* — 18

Ana Mandara | *Viet.* — 22

Bistro Boudin | *Cal.* — 19

Forbes Island | *Amer./Seafood* — 19

Z Gary Danko | *Amer.* — 29

Grandeho Kamekyo | *Japanese* — 23

Hard Rock | *Amer.* — 12

Z In-N-Out | *Burgers* — 22

McCormick | *Seafood* — 20

North Beach Pizza | *Pizza* — 20

Scoma's | *Seafood* — 22

FOREST HILLS/ WEST PORTAL

Bursa Kebab | *Med.* — 22

Chouchou | *French* — 22

Fresca | *Peruvian* — 22

Roti Indian | *Indian* — 22

GLEN PARK

Chenery Park | *Amer.* — 21

Gialina | *Pizza* — 24

La Corneta | *Mex.* — 22

Le P'tit Laurent | *French* — 22

Osha Thai | *Thai* — 21

HAIGHT-ASHBURY/ COLE VALLEY

Alembic	*Eclectic*	22
Asqew Grill	*Cal.*	16
BurgerMeister	*Burgers*	19
Cha Cha Cha	*Carib.*	20
Citrus Club	*Pan-Asian*	21
El Balazo	*Mex.*	19
Eos Rest.	*Asian Fusion/Cal.*	23
Grandeho Kamekyo	*Japanese*	23
Kan Zaman	*Mideast.*	17
La Boulange	*Bakery*	22
Magnolia	*Amer./Southern*	18
Massawa	*African*	19
North Beach Pizza	*Pizza*	20
Pork Store	*Amer.*	22
Zazie	*French*	22

HAYES VALLEY/ CIVIC CENTER

☑ Absinthe	*French/Med.*	22
Arlequin	*Med.*	-
Bar Jules	*Amer.*	24
Bistro Clovis	*French*	21
Blue Bottle	*Cal./Coffee*	23
Brenda's	*Creole/Southern*	24
Caffe Delle Stelle	*Italian*	16
Cav Wine Bar	*Med.*	20
Citizen Cake	*Bakery/Cal.*	21
Delessio Market	*Bakery*	21
Domo Sushi	*Japanese*	23
Espetus	*Brazilian*	22
Essencia	*Peruvian*	19
Frjtz Fries	*Belgian*	18
Hayes St. Grill	*Seafood*	23
Indigo	*Amer.*	19
☑ Jardinière	*Cal./French*	26
La Boulange	*Bakery*	22
Max's	*Deli*	17
Mel's Drive-In	*Diner*	14
Moishe's Pippic	*Deli/Jewish*	18
Patxi's Pizza	*Pizza*	22
Paul K	*Med.*	21
Samovar Tea Lounge	*Tea*	20
Sauce	*Amer.*	19
Sebo	*Japanese*	25
Stacks	*Amer.*	18

Suppenküche	*German*	22
☑ Zuni Café	*Med.*	25

INNER RICHMOND

NEW Academy Cafe	*Eclectic*	21
Bella Trattoria	*Italian*	21
Brother's Korean	*Korean*	23
B Star Bar	*Pan-Asian*	22
Burma Superstar	*Burmese*	25
Giorgio's Pizzeria	*Pizza*	21
Good Luck	*Chinese*	22
Katia's Tea	*Russian*	23
King of Thai	*Thai*	19
Le Soleil	*Viet.*	23
Mandalay	*Burmese*	22
Mel's Drive-In	*Diner*	14
NEW Moss Room	*Cal./Med.*	-
My Tofu	*Korean*	22
Namu	*Cal./Korean*	-
Pagan	*Burmese*	-
Pot de Pho	*Viet.*	18
Q	*Amer.*	19
Richmond Rest.	*Cal.*	26
Roadside BBQ	*BBQ*	17
Troya	*Turkish*	21

INNER SUNSET

Chow/Park Chow	*Amer.*	21
Ebisu	*Japanese*	23
Hotei	*Japanese*	19
Koo	*Asian Fusion*	25
Marnee Thai	*Thai*	23
Naan/Curry	*Indian/Pakistani*	17
Pacific Catch	*Seafood*	20
Pluto's	*Amer.*	19
Pomelo	*Eclectic*	23
San Tung	*Chinese/Korean*	23
Sozai Rest.	*Japanese*	18
Underdog	*Hot Dogs*	20
Yumma's	*Mideast.*	21

JAPANTOWN

Bushi-tei	*Asian Fusion/French*	24
CAFÉ KATi	*Asian Fusion*	21
Isobune	*Japanese*	17
Juban	*Japanese*	19
☑ Kiss Seafood	*Japanese*	28

Maki	*Japanese*	23
Mifune	*Japanese*	17
O Izakaya	*Japanese*	17
Shabu-Sen	*Japanese*	19
Takara	*Japanese*	21

LAUREL HEIGHTS/ PRESIDIO HEIGHTS

Asqew Grill	*Cal.*	16
Ella's	*Amer.*	22
Garibaldis	*Cal./Med.*	22
Pomodoro	*Italian*	17
Rigolo	*French*	16
Sociale	*Italian*	24
☑ Spruce	*Amer.*	25

LOWER HAIGHT

Axum Cafe	*Ethiopian*	20
NEW Bistro St. Germain	*French*	-
Burger Joint	*Burgers*	18
Café du Soleil	*Fench*	19
Indian Oven	*Indian*	23
Kate's Kitchen	*Southern*	22
Memphis Minnie	*BBQ*	20
rnm rest.	*Amer./French*	23
Rosamunde Grill	*German*	25
Thep Phanom	*Thai*	24
Uva Enoteca	*Italian*	20

MARINA

(See map on page 282)

TOP FOOD

Zushi Puzzle	*Japanese*	**G4**	26
A16	*Italian*	**E3**	25
Greens	*Veg.*	**G2**	24
Isa	*French*	**F4**	24
Mamacita	*Mex.*	**E3**	23

LISTING

Ace Wasabi's	*Japanese*	21
Alegrias	*Spanish*	21
Amici's	*Pizza*	20
☑ A16	*Italian*	25
Asqew Grill	*Cal.*	16
Baker St. Bistro	*French*	21
Barney's	*Burgers*	19
Bin 38	*Cal.*	19
Blue Barn Gourmet	*Cal.*	22

Cafe Maritime/East	*Seafood*	21
Circa	*Amer.*	18
Dragon Well	*Chinese*	21
E'Angelo	*Italian*	21
Emporio Rulli	*Dessert/Italian*	22
☑ Greens	*Veg.*	24
Isa	*French*	24
Izzy's Steak	*Steak*	20
Jake's Steaks	*Cheesestks.*	20
Laïola	*Spanish*	20
NEW Let's Be Frank	*Hot Dogs*	-
Mamacita	*Mex.*	23
Mel's Drive-In	*Diner*	14
Nectar Wine	*Cal.*	18
Pacific Catch	*Seafood*	20
Plant Cafe	*Health*	20
Pluto's	*Amer.*	19
Ristorante Parma	*Italian*	23
Three Seasons	*Viet.*	21
NEW Tipsy Pig	*Amer.*	21
Zushi Puzzle	*Japanese*	26

MISSION

(See map on page 284)

TOP FOOD

Tartine	*Bakery*	**D6**	27
Range	*Amer.*	**E6**	26
Delfina	*Italian*	**D6**	26
Chez Spencer	*French*	**B8**	26
Woodward's Gdn.	*Amer./Cal.*	**B7**	25

LISTING

Andalu	*Eclectic*	21
Arinell Pizza	*Pizza*	24
NEW Baby Blues BBQ	*BBQ/Southern*	21
Bar Bambino	*Italian*	23
Bar Tartine	*Med.*	24
Beretta	*Italian*	23
Blowfish Sushi	*Japanese*	20
Blue Plate	*Amer.*	24
Boogaloos	*SW*	20
Burger Joint	*Burgers*	18
Café Gratitude	*Vegan*	16
Cha Cha Cha	*Carib.*	20
Charanga	*Pan-Latin*	21

Menus, photos, voting and more – free at ZAGAT.com

Cha-Ya Veg. | *Japanese/Vegan*	22
Chez Spencer | *French*	26
Conduit | *Amer./French*	22
NEW Corner | *Amer./Italian*	-
Z Delfina | *Italian*	26
Dosa | *Indian*	23
El Balazo | *Mex.*	19
El Metate | *Mex.*	23
Esperpento | *Spanish*	19
Farina | *Italian*	23
NEW Flour + Water | *Italian*	-
Foreign Cinema | *Cal./Med.*	23
Frjtz Fries | *Belgian*	18
Goood Frikin' Chicken | *Mideast.*	18
Herbivore | *Vegan*	15
Jay's | *Cheesestks.*	19
Kiji Sushi Bar | *Japanese*	23
La Corneta | *Mex.*	22
La Cumbre | *Mex.*	19
La Provence | *French*	20
La Taqueria | *Mex.*	25
Limón | *Peruvian*	23
Little Star Pizza | *Pizza*	25
Loló | *Med./Pan-Latin*	22
Luna Park | *Amer./French*	20
Maverick | *Amer.*	24
Medjool | *Med.*	18
Mission Bch. Café | *Cal.*	21
Monk's Kettle | *Cal.*	18
Nihon | *Japanese*	20
Old Jerusalem | *Med./Mideast.*	20
Osha Thai | *Thai*	21
Pakwan | *Pakistani*	22
Pancho Villa | *Mex.*	22
Papalote | *Mex.*	22
Pauline's Pizza | *Pizza*	23
NEW Phat Philly | *Cheesestks.*	20
Picaro | *Spanish*	17
Pizzeria Delfina | *Pizza*	24
Pork Store | *Amer.*	22
Puerto Alegre | *Mex.*	18
Ramblas | *Spanish*	20
Range | *Amer.*	26
Regalito Rosticeria | *Mex.*	21
NEW Saison | *Amer.*	-
NEW Schmidt's | *German*	-

Slow Club | *Amer.*	22
Spork | *Amer.*	21
St. Francis | *Diner*	19
Taqueria Can-Cun | *Mex.*	23
Z Tartine | *Bakery*	27
Ti Couz | *French*	23
Tokyo Go Go | *Japanese*	21
Truly Med. | *Med.*	23
Udupi Palace | *Indian/Veg.*	21
Universal Cafe | *Amer.*	23
Walzwerk | *German*	21
Weird Fish | *Seafood*	21
Woodward's Gdn. | *Amer./Cal.*	25
Yamo | *Burmese*	23
Zeitgeist | *BBQ*	15

NOB HILL

(See map on page 280)

TOP FOOD

Ritz-Carlton Din. Rm. | *French* | **H6**	27
Venticello | *Italian* | **G4**	23
Big 4 | *Amer.* | **H4**	22

LISTING

NEW Aurea | *Cal.*	-
Z Big 4 | *Amer.*	22
Le Club | *Cal./French*	15
Nob Hill Café | *Italian*	21
Z Ritz-Carlton Din. Rm. | *French*	27
Z Tonga | *Pac. Rim/Pan-Asian*	13
Venticello | *Italian*	23

NOE VALLEY

(See map on page 284)

TOP FOOD

Firefly | *Eclectic* | **H2**	25
La Ciccia | *Italian* | **K5**	24
Incanto | *Italian* | **I5**	24
Chloe's Cafe | *Amer.* | **H5**	23
Bacco Ristorante | *Italian* | **H2**	23

LISTING

Alice's | *Chinese*	19
Bacco Ristorante | *Italian*	23
Barney's | *Burgers*	19
NEW Bistro 24 | *Amer.*	-
Chloe's Cafe | *Amer.*	23
NEW Contigo | *Spanish*	19

Eric's	*Chinese*	22
Firefly	*Eclectic*	25
Fresca	*Peruvian*	22
Hamano Sushi	*Japanese*	19
Henry's Hunan	*Chinese*	21
Incanto	*Italian*	24
La Ciccia	*Italian*	24
Le Zinc	*French*	19
Lovejoy's Tea	*Tea*	21
Lupa Trattoria	*Italian*	22
Pomelo	*Eclectic*	23
Pomodoro	*Italian*	17
Savor	*Med.*	18
Toast	*Amer.*	17

NORTH BEACH

(See map on page 280)

TOP FOOD

Coi	*Cal./French*	**F7**	28
House	*Asian Fusion*	**E6**	27
Mama's on Wash.	*Amer.*	**D6**	25
Cafe Jacqueline	*French*	**E6**	25
Tommaso's	*Italian*	**F7**	25

LISTING

Albona Rist.	*Italian*	24
Bocadillos	*Spanish*	22
BurgerMeister	*Burgers*	19
Cafe Jacqueline	*French*	25
Caffè Macaroni	*Italian*	20
Z Coi	*Cal./French*	28
El Raigón	*Argent.*	22
Enrico's	*Amer./Med.*	16
Fior d'Italia	*Italian*	18
Giordano	*Sandwiches*	22
Z House	*Asian Fusion*	27
Iluna Basque	*Spanish*	21
Joe DiMaggio's	*Italian/Steak*	21
Joey & Eddie's	*Italian*	14
King of Thai	*Thai*	19
La Boulange	*Bakery*	22
La Trappe	*Belgian*	18
L'Osteria	*Italian*	23
Mama's on Wash.	*Amer.*	25
Mangarosa	*Brazilian/Italian*	18
Mario's Bohemian	*Italian*	18
Maykadeh	*Persian*	26

Mo's	*Amer.*	20
Naan/Curry	*Indian/Pakistani*	17
North Beach Pizza	*Pizza*	20
North Beach Rest.	*Italian*	22
Pomodoro	*Italian*	17
Rist. Ideale	*Italian*	23
Rose Pistola	*Italian*	22
Tommaso's	*Italian*	25
NEW Tony's Pizza	*Italian*	-
Tratt. Contadina	*Italian*	22
Washington Sq. B&G	*Amer.*	-

OUTER RICHMOND

Ariake	*Japanese*	24
Z Aziza	*Moroccan*	26
Z Chapeau!	*French*	26
Cliff House	*Cal.*	18
Kabuto	*Japanese*	26
Khan Toke	*Thai*	22
Mayflower	*Chinese*	22
Mescolanza	*Italian*	21
Oyaji	*Japanese*	23
Pacific Café	*Seafood*	23
Pagan	*Burmese*	-
Pizzetta 211	*Pizza*	25
Shanghai Dumpling	*Chinese*	23
Z Sutro's	*Cal.*	21
Ton Kiang	*Chinese*	24

OUTER SUNSET

Beach Chalet	*Amer.*	15
Cajun Pacific	*Cajun*	20
Hard Knox	*Southern*	19
King of Thai	*Thai*	19
Marnee Thai	*Thai*	23
Park Chalet	*Cal.*	16
Pizza Place on Noriega	*Pizza*	-
Thanh Long	*Viet.*	24

PACIFIC HEIGHTS

Eliza's	*Chinese*	21
Florio	*French/Italian*	21
Godzila Sushi	*Japanese*	19
La Boulange	*Bakery*	22
Pizzeria Delfina	*Pizza*	24
Rest. Cassis	*French*	22
SPQR	*Italian*	23

Tajine	*Moroccan*	-
Vivande	*Italian*	23
Woodhse.	*Seafood*	21

POLK GULCH
(See map on page 280)

TOP FOOD

Acquerello	*Italian*	**G1**	28
Swan Oyster	*Seafood*	**H1**	26
Harris'	*Steak*	**F1**	25

LISTING

🛿 Acquerello	*Italian*	28
Crustacean	*Euro./Viet.*	23
Harris'	*Steak*	25
🛿 House of Prime	*Amer.*	24
Miller's/Deli	*Deli/Jewish*	22
Naan/Curry	*Indian/Pakistani*	17
Ruth's Chris	*Steak*	23
Shalimar	*Indian/Pakistani*	23
Swan Oyster	*Seafood*	26

POTRERO HILL

Aperto	*Italian*	23
Chez Maman	*French*	22
Chez Papa	*French*	23
El Balazo	*Mex.*	19
Eliza's	*Chinese*	21
Goat Hill Pizza	*Pizza*	18
Grand Pu Bah	*Thai*	18
Hard Knox	*Southern*	19
🆕 Horatius	*Med./Portug.*	-
🆕 Pizza Nostra	*Pizza*	-

PRESIDIO

La Terrasse	*French*	18
Presidio Social	*Amer.*	18
Warming Hut	*Sandwiches*	15

RUSSIAN HILL
(See map on page 280)

TOP FOOD

La Folie	*French*	**E1**	28
Frascati	*Cal./Med.*	**E3**	26
Zarzuela	*Spanish*	**E3**	25

LISTING

Antica Trattoria	*Italian*	22
1550 Hyde	*Cal./Med.*	22
Frascati	*Cal./Med.*	26

Helmand Palace	*Afghani*	23
Hyde St. Bistro	*French*	21
La Boulange	*Bakery*	22
🛿 La Folie	*French*	28
🆕 Lalola Bar	*Spanish*	21
Luella	*Cal./Med.*	22
Matterhorn Swiss	*Swiss*	23
Nick's Tacos	*Mex.*	22
Pesce	*Italian/Seafood*	24
Rist. Milano	*Italian*	22
Street	*Amer.*	21
Sushi Groove	*Japanese*	21
Yabbies Coastal	*Seafood*	21
Zarzuela	*Spanish*	25

SOMA
(See map on page 283)

TOP FOOD

Ame	*Amer.*	**H1**	26
Yank Sing	*Chinese*	**I1, J2**	25
Sentinel	*Sandwiches*	**H1**	25
Mochica	*Peruvian*	**E3**	25
Manora's Thai	*Thai*	**B3**	25

LISTING

Amber	*Indian*	24
🛿 Ame	*Amer.*	26
Anchor & Hope	*Seafood*	21
AsiaSF	*Asian/Cal.*	17
bacar	*Cal./Med.*	23
🆕 Basil Canteen	*Thai*	21
Basil Thai	*Thai*	22
Blue Bottle	*Cal./Coffee*	23
Buca di Beppo	*Italian*	14
Butler & Chef	*French*	20
Caffè Museo	*Italian/Med.*	18
Cha Am Thai	*Thai*	19
Chez Papa	*French*	23
Coco500	*Cal./Med.*	22
Cosmopolitan	*Amer.*	19
Custom Burger	*Burgers*	19
District	*Eclectic*	18
Ducca	*Italian*	20
farmerbrown/skillet	*Soul*	21
Fifth Floor	*Amer./French*	25
🆕 54 Mint	*Italian*	-
Fringale	*Basque/French*	24

Goat Hill Pizza | *Pizza* 18

NEW Heaven's Dog | *Chinese* 21

Henry's Hunan | *Chinese* 21

Koh Samui | *Thai* 21

La Boulange | *Bakery* 22

Le Charm Bistro | *French* 22

Local Kitchen | *Cal./Italian* 20

Luce | *Cal./Italian* 20

Manora's Thai | *Thai* 25

Maya | *Mex.* 21

Mel's Drive-In | *Diner* 14

Mochica | *Peruvian* 25

Mo's | *Amer.* 20

Oola | *Cal.* 20

Orson | *Cal.* 18

Osha Thai | *Thai* 21

Pazzia | *Italian* 23

Rest. LuLu/Petite | *French/Med.* 21

Rist. Umbria | *Italian* 21

NEW RN74 | *French* -

Roy's | *Hawaiian* 23

Salt House | *Amer.* 21

Samovar Tea Lounge | *Tea* 20

Sanraku | *Japanese* 24

Sentinel | *Sandwiches* 25

South Park | *French* 23

supperclub | *Eclectic* 15

Suriya Thai | *Thai* 20

Sushi Groove | *Japanese* 21

Town Hall | *Amer.* 24

Tu Lan | *Viet.* 22

TWO | *Cal.* 19

Vitrine | *Amer.* 23

XYZ | *Amer./Cal.* 19

Z Yank Sing | *Chinese* 25

NEW Zaré/Fly Trap | *Cal./Med.* 22

Zuppa | *Italian* 19

TENDERLOIN

(See map on page 280)

TOP FOOD

Canteen | *Cal.* | **I4** 27

Dottie's | *Diner* | **J4** 25

Bodega Bistro | *Viet.* | **K2** 25

LISTING

A La Turca | *Turkish* 21

Bambuddha | *Pan-Asian* 17

Bodega Bistro | *Viet.* 25

Z Canteen | *Cal.* 27

Dottie's | *Diner* 25

farmerbrown/skillet | *Soul* 21

Osha Thai | *Thai* 21

Pakwan | *Pakistani* 22

Saha | *Mideast.* 25

Saigon Sandwiches | *Sandwiches/Viet.* 25

Sai Jai Thai | *Thai* 25

Shalimar | *Indian/Pakistani* 23

Thai House | *Thai* 23

UPPER FILLMORE

Dosa | *Indian* 23

Elite Cafe | *Amer.* 19

Fresca | *Peruvian* 22

Jackson Fillmore | *Italian* 21

La Méditerranée | *Med./Mideast.* 20

Ten-Ichi | *Japanese* 20

WESTERN ADDITION

Alamo Sq. | *French/Seafood* 20

Bar Crudo | *Seafood* 26

Candybar | *Dessert* 17

Cheese Steak Shop | *Cheesestks.* 23

Delessio Market | *Bakery* 21

Green Chile | *Mex.* 20

Herbivore | *Vegan* 15

Jay's | *Cheesestks.* 19

Little Chihuahua | *Mex.* 23

Little Star Pizza | *Pizza* 25

NEW Metro Café | *Cal.* -

nopa | *Cal.* 25

NEW Nopalito | *Mex.* 23

Papalote | *Mex.* 22

Poleng | *Pan-Asian* 19

1300/Fillmore | *Soul/Southern* 22

Tsunami | *Japanese* 22

Yoshi's SF | *Japanese* 22

East of San Francisco

ALAMEDA

BurgerMeister | *Burgers* 19

Burma Superstar | *Burmese* 25

Cheese Steak Shop | *Cheesestks.* 23

Pappo | *Cal./Med.* 24

ALBANY

Caspers Hot Dogs	*Hot Dogs*	18
Fonda Solana	*Pan-Latin*	23
Nizza La Bella	*French/Italian*	20

BERKELEY

Adagia	*Cal.*	18
Ajanta	*Indian*	25
Amanda's	*Cal./Health*	18
Arinell Pizza	*Pizza*	24
Barney's	*Burgers*	19
Imperial/Berkeley	*Tea*	20
Bette's Oceanview	*Diner*	23
Bistro Liaison	*French*	22
Breads of India	*Indian*	19
Cactus Taqueria	*Mex.*	21
Café Fanny	*French*	23
Café Gratitude	*Vegan*	16
Café Rouge	*French/Med.*	22
César	*Spanish*	22
Cha Am Thai	*Thai*	19
Cha-Ya Veg.	*Japanese/Vegan*	22
Z Cheese Board	*Bakery/Pizza*	26
Cheese Steak Shop	*Cheesestks.*	23
Z Chez Panisse	*Cal./Med.*	28
Z Chez Panisse Café	*Cal./Med.*	27
Corso	*Italian*	24
Digs Bistro	*Amer./Med.*	25
downtown	*Cal./Med.*	19
Everett & Jones	*BBQ*	20
FatApple's	*Diner*	18
NEW Five	*Amer./Cal.*	-
Gioia Pizzeria	*Pizza*	23
Great China	*Chinese*	23
grégoire	*French*	22
Herbivore	*Vegan*	15
Jimmy Bean's	*Diner*	19
Jordan's	*Cal./French*	17
Juan's	*Mex.*	16
Kirala	*Japanese*	25
Lalime's	*Cal./Med.*	26
La Méditerranée	*Med./Mideast.*	20
Lanesplitter Pub	*Pizza*	17
La Note	*French*	21
Le Cheval	*Viet.*	21
Lo Coco's	*Italian*	22

Naan/Curry	*Indian/Pakistani*	17
North Beach Pizza	*Pizza*	20
O Chamé	*Japanese*	24
Picante Cocina	*Mex.*	21
Plearn Thai	*Thai*	21
Rick & Ann's	*Amer.*	21
Z Rivoli	*Cal./Med.*	27
Saul's Rest./Deli	*Deli*	19
Sea Salt	*Seafood*	22
Shen Hua	*Chinese*	22
Tacubaya	*Mex.*	24
Thai Buddhist	*Thai*	19
Tratt. La Siciliana	*Italian*	25
T Rex BBQ	*BBQ*	18
Udupi Palace	*Indian/Veg.*	21
Venezia	*Italian*	18
Venus	*Cal.*	23
Vik's Chaat	*Indian*	24
Z Zachary's Pizza	*Pizza*	24
Zatar	*Med.*	22

CONCORD

El Balazo	*Mex.*	19

DANVILLE

Amber Bistro	*Cal.*	22
Amici's	*Pizza*	20
Blackhawk Grille	*Cal.*	19
Bridges	*Asian/Cal.*	22
Chow/Park Chow	*Amer.*	21
El Balazo	*Mex.*	19
Esin Rest.	*Amer./Med.*	24
Forbes Mill Steak	*Steak*	22
Peasant & Pear	*Med.*	22
Piatti	*Italian*	18

DUBLIN

Amici's	*Pizza*	20
Caspers Hot Dogs	*Hot Dogs*	18
Koi	*Chinese*	23

EL CERRITO

FatApple's	*Diner*	18

EMERYVILLE

Asqew Grill	*Cal.*	16
Bucci's	*Cal./Italian*	21
Pomodoro	*Italian*	17

Townhouse B&G	*Cal.*	21
Trader Vic's	*Polynesian*	17

FREMONT

Pakwan	*Pakistani*	22
Shalimar	*Indian/Pakistani*	23

HAYWARD

Caspers Hot Dogs	*Hot Dogs*	18
Everett & Jones	*BBQ*	20
Pakwan	*Pakistani*	22

LAFAYETTE

NEW Artisan Bistro	*Cal./French*	-
Bo's Barbecue	*BBQ*	23
Cheese Steak Shop	*Cheesestks.*	23
NEW Chevalier	*French*	-
Chow/Park Chow	*Amer.*	21
Duck Club	*Amer.*	19
El Balazo	*Mex.*	19
Metro	*Cal./French*	-
Pizza Antica	*Pizza*	21
Postino	*Italian*	23
Yankee Pier	*New Eng./Seafood*	17

LAKE TAHOE

Bridgetender	*Pub*	19
Café Fiore	*Italian*	25
Christy Hill	*Cal.*	24
Cottonwood	*Eclectic*	21
Dragonfly	*Asian/Cal.*	22
Evan's	*Amer.*	28
Gar Woods	*Amer./Med.*	17
Jake's/Lake	*Cal.*	16
Moody's Bistro	*Amer.*	25
Naked Fish	*Japanese*	21
Pianeta	*Italian*	23
PlumpJack	*Cal./Med.*	23
Red Hut	*Diner*	23
River Ranch	*Cal.*	15
Soule Domain	*Amer.*	22
Sunnyside	*Seafood/Steak*	18
⨔ Wolfdale's	*Cal.*	27

LIVERMORE

Wente Vineyards	*Cal./Med.*	23

OAKLAND

À Côté	*French/Med.*	24
NEW Adesso	*Italian*	-
NEW Barlata	*Spanish*	-
Barney's	*Burgers*	19
BayWolf	*Cal./Med.*	25
Bellanico	*Italian*	23
Blackberry Bistro	*Southern*	19
Breads of India	*Indian*	19
Burma Superstar	*Burmese*	25
Cactus Taqueria	*Mex.*	21
Caffè Verbena	*Cal./Italian*	17
Camino	*Cal./Med.*	22
Caspers Hot Dogs	*Hot Dogs*	18
César	*Spanish*	22
Cheese Steak Shop	*Cheesestks.*	23
Citron	*Cal./French*	23
NEW Commis	*Amer.*	-
Doña Tomás	*Mex.*	23
Dopo	*Italian*	25
Everett & Jones	*BBQ*	20
Fentons Creamery	*Ice Cream*	19
Flora	*Amer.*	23
Garibaldis	*Cal./Med.*	22
grégoire	*French*	22
Home of Chicken	*Southern*	20
⨔ In-N-Out	*Burgers*	22
Koryo BBQ	*Korean*	23
NEW Lake Chalet	*Cal.*	-
Lanesplitter Pub	*Pizza*	17
Le Cheval	*Viet.*	21
Levende	*Eclectic*	19
Lo Coco's	*Italian*	22
Luka's Taproom	*Cal./French*	20
Mama's Royal	*Amer.*	21
Marica	*Seafood*	23
NEW Marzano	*Italian/Pizza*	23
Max's	*Deli*	17
Mezze	*Cal./Med.*	20
NEW Miss Pearl's	*Carib.*	17
Nan Yang	*Burmese*	20
Oliveto Cafe	*Italian*	24
Oliveto Restaurant	*Italian*	25
Ozumo	*Japanese*	24
NEW Penelope	*Cal.*	-
Pho 84	*Viet.*	22

NEW Picán | *Southern*	–	
Pizzaiolo | *Pizza*	25	
Pizza Rustica | *Pizza*	18	
Pomodoro | *Italian*	17	
Rest. Peony | *Chinese*	20	
Scott's | *Seafood*	18	
NEW Sidebar | *Cal.*	20	
Soi4 | *Thai*	23	
Soizic | *Cal./French*	24	
Somerset | *Amer.*	17	
Tamarindo | *Mex.*	24	
Uzen | *Japanese*	24	
Wood Tavern | *Cal.*	25	
Xyclo | *Viet.*	22	
Yoshi's | *Japanese*	20	
Z Zachary's Pizza | *Pizza*	24	

ORINDA

Casa Orinda \| *Italian/Steak* — 18

PLEASANT HILL

Caspers Hot Dogs \| *Hot Dogs* — 18

PLEASANTON

Cheese Steak Shop \| *Cheesestks.* — 23
El Balazo \| *Mex.* — 19

RICHMOND

Caspers Hot Dogs \| *Hot Dogs* — 18
Salute Marina \| *Italian* — 18

SAN RAMON

El Balazo \| *Mex.* — 19
Izzy's Steak \| *Steak* — 20
Max's \| *Deli* — 17
Z Zachary's Pizza \| *Pizza* — 24

WALNUT CREEK

Bing Crosby's \| *Amer.* — 19
Breads of India \| *Indian* — 19
Caspers Hot Dogs \| *Hot Dogs* — 18
Cheese Steak Shop \| *Cheesestks.* — 23
Il Fornaio \| *Italian* — 19
Lark Creek \| *Amer.* — 21
Le Cheval \| *Viet.* — 21
Plearn Thai \| *Thai* — 21
Prima \| *Italian* — 24
Ruth's Chris \| *Steak* — 23

Scott's \| *Seafood* — 18
Va de Vi \| *Eclectic* — 23
Vic Stewart's \| *Steak* — 21

YOSEMITE/ OAKHURST

Z Ahwahnee \| *Amer./Cal.* — 19
Z Erna's Elderberry \| *Cal./French* — 28

North of San Francisco

BODEGA BAY

Duck Club \| *Amer.* — 19

CALISTOGA

All Seasons \| *Cal.* — 20
Brannan's Grill \| *Amer./French* — 20
JoLe \| *Amer.* — 26

CORTE MADERA

Il Fornaio \| *Italian* — 19
Izzy's Steak \| *Steak* — 20
Max's \| *Deli* — 17
Pacific Catch \| *Seafood* — 20

FAIRFAX

Lotus/Anokha \| *Indian* — 25

FORESTVILLE

Z Farmhouse Inn \| *Cal.* — 26
Mosaic \| *Cal.* — 26

GEYSERVILLE

Diavola \| *Italian* — 24
Santi \| *Italian* — 25

GLEN ELLEN/ KENWOOD

Cafe Citti \| *Italian* — 22
fig cafe \| *French* — 24
Kenwood \| *Amer./French* — 23

GUERNEVILLE

Z Applewood Inn \| *Cal.* — 27

HEALDSBURG/ WINDSOR

Barndiva \| *Amer.* — 19
Bistro Ralph \| *Cal./French* — 23
Bovolo \| *Italian* — 24
Charcuterie \| *French* — 22
Z Cyrus \| *French* — 29
Downtown Bakery \| *Bakery* — 25

Dry Creek | *Amer.*	24
Healdsburg B&G | *Amer.*	19
Jimtown Store | *Deli*	18
Z Madrona | *Amer./French*	26
Manzanita | *Cal./Med.*	19
Mirepoix | *French*	26
Ravenous Cafe | *Cal./Eclectic*	22
Osake/Sake 'O | *Cal./Japanese*	23
NEW Scopa | *Italian*	24
Willi's Seafood | *Seafood*	24
Zin | *Amer.*	23

LARKSPUR

E&O Trading | *SE Asian*	19
Emporio Rulli | *Dessert/Italian*	22
Left Bank | *French*	18
Picco | *Italian*	26
Pizzeria Picco | *Pizza*	25
Table Café | *Cal.*	-
NEW Tavern at Lark Creek | *Amer.*	-
Yankee Pier | *New Eng./Seafood*	17

MENDOCINO COUNTY

Albion River Inn | *Cal.*	25
Boonville Hotel | *Cal.*	22
Cafe Beaujolais | *Cal./French*	25
Chapter & Moon | *Amer.*	22
Ledford Hse. | *Cal./Med.*	25
Little River Inn | *Cal./Seafood*	21
MacCallum Hse. | *Cal.*	21
Mendo Bistro | *Amer.*	24
Mendocino Hotel | *Cal.*	18
Moosse Café | *Cal.*	24
955 Ukiah | *Amer./French*	23
Ravens Rest. | *Vegan*	22
Rendezvous Inn | *French*	25
Restaurant | *Amer./Eclectic*	23
Rest. at Stevenswood | *Amer.*	26
St. Orres | *Cal.*	22

MILL VALLEY

Asqew Grill | *Cal.*	16
Avatar's | *Eclectic*	25
Balboa Cafe | *Amer.*	19
Z Buckeye Rdhse. | *Amer./BBQ*	23
Bungalow 44 | *Amer.*	21

Dipsea Cafe | *Amer.*	19
Z El Paseo | *French*	26
Frantoio | *Italian*	21
Harmony Rest. | *Chinese*	22
Z In-N-Out | *Burgers*	22
Joe's Taco | *Mex.*	20
La Boulange | *Bakery*	22
La Ginestra | *Italian*	21
Piatti | *Italian*	18
Piazza D'Angelo | *Italian*	20
Pizza Antica | *Pizza*	21
Robata Grill | *Japanese*	21
Toast | *Amer.*	-

NAPA

Alexis Baking | *Bakery*	22
Angèle | *French*	22
Annalien | *Viet.*	23
Azzurro Pizzeria | *Pizza*	22
BarBersQ | *BBQ*	22
Bistro Don Giovanni | *Italian*	23
Boon Fly Café | *Cal.*	22
Bounty Hunter | *BBQ*	19
Brix | *Cal./Med.*	22
Celadon | *Amer./Eclectic*	24
Cole's Chop Hse. | *Steak*	24
Cuvée | *Amer.*	21
NEW Elements | *Cal./Med.*	22
Z Farm | *Amer.*	24
Folio Enoteca | *Cal./Med.*	16
Fumé Bistro | *Amer.*	22
Hog Island Oyster | *Seafood*	25
Z In-N-Out | *Burgers*	22
Z La Toque | *French*	26
Model Bakery | *Bakery*	20
Napa General | *Cal./Eclectic*	20
Napa Wine Train | *Cal.*	16
Oxbow Wine | *Cal./Med.*	22
Pearl | *Cal.*	23
Pica Pica Maize | *Venezuelan*	25
Rôtisario | *Chicken*	-
Taylor's Auto | *Diner*	22
Z Ubuntu | *Cal./Vegan*	26
Uva Trattoria | *Italian*	23
Zinsvalley | *Amer.*	19
ZuZu | *Spanish*	23

NOVATO

Boca | Argent./Steak — 22
Cacti Grill | SW — 19
La Boulange | Bakery — 22
Lotus/Anokha | Indian — 25
Toast | Amer. — -

OCCIDENTAL

Bistro/Copains | French — 25

PETALUMA

Central Market | Cal./Med. — 24
Cucina Paradiso | Italian — 24
Della Fattoria | Bakery/Eclectic — 24
Risibisi | Italian — 25
Tea Room Café | Amer. — 24
Volpi's Rist. | Italian — 19
Water St. Bistro | French — 23

ROSS

Marché aux Fleurs | French — 25

RUTHERFORD

Z Auberge du Sol. | Cal./French — 26
Rutherford Grill | Amer. — 24

SAN ANSELMO

AVA | Amer. — 22
Cucina Rest. | Italian — 23
NEW Dreamfarm | Amer. — -
Insalata's | Med. — 25
NEW Marinitas | Pan-Latin — 21

SAN RAFAEL

Amici's | Pizza — 20
Barney's | Burgers — 19
Café Gratitude | Vegan — 16
Il Davide | Italian — 21
Las Camelias | Mex. — 18
Lotus/Anokha | Indian — 25
Royal Thai | Thai — 23
Sabor of Spain | Spanish — 19
Sol Food | Puerto Rican — 23
Vin Antico | Italian — 23

SANTA ROSA/ ROHNERT PARK

Betty's Fish | Seafood — 21
Cheese Steak Shop | Cheesestks. — 23
Flavor | Cal./Eclectic — 19

Gary Chu's | Chinese — 20
Hana Japanese | Japanese — 24
John Ash | Cal. — 24
La Gare | Fench — 19
Monti's | Amer./Med. — 21
Osake/Sake 'O | Cal./Japanese — 23
Rosso Pizzeria | Italian/Pizza — 25
Syrah | Cal./French — 25
Willi's Wine | Eclectic — 26
zazu | Amer./Italian — 25

SAUSALITO

Avatar's | Eclectic — 25
Fish | Seafood — 23
Murray Circle | Cal. — 24
Poggio | Italian — 22
Scoma's | Seafood — 22
Z Sushi Ran | Japanese — 28

SEBASTOPOL/ GRATON

Cafe Saint Rose | Cal./Med. — 23
Hopmonk Tav. | Eclectic — 17
K&L Bistro | French — 25
Peter Lowell's | Italian — 22
NEW Pizzavino | Pizza — -
NEW Restaurant Eloise | French/Med. — -
Starlight | Southern — 22
Underwood Bar | Med. — 24
Willow Wood | Eclectic/Med. — 24

SONOMA

Cafe La Haye | Amer./Cal. — 26
Carneros Bistro | Cal. — 23
Della Santina's | Italian — 21
El Dorado | Cal./Med. — 24
Emmy's Spaghetti | Italian — 21
NEW Estate | Cal./Italian — 20
girl & the fig | French — 24
Harvest Moon | Cal./Med. — 24
LaSalette | Portug. — 25
Meritage Martini | Italian — 20
Santé | Cal./French — 25

ST. HELENA

NEW AKA Bistro | Amer. — 21
Cindy's | Amer./Cal. — 24

Cook St. Helena	*Italian*	25
Go Fish	*Eclectic/Seafood*	22
Market	*Amer.*	22
Martini House	*Amer.*	26
Meadowood Grill	*Cal.*	22
☑ Meadowood Rest.	*Cal.*	26
Model Bakery	*Bakery*	20
Pizzeria Tra Vigne	*Pizza*	21
Press	*Amer./Steak*	23
Taylor's Auto	*Diner*	22
☑ Terra	*Amer.*	27
Tra Vigne	*Italian*	24
Wine Spectator	*Cal.*	22

TIBURON

Caprice	*Amer.*	21
Cottage Eatery	*Cal.*	23
Guaymas	*Mex.*	16

VALLEY FORD

Rocker Oysterfellers	*Amer.*	21

WEST MARIN/OLEMA

Drake's	*Cal.*	21
Nick's Cove	*Cal.*	21
Olema Inn	*Cal.*	22
NEW Osteria Stellina	*Italian*	-
Pine Cone Diner	*Diner*	20
Station House	*Cal.*	20

YOUNTVILLE

☑ ad hoc	*Amer.*	26
NEW Bardessono	*Amer.*	23
☑ Bistro Jeanty	*French*	25
☑ NEW Bottega	*Italian*	25
☑ Bouchon	*French*	26
☑ Étoile	*Cal.*	26
☑ French Laundry	*Amer./French*	29
Hurley's	*Cal./Med.*	21
☑ Mustards	*Amer./Cal.*	25
Napa Valley Grille	*Cal.*	21
☑ Redd	*Cal.*	27

South of San Francisco

BIG SUR

Big Sur	*Amer./Bakery*	21
Deetjen's	*Cal.*	22

Nepenthe	*Amer.*	17
☑ Sierra Mar	*Cal./Eclectic*	27

BURLINGAME

Ecco	*Cal./Continental*	23
Il Fornaio	*Italian*	19
Isobune	*Japanese*	17
Juban	*Japanese*	19
Kabul Afghan	*Afghan*	22
Kuleto's	*Italian*	20
La Corneta	*Mex.*	22
Max's	*Deli*	17
Nectar Wine	*Cal.*	18
Roti Indian	*Indian*	22
Stacks	*Amer.*	18
Straits	*Singapor.*	19

CAMPBELL

Buca di Beppo	*Italian*	14
Twist	*Amer./French*	22

CARMEL/ MONTEREY PEN

Anton & Michel	*Continental*	23
Aubergine	*Cal.*	25
Bistro Moulin	*Euro.*	-
Cantinetta Luca	*Italian*	23
Casanova	*French/Italian*	23
Citronelle	*Cal./French*	24
Club XIX	*Cal./French*	23
Duck Club	*Amer.*	19
Estéban	*Spanish*	-
Fandango	*Med.*	23
Fishwife	*Cal./Seafood*	20
Flying Fish	*Cal./Seafood*	24
Forge in Forest	*Pub*	18
Fresh Cream	*French*	25
Grasing's Coastal	*Cal.*	24
Il Fornaio	*Italian*	19
Kurt's Carmel	*Steak*	23
Montrio Bistro	*Cal.*	21
☑ Pacific's Edge	*Amer./French*	25
☑ Passionfish	*Cal./Seafood*	26
Piatti	*Italian*	18
Rio Grill	*Cal.*	21
☑ Roy's	*Hawaiian*	25
Sardine Factory	*Amer./Seafood*	21

Stokes | *Cal./Med.* 21
Tarpy's | *Amer.* 20
TusCA | *Cal./Italian* -

CARMEL VALLEY

Café Rustica | *Cal.* 23
Z Marinus | *French* 27
Will's Fargo | *Seafood/Steak* 22

CUPERTINO

Alexander's | *Japanese/Steak* 25
Amici's | *Pizza* 20
GoChi | *Japanese* 23

HALF MOON BAY/ COAST

Barbara's Fish Trap | *Seafood* 20
Z Cafe Gibraltar | *Med.* 27
Cetrella | *Med.* 20
Chez Shea | *Eclectic* 23
Duarte's Tavern | *Amer.* 21
Flying Fish | *Cal./Seafood* 22
Half Moon Brew | *Pub/Seafood* 16
Mezza Luna | *Italian* 21
Z Navio | *Amer.* 24
Pasta Moon | *Italian* 23
Sam's Chowder | *Seafood* 20
Taqueria 3 Amigos | *Mex.* 19

LOS ALTOS

Chef Chu's | *Chinese* 22
Hunan | *Chinese* 22
Zitune | *Moroccan* 25

LOS GATOS

Cin-Cin Wine | *Eclectic* 23
Dio Deka | *Greek* 25
Forbes Mill Steak | *Steak* 22
Z Manresa | *Amer.* 27
Nick's on Main | *Amer.* 25
Trevese | *Amer.* 23

MENLO PARK

Bistro Vida | *French* 18
Cool Café | *Cal.* -
Duck Club | *Amer.* 19
Flea St. Café | *Amer.* 25
Iberia | *Spanish* 21

Juban | *Japanese* 19
Z Kaygetsu | *Japanese* 28
Left Bank | *French* 18
NEW Madera | *Amer.* -
Marché | *French* 25
Naomi Sushi | *Japanese* 21
Stacks | *Amer.* 18

MILLBRAE

Fook Yuen | *Chinese/Seafood* 22
Z In-N-Out | *Burgers* 22
Mayflower | *Chinese* 22

MILPITAS

Mayflower | *Chinese* 22

MOUNTAIN VIEW

Amber | *Indian* 24
Amici's | *Pizza* 20
Cantankerous | *Seafood* 18
Cascal | *Pan-Latin* 20
Chez TJ | *French* 23
Z In-N-Out | *Burgers* 22
Krung Thai | *Thai* 20
Passage to India | *Indian* 18
NEW Sakoon | *Indian* -
Uncle Frank's | *BBQ* 20
Xanh | *Viet.* 23
Zucca | *Med.* 18

PALO ALTO/ EAST PALO ALTO

Bistro Elan | *Cal./French* 24
Buca di Beppo | *Italian* 14
Café Brioche | *Cal./French* 22
NEW Calafia | *Cal.* 21
Cool Café | *Cal.* -
Z Evvia | *Greek* 26
Fuki Sushi | *Japanese* 22
Hunan | *Chinese* 22
Il Fornaio | *Italian* 19
Jin Sho | *Japanese* 24
NEW Joya | *Nuevo Latino* 18
Junnoon | *Indian* 23
Kanpai | *Japanese* 22
La Strada | *Italian* 21
Lavanda | *Med.* 20

MacArthur Pk. | *Amer.*	16
Mantra | *Cal./Indian*	20
Max's | *Deli*	17
NEW Mayfield | *Bakery/Cal.*	19
Osteria | *Italian*	23
Pampas | *Brazilian*	21
Patxi's Pizza | *Pizza*	22
Pluto's | *Amer.*	19
Quattro | *Italian*	21
Scott's | *Seafood*	18
Shokolaat | *Cal.*	19
St. Michael's | *Cal.*	23
Straits | *Singapor.*	19
Tai Pan | *Chinese*	23
Tamarine | *Viet.*	26
Three Seasons | *Viet.*	21
Trader Vic's | *Polynesian*	17
Zibibbo | *Med.*	19

REDWOOD CITY

Z Chantilly | *French/Italian*	23
NEW Donato | *Italian*	-
John Bentley's | *Cal.*	25
Mandaloun | *Cal./Med.*	20
NEW Martins West | *British*	-
Max's | *Deli*	17
Old Port Lobster | *Seafood*	22
Red Lantern | *SE Asian*	19

REDWOOD SHORES

Amici's | *Pizza*	20
Mistral | *French/Italian*	18

SAN BRUNO

Don Pico's | *Mex.*	23

SAN CARLOS

Izzy's Steak | *Steak*	20
Kabul Afghan | *Afghan*	22

SAN JOSE

Amber | *Indian*	24
Amici's | *Pizza*	20
Arcadia | *Amer.*	21
Blowfish Sushi | *Japanese*	20
Buca di Beppo | *Italian*	14
Cheesecake | *Amer.*	16

Cheese Steak Shop | *Cheesestks.*	23
E&O Trading | *SE Asian*	19
Emile's | *French/Swiss*	22
Eulipia | *Amer.*	24
Il Fornaio | *Italian*	19
Z In-N-Out | *Burgers*	22
Krung Thai | *Thai*	20
Z La Forêt | *Continental/French*	26
La Victoria | *Mex.*	20
NEW LB Steak | *Steak*	-
Left Bank | *French*	18
Z Le Papillon | *French*	27
Morton's | *Steak*	24
Original Joe's | *Amer./Italian*	20
Pizza Antica | *Pizza*	21
Pluto's | *Amer.*	19
Pomodoro | *Italian*	17
Scott's | *Seafood*	18
7 Restaurant | *Amer./French*	21
71 Saint Peter | *Cal./Med.*	22
Sino | *Chinese*	19
Straits | *Singapor.*	19
Taqueria Tlaquepaque | *Mex.*	25
Thea Med. | *Greek/Med.*	20
Yankee Pier | *New Eng./Seafood*	17

SAN MATEO

Amici's | *Pizza*	20
Espetus | *Brazilian*	22
Happy Cafe | *Chinese*	21
Hotaru | *Japanese*	21
La Cumbre | *Mex.*	19
Lure | *Seafood*	20
North Beach Pizza | *Pizza*	20
Pancho Villa | *Mex.*	22
Rist. Capellini | *Italian*	20
Taqueria 3 Amigos | *Mex.*	19
231 Ellsworth | *Amer.*	22
Viognier | *Cal./French*	23

SANTA CLARA

Cheesecake | *Amer.*	16
Dasaprakash | *Indian*	19
Parcel 104 | *Cal.*	23
Piatti | *Italian*	18

SANTA CRUZ/ CAPITOLA

NEW Aquarius | *Amer.*	-
Gabriella Café | *Cal./Italian*	23
Gayle's Bakery | *Bakery*	25
O'mei | *Chinese*	24
Rist. Avanti | *Cal.*	-
Shadowbrook | *Amer./Cal.*	18

SARATOGA

Basin | *Amer.*	21
Z Plumed Horse | *Cal.*	25
Z Sent Sovi | *Cal.*	26

SOUTH SF/ DALY CITY

Basque Cultural | *Spanish*	22
Burger Joint | *Burgers*	18
BurgerMeister | *Burgers*	19

Ebisu | *Japanese*	23
Z In-N-Out | *Burgers*	22
Koi | *Chinese*	23
Yankee Pier | *New Eng./Seafood*	17

SUNNYVALE

Cheese Steak Shop | *Cheesestks.*	23
Dish Dash | *Mideast.*	23
Il Postale | *Italian*	20
Lion & Compass | *Amer.*	20
Shalimar | *Indian/Pakistani*	23
Turmeric | *Indian*	19
Udupi Palace | *Indian/Veg.*	21

WOODSIDE

Bella Vista | *Continental*	19
John Bentley's | *Cal.*	25
Village Pub | *Amer.*	26

LOCATIONS

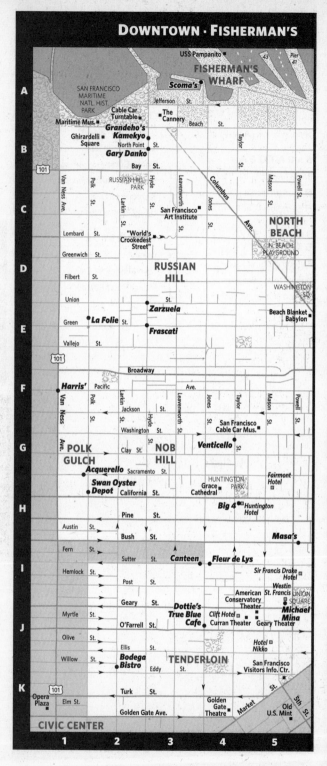

USS Pampanito

43

Pier
41

FISHERMAN'S
WHARF

Scoma's

SAN FRANCISCO
MARITIME
NATL. HIST.
PARK

Jefferson St.

Cable Car
Turntable

The
Cannery

Beach St.

Maritime Mus.

Grandeho's
Kamekyo

North Point St.

Ghirardelli
Square

Gary Danko

Bay St.

Taylor St.

101

Van Ness Ave.

Polk St.

Larkin St.

RUSSIAN HILL
PARK

Hyde St.

Leavenworth St.

Columbus Ave.

Mason St.

Powell St.

San Francisco
Art Institute

Jones St.

NORTH
BEACH

Lombard St.

"World's
Crookedest
Street"

N. BEACH
PLAYGROUND

Greenwich St.

RUSSIAN
HILL

Filbert St.

WASHINGTON
SQ.

Union St.

Zarzuela

La Folie

Green St.

Beach Blanket
Babylon

Frascati

Vallejo St.

101

Broadway

Harris'

Pacific Ave.

Van Ness

Polk St.

Larkin St.

Jackson St.

Leavenworth St.

Jones St.

Taylor St.

Mason St.

Powell St.

Hyde St.

Washington St.

San Francisco
Cable Car Mus.

Ave.

POLK
GULCH

Clay St.

NOB
HILL

Venticello

Acquerello

Sacramento St.

Fairmont
Hotel

Swan Oyster
Depot

California St.

HUNTINGTON
PARK

Grace
Cathedral

Big 4

Huntington
Hotel

Pine St.

Austin St.

Bush St.

Masa's

Fern St.

Sutter St.

Canteen

Fleur de Lys

Hemlock St.

Sir Francis Drake
Hotel

Post St.

Westin
St. Francis

UNION
SQUARE

Geary St.

American
Conservatory
Theater

Myrtle St.

Dottie's
True Blue
Cafe

Clift Hotel

Michael
Mina

O'Farrell St.

Curran Theater

Geary Theater

Olive St.

Ellis St.

Hotel
Nikko

Willow St.

Bodega
Bistro

Eddy St.

TENDERLOIN

San Francisco
Visitors Info. Ctr.

101

Turk St.

Opera
Plaza

Elm St.

Golden Gate Ave.

Golden
Gate
Theatre

Market

Old
U.S. Mint

5th St.

CIVIC CENTER

1   2   3   4   5

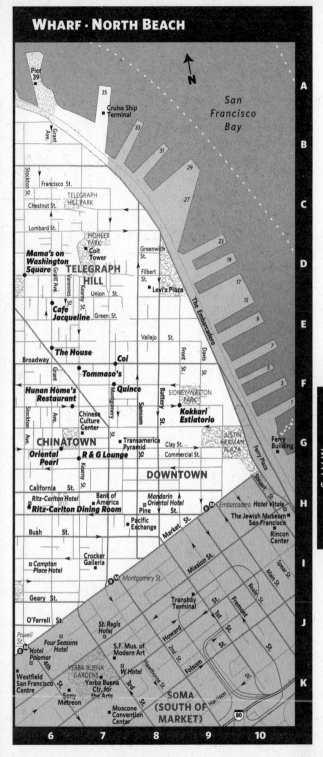

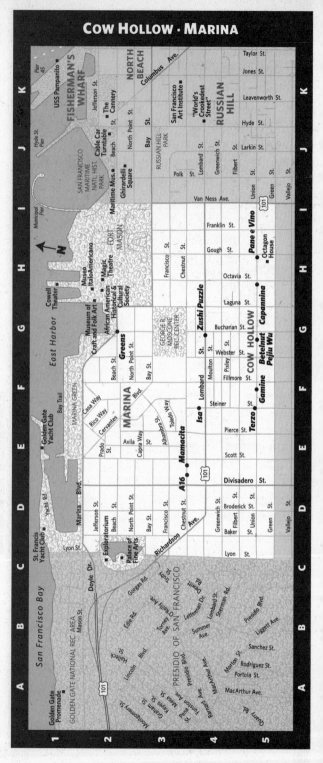

COW HOLLOW · MARINA

San Francisco Bay

Golden Gate Promenade

GOLDEN GATE NATIONAL REC. AREA

St. Francis Yacht Club

Golden Gate Yacht Club

East Harbor

Municipal Pier

Hyde St. Pier

Pier 45

FISHERMAN'S WHARF

USS Pampanito

SAN FRANCISCO MARITIME NATL. HIST. PARK

Maritime Mus.

Ghirardelli Square

Cable Car Turntable

The Cannery

NORTH BEACH

Columbus Ave.

San Francisco Art Institute

"World's Crookedest Street"

RUSSIAN HILL

RUSSIAN HILL PARK

Cowell Theater

Museum of Craft and Folk Art

Magic Theatre

Museo ItaloAmericano

African American Historical & Cultural Society

FORT MASON

MARINA GREEN

Bay Trail

Marina Blvd.

MARINA

Casa Way

Rico Way

Cervantes

Prado

Avila

Capra Way

Alhambra St.

Toledo Way

Greens

Beach St.

North Point St.

Bay St.

Lombard St.

Steiner St.

Pierce St.

Scott St.

Divisadero St.

Greenwich St.

Filbert St.

Baker St.

Broderick St.

Lyon St.

Union St.

Green St.

Vallejo St.

GEORGE R. MOSCONE REC. CENTER

Buchanan St.

Webster St.

Pixley

Fillmore St.

Moulton

Laguna St.

Octavia St.

Gough St.

Franklin St.

Van Ness Ave.

Octagon House

Pane e Vino

Zushi Puzzle

Capannina

Betelnut Pejiu Wu

COW HOLLOW

Gamine

Terzo

Isa

Mamacita

A16

Chestnut St.

Francisco St.

North Point St.

Bay St.

Jefferson St.

Exploratorium

Palace of Fine Arts

Lyon St.

Richardson Ave.

Doyle Dr.

PRESIDIO OF SAN FRANCISCO

Gorgas Rd.

Ruby

DeWitt Rd.

Edie Rd.

O'Reilly Ave.

Torney Ave.

Letterman Dr.

Summer Ave.

Lombard St.

Sherman Rd.

Presidio Blvd.

Liggett Ave.

Sanchez St.

Rodriguez St.

Portola St.

MacArthur Ave.

Lincoln Blvd.

Halleck St.

Graham St.

Mesa St.

Montgomery St.

Pena St.

Barnard Ave.

MacArthur Ave.

Presidio Ave.

Morton St.

Quarry Rd.

Taylor St.

Jones St.

Leavenworth St.

Hyde St.

Larkin St.

Polk St.

Filbert St.

Greenwich St.

Lombard St.

101

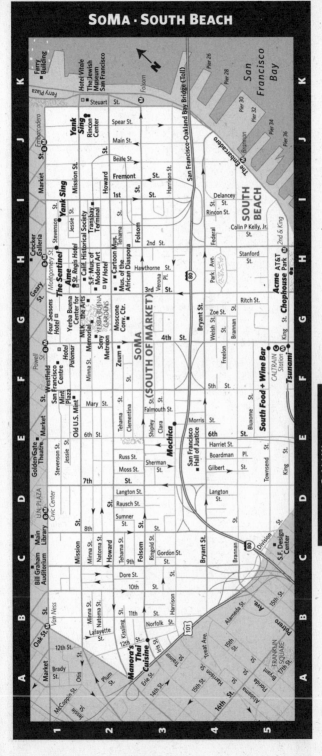

SoMa · South Beach

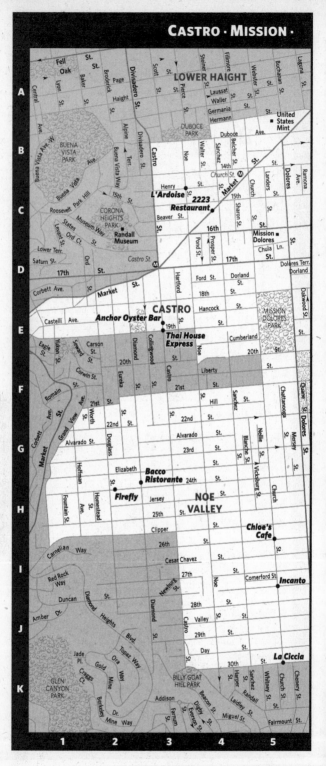

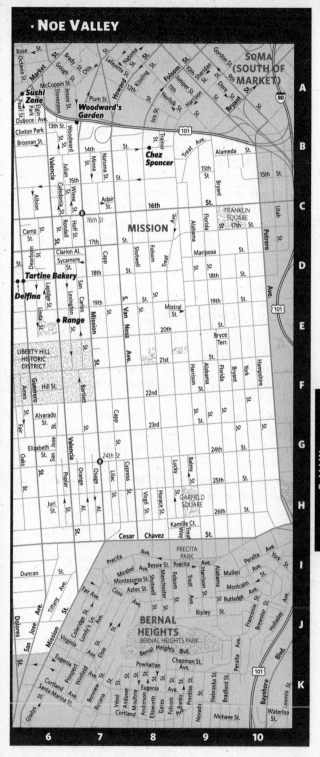

SoMA (SOUTH OF MARKET)

Rose St.
Octavia St.
Market St.
Gough St.
McCoppin St.
Stevenson
Jessie St.
Pearl St.
Eighth Park
Duboce Ave.
Sushi Zone
Brady St.
Otis St.
Lafayette St.
Natoma St.
Howard St.
12th St.
Kissling St.
Plum St.
Woodward's Garden
Folsom St.
10th St. Sheridan
Junper St.
11th St.
Harrison St.
Norfolk St.
9th St.
Dore St.
Bryant St.
Gordon St.

80

13th St.
Clinton Park
Brosnan St.
Valencia St.
Woodward St.
Julian St.
Caledonia St.
14th St.
Minna St.
Natoma St.
Trainor St.
Treat Ave.
Alameda St.
15th St.
Bryant St.
Chez Spencer
15th St.

Albion St.
15th St.
Wiese St.
Adair St.
16th St.
MISSION
Florida St.
FRANKLIN SQUARE
17th St.
Utah St.
Potrero St.

Camp St.
16th St
Rondell St.
Hoff St.
Clarion Al.
Sycamore St.
17th St.
Capp St.
Shotwell St.
Folsom St.
Treat Ave.
Alabama St.
Mariposa St.
18th St.
Florida St.
101

Bedford St.
Tartine Bakery
Delfina
Lapidge St.
Linda St.
18th St.
San Carlos St.
Lexington St.
19th St.
Mission St.
S. Van Ness Ave.
Capp St.
Shotwell St.
Folsom St.
Mistral St.
19th St.
18th St.

Range
20th St.
21st St.
Bryce Terr.
St.

LIBERTY HILL HISTORIC DISTRICT
Guerrero St.
Ames St.
Hill St.
Bartlett St.
Harrison St.
Alabama St.
Florida St.
Bryant St.
York St.
Hampshire St.

Fair St.
Alvarado St.
San Jose Ave.
22nd St.
Capp St.
23rd St.
St.
St.

Oaks St.
Elizabeth St.
Valencia St.
Poplar St.
Orange St.
Osage Al.
24th St
Lilac St.
Cypress St.
Lucky St.
Balmy St.
24th St.
25th St.

Juri St.
Virgil St.
Horace St.
GARFIELD SQUARE
26th St.

Kamille Ct.
Cesar Chavez St.
Treat Way
St.

Duncan St.
PRECITA PARK
Precita Ave.
Peralta Ave.
York St.

Dolores St.
San Jose Ave.
Tiffany Ave.
Mirabel Ave.
Montezuma St.
Coso Ave.
Bessie St.
Manchester St.
Aztec St.
Shotwell St.
Folsom St.
Treat Ave.
Precita Ave.
Harrison St.
Alabama St.
Mullen Ave.
Montcalm St.
Rutledge St.
Ripley St.
Franconia St.
Brewster St.
Holladay Ave.

Mission St.
Fair Ave.
Coleridge St.
Lundy's Ln.
Elsie St.
BERNAL HEIGHTS
BERNAL HEIGHTS PARK
Bernal Heights Blvd.
Peralta Ave.
101
Loomis St.

Jose Ave.
San St.
Virginia Ave.
Eugenia Ave.
Prospect Ave.
Winfield St.
Bonview St.
Elsie St.
Powhattan Ave.
Chapman St.
Ave.

Gladys St.
Cortland Ave.
Santa Marina St.
Becanna St.
Wool St.
Andover St.
Moultrie St.
Anderson St.
Eugenia Ave.
Ellsworth St.
Gates St.
Folsom St.
Banks St.
Prentiss St.
Nevada St.
Nebraska St.
Bradford St.
Bayshore Blvd.
Mohave St.
Waterloo St.

A B C D E F G H I J K

6 7 8 9 10

MAPS

Special Features

Listings cover the best in each category and include names, locations and Food ratings. Multi-location restaurants' features may vary by branch.

BREAKFAST

(See also Hotel Dining)

Alexis Baking | **Napa/N**	22
Bette's Oceanview | **Berkeley/E**	23
Big Sur | **Big Sur/S**	21
Blackberry Bistro | **Oakland/E**	19
Boulette's Larder | **Embarcadero**	25
Butler & Chef | **SoMa**	20
Café Fanny | **Berkeley/E**	23
Chloe's Cafe | **Noe Valley**	23
Dipsea Cafe | **Mill Valley/N**	19
Dottie's | **Tenderloin**	25
Downtown Bakery | **Healdsburg/N**	25
Ella's | **Presidio Hts**	22
Emporio Rulli | **multi.**	22
FatApple's | **multi.**	18
Gayle's Bakery | **Capitola/S**	25
Il Fornaio | **multi.**	19
Jimmy Bean's | **Berkeley/E**	19
Jimtown Store | **Healdsburg/N**	18
Kate's Kitchen | **Lower Haight**	22
Koi | **Daly City/S**	23
La Boulange | **multi.**	22
La Note | **Berkeley/E**	21
Mama's on Wash. | **N Beach**	25
Mama's Royal | **Oakland/E**	21
Mel's Drive-In | **multi.**	14
Model Bakery | **St. Helena/N**	20
Mo's | **multi.**	20
Napa General | **Napa/N**	20
Oliveto Cafe | **Oakland/E**	24
Pork Store | **multi.**	22
Red's Java | **Embarcadero**	16
Rick & Ann's | **Berkeley/E**	21
Rigolo | **Presidio Hts**	16
Rose's Cafe | **Cow Hollow**	22
Savor | **Noe Valley**	18
Sears Fine Food | **Downtown**	19
☑ Tartine | **Mission**	27
Toast | **Noe Valley**	17
Town's End | **Embarcadero**	20
Venus | **Berkeley/E**	23
Water St. Bistro | **Petaluma/N**	23
Willow Wood | **Graton/N**	24
Zazie | **Cole Valley**	22

BRUNCH

☑ Absinthe | **Hayes Valley**	22
☑ Ahwahnee | **Yosemite/E**	19
Alexis Baking | **Napa/N**	22
Americano | **Embarcadero**	18
ANZU | **Downtown**	22
Baker St. Bistro | **Marina**	21
Balboa Cafe | **Cow Hollow**	19
Beach Chalet | **Outer Sunset**	15
Bistro Liaison | **Berkeley/E**	22
Bistro Vida | **Menlo Pk/S**	18
Blackhawk Grille | **Danville/E**	19
☑ Buckeye Rdhse. | **Mill Valley/N**	23
Campton Place | **Downtown**	24
☑ Canteen | **Tenderloin**	27
Carnelian Room | **Downtown**	18
Catch | **Castro**	18
Chez Maman | **Potrero Hill**	22
Chloe's Cafe | **Noe Valley**	23
Chow/Park Chow | **multi.**	21
Citizen Cake | **Hayes Valley**	21
Corso | **Berkeley/E**	24
Delancey St. | **Embarcadero**	17
Dipsea Cafe | **Mill Valley/N**	19
Dottie's | **Tenderloin**	25
Duck Club | **Lafayette/E**	19
Elite Cafe | **Upper Fillmore**	19
Ella's | **Presidio Hts**	22
☑ Erna's Elderberry | **Oakhurst/E**	28
NEW Estate | **Sonoma/N**	20
Fandango | **Pacific Grove/S**	23
fig cafe | **Glen Ellen/N**	24
NEW Five | **Berkeley/E**	-
Foreign Cinema | **Mission**	23
Gabriella Café | **Santa Cruz/S**	23
☑ Garden Court | **Downtown**	20
Garibaldis | **Oakland/E**	22

Gayle's Bakery | **Capitola/S**	25
girl & the fig | **Sonoma/N**	24
Grand Cafe | **Downtown**	19
Z Greens | **Marina**	24
Home | **Castro**	18
Insalata's | **San Anselmo/N**	25
Jordan's | **Berkeley/E**	17
Kate's Kitchen | **Lower Haight**	22
Z La Forêt | **San Jose/S**	26
La Note | **Berkeley/E**	21
Lark Creek | **Walnut Creek/E**	21
Le Zinc | **Noe Valley**	19
Liberty Café | **Bernal Hts**	22
Luna Park | **Mission**	20
NEW Madera | **Menlo Pk/S**	–
NEW Marinitas | **San Anselmo/N**	21
NEW Mayfield | **Palo Alto/S**	19
NEW Metro Café | **W Addition**	–
MoMo's | **S Beach**	17
Z Navio | **Half Moon Bay/S**	24
Nob Hill Café | **Nob Hill**	21
Park Chalet | **Outer Sunset**	16
Piazza D'Angelo | **Mill Valley/N**	20
Picante Cocina | **Berkeley/E**	21
Q | **Inner Rich**	19
NEW Restaurant Eloise | **Sebastopol/N**	–
Rest. LuLu/Petite | **SoMa**	21
Rick & Ann's | **Berkeley/E**	21
Rio Grill | **Carmel/S**	21
Rose's Cafe | **Cow Hollow**	22
Savor | **Noe Valley**	18
Scott's | **multi.**	18
Z Seasons | **Downtown**	26
Slow Club | **Mission**	22
St. Michael's | **Palo Alto/S**	23
Tarpy's | **Monterey/S**	20
NEW Tavern at Lark Creek | **Larkspur/N**	–
NEW Tipsy Pig | **Marina**	21
Toast | **Noe Valley**	17
Town's End | **Embarcadero**	20
Trader Vic's | **Emeryville/E**	17
Tra Vigne | **St. Helena/N**	24
2223 | **Castro**	23
Universal Cafe | **Mission**	23

Venus | **Berkeley/E**	23
Washington Sq. B&G | **N Beach**	–
Wente Vineyards | **Livermore/E**	23
Willow Wood | **Graton/N**	24
Z Yank Sing | **SoMa**	25
Zazie | **Cole Valley**	22
Z Zuni Café | **Hayes Valley**	25

BUSINESS DINING

Acme Chophse. | **S Beach**	20
Alexander's | **Cupertino/S**	25
Alfred's Steak | **Downtown**	22
Amber | **multi.**	24
Z Ame | **SoMa**	26
Americano | **Embarcadero**	18
Anchor & Hope | **SoMa**	21
ANZU | **Downtown**	22
Z Aqua | **Downtown**	26
NEW Aurea | **Nob Hill**	–
bacar | **SoMa**	23
NEW Bardessono | **Yountville/N**	23
Basin | **Saratoga/S**	21
Belden Taverna | **Downtown**	18
Z Big 4 | **Nob Hill**	22
Bing Crosby's | **Walnut Creek/E**	19
Boca | **Novato/N**	22
Z NEW Bottega | **Yountville/N**	25
Z Boulevard | **Embarcadero**	27
Bushi-tei | **Japantown**	24
Café de la Presse | **Downtown**	18
Caffè Verbena | **Oakland/E**	17
Campton Place | **Downtown**	24
Cantankerous | **Mtn View/S**	18
Carnelian Room | **Downtown**	18
Cha Am Thai | **SoMa**	19
Z Chantilly | **Redwood City/S**	23
Chaya | **Embarcadero**	22
Chef Chu's | **Los Altos/S**	22
Chez Papa | **SoMa**	23
Citronelle | **Carmel/S**	24
Cole's Chop Hse. | **Napa/N**	24
Colibrí Mexican | **Downtown**	20
Cool Café | **Palo Alto/S**	–
Cosmopolitan | **SoMa**	19
Dio Deka | **Los Gatos/S**	25
NEW Donato | **Redwood City/S**	–
Ducca | **SoMa**	20

Duck Club	**Menlo Pk/S**	19	Max's	**Oakland/E**	17
E&O Trading	**San Jose/S**	19	Meadowood Grill	**St. Helena/N**	22
Emile's	**San Jose/S**	22		
Z Evvia	**Palo Alto/S**	26	Mexico DF	**Embarcadero**	20
Z Farallon	**Downtown**	24	**NEW** Midi	**Downtown**	-
Fish & Farm	**Downtown**	20	Mijita	**Embarcadero**	20
NEW Five	**Berkeley/E**	-	Mistral	**Redwood Shores/S**	18
5A5 Steak Lounge	**Downtown**	-	Mixt Greens	**Downtown**	22
Flea St. Café	**Menlo Pk/S**	25	MoMo's	**S Beach**	17
Fresh Cream	**Monterey/S**	25	Morton's	**multi.**	24
Fuki Sushi	**Palo Alto/S**	22	**NEW** Moss Room	**Inner Rich**	21
Gaylord India	**Downtown**	18	Muracci's	**Downtown**	21
Z NEW Gitane	**Downtown**	22	Murray Circle	**Sausalito/N**	24
Grand Cafe	**Downtown**	19	O Izakaya	**Japantown**	17
Harris'	**Polk Gulch**	25	One Market	**Embarcadero**	22
NEW Heaven's Dog	**SoMa**	21	Osha Thai	**Glen Pk**	21
Z House of Prime	**Polk Gulch**	24	Osteria	**Palo Alto/S**	23
Iberia	**Menlo Pk/S**	21	Ozumo	**multi.**	24
Il Fornaio	**multi.**	19	Palio d'Asti	**Downtown**	20
Izzy's Steak	**multi.**	20	Pampas	**Palo Alto/S**	21
Jin Sho	**Palo Alto/S**	24	Pazzia	**SoMa**	23
Joe DiMaggio's	**N Beach**	21	Peasant & Pear	**Danville/E**	22
NEW Joya	**Palo Alto/S**	18	**Z** Perbacco	**Downtown**	25
Junnoon	**Palo Alto/S**	23	Picco	**Larkspur/N**	26
Kanpai	**Palo Alto/S**	22	Piperade	**Downtown**	25
Z Kaygetsu	**Menlo Pk/S**	28	**Z** Plumed Horse	**Saratoga/S**	25
Z Kokkari	**Downtown**	27	Poggio	**Sausalito/N**	22
Kuleto's	**Downtown**	20	Ponzu	**Downtown**	20
Kuleto's	**Burlingame/S**	20	Presidio Social	**Presidio**	18
Kyo-Ya	**Downtown**	24	Press	**St. Helena/N**	23
Z La Forêt	**San Jose/S**	26	Quattro	**E Palo Alto/S**	21
Lark Creek Steak	**Downtown**	23	Red Lantern	**Redwood City/S**	19
Lavanda	**Palo Alto/S**	20	Rest. LuLu/Petite	**SoMa**	21
NEW LB Steak	**San Jose/S**	-	Rist. Umbria	**SoMa**	21
Le Central Bistro	**Downtown**	20	**Z** Ritz-Carlton Din. Rm.	**Nob Hill**	27
Z Le Papillon	**San Jose/S**	27	**NEW** RN74	**SoMa**	-
Level III	**Downtown**	18	Roy's	**SoMa**	23
Lion & Compass	**Sunnyvale/S**	20	Ruth's Chris	**Polk Gulch**	23
Luce	**SoMa**	20	Salt House	**SoMa**	21
MacArthur Pk.	**Palo Alto/S**	16	Sam's Grill	**Downtown**	22
NEW Madera	**Menlo Pk/S**	-	Sanraku	**multi.**	24
Z Marinus	**Carmel Valley/S**	27	**Z** Seasons	**Downtown**	26
MarketBar	**Embarcadero**	16	Sens Rest.	**Downtown**	20
NEW Martins West	**Redwood City/S**	-	71 Saint Peter	**San Jose/S**	22
		Shanghai 1930	**Embarcadero**	20
Z Masa's	**Downtown**	28	Silks	**Downtown**	24

Sino | **San Jose/S**	19
South Food/Wine | **S Beach**	21
South Park | **SoMa**	23
St. Michael's | **Palo Alto/S**	23
🅩 Tadich Grill | **Downtown**	23
Tommy Toy's | **Downtown**	23
Townhouse B&G | **Emeryville/E**	21
231 Ellsworth | **San Mateo/S**	22
NEW Urban Tavern | **Downtown**	17
Viognier | **San Mateo/S**	23
Waterfront | **Embarcadero**	18
🅩 Yank Sing | **SoMa**	25
NEW Zaré/Fly Trap | **SoMa**	22
Zibibbo | **Palo Alto/S**	19
🅩 Zuni Café | **Hayes Valley**	25
Zuppa | **SoMa**	19

CATERING

🅩 Acquerello | **Polk Gulch**	28
Adagia | **Berkeley/E**	18
Alexis Baking | **Napa/N**	22
All Seasons | **Calistoga/N**	20
Americano | **Embarcadero**	18
Asqew Grill | **multi.**	16
Barndiva | **Healdsburg/N**	19
Betelnut Pejiu | **Cow Hollow**	22
Bistro Liaison | **Berkeley/E**	22
🅩 BIX | **Downtown**	23
Blowfish Sushi | **multi.**	20
Bocadillos | **N Beach**	22
Boonville Hotel | **Boonville/N**	22
🅩 Buckeye Rdhse. | **Mill Valley/N**	23
CAFÉ KATi | **Japantown**	21
Caffè Verbena | **Oakland/E**	17
César | **Berkeley/E**	22
Cha Cha Cha | **multi.**	20
Charanga | **Mission**	21
Chef Chu's | **Los Altos/S**	22
Chenery Park | **Glen Pk**	21
Chez Papa | **Potrero Hill**	23
Chez Spencer | **Mission**	26
Citron | **Oakland/E**	23
Coco500 | **SoMa**	22
Cool Café | **Palo Alto/S**	-
Cucina Paradiso | **Petaluma/N**	24
Della Santina's | **Sonoma/N**	21
Destino | **Castro**	22

downtown | **Berkeley/E**	19
Ebisu | **Inner Sunset**	23
Emporio Rulli | **Larkspur/N**	22
Eos Rest. | **Cole Valley**	23
🅩 Evvia | **Palo Alto/S**	26
fig cafe | **Glen Ellen/N**	24
Fresca | **multi.**	22
Fringale | **SoMa**	24
Gabriella Café | **Santa Cruz/S**	23
Gayle's Bakery | **Capitola/S**	25
Globe | **Downtown**	20
Grasing's Coastal | **Carmel/S**	24
🅩 Greens | **Marina**	24
Hana Japanese | **Rohnert Pk/N**	24
Iberia | **Menlo Pk/S**	21
Il Davide | **San Rafael/N**	21
Il Fornaio | **San Jose/S**	19
Insalata's | **San Anselmo/N**	25
Jimtown Store | **Healdsburg/N**	18
🅩 Kokkari | **Downtown**	27
La Méditerranée | **multi.**	20
La Strada | **Palo Alto/S**	21
Lavanda | **Palo Alto/S**	20
Left Bank | **multi.**	18
Manzanita | **Healdsburg/N**	19
Marché | **Menlo Pk/S**	25
🅩 Marinus | **Carmel Valley/S**	27
Max's | **Downtown**	17
Memphis Minnie | **Lower Haight**	20
Mochica | **SoMa**	25
Moki's Sushi | **Bernal Hts**	22
Monti's | **Santa Rosa/N**	21
Napa General | **Napa/N**	20
Nick's Tacos | **Russian Hill**	22
Ozumo | **Embarcadero**	24
Piatti | **multi.**	18
Piazza D'Angelo | **Mill Valley/N**	20
Picante Cocina | **Berkeley/E**	21
Pizza Antica | **Lafayette/E**	21
Pizza Rustica | **Oakland/E**	18
Pomelo | **Inner Sunset**	23
Rest. LuLu/Petite | **SoMa**	21
Rick & Ann's | **Berkeley/E**	21
Roy's | **SoMa**	23
Sabor of Spain | **San Rafael/N**	19
Santi | **Geyserville/N**	25

SPECIAL FEATURES

Saul's Rest./Deli | **Berkeley/E** 19

Shalimar | **multi.** 23

St. Michael's | **Palo Alto/S** 23

Straits | **multi.** 19

Town's End | **Embarcadero** 20

Tratt. La Siciliana | **Berkeley/E** 25

Tra Vigne | **St. Helena/N** 24

Truly Med. | **Mission** 23

Village Pub | **Woodside/S** 26

Vivande | **Pacific Hts** 23

Washington Sq. B&G | **N Beach** ⌐

Wente Vineyards | **Livermore/E** 23

Willi's Seafood | **Healdsburg/N** 24

Willi's Wine | **Santa Rosa/N** 26

Z Yank Sing | **SoMa** 25

Yumma's | **Inner Sunset** 21

Zatar | **Berkeley/E** 22

zazu | **Santa Rosa/N** 25

Zibibbo | **Palo Alto/S** 19

Zin | **Healdsburg/N** 23

Zuppa | **SoMa** 19

CELEBRITY CHEFS

NEW Academy Cafe | 21
Charles Phan | **Inner Rich**

Acme Chophse. | *Traci Des Jardins* | 20
S Beach

Z ad hoc | *Thomas Keller* | 26
Yountville/N

Z Ame | *Hiro Sone* | **SoMa** 26

Anchor & Hope | *Mitchell and* 21
Steven Rosenthal | **SoMa**

Arcadia | *Michael Mina* | 21
San Jose/S

Z Aziza | *Mourad Lahlou* | 26
Outer Rich

NEW Barlata | *Daniel Olivella* | ⌐
Oakland/E

B44 | *Daniel Olivella* | **Downtown** 21

Z Bistro Jeanty | *Philippe Jeanty* | 25
Yountville/N

Boca | *George Morrone* | **Novato/N** 22

Bocadillos | *Gerald Hirigoyen* | 22
N Beach

Z **NEW** Bottega | 25
Michael Chiarello | **Yountville/N**

Z Bouchon | *Thomas Keller* | 26
Yountville/N

Z Boulevard | *Nancy Oakes* | 27
Embarcadero

Bushi-tei | 24
Seiji 'Waka' Wakabayashi |
Japantown

Café Fanny | *Alice Waters* | 23
Berkeley/E

Z Canteen | *Dennis Leary* | 27
Tenderloin

Chef Chu's | *Lawrence Chu* | 22
Los Altos/S

Z Chez Panisse | *Alice Waters* | 28
Berkeley/E

Z Chez Panisse Café | 27
Alice Waters | **Berkeley/E**

Cindy's | *Cindy Pawlcyn* | 24
St. Helena/N

Citizen Cake | *Elizabeth Falkner* | 21
Hayes Valley

Citronelle | *Michel Richard* | 24
Carmel/S

Coco500 | *Loretta Keller* | **SoMa** 22

Z Coi | *Daniel Patterson* | **N Beach** 28

Cool Café | *Jesse Cool* | **Palo Alto/S** ⌐

Corso | *Wendy Brucker* | 24
Berkeley/E

Z Cyrus | *Douglas Keane* | 29
Healdsburg/N

Z Delfina | *Craig Stoll* | **Mission** 26

Dry Creek | *Charlie Palmer* | 24
Healdsburg/N

EPIC | *Jan Birnbaum* | **Embarcadero** 20

Z Farallon | *Mark Franz* | 24
Downtown

Flea St. Café | *Jesse Cool* | 25
Menlo Pk/S

Z Fleur de Lys | *Hubert Keller* | 27
Downtown

Z French Laundry | *Thomas Keller* | 29
Yountville/N

Frontera Fresco | *Rick Bayless* | 18
Downtown

Z Gary Danko | *Gary Danko* | 29
Fish. Wharf

Go Fish | *Cindy Pawlcyn* | 22
St. Helena/N

Healdsburg B&G | *Douglas Keane* | 19
Healdsburg/N

NEW Heaven's Dog | 21
Charles Phan | **SoMa**

NEW Il Cane Rosso | *Daniel Patterson* | **Embarcadero** — ⎯

Z Jardinière | *Traci Des Jardins* | **Civic Ctr** — 26

Z La Folie | *Roland Passot* | **Russian Hill** — 28

NEW La Mar | *Gastón Acurio* | **Embarcadero** — 23

Z La Toque | *Ken Frank* | **Napa/N** — 26

NEW LB Steak | *Roland Passot* | **San Jose/S** — ⎯

Z Marinus | *Cal Stamenov* | **Carmel Valley/S** — 27

Martini House | *Todd Humphries* | **St. Helena/N** — 26

Z Masa's | *Gregory Short* | **Downtown** — 28

Z Michael Mina | *Michael Mina* | **Downtown** — 27

Mijita | *Traci Des Jardins* | **Embarcadero** — 20

NEW Miss Pearl's | *Joey Altman* | **Oakland/E** — 17

NEW Moss Room | *Loretta Keller* | **Inner Rich** — 21

Z Mustards | *Cindy Pawlcyn* | **Yountville/N** — 25

Nick's Cove | *Mark Franz* | **Marshall/N** — 21

nopa | *Laurence Jossel* | **W Addition** — 25

Orson | *Elizabeth Falkner* | **SoMa** — 18

Out the Door | *Charles Phan* | **Embarcadero** — 22

Picco | *Bruce Hill* | **Larkspur/N** — 26

Piperade | *Gerald Hirigoyen* | **Downtown** — 25

Pizzeria Delfina | *Craig Stoll* | **multi.** — 24

Pizzeria Picco | *Bruce Hill* | **Larkspur/N** — 25

Z Redd | *Richard Reddington* | **Yountville/N** — 27

Z Ritz-Carlton Din. Rm. | *Ron Siegel* | **Nob Hill** — 27

Z Rivoli | *Wendy Brucker* | **Berkeley/E** — 27

NEW RN74 | *Michael Mina* | **SoMa** — ⎯

Roy's | *Roy Yamaguchi* | **SoMa** — 23

Z Roy's | *Roy Yamaguchi* | **Pebble Bch/S** — 25

Salt House | *Mitchell and Steven Rosenthal* | **SoMa** — 21

Sentinel | *Dennis Leary* | **SoMa** — 25

Sino | *Chris Yeo* | **San Jose/S** — 19

Z Slanted Door | *Charles Phan* | **Embarcadero** — 26

South Food/Wine | *Luke Mangan* | **S Beach** — 21

Straits | *Chris Yeo* | **multi.** — 19

Z Terra | *Hiro Sone* | **St. Helena/N** — 27

Town Hall | *Steven and Mitchell Rosenthal* | **SoMa** — 24

TWO | *David Gingrass* | **SoMa** — 19

Z Waterbar | *Mark Franz* | **Embarcadero** — 20

'wichcraft | *Tom Colicchio* | **Downtown** — 18

Will's Fargo | *Cal Stamenov* | **Carmel Valley/S** — 22

Yoshi's SF | *Shotaro "Sho" Kamio* | **W Addition** — 22

NEW Zinnia | *Sean O'Brien* | **Downtown** — 23

Z Zuni Café | *Judy Rodgers* | **Hayes Valley** — 25

CHILD-FRIENDLY

(Alternatives to the usual fast-food places; * children's menu available)

Z Ahwahnee* | **Yosemite/E** — 19

Alexis Baking | **Napa/N** — 22

Alice's | **Noe Valley** — 19

Alioto's* | **Fish. Wharf** — 18

Amici's* | **multi.** — 20

Aperto* | **Potrero Hill** — 23

Arcadia* | **San Jose/S** — 21

Asqew Grill* | **multi.** — 16

Azzurro Pizzeria | **Napa/N** — 22

Barbara's Fish Trap* | **Princeton Sea/S** — 20

Barney's* | **multi.** — 19

Basque Cultural* | **S San Francisco/S** — 22

Beach Chalet* | **Outer Sunset** — 15

Bellanico | **Oakland/E** — 23

Bette's Oceanview | **Berkeley/E** — 23

Bistro Boudin* | **Fish. Wharf** — 19

Brandy Ho's | **multi.** — 19

Buca di Beppo* | **multi.** — 14

Z Buckeye Rdhse.* | Mill Valley/N	23
Bungalow 44* | Mill Valley/N	21
Burger Joint | multi.	18
Burma Superstar | Inner Rich	25
Cactus Taqueria* | multi.	21
Cafe Citti | Kenwood/N	22
Caffe Delle Stelle | Hayes Valley	16
Caffè Macaroni | N Beach	20
Caffè Museo | SoMa	18
Caspers Hot Dogs | multi.	18
Cetrella* | Half Moon Bay/S	20
Cheesecake* | multi.	16
Chenery Park | Glen Pk	21
Chow/Park Chow* | multi.	21
Cindy's | St. Helena/N	24
Citrus Club | Haight-Ashbury	21
Cook St. Helena | St. Helena/N	25
Cool Café | Palo Alto/S	-
Delancey St. | Embarcadero	17
Dipsea Cafe* | Mill Valley/N	19
Dottie's | Tenderloin	25
Duarte's Tavern* | Pescadero/S	21
El Balazo* | Haight-Ashbury	19
Eliza's | multi.	21
Ella's* | Presidio Hts	22
Emmy's Spaghetti* | Bernal Hts	21
Eric's | Noe Valley	22
FatApple's* | multi.	18
Fentons Creamery* | Oakland/E	19
Fish | Sausalito/N	23
Flavor* | Santa Rosa/N	19
Fog City Diner* | Embarcadero	19
Fook Yuen | Millbrae/S	22
Forbes Mill Steak* | Danville/E	22
Foreign Cinema* | Mission	23
Front Porch* | Bernal Hts	22
Garibaldis* | Oakland/E	22
Gar Woods* | Carnelian Bay/E	17
Giordano | N Beach	22
Giorgio's Pizzeria | Inner Rich	21
Goat Hill Pizza | Potrero Hill	18
Great China | Berkeley/E	23
Great Eastern | Chinatown	21
Guaymas* | Tiburon/N	16
Hard Rock* | Fish. Wharf	12

Healdsburg B&G* | Healdsburg/N	19
Henry's Hunan | multi.	21
Hurley's | Yountville/N	21
Il Fornaio* | multi.	19
Insalata's* | San Anselmo/N	25
Jay's* | multi.	19
Jimmy Bean's* | Berkeley/E	19
Joe's Cable Car | Excelsior	21
Joe's Taco* | Mill Valley/N	20
Juan's | Berkeley/E	16
Juban | multi.	19
Koi | Daly City/S	23
Koryo BBQ | Oakland/E	23
Kuleto's | Downtown	20
Kuleto's* | Burlingame/S	20
La Boulànge | multi.	22
La Cumbre | Mission	19
La Méditerranée* | multi.	20
Lark Creek* | Walnut Creek/E	21
Lark Creek Steak* | Downtown	23
La Taqueria | Mission	25
Left Bank* | multi.	18
Lo Coco's | Berkeley/E	22
Lovejoy's Tea* | Noe Valley	21
Luella | Russian Hill	22
Mama's on Wash. | N Beach	25
Market | St. Helena/N	22
Max's* | multi.	17
Mel's Drive-In* | multi.	14
Mifune | Japantown	17
Model Bakery* | St. Helena/N	20
Mo's* | SoMa	20
Napa General* | Napa/N	20
Napa Valley Grille* | Yountville/N	21
Nepenthe* | Big Sur/S	17
North Beach Pizza | multi.	20
O'mei | Santa Cruz/S	24
Original Joe's* | San Jose/S	20
Pacific Catch* | multi.	20
Pancho Villa | multi.	22
Parcel 104* | Santa Clara/S	23
Park Chalet* | Outer Sunset	16
Piatti* | multi.	18
Picante Cocina* | Berkeley/E	21
Pizza Antica* | multi.	21

Pizza Rustica | **Oakland/E**	18
Pizzeria Tra Vigne* | **St. Helena/N**	21
Pomodoro* | **multi.**	17
Q | **Inner Rich**	19
Quattro* | **E Palo Alto/S**	21
R & G Lounge | **Chinatown**	23
Rest. Peony | **Oakland/E**	20
Rick & Ann's* | **Berkeley/E**	21
Rigolo* | **Presidio Hts**	16
Robata Grill | **Mill Valley/N**	21
Z Roy's* | **Pebble Bch/S**	25
Sam's Chowder* | **Half Moon Bay/S**	20
Saul's Rest./Deli* | **Berkeley/E**	19
Savor* | **Noe Valley**	18
Scoma's* | **multi.**	22
Sears Fine Food | **Downtown**	19
Shen Hua | **Berkeley/E**	22
Taqueria Can-Cun | **multi.**	23
Tarpy's* | **Monterey/S**	20
Taylor's Auto | **multi.**	22
Toast* | **Noe Valley**	17
Tommaso's | **N Beach**	25
Ton Kiang | **Outer Rich**	24
TusCA* | **Monterey/S**	-
Venezia* | **Berkeley/E**	18
Willow Wood | **Graton/N**	24
Yankee Pier* | **multi.**	17
Z Yank Sing | **SoMa**	25
Z Zachary's Pizza | **Oakland/E**	24

CRITIC-PROOF

(Gets lots of business despite so-so food)

Buca di Beppo | **multi.**	14
Hard Rock | **Fish. Wharf**	12
Mel's Drive-In | **multi.**	14

DANCING

AsiaSF | **SoMa**	17
Bambuddha | **Tenderloin**	17
Enrico's | **N Beach**	16
Jordan's | **Berkeley/E**	17
Kan Zaman | **Haight-Ashbury**	17
Le Colonial | **Downtown**	22
Luka's Taproom | **Oakland/E**	20
Shanghai 1930 | **Embarcadero**	20
Z Tonga | **Nob Hill**	13

DELIVERY

Alexis Baking | **Napa/N**	22
Amici's | **multi.**	20
Angkor Borei | **Bernal Hts**	23
Basil Thai | **SoMa**	22
Brandy Ho's | **Chinatown**	19
Dish Dash | **Sunnyvale/S**	23
Gary Chu's | **Santa Rosa/N**	20
Goat Hill Pizza | **SoMa**	18
Henry's Hunan | **SoMa**	21
Insalata's | **San Anselmo/N**	25
Max's | **multi.**	17
North Beach Pizza | **multi.**	20
Pakwan | **Hayward/E**	22
Piatti | **Carmel/S**	18
Pizza Antica | **San Jose/S**	21
Pizza Rustica | **Oakland/E**	18
Swan Oyster | **Polk Gulch**	26
Ton Kiang | **Outer Rich**	24
Zante | **Bernal Hts**	20

DINING ALONE

(Other than hotels and places with counter service)

Z Absinthe | **Hayes Valley**	22
Acme Chophse. | **S Beach**	20
Amanda's | **Berkeley/E**	18
Anchor & Hope | **SoMa**	21
Ariake | **Outer Rich**	24
Arinell Pizza | **multi.**	24
Asqew Grill | **multi.**	16
Avatar's | **Sausalito/N**	25
bacar | **SoMa**	23
Bar Crudo | **W Addition**	26
NEW Barlata | **Oakland/E**	-
Barney's | **San Rafael/N**	19
Bar Tartine | **Mission**	24
Beretta | **Mission**	23
Bette's Oceanview | **Berkeley/E**	23
Z Bistro Jeanty | **Yountville/N**	25
Bistro Ralph | **Healdsburg/N**	23
Blowfish Sushi | **multi.**	20
Blue Barn Gourmet | **Marina**	22
Blue Bottle | **SoMa**	23
Bocadillos | **N Beach**	22
Z Bouchon | **Yountville/N**	26
Z Boulevard | **Embarcadero**	27

SPECIAL FEATURES

Bovolo | **Healdsburg/N**	24
🅩 Buckeye Rdhse. | **Mill Valley/N**	23
Bungalow 44 | **Mill Valley/N**	21
Cafe Bastille | **Downtown**	18
Cafe Citti | **Kenwood/N**	22
Café Claude | **Downtown**	21
Café de la Presse | **Downtown**	18
Café du Soleil | **Lower Haight**	19
Café Gratitude | **multi.**	16
Café Rouge | **Berkeley/E**	22
Candybar | **W Addition**	17
Cascal | **Mtn View/S**	20
Cav Wine Bar | **Hayes Valley**	20
César | **Berkeley/E**	22
Cetrella | **Half Moon Bay/S**	20
Cha Cha Cha | **multi.**	20
Chez Maman | **Potrero Hill**	22
Chez Papa | **Potrero Hill**	23
Chouchou | **Forest Hills**	22
Citizen Cake | **Hayes Valley**	21
Coco500 | **SoMa**	22
🅩 Coi | **N Beach**	28
🅽🅴🆆 Contigo | **Noe Valley**	19
Cook St. Helena | **St. Helena/N**	25
Corso | **Berkeley/E**	24
Cottonwood | **Truckee/E**	21
Cuvée | **Napa/N**	21
Delessio Market | **multi.**	21
Della Fattoria | **Petaluma/N**	24
Domo Sushi | **Hayes Valley**	23
Dosa | **Mission**	23
Duarte's Tavern | **Pescadero/S**	21
E&O Trading | **San Jose/S**	19
Ebisu | **multi.**	23
Emporio Rulli | **Larkspur/N**	22
Enrico's | **N Beach**	16
Eos Rest. | **Cole Valley**	23
🅩 Evvia | **Palo Alto/S**	26
farmerbrown/skillet | **Tenderloin**	21
FatApple's | **multi.**	18
1550 Hyde | **Russian Hill**	22
Firefly | **Noe Valley**	25
Flora | **Oakland/E**	23
Fog City Diner | **Embarcadero**	19
Folio Enoteca | **Napa/N**	16

Forge in Forest | **Carmel/S**	18
Fringale | **SoMa**	24
Frjtz Fries | **multi.**	18
Gamine | **Cow Hollow**	22
Godzila Sushi | **Pacific Hts**	19
Grandeho Kamekyo | **multi.**	23
Grand Pu Bah | **Potrero Hill**	18
Green Chile | **W Addition**	20
grégoire | **Oakland/E**	22
Hamano Sushi | **Noe Valley**	19
Hana Japanese | **Rohnert Pk/N**	24
Hog Island Oyster | **Embarcadero**	25
Home of Chicken | **Oakland/E**	20
Hopmonk Tav. | **Sebastopol/N**	17
Hurley's | **Yountville/N**	21
Kabuto | **Outer Rich**	26
Kanpai | **Palo Alto/S**	22
🅩 Kaygetsu | **Menlo Pk/S**	28
King of Thai | **multi.**	19
Kirala | **Berkeley/E**	25
🅩 Kiss Seafood | **Japantown**	28
Koo | **Inner Sunset**	25
Krung Thai | **San Jose/S**	20
La Boulange | **multi.**	22
Lanesplitter Pub | **multi.**	17
La Note | **Berkeley/E**	21
La Trappe | **N Beach**	18
La Victoria | **San Jose/S**	20
Left Bank | **Menlo Pk/S**	18
Le Zinc | **Noe Valley**	19
Little Chihuahua | **W Addition**	23
Local Kitchen | **SoMa**	20
Mario's Bohemian | **N Beach**	18
MarketBar | **Embarcadero**	16
🅽🅴🆆 Marzano | **Oakland/E**	23
Maverick | **Mission**	24
🅽🅴🆆 Mayfield | **Palo Alto/S**	19
Medjool | **Mission**	18
Mel's Drive-In | **Inner Rich**	14
Meritage Martini | **Sonoma/N**	20
Miller's/Deli | **Polk Gulch**	22
Mission Bch. Café | **Mission**	21
Model Bakery | **Napa/N**	20
Monk's Kettle | **Mission**	18
Muracci's | **Downtown**	21

Menus, photos, voting and more – free at ZAGAT.com

☑ Mustards | **Yountville/N**	25
My Tofu | **Inner Rich**	22
Naan/Curry | **Downtown**	17
Naked Fish | **S Lake Tahoe/E**	21
Naomi Sushi | **Menlo Pk/S**	21
Napa General | **Napa/N**	20
Nectar Wine | **Burlingame/S**	18
Nizza La Bella | **Albany/E**	20
NEW Nopalito | **W Addition**	23
Old Jerusalem | **Mission**	20
Old Port Lobster | **Redwood City/S**	22
Oliveto Cafe | **Oakland/E**	24
Orson | **SoMa**	18
Ottimista | **Cow Hollow**	19
Out the Door | **multi.**	22
Oxbow Wine | **Napa/N**	22
Oyaji | **Outer Rich**	23
Pacific Catch | **multi.**	20
Pakwan | **Fremont/E**	22
Papalote | **multi.**	22
Peter Lowell's | **Sebastopol/N**	22
NEW Phat Philly | **Mission**	20
Pica Pica Maize | **Napa/N**	25
Piccino | **Dogpatch**	24
Pine Cone Diner | **Pt Reyes/N**	20
Piperade | **Downtown**	25
Pizza Place on Noriega | **Outer Sunset**	-
Pizzeria Delfina | **Pacific Hts**	24
Plant Cafe | **Marina**	20
Pluto's | **multi.**	19
Pomodoro | **multi.**	17
Pot de Pho | **Inner Rich**	18
☑ Redd | **Yountville/N**	27
Red Hut | **S Lake Tahoe/E**	23
Regalito Rosticeria | **Mission**	21
rnm rest. | **Lower Haight**	23
Robata Grill | **Mill Valley/N**	21
Rôtisario | **Napa/N**	-
Ryoko's | **Downtown**	22
Osake/Sake 'O | **Healdsburg/N**	23
Samovar Tea Lounge | **multi.**	20
Sebo | **Hayes Valley**	25
Serpentine | **Dogpatch**	21
Shabu-Sen | **Japantown**	19

Shanghai Dumpling | **Outer Rich**	23
Sino | **San Jose/S**	19
Spork | **Mission**	21
SPQR | **Pacific Hts**	23
Suppenküche | **Hayes Valley**	22
☑ Sushi Ran | **Sausalito/N**	28
Sushi Zone | **Castro**	26
Swan Oyster | **Polk Gulch**	26
Table Café | **Larkspur/N**	-
Taqueria Can-Cun | **multi.**	23
Taqueria 3 Amigos | **multi.**	19
Taylor's Auto | **Napa/N**	22
Tea Room Café | **Petaluma/N**	24
Terzo | **Cow Hollow**	23
Ti Couz | **Mission**	23
Toast | **Noe Valley**	17
Tokyo Go Go | **Mission**	21
Town Hall | **SoMa**	24
Tra Vigne | **St. Helena/N**	24
Tres Agaves | **S Beach**	15
T Rex BBQ | **Berkeley/E**	18
Tsunami | **W Addition**	22
Uva Enoteca | **Lower Haight**	20
Viognier | **San Mateo/S**	23
Vivande | **Pacific Hts**	23
Willi's Seafood | **Healdsburg/N**	24
Will's Fargo | **Carmel Valley/S**	22
Woodhse. | **Castro**	21
Xanh | **Mtn View/S**	23
Yamo | **Mission**	23
Yoshi's | **Oakland/E**	20
Yoshi's SF | **W Addition**	22
Zazie | **Cole Valley**	22
Zibibbo | **Palo Alto/S**	19
☑ Zuni Café | **Hayes Valley**	25
Zushi Puzzle | **Marina**	26

ENTERTAINMENT

(Call for days and times of performances)

☑ Ahwahnee | piano | **Yosemite/E**	19
Albion River Inn | piano | **Albion/N**	25
Ana Mandara | jazz | **Fish. Wharf**	22
AsiaSF | gender illusionists | **SoMa**	17
bacar | jazz | **SoMa**	23
Bambuddha | DJ | **Tenderloin**	17

Beach Chalet | jazz | **Outer Sunset** 15

🅩 Big 4 | piano | **Nob Hill** 22

Bing Crosby's | piano | 19
Walnut Creek/E

🅩 BIX | jazz | **Downtown** 23

Blowfish Sushi | DJ | **San Jose/S** 20

Butterfly | jazz | **Embarcadero** 20

Cafe Bastille | jazz | **Downtown** 18

Café Claude | jazz | **Downtown** 21

Cascal | Spanish band | 20
Mtn View/S

Cetrella | jazz | **Half Moon Bay/S** 20

🅩 Cheese Board | jazz/pop | 26
Berkeley/E

Emmy's Spaghetti | DJ | **Bernal Hts** 21

Enrico's | jazz | **N Beach** 16

Everett & Jones | varies | 20
Oakland/E

Foreign Cinema | films | **Mission** 23

🅩 Garden Court | jazz/piano | 20
Downtown

Giordano | varies | **N Beach** 22

Harris' | jazz/piano | **Polk Gulch** 25

Jordan's | jazz | **Berkeley/E** 17

Kan Zaman | belly dancers/DJ | 17
Haight-Ashbury

Katia's Tea | accordion | **Inner Rich** 23

La Note | accordion | **Berkeley/E** 21

Ledford Hse. | jazz | **Albion/N** 25

Levende | DJ | **Oakland/E** 19

Lime | DJ | **Castro** 17

🅩 Marinus | jazz | 27
Carmel Valley/S

Max's | piano/singing waiters | 17
multi.

🅩 Navio | jazz | **Half Moon Bay/S** 24

Olema Inn | jazz | **Olema/N** 22

🅩 Plumed Horse | piano | 25
Saratoga/S

Poleng | dancing/DJ | **W Addition** 19

Rose Pistola | jazz | **N Beach** 22

Santé | piano | **Sonoma/N** 25

Sardine Factory | piano | 21
Monterey/S

Scott's | jazz/piano | **multi.** 18

🅩 Seasons | piano | **Downtown** 26

Shanghai 1930 | jazz | 20
Embarcadero

🅩 Slanted Door | DJ | 26
Embarcadero

Straits | varies | **multi.** 19

Sushi Groove | DJ | **SoMa** 21

🅩 Tonga | live music | **Nob Hill** 13

Townhouse B&G | live music | 21
Emeryville/E

Uva Trattoria | jazz | **Napa/N** 23

Vic Stewart's | piano | 21
Walnut Creek/E

Washington Sq. B&G | piano | –
N Beach

XYZ | DJ | **SoMa** 19

Yoshi's | jazz | **Oakland/E** 20

Yoshi's SF | live music | 22
W Addition

🅩 Zuni Café | pianist | 25
Hayes Valley

FIREPLACES

Adagia | **Berkeley/E** 18

🅩 Ahwahnee | **Yosemite/E** 19

NEW AKA Bistro | **St. Helena/N** 21

Albion River Inn | **Albion/N** 25

Alexander's | **Cupertino/S** 25

🅩 Ame | **SoMa** 26

Anton & Michel | **Carmel/S** 23

🅩 Applewood Inn | 27
Guerneville/N

Asia de Cuba | **Downtown** 20

🅩 Auberge du Sol. | 26
Rutherford/N

Barney's | **Berkeley/E** 19

Bella Vista | **Woodside/S** 19

Betelnut Pejiu | **Cow Hollow** 22

🅩 Big 4 | **Nob Hill** 22

Bing Crosby's | **Walnut Creek/E** 19

Bistro Don Giovanni | **Napa/N** 23

🅩 Bistro Jeanty | **Yountville/N** 25

Boca | **Novato/N** 22

Boonville Hotel | **Boonville/N** 22

Brannan's Grill | **Calistoga/N** 20

Brix | **Napa/N** 22

🅩 Buckeye Rdhse. | **Mill Valley/N** 23

Cafe Citti | **Kenwood/N** 22

Café Gratitude | **Berkeley/E** 16

Caprice | **Tiburon/N** 21

Casanova | **Carmel/S** 23

Casa Orinda	**Orinda/E**	18
Cetrella	**Half Moon Bay/S**	20
Z Chantilly	**Redwood City/S**	23
Chapter & Moon	**Ft Bragg/N**	22
Chez Spencer	**Mission**	26
Chez TJ	**Mtn View/S**	23
Chow/Park Chow	**multi.**	21
Cottonwood	**Truckee/E**	21
Cuvée	**Napa/N**	21
Deetjen's	**Big Sur/S**	22
Della Santina's	**Sonoma/N**	21
Digs Bistro	**Berkeley/E**	25
Dio Deka	**Los Gatos/S**	25
Dipsea Cafe	**Mill Valley/N**	19
Duck Club	**Bodega Bay/N**	19
E&O Trading	**Larkspur/N**	19
El Dorado	**Sonoma/N**	24
Z El Paseo	**Mill Valley/N**	26
EPIC	**Embarcadero**	20
Z Erna's Elderberry	**Oakhurst/E**	28
Estéban	**Monterey/S**	-
Z Étoile	**Yountville/N**	26
Z Evvia	**Palo Alto/S**	26
Fandango	**Pacific Grove/S**	23
Z Farm	**Napa/N**	24
Z Farmhouse Inn	**Forestville/N**	26
5A5 Steak Lounge	**Downtown**	-
Flavor	**Santa Rosa/N**	19
Z Fleur de Lys	**Downtown**	27
Flying Fish	**Carmel/S**	24
Forbes Mill Steak	**Los Gatos/S**	22
Foreign Cinema	**Mission**	23
Forge in Forest	**Carmel/S**	18
Z French Laundry	**Yountville/N**	29
Fresh Cream	**Monterey/S**	25
Gar Woods	**Carnelian Bay/E**	17
Guaymas	**Tiburon/N**	16
Half Moon Brew	**Half Moon Bay/S**	16
Harris'	**Polk Gulch**	25
Home	**Castro**	18
Z House of Prime	**Polk Gulch**	24
Iberia	**Menlo Pk/S**	21
Il Fornaio	**multi.**	19
Izzy's Steak	**Marina**	20
Jake's/Lake	**Tahoe City/E**	16
John Ash	**Santa Rosa/N**	24
John Bentley's	**Woodside/S**	25
Kenwood	**Kenwood/N**	23
Z Kokkari	**Downtown**	27
Kuleto's	**Downtown**	20
NEW Lake Chalet	**Oakland/E**	-
La Terrasse	**Presidio**	18
Z La Toque	**Napa/N**	26
NEW LB Steak	**San Jose/S**	-
Ledford Hse.	**Albion/N**	25
Left Bank	**Larkspur/N**	18
Le Soleil	**Inner Rich**	23
Level III	**Downtown**	18
Lupa Trattoria	**Noe Valley**	22
MacArthur Pk.	**Palo Alto/S**	16
MacCallum Hse.	**Mendocino/N**	21
NEW Madera	**Menlo Pk/S**	-
Z Madrona	**Healdsburg/N**	26
Mandaloun	**Redwood City/S**	20
Z Marinus	**Carmel Valley/S**	27
Martini House	**St. Helena/N**	26
Z Meadowood Rest.	**St. Helena/N**	26
Mendocino Hotel	**Mendocino/N**	18
Metro	**Lafayette/E**	-
Mezza Luna	**Princeton Sea/S**	21
Monti's	**Santa Rosa/N**	21
Moosse Café	**Mendocino/N**	24
Mosaic	**Forestville/N**	26
Murray Circle	**Sausalito/N**	24
Napa General	**Napa/N**	20
Z Navio	**Half Moon Bay/S**	24
Nepenthe	**Big Sur/S**	17
Nick's Cove	**Marshall/N**	21
Z Pacific's Edge	**Carmel/S**	25
Parcel 104	**Santa Clara/S**	23
Park Chalet	**Outer Sunset**	16
Piatti	**multi.**	18
Piazza D'Angelo	**Mill Valley/N**	20
NEW Pickles	**Downtown**	-
Plouf	**Downtown**	22
Z Plumed Horse	**Saratoga/S**	25
PlumpJack	**Olympic Valley/E**	23
Poleng	**W Addition**	19
Postino	**Lafayette/E**	23
Press	**St. Helena/N**	23

SPECIAL FEATURES

Prima | **Walnut Creek/E**	24
Ravenous Cafe | **Healdsburg/N**	22
Ravens Rest. | **Mendocino/N**	22
Rendezvous Inn | **Ft Bragg/N**	25
Rest. at Stevenswood | **Little River/N**	26
Rest. LuLu/Petite | **SoMa**	21
Rio Grill | **Carmel/S**	21
River Ranch | **Tahoe City/E**	15
Rutherford Grill | **Rutherford/N**	24
Salute Marina | **Richmond/E**	18
Santé | **Sonoma/N**	25
Santi | **Geyserville/N**	25
Sardine Factory | **Monterey/S**	21
Z Seasons | **Downtown**	26
Shadowbrook | **Capitola/S**	18
Shanghai 1930 | **Embarcadero**	20
Z Sierra Mar | **Big Sur/S**	27
Soule Domain | **Kings Bch/E**	22
Z Spruce | **Presidio Hts**	25
Stokes | **Monterey/S**	21
St. Orres | **Gualala/N**	22
Sunnyside | **Tahoe City/E**	18
Tarpy's | **Monterey/S**	20
Terzo | **Cow Hollow**	23
Toast | **Novato/N**	-
Townhouse B&G | **Emeryville/E**	21
Troya | **Inner Rich**	21
TusCA | **Monterey/S**	-
Venticello | **Nob Hill**	23
Vic Stewart's | **Walnut Creek/E**	21
Village Pub | **Woodside/S**	26
Viognier | **San Mateo/S**	23
Will's Fargo | **Carmel Valley/S**	22
Wine Spectator | **St. Helena/N**	22
Zibibbo | **Palo Alto/S**	19
Zinsvalley | **Napa/N**	19

HISTORIC PLACES
(Year opened; * building)

1800 | Côté Sud* | **Castro**	19
1800 | Market* | **St. Helena/N**	22
1829 | Cindy's* | **St. Helena/N**	24
1833 | Stokes* | **Monterey/S**	21
1844 | Celadon* | **Napa/N**	24
1848 | La Forêt* | **San Jose/S**	26
1849 | Tadich Grill | **Downtown**	23

1856 | Garden Court* | **Downtown**	20
1857 | Little River Inn* | **Little River/N**	21
1860 | Pizza Antica* | **Lafayette/E**	21
1863 | Cliff House | **Outer Rich**	18
1863 | Sutro's* | **Outer Rich**	21
1864 | Boonville Hotel* | **Boonville/N**	22
1864 | Estate* | **Sonoma/N**	20
1864 | Rocker Oysterfellers* | **Valley Ford/Nt**	21
1867 | Sam's Grill | **Downtown**	22
1870 | Murray Circle* | **Sausalito/N**	24
1875 | La Note* | **Berkeley/E**	21
1876 | Olema Inn* | **Olema/N**	22
1878 | Mendocino Hotel* | **Mendocino/N**	18
1880 | Pianeta* | **Truckee/E**	23
1881 | Il Fornaio* | **Carmel/S**	19
1881 | Madrona* | **Healdsburg/N**	26
1882 | MacCallum Hse.* | **Mendocino/N**	21
1884 | Napa General* | **Napa/N**	20
1884 | Terra* | **St. Helena/N**	27
1886 | Cole's Chop Hse.* | **Napa/N**	24
1886 | Fior d'Italia | **N Beach**	18
1886 | Mendo Bistro* | **Ft Bragg/N**	24
1886 | Willi's Wine* | **Santa Rosa/N**	26
1888 | Bottega* | **Yountville/N**	25
1888 | Bounty Hunter* | **Napa/N**	19
1888 | Tavern at Lark Creek* | **Larkspur/N**	-
1889 | Boulevard* | **Embarcadero**	27
1889 | Pacific Café* | **Outer Rich**	23
1890 | Chez TJ* | **Mtn View/S**	23
1890 | Eureka* | **Castro**	20
1890 | Scoma's* | **Sausalito/N**	22
1893 | Cafe Beaujolais* | **Mendocino/N**	25
1893 | Jimtown Store* | **Healdsburg/N**	18
1894 | Duarte's Tavern* | **Pescadero/S**	21
1894 | Fentons Creamery | **Oakland/E**	19
1895 | Restaurant* | **Ft Bragg/N**	23

Year	Restaurant / Location	Score
1897	Rendezvous Inn*	Ft Bragg/N	25
1900	Axum Cafe*	Lower Haight	20
1900	Bar Tartine*	Mission	24
1900	Central Market*	Petaluma/N	24
1900	Cha Cha Cha*	Mission	20
1900	French Laundry*	Yountville/N	29
1900	La Ginestra*	Mill Valley/N	21
1900	Pauline's Pizza*	Mission	23
1900	Salute Marina*	Richmond/E	18
1902	Santi*	Geyserville/N	25
1904	Moosse Café*	Mendocino/N	24
1904	Paul K*	Hayes Valley	21
1905	Hopmonk Tav.*	Sebastopol/N	17
1906	Coco500*	SoMa	22
1906	Imperial/Berkeley*	Embarcadero	20
1906	Pork Store*	Haight-Ashbury	22
1907	Town Hall*	SoMa	24
1908	Zaré/Fly Trap*	SoMa	22
1909	Campton Place*	Downtown	24
1910	Catch*	Castro	18
1910	Harris'*	Polk Gulch	25
1910	Poleng*	W Addition	19
1910	Rest. LuLu/Petite*	SoMa	21
1912	Swan Oyster	Polk Gulch	26
1913	Balboa Cafe	Cow Hollow	19
1913	Zuni Café*	Hayes Valley	25
1914	Healdsburg B&G*	Healdsburg/N	19
1914	Red's Java*	Embarcadero	16
1915	Jordan's*	Berkeley/E	17
1915	Napa Wine Train*	Napa/N	16
1917	Pacific's Edge*	Carmel/S	25
1917	Tarpy's*	Monterey/S	20
1918	MacArthur Pk.*	Palo Alto/S	16
1918	St. Francis	Mission	19
1919	Albion River Inn*	Albion/N	25
1919	Ana Mandara*	Fish. Wharf	22
1919	Sauce*	Hayes Valley	19
1920	Acquerello*	Polk Gulch	28
1920	Albona Rist.*	N Beach	24
1920	Bistro Vida*	Menlo Pk/S	18
1920	Boogaloos*	Mission	20
1923	Martini House*	St. Helena/N	26
1925	Adagia*	Berkeley/E	18
1925	Alioto's	Fish. Wharf	18
1925	John Bentley's*	Redwood City/S	25
1925	Rist. Capellini*	San Mateo/S	20
1927	Ahwahnee*	Yosemite/E	19
1927	Bella Vista*	Woodside/S	19
1927	Townhouse B&G*	Emeryville/E	21
1928	Alfred's Steak	Downtown	22
1928	Elite Cafe*	Upper Fillmore	19
1929	Aubergine*	Carmel/S	25
1930	Big 4*	Nob Hill	22
1930	Caprice*	Tiburon/N	21
1930	Evan's*	S Lake Tahoe/E	28
1930	Foreign Cinema*	Mission	23
1930	Lalime's*	Berkeley/E	26
1930	Lo Coco's*	Oakland/E	22
1930	Ravenous Cafe*	Healdsburg/N	22
1930	Tea Room Café*	Petaluma/N	24
1932	Casa Orinda*	Orinda/E	18
1933	Luka's Taproom*	Oakland/E	20
1934	Caspers Hot Dogs	multi.	18
1935	Tommaso's	N Beach	25
1936	Gabriella Café*	Santa Cruz/S	23
1937	Buckeye Rdhse.	Mill Valley/N	23
1937	Postino*	Lafayette/E	23
1937	231 Ellsworth*	San Mateo/S	22
1938	Deetjen's*	Big Sur/S	22
1938	Sears Fine Food	Downtown	19
1945	Tonga	Nob Hill	13
1947	Shadowbrook	Capitola/S	18

1949 | House of Prime | **Polk Gulch** 24

1949 | Nepenthe | **Big Sur/S** 17

1949 | Taylor's Auto | **St. Helena/N** 22

1950 | Alexis Baking* | **Napa/N** 22

1950 | Red Hut* | **S Lake Tahoe/E** 23

1952 | Plumed Horse | **Saratoga/S** 25

1953 | Mel's Drive-In* | **Inner Rich** 14

1955 | Breads of India* | 19
Berkeley/E

1956 | Original Joe's | **San Jose/S** 20

1958 | Enrico's | **N Beach** 16

1958 | Yank Sing | **SoMa** 25

1959 | St. Michael's | **Palo Alto/S** 23

1959 | Will's Fargo | 22
Carmel Valley/S

HOTEL DINING

Ahwahnee Hotel
🅩 Ahwahnee | **Yosemite/E** 19

Auberge du Soleil
🅩 Auberge du Sol. | 26
Rutherford/N

Bardessono Hotel & Spa
NEW Bardessono | 23
Yountville/N

Bernardus Lodge
🅩 Marinus | **Carmel Valley/S** 27

Best Western Americania
Custom Burger | **SoMa** 19

Blue Heron Inn, The
Moosse Café | **Mendocino/N** 24

Blue Rock Inn
Left Bank | **Larkspur/N** 18

Boonville Hotel
Boonville Hotel | **Boonville/N** 22

California, Hotel
Millennium | **Downtown** 25

Campton Place Hotel
Campton Place | **Downtown** 24

Carlton Hotel
Saha | **Tenderloin** 25

Carneros Inn
Boon Fly Café | **Napa/N** 22
🅩 Farm | **Napa/N** 24

Casa Madrona
Poggio | **Sausalito/N** 22

Casa Munras Hotel
Estéban | **Monterey/S** -

Cavallo Point Resort
Murray Circle | **Sausalito/N** 24

Château du Sureau
🅩 Erna's Elderberry | 28
Oakhurst/E

Claremont Resort & Spa
Jordan's | **Berkeley/E** 17

Clift Hotel
Asia de Cuba | **Downtown** 20

Commodore Hotel
🅩 Canteen | **Tenderloin** 27

Dina's Garden Hotel
Trader Vic's | **Palo Alto/S** 17

El Dorado Hotel
El Dorado | **Sonoma/N** 24

Fairmont Hotel
🅩 Tonga | **Nob Hill** 13

Fairmont Sonoma Mission Inn
Santé | **Sonoma/N** 25

Farmhouse Inn
🅩 Farmhouse Inn | 26
Forestville/N

Four Seasons Hotel
Quattro | **E Palo Alto/S** 21
🅩 Seasons | **Downtown** 26

Frank, Hotel
Max's | **Downtown** 17

Galleria Park Hotel
NEW Midi | **Downtown** -

Garden Court Hotel
Il Fornaio | **Palo Alto/S** 19

Healdsburg, Hotel
Dry Creek | **Healdsburg/N** 24

Hilton
NEW Urban Tavern | 17
Downtown

Huntington Hotel
🅩 Big 4 | **Nob Hill** 22

Hyatt Highlands Inn
🅩 Pacific's Edge | **Carmel/S** 25

Hyatt Regency Monterey
TusCA | **Monterey/S** -

Inn at Southbridge
Pizzeria Tra Vigne | **St. Helena/N** 21

SPECIAL FEATURES

Stevenswood Lodge
  Rest. at Stevenswood | **Little River/N** 26

St. Orres Hotel
  St. Orres | **Gualala/N** 22

St. Regis
  Z Ame | **SoMa** 26
  Vitrine | **SoMa** 23

Truckee Hotel
  Moody's Bistro | **Truckee/E** 25

Valley Ford Hotel
  Rocker Oysterfellers | **Valley Ford/Nt** 21

Villa Florence Hotel
  Kuleto's | **Downtown** 20

Vintage Ct., Hotel
  Z Masa's | **Downtown** 28

Vitale, Hotel
  Americano | **Embarcadero** 18

Warwick Regis
  La Scene | **Downtown** 18

Waterfront Plaza Hotel
  NEW Miss Pearl's | **Oakland/E** 17

Westin San Francisco
  Ducca | **SoMa** 20

Westin St. Francis
  Z Michael Mina | **Downtown** 27

Westin Verasa
  Z La Toque | **Napa/N** 26

W Hotel
  XYZ | **SoMa** 19

LATE DINING

(Weekday closing hour)

Z Absinthe | 12 AM | **Hayes Valley** 22

NEW Adesso | varies | **Oakland/E** –

Alembic | 12 AM | **Haight-Ashbury** 22

Beretta | 12 AM | **Mission** 23

NEW Bistro 24 | 12 AM | **Noe Valley** –

Z Bouchon | 12:30 AM | **Yountville/N** 26

Brazen Head | 1 AM | **Cow Hollow** 20

Brother's Korean | varies | **Inner Rich** 23

Cafe Maritime/East | 1 AM | **Marina** 21

Caspers Hot Dogs | 11:30 PM | **multi.** 18

NEW Corner | 12 AM | **Mission** –

NEW Flour + Water | 12 AM | **Mission** –

Fonda Solana | 12:30 AM | **Albany/E** 23

Z NEW Gitane | 12 AM | **Downtown** 22

Globe | 1 AM | **Downtown** 20

Great Eastern | 12 AM | **Chinatown** 21

NEW Heaven's Dog | 1 AM | **SoMa** 21

Home | 12 AM | **Castro** 18

Home of Chicken | varies | **Oakland/E** 20

Z In-N-Out | varies | **multi.** 22

King of Thai | varies | **multi.** 19

Koryo BBQ | 12 AM | **Oakland/E** 23

Lanesplitter Pub | varies | **multi.** 17

La Victoria | 2 AM | **San Jose/S** 20

Lime | varies | **Castro** 17

Luka's Taproom | 12 AM | **Oakland/E** 20

Magnolia | 12 AM | **Haight-Ashbury** 18

NEW Marinitas | 12 AM | **San Anselmo/N** 21

Mel's Drive-In | varies | **multi.** 14

Monk's Kettle | 1 AM | **Mission** 18

Naan/Curry | varies | **Downtown** 17

nopa | 1 AM | **W Addition** 25

North Beach Pizza | varies | **N Beach** 20

Oola | 1 AM | **SoMa** 20

Original Joe's | varies | **San Jose/S** 20

Osha Thai | varies | **multi.** 21

Pancho Villa | varies | **Mission** 22

Ryoko's | 2 AM | **Downtown** 22

Sauce | 12 AM | **Hayes Valley** 19

Scala's Bistro | 12 AM | **Downtown** 21

Shalimar | 11:30 PM | **Tenderloin** 23

Taqueria Can-Cun | varies | **Mission** 23

Taqueria 3 Amigos | 12 AM | **San Mateo/S** 19

Thai House | varies | **Tenderloin** 23

Tsunami	12 AM	multi.	22
Zeitgeist	2 AM	Mission	15

MEET FOR A DRINK

☑ Absinthe	Hayes Valley	22
NEW Adesso	Oakland/E	–
NEW AKA Bistro	St. Helena/N	21
Alembic	Haight-Ashbury	22
Alexander's	Cupertino/S	25
Amber Bistro	Danville/E	22
Amber	SoMa	24
Americano	Embarcadero	18
Ana Mandara	Fish. Wharf	22
Anchor & Hope	SoMa	21
Andalu	Mission	21
AsiaSF	SoMa	17
NEW Aurea	Nob Hill	–
bacar	SoMa	23
Balboa Cafe	Cow Hollow	19
Bambuddha	Tenderloin	17
Bar Bambino	Mission	23
NEW Bardessono	Yountville/N	23
NEW Barlata	Oakland/E	–
Barndiva	Healdsburg/N	19
Beach Chalet	Outer Sunset	15
Bellanico	Oakland/E	23
Beretta	Mission	23
Betelnut Pejiu	Cow Hollow	22
☑ Big 4	Nob Hill	22
Bing Crosby's	Walnut Creek/E	19
Bin 38	Marina	19
Bistro/Copains	Occidental/N	25
Bistro Don Giovanni	Napa/N	23
NEW Bistro St. Germain	Lower Haight	–
Bistro Vida	Menlo Pk/S	18
☑ BIX	Downtown	23
Blowfish Sushi	Mission	20
☑ NEW Bottega	Yountville/N	25
☑ Bouchon	Yountville/N	26
☑ Boulevard	Embarcadero	27
Brazen Head	Cow Hollow	20
Bridgetender	Tahoe City/E	19
☑ Buckeye Rdhse.	Mill Valley/N	23
Bungalow 44	Mill Valley/N	21
Butterfly	Embarcadero	20

Cafe Bastille	Downtown	18
Café Claude	Downtown	21
Café de la Presse	Downtown	18
Café Flore	Castro	15
Café Rouge	Berkeley/E	22
Candybar	W Addition	17
Carnelian Room	Downtown	18
Cascal	Mtn View/S	20
Catch	Castro	18
Cav Wine Bar	Hayes Valley	20
Central Market	Petaluma/N	24
César	Berkeley/E	22
Cetrella	Half Moon Bay/S	20
Chaya	Embarcadero	22
Cin-Cin Wine	Los Gatos/S	23
Circa	Marina	18
Citronelle	Carmel/S	24
Colibrí Mexican	Downtown	20
Conduit	Mission	22
Cosmopolitan	SoMa	19
Cottonwood	Truckee/E	21
Cuvée	Napa/N	21
Dio Deka	Los Gatos/S	25
District	SoMa	18
NEW Donato	Redwood City/S	–
Doña Tomás	Oakland/E	23
Dragonfly	Truckee/E	22
Ducca	SoMa	20
E&O Trading	multi.	19
NEW Elements	Napa/N	22
Elite Cafe	Upper Fillmore	19
Enrico's	N Beach	16
Eos Rest.	Cole Valley	23
EPIC	Embarcadero	20
NEW Estate	Sonoma/N	20
Estéban	Monterey/S	–
Eureka	Castro	20
☑ Farallon	Downtown	24
☑ Farm	Napa/N	24
1550 Hyde	Russian Hill	22
NEW 54 Mint	SoMa	–
fig cafe	Glen Ellen/N	24
NEW Five	Berkeley/E	–
5A5 Steak Lounge	Downtown	–
Flora	Oakland/E	23
Florio	Pacific Hts	21

Folio Enoteca | **Napa/N**	16
Fonda Solana | **Albany/E**	23
Foreign Cinema | **Mission**	23
Garibaldis | **multi.**	22
Gar Woods | **Carnelian Bay/E**	17
Z NEW Gitane | **Downtown**	22
Go Fish | **St. Helena/N**	22
Guaymas | **Tiburon/N**	16
Half Moon Brew | **Half Moon Bay/S**	16
NEW Heaven's Dog | **SoMa**	21
Home | **Castro**	18
Hopmonk Tav. | **Sebastopol/N**	17
Hurley's | **Yountville/N**	21
Iberia | **Menlo Pk/S**	21
Jake's/Lake | **Tahoe City/E**	16
Z Jardinière | **Civic Ctr**	26
JoLe | **Calistoga/N**	26
NEW Joya | **Palo Alto/S**	18
Junnoon | **Palo Alto/S**	23
Kan Zaman | **Haight-Ashbury**	17
Z Kokkari | **Downtown**	27
Laïola | **Marina**	20
NEW Lalola Bar | **Russian Hill**	21
NEW La Mar | **Embarcadero**	23
La Terrasse | **Presidio**	18
La Trappe | **N Beach**	18
Lavanda | **Palo Alto/S**	20
Le Colonial | **Downtown**	22
Left Bank | **multi.**	18
Level III | **Downtown**	18
Le Zinc | **Noe Valley**	19
Lime | **Castro**	17
Local Kitchen | **SoMa**	20
Luce | **SoMa**	20
Luka's Taproom | **Oakland/E**	20
Luna Park | **Mission**	20
Lure | **San Mateo/S**	20
NEW Madera | **Menlo Pk/S**	–
Magnolia | **Haight-Ashbury**	18
Mamacita | **Marina**	23
Mantra | **Palo Alto/S**	20
NEW Marinitas | **San Anselmo/N**	21
MarketBar | **Embarcadero**	16
Martini House | **St. Helena/N**	26
NEW Martins West | **Redwood City/S**	–
Medjool | **Mission**	18
Mendocino Hotel | **Mendocino/N**	18
Meritage Martini | **Sonoma/N**	20
Mexico DF | **Embarcadero**	20
Z Michael Mina | **Downtown**	27
NEW Midi | **Downtown**	–
NEW Miss Pearl's | **Oakland/E**	17
MoMo's | **S Beach**	17
Monk's Kettle | **Mission**	18
Montrio Bistro | **Monterey/S**	21
Moody's Bistro | **Truckee/E**	25
Mosaic | **Forestville/N**	26
NEW Moss Room | **Inner Rich**	21
Murray Circle | **Sausalito/N**	24
Z Mustards | **Yountville/N**	25
Nectar Wine | **Burlingame/S**	18
NEW Nettie's | **Cow Hollow**	20
Nihon | **Mission**	20
Nizza La Bella | **Albany/E**	20
nopa | **W Addition**	25
NEW Nopalito | **W Addition**	23
O Izakaya | **Japantown**	17
Oliveto Cafe | **Oakland/E**	24
One Market | **Embarcadero**	22
Orson | **SoMa**	18
Ottimista | **Cow Hollow**	19
Oxbow Wine | **Napa/N**	22
Oyaji | **Outer Rich**	23
Ozumo | **multi.**	24
Palio d'Asti | **Downtown**	20
Park Chalet | **Outer Sunset**	16
Z Perbacco | **Downtown**	25
NEW Picán | **Oakland/E**	–
Picco | **Larkspur/N**	26
Z Plumed Horse | **Saratoga/S**	25
Poleng | **W Addition**	19
Ponzu | **Downtown**	20
Presidio Social | **Presidio**	18
Prima | **Walnut Creek/E**	24
Ramblas | **Mission**	20
Range | **Mission**	26
Z Redd | **Yountville/N**	27
Red Lantern | **Redwood City/S**	19

Menus, photos, voting and more - free at ZAGAT.com

Rest. Cassis | **Pacific Hts**	22
Rest. LuLu/Petite | **SoMa**	21
Rist. Avanti | **Santa Cruz/S**	-
River Ranch | **Tahoe City/E**	15
NEW RN74 | **SoMa**	-
Rose Pistola | **N Beach**	22
Rose's Cafe | **Cow Hollow**	22
Rosso Pizzeria | **Santa Rosa/N**	25
Sardine Factory | **Monterey/S**	21
Sea Salt | **Berkeley/E**	22
Sens Rest. | **Downtown**	20
Serpentine | **Dogpatch**	21
Shanghai 1930 | **Embarcadero**	20
NEW Sidebar | **Oakland/E**	20
Sino | **San Jose/S**	19
Slow Club | **Mission**	22
South Food/Wine | **S Beach**	21
Sozai Rest. | **Inner Sunset**	18
Starlight | **Sebastopol/N**	22
Sunnyside | **Tahoe City/E**	18
Suppenküche | **Hayes Valley**	22
Sushi Groove | **Russian Hill**	21
Tamarine | **Palo Alto/S**	26
NEW Taverna Aventine | **Downtown**	-
NEW Tavern at Lark Creek | **Larkspur/N**	-
Terzo | **Cow Hollow**	23
1300/Fillmore | **W Addition**	22
NEW Tipsy Pig | **Marina**	21
Tokyo Go Go | **Mission**	21
Z Tonga | **Nob Hill**	13
Town Hall | **SoMa**	24
Townhouse B&G | **Emeryville/E**	21
Trader Vic's | **Emeryville/E**	17
Tra Vigne | **St. Helena/N**	24
Tres Agaves | **S Beach**	15
TusCA | **Monterey/S**	-
TWO | **SoMa**	19
2223 | **Castro**	23
Umami | **Cow Hollow**	22
Underwood Bar | **Graton/N**	24
NEW Urban Tavern | **Downtown**	17
Uva Enoteca | **Lower Haight**	20
Va de Vi | **Walnut Creek/E**	23
Vin Antico | **San Rafael/N**	23

Washington Sq. B&G | **N Beach**	-
Z Waterbar | **Embarcadero**	20
NEW Wexler's | **Downtown**	-
Willi's Seafood | **Healdsburg/N**	24
Will's Fargo | **Carmel Valley/S**	22
Wine Spectator | **St. Helena/N**	22
Wood Tavern | **Oakland/E**	25
Xanh | **Mtn View/S**	23
Yoshi's SF | **W Addition**	22
NEW Zaré/Fly Trap | **SoMa**	22
Zibibbo | **Palo Alto/S**	19
Zin | **Healdsburg/N**	23
NEW Zinnia | **Downtown**	23
Z Zuni Café | **Hayes Valley**	25
ZuZu | **Napa/N**	23

NATURAL/ ORGANIC/LOCAL

NEW Academy Cafe | **Inner Rich**	21
Acme Chophse. | **S Beach**	20
Adagia | **Berkeley/E**	18
Z ad hoc | **Yountville/N**	26
Ajanta | **Berkeley/E**	25
NEW AKA Bistro | **St. Helena/N**	21
Amanda's | **Berkeley/E**	18
NEW Aquarius | **Santa Cruz/S**	-
NEW Artisan Bistro | **Lafayette/E**	-
Aubergine | **Carmel/S**	25
AVA | **San Anselmo/N**	22
NEW Bardessono | **Yountville/N**	23
Bar Jules | **Hayes Valley**	24
Barndiva | **Healdsburg/N**	19
Bellanico | **Oakland/E**	23
Bistro/Copains | **Occidental/N**	25
Bistro Don Giovanni | **Napa/N**	23
Blue Barn Gourmet | **Marina**	22
Blue Plate | **Mission**	24
Z NEW Bottega | **Yountville/N**	25
Boulette's Larder | **Embarcadero**	25
Bovolo | **Healdsburg/N**	24
Breads of India | **multi.**	19
Brix | **Napa/N**	22
Butler & Chef | **SoMa**	20
Cafe Beaujolais | **Mendocino/N**	25
Z Cafe Gibraltar | **El Granada/S**	27
Café Gratitude | **multi.**	16
Cafe Saint Rose | **Sebastopol/N**	23

NEW Calafia | **Palo Alto/S**	21
Camino | **Oakland/E**	22
Z Cheese Board | **Berkeley/E**	26
Z Chez Panisse | **Berkeley/E**	28
Z Chez Panisse Café | **Berkeley/E**	27
Chez Shea | **Half Moon Bay/S**	23
Chow/Park Chow | **Inner Sunset**	21
Z Coi | **N Beach**	28
NEW Commis | **Oakland/E**	-
NEW Contigo | **Noe Valley**	19
Cool Café | **Palo Alto/S**	-
Cottage Eatery | **Tiburon/N**	23
Deetjen's | **Big Sur/S**	22
Z Delfina | **Mission**	26
Della Fattoria | **Petaluma/N**	24
Della Santina's | **Sonoma/N**	21
NEW Donato | **Redwood City/S**	-
Doña Tomás | **Oakland/E**	23
Dopo | **Oakland/E**	25
Dosa | **multi.**	23
Dragonfly | **Truckee/E**	22
Drake's | **Inverness/N**	21
Dry Creek | **Healdsburg/N**	24
NEW Elements | **Napa/N**	22
Eos Rest. | **Cole Valley**	23
EPIC | **Embarcadero**	20
Z Erna's Elderberry | **Oakhurst/E**	28
Z Étoile | **Yountville/N**	26
Eureka | **Castro**	20
Z Evvia | **Palo Alto/S**	26
Z Farallon | **Downtown**	24
Z Farm | **Napa/N**	24
farmerbrown/skillet | **multi.**	21
Z Farmhouse Inn | **Forestville/N**	26
1550 Hyde | **Russian Hill**	22
Fifth Floor | **SoMa**	25
fig cafe | **Glen Ellen/N**	24
Firefly | **Noe Valley**	25
Fish | **Sausalito/N**	23
Fish & Farm | **Downtown**	20
Flea St. Café | **Menlo Pk/S**	25
Z Fleur de Lys | **Downtown**	27
NEW Flour + Water | **Mission**	-
Foreign Cinema | **Mission**	23
Z French Laundry | **Yountville/N**	29
Gabriella Café | **Santa Cruz/S**	23

Garibaldis | **multi.**	22
Z Gary Danko | **Fish. Wharf**	29
Gialina | **Glen Pk**	24
Gioia Pizzeria | **Berkeley/E**	23
Globe | **Downtown**	20
Grasing's Coastal | **Carmel/S**	24
Green Chile | **W Addition**	20
Z Greens | **Marina**	24
Harmony Rest. | **Mill Valley/N**	22
Harvest Moon | **Sonoma/N**	24
Hayes St. Grill | **Hayes Valley**	23
NEW Heaven's Dog | **SoMa**	21
Herbivore | **multi.**	15
Imperial/Berkeley | **Embarcadero**	20
Incanto | **Noe Valley**	24
Insalata's | **San Anselmo/N**	25
Z Jardinière | **Civic Ctr**	26
Jimtown Store | **Healdsburg/N**	18
John Ash | **Santa Rosa/N**	24
Junnoon | **Palo Alto/S**	23
Kiji Sushi Bar | **Mission**	23
La Ciccia | **Noe Valley**	24
Z La Folie | **Russian Hill**	28
Laïola | **Marina**	20
Lalime's | **Berkeley/E**	26
Lark Creek | **Walnut Creek/E**	21
Las Camelias | **San Rafael/N**	18
Z La Toque | **Napa/N**	26
Ledford Hse. | **Albion/N**	25
Local Kitchen | **SoMa**	20
Lotus/Anokha | **San Rafael/N**	25
Luella | **Russian Hill**	22
MacCallum Hse. | **Mendocino/N**	21
NEW Madera | **Menlo Pk/S**	-
Z Madrona | **Healdsburg/N**	26
Magnolia | **Haight-Ashbury**	18
Z Manresa | **Los Gatos/S**	27
Marché | **Menlo Pk/S**	25
Marché aux Fleurs | **Ross/N**	25
NEW Marinitas | **San Anselmo/N**	21
Z Marinus | **Carmel Valley/S**	27
MarketBar | **Embarcadero**	16
Martini House | **St. Helena/N**	26
NEW Martins West | **Redwood City/S**	-
NEW Marzano | **Oakland/E**	23

Menus, photos, voting and more - free at ZAGAT.com

Restaurant	Rating
Z Masa's | **Downtown**	28
Maverick | **Mission**	24
Meadowood Grill | **St. Helena/N**	22
Z Meadowood Rest. | **St. Helena/N**	26
Mendo Bistro | **Ft Bragg/N**	24
NEW Midi | **Downtown**	-
Millennium | **Downtown**	25
Mixt Greens | **Downtown**	22
Montrio Bistro | **Monterey/S**	21
Mosaic | **Forestville/N**	26
NEW Moss Room | **Inner Rich**	21
Z Navio | **Half Moon Bay/S**	24
Nick's Cove | **Marshall/N**	21
Nick's Tacos | **Russian Hill**	22
nopa | **W Addition**	25
NEW Nopalito | **W Addition**	23
O Chamé | **Berkeley/E**	24
Olema Inn | **Olema/N**	22
Oliveto Cafe | **Oakland/E**	24
Oliveto Restaurant | **Oakland/E**	25
One Market | **Embarcadero**	22
Oola | **SoMa**	20
NEW Osteria Stellina | **Pt Reyes/N**	-
Pacific Catch | **Marina**	20
Z Pacific's Edge | **Carmel/S**	25
Parcel 104 | **Santa Clara/S**	23
Z Passionfish | **Pacific Grove/S**	26
Pauline's Pizza | **Mission**	23
Pearl | **Napa/N**	23
Peter Lowell's | **Sebastopol/N**	22
Piccino | **Dogpatch**	24
Picco | **Larkspur/N**	26
Pine Cone Diner | **Pt Reyes/N**	20
Pizza Antica | **Lafayette/E**	21
Pizzaiolo | **Oakland/E**	25
NEW Pizzavino | **Sebastopol/N**	-
Pizzeria Picco | **Larkspur/N**	25
Pizzeria Tra Vigne | **St. Helena/N**	21
Pizzetta 211 | **Outer Rich**	25
Plant Cafe | **Marina**	20
Press | **St. Helena/N**	23
Z Quince | **Downtown**	27
Range | **Mission**	26
Ravenous Cafe | **Healdsburg/N**	22
Ravens Rest. | **Mendocino/N**	22
Regalito Rosticeria | **Mission**	21
Rendezvous Inn | **Ft Bragg/N**	25
Rest. at Stevenswood | **Little River/N**	26
NEW Restaurant Eloise | **Sebastopol/N**	-
Richmond Rest. | **Inner Rich**	26
Rist. Avanti | **Santa Cruz/S**	-
Z Ritz-Carlton Din. Rm. | **Nob Hill**	27
Z Rivoli | **Berkeley/E**	27
rnm rest. | **Lower Haight**	23
Rocker Oysterfellers | **Valley Ford/Nt**	21
Osake/Sake 'O | **Healdsburg/N**	23
Santi | **Geyserville/N**	25
Sebo | **Hayes Valley**	25
Serpentine | **Dogpatch**	21
Z Sierra Mar | **Big Sur/S**	27
Z Slanted Door | **Embarcadero**	26
Slow Club | **Mission**	22
Soizic | **Oakland/E**	24
Sol Food | **San Rafael/N**	23
SPQR | **Pacific Hts**	23
Z Spruce | **Presidio Hts**	25
St. Orres | **Gualala/N**	22
Z Sutro's | **Outer Rich**	21
Syrah | **Santa Rosa/N**	25
Table Café | **Larkspur/N**	-
Tacubaya | **Berkeley/E**	24
Tamarine | **Palo Alto/S**	26
Z Tartine | **Mission**	27
NEW Tavern at Lark Creek | **Larkspur/N**	-
Terzo | **Cow Hollow**	23
NEW Tipsy Pig | **Marina**	21
Town Hall | **SoMa**	24
NEW Trademark Grill | **Downtown**	-
Tra Vigne | **St. Helena/N**	24
Trevese | **Los Gatos/S**	23
T Rex BBQ | **Berkeley/E**	18
Twist | **Campbell/S**	22
TWO | **SoMa**	19
2223 | **Castro**	23
Z Ubuntu | **Napa/N**	26
Underdog | **Inner Sunset**	20

SPECIAL FEATURES

Underwood Bar | **Graton/N**	24
Village Pub | **Woodside/S**	26
Viognier | **San Mateo/S**	23
Warming Hut | **Presidio**	15
Water St. Bistro | **Petaluma/N**	23
Weird Fish | **Mission**	21
Wente Vineyards | **Livermore/E**	23
NEW Wexler's | **Downtown**	-)
Willi's Seafood | **Healdsburg/N**	24
Willi's Wine | **Santa Rosa/N**	26
Wine Spectator | **St. Helena/N**	22
Z Wolfdale's | **Tahoe City/E**	27
Woodward's Gdn. | **Mission**	25
Yankee Pier | **San Jose/S**	17
NEW Zaré/Fly Trap | **SoMa**	22
Zatar | **Berkeley/E**	22
zazu | **Santa Rosa/N**	25
Zin | **Healdsburg/N**	23
NEW Zinnia | **Downtown**	23
Z Zuni Café | **Hayes Valley**	25

NOTEWORTHY NEWCOMERS

Academy Cafe | **Inner Rich**	21
Adesso | **Oakland/E**	-)
AKA Bistro | **St. Helena/N**	21
Aquarius | **Santa Cruz/S**	-)
Artisan Bistro | **Lafayette/E**	-)
Aurea | **Nob Hill**	-)
Baby Blues BBQ | **Mission**	21
Bardessono | **Yountville/N**	23
Barlata | **Oakland/E**	-)
Basil Canteen | **SoMa**	21
Bistro St. Germain | **Lower Haight**	-)
Bistro 24 | **Noe Valley**	-)
Z Bottega | **Yountville/N**	25
Calafia | **Palo Alto/S**	21
Chevalier | **Lafayette/E**	-)
Commis | **Oakland/E**	-)
Contigo | **Noe Valley**	19
Corner | **Mission**	-)
Donato | **Redwood City/S**	-)
Dreamfarm | **San Anselmo/N**	-)
Elements | **Napa/N**	22
Estate | **Sonoma/N**	20
54 Mint | **SoMa**	-)
Five | **Berkeley/E**	-)

Flour + Water | **Mission**	-)
Z Gitane | **Downtown**	22
Heaven's Dog | **SoMa**	21
Horatius | **Potrero Hill**	-)
Il Cane Rosso | **Embarcadero**	-)
Joya | **Palo Alto/S**	18
Lake Chalet | **Oakland/E**	-)
Lalola Bar | **Russian Hill**	21
La Mar | **Embarcadero**	23
LB Steak | **San Jose/S**	-)
Let's Be Frank | **Marina**	-)
Madera | **Menlo Pk/S**	-)
Marinitas | **San Anselmo/N**	21
Martins West | **Redwood City/S**	-)
Marzano | **Oakland/E**	23
Mayfield | **Palo Alto/S**	19
Metro Café | **W Addition**	-)
Midi | **Downtown**	-)
Miss Pearl's | **Oakland/E**	17
Moss Room | **Inner Rich**	21
Nettie's | **Cow Hollow**	20
Nopalito | **W Addition**	23
Osteria Stellina | **Pt Reyes/N**	-)
Penelope | **Oakland/E**	-)
Phat Philly | **Mission**	20
Picán | **Oakland/E**	-)
Pickles | **Downtown**	-)
Pizza Nostra | **Potrero Hill**	-)
Pizzavino | **Sebastopol/N**	-)
Restaurant Eloise | **Sebastopol/N**	-)
RN74 | **SoMa**	-)
Saison | **Mission**	-)
Sakoon | **Mtn View/S**	-)
Schmidt's | **Mission**	-)
Scopa | **Healdsburg/N**	24
Showdogs | **Downtown**	-)
Sidebar | **Oakland/E**	20
Taverna Aventine | **Downtown**	-)
Tavern at Lark Creek | **Larkspur/N**	-)
Tipsy Pig | **Marina**	21
Tony's Pizza | **N Beach**	-)
Trademark Grill | **Downtown**	-)
Urban Tavern | **Downtown**	17
Wexler's | **Downtown**	-)
Zaré/Fly Trap | **SoMa**	22
Zinnia | **Downtown**	23

OFFBEAT

Ace Wasabi's | **Marina**	21
Albona Rist. | **N Beach**	24
AsiaSF | **SoMa**	17
Avatar's | **Sausalito/N**	25
Bambuddha | **Tenderloin**	17
Basque Cultural | **S San Francisco/S**	22
Blowfish Sushi | **Mission**	20
Boogaloos | **Mission**	20
Brenda's | **Civic Ctr**	24
Buca di Beppo | **multi.**	14
Café Gratitude | **multi.**	16
Caffè Macaroni | **N Beach**	20
Candybar | **W Addition**	17
Casa Orinda | **Orinda/E**	18
Caspers Hot Dogs | **multi.**	18
Cha Cha Cha | **multi.**	20
Cha-Ya Veg. | **multi.**	22
Destino | **Castro**	22
Don Pico's | **San Bruno/S**	23
Duarte's Tavern | **Pescadero/S**	21
E&O Trading | **Larkspur/N**	19
Fish | **Sausalito/N**	23
Flying Fish | **Carmel/S**	24
Forbes Island | **Fish. Wharf**	19
Home of Chicken | **Oakland/E**	20
Jimtown Store | **Healdsburg/N**	18
Joe's Cable Car | **Excelsior**	21
Kan Zaman | **Haight-Ashbury**	17
Katia's Tea | **Inner Rich**	23
Loló | **Mission**	22
Lovejoy's Tea | **Noe Valley**	21
Matterhorn Swiss | **Russian Hill**	23
Maykadeh | **N Beach**	26
Millennium | **Downtown**	25
Nick's Tacos | **Russian Hill**	22
Orson | **SoMa**	18
Oyaji | **Outer Rich**	23
Puerto Alegre | **Mission**	18
Ravens Rest. | **Mendocino/N**	22
Red's Java | **Embarcadero**	16
Sol Food | **San Rafael/N**	23
St. Orres | **Gualala/N**	22
supperclub | **SoMa**	15
Thai Buddhist | **Berkeley/E**	19
Ⓩ Tonga | **Nob Hill**	13
Trader Vic's | **Emeryville/E**	17
Uncle Frank's | **Mtn View/S**	20
Venezia | **Berkeley/E**	18
Zante | **Bernal Hts**	20

OUTDOOR DINING

(G=garden; P=patio; S=sidewalk; T=terrace; W=waterside)

Ⓩ Absinthe | S | **Hayes Valley**	22
À Côté | P | **Oakland/E**	24
Adagia | P | **Berkeley/E**	18
Alexis Baking | S | **Napa/N**	22
Angèle | P, W | **Napa/N**	22
Anton & Michel | G, P | **Carmel/S**	23
Aperto | S | **Potrero Hill**	23
Ⓩ Applewood Inn | G, T | **Guerneville/N**	27
Ⓩ Auberge du Sol. | T | **Rutherford/N**	26
Baker St. Bistro | S | **Marina**	21
Bambuddha | P, W | **Tenderloin**	17
Barbara's Fish Trap | P, S, W | **Princeton Sea/S**	20
Barndiva | G, P | **Healdsburg/N**	19
Barney's | P | **multi.**	19
Basin | P | **Saratoga/S**	21
Beach Chalet | W | **Outer Sunset**	15
Betelnut Pejiu | S | **Cow Hollow**	22
B44 | S | **Downtown**	21
Bistro Boudin | P, W | **Fish. Wharf**	19
Bistro Don Giovanni | P, T | **Napa/N**	23
Bistro Elan | P | **Palo Alto/S**	24
Ⓩ Bistro Jeanty | P | **Yountville/N**	25
Bistro Liaison | P | **Berkeley/E**	22
Bistro Vida | S | **Menlo Pk/S**	18
Blackhawk Grille | P, T, W | **Danville/E**	19
Blue Bottle | P | **SoMa**	23
Blue Plate | G, P | **Mission**	24
Boca | P | **Novato/N**	22
Bo's Barbecue | T | **Lafayette/E**	23
Ⓩ Bouchon | P | **Yountville/N**	26
Bridges | P | **Danville/E**	22
Brindisi | S | **Downtown**	18
Bucci's | P | **Emeryville/E**	21

Z Buckeye Rdhse. | P | Mill Valley/N — 23

Bungalow 44 | P | Mill Valley/N — 21

Cactus Taqueria | S | Oakland/E — 21

Cafe Bastille | S, T | Downtown — 18

Cafe Citti | P | Kenwood/N — 22

Café Claude | S | Downtown — 21

Café Fanny | P | Berkeley/E — 23

Café Rouge | P | Berkeley/E — 22

Café Tiramisu | S | Downtown — 20

Caffè Museo | S | SoMa — 18

Casanova | P | Carmel/S — 23

Cascal | P | Mtn View/S — 20

Catch | P, S | Castro — 18

Celadon | P | Napa/N — 24

César | P | Berkeley/E — 22

Charanga | P | Mission — 21

Chaya | P, S | Embarcadero — 22

Cheesecake | P, T | Downtown — 16

Chez Maman | S | Potrero Hill — 22

Chez Papa | S | Potrero Hill — 23

Chez Spencer | G, P | Mission — 26

Chez TJ | P | Mtn View/S — 23

Chloe's Cafe | S | Noe Valley — 23

Chow/Park Chow | P, S, T | multi. — 21

Cindy's | P | St. Helena/N — 24

Citron | P | Oakland/E — 23

Club XIX | P, W | Pebble Bch/S — 23

Cole's Chop Hse. | T, W | Napa/N — 24

Cool Café | P | Palo Alto/S — -

Côté Sud | P | Castro — 19

Delancey St. | P, S | Embarcadero — 17

Z Delfina | P | Mission — 26

Della Santina's | G, P | Sonoma/N — 21

Doña Tomás | G, P | Oakland/E — 23

Dopo | S | Oakland/E — 25

Dry Creek | S | Healdsburg/N — 24

Ducca | P | SoMa — 20

Duck Club | P | Menlo Pk/S — 19

El Dorado | P, W | Sonoma/N — 24

Z El Paseo | P | Mill Valley/N — 26

Emporio Rulli | P, S | multi. — 22

Enrico's | P | N Beach — 16

EPIC | P | Embarcadero — 20

Z Étoile | P, T | Yountville/N — 26

Everett & Jones | P, S | multi. — 20

Fentons Creamery | P | Oakland/E — 19

Fish | T, W | Sausalito/N — 23

Flavor | P | Santa Rosa/N — 19

Flea St. Café | P | Menlo Pk/S — 25

Fog City Diner | S | Embarcadero — 19

Fonda Solana | S | Albany/E — 23

Foreign Cinema | P | Mission — 23

Frantoio | G, P | Mill Valley/N — 21

Fumé Bistro | P | Napa/N — 22

Gabriella Café | P | Santa Cruz/S — 23

Gayle's Bakery | P | Capitola/S — 25

girl & the fig | P | Sonoma/N — 24

Grasing's Coastal | P | Carmel/S — 24

grégoire | S | Berkeley/E — 22

Guaymas | P, T, W | Tiburon/N — 16

Hog Island Oyster | P, W | Embarcadero — 25

Home | P | Castro — 18

Hurley's | P | Yountville/N — 21

Iberia | P | Menlo Pk/S — 21

Il Davide | P | San Rafael/N — 21

Il Fornaio | P | multi. — 19

Isa | P | Marina — 24

Jimmy Bean's | S | Berkeley/E — 19

Jimtown Store | P | Healdsburg/N — 18

John Ash | P | Santa Rosa/N — 24

Kenwood | G | Kenwood/N — 23

La Boulange | S | multi. — 22

NEW Lake Chalet | T, W | Oakland/E — -

La Note | P | Berkeley/E — 21

Lark Creek | P | Walnut Creek/E — 21

LaSalette | P | Sonoma/N — 25

La Strada | T | Palo Alto/S — 21

Le Charm Bistro | P | SoMa — 22

Le Colonial | P | Downtown — 22

Left Bank | P, S | multi. — 18

Le Zinc | G | Noe Valley — 19

Lion & Compass | P | Sunnyvale/S — 20

MacCallum Hse. | T | Mendocino/N — 21

Z Madrona | T | Healdsburg/N — 26

Marché aux Fleurs | P | Ross/N — 25

MarketBar | P | Embarcadero — 16

Martini House | P | St. Helena/N — 26

Meadowood Grill | T | St. Helena/N — 22

Ⓩ Meadowood Rest. | T | St. Helena/N 26

Medjool | P | **Mission** 18

Meritage Martini | G, P | Sonoma/N 20

Mezze | S | **Oakland/E** 20

Mistral | P, W | Redwood Shores/S 18

MoMo's | T | **S Beach** 17

Monti's | P | **Santa Rosa/N** 21

Moosse Café | T, W | Mendocino/N 24

Mo's | P | **SoMa** 20

Murray Circle | P | **Sausalito/N** 24

Napa General | T, W | **Napa/N** 20

Napa Valley Grille | P | Yountville/N 21

Nepenthe | P, W | **Big Sur/S** 17

Nizza La Bella | S | **Albany/E** 20

O Chamé | P | **Berkeley/E** 24

Olema Inn | P | **Olema/N** 22

Oliveto Cafe | S | **Oakland/E** 24

Parcel 104 | P | **Santa Clara/S** 23

Park Chalet | G, W | **Outer Sunset** 16

Pasta Moon | P | **Half Moon Bay/S** 23

Pazzia | P | **SoMa** 23

Piatti | P, W | **multi.** 18

Piazza D'Angelo | P | **Mill Valley/N** 20

Picante Cocina | P | **Berkeley/E** 21

Piperade | P | **Downtown** 25

Pizza Antica | P | **multi.** 21

Pizzeria Tra Vigne | P | St. Helena/N 21

Pizzetta 211 | S | **Outer Rich** 25

Plouf | T | **Downtown** 22

PlumpJack | P | **Olympic Valley/E** 23

Poggio | S | **Sausalito/N** 22

Postino | P | **Lafayette/E** 23

Press | P | **St. Helena/N** 23

Prima | P | **Walnut Creek/E** 24

Ravenous Cafe | P | **Healdsburg/N** 22

Red's Java | P, W | **Embarcadero** 16

Rick & Ann's | P | **Berkeley/E** 21

Rose Pistola | S | **N Beach** 22

Rose's Cafe | S | **Cow Hollow** 22

Ⓩ Roy's | P | **Pebble Bch/S** 25

Rutherford Grill | P | **Rutherford/N** 24

Sam's Chowder | P | Half Moon Bay/S 20

Santi | P | **Geyserville/N** 25

Savor | P | **Noe Valley** 18

Scoma's | P, W | **Sausalito/N** 22

Sea Salt | P | **Berkeley/E** 22

71 Saint Peter | P | **San Jose/S** 22

Ⓩ Sierra Mar | T, W | **Big Sur/S** 27

Slow Club | S | **Mission** 22

Sociale | G, P | **Presidio Hts** 24

South Park | S | **SoMa** 23

Straits | P | **multi.** 19

Ⓩ Sushi Ran | P | **Sausalito/N** 28

Tarpy's | P | **Monterey/S** 20

Ⓩ Tartine | S | **Mission** 27

Taylor's Auto | G, P | **multi.** 22

Ti Couz | S | **Mission** 23

Townhouse B&G | P | Emeryville/E 21

Town's End | P | **Embarcadero** 20

Trader Vic's | T | **Palo Alto/S** 17

Tra Vigne | G, T | **St. Helena/N** 24

Trevese | P | **Los Gatos/S** 23

Underwood Bar | P | **Graton/N** 24

Universal Cafe | P | **Mission** 23

Va de Vi | S, T | **Walnut Creek/E** 23

Ⓩ Waterbar | P, W | **Embarcadero** 20

Waterfront | P, W | **Embarcadero** 18

Water St. Bistro | P, W | Petaluma/N 23

Wente Vineyards | P | Livermore/E 23

Willi's Seafood | P | **Healdsburg/N** 24

Willi's Wine | P | **Santa Rosa/N** 26

Wine Spectator | T | **St. Helena/N** 22

Yankee Pier | P, T | **multi.** 17

Yumma's | G | **Inner Sunset** 21

Zazie | G | **Cole Valley** 22

Zibibbo | G, P | **Palo Alto/S** 19

Zinsvalley | P | **Napa/N** 19

Zucca | P | **Mtn View/S** 18

Ⓩ Zuni Café | S | **Hayes Valley** 25

PEOPLE-WATCHING

Ⓩ Absinthe | **Hayes Valley** 22

Ace Wasabi's | **Marina** 21

À Côté | **Oakland/E** 24

Ana Mandara | **Fish. Wharf**	22
Anchor & Hope | **SoMa**	21
Asia de Cuba | **Downtown**	20
AsiaSF | **SoMa**	17
Balboa Cafe | **multi.**	19
Bambuddha | **Tenderloin**	17
NEW Barlata | **Oakland/E**	–
Barndiva | **Healdsburg/N**	19
Bar Tartine | **Mission**	24
Belden Taverna | **Downtown**	18
Beretta | **Mission**	23
Betelnut Pejiu | **Cow Hollow**	22
Bing Crosby's | **Walnut Creek/E**	19
Bin 38 | **Marina**	19
Bistro Don Giovanni | **Napa/N**	23
Z Bistro Jeanty | **Yountville/N**	25
NEW Bistro St. Germain | **Lower Haight**	–
Z BIX | **Downtown**	23
Blowfish Sushi | **Mission**	20
Blue Bottle | **SoMa**	23
Boogaloos | **Mission**	20
Z NEW Bottega | **Yountville/N**	25
Z Bouchon | **Yountville/N**	26
Z Boulevard | **Embarcadero**	27
Bridgetender | **Tahoe City/E**	19
Brix | **Napa/N**	22
Bungalow 44 | **Mill Valley/N**	21
Cafe Bastille | **Downtown**	18
Café Claude | **Downtown**	21
Café de la Presse | **Downtown**	18
Café Flore | **Castro**	15
Candybar | **W Addition**	17
Cascal | **Mtn View/S**	20
Catch | **Castro**	18
Cav Wine Bar | **Hayes Valley**	20
Central Market | **Petaluma/N**	24
César | **Berkeley/E**	22
Cha Cha Cha | **multi.**	20
Chaya | **Embarcadero**	22
Z Chez Panisse Café | **Berkeley/E**	27
Chez Papa | **SoMa**	23
Cin-Cin Wine | **Los Gatos/S**	23
Circa | **Marina**	18
Conduit | **Mission**	22
Cottonwood | **Truckee/E**	21
Dio Deka | **Los Gatos/S**	25
District | **SoMa**	18
NEW Donato | **Redwood City/S**	–
Dosa | **multi.**	23
downtown | **Berkeley/E**	19
Downtown Bakery | **Healdsburg/N**	25
Dragonfly | **Truckee/E**	22
Ducca | **SoMa**	20
E&O Trading | **Larkspur/N**	19
NEW Elements | **Napa/N**	22
Enrico's | **N Beach**	16
EPIC | **Embarcadero**	20
Estéban | **Monterey/S**	–
Z Evvia | **Palo Alto/S**	26
Farina | **Mission**	23
NEW 54 Mint | **SoMa**	–
Fish & Farm | **Downtown**	20
NEW Five | **Berkeley/E**	–
5A5 Steak Lounge | **Downtown**	–
Flea St. Café | **Menlo Pk/S**	25
Flora | **Oakland/E**	23
NEW Flour + Water | **Mission**	–
Folio Enoteca | **Napa/N**	16
Foreign Cinema | **Mission**	23
Frjtz Fries | **multi.**	18
Front Porch | **Bernal Hts**	22
Gar Woods | **Carnelian Bay/E**	17
Z NEW Gitane | **Downtown**	22
Grand Pu Bah | **Potrero Hill**	18
NEW Heaven's Dog | **SoMa**	21
Hog Island Oyster | **Napa/N**	25
Hopmonk Tav. | **Sebastopol/N**	17
Jake's/Lake | **Tahoe City/E**	16
Z Jardinière | **Civic Ctr**	26
Joey & Eddie's | **N Beach**	14
NEW Joya | **Palo Alto/S**	18
Junnoon | **Palo Alto/S**	23
Laïola | **Marina**	20
NEW La Mar | **Embarcadero**	23
NEW LB Steak | **San Jose/S**	–
Le Club | **Nob Hill**	15
Left Bank | **Larkspur/N**	18
Level III | **Downtown**	18
Lime | **Castro**	17
Local Kitchen | **SoMa**	20

Luce | **SoMa**	20
Lure | **San Mateo/S**	20
Magnolia | **Haight-Ashbury**	18
Mamacita | **Marina**	23
NEW Marinitas | **San Anselmo/N**	21
Mario's Bohemian | **N Beach**	18
MarketBar | **Embarcadero**	16
Martini House | **St. Helena/N**	26
NEW Martins West | **Redwood City/S**	-
Maverick | **Mission**	24
NEW Mayfield | **Palo Alto/S**	19
Medjool | **Mission**	18
Mexico DF | **Embarcadero**	20
NEW Midi | **Downtown**	-
Mijita | **Embarcadero**	20
NEW Miss Pearl's | **Oakland/E**	17
Moody's Bistro | **Truckee/E**	25
Z Mustards | **Yountville/N**	25
Nectar Wine | **multi.**	18
NEW Nettie's | **Cow Hollow**	20
Nick's on Main | **Los Gatos/S**	25
Nihon | **Mission**	20
nopa | **W Addition**	25
Oliveto Cafe | **Oakland/E**	24
Orson | **SoMa**	18
Ottimista | **Cow Hollow**	19
Ozumo | **Oakland/E**	24
Pampas | **Palo Alto/S**	21
NEW Picán | **Oakland/E**	-
Picco | **Larkspur/N**	26
Z Plumed Horse | **Saratoga/S**	25
Poesia | **Castro**	20
Poggio | **Sausalito/N**	22
Postino | **Lafayette/E**	23
Quattro | **E Palo Alto/S**	21
Z Redd | **Yountville/N**	27
Red Lantern | **Redwood City/S**	19
Rest. LuLu/Petite | **SoMa**	21
River Ranch | **Tahoe City/E**	15
NEW RN74 | **SoMa**	-
Rose Pistola | **N Beach**	22
Rose's Cafe | **Cow Hollow**	22
Scala's Bistro | **Downtown**	21
Sens Rest. | **Downtown**	20
Serpentine | **Dogpatch**	21

NEW Sidebar | **Oakland/E**	20
Sino | **San Jose/S**	19
South Food/Wine | **S Beach**	21
SPQR | **Pacific Hts**	23
Starlight | **Sebastopol/N**	22
Sunnyside | **Tahoe City/E**	18
supperclub | **SoMa**	15
Sushi Groove | **multi.**	21
Tamarine | **Palo Alto/S**	26
NEW Taverna Aventine | **Downtown**	-
Taylor's Auto | **Napa/N**	22
NEW Tipsy Pig | **Marina**	21
Tokyo Go Go | **Mission**	21
Town Hall | **SoMa**	24
Tra Vigne | **St. Helena/N**	24
Tres Agaves | **S Beach**	15
Tsunami | **W Addition**	22
2223 | **Castro**	23
Umami | **Cow Hollow**	22
NEW Urban Tavern | **Downtown**	17
Uva Enoteca | **Lower Haight**	20
Va de Vi | **Walnut Creek/E**	23
Village Pub | **Woodside/S**	26
Viognier | **San Mateo/S**	23
Z Waterbar | **Embarcadero**	20
Wood Tavern | **Oakland/E**	25
Xanh | **Mtn View/S**	23
Yoshi's SF | **W Addition**	22
NEW Zaré/Fly Trap | **SoMa**	22
Zibibbo | **Palo Alto/S**	19
NEW Zinnia | **Downtown**	23
Z Zuni Café | **Hayes Valley**	25
Zuppa | **SoMa**	19

POWER SCENES

Alexander's | **Cupertino/S**	25
Ana Mandara | **Fish. Wharf**	22
Z Aqua | **Downtown**	26
Arcadia | **San Jose/S**	21
Asia de Cuba | **Downtown**	20
Z Auberge du Sol. | **Rutherford/N**	26
bacar | **SoMa**	23
Balboa Cafe | **Mill Valley/N**	19
Z Big 4 | **Nob Hill**	22
Blackhawk Grille | **Danville/E**	19

Bouchon	**Yountville/N**	26
Boulevard	**Embarcadero**	27
Chaya	**Embarcadero**	22
Chef Chu's	**Los Altos/S**	22
Citronelle	**Carmel/S**	24
Dio Deka	**Los Gatos/S**	25
downtown	**Berkeley/E**	19
EPIC	**Embarcadero**	20
Evvia	**Palo Alto/S**	26
Fifth Floor	**SoMa**	25
Fleur de Lys	**Downtown**	27
Forbes Mill Steak	**multi.**	22
Gary Danko	**Fish. Wharf**	29
Il Fornaio	**Palo Alto/S**	19
Jardinière	**Civic Ctr**	26
Kokkari	**Downtown**	27
Le Central Bistro	**Downtown**	20
Le Colonial	**Downtown**	22
Lion & Compass	**Sunnyvale/S**	20
Martini House	**St. Helena/N**	26
NEW Martins West	**Redwood City/S**	-
Masa's	**Downtown**	28
Michael Mina	**Downtown**	27
NEW Midi	**Downtown**	-
Mistral	**Redwood Shores/S**	18
Morton's	**multi.**	24
One Market	**Embarcadero**	22
Ottimista	**Cow Hollow**	19
Ozumo	**Embarcadero**	24
Parcel 104	**Santa Clara/S**	23
Perbacco	**Downtown**	25
Plumed Horse	**Saratoga/S**	25
Press	**St. Helena/N**	23
Quattro	**E Palo Alto/S**	21
Redd	**Yountville/N**	27
Ritz-Carlton Din. Rm.	**Nob Hill**	27
NEW RN74	**SoMa**	-
Sam's Grill	**Downtown**	22
Seasons	**Downtown**	26
Sens Rest.	**Downtown**	20
Silks	**Downtown**	24
Spruce	**Presidio Hts**	25
Tadich Grill	**Downtown**	23
Tommy Toy's	**Downtown**	23
Town Hall	**SoMa**	24

NEW Urban Tavern	**Downtown**	17
Village Pub	**Woodside/S**	26
Viognier	**San Mateo/S**	23
Waterbar	**Embarcadero**	20
NEW Zinnia	**Downtown**	23
Zuni Café	**Hayes Valley**	25

PRE-THEATER DINING

(Call for prices and times)

ANZU	**Downtown**	22
Indigo	**Civic Ctr**	19
La Scene	**Downtown**	18
Michael Mina	**Downtown**	27
NEW Urban Tavern	**Downtown**	17
Venus	**Berkeley/E**	23

PRIVATE ROOMS

(Restaurants charge less at off times; call for capacity)

Absinthe	**Hayes Valley**	22
Acme Chophse.	**S Beach**	20
À Côté	**Oakland/E**	24
Acquerello	**Polk Gulch**	28
Adagia	**Berkeley/E**	18
Alegrias	**Marina**	21
Alexander's	**Cupertino/S**	25
Alfred's Steak	**Downtown**	22
Ana Mandara	**Fish. Wharf**	22
Andalu	**Mission**	21
Angèle	**Napa/N**	22
Anton & Michel	**Carmel/S**	23
Arcadia	**San Jose/S**	21
Auberge du Sol.	**Rutherford/N**	26
Aubergine	**Carmel/S**	25
Aziza	**Outer Rich**	26
bacar	**SoMa**	23
Barndiva	**Healdsburg/N**	19
Basin	**Saratoga/S**	21
BayWolf	**Oakland/E**	25
Bella Vista	**Woodside/S**	19
Betelnut Pejiu	**Cow Hollow**	22
Big 4	**Nob Hill**	22
Bing Crosby's	**Walnut Creek/E**	19
Bistro Liaison	**Berkeley/E**	22
Blackhawk Grille	**Danville/E**	19
Blue Plate	**Mission**	24
Boca	**Novato/N**	22

Boonville Hotel | **Boonville/N**	22	Hurley's | **Yountville/N**	21
Boulette's Larder | **Embarcadero**	25	Iberia | **Menlo Pk/S**	21
Z Boulevard | **Embarcadero**	27	Il Fornaio | **multi.**	19
Buca di Beppo | **multi.**	14	Incanto | **Noe Valley**	24
Z Buckeye Rdhse. | **Mill Valley/N**	23	Indigo | **Civic Ctr**	19
CAFÉ KATi | **Japantown**	21	Insalata's | **San Anselmo/N**	25
Café Rouge | **Berkeley/E**	22	**Z** Jardinière | **Civic Ctr**	26
Campton Place | **Downtown**	24	John Bentley's | **multi.**	25
Caprice | **Tiburon/N**	21	Kenwood | **Kenwood/N**	23
Carnelian Room | **Downtown**	18	Khan Toke | **Outer Rich**	22
Carneros Bistro | **Sonoma/N**	23	**Z** Kokkari | **Downtown**	27
Casanova | **Carmel/S**	23	Kurt's Carmel | **Carmel/S**	23
Cetrella | **Half Moon Bay/S**	20	**Z** La Folie | **Russian Hill**	28
Cha Cha Cha | **Mission**	20	**Z** La Forêt | **San Jose/S**	26
Z Chantilly | **Redwood City/S**	23	Lalime's | **Berkeley/E**	26
Chaya | **Embarcadero**	22	La Strada | **Palo Alto/S**	21
Chez TJ | **Mtn View/S**	23	Lavanda | **Palo Alto/S**	20
Cindy's | **St. Helena/N**	24	Le Colonial | **Downtown**	22
Citron | **Oakland/E**	23	Left Bank | **multi.**	18
Citronelle | **Carmel/S**	24	**Z** Le Papillon | **San Jose/S**	27
Club XIX | **Pebble Bch/S**	23	Lion & Compass | **Sunnyvale/S**	20
Cosmopolitan | **SoMa**	19	Little River Inn | **Little River/N**	21
Z Cyrus | **Healdsburg/N**	29	MacCallum Hse. | **Mendocino/N**	21
downtown | **Berkeley/E**	19	**Z** Madrona | **Healdsburg/N**	26
Dry Creek | **Healdsburg/N**	24	**Z** Manresa | **Los Gatos/S**	27
Z El Paseo | **Mill Valley/N**	26	Manzanita | **Healdsburg/N**	19
Emile's | **San Jose/S**	22	Marché | **Menlo Pk/S**	25
Eos Rest. | **Cole Valley**	23	**Z** Marinus | **Carmel Valley/S**	27
Z Erna's Elderberry | **Oakhurst/E**	28	Martini House | **St. Helena/N**	26
Eulipia | **San Jose/S**	24	**Z** Masa's | **Downtown**	28
Fandango | **Pacific Grove/S**	23	Maya | **SoMa**	21
Z Farallon | **Downtown**	24	Millennium | **Downtown**	25
Fifth Floor | **SoMa**	25	Montrio Bistro | **Monterey/S**	21
Flea St. Café | **Menlo Pk/S**	25	Morton's | **Downtown**	24
Z Fleur de Lys | **Downtown**	27	**NEW** Moss Room | **Inner Rich**	21
Florio | **Pacific Hts**	21	**Z** Navio | **Half Moon Bay/S**	24
Foreign Cinema | **Mission**	23	North Beach Rest. | **N Beach**	22
Frantoio | **Mill Valley/N**	21	Olema Inn | **Olema/N**	22
Z French Laundry | **Yountville/N**	29	One Market | **Embarcadero**	22
Garibaldis | **Oakland/E**	22	Orson | **SoMa**	18
Gary Chu's | **Santa Rosa/N**	20	Ozumo | **Embarcadero**	24
Z Gary Danko | **Fish. Wharf**	29	**Z** Pacific's Edge | **Carmel/S**	25
girl & the fig | **Sonoma/N**	24	Palio d'Asti | **Downtown**	20
Grand Cafe | **Downtown**	19	Parcel 104 | **Santa Clara/S**	23
Grasing's Coastal | **Carmel/S**	24	**Z** Passionfish | **Pacific Grove/S**	26
Harris' | **Polk Gulch**	25	Pauline's Pizza | **Mission**	23

SPECIAL FEATURES

ⓏPerbacco | **Downtown**	25
Pesce | **Russian Hill**	24
Piatti | **multi.**	18
Piazza D'Angelo | **Mill Valley/N**	20
ⓏPlumed Horse | **Saratoga/S**	25
PlumpJack | **Olympic Valley/E**	23
Poggio | **Sausalito/N**	22
Ponzu | **Downtown**	20
Postino | **Lafayette/E**	23
Press | **St. Helena/N**	23
Prima | **Walnut Creek/E**	24
R & G Lounge | **Chinatown**	23
Rest. LuLu/Petite | **SoMa**	21
Rio Grill | **Carmel/S**	21
ⓏRitz-Carlton Din. Rm. | **Nob Hill**	27
Rose Pistola | **N Beach**	22
Roy's | **SoMa**	23
Ruth's Chris | **Polk Gulch**	23
Santi | **Geyserville/N**	25
Sardine Factory | **Monterey/S**	21
Sauce | **Hayes Valley**	19
Scala's Bistro | **Downtown**	21
Scott's | **multi.**	18
ⓏSeasons | **Downtown**	26
71 Saint Peter | **San Jose/S**	22
Shadowbrook | **Capitola/S**	18
Shanghai 1930 | **Embarcadero**	20
Silks | **Downtown**	24
ⓏSlanted Door | **Embarcadero**	26
Soi4 | **Oakland/E**	23
Soizic | **Oakland/E**	24
ⓏSpruce | **Presidio Hts**	25
St. Orres | **Gualala/N**	22
Straits | **San Jose/S**	19
Tamarine | **Palo Alto/S**	26
Tarpy's | **Monterey/S**	20
ⓏTerra | **St. Helena/N**	27
Ti Couz | **Mission**	23
Tommy Toy's | **Downtown**	23
Town Hall | **SoMa**	24
Trader Vic's | **multi.**	17
Tra Vigne | **St. Helena/N**	24
TusCA | **Monterey/S**	-
231 Ellsworth | **San Mateo/S**	22
2223 | **Castro**	23
Vic Stewart's | **Walnut Creek/E**	21

Village Pub | **Woodside/S**	26
Viognier | **San Mateo/S**	23
ⓏWaterbar | **Embarcadero**	20
Wente Vineyards | **Livermore/E**	23
ⓏYank Sing | **SoMa**	25
Zarzuela | **Russian Hill**	25
Zibibbo | **Palo Alto/S**	19
Zinsvalley | **Napa/N**	19
Zuppa | **SoMa**	19

PRIX FIXE MENUS

(Call for prices and times)

ⓏAbsinthe | **Hayes Valley**	22
ⓏAcquerello | **Polk Gulch**	28
Ⓩad hoc | **Yountville/N**	26
Ajanta | **Berkeley/E**	25
Alamo Sq. | **W Addition**	20
Amber Bistro | **Danville/E**	22
Ana Mandara | **Fish. Wharf**	22
ⓏAqua | **Downtown**	26
ⓏAuberge du Sol. | **Rutherford/N**	26
Aubergine | **Carmel/S**	25
Axum Cafe | **Lower Haight**	20
ⓏAziza | **Outer Rich**	26
Baker St. Bistro | **Marina**	21
Basque Cultural | **S San Francisco/S**	22
B44 | **Downtown**	21
Bistro Liaison | **Berkeley/E**	22
NEW Bistro St. Germain | **Lower Haight**	-
ⓏBIX | **Downtown**	23
Boonville Hotel | **Boonville/N**	22
Bridges | **Danville/E**	22
Brother's Korean | **Inner Rich**	23
Cafe Bastille | **Downtown**	18
ⓏCafe Gibraltar | **El Granada/S**	27
Caffe Delle Stelle | **Hayes Valley**	16
Capannina | **Cow Hollow**	24
Caprice | **Tiburon/N**	21
Carnelian Room | **Downtown**	18
Casanova | **Carmel/S**	23
ⓏChapeau! | **Outer Rich**	26
Charcuterie | **Healdsburg/N**	22
ⓏChez Panisse | **Berkeley/E**	28
ⓏChez Panisse Café | **Berkeley/E**	27
Chez Spencer | **Mission**	26

Chez TJ | **Mtn View/S**	23	Le Zinc | **Noe Valley**	19
Citron | **Oakland/E**	23	MacCallum Hse. | **Mendocino/N**	21
Côté Sud | **Castro**	19	⚡ Madrona | **Healdsburg/N**	26
Cuvée | **Napa/N**	21	⚡ Manresa | **Los Gatos/S**	27
⚡ Cyrus | **Healdsburg/N**	29	Market | **St. Helena/N**	22
Dry Creek | **Healdsburg/N**	24	MarketBar | **Embarcadero**	16
Duck Club | **Lafayette/E**	19	Martini House | **St. Helena/N**	26
E&O Trading | **multi.**	19	⚡ Masa's | **Downtown**	28
Ecco | **Burlingame/S**	23	Maya | **SoMa**	21
Emile's | **San Jose/S**	22	Meadowood Grill | **St. Helena/N**	22
⚡ Erna's Elderberry | **Oakhurst/E**	28	⚡ Meadowood Rest. | **St. Helena/N**	26
Espetus | **Hayes Valley**	22		
⚡ Étoile | **Yountville/N**	26	⚡ Michael Mina | **Downtown**	27
⚡ Farallon | **Downtown**	24	Millennium | **Downtown**	25
1550 Hyde | **Russian Hill**	22	Mirepoix | **Windsor/N**	26
Firefly | **Noe Valley**	25	⚡ Navio | **Half Moon Bay/S**	24
⚡ Fleur de Lys | **Downtown**	27	One Market | **Embarcadero**	22
⚡ French Laundry | **Yountville/N**	29	⚡ Pacific's Edge | **Carmel/S**	25
Garibaldis | **multi.**	22	Pakwan | **Hayward/E**	22
⚡ Gary Danko | **Fish. Wharf**	29	Parcel 104 | **Santa Clara/S**	23
girl & the fig | **Sonoma/N**	24	Piperade | **Downtown**	25
Grand Pu Bah | **Potrero Hill**	18	⚡ Plumed Horse | **Saratoga/S**	25
Grasing's Coastal | **Carmel/S**	24	Ponzu | **Downtown**	20
⚡ Greens | **Marina**	24	⚡ Ritz-Carlton Din. Rm. | **Nob Hill**	27
Hana Japanese | **Rohnert Pk/N**	24	rnm rest. | **Lower Haight**	23
Hurley's | **Yountville/N**	21	Roy's | **SoMa**	23
Hyde St. Bistro | **Russian Hill**	21	Sanraku | **Downtown**	24
Il Davide | **San Rafael/N**	21	Santé | **Sonoma/N**	25
Indigo | **Civic Ctr**	19	Scoma's | **Fish. Wharf**	22
Isa | **Marina**	24	⚡ Seasons | **Downtown**	26
Isobune | **Burlingame/S**	17	⚡ Sent Sovi | **Saratoga/S**	26
⚡ Jardinière | **Civic Ctr**	26	71 Saint Peter | **San Jose/S**	22
Jimmy Bean's | **Berkeley/E**	19	Shanghai 1930 | **Embarcadero**	20
Junnoon | **Palo Alto/S**	23	⚡ Sierra Mar | **Big Sur/S**	27
K&L Bistro | **Sebastopol/N**	25	Silks | **Downtown**	24
Kan Zaman | **Haight-Ashbury**	17	⚡ Slanted Door | **Embarcadero**	26
Kyo-Ya | **Downtown**	24	South Food/Wine | **S Beach**	21
⚡ La Forêt | **San Jose/S**	26	South Park | **SoMa**	23
La Provence | **Mission**	20	St. Orres | **Gualala/N**	22
La Strada | **Palo Alto/S**	21	Syrah | **Santa Rosa/N**	25
La Terrasse | **Presidio**	18	Tajine | **Pacific Hts**	-
⚡ La Toque | **Napa/N**	26	Tarpy's | **Monterey/S**	20
Lavanda | **Palo Alto/S**	20	Tommy Toy's | **Downtown**	23
Le Charm Bistro | **SoMa**	22	Ton Kiang | **Outer Rich**	24
Ledford Hse. | **Albion/N**	25	Town's End | **Embarcadero**	20
⚡ Le Papillon | **San Jose/S**	27	231 Ellsworth | **San Mateo/S**	22

SPECIAL FEATURES

Unicorn Pan Asian | **Downtown** 23

Vik's Chaat | **Berkeley/E** 24

🛛 Waterbar | **Embarcadero** 20

Yankee Pier | **Larkspur/N** 17

Zazie | **Cole Valley** 22

Zibibbo | **Palo Alto/S** 19

Zitune | **Los Altos/S** 25

Zucca | **Mtn View/S** 18

QUIET CONVERSATION

🛛 Acquerello | **Polk Gulch** 28

Alexander's | **Cupertino/S** 25

🛛 Applewood Inn | **Guerneville/N** 27

Arcadia | **San Jose/S** 21

🛛 Auberge du Sol. | **Rutherford/N** 26

Aubergine | **Carmel/S** 25

BayWolf | **Oakland/E** 25

Bella Vista | **Woodside/S** 19

Bushi-tei | **Japantown** 24

Cafe Jacqueline | **N Beach** 25

Campton Place | **Downtown** 24

Casanova | **Carmel/S** 23

🛛 Chantilly | **Redwood City/S** 23

🛛 Chez Panisse | **Berkeley/E** 28

Chez TJ | **Mtn View/S** 23

Citronelle | **Carmel/S** 24

Cottage Eatery | **Tiburon/N** 23

🛛 Cyrus | **Healdsburg/N** 29

Duck Club | **multi.** 19

Ecco | **Burlingame/S** 23

🛛 El Paseo | **Mill Valley/N** 26

Emile's | **San Jose/S** 22

NEW Estate | **Sonoma/N** 20

🛛 Farmhouse Inn | **Forestville/N** 26

Fifth Floor | **SoMa** 25

NEW Five | **Berkeley/E** -

Flea St. Café | **Menlo Pk/S** 25

🛛 Fleur de Lys | **Downtown** 27

Forbes Mill Steak | **multi.** 22

🛛 Gary Danko | **Fish. Wharf** 29

Kyo-Ya | **Downtown** 24

Lalime's | **Berkeley/E** 26

L'Ardoise | **Castro** 24

🛛 La Toque | **Napa/N** 26

Le Club | **Nob Hill** 15

🛛 Le Papillon | **San Jose/S** 27

Lovejoy's Tea | **Noe Valley** 21

Luce | **SoMa** 20

🛛 Madrona | **Healdsburg/N** 26

🛛 Manresa | **Los Gatos/S** 27

Marché | **Menlo Pk/S** 25

Marché aux Fleurs | **Ross/N** 25

🛛 Masa's | **Downtown** 28

🛛 Meadowood Rest. | **St. Helena/N** 26

Mescolanza | **Outer Rich** 21

Morton's | **San Jose/S** 24

NEW Moss Room | **Inner Rich** 21

Murray Circle | **Sausalito/N** 24

O Chamé | **Berkeley/E** 24

🛛 Pacific's Edge | **Carmel/S** 25

🛛 Plumed Horse | **Saratoga/S** 25

Postino | **Lafayette/E** 23

Quattro | **E Palo Alto/S** 21

🛛 Quince | **Downtown** 27

Richmond Rest. | **Inner Rich** 26

Scott's | **Palo Alto/S** 18

🛛 Seasons | **Downtown** 26

Silks | **Downtown** 24

Soizic | **Oakland/E** 24

Soule Domain | **Kings Bch/E** 22

Stokes | **Monterey/S** 21

St. Orres | **Gualala/N** 22

Terzo | **Cow Hollow** 23

Trevese | **Los Gatos/S** 23

NEW Urban Tavern | **Downtown** 17

NEW Zaré/Fly Trap | **SoMa** 22

NEW Zinnia | **Downtown** 23

RAW BARS

🛛 Absinthe | **Hayes Valley** 22

Acme Chophse. | **S Beach** 20

🛛 Ame | **SoMa** 26

Anchor Oyster | **Castro** 23

🛛 Aqua | **Downtown** 26

bacar | **SoMa** 23

Bar Crudo | **W Addition** 26

Bistro Vida | **Menlo Pk/S** 18

🛛 Bouchon | **Yountville/N** 26

Cafe Maritime/East | **Marina** 21

Café Rouge | **Berkeley/E** 22

Central Market | **Petaluma/N**	24
Ⓩ Farallon | **Downtown**	24
Fish | **Sausalito/N**	23
Fog City Diner | **Embarcadero**	19
Foreign Cinema | **Mission**	23
Fresca | **Noe Valley**	22
Go Fish | **St. Helena/N**	22
Grand Cafe | **Downtown**	19
Grand Pu Bah | **Potrero Hill**	18
Hog Island Oyster | **multi.**	25
Luka's Taproom | **Oakland/E**	20
Meritage Martini | **Sonoma/N**	20
Metro | **Lafayette/E**	-
Monti's | **Santa Rosa/N**	21
Nick's Cove | **Marshall/N**	21
Pesce | **Russian Hill**	24
Quattro | **E Palo Alto/S**	21
Rest. LuLu/Petite | **SoMa**	21
Sea Salt | **Berkeley/E**	22
Station House | **Pt Reyes/N**	20
Ⓩ Sushi Ran | **Sausalito/N**	28
Swan Oyster | **Polk Gulch**	26
Ⓩ Waterbar | **Embarcadero**	20
Willi's Seafood | **Healdsburg/N**	24
Woodhse. | **Castro**	21
Yabbies Coastal | **Russian Hill**	21
Yankee Pier | **multi.**	17
Zibibbo | **Palo Alto/S**	19
Ⓩ Zuni Café | **Hayes Valley**	25

ROMANTIC PLACES

Ⓩ Acquerello | **Polk Gulch**	28
Ⓩ Ahwahnee | **Yosemite/E**	19
Albion River Inn | **Albion/N**	25
Alexander's | **Cupertino/S**	25
Amber | **SoMa**	24
Ana Mandara | **Fish. Wharf**	22
Anton & Michel | **Carmel/S**	23
Ⓩ Applewood Inn | **Guerneville/N**	27
Ⓩ Auberge du Sol. | **Rutherford/N**	26
Aubergine | **Carmel/S**	25
Ⓩ Aziza | **Outer Rich**	26
Barndiva | **Healdsburg/N**	19
Bella Vista | **Woodside/S**	19
Ⓩ Big 4 | **Nob Hill**	22

Bing Crosby's | **Walnut Creek/E**	19
Bistro Clovis | **Hayes Valley**	21
Bistro/Copains | **Occidental/N**	25
Bistro Elan | **Palo Alto/S**	24
Bistro Vida | **Menlo Pk/S**	18
Ⓩ NEW Bottega | **Yountville/N**	25
Ⓩ Boulevard | **Embarcadero**	27
Brix | **Napa/N**	22
Bushi-tei | **Japantown**	24
Cafe Beaujolais | **Mendocino/N**	25
Cafe Jacqueline | **N Beach**	25
Candybar | **W Addition**	17
Caprice | **Tiburon/N**	21
Carnelian Room | **Downtown**	18
Casanova | **Carmel/S**	23
Cav Wine Bar | **Hayes Valley**	20
Ⓩ Chantilly | **Redwood City/S**	23
Ⓩ Chapeau! | **Outer Rich**	26
Ⓩ Chez Panisse | **Berkeley/E**	28
Chez Spencer | **Mission**	26
Chez TJ | **Mtn View/S**	23
Christy Hill | **Tahoe City/E**	24
Citron | **Oakland/E**	23
Citronelle | **Carmel/S**	24
Ⓩ Coi | **N Beach**	28
Cool Café | **Palo Alto/S**	-
Cottage Eatery | **Tiburon/N**	23
Ⓩ Cyrus | **Healdsburg/N**	29
Deetjen's | **Big Sur/S**	22
NEW Donato | **Redwood City/S**	-
Ducca | **SoMa**	20
Duck Club | **multi.**	19
Ecco | **Burlingame/S**	23
Ⓩ El Paseo | **Mill Valley/N**	26
Emile's | **San Jose/S**	22
Ⓩ Erna's Elderberry | **Oakhurst/E**	28
NEW Estate | **Sonoma/N**	20
Ⓩ Étoile | **Yountville/N**	26
Ⓩ Farmhouse Inn | **Forestville/N**	26
Fifth Floor | **SoMa**	25
Flea St. Café | **Menlo Pk/S**	25
Ⓩ Fleur de Lys | **Downtown**	27
Forbes Island | **Fish. Wharf**	19
Forge in Forest | **Carmel/S**	18
Ⓩ French Laundry | **Yountville/N**	29
Fresh Cream | **Monterey/S**	25

Gabriella Café | **Santa Cruz/S**	23
Z Garden Court | **Downtown**	20
Z Gary Danko | **Fish. Wharf**	29
Z NEW Gitane | **Downtown**	22
Harvest Moon | **Sonoma/N**	24
Incanto | **Noe Valley**	24
Indigo | **Civic Ctr**	19
Z Jardinière | **Civic Ctr**	26
John Ash | **Santa Rosa/N**	24
John Bentley's | **Woodside/S**	25
Katia's Tea | **Inner Rich**	23
Khan Toke | **Outer Rich**	22
La Corneta | **Burlingame/S**	22
Z La Folie | **Russian Hill**	28
Z La Forêt | **San Jose/S**	26
Lalime's | **Berkeley/E**	26
NEW La Mar | **Embarcadero**	23
La Note | **Berkeley/E**	21
L'Ardoise | **Castro**	24
Z La Toque | **Napa/N**	26
Le Club | **Nob Hill**	15
Z Le Papillon | **San Jose/S**	27
Level III | **Downtown**	18
Little River Inn | **Little River/N**	21
Luce | **SoMa**	20
MacCallum Hse. | **Mendocino/N**	21
NEW Madera | **Menlo Pk/S**	-
Z Madrona | **Healdsburg/N**	26
Mantra | **Palo Alto/S**	20
Marché aux Fleurs | **Ross/N**	25
Z Marinus | **Carmel Valley/S**	27
Martini House | **St. Helena/N**	26
Z Masa's | **Downtown**	28
Matterhorn Swiss | **Russian Hill**	23
Z Meadowood Rest. | **St. Helena/N**	26
Medjool | **Mission**	18
Z Michael Mina | **Downtown**	27
Moosse Café | **Mendocino/N**	24
NEW Moss Room | **Inner Rich**	21
Murray Circle | **Sausalito/N**	24
Napa Wine Train | **Napa/N**	16
Nick's Cove | **Marshall/N**	21
O Chamé | **Berkeley/E**	24
Olema Inn | **Olema/N**	22
Ozumo | **Oakland/E**	24

Z Pacific's Edge | **Carmel/S**	25
Pampas | **Palo Alto/S**	21
Peasant & Pear | **Danville/E**	22
Pianeta | **Truckee/E**	23
Picco | **Larkspur/N**	26
Z Quince | **Downtown**	27
Rest. at Stevenswood | **Little River/N**	26
Risibisi | **Petaluma/N**	25
Z Ritz-Carlton Din. Rm. | **Nob Hill**	27
River Ranch | **Tahoe City/E**	15
Z Roy's | **Pebble Bch/S**	25
Salute Marina | **Richmond/E**	18
Sea Salt | **Berkeley/E**	22
Z Sent Sovi | **Saratoga/S**	26
71 Saint Peter | **San Jose/S**	22
Shadowbrook | **Capitola/S**	18
Shokolaat | **Palo Alto/S**	19
Z Sierra Mar | **Big Sur/S**	27
Silks | **Downtown**	24
Slow Club | **Mission**	22
Soizic | **Oakland/E**	24
Soule Domain | **Kings Bch/E**	22
Starlight | **Sebastopol/N**	22
St. Michael's | **Palo Alto/S**	23
Stokes | **Monterey/S**	21
St. Orres | **Gualala/N**	22
Sunnyside | **Tahoe City/E**	18
supperclub | **SoMa**	15
NEW Tavern at Lark Creek | **Larkspur/N**	-
Z Terra | **St. Helena/N**	27
Terzo | **Cow Hollow**	23
1300/Fillmore | **W Addition**	22
Trevese | **Los Gatos/S**	23
Twist | **Campbell/S**	22
Venticello | **Nob Hill**	23
Viognier | **San Mateo/S**	23
Wente Vineyards | **Livermore/E**	23
Z Wolfdale's | **Tahoe City/E**	27
Woodward's Gdn. | **Mission**	25
Zarzuela | **Russian Hill**	25

SENIOR APPEAL

Acme Chophse. | **S Beach**	20
Z Acquerello | **Polk Gulch**	28
Alfred's Steak | **Downtown**	22

Alioto's	**Fish. Wharf**	18	**NEW** Urban Tavern	**Downtown**	17
Anton & Michel	**Carmel/S**	23	Vic Stewart's	**Walnut Creek/E**	21
NEW Aurea	**Nob Hill**	-	**Z** Waterbar	**Embarcadero**	20
Bella Vista	**Woodside/S**	19	**NEW** Zaré/Fly Trap	**SoMa**	22
Z Big 4	**Nob Hill**	22		

SINGLES SCENES

Bing Crosby's	**Walnut Creek/E**	19
Cantankerous	**Mtn View/S**	18
Caprice	**Tiburon/N**	21
Z Chantilly	**Redwood City/S**	23
Christy Hill	**Tahoe City/E**	24
Citronelle	**Carmel/S**	24
Cole's Chop Hse.	**Napa/N**	24
Cook St. Helena	**St. Helena/N**	25
Z Cyrus	**Healdsburg/N**	29
Duck Club	**multi.**	19
Emile's	**San Jose/S**	22
EPIC	**Embarcadero**	20
NEW Estate	**Sonoma/N**	20
Eulipia	**San Jose/S**	24
Fior d'Italia	**N Beach**	18
Z Fleur de Lys	**Downtown**	27
Forbes Mill Steak	**multi.**	22
Z Garden Court	**Downtown**	20
Harris'	**Polk Gulch**	25
Hayes St. Grill	**Hayes Valley**	23
Z House of Prime	**Polk Gulch**	24
Izzy's Steak	**Marina**	20
Joe DiMaggio's	**N Beach**	21
La Ginestra	**Mill Valley/N**	21
Lalime's	**Berkeley/E**	26
NEW LB Steak	**San Jose/S**	-
Le Central Bistro	**Downtown**	20
Z Masa's	**Downtown**	28
Z Meadowood Rest.	**St. Helena/N**	26
Morton's	**multi.**	24
North Beach Rest.	**N Beach**	22
Z Plumed Horse	**Saratoga/S**	25
Z Rotunda	**Downtown**	19
Sardine Factory	**Monterey/S**	21
Scoma's	**Fish. Wharf**	22
Sens Rest.	**Downtown**	20
Soule Domain	**Kings Bch/E**	22
Z Tadich Grill	**Downtown**	23
Trevese	**Los Gatos/S**	23
TusCA	**Monterey/S**	-

Ace Wasabi's	**Marina**	21
Anchor & Hope	**SoMa**	21
Andalu	**Mission**	21
Asia de Cuba	**Downtown**	20
Balboa Cafe	**multi.**	19
Bambuddha	**Tenderloin**	17
NEW Barlata	**Oakland/E**	-
Barndiva	**Healdsburg/N**	19
Beach Chalet	**Outer Sunset**	15
Beretta	**Mission**	23
Betelnut Pejiu	**Cow Hollow**	22
Bin 38	**Marina**	19
Z BIX	**Downtown**	23
Blowfish Sushi	**Mission**	20
Blue Plate	**Mission**	24
Butterfly	**Embarcadero**	20
Cafe Bastille	**Downtown**	18
Café Claude	**Downtown**	21
Café Flore	**Castro**	15
Cascal	**Mtn View/S**	20
Catch	**Castro**	18
Cha Cha Cha	**multi.**	20
Cin-Cin Wine	**Los Gatos/S**	23
Conduit	**Mission**	22
Cosmopolitan	**SoMa**	19
Cottonwood	**Truckee/E**	21
Custom Burger	**SoMa**	19
District	**SoMa**	18
Dosa	**Upper Fillmore**	23
Dragonfly	**Truckee/E**	22
E&O Trading	**multi.**	19
Elite Cafe	**Upper Fillmore**	19
Emmy's Spaghetti	**Bernal Hts**	21
5A5 Steak Lounge	**Downtown**	-
Flora	**Oakland/E**	23
Foreign Cinema	**Mission**	23
Frjtz Fries	**multi.**	18
Gar Woods	**Carnelian Bay/E**	17
Z NEW Gitane	**Downtown**	22
Grand Pu Bah	**Potrero Hill**	18

Guaymas | **Tiburon/N**	16
Half Moon Brew | **Half Moon Bay/S**	16
NEW Heaven's Dog | **SoMa**	21
Home | **Castro**	18
Hopmonk Tav. | **Sebastopol/N**	17
Jake's/Lake | **Tahoe City/E**	16
NEW Joya | **Palo Alto/S**	18
Junnoon | **Palo Alto/S**	23
Kan Zaman | **Haight-Ashbury**	17
Laïola | **Marina**	20
La Trappe | **N Beach**	18
Le Club | **Nob Hill**	15
Level III | **Downtown**	18
Lime | **Castro**	17
Local Kitchen | **SoMa**	20
Luce | **SoMa**	20
Luna Park | **Mission**	20
Magnolia | **Haight-Ashbury**	18
NEW Martins West | **Redwood City/S**	-
Medjool | **Mission**	18
NEW Miss Pearl's | **Oakland/E**	17
MoMo's | **S Beach**	17
Monk's Kettle | **Mission**	18
Moody's Bistro | **Truckee/E**	25
Nectar Wine | **multi.**	18
NEW Nettie's | **Cow Hollow**	20
Nihon | **Mission**	20
Orson | **SoMa**	18
Ottimista | **Cow Hollow**	19
Ozumo | **multi.**	24
Poesia | **Castro**	20
Poleng | **W Addition**	19
Puerto Alegre | **Mission**	18
Quattro | **E Palo Alto/S**	21
Ramblas | **Mission**	20
Red Lantern | **Redwood City/S**	19
River Ranch | **Tahoe City/E**	15
rnm rest. | **Lower Haight**	23
Rose Pistola | **N Beach**	22
Serpentine | **Dogpatch**	21
7 Restaurant | **San Jose/S**	21
Sino | **San Jose/S**	19
Slow Club | **Mission**	22
South Food/Wine | **S Beach**	21

Starlight | **Sebastopol/N**	22
Sunnyside | **Tahoe City/E**	18
Sushi Groove | **multi.**	21
NEW Taverna Aventine | **Downtown**	-
Ti Couz | **Mission**	23
NEW Tipsy Pig | **Marina**	21
Tokyo Go Go | **Mission**	21
Tres Agaves | **S Beach**	15
Tsunami | **W Addition**	22
2223 | **Castro**	23
Umami | **Cow Hollow**	22
Universal Cafe | **Mission**	23
Xanh | **Mtn View/S**	23
Zibibbo | **Palo Alto/S**	19
NEW Zinnia | **Downtown**	23
Z Zuni Café | **Hayes Valley**	25

SLEEPERS

(Good food, but little known)

Ariake | **Outer Rich**	24
Bardessono | **Yountville/N**	23
Café Fiore | **S Lake Tahoe/E**	25
Cafe Saint Rose | **Sebastopol/N**	23
Carneros Bistro | **Sonoma/N**	23
Chez Shea | **Half Moon Bay/S**	23
Club XIX | **Pebble Bch/S**	23
Cottage Eatery | **Tiburon/N**	23
Digs Bistro | **Berkeley/E**	25
Eulipia | **San Jose/S**	24
Evan's | **S Lake Tahoe/E**	28
Harvest Moon | **Sonoma/N**	24
Jai Yun | **Chinatown**	23
Jin Sho | **Palo Alto/S**	24
JoLe | **Calistoga/N**	26
Katia's Tea | **Inner Rich**	23
Kiji Sushi Bar | **Mission**	23
Koryo BBQ | **Oakland/E**	23
Kurt's Carmel | **Carmel/S**	23
Le Soleil | **Inner Rich**	23
Little Chihuahua | **W Addition**	23
Marica | **Oakland/E**	23
Maykadeh | **N Beach**	26
Nick's on Main | **Los Gatos/S**	25
Pappo | **Alameda/E**	24
Pearl | **Napa/N**	23
Pianeta | **Truckee/E**	23

Pica Pica Maize | **Napa/N**	25
Piccino | **Dogpatch**	24
Piqueo's | **Bernal Hts**	24
Red Hut | **S Lake Tahoe/E**	23
Restaurant | **Ft Bragg/N**	23
Rest. at Stevenswood | **Little River/N**	26
Risibisi | **Petaluma/N**	25
Ristorante Parma | **Marina**	23
Sai Jai Thai | **Tenderloin**	25
Santé | **Sonoma/N**	25
Scopa | **Healdsburg/N**	24
Taqueria Tlaquepaque | **San Jose/S**	25
Tea Room Café | **Petaluma/N**	24
Uzen | **Oakland/E**	24
Vin Antico | **San Rafael/N**	23
Vitrine | **SoMa**	23
Water St. Bistro | **Petaluma/N**	23
Yamo | **Mission**	23

TASTING MENUS

☑ Acquerello | **Polk Gulch**	28
Alexander's | **Cupertino/S**	25
☑ Ame | **SoMa**	26
☑ Applewood Inn | **Guerneville/N**	27
☑ Aqua | **Downtown**	26
☑ Auberge du Sol. | **Rutherford/N**	26
Aubergine | **Carmel/S**	25
☑ Aziza | **Outer Rich**	26
Bushi-tei | **Japantown**	24
☑ Cafe Gibraltar | **El Granada/S**	27
Carnelian Room | **Downtown**	18
Chez Spencer | **Mission**	26
Chez TJ | **Mtn View/S**	23
Citron | **Oakland/E**	23
Club XIX | **Pebble Bch/S**	23
☑ Coi | **N Beach**	28
Côté Sud | **Castro**	19
☑ Cyrus | **Healdsburg/N**	29
Dosa | **multi.**	23
Dry Creek | **Healdsburg/N**	24
Ecco | **Burlingame/S**	23
Eiji | **Castro**	-
☑ El Paseo | **Mill Valley/N**	26

Emile's | **San Jose/S**	22
☑ Étoile | **Yountville/N**	26
Fifth Floor | **SoMa**	25
Fior d'Italia | **N Beach**	18
☑ French Laundry | **Yountville/N**	29
☑ Gary Danko | **Fish. Wharf**	29
Hana Japanese | **Rohnert Pk/N**	24
☑ Jardinière | **Civic Ctr**	26
Jin Sho | **Palo Alto/S**	24
Juban | **multi.**	19
Kanpai | **Palo Alto/S**	22
☑ Kaygetsu | **Menlo Pk/S**	28
Kiji Sushi Bar | **Mission**	23
☑ Kiss Seafood | **Japantown**	28
Koi | **Daly City/S**	23
Kyo-Ya | **Downtown**	24
☑ La Folie | **Russian Hill**	28
☑ La Forêt | **San Jose/S**	26
☑ La Toque | **Napa/N**	26
☑ Le Papillon | **San Jose/S**	27
MacCallum Hse. | **Mendocino/N**	21
☑ Madrona | **Healdsburg/N**	26
☑ Manresa | **Los Gatos/S**	27
Marché | **Menlo Pk/S**	25
☑ Marinus | **Carmel Valley/S**	27
Martini House | **St. Helena/N**	26
☑ Masa's | **Downtown**	28
☑ Meadowood Rest. | **St. Helena/N**	26
Meritage Martini | **Sonoma/N**	20
☑ Michael Mina | **Downtown**	27
Millennium | **Downtown**	25
Murray Circle | **Sausalito/N**	24
☑ Navio | **Half Moon Bay/S**	24
☑ Pacific's Edge | **Carmel/S**	25
Parcel 104 | **Santa Clara/S**	23
☑ Plumed Horse | **Saratoga/S**	25
Prima | **Walnut Creek/E**	24
☑ Redd | **Yountville/N**	27
Rendezvous Inn | **Ft Bragg/N**	25
Rest. at Stevenswood | **Little River/N**	26
Richmond Rest. | **Inner Rich**	26
☑ Ritz-Carlton Din. Rm. | **Nob Hill**	27
Sanraku | **Downtown**	24
Santé | **Sonoma/N**	25

☑ Seasons | **Downtown**	26
☑ Sent Sovi | **Saratoga/S**	26
71 Saint Peter | **San Jose/S**	22
Silks | **Downtown**	24
Syrah | **Santa Rosa/N**	25
Tommy Toy's | **Downtown**	23
Trevese | **Los Gatos/S**	23
231 Ellsworth | **San Mateo/S**	22
XYZ | **SoMa**	19

TEEN APPEAL

Amici's | **multi.**	20
Asqew Grill | **multi.**	16
Barney's | **multi.**	19
Beach Chalet | **Outer Sunset**	15
Buca di Beppo | **multi.**	14
Burger Joint | **multi.**	18
BurgerMeister | **multi.**	19
Cactus Taqueria | **multi.**	21
Cheesecake | **multi.**	16
Custom Burger | **SoMa**	19
Ebisu | **S San Francisco/S**	23
El Balazo | **multi.**	19
FatApple's | **multi.**	18
Fentons Creamery | **Oakland/E**	19
Fog City Diner | **Embarcadero**	19
Frontera Fresco | **Downtown**	18
Gar Woods | **Carnelian Bay/E**	17
Goat Hill Pizza | **Potrero Hill**	18
Hard Rock | **Fish. Wharf**	12
Jake's/Lake | **Tahoe City/E**	16
Jake's Steaks | **Marina**	20
Joe's Cable Car | **Excelsior**	21
La Corneta | **multi.**	22
La Victoria | **San Jose/S**	20
Little Chihuahua | **W Addition**	23
MacArthur Pk. | **Palo Alto/S**	16
Max's | **multi.**	17
Mel's Drive-In | **multi.**	14
Miller's/Deli | **Polk Gulch**	22
Mo's | **multi.**	20
Park Chalet | **Outer Sunset**	16
Pauline's Pizza | **Mission**	23
Picante Cocina | **Berkeley/E**	21
Pizza Antica | **Lafayette/E**	21
NEW Pizza Nostra | **Potrero Hill**	-

Pizza Place on Noriega | **Outer Sunset**	-
Pizzeria Picco | **Larkspur/N**	25
Plant Cafe | **Marina**	20
Rosso Pizzeria | **Santa Rosa/N**	25
Rutherford Grill | **Rutherford/N**	24
Sardine Factory | **Monterey/S**	21
Shen Hua | **Berkeley/E**	22
Sunnyside | **Tahoe City/E**	18
Taylor's Auto | **St. Helena/N**	22
☑ Tonga | **Nob Hill**	13

THEME RESTAURANTS

Bing Crosby's | **Walnut Creek/E**	19
Buca di Beppo | **multi.**	14
Hard Rock | **Fish. Wharf**	12
Joe DiMaggio's | **N Beach**	21
Max's | **multi.**	17
NEW Miss Pearl's | **Oakland/E**	17
Napa Wine Train | **Napa/N**	16
supperclub | **SoMa**	15

TRENDY

Ace Wasabi's | **Marina**	21
À Côté | **Oakland/E**	24
Amber Bistro | **Danville/E**	22
Amber | **multi.**	24
☑ Ame | **SoMa**	26
Anchor & Hope | **SoMa**	21
☑ Aqua | **Downtown**	26
Asia de Cuba | **Downtown**	20
☑ A16 | **Marina**	25
Balboa Cafe | **Cow Hollow**	19
Bambuddha | **Tenderloin**	17
NEW Barlata | **Oakland/E**	-
Barndiva | **Healdsburg/N**	19
Bar Tartine | **Mission**	24
Bellanico | **Oakland/E**	23
Beretta | **Mission**	23
Betelnut Pejiu | **Cow Hollow**	22
Bing Crosby's | **Walnut Creek/E**	19
Bin 38 | **Marina**	19
Bistro Don Giovanni | **Napa/N**	23
☑ BIX | **Downtown**	23
Blowfish Sushi | **Mission**	20
Blue Bottle | **SoMa**	23

Blue Plate	**Mission**	24	Fonda Solana	**Albany/E**	23
Bocadillos	**N Beach**	22	Foreign Cinema	**Mission**	23
Boogaloos	**Mission**	20	Fringale	**SoMa**	24
Z NEW Bottega	**Yountville/N**	25	Frjtz Fries	**multi.**	18
Z Bouchon	**Yountville/N**	26	Front Porch	**Bernal Hts**	22
Z Boulevard	**Embarcadero**	27	Garibaldis	**Oakland/E**	22
Z Buckeye Rdhse.	**Mill Valley/N**	23	girl & the fig	**Sonoma/N**	24
Bungalow 44	**Mill Valley/N**	21	**Z NEW** Gitane	**Downtown**	22
Café Fanny	**Berkeley/E**	23	Globe	**Downtown**	20
Café Flore	**Castro**	15	Go Fish	**St. Helena/N**	22
Café Rouge	**Berkeley/E**	22	Grand Pu Bah	**Potrero Hill**	18
Candybar	**W Addition**	17	**NEW** Heaven's Dog	**SoMa**	21
Cascal	**Mtn View/S**	20	Hopmonk Tav.	**Sebastopol/N**	17
Cav Wine Bar	**Hayes Valley**	20	Iluna Basque	**N Beach**	21
César	**Berkeley/E**	22	Isa	**Marina**	24
Cetrella	**Half Moon Bay/S**	20	Jake's/Lake	**Tahoe City/E**	16
Cha Cha Cha	**multi.**	20	**Z** Jardinière	**Civic Ctr**	26
Charanga	**Mission**	21	**NEW** Joya	**Palo Alto/S**	18
Chaya	**Embarcadero**	22	Junnoon	**Palo Alto/S**	23
Z Chez Panisse Café	**Berkeley/E**	27	Laïola	**Marina**	20
Chez Papa	**multi.**	23	La Trappe	**N Beach**	18
Cindy's	**St. Helena/N**	24	Le Club	**Nob Hill**	15
Coco500	**SoMa**	22	Level III	**Downtown**	18
Conduit	**Mission**	22	Lime	**Castro**	17
Corso	**Berkeley/E**	24	Limón	**Mission**	23
Custom Burger	**SoMa**	19	Local Kitchen	**SoMa**	20
Z Delfina	**Mission**	26	Luna Park	**Mission**	20
Doña Tomás	**Oakland/E**	23	Mamacita	**Marina**	23
Dosa	**multi.**	23	Mantra	**Palo Alto/S**	20
downtown	**Berkeley/E**	19	Martini House	**St. Helena/N**	26
Dry Creek	**Healdsburg/N**	24	**NEW** Martins West	**Redwood City/S**	–
Ducca	**SoMa**	20		
E&O Trading	**Larkspur/N**	19	Maverick	**Mission**	24
Ebisu	**Inner Sunset**	23	Medjool	**Mission**	18
Emmy's Spaghetti	**Bernal Hts**	21	Mexico DF	**Embarcadero**	20
Enrico's	**N Beach**	16	**NEW** Miss Pearl's	**Oakland/E**	17
Eos Rest.	**Cole Valley**	23	**Z** Mustards	**Yountville/N**	25
Estéban	**Monterey/S**	–	Naked Fish	**S Lake Tahoe/E**	21
Z Evvia	**Palo Alto/S**	26	Nectar Wine	**Burlingame/S**	18
Z Farallon	**Downtown**	24	Nihon	**Mission**	20
Farina	**Mission**	23	nopa	**W Addition**	25
farmerbrown/skillet	**Tenderloin**	21	Orson	**SoMa**	18
5A5 Steak Lounge	**Downtown**	–	Osha Thai	**multi.**	21
Flea St. Café	**Menlo Pk/S**	25	Ottimista	**Cow Hollow**	19
Flora	**Oakland/E**	23	Ozumo	**multi.**	24
NEW Flour + Water	**Mission**	–	Piazza D'Angelo	**Mill Valley/N**	20

NEW Picán | **Oakland/E**	–
Picco | **Larkspur/N**	26
Piperade | **Downtown**	25
Pizza Antica | **San Jose/S**	21
Pizzeria Delfina | **Mission**	24
Pizzeria Picco | **Larkspur/N**	25
Plouf | **Downtown**	22
Poggio | **Sausalito/N**	22
Poleng | **W Addition**	19
Postino | **Lafayette/E**	23
Press | **St. Helena/N**	23
Red Lantern | **Redwood City/S**	19
Rest. LuLu/Petite | **SoMa**	21
rnm rest. | **Lower Haight**	23
Rose Pistola | **N Beach**	22
Rose's Cafe | **Cow Hollow**	22
Salt House | **SoMa**	21
Santi | **Geyserville/N**	25
NEW Scopa | **Healdsburg/N**	24
Sebo | **Hayes Valley**	25
Serpentine | **Dogpatch**	21
NEW Sidebar | **Oakland/E**	20
Sino | **San Jose/S**	19
Z Slanted Door | **Embarcadero**	26
Slow Club | **Mission**	22
South Food/Wine | **S Beach**	21
Spork | **Mission**	21
SPQR | **Pacific Hts**	23
Z Spruce | **Presidio Hts**	25
Starlight | **Sebastopol/N**	22
supperclub | **SoMa**	15
Sushi Groove | **multi.**	21
Tamarine | **Palo Alto/S**	26
Terzo | **Cow Hollow**	23
1300/Fillmore | **W Addition**	22
Ti Couz | **Mission**	23
NEW Tipsy Pig | **Marina**	21
Tokyo Go Go | **Mission**	21
Town Hall | **SoMa**	24
Trader Vic's | **multi.**	17
Tres Agaves | **S Beach**	15
Tsunami | **W Addition**	22
TWO | **SoMa**	19
2223 | **Castro**	23
Umami | **Cow Hollow**	22
Underwood Bar | **Graton/N**	24
Universal Cafe | **Mission**	23
NEW Urban Tavern | **Downtown**	17
Uva Enoteca | **Lower Haight**	20
Village Pub | **Woodside/S**	26
Z Waterbar | **Embarcadero**	20
Willi's Seafood | **Healdsburg/N**	24
Wood Tavern | **Oakland/E**	25
Xanh | **Mtn View/S**	23
Xyclo | **Oakland/E**	22
XYZ | **SoMa**	19
Yoshi's SF | **W Addition**	22
Zibibbo | **Palo Alto/S**	19
NEW Zinnia | **Downtown**	23
Z Zuni Café | **Hayes Valley**	25
Zuppa | **SoMa**	19
ZuZu | **Napa/N**	23

VALET PARKING

Z Absinthe | **Hayes Valley**	22
Acme Chophse. | **S Beach**	20
Z Ahwahnee | **Yosemite/E**	19
Albona Rist. | **N Beach**	24
Amber Bistro | **Danville/E**	22
Z Ame | **SoMa**	26
Americano | **Embarcadero**	18
Ana Mandara | **Fish. Wharf**	22
Andalu | **Mission**	21
ANZU | **Downtown**	22
Z Aqua | **Downtown**	26
NEW Aquarius | **Santa Cruz/S**	–
Arcadia | **San Jose/S**	21
Asia de Cuba | **Downtown**	20
Z Auberge du Sol. | **Rutherford/N**	26
Aubergine | **Carmel/S**	25
NEW Aurea | **Nob Hill**	–
Z Aziza | **Outer Rich**	26
bacar | **SoMa**	23
Balboa Cafe | **Cow Hollow**	19
NEW Bardessono | **Yountville/N**	23
Z Big 4 | **Nob Hill**	22
Bing Crosby's | **Walnut Creek/E**	19
Z BIX | **Downtown**	23
Blowfish Sushi | **San Jose/S**	20
Z Boulevard | **Embarcadero**	27
Bridges | **Danville/E**	22

Z Buckeye Rdhse. | **Mill Valley/N**	23	Kuleto's | **Downtown**	20
Cafe Maritime/East | **Marina**	21	Kuleto's | **Burlingame/S**	20
Campton Place | **Downtown**	24	Kyo-Ya | **Downtown**	24
Casa Orinda | **Orinda/E**	18	Z La Folie | **Russian Hill**	28
Catch | **Castro**	18	La Scene | **Downtown**	18
Cha Am Thai | **SoMa**	19	Z La Toque | **Napa/N**	26
Z Chantilly | **Redwood City/S**	23	NEW LB Steak | **San Jose/S**	-
Chaya | **Embarcadero**	22	Le Cheval | **Oakland/E**	21
Cheesecake | **Santa Clara/S**	16	Le Club | **Nob Hill**	15
Club XIX | **Pebble Bch/S**	23	Level III | **Downtown**	18
Z Coi | **N Beach**	28	Lion & Compass | **Sunnyvale/S**	20
Cole's Chop Hse. | **Napa/N**	24	Luce | **SoMa**	20
Crustacean | **Polk Gulch**	23	MacArthur Pk. | **Palo Alto/S**	16
Delancey St. | **Embarcadero**	17	Mangarosa | **N Beach**	18
Dio Deka | **Los Gatos/S**	25	NEW Marinitas | **San Anselmo/N**	21
Ducca | **SoMa**	20	Z Marinus | **Carmel Valley/S**	27
Duck Club | **Lafayette/E**	19	Z Masa's | **Downtown**	28
Ecco | **Burlingame/S**	23	Matterhorn Swiss | **Russian Hill**	23
Elite Cafe | **Upper Fillmore**	19	Maykadeh | **N Beach**	26
El Raigón | **N Beach**	22	Medjool | **Mission**	18
Emile's | **San Jose/S**	22	Mexico DF | **Embarcadero**	20
EPIC | **Embarcadero**	20	Z Michael Mina | **Downtown**	27
Z Evvia | **Palo Alto/S**	26	Millennium | **Downtown**	25
Z Farallon | **Downtown**	24	NEW Miss Pearl's | **Oakland/E**	17
Farina | **Mission**	23	MoMo's | **S Beach**	17
Fifth Floor | **SoMa**	25	Morton's | **multi.**	24
Fior d'Italia | **N Beach**	18	Z Navio | **Half Moon Bay/S**	24
5A5 Steak Lounge | **Downtown**	-	Nob Hill Café | **Nob Hill**	21
Z Fleur de Lys | **Downtown**	27	North Beach Rest. | **N Beach**	22
Florio | **Pacific Hts**	21	O Izakaya | **Japantown**	17
Foreign Cinema | **Mission**	23	One Market | **Embarcadero**	22
Garibaldis | **multi.**	22	Ozumo | **Embarcadero**	24
Z Gary Danko | **Fish. Wharf**	29	Z Pacific's Edge | **Carmel/S**	25
Grand Cafe | **Downtown**	19	Parcel 104 | **Santa Clara/S**	23
Harris' | **Polk Gulch**	25	Z Perbacco | **Downtown**	25
Hayes St. Grill | **Hayes Valley**	23	Picco | **Larkspur/N**	26
Home | **Castro**	18	Pizzeria Picco | **Larkspur/N**	25
Z House of Prime | **Polk Gulch**	24	Z Plumed Horse | **Saratoga/S**	25
Hunan | **Chinatown**	22	Poggio | **Sausalito/N**	22
Il Fornaio | **multi.**	19	Postino | **Lafayette/E**	23
Insalata's | **San Anselmo/N**	25	Prima | **Walnut Creek/E**	24
Z Jardinière | **Civic Ctr**	26	Quattro | **E Palo Alto/S**	21
Joe DiMaggio's | **N Beach**	21	Z Quince | **Downtown**	27
Joey & Eddie's | **N Beach**	14	Rest. LuLu/Petite | **multi.**	21
Jordan's | **Berkeley/E**	17	Rist. Capellini | **San Mateo/S**	20
Z Kokkari | **Downtown**	27	Z Ritz-Carlton Din. Rm. | **Nob Hill**	27

rnm rest. | **Lower Haight**	23
Rose Pistola | **N Beach**	22
☑ Roy's | **Pebble Bch/S**	25
Ruth's Chris | **multi.**	23
Santé | **Sonoma/N**	25
Scoma's | **Fish. Wharf**	22
Scott's | **Walnut Creek/E**	18
☑ Seasons | **Downtown**	26
Shanghai 1930 | **Embarcadero**	20
☑ Sierra Mar | **Big Sur/S**	27
Silks | **Downtown**	24
☑ Slanted Door | **Embarcadero**	26
☑ Spruce | **Presidio Hts**	25
Straits | **Downtown**	19
Sunnyside | **Tahoe City/E**	18
Suppenküche | **Hayes Valley**	22
supperclub | **SoMa**	15
NEW Tavern at Lark Creek | **Larkspur/N**	-
Terzo | **Cow Hollow**	23
Thanh Long | **Outer Sunset**	24
Tokyo Go Go | **Mission**	21
Tommy Toy's | **Downtown**	23
Townhouse B&G | **Emeryville/E**	21
Trader Vic's | **Emeryville/E**	17
TWO | **SoMa**	19
231 Ellsworth | **San Mateo/S**	22
☑ Ubuntu | **Napa/N**	26
NEW Urban Tavern | **Downtown**	17
Venticello | **Nob Hill**	23
Vitrine | **SoMa**	23
☑ Waterbar | **Embarcadero**	20
Waterfront | **Embarcadero**	18
Wente Vineyards | **Livermore/E**	23
Wine Spectator | **St. Helena/N**	22
XYZ | **SoMa**	19
Yankee Pier | **multi.**	17
Zazil Coastal | **Downtown**	18
Zibibbo | **Palo Alto/S**	19
NEW Zinnia | **Downtown**	23
☑ Zuni Café | **Hayes Valley**	25

VIEWS

☑ Ahwahnee | **Yosemite/E**	19
Albion River Inn | **Albion/N**	25
Alioto's | **Fish. Wharf**	18

Americano | **Embarcadero**	18
Angèle | **Napa/N**	22
☑ Applewood Inn | **Guerneville/N**	27
☑ Auberge du Sol. | **Rutherford/N**	26
Barbara's Fish Trap | **Princeton Sea/S**	20
Barndiva | **Healdsburg/N**	19
Beach Chalet | **Outer Sunset**	15
Bella Vista | **Woodside/S**	19
Imperial/Berkeley | **Berkeley/E**	20
Big Sur | **Big Sur/S**	21
Bistro Boudin | **Fish. Wharf**	19
Bistro Don Giovanni | **Napa/N**	23
Blackhawk Grille | **Danville/E**	19
Boulette's Larder | **Embarcadero**	25
Bridgetender | **Tahoe City/E**	19
Brix | **Napa/N**	22
Cafe Beaujolais | **Mendocino/N**	25
☑ Cafe Gibraltar | **El Granada/S**	27
Caprice | **Tiburon/N**	21
Carnelian Room | **Downtown**	18
Chapter & Moon | **Ft Bragg/N**	22
Chaya | **Embarcadero**	22
Cheesecake | **Downtown**	16
Chez TJ | **Mtn View/S**	23
Christy Hill | **Tahoe City/E**	24
Cliff House | **Outer Rich**	18
Club XIX | **Pebble Bch/S**	23
Cool Café | **Palo Alto/S**	-
Cottonwood | **Truckee/E**	21
Cucina Paradiso | **Petaluma/N**	24
Delancey St. | **Embarcadero**	17
Dragonfly | **Truckee/E**	22
Drake's | **Inverness/N**	21
Dry Creek | **Healdsburg/N**	24
Duck Club | **multi.**	19
Enrico's | **N Beach**	16
Eos Rest. | **Cole Valley**	23
EPIC | **Embarcadero**	20
☑ Erna's Elderberry | **Oakhurst/E**	28
☑ Étoile | **Yountville/N**	26
☑ Farmhouse Inn | **Forestville/N**	26
Fish | **Sausalito/N**	23
Frascati | **Russian Hill**	26

Fresh Cream | **Monterey/S**	25
Gar Woods | **Carnelian Bay/E**	17
Z Greens | **Marina**	24
Guaymas | **Tiburon/N**	16
Half Moon Brew | **Half Moon Bay/S**	16
Hog Island Oyster | **Embarcadero**	25
NEW Il Cane Rosso | **Embarcadero**	-
Il Fornaio | **Carmel/S**	19
Jake's/Lake | **Tahoe City/E**	16
Joey & Eddie's | **N Beach**	14
John Ash | **Santa Rosa/N**	24
Jordan's | **Berkeley/E**	17
Kenwood | **Kenwood/N**	23
Z La Forêt | **San Jose/S**	26
NEW La Mar | **Embarcadero**	23
La Terrasse | **Presidio**	18
Le Charm Bistro | **SoMa**	22
Ledford Hse. | **Albion/N**	25
Lion & Compass | **Sunnyvale/S**	20
Little River Inn | **Little River/N**	21
NEW Madera | **Menlo Pk/S**	-
Mama's on Wash. | **N Beach**	25
Z Marinus | **Carmel Valley/S**	27
McCormick | **Fish. Wharf**	20
Meadowood Grill | **St. Helena/N**	22
Z Meadowood Rest. | **St. Helena/N**	26
Medjool | **Mission**	18
Mendocino Hotel | **Mendocino/N**	18
Mezza Luna | **Princeton Sea/S**	21
Mijita | **Embarcadero**	20
Mistral | **Redwood Shores/S**	18
MoMo's | **S Beach**	17
Moosse Café | **Mendocino/N**	24
Mo's | **SoMa**	20
Napa General | **Napa/N**	20
Napa Valley Grille | **Yountville/N**	21
Napa Wine Train | **Napa/N**	16
Z Navio | **Half Moon Bay/S**	24
Nepenthe | **Big Sur/S**	17
One Market | **Embarcadero**	22
Ozumo | **Embarcadero**	24
Z Pacific's Edge | **Carmel/S**	25
Park Chalet | **Outer Sunset**	16
Picco | **Larkspur/N**	26
Pizzeria Picco | **Larkspur/N**	25
Press | **St. Helena/N**	23
Ravens Rest. | **Mendocino/N**	22
Red's Java | **Embarcadero**	16
Rest. at Stevenswood | **Little River/N**	26
River Ranch | **Tahoe City/E**	15
Z Rivoli | **Berkeley/E**	27
Z Rotunda | **Downtown**	19
Z Roy's | **Pebble Bch/S**	25
Salute Marina | **Richmond/E**	18
Sam's Chowder | **Half Moon Bay/S**	20
Scoma's | **multi.**	22
Scott's | **Oakland/E**	18
Shadowbrook | **Capitola/S**	18
Z Sierra Mar | **Big Sur/S**	27
Z Slanted Door | **Embarcadero**	26
St. Orres | **Gualala/N**	22
Z Sutro's | **Outer Rich**	21
Trader Vic's | **multi.**	17
TusCA | **Monterey/S**	-
Venticello | **Nob Hill**	23
Z Waterbar | **Embarcadero**	20
Waterfront | **Embarcadero**	18
Water St. Bistro | **Petaluma/N**	23
Wente Vineyards | **Livermore/E**	23
Wine Spectator | **St. Helena/N**	22
Z Wolfdale's | **Tahoe City/E**	27
zazu | **Santa Rosa/N**	25

VISITORS ON EXPENSE ACCOUNT

Z Acquerello | **Polk Gulch**	28
Alexander's | **Cupertino/S**	25
Z Aqua | **Downtown**	26
Z Auberge du Sol. | **Rutherford/N**	26
Aubergine | **Carmel/S**	25
NEW Bardessono | **Yountville/N**	23
Z NEW Bottega | **Yountville/N**	25
Z Boulevard | **Embarcadero**	27
Campton Place | **Downtown**	24
Carnelian Room | **Downtown**	18
Z Chez Panisse | **Berkeley/E**	28
Chez TJ | **Mtn View/S**	23
Citronelle | **Carmel/S**	24
Club XIX | **Pebble Bch/S**	23
Z Cyrus | **Healdsburg/N**	29

Deetjen's | **Big Sur/S**	22
Dry Creek | **Healdsburg/N**	24
EPIC | **Embarcadero**	20
Z Erna's Elderberry | **Oakhurst/E**	28
Eulipia | **San Jose/S**	24
Z Evvia | **Palo Alto/S**	26
Fifth Floor | **SoMa**	25
Flea St. Café | **Menlo Pk/S**	25
Z Fleur de Lys | **Downtown**	27
Forbes Mill Steak | **Los Gatos/S**	22
Z French Laundry | **Yountville/N**	29
Fresh Cream | **Monterey/S**	25
Z Gary Danko | **Fish. Wharf**	29
Z Greens | **Marina**	24
Harris' | **Polk Gulch**	25
Z Jardinière | **Civic Ctr**	26
John Ash | **Santa Rosa/N**	24
Z Kaygetsu | **Menlo Pk/S**	28
Z Kokkari | **Downtown**	27
Kyo-Ya | **Downtown**	24
Z La Folie | **Russian Hill**	28
Z La Forêt | **San Jose/S**	26
Z La Toque | **Napa/N**	26
Z Manresa | **Los Gatos/S**	27
Z Marinus | **Carmel Valley/S**	27
Z Masa's | **Downtown**	28
McCormick | **Fish. Wharf**	20
Z Meadowood Rest. | **St. Helena/N**	26
Z Michael Mina | **Downtown**	27
NEW Midi | **Downtown**	-
Morton's | **Downtown**	24
Napa Wine Train | **Napa/N**	16
Oliveto Restaurant | **Oakland/E**	25
Orson | **SoMa**	18
Z Pacific's Edge | **Carmel/S**	25
Z Plumed Horse | **Saratoga/S**	25
Press | **St. Helena/N**	23
Z Ritz-Carlton Din. Rm. | **Nob Hill**	27
Roy's | **SoMa**	23
Z Roy's | **Pebble Bch/S**	25
Santé | **Sonoma/N**	25
Z Seasons | **Downtown**	26
Z Sent Sovi | **Saratoga/S**	26
71 Saint Peter | **San Jose/S**	22
Shanghai 1930 | **Embarcadero**	20

Z Sierra Mar | **Big Sur/S**	27
Silks | **Downtown**	24
Sino | **San Jose/S**	19
Tommy Toy's | **Downtown**	23
Village Pub | **Woodside/S**	26
Z Waterbar | **Embarcadero**	20
NEW Zinnia | **Downtown**	23

WINE BARS

All Seasons | **Calistoga/N**	20
Z A16 | **Marina**	25
NEW Aurea | **Nob Hill**	-
bacar | **SoMa**	23
Bar Bambino | **Mission**	23
Bar Tartine | **Mission**	24
Bin 38 | **Marina**	19
NEW Bistro St. Germain | **Lower Haight**	-
Bocadillos | **N Beach**	22
Bounty Hunter | **Napa/N**	19
Candybar | **W Addition**	17
Cantinetta Luca | **Carmel/S**	23
Carneros Bistro | **Sonoma/N**	23
Cav Wine Bar | **Hayes Valley**	20
Cucina Paradiso | **Petaluma/N**	24
Cucina Rest. | **San Anselmo/N**	23
District | **SoMa**	18
NEW Elements | **Napa/N**	22
Z El Paseo | **Mill Valley/N**	26
Eos Rest. | **Cole Valley**	23
Z Étoile | **Yountville/N**	26
1550 Hyde | **Russian Hill**	22
fig cafe | **Glen Ellen/N**	24
Folio Enoteca | **Napa/N**	16
Frascati | **Russian Hill**	26
girl & the fig | **Sonoma/N**	24
Incanto | **Noe Valley**	24
Kuleto's | **Downtown**	20
Z La Toque | **Napa/N**	26
Le Zinc | **Noe Valley**	19
Liberty Café | **Bernal Hts**	22
Martini House | **St. Helena/N**	26
Maverick | **Mission**	24
Millennium | **Downtown**	25
Mosaic | **Forestville/N**	26
Napa General | **Napa/N**	20
Napa Wine Train | **Napa/N**	16

Nectar Wine | **multi.**	18
Ottimista | **Cow Hollow**	19
Picco | **Larkspur/N**	26
Prima | **Walnut Creek/E**	24
Rest. LuLu/Petite | **SoMa**	21
Richmond Rest. | **Inner Rich**	26
Rist. Avanti | **Santa Cruz/S**	–
NEW RN74 | **SoMa**	–
Rosso Pizzeria | **Santa Rosa/N**	25
Sabor of Spain | **San Rafael/N**	19
Sociale | **Presidio Hts**	24
South Food/Wine | **S Beach**	21
Starlight | **Sebastopol/N**	22
Z Sushi Ran | **Sausalito/N**	28
Uva Enoteca | **Lower Haight**	20
Va de Vi | **Walnut Creek/E**	23
Vin Antico | **San Rafael/N**	23
Viognier | **San Mateo/S**	23
Vivande | **Pacific Hts**	23
Wente Vineyards | **Livermore/E**	23
Willi's Seafood | **Healdsburg/N**	24
Willi's Wine | **Santa Rosa/N**	26
Yabbies Coastal | **Russian Hill**	21
Zibibbo | **Palo Alto/S**	19
Zin | **Healdsburg/N**	23
ZuZu | **Napa/N**	23

WINNING WINE LISTS

Z Absinthe | **Hayes Valley**	22
Acme Chophse. | **S Beach**	20
À Côté | **Oakland/E**	24
Z Acquerello | **Polk Gulch**	28
Albion River Inn | **Albion/N**	25
Alembic | **Haight-Ashbury**	22
Alexander's | **Cupertino/S**	25
Alioto's | **Fish. Wharf**	18
All Seasons | **Calistoga/N**	20
Z Ame | **SoMa**	26
Angèle | **Napa/N**	22
Anton & Michel | **Carmel/S**	23
Z Aqua | **Downtown**	26
Z A16 | **Marina**	25
Z Auberge du Sol. | **Rutherford/N**	26
Aubergine | **Carmel/S**	25
NEW Aurea | **Nob Hill**	–

bacar | **SoMa**	23
Balboa Cafe | **Mill Valley/N**	19
Bar Bambino | **Mission**	23
NEW Bardessono | **Yountville/N**	23
NEW Barlata | **Oakland/E**	–
Bar Tartine | **Mission**	24
BayWolf | **Oakland/E**	25
Bella Vista | **Woodside/S**	19
Beretta | **Mission**	23
Bin 38 | **Marina**	19
Bistro Clovis | **Hayes Valley**	21
Bistro Don Giovanni | **Napa/N**	23
Bistro Ralph | **Healdsburg/N**	23
Blackhawk Grille | **Danville/E**	19
Bocadillos | **N Beach**	22
Z NEW Bottega | **Yountville/N**	25
Z Bouchon | **Yountville/N**	26
Z Boulevard | **Embarcadero**	27
Bridges | **Danville/E**	22
Brix | **Napa/N**	22
Butterfly | **Embarcadero**	20
CAFÉ KATi | **Japantown**	21
Cafe La Haye | **Sonoma/N**	26
Camino | **Oakland/E**	22
Campton Place | **Downtown**	24
Cantinetta Luca | **Carmel/S**	23
Carnelian Room | **Downtown**	18
Carneros Bistro | **Sonoma/N**	23
Casanova | **Carmel/S**	23
Cav Wine Bar | **Hayes Valley**	20
Celadon | **Napa/N**	24
Central Market | **Petaluma/N**	24
César | **Berkeley/E**	22
Cetrella | **Half Moon Bay/S**	20
Z Chapeau! | **Outer Rich**	26
Z Chez Panisse | **Berkeley/E**	28
Z Chez Panisse Café | **Berkeley/E**	27
Chez Papa | **SoMa**	23
Chez TJ | **Mtn View/S**	23
Citron | **Oakland/E**	23
Citronelle | **Carmel/S**	24
Club XIX | **Pebble Bch/S**	23
Cole's Chop Hse. | **Napa/N**	24
NEW Contigo | **Noe Valley**	19
Côté Sud | **Castro**	19
Cottage Eatery | **Tiburon/N**	23

Cuvée	**Napa/N**	21
Z Cyrus	**Healdsburg/N**	29
Dio Deka	**Los Gatos/S**	25
District	**SoMa**	18
NEW Donato	**Redwood City/S**	–
downtown	**Berkeley/E**	19
NEW Dreamfarm	**San Anselmo/N**	–
Dry Creek	**Healdsburg/N**	24
NEW Elements	**Napa/N**	22
Z El Paseo	**Mill Valley/N**	26
Emile's	**San Jose/S**	22
Eos Rest.	**Cole Valley**	23
EPIC	**Embarcadero**	20
Z Erna's Elderberry	**Oakhurst/E**	28
NEW Estate	**Sonoma/N**	20
Z Étoile	**Yountville/N**	26
Fandango	**Pacific Grove/S**	23
Z Farallon	**Downtown**	24
Z Farm	**Napa/N**	24
Z Farmhouse Inn	**Forestville/N**	26
1550 Hyde	**Russian Hill**	22
Fifth Floor	**SoMa**	25
NEW 54 Mint	**SoMa**	–
fig cafe	**Glen Ellen/N**	24
NEW Five	**Berkeley/E**	–
Flea St. Café	**Menlo Pk/S**	25
Z Fleur de Lys	**Downtown**	27
Folio Enoteca	**Napa/N**	16
Forbes Mill Steak	**multi.**	22
Z French Laundry	**Yountville/N**	29
Gabriella Café	**Santa Cruz/S**	23
Z Gary Danko	**Fish. Wharf**	29
girl & the fig	**Sonoma/N**	24
Grasing's Coastal	**Carmel/S**	24
Z Greens	**Marina**	24
Incanto	**Noe Valley**	24
Indigo	**Civic Ctr**	19
Z Jardinière	**Civic Ctr**	26
John Ash	**Santa Rosa/N**	24
JoLe	**Calistoga/N**	26
Kenwood	**Kenwood/N**	23
Z Kokkari	**Downtown**	27
Kuleto's	**Downtown**	20
Kuleto's	**Burlingame/S**	20
Kurt's Carmel	**Carmel/S**	23

Z La Folie	**Russian Hill**	28
Z La Forêt	**San Jose/S**	26
Laïola	**Marina**	20
NEW La Mar	**Embarcadero**	23
Lark Creek Steak	**Downtown**	23
LaSalette	**Sonoma/N**	25
Z La Toque	**Napa/N**	26
Lavanda	**Palo Alto/S**	20
NEW LB Steak	**San Jose/S**	–
Ledford Hse.	**Albion/N**	25
Z Le Papillon	**San Jose/S**	27
Liberty Café	**Bernal Hts**	22
Local Kitchen	**SoMa**	20
Luce	**SoMa**	20
Luella	**Russian Hill**	22
Z Madrona	**Healdsburg/N**	26
Z Manresa	**Los Gatos/S**	27
Manzanita	**Healdsburg/N**	19
Marché	**Menlo Pk/S**	25
NEW Marinitas	**San Anselmo/N**	21
Z Marinus	**Carmel Valley/S**	27
Martini House	**St. Helena/N**	26
NEW Martins West	**Redwood City/S**	–
Z Masa's	**Downtown**	28
Meadowood Grill	**St. Helena/N**	22
Z Meadowood Rest.	**St. Helena/N**	26
Mendo Bistro	**Ft Bragg/N**	24
Z Michael Mina	**Downtown**	27
Millennium	**Downtown**	25
Monk's Kettle	**Mission**	18
Monti's	**Santa Rosa/N**	21
Montrio Bistro	**Monterey/S**	21
Mosaic	**Forestville/N**	26
NEW Moss Room	**Inner Rich**	21
Z Mustards	**Yountville/N**	25
Naomi Sushi	**Menlo Pk/S**	21
Napa Valley Grille	**Yountville/N**	21
Napa Wine Train	**Napa/N**	16
Z Navio	**Half Moon Bay/S**	24
Nectar Wine	**Burlingame/S**	18
Nick's Cove	**Marshall/N**	21
955 Ukiah	**Mendocino/N**	23
North Beach Rest.	**N Beach**	22
Oliveto Cafe	**Oakland/E**	24

SPECIAL FEATURES

Z Marinus	27
Z Pacific's Edge	25
El Granada	
Z Cafe Gibraltar	27
Forestville	
Z Farmhouse Inn	26
Mosaic	26
Fort Bragg	
Mendo Bistro	24
Rendezvous Inn	25
Geyserville	
Santi	25
Graton	
Underwood Bar	24
Gualala	
St. Orres	22
Half Moon Bay	
Cetrella	20
Z Navio	24
Healdsburg	
Z Cyrus	29
Dry Creek	24
Z Madrona	26
Willi's Seafood	24
Kenwood	
Kenwood	23
Larkspur	
Emporio Rulli	22
Little River	
Little River Inn	21
Livermore	
Wente Vineyards	23
Los Gatos	
Z Manresa	27
Mendocino	
Cafe Beaujolais	25
MacCallum Hse.	21
Menlo Park	
Flea St. Café	25
Z Kaygetsu	28
Marché	25
Mill Valley	
Z Buckeye Rdhse.	23
Monterey	
Montrio Bistro	21

Stokes	21
Tarpy's	20
Mountain View	
Chez TJ	23
Napa	
Angèle	22
Celadon	24
Z Mustards	25
Oakhurst	
Z Erna's Elderberry	28
Oakland	
À Côté	24
BayWolf	25
Oliveto Restaurant	25
Z Zachary's Pizza	24
Pacific Grove	
Fandango	23
Palo Alto	
Cool Café	-
Z Evvia	26
Junnoon	23
Mantra	20
Tamarine	26
Pebble Beach	
Z Roy's	25
Pescadero	
Duarte's Tavern	21
Rohnert Park	
Hana Japanese	24
Rutherford	
Z Auberge du Sol.	26
Z La Toque	26
San Anselmo	
Insalata's	25
San Jose	
Arcadia	21
Emile's	22
Z La Forêt	26
Z Le Papillon	27
San Mateo	
Lure	20
Viognier	23
Santa Rosa	
John Ash	24
Willi's Wine	26

SPECIAL FEATURES

ALPHABETICAL PAGE INDEX

All places are in San Francisco unless otherwise noted (East of San Francisco=E; North of San Francisco=N; South of San Francisco=S).

Visit ZAGAT.mobi from your mobile phone

337

ALPHA INDEX

Wine Vintage Chart

This chart, based on our 0 to 30 scale, is designed to help you select wine. The ratings (by **Howard Stravitz,** a law professor at the University of South Carolina) reflect the vintage quality and the wine's readiness to drink. We exclude the 1991–1993 vintages because they are not that good. A dash indicates the wine is either past its peak or too young to rate. Loire ratings are for dry white wines.

Whites	89	90	94	95	96	97	98	99	00	01	02	03	04	05	06	07
French:																
Alsace	24	25	24	23	23	22	25	23	25	26	22	21	24	25	24	-
Burgundy	23	22	-	27	26	23	21	25	25	24	27	23	26	27	25	23
Loire Valley	-	-	-	-	-	-	-	-	24	25	26	22	23	27	24	-
Champagne	26	29	-	26	27	24	23	24	24	22	26	21	-	-	-	-
Sauternes	25	28	-	21	23	25	23	24	24	29	25	24	21	26	23	27
California:																
Chardonnay	-	-	-	-	-	-	-	24	23	26	26	25	26	29	25	-
Sauvignon Blanc	-	-	-	-	-	-	-	-	-	-	-	26	27	26	27	26
Austrian:																
Grüner Velt./ Riesling	-	-	-	25	21	26	26	25	22	23	25	26	26	25	24	-
German:	26	27	24	23	26	25	26	23	21	29	27	24	26	28	24	-

Reds	89	90	94	95	96	97	98	99	00	01	02	03	04	05	06	07
French:																
Bordeaux	25	29	21	26	25	23	25	24	29	26	24	26	24	28	25	23
Burgundy	24	26	-	26	27	25	22	27	22	24	27	25	24	27	25	-
Rhône	28	28	23	26	22	24	27	26	27	26	-	26	24	27	25	-
Beaujolais	-	-	-	-	-	-	-	-	-	-	22	24	21	27	25	23
California:																
Cab./Merlot	-	28	29	27	25	28	23	26	-	27	26	25	24	26	23	-
Pinot Noir	-	-	-	-	-	-	-	24	23	25	28	26	27	25	24	-
Zinfandel	-	-	-	-	-	-	-	-	-	25	23	27	22	23	23	-
Oregon:																
Pinot Noir	-	-	-	-	-	-	-	-	-	-	27	25	26	27	26	-
Italian:																
Tuscany	-	25	23	24	20	29	24	27	24	27	-	25	27	25	24	-
Piedmont	27	27	-	-	26	27	26	25	28	27	-	24	23	26	25	24
Spanish:																
Rioja	-	-	26	26	24	25	-	25	24	27	-	24	25	26	24	-
Ribera del Duero/Priorat	-	-	26	26	27	25	24	25	24	27	20	24	27	26	24	-
Australian:																
Shiraz/Cab.	-	-	24	26	23	26	28	24	24	27	27	25	26	26	24	-
Chilean:	-	-	-	-	-	24	-	25	23	26	24	25	24	26	25	24

7 20613 06174 7

ZAGATMAP

San Francisco Transit Map

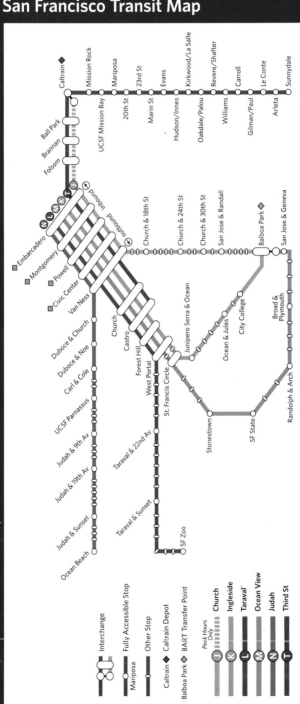

Legend:

- ⬯ Interchange
- ◯ Fully Accessible Stop — Mariposa
- ● Other Stop
- ◆ Caltrain Depot — Caltrain
- ◆ BART Transfer Point — Balboa Park

Peak Hours Only

- **J** Church
- **K** Ingleside
- **L** Taraval
- **M** Ocean View
- **N** Judah
- **T** Third St

Most Popular Restaurants

Map coordinates follow each name. Sections A–G show the City of San Francisco (see adjacent map). Sections H–O show the Greater Bay area and outlying regions (see reverse side of map).

1. Gary Danko (A-5)
2. Boulevard (C-8)
3. French Laundry (J-3)
4. Slanted Door (B-8)
5. Chez Panisse (L-3)
6. Cyrus (J-2)
7. Kokkari Estiatorio (B-7)
8. Zuni Café (E-5)
9. Chez Panisse Café (L-3)
10. A16 (B-3)
11. Michael Mina* (C-6)
12. Delfina (F-5)
13. Yank Sing (C-7, C-8)
14. Aqua (C-7)
15. Bouchon (J-3)
16. In-N-Out† (A-6)
17. Fleur de Lys (C-6)
18. Quince (C-5)
19. Auberge du Soleil (J-3)
20. Perbacco (C-7)
21. Tadich Grill (C-7)
22. Farallon (C-6)
23. Jardinière (D-5)
24. Bistro Jeanty (J-3)
25. Absinthe (E-5)
26. Chapeau! (D-1)
27. Ritz-Carlton Dining Room (C-6)
28. Acquerello (C-5)
29. Evvia (L-3)
30. House of Prime Rib (C-5)
31. ad hoc (J-3)
32. Greens (A-4)
33. Mustards Grill (J-3)
34. Buckeye Roadhouse (K-3)
35. Redd (J-3)
36. Zachary's Pizza† (L-3)
37. Aziza (D-1)
38. Ame (C-7)
39. BIX (B-7)
40. Manresa* (M-4)
41. Scoma's (A-6, L-3)
42. Sushi Ran (L-3)
43. La Folie (B-5)
44. Chow/Park Chow† (F-5)
45. Hog Island Oyster (B-8, K-3)
46. Burma Superstar† (D-2)
47. Amber India† (L-3)
48. Tartine Bakery* (F-5)
49. Foreign Cinema (G-5)
50. Range (G-5)

---

*Indicates tie with above   † Indicates multiple branches